W9-BCT-324

CURRENT TRENDS & ISSUES

TODAY'S TECHNOLOGY FOR LEARNING DISABILITIES

**Focus On**

**Activities**

**Effective Practices**

**FOR LEARNING DISABILITIES**

THIRD EDITION

# Learning Disabilities

## Foundations, Characteristics, and Effective Teaching

**Daniel P. Hallahan**
*University of Virginia*

**John W. Lloyd**
*University of Virginia*

**James M. Kauffman**
*University of Virginia*

**Margaret Weiss**
*Virginia Polytechnic University*

**Elizabeth A. Martinez**
*Council for Exceptional Children*

371.9
L438h
2005

PEARSON

Boston    New York    San Francisco
Mexico City    Montreal    Toronto    London    Madrid    Munich    Paris
Hong Kong    Singapore    Tokyo    Cape Town    Sydney

N.C. WESLEYAN COLLEGE
ELIZABETH BRASWELL PEARSALL LIBRARY

*Executive Editor:* Virginia Lanigan
*Development Editor:* Alicia Reilly
*Series Editorial Assistant:* Scott Blaszak
*Executive Marketing Manager:* Amy Cronin Jordan
*Senior Production Editor:* Annette Pagliaro
*Editorial Production:* Trinity Publishers Services
*Composition Buyer:* Linda Cox
*Manufacturing Buyer:* Andrew Turso
*Cover Administrator:* Linda Knowles
*Photo Research:* PoYee Oster, Photoquick Research
*Text Design:* Denise Hoffman
*Composition:* Omegatype Typography, Inc.

For related titles and support materials, visit our online catalog at www.ablongman.com.

Copyright © 2005, 1999, 1996 Pearson Education, Inc.

All rights reserved. No part of the material protected by this copyright notice may be reproduced or utilized in any form or by any means, electronic or mechanical, including photocopying, recording, or by any information storage and retrieval system, without written permission from the copyright owner.

To obtain permission(s) to use material from this work, please submit a written request to Allyn and Bacon, Permissions Department, 75 Arlington Street, Boston, MA 02116 or fax your request to 617-848-7320.

Between the time Website information is gathered and then published, it is not unusual for some sites to have closed. Also, the transcription of URLs can result in unintended typographical errors. The publisher would appreciate notification where these errors occur so that they may be corrected in subsequent editions.

**Library of Congress Cataloging-in-Publication Data**

Learning disabilities: Fsoundations, characteristics, and effective teaching / Daniel P. Hallahan . . . [et al.].—3rd ed.

  p. cm.

   Rev. ed. of: Introduction to learning disabilities / Daniel P. Hallahan, James M. Kauffman, John Wills Lloyd. 2nd ed. c1999.

 Includes bibliographical references and index.

 ISBN 0-205-38867-1

   1. Learning disabilities. 2. Learning disabilities—United States. 3. Learning disabled—Education. 4. Learning disabled—Education—United States. I. Hallahan, Daniel P., 1944– II. Hallahan, Daniel P., 1944– Introduction to learning disabilities.

LC4704.H34 2005
371.9—dc22

2004040039

Printed in the United States of America

10 9 8 7 6 5 4 3   RRD-VA 08 07 06 05

**Photo Credits:** p. 1, T. Lindfors; p. 42, Alan Carey/The Image Works; p. 51, Warren Anatomical Museum, Harvard Medical School; p. 64, Mark C. Burnett/Stock Boston; p. 108, Robin L. Sachs/PhotoEdit; p. 142, Francisco Cruz/SuperStock; p. 166, Sonda Dawes/The Image Works; p. 194, Ellen Senisi/The Image Works; pp. 222, 258, David Young Wolff/PhotoEdit; p. 270, ERICA, Inc.; p. 294, Brownie Harris/Corbis; p. 324, John Henley/Corbis; p. 360, T. Lindfors; p. 406, David Young Wolff/Getty Images; p. 450, LWA-Dann Tardif/Corbis; p. 488, T. Lindfors.

# CONTENTS

# 3 Eligibility for Special Education Services    65

# 4 Parents and Families    109

## Prevention and Intervention in Early Childhood    143

## Transition Programming in Adolescence and Adulthood    167

## 7   Social, Emotional, and Behavioral Problems   195

# Cognition, Metacognition, and Memory in Students with Learning Disabilities      223

# Attention Deficit Hyperactivity Disorder      259

## 12　Students Who Experience Difficulties with Reading　361

# 13 Students Who Experience Difficulties with Writing      407

This text is a thorough introduction to the field of learning disabilities across the life span, from early childhood to adulthood. We have written the text for undergraduate and graduate courses in learning disabilities, but also as a reference for teaching and professional practice throughout your career. We have attempted to strike a good balance between foundational information and practical tools that you can use readily with your own students.

## Topical Updates, New Materials, and Organizational Changes in This Edition

The field of learning disabilities is often characterized by challenges and contradictions. Indeed, these challenges and contradictions are one reason we continue to find it so fascinating. As in previous editions, research and the important trends in the field are emphasized continually. For example, this new edition delves into:

- **Reauthorization of IDEA.** As this book goes to press, the reauthorization of IDEA has not yet passed Congress. However, we have monitored the critical changes being proposed for learning disabilities, changes that most who are close to the process feel confident will be included in the final legislation (in particular those related to eligibility).
- **Inclusionary practices.** We present the most current research and practices on how to accommodate students with learning disabilities in general education classrooms.
- **Technological advances.** We present the most recent technological innovations pertaining to identifying and teaching students with learning disabilities.

The third edition introduces **three new chapters:**

*NEW! Chapter 3—Eligibility for Special Education Services* This chapter focuses on the laws, definitions, identification, and eligibility topics related to learning disabilities. The new edition integrates the eligibility process with related assessment concepts and includes the most recent information about response-to-intervention as an alternative means to eligibility determination.

*NEW! Chapter 9—Attention Deficit Hyperactivity Disorder* Because of the extensive overlap of learning disabilities with attention deficit hyperactivity disorder (ADHD), this edition includes a new chapter on ADHD—its causes, characteristics, and treatment.

*NEW! Chapter 15—Participation in General Education Classrooms for Students with Learning Disabilities* This chapter considers students with learning disabilities in the general education classroom and includes information about planning for, accommodating, and adapting instruction to include students with learning disabilities.

We have made substantial **organizational changes to this edition** as well. For example, whereas in the previous edition we had a chapter on Assessment and one on Service Delivery Models, in this edition we have combined some of their content into the new chapter on Eligibility for Special Education Services. We believe this offers the reader a more succinct presentation of critical issues pertaining to eligibility. Also, we have placed the updated chapter on Educational Approaches immediately preceding the chapters focused on academic areas.

## Text Features

As in previous editions, each chapter includes a variety of recurring features to enhance your understanding, extend and apply your learning, and spark further interest in the topics being presented. We have added a number of new features in this edition, and we have expanded the number of popular features retained from previous editions.

*NEW!* ***Case Studies: Shannon and Jamal*** In Chapter 1, we introduce the reader to two cases of students with learning disabilities: Shannon—a 14-year-old white girl in the eighth grade—and Jamal—a 6-year-old African American boy in first grade. Each hypothetical case is a composite of cases of real students whom we, the authors, have known. We then refer to these cases throughout the text to delineate, clarify, and/or expand key concepts presented in each chapter. Quotes from Jamal and Shannon, as well as their parents and key professionals, provide a real-world context for the experience of students with learning disabilities. Marginal names—either **Shannon** or **Jamal**—provide an easy visual reference wherever the cases are discussed. More extensive case files are available on the Companion Website—www.ablongman.com/hallahanLD3e.

Shannon
Jamal

*NEW!* ***Case Connections*** A separate feature in every chapter focuses in depth on a particular issue having to do with Shannon and/or Jamal and relates this issue to the overall content of the chapter, including concrete, practical examples of school-home communication, transition planning, teacher interviews, student self-explanations, and so on.

*NEW!* ***Reflections on the Cases*** At the end of each chapter, we offer a few questions that provide an opportunity for readers to consider in more depth issues raised by the cases of Jamal and/or Shannon.

*NEW!* ***Focus on → Strategies and Activities for Teachers*** Created by Dr. Kristin L. Sayeski, University of Virginia, these sections at the very end of Chapters 4, 8, 9, and 11 through 15 provide quick, easy-to-apply teaching strategies and activities that are particularly beneficial for students with learning disabilities. All are based on empirically validated practices and are designed to be "classroom-ready"— great for beginning teachers!

*NEW! CEC Knowledge and Skills*   The Council for Exceptional Children (CEC) is an international organization that provides resources to special education professionals and advocates for the rights and responsibilities of special education students, families, and professionals. Because the CEC Standards are becoming so important to the profession, including the certification and licensure process, this text is aligned with CEC Standards via the following new features, created by Dr. Candice Haas Hollingsead, Andrews University.

*Council for Exceptional Children*

- **CEC Knowledge and Skills Discussed in This Chapter** opens each chapter and highlights the key topics in each chapter as they relate to CEC Standards.
- **CEC Knowledge Check** questions in the margin link the content of the text to CEC standards.
- **Portfolio-Building Activity: Demonstrating Your Knowledge of the CEC Content Standards** at the end of each chapter is a cumulative activity allowing you to apply the information you have learned in the chapter to develop a professional portfolio that reflects the knowledge and skills that CEC recommends for all teachers of students with learning disabilities.
- **CEC Professional Standards Appendix** at the end of the book is a comprehensive reference to the CEC Common Core Standards and the Learning Disability Knowledge and Skills Bases.

*Effective Teaching Practices for Learning Disabilities*   provide clear, easy-to-grasp explanations and how-to information on the latest empirically validated teaching approaches for students with learning disabilities. (11 chapters)

*Today's Technology for Learning Disabilities*   highlight technological advances or useful Websites for students with learning disabilities and their teachers. (13 chapters)

*Multicultural Considerations*   introduce issues pertaining to cultural differences versus disabilities, and prepare students to teach in today's diverse classrooms. (14 chapters)

*Current Trends and Issues*   succinctly capture the essence of critical themes, ethical questions, and topics in the field, providing an excellent vehicle for classroom discussions. (15 chapters)

*Effective Study Tools:*
- Chapter Opening Outlines
- Marginal Definitions of Key Terms and Concepts
- Question-Answer Summaries

## Supplements for Students and Instructors

- **Instructor's Manual with Test Bank.** The instructor's manual provides a variety of teaching tools and ideas for each chapter. Included as well are Assessment Rubrics for the CEC Portfolio Building Activities that conclude each chapter. The Test Bank contains an assortment of multiple-choice, short-answer, and essay questions.
- **PowerPoint Presentation.** Designed specifically for adopting instructors of this text, the PowerPoint Presentation consists of a series of slides, organized by chapter, that can be shown as is or used to make overhead transparencies.
- **Companion Website** (www.ablongman.com/hallahanLD3e). This valuable interactive study tool contains a wealth of online assets to help students better learn and understand the text content. Its many features include an online study guide for each chapter, live Weblinks of helpful online resources related to chapter topics, and other material to extend and further clarify in-text features (such as the end-of-chapter portfolio-building activities). Also included are extensive case files on Shannon and Jamal, the students profiled throughout the text. As an added convenience, there is a full text correlation to CEC Knowledge and Skills for teachers of students with learning disabilities.

www.ablongman.com/
hallahanLD3e

## Acknowledgments

Once again, we are indebted to our editor, Virginia Lanigan. Her faith in our ability to pull off a major revision, including new authors, chapters, and a reorganization based on cases, was either foolhardy or brilliant. You, the reader, will be the final judge, but we are confident that it was the latter. In particular, she helped us take full pedagogical advantage of the cases of Jamal and Shannon by her numerous suggestions and her willingness to go to bat for ratcheting up the design of the book. We thank Alicia Reilly, too, for helping us conceptualize the reorganization. But we are most appreciative of her being such a nice taskmaster. Her oversight brought cohesion to a complicated array of chapters, features, supplements, and, especially, personalities.

We thank our reviewers: Ann B. Welch, Bridgewater College; Bettie J. Willingham, Barton College; Gaby van der Giesson, Fairmont State College; Susan Gurganus, College of Charleston; Mariann W. Tillery, High Point University; Ana Maria Pazos-Rego, Kent State University; Theodore G. Schoneberger, California State University, Stanislaus; Monica A. Lambert, Appalachian State University; Marilyn L. Scheffler, University of Nebraska; Vincent J. Varrassi, Fairleigh Dickenson University; Kimberly Fields, Albany State University; and Gholam Kibria, Delaware State University.

Thanks also to Stephen Byrd, doctoral student in special education at the University of Virginia. His relentless tracking down of permissions and articles is much appreciated.

Finally, thanks to John and Evelyn Ward of Trinity Publishers Services. They did an amazing job of readying the manuscript under an extremely tight deadline.

# Learning Disabilities

## What Are Individuals with Learning Disabilites Like?
- Jamal
- Shannon

## Why Is It Important to Understand Learning Disabilites?
- Most Teachers Will Have Students with Learning Disabilities
- Understanding Learning Disabilities Helps Us Understand Learning
- Many Students with Learning Disabilities Can Contribute Valuably to Society

## Why Are Learning Disabilities Controversial?
- Defining Learning Disabilities Has Been Difficult

- Discrepancy between Ability and Achievement Is Controversial
- Criteria Used to Determine Eligibility for Special Education Vary
- Learning Disability as a Construct

## How Many People Have Learning Disabilities?
- Demographics of People with Learning Disabilities
- Association with Other Disabilities

## Who Works with People Who Have Learning Disabilities?

## Can Learning Disabilities Be Overcome?
- A Critical Need for Effective Teaching
- Learning Disabilities Are Life-Span Problems

Council for Exceptional Children

See Companion Website for detailed correlations between chapter content and Council for Exceptional Children Standards; **www.ablongman.com/ hallahanLD3e**

**CEC Knowledge and Skills Discussed in This Chapter**

**1** The foundational development of the construct called "learning disability."

**2** How the definition of learning disabilities has developed over the years and continues to change.

**3** How the development of the learning disability definition has affected schools.

**4** The medical, legal, and ethical issues relating the definition to the identification of individuals as learning disabled, especially in the areas of gender equity and cultural/linguistic differences.

**5** The relationship between definition and potential causes or etiology of the disability.

**6** Consideration of ultimate goals, costs, and optimal student outcomes to determine effective methodologies.

# Basic Concepts

> I guess I'm going to have to understand a lot about learning
> disabilities now.
>
> *Irene Smith, Jamal's mother*

Almost everyone understands learning disabilities in an informal sense. However, students who have learning disabilities, teachers, school administrators, parents, speech pathologists, psychologists, physicians, and many others need to understand the term *learning disability* in a more formal way. They need to know that learning disability is a distinct category of special education, that it has legal status based on U.S. federal and state law (and similar laws in other countries), and that there is a substantial body of research about it. They should have fundamental knowledge of the characteristics of individuals with learning disabilities, the causes of learning disabilities, how to assess learning disabilities, teaching methods for treating learning disabilities, and the long-term outcomes for individuals who have learning disabilities.

When told that her son Jamal had a diagnosis of learning disability, Mrs. Smith wanted answers to a lot of questions. What caused this disability? How might it have been prevented? What is it like to have a learning disability? What can be done about it? How will this disability change my interaction with my child? Can he learn anything? Does this mean my child will not graduate from high school? Will he ever be able to take care of himself? What kind of job will my child be able to get and keep?

Jamal

Learning disability is one of many differences characteristic of people in contemporary society. Other differences include intellectual *giftedness, cerebral palsy,* athletic prowess, *emotional* or *behavioral problems,* musical ability, *mental retardation, deafness,* artistic talent, *blindness,* and so forth (Hallahan & Kauffman, 2003). If we observe differences only in behavior, not in physical appearance, we may wonder whether the disability is real or imagined. We may also wonder whether our ignorance or bias is confusing the issue. To many people, learning disabilities seem less tangible than some other disabilities (e.g., cerebral palsy), and therefore some may wonder whether learning disabilities actually exist.

Teachers and those preparing to be teachers are likely to have other questions. If I have a student with a learning disability, what am I supposed to know about such students? What causes these disabilities? What are my responsibilities in such cases? How do I decide the best ways to teach this student? Where can I turn for help? What works for such students? Will I really be able to help this student? Because learning disabilities are by far the most prevalent of student disabilities, these questions are most likely to be prompted by an encounter with a student who has a learning disability.

Finding the answers to such questions depends on gaining a basic understanding of underlying issues facing the field of learning disabilities. These issues are undoubtedly some of the most complex and challenging in all of education. They form the core of understanding learning disabilities. In this chapter, the authors introduce cases showing what learning disabilities are like, consider why studying learning disabilities is important, describe problems that impede progress in understanding learning disabilities, and discuss ideas that help to organize what we know about learning disabilities.

## What Are Individuals with Learning Disabilities Like?

Jamal

Shannon

Like everyone else, each individual with a learning disability is unique. People with learning disabilities are not a type; they are individuals who, for whatever reason, require specialized instruction and access to accommodations and other adaptations that will permit them to succeed. To help show how different individuals with learning disabilities can be from one another, we refer to two students' stories throughout this book. In this section, we introduce Jamal, the son of Irene Smith (see the quote at the beginning of this chapter), and Shannon, the daughter of Daniel and Kerri Ireland. In this and subsequent chapters you will find references to Jamal and Shannon. On the Website for this book (www.ablongman.com/hallahanLD3e) are school records and other information that provide a more comprehensive perspective on the cases of these students.

## Jamal

Jamal

Jamal Smith was six years old and in first grade at Hereford Elementary School when we documented his story. He talked a lot about TV shows, dinosaurs, and rockets. He had recently developed an interest in space travel and very quickly was able to name all of the planets in the solar system. He was good at sports, a natural leader, liked by most of his peers, and unusually happy. When his teacher started a lesson, he was usually one of the most eager students. He followed directions right away, volunteered to answer the first questions the teacher asked, and tried to help his fellow students. On the playground, he helped organize games, was relied on as an arbiter by other students, and often was the star of his team.

His teacher, Alice Hamilton, observed that "he is a bright boy, but he just doesn't get some things. He can talk your ear off about things that he knows, but he's got no clue in reading." She noted that he sometimes seemed impatient during lessons that she was presenting, as if he already knew the content and wanted to learn about something else. "It's as if he's way ahead of me," she said. "He'll pick up on what I'm doing and seem to have an instant understanding of it. Then he's ready to move on."

Ms. Hamilton was so concerned about Jamal's performance early in first grade that she contacted Jamal's mother, Irene Smith. The two women knew each other from meetings two years earlier when Ms. Hamilton had taught Patricia, Jamal's older sister. Ms. Hamilton remembered that Patricia had been a good student, not a star, but quite capable of earning passing grades.

They met, and Ms. Hamilton explained her concern: "Jamal seems really bright, but I'm worried that he's not keeping up in reading. I have kids who are taking to reading like a duck to water, but I'm afraid Jamal could be sinking. He seems too smart to have trouble. He knows so much. He's so verbal. So I want to know whether or not you see this, too."

Jamal's mother was shocked. She did not see the problem. She explained, "Of course, I don't know much, but he can read whole books to me. He doesn't have any reading problem."

"Well, I've seen him read one or two whole books very well," replied Ms. Hamilton. "However, when I ask him to read the same words that are in the book when they are on other pages or I write them on paper, he just can't do it. I think he might have memorized the books he can read."

"Oh, really?" asked Mrs. Smith.

"Yes, really. I also gave some simple tests to Jamal, and he can't do things that lots of kindergartners can do," Ms. Hamilton told Mrs. Smith. "He can't take words apart into syllables or take sounds and blend them together into words."

"Are you saying he's retarded? He's not retarded," said Mrs. Smith quickly.

"No! He's a bright boy. That's what worries me." Ms. Hamilton continued, "If he has problems, I think we should catch them now. It's not that he's mentally retarded, it's that he has some specific learning problems. And they're problems that can be helped. We just need to get the help."

"Well, what does it take to get the help?" asked Mrs. Smith.

"We've already tried some things," Ms. Hamilton replied. "We gave him extra reading time and some special attention, but that hasn't taken care of things. He still didn't take off."

"I think we need an evaluation for special education," said Ms. Hamilton. "That means that some people will give some tests to Jamal and they'll report what they find to a team of people. And you'll be part of the team. If the team says, 'learning disability,' then Jamal can get special education. That means he can get special help with his learning problems."

"Well, I don't understand much of anything about this." Mrs. Smith shook her head. "But, I guess I'm going to have to understand a lot about learning disabilities now."

Several months later, as you will learn in subsequent chapters, Jamal was identified as eligible for special education because of his problems with some components of early reading. The decision to grant him special education services was not an easy one, and what happened along the way is instructive. Some members of the educational team charged with responding to the problems Jamal was experiencing were reluctant to apply the label of learning disability. Jamal's teacher advocated strongly that he be eligible for special education, but the school psychologist recommended delaying the eligibility decision.

## Shannon

Shannon

Shannon Ireland's case is different from Jamal's. Jamal was popular, but Shannon was shy. Shannon was good at art, and Jamal excelled in sports. Shannon's case began in an earlier era of special education, when some ways of providing services were more popular than today. It also is different because, of course, Shannon's problems were different. She was a different person.

Shannon was fourteen and in the eighth grade at Bishop Memorial Middle School when we wrote this book. When she was in third grade, a team of professionals decided that Shannon was eligible for special education because of a learning disability. Shannon's special education teacher during elementary school was Peter Martens. He remembered Shannon as "sort of shy and 'spacey.' But as long as I kept her engaged, kept involving her, she learned like a champ."

During the elementary grades, Shannon had problems in virtually every academic area. She also had a quiet demeanor and a tendency to lose focus on class activities. After several years of Mr. Martens's intensive remedial instruction, Shannon learned to read and understand what she read, to spell reasonably, and to compose essays and poems. She continued to have trouble with mathematics, lagging behind her classmates, and she never really broke out of her shyness. As you will learn later (Chapter 9), Shannon also had a second disability—attention deficit hyperactivity disorder (ADHD)—that became more apparent as she progressed into less structured educational situations.

To help you get to know Shannon, we have two documents. The first is an excerpt from a letter from Mrs. Ireland, and the second is a statement by Shannon herself (see the Case Connections box on page 6). In one part of a letter to a university professor written when Shannon was in middle school, Shannon's mother wrote about Shannon's school history and her continuing problems with math.

> I will always be grateful to Pete Martens, Shan's first special education teacher. Of course, Danny and I both wish that Pete could have taken care of her math problems the same as he took care of her reading. But, you know, you can't have everything, and we're just thankful that she can read and write now. At least she'll be able to get through high

school and maybe get some college. And there are lots of jobs that she could do that don't require math.

Anyway, in second and third grade, before she got into Pete's class, she thought she was dumb and that nobody liked her. Then he made her work really hard and she started to catch on. She started learning and feeling better about herself. He told her, "You're just going to have to work harder at some things. Just like some people would have to work really hard on drawing, but drawing's easy for you." Actually, I think it was the phonics he made her learn.

Now she's in middle school and, next year, high school. She's still worried about not being popular, that she doesn't have many friends. Of course, the ADHD is a struggle for her. And, also, she still has trouble with math. She can do her basic facts now pretty well, but it's all gotten a lot harder with algebra coming on. First it was just story problems, but now they want her to do pretty complicated math. We just want her to be able to get a diploma, so we're keeping with it.

## Why Is It Important to Understand Learning Disabilities?

Appreciation for the individuality of students who, like Shannon and Jamal, have learning disabilities is one of the most important concepts teachers can learn. Accepting differences or variations in student performance and altering instruction so that students who have different needs will have successful outcomes is the goal of teaching students with learning disabilities. The goal of teachers—regardless of whether they teach in general or special education and whether they work exclusively with students with learning disabilities, those who have no disabilities, or those who have more substantial disabilities—should be to meet the unique needs of their students. Perhaps the most important concept that the study of learning disabilities has contributed to education is that individuals have different strengths and weaknesses and those strengths and weaknesses should be taken into account in planning and providing education for them. Education needs to be flexible and adapt to students' characteristics.

In addition to the philosophical benefits of treating individuals as unique learners, there are other reasons it is important to understand learning disabilities. In the next few sections, we explain some of these reasons.

Council for
Exceptional
Children

**CEC Knowledge Check**
What is the major goal of teachers who work in the field of special education?
CC1K1, CC1S1

### Most Teachers Will Have Students with Learning Disabilities

As we show in a subsequent section, more than 5% of school-aged children are identified as having learning disabilities. Teachers in the primary or elementary

CASE
CONNECTIONS

Shannon

## Shannon's Reflections on Learning Disabilities

In an essay she wrote on her own when she was in eighth grade, Shannon described her feelings about having a learning disability.

I think there are people in this world with disabilities that are treated unfairly. I have learning disabilities in math (story problems mostly) that I have always had as long as I can remember. I did not think it was important for me to be good in everything and I have to work really very hard in other subjects so I don't have all the time in the world. Now I feel it is unfair if I have to take the exit exam to get my diploma because I just know I won't do good in the math part and then I won't get that diploma and then what am I going to do?

People should have a chance. Just because you have a disability doesn't mean you can't learn. It just seems like if you have a disability then they figure you are a failure. Well, I'm *not.* I have to work hard, but I can learn.

I know about my disabilities. It's called dyscalculia and it means "disability in calculating" but I can calculate pretty good. I'm not real fast, but I can do it if you give me the time or if somebody would show me how to make those calculators work I could be faster maybe. I have trouble with making equations and factors and multiplying fractions. Dyscalculia isn't as popular or known as dyslexia which they thought I had too. Dyscalculia is important though because if it keeps me from getting a diploma that would be terrible injustice.

So I think they should let me have extra time on the test and let me use calculators. What would they think if they had to do something that their whole life depended on it and they weren't good at it? Well that is what it feels like to me.

As would most early adolescents, when Shannon wrote this statement she still saw the world in terms of personal fairness. From reading it, you may already have ideas about her skill with written expression, her attitude, and her ability. As you read this text, you will learn more about her, and some of those ideas probably will change. Even though you may already know a lot about them, we hope you will come to understand learning disabilities in a more complete way.

grades who have 20 to 25 students in their classes will have at least one and perhaps two or more students who have learning disabilities. If they share students with other teachers (for example, by grouping students for arithmetic instruction), this number may increase.

Teachers in the secondary grades, where students move from class to class, will have even more students with learning disabilities in their classes. Secondary teachers may have as many as six or seven class periods per day with 20 to 25 or even 30 students in each period. If the school in which these teachers work identifies 5% of its students as having learning disabilities, these teachers may have six or more students with learning disabilities.

It is important for those who teach these students to know about the nature, causes, assessment, and treatment of learning disabilities. Teachers who work primarily with students who have other disabilities, such as emotional or behavior disorders, also will benefit from knowing about learning disabilities, because these students often will have learning characteristics that are similar to those of students with learning disabilities. One of the most helpful ways to lessen behavior problems is to address the academic learning performance of students with emotional or behavior disorders (Kauffman, 2005).

For general educators—those who teach regular classes of elementary students or content classes composed of secondary students—one consequence of having students with disabilities is that they will become members of a team who collaborate to address the educational problems of those students. They will have to become familiar with these students' **individualized education programs**—the **IEP,** as it is called, is a document that describes special practices needed by students because of their unique educational needs. Teachers will need to adjust their teaching to align with the requirements of the IEP.

**individualized education program (IEP)**  a written agreement of educators and parents, required by IDEA, that includes statements about the student's education needs and the special education and related services that will be provided

## Understanding Learning Disabilities Helps Us Understand Learning

When explaining a concept, it is often helpful to illustrate both what the concept is and what it is not. For example, we might explain that citrus fruits share certain features with but are different in certain ways from fruits that fit in other categories (berries, drupes, pomes). Similarly, understanding a complex concept such as "learning" means being able to explain what learning is not, what happens when learning does not happen. In this way, studying learning disabilities—when learning does not happen in the usual ways—helps us understand normal learning. Learning disabilities has provided a stimulus for research that has benefited not just students with learning disabilities but also students who have not been identified as having learning disabilities (Gerber, 2000).

Research on preventing reading problems illustrates the reciprocal relationship between research on learning and not learning. Because reading problems are common among students with learning disabilities, scholars in the field of learning disabilities have studied ways of preventing reading problems from the inception of the field through today (Blachman, Tangel, Ball, Black, & McGraw, 1999; Coyne, Kame'enui, & Simmons, 2001; de Hirsch, Jansky, & Langford, 1966; Liberman, 1971; Liberman, Shankweiler, Fischer, & Carter, 1974; Torgesen, 2002b; Vaughn, Levy, Coleman, & Bos, 2002; Vellutino, Steger, & Kandel, 1972). These researchers have found that certain component skills and teaching procedures are critical to learning to read and that many students with learning disabilities lack these skills. If young children do not have these critical skills or are not taught them, they are likely to fail in the beginning stages of reading. Once they have begun to fail, it is difficult for them to catch up with their peers. (We explain more about these skills in later chapters on spoken language and reading.)

By conducting many studies that helped identify these missing skills in early reading over more than 30 years' time, learning disabilities scholars have contributed to educators' and psychologists' understanding of normal reading development. Their contributions are apparent in the report of the National Reading Panel (2000), an extensive report on early reading instruction. Dozens of studies conducted by researchers associated with learning disabilities were included in the panel's report or appeared in journals such as *Learning Disabilities: Research and Practice, Learning Disability Quarterly,* and *Journal of Learning Disabilities,* as well as other publications primarily associated with special education.

### Many Students with Learning Disabilities Can Contribute Valuably to Society

Popular discussions of learning disabilities, such as those one finds on the Internet (e.g., www.dyslexiaonline.org), often identify accomplished people (for example, inventor Thomas Edison, physicist Albert Einstein, entertainer Whoopi Goldberg, business tycoon Charles Schwab) as having learning disabilities. As we discuss later in this and other chapters, even when educators have extensive assessment data, it is very difficult to determine whether an individual has a learning disability. We do not have the assessment data needed to determine whether many of the historical and popular figures said to have had learning disabilities actually had learning disabilities. Therefore, absent independent diagnostic data, it is especially difficult to identify a historical figure or even a contemporary celebrity as having a learning disability.

Nevertheless, teachers and others sometimes point to these notable individuals to show that those who have learning problems can also produce great accomplishments. These teachers may believe that these examples can motivate students with learning disabilities to try harder and achieve more. We question whether such an approach produces better outcomes for students with disabilities. If learning disability means "lazy and dumb," then motivating students will be critically important. Although motivating students is an important part of teaching, we doubt that it is the most important part of teaching students with learning disabilities.

It is clear that, learning disability or not, individuals such as Edison can overcome personal difficulties and contribute significantly to society. This is true for many individuals who have had learning disabilities and yet have gone on to have successful careers in many areas. Although not all will achieve the prominence of a Charles Schwab, these individuals can find quiet success in holding a good job, raising a fine family, contributing to their communities, and succeeding socially.

## Why Are Learning Disabilities Controversial?

Probably more than any other category of special education, learning disabilities has been the subject of dispute and debate. Stanovich described the contentious history of learning disabilities:

The field of learning disabilities . . . has a checkered history that is littered with contention, false starts, fads, dead ends, pseudoscience, and just a little bit of hard-won progress. It seems as though the field is constantly getting into scrapes, is always on probation, is never really secure. Why is this? (Stanovich, 1988, p. 210)

In asking this question, Stanovich was reflecting over the relatively brief time period—fewer than 30 years when he posed it—that scholars have studied learning disabilities. During that time, many people have made outstanding contributions to learning disabilities. The five people described in Figure 1.1 (pages 10–11) were among the earliest contributors. They, along with many who followed them, have helped put learning disabilities on a more solid, scientific footing. This hard-won progress was made despite ongoing controversy.

Controversy has enlivened discussion about learning disability since the inception of the field, even before Samuel Kirk, speaking to a group of parents in Chicago in 1963, suggested *learning disability* as the term for referring to children who were having difficulty in school but who were not considered disabled by mental retardation or emotional disturbance. As Kirk put it:

Recently I have used the term "learning disability" to describe a group of children who have disorders in development, in language, speech, reading, and associated communication skills needed for social interaction. In this group I do not include children who have sensory handicaps such as blindness or deafness, because we have methods of managing and training the deaf and the blind. I also exclude from this group children who have generalized mental retardation. (Kirk, 1963)

In earlier decades, these children's difficulties had been variously categorized as mild exogenous mental retardation (mild mental retardation caused by brain injury), minimal brain dysfunction (behavioral abnormalities similar to but less severe than those caused by brain injury, although brain damage cannot be verified), dyslexia (extreme difficulty in reading), perceptual impairment (persistent difficulty in making sense of sensory stimulation), hyperactivity (excessive motor behavior and inattention), and slow learning (a child whose intelligence is not far enough below average to indicate mental retardation) (Hallahan & Cruickshank, 1973; Hallahan & Kauffman, 1977; Hallahan & Mercer, 2002; Mann, 1979; Wiederholt, 1974). The complexities inherent in these and other terms were eventually distilled into the concept of learning disabilities.

So why is providing special education for students who do not have obvious physical disabilities, mental retardation, or other disorders but who do have clear underachievement such a problem? To begin with, much of the difficulty lies in the problem of defining learning disabilities. Although the layperson may have a general idea of what the term means, there are substantial disagreements among professionals of the many disciplines concerned with learning disabilities about precisely how the term is defined.

There are both theoretical and practical reasons that it is important to define phenomena, including categories of special education. The theoretical reasons include the idea that unless one can define something in clear terms, one does not really know that thing (Forness & Kavale, 1997; Hammill, 1990). The practical

### William M. Cruickshank

Cruickshank's career in special education spanned 46 years. He served on the faculty of both Syracuse University and the University of Michigan. In the late 1950s, he directed a federally funded research project establishing classes in the Montgomery County (Maryland) public schools that were recognized by many as the first organized attempt to teach students with learning disabilities in public schools. He was also one of the early pioneers in the notion of interdiscliplinary cooperation and fought to ensure that special educators would have equal footing with other professionals. In 1978, he founded the International Academy for Research in Learning Disabilities.

### Samuel Orton

Orton was a specialist in neurology and neuropathology. He theorized that dyslexia was attributable to some form of brain injury and that special techniques were required to instruct those with dyslexia. Orton felt that nearly all dyslexic symptoms could be explained by mixed dominance of the cerebral hemispheres and that the mixed dominant state of the brain was transferred hereditarily. In one of his most influential books, *Reading, Writing, and Speech Problems of Children* (1937), he described a systematic phonics program reinforced with kinesthetic aids (letter tracing). He coined the term *strephosymbolia,* which he described as "word blindness."

### Katrina de Hirsch

De Hirsch adopted some of Orton's thinking as a starting point for her own discussion of children with "specific dyslexia," or what Orton would have called "strephosymbolia." She studied in Buenos Aires, attended the University of Frankfurt am Main, and went on to pursue a degree in speech pathology at London's Hospital for Nervous Diseases. She believed that disorders of speech in children can be placed on a continuum of language dysfunction. At Columbia-Presbyterian Medical Center she started the first language disorder clinic in this country. Her thinking in the 1950s and 1960s overlapped with other perceptual-motor theorists in that she believed that for students with reading disabilities who can be predicted to fail, formal reading instruction should not take place until success has been achieved with perceptual-motor and oral language instruction.

**FIGURE 1.1** Continued

### Samuel Kirk

One of the most significant figures in learning disabilities, Kirk became deeply involved in the language disabilities of children rather late in his career. He was employed as a psychologist at the Wayne County Training School and simultaneously enrolled in courses at the University of Michigan. After 15 years of clinical experience, graduate work by students, and field testing, he and his colleagues produced the landmark test *Illinois Test of Psycholinguistic Abilities* (ITPA) in 1968. Although the ITPA was first conceptualized as a diagnostic test in the area of mental retardation, it became one of the primary tests identified with learning disabilities. The term *learning disabilities* has been attributed to Kirk, who used it in public during a presentation to a group of parents at the first conference of the Association for Children with Learning Disabilities in 1963.

### Barbara Bateman

Bateman began her career in special education as a teacher of children with multiple disabilities. While at the University of Illinois, where she received her Ph.D. in special education, she worked extensively with Samuel Kirk, publishing a paper in 1962 that was among the first to use the term *learning disabilities* in its title. After working for many years in instructional aspects of teaching students with disabilities, she began to focus her attention on special education law and received her law degree from the University of Oregon Law School in 1976. In more recent years, her book *Better IEPs* (Bateman & Linden, 1998) has informed teachers how to write legally correct, instructionally relevant IEPs.

*Source:* Photographs of Cruickshank, Orton, and Kirk are from *Introduction to Learning Disabilities* by T. Lovitt, 1989, Boston: Allyn and Bacon. Copyright 1989 by Allyn & Bacon. Reprinted by permission. Photograph of de Hirsch is from *Psychoeducational Foundations of Learning Disabilities* by D. Hallahan and W. Cruickshank, 1973, Englewood Cliffs, NJ: Prentice-Hall. Copyright 1973 by Prentice-Hall. Reprinted by permission. Photograph of Bateman is courtesy of Barbara Bateman.

Council for Exceptional Children

**CEC Knowledge Check**

Of the five influential leaders in the early development of learning disabilities, which two are the most important? Support your choices. LD1K1

considerations pertain to legislation, funding, identification, research, and treatment. When advocating for funds and legislation with lawmakers, it helps to be able to articulate clearly for whom the funds and legislation are intended. Definitions aid clear communication; if people have markedly different definitions of learning disability when they talk, the chances of miscommunication increase. As legal statements, definitions lead to criteria for determining who is eligible for, in this case, learning disabilities services; clear definitions produce clearer criteria which, in turn, lead to more consistent eligibility decisions. Definitions also affect our estimates about how many individuals might have a disability. If a clear, easily communicated definition produces consistent criteria, then we can expect that a count of how many individuals have been found eligible for services will be more precise than when a count is based on an ambiguous definition.

## Defining Learning Disabilities Has Been Difficult

Today, people from nearly every walk of life recognize the term *learning disability*. Learning disability is one of 13 specific categories in special education, is defined by federal and state laws, and is a specialization for which teachers in many states must obtain special teaching certification. In some parts of the world, the term *learning disability* is equivalent to the U.S. term *mild mental retardation* or includes what in the United States would be called "behavior disorders" (Opp, 2001; Stevens & Werkoven, 2001). However, the concept of learning disabilities as referring to below-average achievement that is not explained by other intellectual or sensory factors has gained almost complete acceptance among educators and the general public in the United States and many other foreign countries (Mazurek & Winzer, 1994; Winzer, 1993). Although it is widely accepted, the concept of learning disabilities is not yet completely formed. Like other complex but useful concepts, it repeatedly requires refinement (see Bradley, Danielson, & Hallahan, 2002; Kavale & Forness, 1985, 1992; Lyon et al., 2001; Moats & Lyon, 1993; Torgesen, 1991).

To say that considerable debate has surrounded the issue of defining learning disabilities is an understatement. At least 11 definitions have enjoyed some degree of official status in the field (Hammill, 1990), and professional and federal committees have convened to write a definition that is acceptable to the various constituencies. During the early 2000s, the President's Commission on Excellence in Special Education (2002) conducted hearings about special education that influenced the changes in special education law debated in 2003 by the U.S. Congress. The definition of learning disabilities and how states implemented it was one of the most controversial areas examined by the President's Commission. Understanding how the definition of learning disability has evolved provides context for how learning disability is defined today.

### Definitions of Learning Disability Have Changed

When he spoke to the meeting of parents, professors, and others in Chicago in 1963, Kirk recommended that the group adopt the term *learning disability* to identify the children about whom they were concerned. Kirk argued that the term *learning disability* was the best choice of various alternatives, some of which Kirk said referred to causes of problems (e.g., such as the terms *brain injury* or *minimal brain dysfunction*) or that referred to behavioral manifestations of the problems (e.g., the terms *hyperkinetic behavior* or *perceptual disorder*). Kirk said that the term *learning disability* placed the emphasis on problems that could be assessed and changed. The group followed Kirk's recommendation and formed an organization called the Association for Children with Learning Disabilities (ACLD). This group later renamed itself the Association for Children and Adults with Learning Disabilities and, most recently, the Learning Disabilities Association of America (LDA). Consisting of both parents and professionals, LDA is the major organizational voice for parents of children with learning disabilities.

Although Kirk is often said to have coined the term *learning disability* in his speech to the people who would form the ACLD, the term had been used earlier (Hodges & Balow, 1961; Kirk & Bateman, 1962; Thelander, Phelps, & Walton, 1958). In the 1962 edition of his influential introductory text on exceptional children, Kirk defined learning disability as follows:

> A learning disability refers to a retardation, disorder, or delayed development in one or more of the processes of speech, language, reading, writing, arithmetic, or other school subject resulting from a psychological handicap caused by a possible cerebral dysfunction and/or emotional or behavioral disturbances. It is not the result of mental retardation, sensory deprivation, or cultural and instructional factors. (Kirk, 1962, p. 263)

Five components in Kirk's definition have appeared in many of the definitions that followed it:

1. subaverage achievement (reading, writing, arithmetic) or achievement-related behavior (speech or language)
2. intra-individual differences—the possibility that the subaverage achievement or achievement-related behavior occurs in only one or some areas, with average or above-average achievement in the other areas
3. reference to *psychological processing problems* as causal factors or at least as correlated factors
4. suggestion of *cerebral dysfunction* as a possible causal factor
5. exclusion of other disabling conditions (e.g., *mental retardation*) and environmental conditions as causal factors.

As various groups and individuals grappled with defining learning disability, other components emerged, too. These included:

1. life-span problems—the idea that learning disabilities persist into adulthood
2. social relations problems—that learning disability may also affect behavior in social situations and even that social problems may be a form of learning disability
3. *comorbidity*—the possibility that learning disabilities may occur in combination with other conditions or individual attributes (especially giftedness or serious emotional disturbance).

Kirk's initial definition of learning disability was the first of many efforts to define the phenomenon, with subsequent definitions changing the emphasis on one or another of the components and adding or omitting components. Table 1.1 (pages 14–15) lists a few of the many definitions that have been offered since Kirk's early effort to define the term and shows how each definition emphasized different components.

**TABLE 1.1** Definitions of Learning Disabilities and Their Common and Unique Features

| | |
|---|---|
| Kirk (1962, p. 263) | A learning disability refers to a retardation, disorder, or delayed development in one or more of the processes of speech, language, reading, writing, arithmetic, or other school subject resulting from a psychological handicap caused by a possible cerebral dysfunction and/or emotional or behavioral disturbances. It is not the result of mental retardation, sensory deprivation, or cultural and instructional factors. |
| Bateman (1965, p. 220) | Children who have learning disorders are those who manifest an educationally significant discrepancy between their estimated intellectual potential and actual level of performance related to basic disorders in the learning process, which may or may not be accompanied by demonstrable central nervous system dysfunction and which are not secondary to generalized mental retardation, educational or cultural deprivation, severe emotional disturbance, or sensory loss. |
| NACHC (U.S. Office of Education, 1968, p. 3) | Children with special (specific) learning disabilities exhibit a disorder in one or more of the basic psychological processes involved in understanding or in using spoken and written language. These may be manifested in disorders of listening, thinking, talking, reading, writing, spelling or arithmetic. They include conditions which have been referred to as perceptual handicaps, brain injury, minimal brain dysfunction, dyslexia, developmental aphasia, etc. They do not include learning problems that are due primarily to visual, hearing or motor handicaps, to mental retardation, emotional disturbance, or to environmental disadvantage. |
| 94–142 (U.S. Office of Education, 1977, p. 65083) | The term "specific learning disability" means a disorder in one or more of the basic psychological processes involved in understanding or in using language, spoken or written, which may manifest itself in an imperfect ability to listen, speak, read, write, spell, or to do mathematical calculations. The term includes such conditions as perceptual handicaps, brain injury, minimal brain dysfunction, dyslexia and developmental aphasia. The term does not include children who have learning disabilities which are primarily the result of visual, hearing, or motor handicaps, or mental retardation, or emotional disturbance, or of environmental, cultural, or economic disadvantage. |
| NJCLD (Hammill, Leigh, McNutt, & Larsen, 1981) | "Learning disabilities" is a generic term that refers to a heterogeneous group of disorders manifested by significant difficulties in the acquisition and use of listening, speaking, reading, writing, reasoning, or mathematical abilities. These disorders are intrinsic to the individual and presumed to be due to central nervous system dysfunction. Even though a learning disability may occur concomitantly with other handicapping conditions (e.g., sensory impairment, mental retardation, social and emotional disturbance) or environmental influences (e.g., cultural differences, insufficient-inappropriate instruction, psychogenic factors), it is not the direct result of those conditions or influences. |
| LDA (Association for Children with Learning Disabilities, 1986, p. 15) | Specific Learning Disabilities is a chronic condition of presumed neurological origin which selectively interferes with the development, integration, and/or demonstration of verbal and/or nonverbal abilities. Specific Learning Disabilities exists as a distinct handicapping condition and varies in its manifestations and in degree of severity. Throughout life, the condition can affect self-esteem, education, vocation, socialization, and/or daily living activities. |

TABLE 1.1  Continued

IDEA (Individuals with Disabilities Education Act Amendments of 1997, Sec. 602(26), p. 13)

A. IN GENERAL—The term "specific learning disability" means a disorder in one or more of the basic psychological processes involved in understanding or in using language, spoken or written, which disorder may manifest itself in imperfect ability to listen, think, speak, read, write, spell, or do mathematical calculations.

B. DISORDERS INCLUDED—Such term includes such conditions as perceptual disabilities, brain injury, minimal brain dysfunction, dyslexia, and developmental aphasia.

C. DISORDERS NOT INCLUDED—Such term does not include a learning problem that is primarily the result of visual, hearing, or motor disabilities, of mental retardation, of emotional disturbance, or of environmental, cultural, or economic disadvantage.

| Definition | Subaverage Achievement | Intra-individual Differences | Process Deficits | CNS Dysfunction | Discrepancy | Exclusion of Other Disabilities | Life-span Problem |
|---|---|---|---|---|---|---|---|
| Kirk | • | • | • | • |  | • |  |
| Bateman | • | • | • | • | • | • |  |
| NACHC | • | • | • |  |  | • |  |
| 94–142 | • | • | • |  |  | • |  |
| NJCLD | • |  |  | • |  |  |  |
| LDA | • | • | • | • |  |  | • |
| IDEA | • | • | • |  |  | • |  |

The upper panel shows the definitions, with a label for each. The lower panel shows which components appeared in each labeled definition. Following is a brief discussion of the important aspects identified in definitions of learning disabilities:

*Achievement Deficits*  From the beginning of interest in learning disabilities, there has been an emphasis on problems in achievement. As a hallmark of learning disabilities, achievement deficits are important, but not all students who have low achievement necessarily have learning disabilities. Some students with other disabilities, especially emotional or behavior disorders and mental retardation, have below-average achievement. However, it very unlikely that a student with above-average achievement would be identified as having a learning disability. (We discuss achievement problems in almost every chapter of this book.)

*Intra-individual Differences*  A student may have especially marked achievement deficits in only one or in multiple areas. This aspect of learning disability distinguishes it from mental retardation, in which one would expect lowered performance across the range of academic areas. Some people regard intra-individual differences as related to ability and achievement, postulating an **ability-achievement discrepancy** (an idea discussed more fully in a subsequent section). We discuss

Council for Exceptional Children

**CEC Knowledge Check**
What point is unique to the Bateman definition? How has this definition affected the identification of students with learning disabilities? CC1K1

**ability-achievement discrepancy**  the discrepancy between a person's potential for achievement based on intellectual ability and his or her actual achievement

intra-individual differences in many chapters, especially those having to do with eligibility and identification (Chapter 3) and the academic areas (Chapters 11 through 14).

***Psychological Processing Problems*** The concept of psychological processes dominated discussions in the 1960s and 1970s. Early authorities in learning disabilities believed that certain deficits in how children received, organized, and expressed auditory (verbal) and visual information were closely related to their learning problems and might even be at the root of those problems. Because these deficits were hard to assess reliably and because improving children's performance on them rarely resulted in improved achievement, the idea of processes was controversial and ultimately discarded (Hallahan & Cruickshank, 1973; Mann, 1979). More recently, however, educators have come to understand that there are precursor skills for some areas of academic achievement that appear very similar to some of the psychological processes discussed in the early days of learning disabilities. For example, *phonemic awareness,* which is often considered a psychological process, is important in reading and spelling (Torgesen, 2002a). We discuss some of the modern processes of importance in the chapters about cognitive, metacognitive, and motivational problems (Chapter 8) and the academic areas (Chapters 11 through 14).

***Neurological Deficits*** Throughout the history of learning disabilities, authorities have grappled with the idea that the behavioral problems referred to in Kirk's definition are, in fact, the consequence of minor variations in neurological functioning. The idea is appealing because we know that conditions with identifiable neurological bases, such as cerebral palsy, often are accompanied by anomalies in learning and behavior. However, until recently, scientists have not been able to measure subtle neurological differences consistently. Furthermore, were those differences actually found to cause learning disabilities, there would probably be few implications for teaching. We examine the important role of neurological deficits in learning disabilities in the chapter on causes of learning disabilities (Chapter 2).

***Exclusion*** When the field of learning disabilities was emerging in the 1960s, there was strong pressure to distinguish it from other already-recognized disabilities. Parents and others wanted to make it clear that children's problems were not the result of other handicapping conditions. These children did not have mental retardation, emotional disturbance, cerebral palsy, or other problems. They had academic underachievement that could not be explained by other disabilities (Kavale, 2002). As a result, many definitions of learning disabilities incorporated phrasing that defined learning disability by excluding other problems. For some authorities (e.g., Henley, Ramsey, & Algozzine, 1996), a definition by exclusion was unacceptable, and this became a reason to doubt whether learning disabilities were real problems.

***Life-span Problems*** Most early efforts in the area of learning disabilities were focused on preventing learning problems in young children, but many in the field came to recognize that even though prevention was an important goal, it was not practiced (Kauffman, 1999). Furthermore, some students' disabilities did not become obvious until they were older. For example, Shannon's attention problems probably were masked during her first few years of school by an absence of requirements for self-sustained attention and then, during her middle elementary years, by the fact that her teacher used highly engaging techniques of instruction so that her attention problems were mitigated. But will she have attention problems as an adult? Some accounts indicate that despite successful remedial instruction, individuals with learning disabilities continue to have problems as adults (Reiff, Gerber, & Ginsberg, 1997). In addition, some children who have no obvious problems prior to school entry turn out to have learning disabilities. We discuss the problems of individuals with learning disabilities outside of the usual K–12 schooling period in Chapters 5 and 6.

 Shannon

**Social Relations Problems**  Because of the emphasis on academic problems in learning disabilities, related problems in social relations were often overlooked. As it happens, such problems often are related. Early on, Bryan (1974a, b) showed that many individuals with learning disabilities were both less popular than their peers and communicated in ways that provoked enmity from them. As a result, we have come to understand that some students with learning disabilities may lack the social graces to permit them to relate with their peers and others (Wong & Donahue, 2002). Thus, many authorities now contend that the definition of learning disabilities should include problems in social relations. We address social-emotional problems in Chapter 7 and also in Chapter 11, where we discuss verbal language problems.

**Comorbidity**  When two problems or disabilities occur together in the same person, they are said to be *comorbid.* Given the emphasis on academic problems in learning disabilities, some might expect that learning disabilities would not overlap with other disabilities. This is not the case. Some children have disabilities in only one academic area, but others have problems in more than one area (e.g., Fuchs & Fuchs, 2002). This was the situation for Shannon when she was in elementary school, but instruction focused more strongly on correcting her problems in reading than in arithmetic. Furthermore, students with learning disabilities may have other handicapping conditions as well; this was also the case with Shannon, who had attention deficit hyperactivity disorder. Also, authorities in gifted education have discussed the potential for students with exceptional talents to have learning disabilities (Brody & Mills, 1997). The topic of comorbidity reappears in later chapters on social behavior (Chapter 7) and attention and ADHD (Chapter 9). All of these factors have affected how learning disabilities have been defined in the past and have profound influences on how learning disabilities are defined now.

### Today's Definition of Learning Disability

In 2000, the U.S. Department of Education Office of Special Education Programs (OSEP) convened a group of 18 educators to reexamine the problem of defining learning disabilities with the purpose of providing a basis for future legislation. The focus of the meeting was to commission a set of papers on issues related to the definition of learning disabilities and to plan a later meeting. The issues addressed included detailed treatments of historical perspectives, classification approaches, ability-achievement discrepancy, and other topics. In August 2001, OSEP invited authors of the papers, authors of responses to the papers, and representatives of organizations and agencies interested in learning disabilities to a meeting on learning disabilities called "Building a Foundation for the Future" (also known as the "LD Summit"). After the summit, a subgroup of researchers met and developed consensus statements about selected issues. In one of those statements, the group reaffirmed the concept of learning disabilities.

Council for Exceptional Children

**CEC Knowledge Check**

Develop your own definition of learning disabilities; include the five major points from Kirk's definition as well as other issues.

CC1S1, LD1K5

> Strong converging evidence supports the validity of the concept of specific learning disabilities (SLD). The evidence is particularly impressive because it converges across different indicators and methodologies. The central concept of SLD involves disorders of learning and cognition that are intrinsic to the individual. SLD are specific in the sense that these disorders each significantly affect a relatively narrow range of academic and performance outcomes. SLD may occur in combination with other disabling conditions, but they are not due primarily to other conditions, such as mental retardation, behavioral disturbance, lack of opportunities to learn, or primary sensory deficits. (Bradley et al., 2002, p. 792)

U.S. federal and state legislation has influenced learning disabilities in many ways, and major laws have had substantial effects on today's definition of learning disabilities (Martin, Martin, & Terman, 1996). Table 1.2 shows many of the major laws and their relation to the definition of learning disabilities. As shown in the table, in 2003–2004 the U.S. Congress debated the fundamental law governing special education. Congress considered leaving the formal definition essentially unchanged. However, Congress proposed that the U.S. Department of Education Office of Special Education and Rehabilitative Services (OSERS) test alternative ways to identify students with learning disabilities. The legislators proposed this action because of intense controversy over the issue about whether a discrepancy between children's ability and their achievement is an appropriate basis for deciding if a student should receive special education services.

## Discrepancy between Ability and Achievement Is Controversial

Given the historical importance of unexpected underachievement in defining learning disabilities, it may seem surprising that there is controversy about the concept of a discrepancy between ability and achievement and the use of such discrepancy in identifying who is eligible for special education (Hallahan & Mercer, 2002; Kavale, 2002). However, the topic has been widely discussed, especially since the 1980s.

### Concerns about the Concept of Discrepancy

Researchers have pointed to at least four problems inherent in the ability-achievement discrepancy concept. First, the concept of ability, as measured by intelligence tests, is fraught with problems. Disputes regarding the definition and measurement

## TABLE 1.2   Legislative Milestones Affecting Learning Disabilities

| YEAR | LAW | NAME | FEATURES |
|---|---|---|---|
| 1975 | PL 94-142 | Education for All Handicapped Children Act | Mandated a free, appropriate public education (FAPE) for all children, including those with learning disabilities; provided for Individual Education Plans (IEPs); ensured due process rights; provided a funding mechanism. |
| 1983 | PL 98-199 | Education of the Handicapped Act (amendments) | Reauthorized the act, changing its name slightly, and established special projects in transition to work, early childhood, and support of parents. |
| 1986 | PL 99-457 | Education of the Handicapped Act (amendments) | Extended the time for early intervention, making special education services available to preschoolers. |
| 1990 | PL 101-476 | Individuals with Disabilities Education Act (IDEA) | Amended EHA and changed its name. Also required that assistive technology and transition plans be part of educational plans and added other areas of disability to the list of those recognized by the U.S. federal government. |
| 1992 | PL 102-119 | Individuals with Disabilities Education Act (amendments) | Reauthorized the law and placed even greater emphasis on early intervention for preschool children. |
| 1997 | PL 105-17 | IDEA Amendments of 1997 | Reauthorized the law and increased influence of parents. |
| 2004 | pending | Improving Education Results for Children with Disabilities Act | Allow determination of eligibility through mechanisms such as response to scientific, research-based intervention. |
| | | | Require that IEPs contain statements of measurable annual goals and how progress toward them will be measured rather than benchmarks or short-term objectives. |

of intelligence have been characteristic of the field since Alfred Binet constructed the first IQ test at the beginning of the 20th century. Issues surrounding the concept of intelligence have increased in intensity over the years. As one researcher put it, "The decision to base the definition of a reading disability on a discrepancy with measured IQ is . . . nothing short of astounding. Certainly one would be hard-pressed to find a concept more controversial than intelligence in all of psychology" (Stanovich, 1989, p. 487). And as others have stated:

It seems unfortunate that the LD field has placed so much emphasis on intelligence in attempting to define LD. The concept of intelligence, itself, is fraught with difficulties, and they become magnified when applied to LD. Intelligence is not as fundamental to LD as has been believed. The LD concept needs to be examined in its own right, not built on another extant, but shaky, concept. Despite its longer history, and the comfort of its familiarity, intelligence is a relatively minor player in the complex

Council for
Exceptional
Children

**CEC Knowledge Check**
What do you think is the most important federal special education law? Why?
LD1K3, LD1K4

amalgam of what is termed *LD*. It seems appropriate that the alliance be broken and the LD field begin to seek its own identity. (Kavale & Forness, 1995a, p. 186)

One of the problems with intelligence tests (and many achievement tests, too) is that they focus on the end product of learning (Meltzer, 1994). These tests provide a score but provide little information on what processes and strategies the individual taking the test used or did not use to arrive at that score. Some students may get the right answer for the wrong reason—they follow a mistaken rule that accidentally leads to the correct answer.

Second, some researchers have pointed out that the intelligence of students with learning disabilities may be underestimated by IQ tests because, to a certain extent, IQ depends on achievement (Siegel, 1989; Stanovich, 1989). In part, intelligence tests assess what a person has learned in comparison to what others have learned by a similar age. If IQ is used when determining a discrepancy, then one is basically comparing one form of achievement test to another form of achievement test.

**Matthew effect**  the idea that the rich get richer while the poor get poorer; for example, in reading, students who develop reading skills early will have an advantage in learning about the world and will, therefore, do better on tests of intelligence

Most people have come to accept the idea of a **Matthew effect.** A Matthew effect refers to the idea of the rich getting richer and the poor getting poorer. Those who know more are able to learn more in the future. (It is derived from Matthew XXV:29 in the Bible: "For unto every one that hath shall be given, and he shall have abundance; but from him that hath not shall be taken away even that which he hath.") With reference to intelligence, a Matthew effect dictates that students who are better readers will have a better chance to learn from what they read than will poor readers, because better readers will not be laboring with the decoding aspects of reading. They will have more time to expand their vocabularies and comprehend more complex concepts, which will result in their better performance on intelligence tests (Stanovich, 1986). The implication for learning disabilities is that the poor reading skills of children with disabilities may lead to poorer performance on intelligence tests; their resulting lower IQs will reduce the discrepancy between IQ and achievement, making it more difficult for them to qualify as having a learning disability.

Third, discrepancies between IQ and achievement, once considered a hallmark of learning disabilities, may not reliably discriminate among students identified as having learning disabilities and similar students who have not been identified as having learning disabilities (Fletcher et al., 2002). Comparisons of students with discrepancies between IQ and achievement (i.e., average IQ and low achievement in reading) and those poor readers who do not have discrepant achievement and IQ (i.e., lower IQ and low achievement in reading) show that they lack similar skills in early reading. Both groups need to learn the same skills (discussed in Chapter 12), regardless of whether they had IQ-achievement discrepancies (Fletcher, Francis, Rourke, Shaywitz, & Shaywitz, 1992; Fletcher et al., 1994; Fletcher et al., 2002; Pennington, Gilger, Olson, & DeFries, 1992; Stanovich & Siegel, 1994). At best, results comparing the two groups are mixed. Furthermore, research on one of the most important skills for learning to read—phonemic awareness (see Chapter 12)—has found the two groups to be more similar than different (Stanovich & Siegel, 1994).

Fourth, using a discrepancy makes it difficult to identify students in the early grades as having a learning disability, because they are not yet old enough to have demonstrated a discrepancy (Kavale, 2002; Mather & Roberts, 1994; Sawyer & Bernstein, 2002). Some authorities in learning disabilities call this a "wait-to-fail model," because children must suffer through months or even years of problems before they can be found eligible for special education. In the first grade, for example, the average child has only begun to master the rudiments of reading and math. In the case of a first-grader such as Jamal, who is smart but has academic problems, the problems may be obvious. But for children who have average or even slightly below-average IQs, the narrow range between where they should be and where they actually are functioning makes it difficult to establish a discrepancy. Some teachers are concerned that even when they are sure a student has a learning disability, they must wait until the next year for the child to score low enough in achievement.

**Council for Exceptional Children**

**CEC Knowledge Check**

How have theoretical objections of discrepancy contributed to the formation of special education and to issues in the field, especially nondiscriminatory referral and assessment? CC1K1, CC1K6, LD1K1, LD1K2, LD1K4

## Concerns about the Methods for Establishing a Discrepancy

Professionals have used various methods to determine a discrepancy between ability and achievement. For many years, they used a very simple method of comparing the mental age obtained from an IQ test to the grade-age equivalent taken from a standardized achievement test. A difference of two years between the two test results was frequently used as an indicator of a discrepancy. This method has largely been abandoned because, for one thing, there are statistical problems in computing grade-equivalent scores. Furthermore, two years below grade level is not an equally serious discrepancy at every grade level. For example, a child who tests two years below grade 8 has a less severe deficit than one who tests two years below grade 4.

As an alternative, some local education agencies (LEAs) compare standard scores. Standard scores have a mean of 100 and a standard deviation of 15, so a standard score of 85 would be one standard deviation below the average. Most IQs are standard scores, and most achievement tests yield a standard score, too. So, for example, if an LEA's rules say that to be identified as having a learning disability, there must be a discrepancy of 22 standard score points, then a student with an IQ of 103 would have to have a standard score of 81 in some area to qualify. Comparing standard scores avoids the problems of using grade equivalents but does not avoid other problems with relying on discrepancy. For example, there is no objective standard for how large a discrepancy must be to establish learning disability. Also, directly comparing standard scores still involves tying learning disability to the questionable construct of IQ.

Table 1.3 (page 22) shows selected scores for Jamal and Shannon. Shannon's full-scale IQ (FSIQ—the measure usually used in comparing standard scores) of 94 may not qualify her for services when compared to her score of 83 in math, her lowest area of achievement. Jamal's FSIQ is high enough that his reading score would be considered discrepant by many LEAs.

 Jamal

 Shannon

Beginning in the late 1970s and early 1980s, many state education agencies (SEAs) and LEAs began to adopt different formulas for identifying IQ-achievement discrepancies. Most of the early formulas were statistically flawed, however. They did not take into account the strong statistical relationship between tested IQ and tested achievement. The U.S. federal government even proposed a formula in the

| TABLE 1.3 | Examples of Scores Illustrating Ability-Achievement Discrepancy | |
|---|---|---|
| STUDENT | IQ | LOWEST ACHIEVEMENT STANDARD SCORE (AREA) |
| Jamal | 105 | 90 (reading) |
| Shannon | 94 | 83 (mathematics) |

**Council for Exceptional Children**

**CEC Knowledge Check**

Why do you think using discrepancy formulas can be of ethical concern?
CC8K2, CC8S6

rules for implementing PL 94-142, but it was immediately criticized and abandoned (Lloyd, Sabatino, Miller, & Miller, 1977). Some have advocated the use of formulas that correct for the relationship between IQ and achievement; these are referred to as *regression-based discrepancy formulas.*

On the surface, regression-based formulas appear objective and professional, but they have problems as well. They still use IQ, require that some arbitrary cutoff score be set, and encourage people to make what are nuanced, human decisions solely on a statistical basis. For these and other reasons, many have questioned the wisdom of using even statistically adequate formulas (Board of Trustees of the Council for Learning Disabilities, 1986).

### Consensus about Discrepancy

Overall, researchers appear to have reservations, although not unanimous reservations, about the usefulness of discrepancy (Fletcher et al., 2002; Kavale, 2002; Speece & Shekitka, 2002, Scruggs & Mastropieri, 2002). Even when OSEP convened the LD Summit to reexamine the problem of defining learning disabilities, the issue of discrepancy was the one area on which there was a divided opinion among the experts.

> Today there is considerable disagreement among practitioners and researchers alike on the usefulness of the discrepancy approach. Although many IDEA stakeholders in the field reject the use of the discrepancy approach because it does not identify the students they believe are in most need of services, many others continue to depend on psychometric tests as a way of corroborating their clinical judgment. The majority of researchers [attending the consensus meeting] agreed that use of IQ tests is neither necessary nor sufficient as a means of classifying students with SLD. However, a minority viewpoint cautioned that the field of SLD could be compromised by eliminating the discrepancy approach because it may be an appropriate marker for unexpected underachievement, which is one measure of SLD. (Bradley et al., 2002, p. 797)

The concept of discrepancy has provided a foundation for learning disabilities throughout most of the brief history of the area of study, and given its historical place in the fabric of learning disabilities, discrepancy will always be a part of the concept of learning disability. Although it does not formally appear in recent or current definitions of learning disabilities, the concept of discrepancy is still familiar and intuitively sensible to many teachers of students who need special education services. The idea of unexpected underachievement serves to distinguish learning disabilities from mental retardation. For these reasons, it is likely that the concept of discrepancy will continue to be associated with learning disabilities.

## Criteria Used to Determine Eligibility for Special Education Vary

The criteria used in determining eligibility for special education are perhaps more important than the definition itself. Formal definitions are often the work of scholars and thus may be more academic and less applicable than definitions needed by practitioners. Practitioners, in contrast, apply rules, guidelines, criteria, and definitions flexibly so that they can meet the needs of individual students or the policies of their agencies.

The majority of states use a definition based on the U.S. federal definition. Though the definition does not explicitly mandate use of discrepancy, states have historically adopted criteria that refer to an ability-achievement discrepancy (Mercer, Jordan, Allsopp, & Mercer, 1996). In the United States, because education is primarily a function of state governments rather than the federal government, rules developed by state educational agencies are usually implemented by local education agencies. To be sure, state rules often are based on federal rules, allowing states to receive federal funds, but states can write their own criteria for determining eligibility.

The exact mechanisms used for identification have varied from state to state and are often quite detailed. To illustrate, Iowa published a 52-page, single-spaced document describing procedures to be used in determining eligibility (Learning Disability Study Group, 1997). Wisconsin provided explicit directions for computing a grade score to be used in determining whether a severe discrepancy exits (Wisconsin Department of Public Instruction, 2002). With the changes in U.S. laws, these mechanisms will be in flux for several years after 2004.

Researchers have examined the way that state and local educational agencies determine whether students are eligible for special education because of learning disabilities. A teacher's decision to refer a student for eligibility assessment—as Ms. Hamilton referred Jamal—is a critical step in the process (Gerber & Semmel, 1984; Ysseldyke, Algozzine, & Epps, 1983; Zigmond, 1993). When a general education teacher considers a student hard to teach, this makes it clear that there is a problem.

Jamal

Teachers usually attempt to solve learning problems prior to recommending a formal evaluation for eligibility. Jamal's teacher informally tested alternative methods to address his problems with important prereading skills. ("We've already tried some things," Ms. Hamilton told Mrs. Smith. "We gave him extra reading time and some special attention, but that hasn't taken care of things. He still didn't take off.") If the general education teacher has already tried prereferral interventions, the probability of a disability becomes even greater.

When instruction usually available in general education classrooms is not sufficient and simple supplements have not solved learning problems, schools often use more formal ways of addressing the situation. Since at least the late 1970s, schools have sought ways of serving students with learning disabilities without having to identify them as needing special services, often by providing special interventions prior to beginning the referral that leads to evaluation and then to a decision about eligibility (e.g., Chalfant, Pysh, & Moultrie, 1979). The concept of intervening prior to referral appeals to many. When it works, it provides a simple solution to problems, builds competence in general education, prevents a student from being labeled as having a disability, and reduces expenses for evaluation and special education.

Over the years, efforts to intervene early have been known by different terms: *child-study team, consultative teacher model, prereferral intervention, teacher assistance team.* These approaches presume that lesser learning problems can be differentiated from learning disabilities by making adjustments in the general education environment. In the late 1990s and early 2000s, updated versions of these approaches were discussed extensively by authorities in learning disabilities (Gresham, 2002; Fuchs & Fuchs, 1998; McNamara & Hollinger, 1997, 2002; Marston, 2002; Sheridan, Welch, & Orme, 1996; Thomas & Grimes, 1995; Vaughn & Fuchs, 2003). When it considered excusing schools from using discrepancy in determining eligibility, the U.S. Congress recommended more extensive study of an even more formal method of prereferral intervention called "responsiveness to intervention."

### Responsiveness to Intervention

There are two broad approaches that authorities in learning disabilities have discussed under the label of *responsiveness to intervention* (or responsiveness to treatment) (Fuchs, Mock, Morgan, & Young, 2002). One of these approaches emphasizes a consultation process in which teams of educators collaborate to identify ways of solving problems experienced by individual children (e.g., Gresham, 2002). The plans these teams develop are implemented and monitored, and if these plans do not work, then students are evaluated for eligibility for special education. The second approach emphasizes provision of a standard curriculum, with supplemental instruction for students who do not respond to the main curriculum. For students who still struggle after receiving supplemental instruction, referral for special education evaluation is the next stage, with the possibility that these students will be found eligible. Although we return to the details of such administrative plans in Chapter 3 on eligibility, we illustrate them here to help explain some of the controversies in learning disabilities.

**Behavioral Consultation**   The first approach—*behavioral consultation*—draws heavily on approaches that have been advocated since the 1970s (e.g., Chalfant et al., 1979; Heron & Catera, 1980) and for which preliminary research support was weak (Lloyd, Cawley, Kohler, & Strain, 1988). In these approaches, schools (1) identify students who are struggling, (2) provide different degrees of specialized instruction within the education situation, and (3) monitor these students' progress before and after they receive specialized instruction. If specialized instruction works (based on comparison of progress before and after the onset of that instruction), then these students continue to receive instruction under the general educational model prevailing in their school. If that instruction does not work, then the school may develop a new plan for even more specialized instruction or may initiate evaluation for special education. Some advocates of this approach place greater emphasis on form-

Council for
Exceptional
Children

**CEC Knowledge Check**
What relationship exits between special education and the organization and function of educational agencies?
CC1K3, LD1K1, LD1K2

ing consultative relationships among general and special educators, but others place more emphasis on modifications of curricula and instruction (Gresham, 2002; McNamara & Hollinger, 1997; Sheridan, Eagle, Cowan, & Mickelson, 2001).

Advocates of the behavioral consultation approach contend that it permits delivery of instruction that is expressly tailored to students' needs but does not require that they be labeled as having learning disabilities. One of the foundations of this approach is assessing students' performance on tasks closely related to the curriculum and assessing it frequently and objectively—a method frequently called *curriculum-based assessment* or *curriculum-based measurement;* curriculum-based measurement has well-documented advantages (Fuchs & Fuchs, 1986). According to advocates, another advantage is that only those students who do not respond to treatment after one or more specialized interventions are evaluated for eligibility, with the result that fewer students are identified as having learning disabilities and thus more are spared the possible stigma of having a label. Advocates also suggest that officially designating fewer students as having learning disabilities will save money (see McNamara & Hollinger, 1997; Sheridan et al., 2002).

***Standardized Protocol*** Whereas the behavioral consultation approach addresses problems across the academic domains and the age span, the second approach— standardizing the protocol or curriculum—operates more from a preventive stance, emphasizing early reading performance. Advocates of a *standardized protocol* are especially concerned about whether young children who have problems in important areas such as phonological processing (the kinds of problems that Jamal was experiencing) might be easily helped before their problems develop into more substantial deficits that can be labeled dyslexia. By the time this happens and they are then eligible for special education services, these students may be too old to have their problems corrected in a timely fashion.

As do their colleagues who support a behavioral consultation model, supporters of the standardized curriculum approach recommend that special education not be provided until after students have fallen through a cascade of less restrictive alternatives. This approach requires that schools adopt curricula that are documented as very effective. A key feature of laws passed in the United States in the early 2000s (for example, "No Child Left Behind" and "Improving Education Results for Children with Disabilities") is that they emphasized "scientifically based reading" instruction. To receive federal funding, state and local education agencies needed to show that kindergarten through third-grade teachers had available and knew how to use curricula that had documented effectiveness and that they would receive help in how to adapt materials and methods to meet the instructional needs of students who were not making adequate progress. Ideally, schools would put into operation the most effective curricula they could find. They would provide a safety net composed of more intensive and supplemental help on specific skills in early reading for those who did not benefit from the main curriculum. For those who continued to fail, there would be the option of special education evaluation.

Critics of the standard curriculum approach have pointed out that it is also a wait-to-fail model. Because some students' problems may be obvious early in their school years, it may be better to establish eligibility right away for them. Jamal's

**CEC Knowledge Check**
What are the positive aspects of using the behavioral consultation model for responsiveness to intervention?
LD1K3, LD1K4, LD1K5

**CEC Knowledge Check**
What are the positive aspects of using the standardized protocol model for responsiveness to intervention?
LD1K3, LD1K4, LD1K5

**Council** for **Exceptional Children**

**CEC Knowledge Check**
What is the main criticism of the standardized protocol model?
LD1K3, LD1K4, LD1K5

general education teacher thought this was true for Jamal, but as you will see in Chapter 3, other school personnel were reluctant to identify him as having a learning disability. Delays raise the chance of continued failure, exacerbating the problems students have. The International Dyslexia Association noted, "Using response-to-instruction as the criterion for identification is hazardous because it may prolong the process of identification and deny needed services to children who are clearly at risk" (Dickman, Hennesy, Moats, Rooney, & Toomey, 2002, p. 17).

The jury is still out about how useful response-to-treatment approaches will prove to be. Whereas these methods have great appeal, we need to know more about their promises and pitfalls (Vaughn & Fuchs, 2003a). Will students who receive these treatments no longer require special assistance? Will many still need later special education? How many will be helped? How many will still require special education? For those who do, will the delay in eligibility be detrimental? These are questions that researchers will study over the next few years.

### Eligibility in Practice

Jamal

Shannon

When a team of professionals meets to decide whether an individual is eligible for special education, the members examine assessment data and reports (such as those for Jamal and Shannon, provided on the Website) to inform their judgment. The team also examines why prereferral interventions that have been used may not have been successful. Research has consistently shown that the procedures used by these teams vary from place to place, are sometimes inconsistent with rules and regulations, and often result in the identification of students as learning disabled who have such low IQs (below 75 and even below 60) that they might reasonably have been considered to have mild or moderate mental retardation (Bocian, Beebe, MacMillan, & Gresham, 1999; Gottlieb, Alter, Gottlieb, & Wishner, 1994; MacMillan, Gresham, Siperstein, & Bocian, 1996; Schrag, 2000).

Evidence such as this has led authorities to question whether the issue of definition is as important as the issue of consistency in criteria used to determine eligibility (MacMillan & Siperstein, 2002; Scruggs & Mastropieri, 2002). Sadly, such questions often become an indictment of practitioners. Educators should not assume that inconsistencies between academic models and practice mean that the practice is wrong and the models are right. The factors that influence the decisions of these different groups are not the same, so we should expect some discrepancy between them (Gerber, 2000).

Another reason for the inconsistencies in definitions of learning disabilities used by researchers and practitioners is that the two groups have different purposes in defining the phenomenon (Lloyd, Hallahan, & Kauffman, 1980; MacMillan & Speece, 1999). Although researchers seek clarity and consistency, teachers and others are confronted with murky and irregular phenomena that demand immediate resolution and do not fall into neat categories.

> The science and practice of learning disabilities appear to be headed in two different directions. Schools serve children as LD who exhibit extremely low achievement and do not necessarily meet IQ-achievement discrepancy standards. Researchers may use sample selection procedures that bear no resemblance to the children served by the

schools, or depend on school-identified samples that vary in unknown ways. In either case, the results of research studies employing either approach to samples have limited external validity for practitioners. (MacMillan & Speece, 1999, pp. 124–125)

Because of changes in U.S. laws, state and local education agencies are revising their procedures for identifying students as having learning disabilities. Some agencies may have adopted more formal response-to-treatment systems, some may continue to use ability-achievement discrepancy methods, and some may depend on the clinical judgment of the members of an eligibility team. Whatever system is in place, it is important for teachers to proceed carefully.

Given all the false starts and contention in learning disabilities, it should be no surprise that problems in the criteria for determining who is eligible for special education because of learning disabilities have led some people to criticize learning disabilities as a manufactured crisis, an illusion. According to this view, learning disabilities is a social construct, a consequence of our social system.

## Learning Disability as a Construct

Many critics have asked whether learning disabilities is a real phenomenon or whether it is instead socially constructed, an outgrowth of the demands, perceptions, values, and judgments of those who are involved with these students (Carrier, 1986; Coles, 1987; Finlan, 1994). One view is that students with learning disabilities are different from most people in ways that are relatively constant across social contexts. In this view, the assumption is that the primary causes of learning disabilities are biological, or neurological. We examine neurological and other possible causes of learning disability in Chapter 2. Another view is that learning disabilities are largely created by social demands and expectations—in other words, constructed by social contexts. In this view the assumption is that the primary causes of learning disabilities are social circumstances, including the demands of schooling and employment.

Few would suggest that the problems we call learning disabilities are entirely a function of either neurological dysfunction or environmental structure and expectations. Virtually all would acknowledge that learning disability is a concept constructed in the social context of the expectations and demands of school, employment, and other aspects of community life and that this concept serves important social and political purposes.

In an extreme view, the act of testing or measuring students' performance brings into existence the problem of learning disabilities. If we did not measure students' performance in such areas as spelling, we would never have to confront the fact that some students spell more accurately—and thus obtain higher scores—than others. If we did not know that some had especially low scores, we would never need to provide them remedial help. Further, if we did not set cutoff points on measures of performance, we would not have to designate students who need help, who have learning disabilities.

People differ substantially in their attitudes about the social criteria chosen for defining learning disabilities. Some think that because the criteria for the definitions

Council for
Exceptional
Children

**CEC Knowledge Check**
How do critics of the learning disabilities field attempt to discredit the labeling of students with learning difficulties?
CC1K1

are arbitrary and can be changed at will, the social construction of the category is indefensible. Others point out that the arbitrary nature of the criteria by which many categories (e.g., citizen, person of voting age, poor, at-risk) are socially constructed cannot be avoided (Kauffman, 1989).

The fact that social and cultural expectations and purposes help shape the definition of learning disabilities has led some to see learning disabilities as an "imaginary disease" (Finlan, 1994) or as a category designed to maintain school programs stratified by race and class (e.g., Sleeter, 1986; see Kavale & Forness, 1987a, for a critique). Although acknowledging that social and political forces are important in defining learning disabilities, others see the social construction of this special education category as overwhelmingly beneficial to the children who are identified, because they can receive important special services with minimal stigma (e.g., Kavale & Forness, 1985; Moats & Lyon, 1993; Singer, 1988; Singer & Butler, 1987). As Moats and Lyon noted, "LD in the United States appears to be a systemic problem: It is an educational category into which children are channeled when the learning-teaching interaction is no longer productive or rewarding for one or both parties" (1993, p. 284). Still others argue that using teacher requests for help with a specific child as the criteria for the need for special education is both reasonable and humane (e.g., Gerber & Semmel, 1984). No doubt controversy will continue to surround the question of how much learning disabilities are a function of social demands and expectations and the social, political, and educational interests that are at play.

## How Many People Have Learning Disabilities?

According to the most recent reports by the U.S. federal government, public schools have identified nearly three million (2,887,217) students ages 6 through 21 as having learning disabilities. Approximately 5.5% of students in the school years (ages 6 to 17) need special education due to learning disabilities (U.S. Department of Education, 2002b). Actually, this percentage is likely a slight underestimate of all cases of learning disabilities, because the numerator consists of the number of students identified by public schools, whereas the denominator includes all persons in the United States, including those in private schools. Because there are undoubtedly students in private schools who have learning disabilities but are not identified as such by the public schools, we can assume that the number in the numerator does not represent all students with learning disabilities.

Since 1976/1977, when the federal government started keeping data on students served in special education, the number of students ages 6 to 21 years identified as having learning disabilities has more than tripled. In addition, those with learning disabilities now represent over half of all students identified as disabled. Figure 1.2 shows the phenomenal growth in the proportion of students with learning disabilities relative to all students with disabilities.

Many authorities have expressed alarm at the rapid growth of students identified as having learning disabilities. Critics claim that learning disabilities is an ill-defined category and includes many students who only need better instruction from

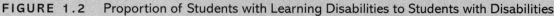

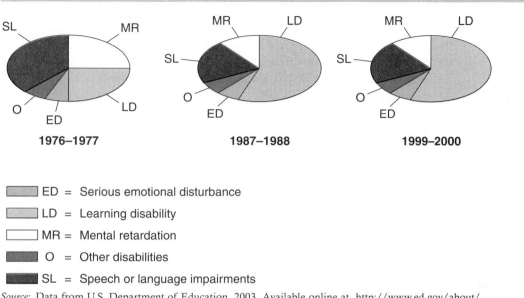

| 1976–1977 | 1987–1988 | 1999–2000 |

ED = Serious emotional disturbance

LD = Learning disability

MR = Mental retardation

O = Other disabilities

SL = Speech or language impairments

*Source:* Data from U.S. Department of Education, 2003. Available online at http://www.ed.gov/about/reports/annual/oesp/

general education teachers (Algozzine & Ysseldyke, 1983; Lyon et al., 2001). Even defenders are concerned that much of this growth is unwarranted and indicative of confusion over definition and diagnostic criteria, especially within the area of mental retardation (Macmillan, Siperstein, & Gresham, 1996). They fear that many children are being misdiagnosed and that the resulting increase in those identified as learning disabled has provided ammunition for critics, thereby jeopardizing services for students who do need help.

Some researchers have indicated that the fact that it is virtually impossible to differentiate between low-achieving students and those classified as having learning disabilities shows that the definition is too loose (e.g., Algozzine & Ysseldyke, 1983; Ysseldyke, Algozzine, Shinn, & McGue, 1982). Others have analyzed the same data and concluded that this is a serious misstatement (Kavale, Fuchs, & Scruggs, 1994). They point out that much of the critics' case is based on the idea that the ability-achievement discrepancy should be used as the most important criterion for classification as learning disabled.

Although it is logical to suspect misdiagnosis as the main cause of the growth of learning disabilities, there is a paucity of research support. Some have noted that the increase in learning disabilities has occurred in almost direct proportion to the decrease in the number of students identified as mentally retarded (Macmillan et al., 1996; see Figure 1.2). These researchers have hypothesized that political and social forces have led to a greater reluctance to identify children as mentally retarded; those children who would formerly have been so labeled are now identified as learning disabled. Helping to bring about this shift in diagnosis was the American Association on Mental Retardation's 1973 decision to change its definition of mental retardation to include an IQ cutoff of about 70 to 75 rather than 85.

Not all professionals consider the increase in prevalence unwarranted. There may be valid reasons for some of the growth (Hallahan, 1992). First, because the field of learning disabilities was relatively new when the federal government started keeping prevalence data in 1976, it may have taken professionals a few years to decide how to place children in this new category. Second, the social-cultural changes that have occurred since 1968 may have heightened children's vulnerability to developing learning disabilities. For example, an increase in poverty has placed more children at risk for biomedical problems, including central nervous system dysfunction (Baumeister, Kupstas, & Klindworth, 1990).

Social and cultural risks exist in addition to biological risks. Families, whether or not in poverty, are experiencing greater degrees of psychological stress. For example, a study of leisure arrived at the following conclusions:

> Americans are starved for time. Since 1969, the annual hours of work of employed Americans have risen markedly—by approximately 140 hours, or more than an additional three weeks. This increase includes both hours on the job and time spent working at home. As a result, leisure, or free time, has declined as well. Increasing numbers of people are finding themselves overworked, stressed out, and heavily taxed by the joint demands of work and family life. (Leete-Guy & Schor, 1992, p. 1)

Stress on parents may result in their being less able to provide the social support necessary to help their children, who themselves are living under an increasing amount of stress. The result may be that children who in a previous time would have gotten by in their schoolwork with a less stressful lifestyle and more support are now experiencing failure.

In addition to the rapid growth in the percentage of students identified as having learning disabilities, there is substantial variation from jurisdiction to jurisdiction in the percentage of students so identified. For example, as shown in Figure 1.3, some states identify about 2% of their students but others identify over 9% of their students as having learning disabilities. One explanation for this variation is that states and localities use different criteria for determining eligibility. Another explanation is that the variation may reflect true differences based, perhaps, on differences in risk factors (environmental toxins, socio-economic status) or quality of preventative services available to families and schools. Probably neither explanation fully accounts for the differences; both factors in combination with other explanations probably are responsible.

Both the growth and variation in the percentage of students identified as having learning disabilities have given fuel to the controversial nature of learning disabilities as an educational category. Another factor that has caused concern is the possibility that some groups—particularly males and children of African American heritage—may be overrepresented among the children identified as having learning disabilities.

**Council for Exceptional Children**

**CEC Knowledge Check**

What factors have caused an increase in the number of students with learning disabilities over the last 30 years? CC1K1, CC1K3

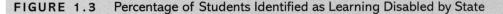

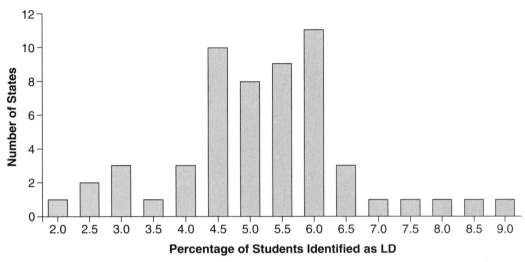

*Note:* Includes other governmental units such as the District of Columbia.

*Source:* Data from U.S. Department of Education, 2003. Available online at http://www.ed.gov/about/reports/annual/oesp/

## Demographics of People with Learning Disabilities

Learning disabilities occur across a wide spectrum of the population—among people of both genders, all ethnic groups, young and old, rich and poor, the socially prominent and the obscure, the socially successful and unsuccessful, those who are admired and those who are reviled, and among those of nearly every conceivable category of human being. As we have already discussed, individuals with learning disabilities are also a very diverse group in terms of the types and degrees of abilities and disabilities they have.

A persistent question about the diversity of students identified as having learning disabilities is whether certain groups are disproportionately represented. For example, are certain groups—students of color, those who are poor, or those of some other group—over- or underrepresented in the population of students with learning disabilities? Likewise, are students of one gender more likely to be identified as learning disabled? And if there is disproportionate representation by ethnicity or gender, is this due to bias or discrimination, or are there reasonable explanations for the disproportionate representation? These questions are not trivial, for if disproportional representation is found to be the result of reprehensible practices that reflect bias or discrimination, then students are being mistreated, and these practices must be corrected. However, if disproportional representation is due to causal factors external to the school, such as poverty and its attendant disadvantages (in the case of ethnic disproportionality) or biological causes (in the case of gender disproportionality), then insisting on strictly proportional representation would be discriminatory in that it would deny appropriate services to students who would otherwise be qualified to receive them, which is another form of mistreatment (see Hallahan & Kauffman, 2003, for further discussion).

### Ethnicity

Educators in the United States do not have conclusive evidence about whether there is disproportional representation of ethnic groups among students with learning disabilities. Whereas there is strong evidence of overrepresentation of African American students in other categories of special education (e.g., mental retardation), the evidence of overrepresentation of certain groups is not strong in learning disabilities (Donovan & Cross, 2002; MacMillan & Reschly, 1998; Oswald, Coutinho, Best, & Singh, 1999). A U.S. government report showed roughly equivalent representation of African Americans and Hispanics in the learning disabilities category. This survey found that the prevalence of learning disabilities in white students, African American students, and Hispanic students was 5.3%, 5.8%, and 5.3%, respectively (U.S. Department of Education, 1996). More recently, the President's Commission on Excellence in Special Education (2002) found no clear evidence for overrepresentation of students from minority groups among those who have learning disabilities. Although U.S. society's concerns often reflect greater concern about other ethnic groups, it is important to note that there is evidence suggesting that Native Americans may be overrepresented in learning disabilities (Donovan & Cross, 2002).

The U.S. federal government provides data about the ethnicity of children receiving special education services. Table 1.4 shows the proportion of children of various ethnic groups according to type of disability. Using for comparison the overall percentage shown in the right-most column, the proportions of children from different ethnic groups who are identified as learning disabled are close to what one would expect. However the proportion of Hispanic children who are identified as learning disabled is about 10% higher than expected.

If educators found clear overrepresentation of some ethnic groups and underrepresentation of other ethnic groups in learning disabilities, they would surely want to know why this occurred. This was the issue examined in an earlier report by the U.S. government on ethnic representation in special education:

> Some have argued that racial discrimination is the culprit. Others have pointed out that professionals, such as school psychologists, are inadequately prepared to assess the capabilities of minority students. These may indeed be factors, but why would Hispanic students be underrepresented in the learning disability category? Furthermore, if racial bias were the sole explanation, how could it account for the fact that African Americans are also overrepresented in categories such as visual impairment and hearing impairment? "[I]t is possible that black youth were more likely than their white counterparts to have experienced poor prenatal, perinatal, or postnatal health care and early childhood nutrition which may have resulted in actual disabilities" (U.S. Department of Education, 1992, p. 15).

Determining whether there is disproportional representation of various ethnic groups among students with learning disabilities is related to the matter of identifi-

Council for
Exceptional
Children

**CEC Knowledge Check**
What are the definition and identification issues in the field of learning disabilities for individuals from culturally diverse backgrounds?
CC1K5

**TABLE 1.4**  Percentage of Students Ages 6 through 21 Served under IDEA by Disability and Race/Ethnicity, during the 2000–2001 School Year

| DISABILITY | AMERICAN INDIAN/ ALASKA NATIVE | ASIAN/ PACIFIC ISLANDER | BLACK (NON-HISPANIC) | HISPANIC | WHITE (NON-HISPANIC) | ALL STUDENTS SERVED |
|---|---|---|---|---|---|---|
| Specific learning disabilities | 56.3 | 43.2 | 45.2 | 60.3 | 48.9 | 50.0 |
| Speech or language impairments | 17.1 | 25.2 | 15.1 | 17.3 | 20.8 | 18.9 |
| Mental retardation | 8.5 | 10.1 | 18.9 | 8.6 | 9.3 | 10.6 |
| Emotional disturbance | 7.5 | 5.3 | 10.7 | 4.5 | 8.0 | 8.2 |
| Multiple disabilities | 2.5 | 2.3 | 1.9 | 1.8 | 1.8 | 2.1 |
| Hearing impairments | 1.1 | 2.9 | 1.0 | 1.5 | 1.2 | 1.2 |
| Orthopedic impairments | 0.8 | 2.0 | 0.9 | 1.4 | 1.4 | 1.3 |
| Other health impairments | 4.1 | 3.9 | 3.7 | 2.8 | 5.9 | 5.1 |
| Visual impairments | 0.4 | 0.8 | 0.4 | 0.5 | 0.5 | 0.4 |
| Autism | 0.6 | 3.4 | 1.2 | 0.9 | 1.4 | 1.4 |
| Deaf-blindness | 0.0 | 0.0 | 0.0 | 0.0 | 0.0 | 0.0 |
| Traumatic brain injury | 0.3 | 0.3 | 0.2 | 0.2 | 0.3 | 0.3 |
| Developmental delay | 0.7 | 0.6 | 0.7 | 0.2 | 0.6 | 0.5 |
| All disabilities | 100.0 | 100.0 | 100.0 | 100.0 | 100.0 | 100.0 |

*Note:* Does not include data for New York State

*Source:* U.S. Department of Education. (2002b) *Twenty-Fourth Annual Report to Congress on the Implementation of the Individuals with Disabilities Education Act.* Washington, DC: U.S. Department of Education, Office of Special Education Programs. Page II-22

cation of students as having learning disabilities. One might suspect that changing the criteria for eligibility might alter the ratio of students from different ethnic groups who are identified, but changes in the criteria for eligibility apparently do not equalize the proportion of white and African American students identified (Colarusso, Keel, & Dangel, 2001).

Even though students from different ethnic groups may not be disproportionaly identified as having learning disabilities, there is also the possibility that they may be treated differently within the system of special education. It might be that children with Hispanic heritage might have IEPs that are systematically different than children of African American or European American heritage. As shown in the Multicultural Considerations box on page 34, the measurement practices of school psychologists may not take into account children's ethnic backgrounds. Or, perhaps, students with learning disabilities who have one ethnic background are more likely to receive most of their schooling in the educational mainstream than other students with learning disabilities. We have only preliminary evidence on this

Council for Exceptional Children

**CEC Knowledge Check**
How do culturally and linguistically diverse backgrounds influence the definition and identification of learning disabilities?
CC1K5

## Are School Psychologists Adequately Trained to Assess Ethnically Diverse Students?

The school psychologist often plays a critical role on the team of professionals determining the eligibility of students for special education services. Scores obtained on standardized achievement and ability tests, administered and interpreted by a school psychologist, can often make the difference between a student being identified as having a learning disability or not. Unfortunately, some school psychologists are not prepared to make valid assessments in the case of children from ethnically diverse backgrounds. For example, 83% of school psychologists surveyed described their training as less than adequate to assess culturally and linguistically diverse students (Ochoa, Rivera, & Ford, 1997).

There is additional evidence that this lack of training leaves school psychologists at a loss considering cultural and linguistic issues in their testing. Researchers asked 671 school psychologists who had conducted assessments of bilingual children and children with limited English proficiency (LEP) the following open-ended question: "As a school psychologist, what criteria/standards do you use to rule out environmental, cultural, economic disadvantaged factors when determining LD eligibility when a LEP or bilingual student displays a severe discrepancy between intelligence and achievement or between grade levels?" (Ochoa, Rivera, & Powell, 1997). The results were extremely disappointing from a multicultural perspective. Few school psychologists said they considered the length of time or the number of years the student had lived in the United States, the home language of the student, or the student's performance in comparison with other bilingual and LEP students. None took into account the educational level of the parents or the level of literacy in the home.

The open-ended nature of the questionnaire may have underestimated the actual degree to which school psychologists take into account cultural and linguistic factors when doing their assessments. Perhaps they were not able to recall all the variables they consider when interpreting their tests. If given a questionnaire listing a variety of factors, perhaps more of them would have stated that they use the factors listed. Nonetheless, it is perplexing that so few school psychologists readily identified what should be obvious mitigating cultural and linguistic factors.

Council for
Exceptional
Children

**CEC Knowledge Check**

What is the result of not taking cultural and linguistic factors into consideration when assessing students for eligibility? Assess your own cultural bias. Is there any possibility that you could make the same mistake when assessing students for eligibility?
CC1K5, CC1K8, CC1K10, CC9K1

matter, and it indicates that although there are clear patterns showing that some students receive special education in more restrictive settings than other students, the pattern has to do with other variables (e.g., how substantial children's problems are), not with the children's ethnic background (Hosp & Reschly, 2002).

### Gender

Since the earliest days of the field of learning disabilities, researchers and practitioners have noted a disproportionate number of boys identified as having learning disabilities. Some studies have found that boys so identified outnumber girls by about 3 or 4 to 1. Data collected by the federal government are only for ages 13 to 21 years, but they are essentially in agreement with other studies in finding that 73% of students identified as having learning disabilities are males (U.S. Department of Education, 1992). However, recent data from the Special Education Elementary Longitudinal Study show that in first through eighth grade, boys outnumber girls about 2 to 1 in learning disabilities (Wagner, Marder, Blackorby, & Cardoso, 2002).

The evidence showing overrepresentation of boys has prompted authorities to seek explanations for the apparent difference. Some authorities have pointed to the possibility of greater biological vulnerability for boys as an explanation for this gender difference. Boys are at greater risk than girls for a variety of biological abnormalities, and their infant mortality rate is higher than that of girls.

Other authorities have raised the issue of possible bias in referral and assessment procedures, suggesting that boys might be more likely to be referred because they are more likely to exhibit behaviors that are bothersome to teachers, such as hyperactivity. Research results on gender bias are mixed. One team of investigators found no evidence of gender bias (Clarizio & Phillips, 1986). But researchers in two other studies concluded that their data showed a bias toward identifying more males as having learning disabilities (Leinhardt, Seewald, & Zigmond, 1982; Shaywitz, Shaywitz, Fletcher, & Escobar, 1990). However, more boys than girls are identified as having disabilities even among infants and toddlers and across most categories of disabilities, so the high proportion of boys among students with learning disabilities cannot be solely the result of bias in identification (Hebbeler et al., 2001; Wagner et al., 2002).

Shaywitz et al. (1990) compared a sample of students identified by schools as reading disabled to an epidemiological sample on the discrepancies between IQ and reading achievement. The children in the latter sample were part of a longitudinal study in which virtually all children entering kindergarten in target schools were identified for testing. The ratio of boys to girls was about 4 to 1 in the school-identified sample, but it was about 1 to 1 in the epidemiological sample. Shaywitz et al. also found that, in contrast to the epidemiological sample, the school-identified group exhibited more behavior problems than a control group of nondisabled students. One possible criticism of this study is that the researchers relied solely on a discrepancy between ability and achievement to arrive at a diagnosis of "true" reading disability.

More research is needed about whether the greater number of males identified for learning disabilities is due to bias. The findings of Shaywitz et al. (1990) are provocative, especially the data showing that school-identified students with reading disabilities show a greater degree of behavioral problems that might prompt teachers to refer them for testing in order to get them out of their classrooms. Our best guess at this point is that some bias does exist, but that the biological vulnerability of males also plays a role. For example, the federal government's figures indicate that all disabilities are more prevalent in males, including conditions that are difficult to imagine as resulting from referral or assessment bias, such as hearing impairment (53% are males), orthopedic impairment (54% are males), and visual impairment (56% are males) (U.S. Department of Education, 1992).

## Association with Other Disabilities

Once an individual is said to have a particular disability, the great temptation is to assume that the label we have chosen summarizes all of the difficulties or tells us what the problem really is. In fact, it is possible for people to have a combination of disabilities and special talents. Historically, every field of disability has sought

Council for
Exceptional
Children

**CEC Knowledge Check**

Do you think educators and other school professionals should be held responsible for gender inequity within the learning disability label as part of the referral process? If so, how might this be accomplished? CC1K4, LD1K4

Council for
Exceptional
Children

**CEC Knowledge Check**

What etiological factors contribute to the increasing numbers of children labeled learning disabled? Could this be related to medical or neurobiological coexisting factors? If so, how? What might be the educational implications? LD2K1, LD2K2, LD3K1

diagnostic purity—clear distinctions between a particular disability and all other categories. But that diagnostic purity has routinely proven elusive.

Research on disabilities of all kinds, including learning disabilities, has shown that they often come in multiples; that is, some involve more than one disability. Some authorities have estimated, for example, that about half of children who meet the criteria for one disability diagnosis also meet those for one or more other disorders (de Mesquita & Gilliam, 1994; Rosenberg, 1997). When one or more disabilities occur in the same person, they are referred to as **comorbid conditions.**

**comorbid conditions**
two or more conditions (diseases, disabilities) occurring at the same time in a person

Comorbidity is often due to at least two factors. First, causal agents are frequently not particular about what part of the human organism they attack. For example, if a fetus does not have enough oxygen during birth (if the umbilical cord becomes wrapped around the neck and cuts off the oxygen supply), the result can be brain damage. It is virtually impossible to predict whether this damage will be localized or widespread. The more widespread, the more likely the child will have more than one disability. Second, the human organism is extremely complex and is made up of a seemingly infinite number of interrelated functions. When one function is affected, others are also likely to be altered. For example, when there is a hearing impairment, speech is likely to be affected. When there is attention deficit hyperactivity disorder, off-task behavior during instruction may result in a learning disability.

Learning disabilities can co-occur with virtually any other disability as well as with giftedness. Two of the most common conditions that occur concomitantly with learning disabilities are attention deficit hyperactivity disorder and serious emotional disturbance, or behavior disorders. In each case, it is often difficult to determine whether one condition is causing the other or whether each occurs independently. Researchers are just beginning to address the many issues of comorbidity and learning disabilities. (A special issue of *Journal of Learning Disabilities* was devoted to this topic. See Rosenberg, 1997.)

## Who Works with People Who Have Learning Disabilities?

There are over 350,000 special education teachers in the United States, and a significant portion of them work with students who have learning disabilities (U.S. Department of Education, 2002b). Because most students with learning disabilities spend a significant portion of their school time in general education classrooms, they also are of concern to teachers in the elementary grades as well as secondary school teachers who specialize in specific subject areas.

Although it is easy to think of learning disabilities as the domain of educators, a diverse array of professionals is concerned with learning disabilities. For this reason, it is often the case that teachers and parents have contact with people from many disciplines outside of education.

In their day-to-day work, teachers are likely to see not just other teachers and administrators, but also speech-language pathologists and even occupational or physical therapists. From time to time, they may have contact with psychologists, attorneys, pediatricians, social workers, and many others.

Researchers concerned with learning disabilities also come from a similarly diverse group of professions. Studies and articles about learning disabilities appear in the journals of educators of many stripes (special, general, reading, physical, preschool, and postsecondary). In addition, physicians, speech pathologists, audiologists, psychologists, and others also conduct and report research about students with learning disabilities.

Because learning disabilities are primarily apparent in educational settings, we consider educators' roles to be the most important professional roles in the field. Nevertheless, it is important for educators, especially special educators, to know at least foundational concepts in other areas so that they can draw relevant concepts from those disciplines, help parents understand those concepts, and communicate clearly with representatives of those other disciplines. Our concern about understanding relevant concepts is manifested in our discussion in later chapters, such as those on the causes of learning disabilities, the problems of learning disabilities outside the K–12 grades, and so forth.

## Can Learning Disabilities Be Overcome?

People naturally want to prevent disabilities, hope for a cure for any disability, or at least an intervention that will minimize it so they are not handicapped in ordinary life activities. These are core concepts in prevention (see the Current Trends and Issues box on page 38). If the disability involves academic learning and social behavior—things that seem to be under voluntary control and to the average person seem easily learned—then hope is redoubled that proper remedial training can make these difficulties disappear. Of all the various disabilities, therefore, learning disabilities are most vulnerable to the often-mistaken assumption that they can be cured, that they will not last a lifetime.

The early years of research and intervention in nearly every category of disability have been characterized by a search for and claims of a cure or something very near it. In fact, promoters of numerous interventions for almost every disability have claimed that their approach produces nearly miraculous effects, but these claims cannot be substantiated by careful scientific research. The strength of the appeal of these claims is in large measure a result of people's desire to avoid confronting a developmental disability that will persist over the individual's life span. The field of learning disabilities has had its share of excessive claims and quack treatments (Worrall, 1990). Students with disabilities should not be subjected to untested and potentially harmful practices.

### A Critical Need for Effective Teaching

Although learning disabilities cannot be overcome in the sense of being cured, persons with learning disabilities can learn strategies that greatly diminish their disabilities' negative impact—perhaps as exemplified by the renowned individuals discussed earlier. And great strides have been made in developing instructional methods since, for example, the pioneering efforts of Cruickshank, Strauss, and

## Prevention

One of the first questions many people ask about learning disabilities, as with other conditions including medical and psychological disorders, is whether the problems students experience could have been prevented. Prevention is an attractive concept because it holds the promise of benefits, not just for the individuals who experience the disorders, but also for others close to the individual (e.g., family members) and society in general (e.g., a reduction of costs for later services). Thus, few people would oppose efforts to prevent learning disabilities. As attractive as it is, however, prevention is difficult to accomplish and uncommon in special education (Kauffman, 1997; Pianta, 1990).

Authorities in most areas discuss three different levels of prevention: primary, secondary, and tertiary.

### Primary Prevention: Keep It from Happening.

Primary prevention efforts are usually aimed at promoting desirable future outcomes in virtually all of the population of individuals who may or may not develop the problem or disorder. For example, in hopes of preventing disease and early death, physicians encourage people to lead healthy lifestyles—to eat healthy foods, exercise, avoid risky behaviors such as smoking, wear seat belts, and so forth. Similarly, public health officials recommend that communities add fluoride to drinking water supplies in hopes of preventing or lessening tooth decay. By analogy, education should apply the most effective instructional practices available in hopes of preventing learning disabilities.

Such reasoning was part of the driving force behind the U.S. federal government's funding of the Reading First program (http://www.ed.gov/offices/OESE/readingfirst/). The Reading First program (and Early Reading First, too) aimed to provide support to state education agencies for making grants to local education agencies so that the LEAs could obtain instructional materials and supplies as well as inservice for teachers so that they could teach reading based on high-quality research about effective reading instruction.

Primary prevention does not always work, however. Sometimes the preventive measures are not applied faithfully or sufficiently. Or sometimes some people respond to the preventive measures but others are disposed to the condition and they will "get it" no matter what is done.

This does not mean that we should not attempt primary prevention efforts, as they may still keep many from suffering the consequences of the condition. Later chapters in this book describe the most effective methods of teaching in general education that can help prevent many students' learning disabilities.

### Secondary Prevention: Catch It Early and Stop It Right Away.

Secondary prevention efforts focus on early detection of problems and then on stopping or slowing the progress of the condition. In medicine, routine screenings for prostate or breast cancer are examples of early detection efforts. Physicians believe that if they catch the cancer early, they can treat it and prevent subsequent problems.

In education, schools often test students with simple screening measures to identify those learners who may have problems. For example, the state of Virginia has a Phonological Awareness and Literacy Screening program in which teachers assess nearly all children in the primary grades to identify those who are most at risk of failing in the early stages of reading; schools receive extra funds to provide supplemental instruction in hopes of preventing later reading problems (Invernizzi, Meier, Juel, & Swank, 1997). In this book we shall introduce you to powerful methods of screening and early intervention for learning disabilities.

### Tertiary Prevention: Treat It Aggressively and Minimize the Consequences.

Tertiary prevention aims to reduce or stop an existing problem or condition from getting worse. When people have diabetes, for example, they must control their diet, exercise, and administer insulin (either as a pill or injection). If people with diabetes do not take such steps, they may have periods of shock or even have limbs amputated. Tertiary prevention is equivalent to treatment or intervention.

When students have learning disabilities, they already have clearly established problems. If they have been in schools providing primary or secondary prevention (or both), they probably have very serious problems. They must receive instruction that corrects for the imbalance in their skills and that uses the most effective intervention methods available. In this book, you will learn about those methods.

their colleagues (cf. Cruickshank, Bentsen, Ratzeburg, & Tannhauser, 1961; Werner & Strauss, 1941; see Weiss & Lloyd, 2001), whose interventions consisted largely of controlling extraneous stimuli and providing a reliable structure of routines.

Researchers have been devising and refining instructional procedures that are more effective than earlier strategies. Among the major approaches we discuss in subsequent chapters are *cognitive training* (which includes procedures such as self-monitoring or self-instruction), *mnemonics* (which includes the use of key words and other ways of assisting memory), *Direct Instruction* (which includes careful sequences of instruction, rapid and frequent responding, and immediate feedback and correction of errors), *metacomprehension training* (which provides students with strategies for thinking about remembering the major points in the material being read), and *scaffolded instruction* (which includes gradual reduction of assistance and reciprocal teaching). Although they vary in the specific skills taught and how they are related to the curriculum areas being taught, these approaches are all systematic procedures for teaching task-approach skills to students with learning disabilities so they can apply these skills in their actual academic situations.

Still, special education for students with learning disabilities will need to have certain features. As Zigmond described it,

> [It] is, first and foremost, instruction focused on individual need. It is carefully planned. It is intensive, urgent, relentless, and goal directed. It is empirically supported practice, drawn from research. To provide special education means to set priorities and select carefully what needs to be taught. It means teaching something special and teaching it in a special way. To provide special education means using the techniques and procedures described by Howell and Davidson [1997] for defining the special education curriculum appropriate for each student that will be designated on the annual IEP. To provide special education means monitoring each student's progress in the manner described by Deno [1997], and taking responsibility for changing instruction when the monitoring data indicate that sufficient progress is not being made. (1997, pp. 384–385)

We believe that special educators must provide instruction based on the very best research available. The instruction that special educators provide must be adapted to meet the individual needs of their students. In this book, we do not advocate a "learning disabilities program." We recommend an approach to serving individuals with learning disabilities that is based on making sure that students initially receive the most effective instruction available and that those who are not progressing according to reasonably accepted criteria under those conditions are then eligible for additional services—possibly prereferral services and, at least, special education services that are "intensive, urgent, relentless, and goal directed" (Zigmond, 1997, p. 384).

## Learning Disabilities Are Life-Span Problems

There is increasing evidence that learning disabilities are truly developmental and not curable in the sense that a disease or unfortunate life circumstance might be.

**CEC Knowledge Check**

Of the three levels of prevention, which will teachers of students with learning disabilities most often use? Which do you think would be the most cost-effective? Which might provide the most optimal student outcomes? CC1K1, CC1K4

**CEC Knowledge Check**

What is the ultimate goal in teaching the five strategic learning methods to students with learning disabilities? CC4S1

There is diminishing support for the assumption that with proper intervention, learning disabilities can be reduced from a true developmental disability to a passing inconvenience. Nevertheless, the myth persists that most children with learning disabilities will outgrow these disabilities as adults. In fact, learning disabilities tend to endure into adulthood. Most successful adults who had learning disabilities as children continue to have specific difficulties, must learn strategies to cope with their problems, and must show extraordinary perseverance (Reiff et al., 1997).

This book is about how teachers and others concerned about students with learning disabilities can develop an understanding of learning disabilities as a field of study. Although they may not be readily recognized in the early years, learning disabilities extend across the life span. They are closely associated with bioneurological differences among people, and they may manifest themselves in one or more areas of human endeavor, including cognition, attention, social behavior and related social factors such as self-concept, language, and—especially—academic learning. As the field has matured, researchers have built a strong body of evidence showing that effective methods can address these problems. Teachers and others can help individuals with learning disabilities achieve at levels that allow them to live satisfying and fulfilling lives.

**Council for Exceptional Children**

**CEC Content Standards**

1. Foundations
2. Development and Characteristics of Learners
3. Individual Learning Differences
9. Professional and Ethical Practice

## PORTFOLIO-BUILDING ACTIVITY

### Demonstrating Mastery of the CEC Standards

Applying the information you have learned in Chapter 1, you can begin to develop your own personal perspective of the special education/learning disabilities field. This perspective will grow and develop as you engage in further study. Compose an initial draft of your Personal Philosophy of Special Education paper that addresses the following:

- What are the historical theories, who are the major contributors, and what are the relevant federal laws underlying the field of learning disabilities?

- How do these theories interact with the dynamic development of the learning disabilities definitions over time?

- What has been and will be the impact of these definitions on legal, ethical, and education policies and procedures?

- What are the issues of definition relative to personal society, family, culture, and label bias?

- Do you understand and how do you respect the heterogeneity of label characteristics in terms of development and lifelong effects?

# SUMMARY

### Why is it important to understand learning disabilities?

- Most teachers will have students with learning disabilities.
- Understanding learning disabilities helps understand normal learning.
- Many individuals with learning disabilities can contribute valuably to society.

### Why are learning disabilities controversial?

- Defining learning disabilities has been and continues to be difficult.
- Discrepancy between ability and achievement, a difference often used to characterize learning disabilities, has been controversial.
- The criteria used to identify students as eligible for special education because of learning disabilities have varied greatly and may have been applied inconsistently.
- Learning disability is a construct rather than a clear entity.

### How many people have learning disabilities?

- More than 5% of the U.S. school-age population are identified as having learning disabilities, and this represents about half of all students who are identified as needing special education.

- Although males are more likely to be identified as having learning disabilities than females, students with learning disabilities come from all ethnic backgrounds, ages, and social groups.
- Learning disabilities sometimes co-occur with other problems and disabilities.

### Who works with people who have learning disabilities?

- School personnel other than special education teachers work with students with learning disabilities. These people include general education teachers, psychologists, and other specialists.
- Professionals from outside the schools (e.g., pediatricians) are also concerned with learning disabilities.

### Can leaning disabilities be overcome?

- There are no simple remedies or easy cures for learning disabilities.
- Although their problems cannot be eliminated, given powerful instruction, students with learning disabilities can learn most skills and subjects.
- Learning disabilities are usually life-span problems. Most adults who had learning disabilities as children continue to experience some problems later in their lives.

## REFLECTIONS ON THE CASES

1. Jamal's mother remarked that she would have to learn a lot about learning disabilities. How much do you think people in the general public know about learning disabilities? What misconceptions might people in the general public have about learning disabilities?

2. Shannon's mother said she gave "all the credit" to Shannon's first special education teacher. How accountable do you think general education teachers should be for the progress of their students? Should there be different levels of accountability when teachers teach students who have learning disabilities?

3. Do you think it was wise for Ms. Hamilton, Jamal's first-grade teacher, to advocate strongly for Jamal receiving special education services? Should she have done something else?

4. Shannon expressed concern about being able to use a calculator and to have extra time to complete tests on mathematics. Is it fair for some, but not all, students to have such accommodations?

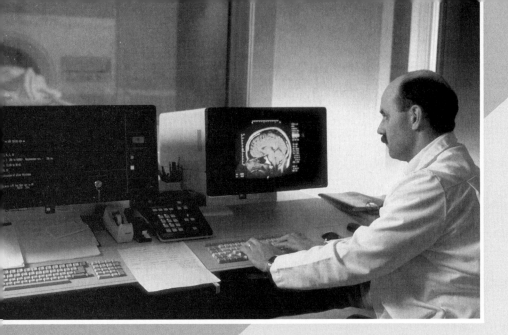

## What Causes Learning Disabilities?
- Historical Context
- Reluctance to Accept Neurological Causes
- Toward an Acceptance of Neurological Causes

## How Does the Brain Function?
- Neurons Send and Receive Messages
- Different Parts of the Brain Have Different Functions
- Left and Right Hemispheres

## How Can We Infer Neurological Dysfunction?
- Postmortem Studies
- Neuroimaging Studies
- Right-Hemisphere Brain Dysfunction

## What Factors Contribute to Neurological Dysfunction?
- Hereditary Factors
- Teratogenic Factors
- Medical Factors
- Environmental Factors

## What Should Educators Keep in Mind Regarding Causes?

**Council for Exceptional Children**

See Companion Website for detailed correlations between chapter content and Council for Exceptional Children Standards; **www.ablongman.com/ hallahanLD3e**

### CEC Knowledge and Skills Discussed in This Chapter

**1** The physiological causes of learning disabilities.

**2** The effects a learning disability can have on an individual's life.

**3** Communication about the causes of learning disabilities with the families and individuals who have been labeled with learning disabilities.

**4** How the foundational philosophies and learning disability theories inform identification, curriculum development, and educational practices.

# Causes of Learning Disabilities

Jamal's dad, who died a few years ago, had lots of trouble in school. I remember him telling me how he could do pretty well in subjects as long they didn't require a lot of reading. The school people weren't really on the ball, so he didn't get much help. Finally, one of his teachers, I think it was in middle school, got him referred. Come to find out he had dyslexia. So when Jamal started having trouble in reading I wondered whether he'd gotten it from his father. I asked the special education teacher. Sure enough, she said reading problems can be inherited. But there's no real test to tell for sure. She also said that there's a pretty good chance that his problems are due to some kind of dysfunction in his brain.

*Irene Smith, Jamal's mother*

One of the most frustrating things plaguing the field of learning disabilities since its inception is the question of **etiology**—that is, what causes learning disabilities. The field was founded on the premise that there is a neurological basis to learning disabilities. But much of the early work was based on clinical guesswork because of the relatively unsophisticated techniques being used to measure neurological status back in the 1960s and 1970s. Much preliminary work in this area was speculative, so many professionals were skeptical about the validity of claims that learning disabilities were the result of neurological problems. By the early 1990s, the picture began to change as researchers developed more and more sophisticated computerized imaging techniques and other methods that could detect brain abnormalities with reasonable reliability. Today, most authorities subscribe to the view that learning disabilities emanate from some kind of differences in brain structure or functioning, and the most widely used definitions suggest that the causes are neurological rather than environmental.

**etiology** cause of a disability or abnormal condition

Current research also suggests that learning disabilities can be inherited. This does not mean that a parent with learning disabilities is guaranteed to have offspring with learning disabilities. But it does mean that a child of a parent with learning disabilities does run some risk of also having learning disabilities. Just how much risk there is scientists are not yet able to say. Neither, as Jamal's special education teacher said to Jamal's mother (see the opening quote), are they able to say for sure that the learning disability is inherited. There are still many unanswered questions regarding causes of learning disabilities. But as you will soon see, researchers have made substantial progress in pinning down causal factors since the early days of the field.

## What Causes Learning Disabilities?

### Historical Context

**neurological dysfunction** a condition wherein a person's behavior (e.g., learning, attention, and so forth) is affected by abnormal functioning of the brain; the exact abnormal functioning is as yet poorly understood

**aphasia** a condition that results in problems in speech production and/or comprehension due to an injury to the brain

**dyslexia** severe impairment in the ability to read that is generally thought to be due to neurological factors

**word blindness** a term used at the beginning of the 20th century (but no longer in use) to describe persons with severe reading impairment

One reason for a presumption of **neurological dysfunction** in learning disabilities is that there is often no other plausible explanation for the child's failure to learn. Another reason is that the field emerged gradually from the work of physicians who identified symptoms of known brain injury that were in many respects similar to the behavior of people who had learning disabilities but who did not have confirmed damage to their brains.

When neurology and ophthalmology were developing as medical specialties in the 19th and early 20th centuries, physicians began describing problems in understanding and using spoken and written language that were associated with damage to specific areas of the brain. Pierre Paul Broca and Carl Wernicke were 19th-century European physicians who identified particular areas of the brain that control speaking and understanding spoken language. Their work laid the foundation for understanding the speech and language problems termed **aphasia.** Other late 19th- and early 20th-century physicians researched reading disabilities that they called **dyslexia,** a term introduced by German ophthalmologist R. Berlin, or **word blindness,** a phrase invented by Scottish ophthalmologist James Hinshelwood at the beginning of the 20th century.

Another neurologist who had an important influence on the development of learning disabilities and the presumption of neurological dysfunction was Samuel Orton. He believed that reading disability was a result of mixed dominance of the cerebral hemispheres—meaning that neither side of the brain was clearly in control—which led to a breakdown in perceptual-motor abilities (Orton, 1937). He theorized that mixed dominance was inherited and led to perceptual reversals (e.g., reading "was" for "saw").

Although Orton's theory of mixed dominance has since been disproved, his educational theories have led to the development of systematic instructional procedures in reading, spelling, and handwriting (Gillingham & Stillman, 1965), and his work lives on in the International Dyslexia Association. His theories also influenced speech-language and hearing specialists such as Katrina de Hirsch and Helmer Myklebust, whose methods were prominent in the 1960s and 1970s (de Hirsch, Jansky, & Langford, 1966; Johnson & Myklebust, 1967; Myklebust, 1973).

Council for Exceptional Children

**CEC Knowledge Check**

The historical foundations of the field of learning disabilities fall into three basic philosophical camps: disorders of spoken and written language, disorders of perceptual-motor process, and disorders of speech-language and hearing. Who are additional major contributors in each of these perspectives? LD1K1, LD1K2

### Reluctance to Accept Neurological Causes

Even though many of today's professionals believe that learning disabilities are neurologically based and even though the most popular definitions of learning disabilities reflect a neurological basis for learning disabilities, the field was originally slow to embrace neurological dysfunction as a viable causal factor. There were at least two reasons why researchers and practitioners may have been skeptical about a neurological basis for learning disabilities: (1) the questionable accuracy of early neurological measures and (2) the emphasis on behaviorism and environmentalism.

## Problems of Inaccurate Measurement of Neurological Dysfunction

Many authorities rightfully questioned the reliability and validity of the standard tests neurologists used to diagnose neurological dysfunction in children with learning disabilities because in the 1960s and 1970s these tools were relatively crude. For example, in both research and clinical practice, neurologists still relied heavily upon the measurement of **soft neurological signs,** largely behavioral indices such as poor balance, poor visual-perceptual skills, poor fine motor coordination, distractibility, and clumsiness. Although these signs are prevalent in people with obvious cases of brain injury, they are not always accurate indicators of more subtle cases of brain dysfunction—the kind of cases that are likely to be learning disabled.

## Emphasis on Behaviorism and Environmentalism

A second reason professionals were hesitant to look to neurology for answers to causal questions was the popularity of behaviorism and environmentalism in the social sciences in the 1960s and 1970s (Pinker, 2002). **Behaviorism** is a philosophical orientation to psychology that stresses the study of observable behaviors instead of nonobservable mental events. It is closely linked to learning theory, which postulates that all behavior is learned and is shaped by rewards and punishments.

Intimately tied to behaviorism and learning theory, **environmentalism** holds that one's learning environment is crucial to psychological development. The 1960s was the heyday of the environmentalist position in child psychology relative to causes of learning and personality development. Several researchers contributed to the dominance of the environmentalist position. In 1961, J. McVicker Hunt published *Intelligence and Experience,* in which he reviewed several studies, many on lower animals, which demonstrated the devastating impact that lack of experiences could have on development. In this same vein, Rosenzweig (1966) published an influential study comparing rats placed in stimulus-"enriched" cages (e.g., numerous paraphernalia for exploratory activity) with those placed in cages devoid of stimuli. He found differential effects on brain structure and chemistry in that the former had thicker cortexes and more acetylcholine, a chemical important for learning.

With the optimism created by environmentalists, social scientists pushed for early intervention programs designed to reverse the negative effects of poverty on the intellectual development of young children. For example, Head Start, aimed at providing health and educational services for preschoolers from impoverished backgrounds, was instituted as part of President Lyndon Johnson's War on Poverty.

Some professionals used the behaviorists' and environmentalists' positions to point to another possible cause of learning disabilities in children—poor teaching, sometimes referred to as "dyspedagogia" (*dys* = poor, *pedagogia* = teaching) (Cohen, 1971). Researchers pointed out that teachers often spend an appallingly low percentage of their time actually engaged in reading instruction and that this and other poor instructional practices over a period of years can result in students developing learning disabilities.

**soft neurological signs** behavioral indicators of neurological dysfunction, such as poor balance, poor visual-perceptual skills, and distractibility; although often present in persons with documented brain injury, these signs do not always mean a person has brain injury or brain dysfunction

**behaviorism** a theoretical approach that stresses the importance of observing and measuring observable behaviors rather than nonobservable mental events; closely linked to learning theory and environmentalism

**environmentalism** a theoretical approach that posits that what individuals encounter in their environment determines what they learn and how they behave

Council for Exceptional Children

**CEC Knowledge Check**
In your words, define the "nature etiology" and "nurture etiology" of learning disabilities.
CC1K1, LD1K1, LD2K1

## Toward an Acceptance of Neurological Causes

Several factors have helped make professionals generally more favorably inclined toward neurological explanations of learning disabilities, chiefly the decrease in the popularity of behaviorism and environmentalism and the increase in the utility of neurological measures.

### Decrease in Popularity of Behaviorism and Environmentalism

Although many authorities still think that behaviorism is an important theoretical position, several have swung to a more cognitive perspective (see Schulz, 1994). Cognitive psychologists recognize nonobservable thought processes as legitimate for scientific inquiry. And more and more cognitive psychologists are blending their work with that of neurologists, making connections between thought processes in the brain and their neurological underpinnings (Pinker, 2002). Similarly, although environmentalism is still seen as a viable position by most working in the fields of education and psychology, some of the unbridled optimism of its early proponents has been tempered by the less than overwhelmingly positive results of early intervention programs. Intervening to remedy the devastating effects of poverty on child development has proved more difficult than was at first assumed. The disillusionment with behaviorism and environmentalism as causal explanations of learning problems has thus left a void that work in the neurological arena has started to fill.

### Technological Advances in Neurological Research

Probably the major reason professionals are now more persuaded that neurological dysfunction is a viable causal factor in many cases of learning disabilities is the advances in neurological research. Starting in the late 1980s, neurological researchers began to make substantial progress in identifying neurological factors as underlying learning disabilities. Much of this progress has been due to advances in computerized neurological measures. Such techniques as **magnetic resonance imaging (MRI), positron emission tomography (PET-scan),** and **functional magnetic resonance imaging (fMRI)** have expanded the area of brain research. (See the Today's Technology box on page 47.) Although expense has thus far kept these techniques from being widely used to diagnose individual cases of learning disabilities in clinical practice, they have allowed researchers to begin to build a case for the importance of neurological dysfunction in many cases of learning disabilities. Before discussing the use of these procedures to determine neurological causes of learning disabilities, we present the basic anatomy of the brain and some of the functions performed by its major parts.

## How Does the Brain Function?

### Neurons Send and Receive Messages

Neurons are the most important cells in the human nervous system, being responsible for sending and receiving information in the brain. Most **neurons** consist of

**magnetic resonance imaging (MRI)** a neuroimaging technique that uses radio waves to produce cross-sectional images of the brain

**positron emission tomography (PET-scan)** a computerized method for measuring blood flow in the brain; during a cognitive task, a low amount of radioactive dye is injected in the brain; the dye collects into active neurons, indicating which areas of the brain are active

**functional magnetic resonance imaging (fMRI)** an adaptation of the MRI (magnetic resonance imaging) used to detect changes in the brain while it is in an active state that, unlike the PET-scan, does not involve the use of radioactive materials

**neurons** brain cells responsible for sending and receiving information

**soma** the cell body, composed of the nucleus and material that supports the functioning of the neuron

**dendrites** treelike projections of the neuron that receive messages from the environment and other neurons

TODAY'S TECHNOLOGY

FOR LEARNING DISABILITIES

## Computerized Imaging and the Brain

A number of recent technological advances in X-ray techniques and computers allow researchers and clinicians to obtain better images of the living brain. Three such techniques are magnetic resonance imaging, positron emission tomography, and functional magnetic resonance imaging.

### Magnetic Resonance Imaging

In magnetic resonance imaging (MRI), a scanner sends a strong magnetic field through the head. The magnetic field causes changes in the orientation of hydrogen atoms, which are detected by the scanner. Because various neural structures contain different amounts of hydrogen, the scanner detects these differences and uses these data to formulate photographs of slices of the brain.

### Positron Emission Tomography

Whereas an MRI is usually used with people when they are at rest, positron emission tomography (PET-scan) can be used to take pictures of the brain while a person is engaged in various activities. It is thus a way of viewing the brain in an active state. PET-scans detect changes in metabolic activity in various parts of the brain. The person is usually injected with a substance of low radioactivity that is similar to glucose. Along with blood, the substance collects in active brain neurons and can be detected by a scanner. While the person performs a task, such as reading or memorizing, the PET-scan can detect which areas of the brain are activated because the radioactive substance is transported to them.

### Functional Magnetic Resonance Imaging

Like the PET-scan, functional magnetic resonance imaging (fMRI) can be used to detect changes in the brain while it is in an active state. With the fMRI, one can record the metabolism of the brain as a person engages in a cognitive task. Unlike the PET-scan, the fMRI has the advantage of not involving the use of radioactive materials.

---

four structures: (1) the cell body, or soma, (2) dendrites, (3) the axon, and (4) terminal buttons. These structures allow neurons to communicate with one another (Pinel, 2000).

The **soma** contains the nucleus and material that supports the functioning of the neuron. **Dendrites** are treelike projections that receive messages from the environment (e.g., sights, sounds, smells) or from other neurons. They receive messages from other neurons through the other neurons' axon and terminal buttons. The **axon** is a long, tubelike extension of the neuron that carries messages to the dendrites of other neurons. These electrical-chemical messages are transported from the axon to the dendrites via **terminal buttons**—buttonlike structures that secrete chemicals (**neurotransmitters**) into the **synapse,** a small gap between the axon and the dendrite. The axon is covered and insulated by a **myelin sheath,** a fatty tissue. The particular neurotransmitter secreted helps determine whether a neuron will receive the message from another neuron and then send it to other neurons. Figure 2.1 (page 48) presents an overview of how electrical-chemical messages are carried from one neuron to another over the synapse.

Our explanation of neuronal communication is brief and necessarily simplified. The fact that scientists have estimated that there are over 60 trillion synapses in the human brain makes the study of the structure and function of neurons extremely complicated (Shepard & Koch, 1990).

**axon** a long, tubelike extension of the neuron that carries messages to the dendrites of other neurons

**terminal buttons** buttonlike structures at the end of the axon that secrete a neurotransmitter into the synapse

**neurotransmitters** chemicals secreted by the terminal buttons that transport electrical-chemical messages from the axon to the dendrites of neurons; the particular neurotransmitter secreted helps determine how neurons send and receive messages

**synapse** a small gap between the axon and the dendrite

**myelin sheath** a fatty tissue that covers and insulates axons

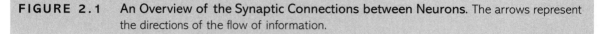

**FIGURE 2.1**  An Overview of the Synaptic Connections between Neurons. The arrows represent the directions of the flow of information.

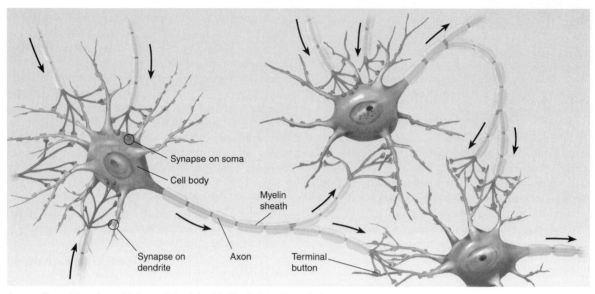

*Source:* From *Physiology of Behavior,* 7th ed. (p. 30, Fig. 2.4) by N. R. Carlson, 2001, Boston: Allyn and Bacon. Copyright © 2001 by Pearson Education. Reprinted by permission of the publisher.

## Different Parts of the Brain Have Different Functions

Neurologists have identified several areas of the brain they think are responsible for different functions (e.g., sensory, motor, language, cognition, and emotion). But because of the brain's complexity, neuroscientists do not always agree on the specificity of some of these brain-behavior connections. Not only is there sometimes disagreement about whether a certain behavior is controlled by one or another part of the brain, but there can also be dispute about whether one or several parts of the brain are implicated. Furthermore, one part of the brain can take over certain functions for a damaged portion of the brain. Because of these disagreements, we present only those basic brain-function relationships most neurologists agree upon.

Neurologists commonly refer to the brain as being divided into the brain stem, cerebellum, and cerebral cortex, with the last consisting of four types of lobes: frontal, parietal, occipital, and temporal. The cerebral cortex has a left and a right hemisphere, both of which contain all four kinds of lobes. In other words, there are a left and right frontal lobe, a left and right parietal lobe, and so forth. Figure 2.2A depicts a top view of the brain, showing both hemispheres; Figure 2.2B shows a side view of the left hemisphere, the cerebellum, and the brain stem.

**brain stem**   the part of the brain supporting the cerebral cortex and connecting it to the spinal cord; regulates survival reflexes such as respiration and heart rate

### Brain Stem

The two hemispheres of the cerebral cortex rest on the **brain stem,** which serves as a connection to the spinal cord. The brain stem regulates important survival reflexes such as respiration and heart rate.

FIGURE 2.2

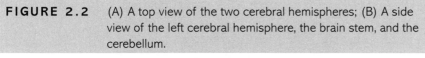

(A) A top view of the two cerebral hemispheres; (B) A side view of the left cerebral hemisphere, the brain stem, and the cerebellum.

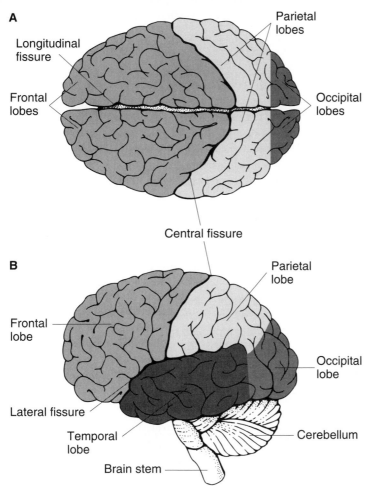

**A**

Longitudinal fissure

Frontal lobes

Parietal lobes

Occipital lobes

Central fissure

**B**

Frontal lobe

Parietal lobe

Occipital lobe

Lateral fissure

Temporal lobe

Cerebellum

Brain stem

*Source:* Adapted from *Biopsychology,* 4th ed. (p. 72, Fig. 3.2) by J. P. J. Pinel, 2000, Boston: Allyn and Bacon. Copyright © 2000 by Pearson Education. Reprinted by permission of the publisher.

## *Cerebellum*

The **cerebellum,** located beneath the cerebral cortex and adjoining the brain stem, is more complex than its size suggests. Though comprising only about 10% of the brain's mass, it contains more than half its neurons (Pinel, 2000). The cerebellum regulates several behaviors having to do with movement (e.g., balance, gait, speech, eye movements). Damage to this area of the brain can result in profound difficulties in controlling a variety of movements. Following is an example of a common test neurologists use to assess functioning of the cerebellum, which you can try:

**cerebellum** the part of the brain below the cerebral cortex next to the brain; regulates several behaviors having to do with movement

Have a friend place his or her finger in front of your face, about three-quarters of an arm's length away. While your friend slowly moves his or her finger around to serve as a moving target, alternately touch your nose and your friend's finger as rapidly as you can. If your cerebellum is normal, you can successfully hit your nose and your friend's finger without too much trouble. People with lateral cerebellar damage have great difficulty; they tend to miss the examiner's hand and poke themselves in the eye. (Carlson, 2001, pp. 266–267)

### Cerebral Cortex

**cerebral cortex** the layer of tissue covering the cerebral hemispheres of the brain; divided into four types of lobes for each hemisphere (frontal, parietal, occipital, and temporal) that regulate motor movements, executive functions, and emotions; bodily sensations and visual perception; visual functions; and attention, memory, and language, respectively

A layer of tissue covering the cerebral hemispheres, the **cerebral cortex** is divided into four types of lobes: frontal, parietal, occipital, and temporal. The cerebral cortex is deeply furrowed (cortex means "bark"), which greatly increases the surface area of the brain. In fact, about two-thirds of the cortex's surface is contained in the creases (Carlson, 2001). The largest grooves are called "fissures." The central fissure divides the frontal lobe from the parietal lobe, and the lateral fissure separates the temporal lobe from the frontal and parietal lobes. (See Figure 2.2A and B.)

### Frontal Lobes of the Cerebral Cortex

**frontal lobes** two lobes located in the front of the brain; responsible for executive functions

Although the **frontal lobes** are responsible for some motor movements, they are perhaps best known for being instrumental in the regulation of one's behavior. Psychologists refer to self-regulation, or the ability to control one's emotions and to problem solve, as being a part of a person's **executive functions.**

**executive functions** the ability to regulate one's behavior through working memory, inner speech, control of emotions and arousal levels, and analysis of problems and communication of problem solutions to others

The first inkling that the frontal lobes play a crucial role in executive functions came from the celebrated case of Phineas Gage, a dynamite worker in the mid 1800s who had a steel rod accidentally propelled through his cheek and out the top of his head, passing through the front part of the frontal lobes (Figure 2.3). Miraculously, Gage survived; however, he suffered serious alterations in personality. He was no longer the industrious, energetic worker he had been before the accident. He was now "childish, irresponsible, and thoughtless of others. He was unable to make or carry out plans, and his actions appeared to be capricious and whimsical" (Carlson, 2001, p. 347).

**prefrontal lobes** the forward part of the frontal lobes that may be implicated in the control of emotions

The front part of the frontal lobes, the **prefrontal lobes,** have also been implicated in the control of emotions. The outmoded prefrontal lobotomy—which severed the connections between the prefrontal lobes and the rest of the brain—was intended as a cure for psychiatric patients who were under severe emotional distress and anguish. Over 40,000 prefrontal lobotomies were performed in the middle part of the 20th century, and its developer was awarded the Nobel Prize in physiology (Pinel, 2000). After several years of careful study, however, researchers concluded that the side effects of prefrontal lobotomies were too devastating, and the surgery was discontinued. They left people childish and irresponsible, almost totally indifferent to the consequences of their actions. Their pathological emotions were gone, but so were their normal ones (Carlson, 2001).

### Parietal Lobes of the Cerebral Cortex

**parietal lobes** the lobes of the cerebral cortex involved in the integration of bodily sensations and visual perceptions

The **parietal lobes** are involved in the integration of bodily sensations and visual perception. Neurologists think that the parietal lobes are crucial to the ability to perceive objects as integrated entities:

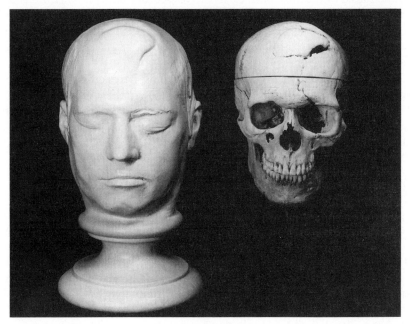

*Source:* From the Warren Anatomical Museum, Harvard Medical School. Reprinted by permission.

An object affects different senses, yet we perceive the object as one whole. A cat is furry, purrs, and projects a visual image. Although these sensations travel along different pathways, we perceive only one cat. If there are defects in visuo-spatial centers [of the parietal lobes], the person has difficulty mapping different sensations involved in the same object. She will perceive the cat visually and hear purring but cannot coordinate these two perceptions. (Haberlandt, 1996, p. 51)

### Occipital Lobes of the Cerebral Cortex

Although other parts of the brain are also involved, the **occipital lobes** are primarily dedicated to various aspects of visual perception. Damage to the occipital lobes, for example, can result in a condition known as *visual agnosia,* which is the inability to recognize common objects even though one may have normal visual acuity.

**occipital lobes**  the lobes of the cerebral cortex dedicated to various aspects of visual perception

### Temporal Lobes of the Cerebral Cortex

The **temporal lobes** serve a variety of important functions related to learning, being involved in attention, memory, and language production and expression. Because of their significance for learning, there has been much speculation about their role in learning disabilities, as discussed in more detail in the next section.

**temporal lobes**  the lobes of the cerebral cortex involved in attention, memory, and language production and reception

## Left and Right Hemispheres

**left and right hemispheres**
the two cerebral hemi-
spheres of the brain, each
of which receives sensory
information from and con-
trols movement of the
opposite side of the body;
in most people, especially
right-handers, the left hemisphere is more important
for language production
and comprehension than
the right hemisphere

The **left and right hemispheres** of the brain are relatively distinct with regard to their functions. For the most part, each receives sensory information from and controls movement of the opposite side of the body. For example, objects presented in the left visual field are perceived in the right hemisphere, sounds heard by the right ear are perceived in the left hemisphere, and movement of the left hand is controlled by the right hemisphere.

Another important way in which the two hemispheres differ is with respect to language. In most people, the left hemisphere is more important for language production and comprehension than the right hemisphere. In over 90% of right-handed individuals, the left hemisphere is specialized for language; in about 70% of left-handed individuals, the left hemisphere is specialized for language (Milner, 1974, cited in Pinel, 2000).

### Broca's and Wernicke's Areas

**aphasia**   a condition that
results in problems in
speech production and/or
comprehension due to an
injury to the brain

**Broca's area**   part of the
brain's left frontal lobe
associated with the ability
to speak

**Wernicke's area**   part of
the left temporal lobe associated with the ability to
comprehend language

Two researchers working in the 19th century were instrumental in drawing attention to the left hemisphere's role in language. Paul Broca performed postmortem examinations of the brains of several persons who had exhibited **aphasia**—severe problems in speaking—and found they all had damage to an area in the left frontal lobe. Several years later, Carl Wernicke identified an area in the left temporal lobe that he hypothesized was largely responsible for speech comprehension. These areas have come to be known, respectively, as **Broca's area** and **Wernicke's area** (Figure 2.4).

Subsequent research has shown that it is not always possible to predict precisely the type of language problem a person will have based on Broca's or Wernicke's area (Pinel, 2000). Documented damage to these areas does not always result in the same kinds of speech problems, and there have been cases of surgical removal of these areas with little disruption of speech production or comprehension. Furthermore, there is evidence that the right hemisphere is also responsible for certain aspects of language and communication. For example, the ability to convey and recognize emotion in one's tone of voice is largely a right-hemisphere activity (Carlson, 2001; Pinel, 2000).

Even though it is dangerous to predict in individual cases the connections between specific brain areas and specific behaviors, the weight of the evidence since the time of Broca and Wernicke indicates that, for most people, the left hemisphere is primarily responsible for many important aspects of language, especially for those who are right-handed. Several methods have been used in pointing to the dominance of the left hemisphere for language. For example, patients who are about to undergo surgery that might affect speech are often given an anesthetic first in the artery leading to the one hemisphere and then, after the anesthetic has worn off, in the artery leading to the other hemisphere. Researchers have noted that, for the overwhelming majority of right-handed people and for the majority of left-handed people, the anesthetization of the left hemisphere results in an inability to speak.

### Split-Brain Studies

**split-brain studies**
studies of the effects on
patients of a surgical procedure that severs the area
between the two hemi-
spheres of the brain

Perhaps the most dramatic demonstrations of the differential abilities of the left and right hemispheres have been the much celebrated **split-brain studies** (Gazzaniga &

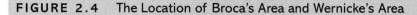

**FIGURE 2.4** The Location of Broca's Area and Wernicke's Area

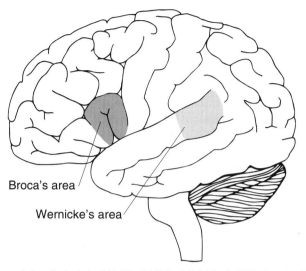

Broca's area

Wernicke's area

*Source:* From *Biopsychology,* 2nd ed. (p. 514, Fig. 16.2) by J. P. J. Pinel, 2000, Boston: Allyn and Bacon. Copyright © 2000 by Pearson Education. Reprinted by permission of the publisher.

LeDoux, 1978; Sperry, 1964). Split-brain studies came about as the result of a surgical procedure performed on patients with severe cases of epilepsy. In these patients, neurons in one hemisphere stimulate neurons in the other hemisphere, creating seizures so intense that they are not controllable by drugs. Severing the area between the two hemispheres reduces the number of seizures by prohibiting the neurons in one hemisphere from setting off those in the other hemisphere.

Split-brain patients provide testimony to the fact that the two brain hemispheres are primarily responsible for different functions. For example, one of the first things these patients say is that their left hand seems to have "a mind of its own" (Carlson, 2001, p. 5). They may be intently reading a book (a left-hemisphere activity) they are holding in their left hand when suddenly the left hand puts the book down. This occurs because their left hand is controlled by their right hemisphere, and the right hemisphere, not being able to read, gets bored.

Researchers have tested split-brain patients using a variety of laboratory tasks. In one typical procedure, the picture of a common object, such as a ball, is flashed to the right or left visual field of these individuals, and their responses are compared. When it is shown to the right visual field, these patients say they see a ball because it is seen by the left hemisphere, the hemisphere in control of speech. With eyes closed, they can also pick out the ball from among several objects using the right hand. They pick out the ball at a chance level of performance, however, when using the left hand. When objects are shown to the left visual field, the results are the opposite. When the ball is shown to the left visual field and hence the right hemisphere, these patients usually say they do not see anything. With eyes closed, however, the left hand, which is controlled by the right hemisphere, is able to pick out the ball from among several objects; but the right hand, which is controlled by the left hemisphere, does no better than chance.

## How Can We Infer Neurological Dysfunction?

Historically, much of the rationale for implicating neurological dysfunction as a cause of learning disabilities has been inferential. Neurologists and other professionals have noted that many of the behaviors and learning problems of people with obvious and well-documented brain injury are also present, although sometimes to a less pervasive degree, in children with learning disabilities. In other words, the types of learning problems and behavioral deviations that occur in those who have brain tumors or who have had strokes or head wounds are also present in some children with learning disabilities. For example, virtually all the behaviors noted previously as associated with damage to the cerebellum and the cerebral cortex are also evident in some children with learning disabilities. These range from problems of movement associated with damage to the cerebellum to attention, language, and memory difficulties associated with damage to the temporal lobes.

Inferring neurological dysfunction in children with learning disabilities from what we know about the behavior of documented cases of brain injury, however, has its limitations. Without some more direct measure of brain structure or functioning, we cannot be sure whether the behavioral or learning problems of the child with learning disabilities are due to the same causes as those of individuals with documented brain injury.

More direct methods of determining whether learning disabilities are the result of neurological dysfunction include postmortem studies and, more recently, neuro-imaging studies. Although such studies have not been definitive, they strongly indicate that learning disabilities, especially reading disabilities, are neurologically based.

### Postmortem Studies

The first evidence suggesting that neurological abnormalities are present in people with dyslexia came from autopsies. Galaburda and Geschwind and their colleagues conducted more than a dozen autopsies on the brains of individuals who had dyslexia and compared them with results of over a hundred autopsies performed on brains of persons (infancy through adulthood) who were not dyslexic (Galaburda & Kemper, 1979; Galaburda, Menard, & Rosen, 1994; Galaburda, Sherman, Rosen, Aboitiz, & Geschwind, 1985; Geschwind & Levitsky, 1968; Humphreys, Kaufmann, & Galaburda, 1990).

Although the number of cases of persons with dyslexia studied by Galaburda and Geschwind was relatively small, their findings were consistent. They found that in the majority of nondyslexic brains, a section of the left temporal lobe was larger than the same area in the right hemisphere. This area, which includes a large portion of Wernicke's area (see Figure 2.4), is referred to as the **planum temporale.** The results for those who were dyslexic were different; in the majority of cases, the planum temporales in the left and right hemispheres were the same size or the planum temporale in the right hemisphere was bigger than that in the left hemisphere.

**planum temporale**  a portion of the brain in Wernicke's area in the left temporal lobe that research suggests is affected in persons with dyslexia

## Neuroimaging Studies

As we noted earlier (see the Today's Technology box on page 47), neuroimaging methods are now being used by researchers to provide information on brain structure and function, with MRIs being used for the former and PET-scans and fMRIs being used for the latter. Although still too experimental to be used clinically to diagnose learning disabilities, researchers have found significant differences in both structure and function between the brains of those with and without dyslexia. Although a few studies have found the same asymmetrical differences between the left and right hemispheres that Galaburda and Geschwind found, several have not. At this point, most authorities have concluded that neuroimaging studies have failed to lend substantial support to Galaburda and Geschwind's conclusions (Habib, 2000).

Even though Galaburda and Geschwind's findings of differences in left-right hemisphere symmetry may be questionable, what is without question is that several independent research teams have found structural and functional differences between persons with and without dyslexia (Grigorenko, 2001; Habib, 2000). Although these researchers have not always found the exact same areas of the brain to be implicated, there has been enough consistency to draw the following conclusions:

1. The left hemisphere of the brain is more often the site of the dysfunction. However, some researchers have also found differences in the right hemisphere between persons with and without dyslexia.
2. Research has been fairly, but by no means totally, consistent in pointing to the following locations as dysfunctional: Broca's area, planum temporale, Wernicke's area, angular gyrus (an area immediately behind Wernicke's area). (See Figure 2.4.)
3. Research has been less consistent in pointing to the following locations as dysfunctional: occipital lobes, parietal lobes (see Figure 2.2), **corpus callosum** (a band of nerve fibers that connects the two hemispheres of the brain).

**corpus callosum** a band of nerve fibers that connects the two hemispheres of the brain

The evidence gathered thus far indicates that it is unlikely that dysfunction of only one specific area of the brain is responsible for reading disabilities. It is much more likely that more than one area of the brain is involved and that specific sites of dysfunction vary from one person to the next. Furthermore, it is likely that the specific types of reading problems are linked generally to different areas of the brain. For example, there is fairly strong evidence linking the ability to blend and break apart sounds, or phonemes, in words to activity in the left temporal lobe. Referred to as **phonological awareness,** these abilities are considered the building blocks of learning to read. (We discuss phonological awareness more fully in Chapter 12 on reading.)

**phonological awareness** the ability to blend sounds, segment the sounds of words, rhyme, and in other ways manipulate the sounds of spoken words

## Right-Hemisphere Brain Dysfunction

Most neurological research in learning disabilities has focused on dyslexia, or severe reading disabilities. And for this reason most of the research has focused on the impact of the left hemisphere on brain dysfunction. This is not surprising, given the

**nonverbal learning disabilities** disabilities that manifest in problems in math, self-regulation, and particularly social functioning

Council for Exceptional Children

**CEC Knowledge Check**

If left-brain dysfunction impacts a child's life differently than right-brain dysfunction, how, in your opinion, would this theory and research information impact curriculum and instruction for such children? CC7K1

Shannon

importance of the left hemisphere for language and the fact that many persons with learning disabilities have language and reading problems. Some researchers, however, have posited that persons who have a dysfunctional right hemisphere exhibit what is referred to as **nonverbal learning disabilities** (Myklebust, 1975; Rourke, 1989, 1995; Semrud-Clikeman & Hynd, 1990). This term is somewhat of a misnomer, because persons with nonverbal learning disabilities often display subtle problems with using language, especially in social situations (Rourke & Tsatsanis, 1996).

In the perceptual realm, individuals with nonverbal learning disabilities have difficulties with visual-spatial and tactual tasks. In the cognitive arena, they often have difficulty in math and in self-regulation and organization. Terms such as *spacy* and *in a fog* are often used to characterize these children (Denckla, 1993).

But the social area is where persons with nonverbal learning disabilities encounter their most significant problems. They are often socially inept, showing deficits in their ability to interpret the social behavior of others and to understand the impact of their own immature behavior on them. These deficits are especially pronounced in novel situations. Even though some may be academically competent, adults with nonverbal learning disabilities often have trouble holding a job because of their problems in social interaction. Some authorities see these persons as being at risk for depression and suicide (Bender, Rosenkrans, & Crane, 1999).

As we note in Chapter 7 (Social, Emotional, and Behavioral Problems), Shannon has a tendency toward depression and has had difficulties in making and keeping friends. These observations, coupled with the fact that her major academic problems lie in math (see Chapter 14 on math disabilities), make her a prime candidate for being considered as having nonverbal learning disabilities. The excerpt from Shannon's special education teacher's report (see the Case Connections box on page 57) also suggests that she has nonverbal learning disabilities.

## What Factors Contribute to Neurological Dysfunction?

There are a variety of reasons why an individual might have neurological dysfunction. These fall under the headings of (1) hereditary, (2) teratogenic, (3) medical, and (4) environmental factors.

### Hereditary Factors

Professionals have long surmised that heredity plays a significant role in many cases of learning disabilities. The authors of some of the first reported cases of reading disability, for example, noted that children with reading disabilities often had relatives who were reading disabled (Hinshelwood, 1907; Stephenson, 1907; Thomas, 1905). Genetics researchers have used two types of studies to look at the issue of whether the condition of learning disabilities is inherited: familiality and heritability.

# Excerpt From Shannon's Educational Evaluation

The following is an excerpt from the educational evaluation conducted by Martin Schein, Shannon's eighth-grade special education teacher. This report was part of Shannon's reevaluation to determine her eligibility for special education services. This particular excerpt was the introduction to a more extensive report that detailed scores on a variety of educational tests.

Shannon is currently an eighth-grader at Martin Luther King, Jr., Middle School. She receives one period of resource assistance daily and one period of collaborative math daily. Her academic grades are: English language arts A−, social studies A, earth science D, and math D. Her science grade was low because Shannon did not do well on tests. Her teacher reports that she has problems grasping new concepts and applying learned facts to new situations. Although she pays attention in class during direct instruction, she is very unengaged when involved in cooperative learning activities. Her math teacher reports that basic math facts and sequential operations are especially weak. She is attentive some of the time, somewhat disorganized, but turns assignments in on time in math. Shannon's social studies teacher reports that she actively participates in class discussions and seems eager to learn more about the subject matter. Her English teacher reports that she likes creative writing and expressing her opinions about what she has read but still has problems with some mechanics in writing.

I reinforce whatever skills the language arts teacher is trying to teach. In resource, Shannon uses her time wisely; however, sometimes she complains because she wants to use the class as a study hall instead of a time to get extra drill and practice in her weak areas. Left on her own, though, she seems to forget what she is doing and dawdles and daydreams.

Classroom observations reveal that Shannon sometimes experiences anxiety when taking a test. For example, when given a science test, she missed several questions on the first try. After experiencing some success, she was able to go back and correct some of her mistakes.

## Familiality

Familiality is said to be operating when a particular condition, such as a reading disability, occurs at a greater than chance rate in a family. In other words, **familiality** is the tendency for something to "run in a family."

**familiality** when a condition, such as reading disability, occurs at a greater-than-chance rate in family relatives

The turn-of-the-century researchers, noted previously, who found evidence of familiality were working with small numbers of cases. In more current studies, researchers have used larger samples to document that reading disability is, indeed, a familial condition (Grigorenko, 2001; Hallgren, 1950; Pennington, 1990). Generally, researchers have found around 35 to 45% of first-degree relatives of children with learning disabilities also have reading disabilities. They have also found evidence for approximately the same degree of familiality for speech and language disorders (Beichtman, Hood, & Inglis, 1992; Lewis, 1992) and spelling disability (Schulte-Korne, Deimel, Muller, Gutenbrunner, & Remschmidt, 1996).

In the quote at the beginning of the chapter, Jamal's mother speculated that Jamal may have inherited his learning disability from his father. Over time, she found out that there was even more evidence that Jamal may have inherited his learning disability from his father's side of the family:

 Jamal

> I think it was about a year after Jamal's father, Robert, died. His family had a reunion, and we were all sitting around chatting about our childhoods. It was then that I found out that several of Robert's relatives had had learning problems of some kind or other, usually involving reading. His older brother, Clay, admitted that he still has problems reading. He figures that if he had been a kid, today, he'd have definitely been identified as learning disabled. But back then in the 1960s, in the school he was attending, they didn't have classes for students with learning disabilities. A couple of Robert's uncles also owned up that they, too, had had trouble with academics.
>
> *Irene Smith, Jamal's mother*

Familiality, however, is not proof of heritability. Learning disabilities may run in families for environmental reasons. For example, one cannot rule out the possibility that parents who have learning disabilities might cause their children to have learning disabilities by the way they raise them. Likewise, siblings may be more likely to have learning disabilities because they share relatively similar environments. In the case of Jamal, however, given the large number of family members with apparent learning disabilities, it is probably a good guess that his condition is inherited.

### Heritability

**heritability**  the degree to which a condition is genetically transmitted; often estimated by comparing the rate of the condition in monozygotic and dizygotic pairs of twins, one of whom has the condition

**monozygotic twins**  twins from the same egg

**dizygotic twins**  twins from two different eggs

The most common way to test for the **heritability** of a condition—the degree to which it is genetically transmitted—is to compare its prevalence in monozygotic (MZ) and dizygotic (DZ) twins. **Monozygotic twins** come from the same egg and share the same genetic characteristics; **dizygotic twins** come from two separate eggs and share the same genetic characteristics as do other siblings. In the case of reading disabilities, for instance, the researcher first finds a group of individuals with reading disabilities who are members of MZ twin pairs and compares them with a group of individuals with reading disabilities who are members of DZ twin pairs. If reading disability is heritable, the proportion of cases in which both twins are reading disabled should be higher in the MZ group than in the DZ group because the MZ twins come from the same egg and share more genetic material than do the DZ twins.

Researchers have consistently found a greater degree of concordance for reading disabilities and speech and language disorders in MZ twins than in DZ twins. For example, in a major study of genetics and learning disabilities, the Colorado

Reading Project, 53 of 99 (54%) MZ pairs and 23 of 73 (32%) DZ pairs were concordant for reading disabilities (DeFries, Gillis, & Wadsworth, 1993). In another study, 24 of 32 (75%) MZ pairs and 8 of 25 (32%) DZ pairs were concordant for speech and language disorders (Lewis & Thompson, 1992). In a study of MZ and DZ nondisabled readers, a high degree of heritability was also found on an oral reading measure (Reynolds et al., 1996).

### Molecular Genetics

Researchers are also tackling the issue of whether specific genes can be identified with reading disabilities. It is the dream of many geneticists to isolate the gene or genes responsible for reading disabilities. But how realistic is this goal? After all, the human body contains approximately 30,000 genes (Human Genome Project Information, 2003). However, given the rapid advances in the field of molecular genetics, the goal appears more attainable than it did just a few short years ago. Considerable research has focused on the genes connected to two chromosomes in particular—Chromosome 6 and Chromosome 15. At this point, there is substantial reason to suspect that genes connected to these two chromosomes may play a role in the hereditary transmission of reading disabilities (Grigorenko, Wood, Meyer, & Pauls, 2000; Kaplan et al., 2002; Petryshen et al., 2001; Schulte-Korne, 2001).

As researchers hone in on particular genes responsible for reading disabilities, a whole host of ethical issues emerge. (See the Current Trends and Issues box on page 60.)

## Teratogenic Factors

Teratogens are agents that can cause abnormal growth or malformation in the fetus. A variety of chemicals has been implicated as **teratogens.** We briefly discuss three of them: alcohol, cocaine, and lead.

Probably the most common teratogen affecting mental development is alcohol. A pregnant woman who drinks excessively runs the risk of having a baby with **fetal alcohol syndrome.** Although this is most often associated with mental retardation, brain damage, hyperactivity, anomalies of the face, and heart abnormalities, some have speculated that in smaller concentrations alcohol might result in more subtle neurological problems that lead to learning disabilities.

Some researchers have also concluded that crack cocaine use by expectant mothers can cause neurological damage in the developing fetus (Greer, 1990). Although not all authorities agree on whether crack cocaine results in learning problems, at this point, it is reasonable to be on the alert for learning disabilities and other behavioral problems in children born to mothers using crack cocaine.

We have long known that lead ingestion can result in brain damage. When lead-based paint was commonly used, researchers found that infants and young children who ate paint chips suffered brain damage and mental retardation (Byers & Lord, 1943; Smith, Baehner, Carney, & Majors, 1963). Lead-based paint is now banned, but researchers have been studying the effects of lower levels of lead that can result from living near lead smelters or other toxic sites. They have found that children exposed prenatally and postnatally to lead run the risk of exhibiting developmental problems (Feldman & White, 1992; Leviton et al., 1993; Minder, Das-Smaal, Brand, & Orlebeke, 1994).

Council for
Exceptional
Children

**CEC Knowledge Check**
Do you believe educators should communicate etiology of learning disabilities information to parents or not? If so, why? Or if not, why not?
CC10S10

**teratogens**  agents that can cause abnormal growth or malformation in the fetus

**fetal alcohol syndrome**  a syndrome associated with mental retardation, brain damage, anomalies of the face, hyperactivity, and heart failure that affects children of women who drank alcohol excessively when pregnant

## CURRENT TRENDS & ISSUES

# Reading Disabilities, Genes, and Ethical Issues

If researchers do find the gene or genes responsible for reading disabilities, this opens up the door for early diagnosis, even prenatally, of reading disabilities. As one researcher has put it:

> If dyslexia genes can be located, a molecular test of reading and spelling disorder would allow earlier diagnosis of children at risk. This in turn would offer the opportunity for very early intervention, at a time when the language areas are at an earlier, more plastic stage of development. (Schulte-Korne, 2001, p. 994)

Such early diagnosis, of course, also raises ethical issues. For example, might parents wish to abort a fetus because it has a defective gene or genes for reading? Or might parents wish to take advantage of some kind of gene replacement therapy if it was available? These same issues have been raised with respect to the area of mental retardation. The following is an excerpt of a speech delivered to Arc, a major parent organization for persons with mental retardation, but it is also applicable to learning disabilities.

A number of arguments are offered against gene therapy, including the concern about the potential for harmful abuse if we don't distinguish between good and bad uses of gene therapy. The eugenics movement of the 1920s to the 1940s found people with mental retardation being involuntarily sterilized. . . . Another concern is that in mental retardation gene-therapy research, many candidates are likely to be children who are too young or too disabled to understand ramifications of the treatment. Finally, gene therapy is very expensive and may never be sufficiently cost-effective to merit high social priority. Opponents say that if those who can afford gene therapy are the only ones to receive it, the distribution of desirable biological traits will widen the differences among various socioeconomic groups. (Davis, 1997)

As with almost any advance in technology that affects human lives, the issues are complex and challenging. As research closes in on finding specific genetic conditions that may cause learning disabilities, researchers and practitioners will need to be vigilant to potential abuses.

---

Council for Exceptional Children

**CEC Knowledge Check**

If a reading disability or dyslexia gene were found, would the benefits outweigh the possible misuse? What would be some of the ethical misuses of gene therapy? What should be the response of the LD professional?
CC1S1, LD2K1, LD2K2, LD9S2

## Medical Factors

There are myriad medical conditions that can contribute to children's problems. The following are sometimes associated with learning disabilities:

- *Premature birth* places children at risk for neurological damage, learning disabilities, and other disabling conditions. One study found that 19% of prematurely born children with very low birthweight had learning disabilities (Ross, Lipper, & Auld, 1991).
- *Diabetes* can lead to neuropsychological problems and learning disabilities. One team of authorities concluded that children with early onset of diabetes (before 5 years of age) are candidates for learning disabilities (Rovet, Ehrlich, Czuchta, & Akler, 1993).
- *Meningitis,* an infection of the brain caused by a variety of viral or bacterial agents, can result in brain damage. There is evidence that this brain damage can lead to learning problems (Taylor & Schatschneider, 1992).
- *Cardiac arrest,* although occurring rarely in children, can lead to loss of oxygen and blood flow to the brain, which results in brain damage. Children who had suffered a cardiac arrest were found to have a variety of deficits on neuropsychological, achievement, and adaptive behavior measures (Morris, Krawiecki, Wright, & Walter, 1993).

- *Pediatric AIDS* is rapidly becoming the major infection that babies can contract from their mothers (Armstrong, Seidel, & Swales, 1993). The effects of pediatric AIDS are not always easy to disentangle from other social and physical causes (e.g., neglect, malnutrition, drug and alcohol addiction), but there is strong evidence that pediatric AIDS can result in neurological damage.

## Environmental Factors

The role the environment may play in causing learning disabilities has already been noted. For example, extremely poor parenting or teaching can put children at risk for developing learning difficulties. In addition to having a direct negative influence on learning, the environment can also have an indirect impact on learning by creating situations in which brain dysfunction is more likely. Poor socioeconomic conditions are linked with a host of factors (e.g., malnutrition, poor prenatal and postnatal health care, teenage pregnancy, substance abuse) that can put children at risk for neurological dysfunction. And, unfortunately, there is strong evidence that, since the mid to late 1970s, increasing numbers of children and their mothers are living in poverty.

## What Should Educators Keep in Mind Regarding Causes?

From an educator's viewpoint, it is important to keep the significance of causal factors in its proper perspective. Knowing the exact cause of a learning disability is of only limited utility to teachers and other educators. For example, knowing that a particular student does or does not have neurological dysfunction is largely irrelevant to how one teaches that student. Furthermore, in considering individual cases, we are rarely able to determine definitively the cause or causes of someone's learning disability because there are no foolproof tests, procedures, or examinations that provide quick and easy answers to the complicated question of causal factors. Nonetheless, as well-rounded professionals able to communicate with professionals from other fields, as well as with parents, teachers have a responsibility to keep abreast of research on causal factors of learning disabilities.

**Council for Exceptional Children**

**CEC Knowledge Check**

There are a number of serious medical factors associated with learning disabilities. Brainstorm what additional effects these conditions can have on a child's life and on the rest of the family. CC3K1, LD2K2

**Council for Exceptional Children**

**CEC Knowledge Check**

Looking back at the USOE definition, if you believe in the "nurture" philosophy of etiology, what factors might cause you to mislabel a child with the label "learning disabled"? LD2K1, LD8K2

---

**PORTFOLIO-BUILDING ACTIVITY**

### Demonstrating Mastery of the CEC Standards

Use the information you have learned in this chapter to refine your Personal Philosophy of Special Education paper in the area of learning disabilities, which you started in Chapter 1. Revise your draft to demonstrate your perspectives on the following issues:

- Discuss the historical and philosophical contributions of neurological (nature) versus behavioral/environmental (nurture) perspectives, including its three major contributors (Hinshelwood, Orton, and Myklebust).

- Discuss your philosophical position regarding the etiology of learning disabilities (i.e., nature versus nurture).

**Council for Exceptional Children**

**CEC Content Standards**

1. Foundations
2. Development and Characteristics of Learners
3. Individual Learning Differences

- Relate why it is important for you as an educator to understand learning disability etiology and relationships in your interactions with students and families.

- Describe how technology and research advancement may affect future definitions and identification procedures.

# SUMMARY

### What causes learning disabilities?

- The field of learning disabilities grew out of a medical and clinical assumption that neurological factors were the basis of learning disabilities. The work of Broca and Wernicke in the 19th century, which identified particular areas of the brain as controlling speaking and understanding of language, laid the groundwork for later work on dyslexia. In the early 20th century, clinicians noted the similarities between children with dyslexia or other learning disabilities and persons with documented brain damage.

- The field was slow to accept neurological dysfunction as a viable causal factor because of the questionable accuracy of neurological measures and the popularity of behaviorism and environmentalism.

- In recent years, professionals have generally taken a more favorable view of neurological explanations of learning disabilities. There has been a decrease in the popularity of behaviorism and environmentalism because intervening to remedy the effects of poverty on child development has been difficult. Furthermore, advances in neurological measures, such as MRIs, PET-scans, and fMRIs, have probably been the most influential reason for the resurgence of interest in exploring neurological factors in learning disabilities.

### How does the brain function?

- Neurons send and receive messages. Neurons consist of a soma (cell body), dendrites (projections that receive messages), and an axon, with its terminal buttons that secrete chemical neurotransmitters into the synapse (a small gap between the axon and dendrite).

- Different parts of the brain have different functions. The brain is commonly divided into the following areas, each of which is generally responsible for different functions:
  - brain stem—regulates survival reflexes such as heart rate and respiration

- cerebellum—regulates several behaviors related to movement, including balance, gait, speech, and eye movements
- cerebral cortex—composed of the frontal lobes (responsible for some motor movements and executive functions), prefrontal lobes (foreparts of the frontal lobes that are implicated in control of emotions), parietal lobes (involved in the integration of bodily sensations and visual perceptions), occipital lobes (primarily dedicated to visual perception, in conjunction with other parts of the brain), and temporal lobes (involved in attention, memory, and language production and reception)

- The left and right hemispheres of the brain are relatively distinct with regard to their functions. For the most part, each receives information and controls movement of the opposite side of the body. In most people, especially those who are right-handed, the left hemisphere is more important for language production and comprehension than the right hemisphere.
  - Broca's area and Wernicke's area are two parts of the left hemisphere associated with language (production and comprehension, respectively). However, damage to these areas does not always result in the same kinds of problems, and there is evidence that the right side of the brain is responsible for some aspects of language and communication.
  - Split-brain studies involve surgical procedures performed on patients with severe epilepsy in which the number of seizures experienced is reduced by severing the area between the two hemispheres. These studies have resulted in dramatic demonstrations of the differential abilities of the two hemispheres.

### How can we infer neurological dysfunction in children?

- Historically, neurological dysfunction in children with learning disabilities has been largely inferred from what we know about the behavior of people with documented brain injury. This approach has its limitations, however, because it does not involve direct measures of brain function or structure.

- More recently, researchers, using postmortem studies and neuroimaging technology (MRI, PET-scan, and fMRI) comparing persons with and without dyslexia, have concluded that
  - the left hemisphere of the brain is more often the site of the dysfunction. However, some researchers have also found differences in the right hemisphere between persons with and without dyslexia.
  - research has been fairly, but not totally, consistent in pointing to dysfunction in the following locations of the brain: Broca's area, planum temporale, Wernicke's area, angular gyrus (an area immediately behind Wernicke's area).
  - research has been less consistent in pointing to the following locations as dysfunctional: occipital lobes, parietal lobes (see Figure 2.2, page 49), corpus callosum (a band of nerve fibers that connects the two hemispheres of the brain).
- Even though many researchers have pointed to the left hemisphere as involved in learning disabilities, there is also evidence that a dysfunctional right hemisphere may be the cause of nonverbal learning disabilities. Nonverbal learning disabilities may include difficulties with visual-spatial and tactual tasks, math, and self-regulation and organization. The most significant problems for people with nonverbal learning disabilities may be in the social area, in which they may exhibit poor social perception and judgment.

### What factors contribute to neurological dysfunction?

- Hereditary factors may play a role. Researchers have used two types of studies to investigate the genetic basis of learning disabilities:
  - Familiality, in which a learning disability occurs at a greater than chance rate in a family, has been found in some studies. But familiality is not proof of heritability, because learning disabilities may occur in a family for environmental reasons.
  - Heritability studies often compare the prevalence of a condition in monozygotic versus dizygotic twins. MZ twins share more genetic material than do DZ twins. If learning disabilities are inherited, when one twin has learning disabilities, there should be more cases of the other twin also having learning disabilities in MZ than in DZ twins. Research has consistently found this to be the case.
- Teratogenic factors may play a role. Teratogens are agents that cause abnormal growth or malformation of the fetus. The following are some examples:
  - Alcohol is probably the most common teratogen that can affect mental development. Authorities speculate that fetal alcohol syndrome, although most often associated with mental retardation, may result in learning disabilities if the alcohol is in smaller concentrations.
  - Crack cocaine use by expectant mothers may also cause neurological damage to a developing fetus, but opinions vary about long-term exposure as a cause of learning disabilities.
  - Ingestion of lead can result in brain damage, and we cannot rule out prenatal exposure as a cause of some cases of learning disabilities.
- Medical factors may play a role. Some examples are premature birth, diabetes, meningitis, cardiac arrest, and pediatric AIDS.
- Environmental factors can have an indirect effect on neurological development by creating situations in which brain dysfunction is more likely to occur. For example, poor socioeconomic conditions are linked to many factors that put children at risk for neurological disorders.

### What should educators keep in mind regarding causes?

- In individual cases, we are rarely able to determine definitively the cause of someone's learning disability.

## REFLECTIONS ON THE CASES

1. Should Jamal's mother inform him of the possible hereditary basis of his condition? What advice, if any, should she give him?

2. How important is it for teachers to know the causes of Jamal's and Shannon's learning disability?

## What Laws Govern the Delivery of Special Education?
- How Is Special Education Defined?
- Definition and Practice of Special Education
- Other Components of Special Education

## How Is a Learning Disability Defined in IDEA?

## What Is the Traditional Eligibility Process?
- Prereferral Strategies
- Referral for Special Education Evaluation
- Evaluation
- Eligibility Decision

## What Is an Alternative Eligibility Process?
- How Does Response-to-Treatment Work?
- Issues around the Response-to-Treatment Process

## What Is an Individualized Education Program?
- Components of the Individualized Education Program
- Special Education Service Delivery

Council for Exceptional Children

See Companion Website for detailed correlations between chapter content and Council for Exceptional Children Standards; www.ablongman.com/hallahanLD3e

### CEC Knowledge and Skills Discussed in This Chapter

1. Laws and due process rights related to screening, prereferral, referral, assessment, eligibility, and placement for individuals who may have learning disabilities.

2. Practical use of the learning disability definition—what it means in terms of who will qualify for services, and what the advantages/disadvantages to changing the definition might be.

3. Nonbiased standards of ethical responsibility in the use of assessment as part of advocating for appropriate eligibility, programming, and placement services for individuals with learning disabilities, with consideration of diversity factors.

4. Interventions, services, integrative supports, accommodations, and modifications supported by research that connect to the cognitive, social, emotional, academic, and other needs of students with learning disabilities

5. Effective parental communication to facilitate ongoing IEP and education team participation.

# Eligibility for Special Education Services

**3**

What was it like? It was intimidating, I'll tell you. I was sitting in that room with all those school people around the table and just me. I felt outnumbered. And they were talking about my boy, my son and what was going to happen to him. I wanted to cry.

*Irene Smith, Jamal's mother*

Students with learning disabilities who are experiencing difficulties in school may be eligible to receive special education services. In order to receive these services, the student must go through the eligibility process as outlined in the Individuals with Disabilities Education Act (IDEA). Before any special education services are provided, a student must be determined to have a disability and to need special education services in order to be successful in school (IDEA S. 1248, 2003). As you read in Chapter 1, the **eligibility process** includes a series of steps and evaluation. Once a student is determined eligible for services, an **individualized education program (IEP)** is developed and implemented. As evidenced by Mrs. Smith's statement, the eligibility process can often be overwhelming for parents and others. In this chapter, we give an overview of special education law, describe traditional and alternative methods of determining eligibility, and outline the components of the IEP. Throughout the chapter, we will identify issues related to these topics.

**eligibility process** the referral, evaluation, and decision steps through which students must go to determine if they have a disability

**individualized education program (IEP)** a written agreement of educators and parents, required by IDEA, that includes statements about the student's education needs and the special education and related services that will be provided

## What Laws Govern the Delivery of Special Education?

The primary law governing special education services is the Individuals with Disabilities Education Act. This federal law, initially passed in 1975, was revised in 1990, 1997, and 2003. State laws also govern special education, but they must conform to the requirements of IDEA.

When we refer to IDEA requirements, we include not only what is written in the actual law (the statute), but also what is written in the federal regulations related to the law. These federal regulations have the same force as the law, and courts require that schools implement the regulations as if they were written into the law itself (cf. Bateman, 1996; Yell, 1998).

IDEA and accompanying federal regulations require first and foremost that every student with a disability be provided a **free and appropriate public education (FAPE).** FAPE is the central issue of the federal law; without it, the other requirements of the law are irrelevant. That is, none of the other requirements of the law can be interpreted for an individual case until the FAPE requirement has been satisfied. Moreover, FAPE and other requirements of IDEA must be determined on an individual basis. A state or school system cannot make generalizations about FAPE and other requirements of the law that apply across the board to all students.

The "free" aspect of the law means that the parent or guardian cannot be charged for the special services that the student requires; the education must be provided at public expense. The "public" means in public schools or facilities. However, public funds may be used to send the student to a private school if that is required to ensure that the student receives an appropriate education.

The special education provided under IDEA must be "appropriate," which is a difficult term to interpret in some circumstances. The law refers to education designed to meet the individual ("unique") needs of the student with disabilities. Whatever instructional methods, materials, equipment, or type of educational environment is required for the student to learn must be provided. Educators may not, under IDEA, assume that all students with a particular category of disability (e.g., learning disability) will have the same educational needs or that education will be appropriate because it is designated for a particular category. The requirement is clearly that appropriateness be judged on a case-by-case basis (Bateman, 1996; Yell, 1998).

IDEA outlines the process and safeguards for special education, from determining eligibility to providing services. In order to receive federal funding for special education, state education agencies (SEAs) and local education agencies (LEAs) must comply with its requirements.

## How Is Special Education Defined?

IDEA defines *special education* as "specially designed instruction, at no cost to the parents, to meet the unique needs of a child with a disability" (IDEA, S.1248, 2003). It involves special instruction designed to address special problems in teaching and learning. The special problems may have to do with a wide variety of disabilities, including physical, sensory, cognitive, speech and language, emotional/behavioral, or academic problems or combinations of all of these.

Students with learning disabilities may require special education primarily, but often not exclusively, because of problems in their learning of academic tasks for reasons that are often obscure but may involve neurological anomalies. These students need special instruction—something different from what can be provided by general education. They also may need related services (e.g., speech therapy) that will help them obtain and benefit from special education.

**free and appropriate public education (FAPE)** education that is appropriate to students with disabilities and is free of cost to the parents or guardians of the student

Council for Exceptional Children

CEC Knowledge Check

What legal protections exist for students with learning disabilities to receive a free and appropriate education? LD1K3

## Definition and Practice of Special Education

Education reformers have sometimes suggested that special education is little or nothing more than good general education. The contention is that if general education were transformed in certain ways, it could address the individual needs of every child and so be special for all (Thomas, 1994). However, as others have pointed out, education cannot be truly special for all any more than other services provided to the public at large can be specially designed for everyone, except in the most superficial sense (Dupre, 1997; Kauffman & Hallahan, 1997). Moreover, when special education is practiced as it should be, it is different from general education along several critical dimensions of instruction (Fuchs & Fuchs, 1995a). At a minimum, these instructional differences involve the training and support teachers receive, class or group size and composition, degree of individualization and teacher direction, accuracy and scope of pupil assessment, precision of implementation of instructional strategies, closeness of monitoring of instructional progress, and **empirical validation** of teaching practices.

### Teacher Training and Support

Special education teachers receive additional training that informs them of the nature and characteristics of the disabilities of their students and the instructional and behavior management practices that will be most effective with them. Appropriate special education teacher training offers skills in addition to those taught in general education teacher preparation and helps special educators understand how their role is different from and complements the role of general education teachers (Kauffman, 1994). Teacher training alone is not enough to produce viable special education. A professional infrastructure of support services, including consultation, supervision, curriculum, instructional materials, and paraprofessional assistance, is required to enhance teaching practice (Heward, 2003; Vaughn, Bos, & Schumm, 1997; Worrall & Carnine, 1994).

### Class or Group Size and Composition

The **pupil-teacher ratio** is lower in special than in general education instructional settings. This is achieved by congregating students with special instructional needs in special schools, classes, or resource rooms or by adding a consulting teacher or co-teacher to work with a general education teacher in a general class. The class or group size in which instruction is offered is necessarily smaller in special education to allow for the degree of individualization required to meet extraordinary instructional problems. Moreover, although **heterogeneous grouping** is popular in general education and has advantages for some school activities, effective instruction of students with special learning problems may require teaching small groups of students with similar skills in the curriculum being taught. Thus, special education may involve not just lower pupil-teacher ratios, but also **homogeneous grouping** of students for instruction in specific skill areas (Grossen, 1993b).

### Individualization and Teacher Direction

All good general education teachers individualize instruction to the extent possible, given the limits of their time and efforts in teaching a relatively large, heterogeneous

Council for
Exceptional
Children

**CEC Knowledge Check**
If general education used empirically validated teaching practices, could the majority of students with learning disabilities be successful in general education? Defend your answer.
CC7K1

**empirical validation**
identifying effective techniques through rigorous scientific study

**pupil-teacher ratio** the ratio of the number of students to the number of teachers

**heterogeneous grouping** placing students in groups by characteristics other than achievement; a group may include students of all achievement levels

**homogeneous grouping** placing students in groups by their achievement level (e.g., students who are above grade level in reading are in one group, students below grade level in another group)

group of students. In special education, the degree of individualization is necessarily higher, as reflected in the IEP that must be written for each child. The required individualization extends to assessing, planning, instructing, and monitoring progress. In addition, instructional materials that are adequate for most students but unusable for students with particular problems may need to be specially adapted. Besides individual attention, special education may require a higher level of teacher direction. Although many or most students in general education may be successful in directing much of their own learning, effective special education often requires that the teacher be more directive and offer more explicit instruction (Grossen, 1993a; Heward, 2003).

### Assessment

Students in general education are routinely assessed, but those in special education require closer scrutiny than can be afforded for all students. The assessment required in special education is broader in scope and more detailed than that required for the successful practice of general education. In special education, teachers must assess all areas of known or suspected disability. They must also give more careful attention to the analysis of students' errors, the patterns of relative strength and weakness, and the effects of particular instructional and behavior management practices than is necessary in general education.

### Instructional Precision

Instruction in general education is, of necessity, designed for typical learners—the vast majority of students. As such, it need not be controlled as precisely as in special education. Questioning, sequencing, pacing, opportunity to respond, wait time, positive and negative examples, repetition, feedback, reinforcement of desired behavior and academic performance, and other instructional elements must be used with greater precision by special than by general educators. Many of the same basic instructional procedures used in general education apply to special education and vice versa, but in special education, there is less room for error in instruction, because these students will not learn given the typical instructional procedures and level of precision that are successful with most students (Swanson, 2000).

### Progress Monitoring

**progress monitoring** the assessment and display of a student's performance in an academic or behavioral skill over time

In general education, student progress need not be monitored as closely as in special education. Special educators must be aware daily, if not moment to moment, of the progress individual students are making. Close **progress monitoring** is essential to avoid small instructional errors that can lead to later catastrophes in learning for students with special problems. Competent general education teachers may assess their students' progress once a week and run relatively little risk of losing touch with their students' learning. This is not the case with special education teachers, who must be more finely attuned to their students' headway.

### Empirical Validation

General, as well as special, education instructional practices have sometimes been based on fads, not derived from careful field tests and scientific confirmation of their effectiveness (Carnine, 1993). The best practices in special education are derived from research and development and have been empirically validated through careful field tests. Progress in special education depends on the accumulation of scientific evidence that its methods are effective (Kauffman, 1993b). Empirical validation has been one of the hallmarks of the competent practice of special education (Fuchs & Fuchs, 1995b).

The features of special education described above have not always characterized the practice of special education, which has too often been poorly implemented (Kauffman, 1994). However, when special education does have these features, it can and does work because it is truly special (Fuchs & Fuchs, 1995a,b). General education teachers can also tailor some of these features to accommodate students who have special needs (Schumm & Vaughn, 1992). Although general education practices can and should be substantially improved, special instruction will nonetheless be required to address the problems of students and teachers for whom general education has been inadequate. Moreover, at present, there appear to be large gaps between general education teachers' beliefs and their practices and skills in accommodating the needs of students with learning disabilities. Special education in the context of general education—or general education that actually meets the needs of students with learning disabilities—is likely quite rare (Schumm, Vaughn, Gordon, & Rothlein, 1994).

## Other Components of Special Education

### Related Services

**Related services** are those services necessary to allow a student to benefit from special education. These must be provided as needed for all students who receive special education. For example, transportation to and from the location at which special education is offered is a related service that cannot be withheld. Physical and occupational therapies, recreation, speech and language therapy, psychological services, counseling, and medical diagnostic services may also be related services. Special education must be delivered in such a way that related services are made available at no cost to the student's parents.

### Continuum of Alternative Placements

IDEA envisions an array of plans and variations of service delivery arrangements suited to students' particular needs. The law does not allow schools to employ only one or two service delivery options, but instead requires a continuum of alternatives ranging from placement in general classes to placement in residential schools.

Most school systems are constantly seeking to improve how they group and instruct students to deliver the special services that those with disabilities need to be successful in school. Special educators are also looking for ways to combine a variety of instructional approaches with all the service delivery options. Strategies such as peer tutoring and cooperative learning, for example, are often suggested as approaches that can help to make teaching more successful. Direct Instruction, on the other hand, may be a particularly effective approach for most students with learning disabilities, but it is seldom feasible to provide it in the context of a general

Council for Exceptional Children

**CEC Knowledge Check**
Considering the seven features of special education, what is your position on providing educational services for students with learning disabilities? Defend your answer.
CC9S2, CC9S11, LD9K1

**related services** the developmental, corrective, and other supportive services required to assist a child with a disability to benefit from special education (e.g., transportation)

Council for Exceptional Children

**CEC Knowledge Check**
What related services might students with learning disabilities need in school? Who is responsible for service payment?
CC9S3, LD9K1

**CEC Knowledge Check**

Why is the place that
students with learning
disabilities receive their
education such an im-
portant issue?
CC1K6, LD1K4

classroom in which student-directed learning is the norm. Direct Instruction "in-cludes effective instructional design principles and teaching behaviors incorporated into a set of published instructional programs" (Marchand-Martella, Slocum, & Martella, 2004, p. 16). Clearly, some instructional approaches are more feasible than others in some service delivery models. Some are more workable than others for different grade levels. The problems of finding the right combinations of in-structional methods and service delivery systems for students of different ages and disabilities—not to mention the demands of individualization—contribute to the controversy surrounding service delivery issues.

These characteristics make special education qualitatively and quantitatively different from general education. In order to receive special education services, a student must be a student with a disability. We now turn to how IDEA defines a learning disability.

## How Is Learning Disability Defined in IDEA?

**conceptual definition** a
definition that identifies a
concept but does not give
guidelines for how to put it
into practice

**operationalize** to put
into practice

As you read in Chapter 1, there has been debate over the definition of a learning dis-ability. Although there are some variations, the **conceptual definition** of a learning disability has remained relatively stable throughout its history. The debate generally revolves around how the definition is **operationalized,** or put into practice. Most local education agencies (LEAs) use the definition of a learning disability found in IDEA. That definition has not changed since the passing of P.L. 94-142 in 1975. The conceptual definition of a learning disability according to IDEA is:

> (A) IN GENERAL—The term "specific learning disability" means a disorder in one or more of the basic psychological processes involved in understanding or in using language, spoken or written, which disorder may manifest itself in imperfect ability to listen, think, speak, read, write, spell, or do mathematical calculations.
> (B) DISORDERS INCLUDED—Such term includes such conditions as perceptual disabilities, brain injury, minimal brain dysfunction, dyslexia, and developmental aphasia.
> (C) DISORDERS NOT INCLUDED—Such term does not include a learning prob-lem that is primarily the result of visual, hearing, or motor disabilities, of mental re-tardation, of emotional disturbance, or of environmental, cultural, or economic disadvantage. (IDEA, S.1248, 2003, sec. 602(29))

However, the federal regulations written for the 1997 reauthorization of IDEA include the following for how to operationalize that definition:

**severe discrepancy** a difference between a student's
ability and achievement
levels that cannot be
explained by chance

> (1) the child does not achieve commensurate with his or her age and ability levels in one or more of the areas listed in paragraph (2) of this section, if provided with learning experiences appropriate for the child's age and ability levels; and
> (2) the team finds that a child has a **severe discrepancy** between achievement and intellectual ability in one or more of the following areas:
>     i. Oral expression.
>     ii. Listening comprehension.

     iii. Written expression.
     iv. Basic reading skill.
      v. Reading comprehension.
     vi. Mathematics calculation.
    vii. Mathematics reasoning.

(b) The team may not identify a child as having a specific learning disability if the severe discrepancy between ability and achievement is primarily the result of—

    (1) a visual, hearing or motor impairment;
    (2) mental retardation;
    (3) emotional disturbance; or
    (4) environmental, cultural or economic disadvantage.

(U.S. Department of Education, 1999, p. 12457)

Using these guidelines for determining a learning disability, LEAs would use traditional assessment methods to determine if (1) a child is not achieving commensurate with others of the same age and ability, (2) a discrepancy between ability and achievement (e.g., IQ and academic achievement) exists, and (3) the discrepancy is not due to the factors listed.

Alternatively, in the most recent reauthorization of IDEA, LEAs are being given the option of considering alternative methods of determining eligibility,

> (A) IN GENERAL—Notwithstanding section 607(b), when determining whether a child has a specific learning disability as defined in section 602(29) a local educational agency shall not be required to take into consideration whether the child has a severe discrepancy between achievement and intellectual ability in oral expression, listening comprehension, written expression, basic reading skill, reading comprehension, mathematical calculation, or mathematical reasoning.
>
> (B) ADDITIONAL AUTHORITY—In determining whether a child has a specific learning disability, a local educational agency may use a process that determines if a child responds to scientific, research-based intervention. (IDEA, S.1248, 2003, Sec. 614(b)(6))

This alternative method is generally referred to as a **response-to-intervention** or **response-to-treatment** approach in which schools provide differing levels and types of instruction for students who are not achieving. The levels and types of instruction become more intensive as students do not progress, and the final several levels are generally provided for through special education. We will review this alternative method in a subsequent section of the chapter.

This response-to-treatment alternative method of determining a learning disability has come about for two main reasons. First, there is great variability in the identification of learning disabilities among local school districts or local education agencies (MacMillan & Siperstein, 2002). In other words, LEAs operationalize the definition of a learning disability, even with the federally mandated criteria, in a variety of ways. (See the Current Trends and Issues box on pages 72–73 for more detail.) Some LEAs rely almost solely on a discrepancy between measured ability and achievement, using discrepancy formulas based on grade or age equivalents, standard score, regression analyses, or others (Kavale, 2002). In all LEAs, the subjectivity of professional judgment is introduced at multiple levels within the eligibility

**response-to-intervention** (or **response-to-treatment**) a method to determine whether a student is a student with a disability by providing various levels of instructional intervention that become more intensive if the student does not improve in achievement level (e.g., if a student is not achieving in reading, more intensive instruction may be implemented; if the student continues to fail, the student may be determined eligible for special education services)

## Operationalizing a Severe Discrepancy: Keeping Things in Perspective

Discrepancy is the operational definition of underachievement and, when present, reliably and appropriately documents the presence of underachievement, not LD. With the valid assumption that LD and underachievement are not equivalent, the task becomes one of deciding what other factors need to be considered before there is confidence that LD has been determined. (Kavale, 2002, p. 407)

Even though a severe discrepancy is but one factor in the definition, it has become the primary issue of debate in the identification of learning disabilities (see Bradley, Danielson, & Hallahan, 2002). In point of fact, studies suggest that up to one-third of the school-identified students with learning disabilities do not exhibit a severe discrepancy. Other factors introduced by the team of decision makers (e.g., less stigma with learning disabilities than mental retardation, the need for help for a student when nothing is available but special education) may ultimately determine identification (Kavale, 2002).

Researchers, practitioners, and others have criticized the severe discrepancy concept for many reasons; one is that there is much variability in how it is operationalized.

There have been four major ways in which the ability-achievement discrepancy has been put into practice:

1. **Grade-level deviations.** An expected grade-level performance is compared to an actual grade-level performance and a difference determined. For example, Henry is in fifth grade and scores a second-grade equivalent on an achievement test given. There would then be a three-grade-level discrepancy between his expected and actual grade-level performance. This method presents difficulties because of the way grade-level equivalents are interpolated and because of the differences in meaning at different grade levels (e.g., a one-year discrepancy at second grade may mean more than a one-year discrepancy at seventh grade).
2. **Expectancy formulas.** These formulas combine many variables, such as chronological age, IQ, grade age, or years in school. These formulas have been criticized because of the influence of measurement and regression on the scores they produce (Kavale, 2002).
3. **Standard score methods.** These methods usually involve the comparison of standard scores from IQ

Council for
Exceptional
Children

**CEC Knowledge Check**
What might a new learning disability definition mean in terms of clearly defining who has a learning disability and who does not? Will this change alter the number of students that special education teachers need to reach/teach (at-risk vs. labeled)?
CC2K5, CC5S7, LD1K5, LD7K3

process (i.e., referral, assessment, and eligibility decision). Though this was part of the original intent of the definition (Bateman, 1965, as cited in Lloyd, 2002), it adds to the variability. It may also play a part in the decision to serve students who are having difficulties achieving in school as students with learning disabilities even though they do not fit the criteria (MacMillan & Siperstein, 2002). Also, the use of different assessment devices may affect the outcome of eligibility decisions (Kavale, 2002).

Second, some researchers have argued that there is little evidence to suggest a reliable difference between students identified as having a learning disability in reading through a discrepancy model and those who are low achieving in reading skills but do not have an IQ-ability discrepancy (Fletcher et al., 2002). The argument in this area has been supported mainly by studies of early reading performance and has not been explored in other areas. Proponents of this argument state that there are many problems with using discrepancy to identify students with learning disabilities, such as where to set the cutoff score, how to adjust for measurement error, how to determine the reliability of decisions, and how to collect multiple data points. They also argue that IQ tests are not needed and that the concept of a "slow learner" is not useful (Fletcher et al., 2002).

tests and tests of achievement. These tests generally have a mean of 100 and a standard deviation of 15 points. For example, a student may have a full-scale IQ standard score of 105 and a basic reading standard score of 85, a discrepancy of 15 points. This method is more statistically viable than the two described before but still has its problems. The assumption in direct comparison is that the IQ and achievement scores are directly correlated (1.0) when the correlation is actually about 0.60, which injects statistical regression (i.e., those with extreme scores on the first test will get a score closer to the population mean on the second test).

4. **Regression methods.** In order to correct for the problems in the standard score method, regression methods were developed. In these methods, calculations are completed using the standard deviation and correlation of the measures to account for the regression to the mean of student scores. For example, if a student has an IQ of 115, then the regression method builds a confidence interval around the expected score of 108 (88.17–128.03). If the student scores within this range on the achievement components, then no severe discrepancy exists. Though this is the most statistically viable approach to determining discrepancy, it

is difficult to implement because of the calculations necessary.

Even if schools use similar methods to determine discrepancies, the teams may come to different identification conclusions, because the standards for determining a severe discrepancy vary. For example, one district may say a severe discrepancy exists if there is a one standard deviation discrepancy in scores (usually 15 points); another district may use a two-standard-deviation cutoff point. Different assessment methods and different tests may also be used, and therefore different discrepancies exist because of differing measurement error.

These are but a few of the reasons that debate has begun about using a response-to-treatment alternative for identifying students with learning disabilities. Perhaps a combination of the IQ-achievement discrepancy and the response-to-treatment model may provide the best identification process (Kavale, 2002). More research is necessary in both how discrepancy identifies students with learning disabilities from their nondisabled but low-achieving peers and how effective response-to-treatment approaches are.

Council for Exceptional Children

**CEC Knowledge Check**
In your opinion, is it one model or the other, or a combination of both? Defend your answer.
LD1K5, CC9S2

The debate about definition and how the definition is operationalized continues to be heated. We return to this debate after outlining the methods of eligibility determination. In the next sections of this chapter, we describe the traditional eligibility process mandated in IDEA and the alternative eligibility process, currently referred to as response-to-treatment, that is included in the most recent reauthorization of IDEA.

## What Is the Traditional Eligibility Process?

The purpose of the eligibility process, whether traditional or alternative, is to determine if a student is a student with a disability and to identify the educational needs of the student. The traditional eligibility process has several steps, including (1) **referral** or request for evaluation, (2) evaluation procedures, and (3) eligibility determination. In addition, each LEA may set up procedures for helping teachers and students before a referral is made. The process is both time and labor intensive in order to ensure the protection of student rights and the collection of appropriate data.

**referral** a formal request to evaluate a student to determine if that student is a student with a disability

## Prereferral Strategies

IDEA requires that schools make efforts to identify all students with disabilities, and teachers have a legal responsibility to refer any student they suspect of having a disability. Nevertheless, procedures designed to prevent unnecessary and inappropriate referrals are both legal and professionally desirable. Nearly all schools have instituted **prereferral strategies** of some type. Typically, these approaches involve groups of teachers and other professional personnel (e.g., school psychologist, social worker) called **child study teams,** student assistance teams, teacher assistance teams, and so on. A teacher having problems teaching or managing the behavior of a student asks for the assistance of the team. The team then helps the teacher implement and monitor alternative instructional or behavior management methods. Only after these alternative approaches have been implemented and have failed to resolve the problems is the student referred to an evaluation team consisting of representatives from the medical, psychological, social, and educational arenas for evaluation of eligibility for special education.

Before concluding that a referral is appropriate, the student's teacher must take certain actions. The teacher must discuss the problems with the student's parent or guardian. Referral should never come as a surprise to the student's parent. The teacher must also document the student's academic or behavioral difficulties and the effects of reasonable attempts to resolve them. This means that the teacher must keep careful, systematic records not only of the student's achievement and behavior, but also of what interventions were tried and how the student responded.

Hasty referrals and those for problems that can be resolved without special education are not justifiable. However, undue delay in referral in the face of clear indications that the student may have a disability and need special education is unprofessional and illegal, even if prereferral interventions are being implemented. Referral does not, of course, guarantee that the student will be found eligible for special education. In Jamal's case, few prereferral strategies were attempted by the general educator. The school psychologist thought this was an important consideration.

**prereferral strategies** instructional or organizational strategies that attempt to help a student achieve before a referral is made for special education evaluation

**child study teams** groups of teachers, parents, and other professionals who provide guidance in helping solve a child's academic or behavioral difficulties before making a referral for special education evaluation

Council for Exceptional Children

**CEC Knowledge Check**
What are the two procedures that must occur before a student can receive a formal evaluation to be considered for services in special education? Who is an essential partner to the process? Is there ever an exception to one of the requirements?
CC1K6, LD1K4, CC8K3

---

Jamal

One of the issues in the case of Jamal, as I see it, is the fact that the teacher did not try many prereferral interventions before referring him for special education evaluation. Ms. Hamilton, his teacher, described Jamal as having difficulties in phonemic awareness, completing assignments, and following directions. She stated that she "gave him extra reading time and some special attention" but that was it. In addition, I see some behavior issues present in Jamal, particularly the talking back and recruiting other students to misbehave when the teacher asks him to do tasks he doesn't feel good about. I think he has issues surrounding his mother, his deceased father, and his performance in school.

*Maria Rivera, school psychologist*

## Referral for Special Education Evaluation

If prereferral strategies are not successful, a parent, teacher, or other person may formally request that the LEA conduct an evaluation to determine if a student is a student with a disability. The request is a formal document that is forwarded to the designated administrator in the LEA with the signature of the requestor. It is at this point that the rules and regulations under IDEA bind the LEA to complete certain steps with **procedural safeguards** for the student and family.

Once the formal request is received by the LEA, the designated administrator must make a decision as to whether an evaluation will be conducted. The administrator considers documentation of a student's performance in the classroom and strategies attempted to help the student in making the decision. Once the decision is made, the LEA notifies the parents of the decision and the reasons for the decision. If the LEA decides against evaluation, no assessments are completed. If the LEA decides to conduct an evaluation, a team of professionals—usually including a school psychologist, teacher of students with learning disabilities, general educator, administrator, and others—meet with the parent to review existing evaluation data and decide what additional evaluation data will be needed, who is responsible for collecting those data, and what the timeline will be. Before any assessments can be conducted, the LEA must make sure the parent understands the evaluation purpose and what assessments will be given. The parent must agree with the LEA's decision and give permission before the evaluation is undertaken.

Referral of students for evaluation for special education is a topic about which many complaints have been lodged. The most frequent are that teachers are too quick to refer students for evaluation and that the reasons for referral are more often misperceptions of the student's behavior, perhaps created by cultural or gender bias, than the student's actual learning difficulties (Patton, 1998; see also Ysseldyke, Algozzine, & Thurlow, 1992, pp. 187–188, 371). However, referrals might be interpreted to mean that the teacher genuinely needs assistance (Gerber & Semmel, 1984), and some studies of referral have found that students' academic problems, not misbehavior, are the primary reasons for referral (e.g., Lloyd, Kauffman, Landrum, & Roe, 1991). Other research has indicated that teachers' concern about students' performance leading to referrals does not appear to be racially or gender biased (e.g., MacMillan, Gresham, Lopez, & Bocian, 1996). Ultimately, "the referral decision is grounded in the child's absolute level of achievement [in comparison to his classroom peers] rather than comparing it to an expected level of achievement based on the individual child's aptitude or achievement in other subjects" (MacMillan & Siperstein, 2002, p. 294).

The referral process has been criticized not only because too many students are referred, but also because most referrals do eventually result in the student's being found eligible for special education services. In a survey of directors of special education, one team of researchers found that 73% of students who were referred were found eligible for special education (Algozzine, Christenson, & Ysseldyke, 1982). These and similar findings have led some to criticize referral and placement practices, particularly for learning disabilities, and to suggest that referral and placement rates are unjustifiably high (Ysseldyke et al., 1983; Ysseldyke et al., 1992). However, no one has suggested an ideal rate of referral (e.g., that 1% of students

**procedural safeguards**
processes outlined by IDEA that ensure the rights of the student and child in the special education process (e.g., the parent must give permission for evaluation procedures)

Council for Exceptional Children

**CEC Knowledge Check**
What are the rights and responsibilities of LEAs and parent(s) or guardian(s) in the referral for special education evaluation?
CC1K4, CC1K6, LD1K4, CC8K3

Council for Exceptional Children

**CEC Knowledge Check**
The findings on referral to eligibility are mixed. What is your opinion on the issue? What is your rationale?
CC8K2, CC9S2

should be referred each year) or an ideal ratio of referred to eligible students (e.g., 2 to 1, meaning that one student would be found eligible for each two referred).

## Evaluation

In traditional eligibility determination, LEAs assess students to determine if they are not achieving commensurate with their ability or age level and if a severe discrepancy exists between ability and achievement in the areas of oral expression, listening comprehension, written expression, basic reading skill, reading comprehension, mathematics calculation, and mathematics reasoning. In addition, the LEA must complete an observation of the student in the classroom, a vision and hearing screening, and other measures to rule out mental retardation, emotional disturbance, and environmental, cultural, or economic disadvantage as reasons for the difficulty in school. Again, the purpose of the evaluation is to determine if the student has a disability and to identify the educational needs of the student.

In order to determine the above, the evaluation of a student includes many measures. In addition to the data already collected about a student and the student's academic history, standardized, norm-referenced tests; informal, classroom-based measures; and vision and hearing screenings are generally administered and observations are made in the classroom. Whatever assessments are decided upon, the LEA is responsible for having enough data at the eligibility meeting to make decisions about the criteria for a specific learning disability. Therefore, evaluations of students usually include assessments across multiple domains of skill and strategies of data collection.

### Domains of Assessment

Specific domains of performance, including aptitude, intelligence, attitude, and a variety of abilities related to sensory and social perception, should be assessed. These domains may also involve the basic processes or curriculum areas in which learning disabilities may be suspected or confirmed. Each domain presents unique challenges in conceptualizing the problem of poor performance as well as unique difficulties in measuring the characteristics and abilities deemed most important. However, as will become apparent in this discussion, these domains are interrelated. That is, problems in one may be intimately connected to problems in others. For example, we cannot assess language without attention to cognition, socialization, and the learning environment. Assessment of mathematical abilities requires attention to cognitive and language skills as well.

The following subsections provide a brief overview of the domains of assessment that we discuss in more detail in other chapters. Although we do not address every possible area of the typical school curriculum (which includes science, health and physical education, and other areas of instruction), the domains covered here provide the basis for identifying learning disabilities and for designing interventions with implications for all aspects of the curriculum.

**Language Abilities** Language, more than any other area of performance, is critical to human interaction. **Communication**—the ability to decode (receive and un-

Council for Exceptional Children

**CEC Knowledge Check**
What is the purpose of a formal special education evaluation?
CC8K2, CC8K3

**communication**   the ability to decode (receive and understand) and encode (express and send) messages

derstand) and encode (express and send) messages—is at the heart of language. **Language** is the communication of ideas by an arbitrary code or system of symbols. Because language difficulties are increasingly seen as the basis of most learning disabilities, classroom teachers are expected to master the basic concepts underlying language development, language disorders, and instruction designed for students with language disabilities. In order to assess students' language competencies and particular problems, teachers must understand how language develops and how spoken and written languages interrelate. They must also understand how language learning communities vary and how to distinguish cultural differences in language from language disabilities (van Keulen, Weddington, & DeBose, 1998). In most cases, if spoken language is involved, the teacher can count on the help of a speech-language pathologist in the evaluation. The speech-language pathologist generally has an in-depth knowledge of the components of language and of language development. The language problems related to learning disabilities may involve oral language or written language. Some students with learning disabilities have pervasive language problems involving all aspects of language usage. Others have difficulties primarily in one aspect of language, such as reading or writing.

*Mathematics Abilities*  The domain of mathematics learning is very broad and includes basic concepts related to **numeracy,** computational skills, and problem solving requiring reasoning about quantities. Computational and reasoning skills may be applied to whole numbers or fractions, money, a variety of types of measurement, algebraic equations, geometry, and more advanced areas of mathematics. As with language, the teacher assessing difficulties in mathematics must be able to identify precisely what the student knows and does not know and be able to understand what concepts and skills are prerequisites for learning more complex ideas and competencies (Smith & Rivera, 1991). The most fundamental concepts and skills in the mathematics domain are often those with which students with learning disabilities have problems (see Taylor, 1997, for further discussion).

*Cognitive Abilities*  We generally refer to pervasive disabilities in cognition as mental retardation. Individuals with learning disabilities have adequate cognitive skills in most areas but difficulty with specific cognitive tasks, such as deploying their attention or processing specific types of information. Cognition includes a wide variety of **information-processing** skills, including perception, attention, memory, comprehension, and guidance of one's own thinking (see Conte, 1991; Swanson & Cooney, 1991; Taylor, 1997; Wong, 1991). One or more of these processes (e.g., attention) may be impaired across all types of academic tasks, leaving the individual with inadequate task-approach skills even though the other cognitive processes are intact. Alternatively, an individual may have difficulty processing information only in a particular area, such as a poor ability to remember words or word sounds even though memory for other information is unimpaired.

*Social Skills*  Learning disabilities have always been seen primarily as problems of academic performance. However, problems in social relationships have always been associated with academic inadequacy. Some individuals with learning disabilities

**language**  the communication of ideas by an arbitrary code or system of symbols

Council for Exceptional Children

**CEC Knowledge Check**
When assessing oral and written language as part of the evaluation process, whose expertise might the special education teacher draw on, and what must be carefully guarded against?
CC6K3, CC8S6, LD8K2

**numeracy**  pertaining to numbers and counting

Council for Exceptional Children

**CEC Knowledge Check**
How would difficulty in information processing be exhibited when a student with a learning disability tries to have a conversation or read a book aloud?
LD3K3

**information-processing** a theory of how information is learned or remembered in the brain, including components of sensory register, short-term memory, working memory, and long-term memory

**CEC Knowledge Check**

Do students with learning disabilities sometimes have social skills deficits? Or is this a coexisting characteristic of a behavior disorder?
LD2K3, LD3K1

**CEC Knowledge Check**

Why are environmental factors part of the evaluation process? Refer back to the current IDEA learning disability definition.
LD1K5, CC8K2, CC9S4

**CEC Knowledge Check**

Evaluation of students for special education services can result in mislabeling. Some of the reasons can be the assessment instruments themselves. Explain this statement.
CC8K4, LD8K1, LD8K2

**valid**   whether a test or assessment device actually measures what it purports to measure

**reliable**   whether a test or assessment device can provide similar results on each administration

**neuropsychological assessment**   assessment of neurological signs and processes related to brain dysfunction, such as motor skills and memory

have excellent social skills, but many have very poor social skills and consequently experience serious social problems (Bryan, 1991; Taylor, 1997). Many students with learning disabilities have emotional or behavioral problems, and a substantial percentage of these can be said to have a coexisting emotional or behavioral disorder. Thus, assessment of social perceptions and interactions is a critical aspect of the assessment of learning disabilities.

***Environmental Factors***   Learning problems do not exist without a context or environment. An important aspect of the assessment of learning disabilities is finding out whether an inadequate environment could be the primary cause of the student's difficulty or a factor contributing significantly to inadequate performance (see Lloyd & Blandford, 1991; Taylor, 1997; Ysseldyke & Christenson, 1987). The learning environment includes the physical space (classroom arrangement, work areas) and the things (desks, tables, instructional materials, equipment) and people (pupils, teachers, other adults) in it. It also includes the home, community, and culture in which the student lives. The social aspect of a learning environment is defined by the emotional tone or climate of the classroom and the interactions among pupils and adults. The instructional environment must also be assessed, including such variables as the amount of time allocated to instruction, the difficulty and interest level of tasks, the sequence in which tasks are presented, the pace of instruction, the frequency of opportunities to respond, and the structure of expectations and rewards.

### Strategies of Assessment

Assessing learning disabilities requires that we assess an individual student's academic and social learning. However, besides finding out what a student knows or can do, we also must have a basis for comparing the student's performance to what we assume is "normal" or typical for students similar in age, gender, cultural group, intelligence, and opportunities to learn. The same strategies are used to assess learning disabilities and all students' learning, but particular attention is paid in the former to how performance in specific areas differs from what the student's other characteristics lead us to expect.

Regardless of the assessment strategy being considered, basic concepts of measurement must be applied to its evaluation. We must ask whether the measurement we obtain is **valid:** Did I measure what I intended? We must also ask whether the measurement is **reliable:** Could I or someone else obtain the same result again? Validity and reliability are psychometric concepts that raise complex issues beyond the scope of our discussion here (see Taylor, 1997; Wallace, Larsen, & Elksnin, 1992, for further discussion). The important point is that the accuracy (validity) and dependability (reliability) of measurement are critical issues in the selection and use of any assessment strategy.

***Neuropsychological Assessment***   Historically, learning disabilities have been linked to neurological factors. Assessment that attempts to link neurological problems to psychological characteristics is called **neuropsychological assessment.** This assessment strategy usually involves giving a battery of tests assumed to measure a variety of processes known to be affected by brain dysfunction. For example, the tests might measure muscle tone, posture and gait, motor skills and coordination, auditory and visual perception, memory, attention, receptive and expressive language, cognition, and academic achievement. However, these tests do not measure neurological functioning directly. Furthermore, many neuropsychological test batteries are of questionable reliability and validity for measuring learning disabilities (Obrzut & Bolick, 1991). Many neuropsychological test batteries were designed for use with adults with known brain damage, and the downward extension of these tests to children makes their appropriateness all the more questionable because of the developmental differences between children and adults in neurological and psychological functioning.

The sophistication, glamour, and mystery of the neurosciences and psychological testing lead many people to exaggerate the reliability and validity of neuropsychological assessment and overvalue its usefulness for teachers. A complete neurological assessment can be done only by a physician, usually one with special training in neurology. A neuropsychological (or psychoneurological) assessment, however, might be done by a psychologist specializing in brain-behavior relationships. Very few (if any) teachers can do neuropsychological testing competently, but teachers should know about the kinds of tests given and their implications for selecting educational methods.

*Contextual Assessment* Comprehensive and competent assessment of students with learning disabilities involves more than testing or measuring specific performance outcomes of instruction. It also requires **contextual assessment,** or attention to context, to the student as a person living in various environments. The student's perceptions and thoughts about the environment of the school and classroom, the objective characteristics of the learning environment itself, and other aspects of the student's life outside of school must be assessed. Assessing these contexts usually involves interviewing the student and others and directly observing the student in various contexts.

A thorough contextual assessment may also require researching school records to determine the history of the student's problems. Such a search can often be highly informative about the social and academic contexts that the student has experienced. Some teachers may avoid looking at a student's records because they do not want to be biased by what others have said. However, a systematic search of archival records may turn up information that will help the teacher anticipate problems, avoid mistakes that others have made, and choose strategies with a higher probability of success (see Walker, Block-Pedego, Todis, & Severson, 1991). Fear of bias must not prevent teachers from using the information available to them.

One means of obtaining important information about students and their environments is interviewing them and significant others in their lives (Lopez-Reyna & Bay, 1997). Getting students who have academic or social trouble in school to speak candidly is no minor feat (Hughes & Baker, 1990; Kauffman, 1997). Extracting accurate and relevant information from interviews requires keen judgment and excellent communication skills (Morgan & Jenson, 1988), as does interviewing parents and school personnel. But skillful interviews can reveal much that is useful

**Council for Exceptional Children**

**CEC Knowledge Check**
Will you, as a special education teacher, be administering or interpreting a neuropsychological assessment? Is it worthwhile to include this on the list of completed assessments in the formal evaluation process? Why, or why not?
CC8K4, CC8S1

**contextual assessment** an assessment of the context in which the student functions both in school and in other settings

**Council for Exceptional Children**

**CEC Knowledge Check**
Why is it valuable to gather relevant background information in the evaluation process?
CC8S1

in planning for teaching, such as the students' most and least preferred activities, students' thoughts about their capabilities, and parents' ability and willingness to supervise homework activities.

Observations can add significantly to the information obtained through interviews. Sometimes there are important discrepancies between what individuals say in interviews and what we find through observation. Moreover, direct observation of the student's behavior in the classroom and other settings (hallways, cafeteria, playground) can provide more precise measurement of academic and social problems. Classroom observations can also be the basis for assessment of the learning environment, helping to pinpoint ways in which the environment might be altered to address the student's learning problems. To be most helpful, observations of the student and the environment must be carefully planned and systematic so that behavior and environmental conditions are defined precisely, appropriate samples of activity are obtained, and results are presented understandably (see Alberto & Troutman, 2003; Kerr & Nelson, 1998).

Skillful teachers take note of errors that students repeat. The pattern of mistakes a student makes, whether on an academic task or in a social situation, often provides the key to successful instruction (Colvin, Sugai, & Patching, 1993; Lopez-Reyna & Bay, 1997; Taylor, 1997). When teachers can anticipate student errors, they can devise plans to help students learn to avoid these errors. Teachers and other professionals can conduct error analyses on any aspect of the assessment process. For example, a standardized reading test may provide standard scores and grade equivalents, but the administrator can also evaluate the pattern of mistakes and conclude that the student does not decode medial vowels correctly or does not know multiplication facts. Error analysis is particularly useful in developing instructional objectives.

***Standardized Testing*** The tests educators are interested in are most often measures of skill, knowledge, or aptitude related to school success. **Standardized testing** involves tests that include set procedures for administration, objective scoring criteria, and a specific frame of reference for interpreting scores. Standardized tests may be designed for administration to individuals or groups.

Set procedures for administration mean that the test instructions (including any time limits that are set) and materials (as well as examiner responses to questions) are fixed. Standardized tests usually have detailed manuals that state exactly how they are to be given, including exactly what the examiner is to say. The purpose of having set procedures is to make the testing conditions as consistent as possible so that fair comparisons can be made among the scores of the people taking the test. Set procedures for administration are important for all types of standardized tests, including those with multiple-choice answers, and for other forms of standardized assessment, such as rating scales or direct observation.

Objective scoring criteria are obvious when there is only one correct answer to a test item. For items having more than one possible right answer and those for which some responses might be better than others, specific criteria are needed for making judgments. Adequately standardized tests have manuals with explicit scoring criteria to use in judging answers; these criteria make the scoring process more objective and reliable.

**CEC Knowledge Check**

Why is observation information valuable to the evaluation process? CC5K1

**CEC Knowledge Check**

How can special education teachers use student errors to help improve instruction? LD4S6

**standardized testing** tests that include set procedures for administration, objective scoring criteria, and a specific frame of reference for interpreting scores

A specific frame of reference for interpreting scores means there is a comparison group, standard, or expectation for use in judging what the test scores mean. The frame of reference may be a specific normative group (as for norm-referenced tests), a specific performance criterion (as for criterion-referenced tests), or a specific way of evaluating answers (as for nonreferenced tests). (See Figure 3.1 on page 82.) In interpreting standardized test scores, we must always keep in mind the way the standardization sample—the group to whom the student is being compared on the test— was selected. If the comparison group is substantially different in demographic characteristics (e.g., region of the country, age, sex, socioeconomic level, ethnicity), then the norms or performance criteria used for comparison may be misleading.

Standardized testing can provide an indispensable picture of how a student's performance under standard testing conditions compares to that of others or to a specified criterion. Knowing how a student compares to others is valuable in determining whether the student's performance is adequate to meet social expectations. Standardized tests can also provide useful information about how a student approaches problems under specified conditions. The information from standardized tests can thus help teachers aim initial instruction at the right academic targets (see Hammill & Bryant, 1991; Taylor, 1997). Furthermore, teachers appear to rely heavily on standardized tests in assessing learning disabilities (Lopez-Reyna, Bay, & Patrikakou, 1996).

However, standardized testing has limitations. It is not very useful in guiding instruction. It has been criticized as offering misleading information regarding students' capabilities, being biased or unfair to certain groups, distracting attention from instruction, and being an exorbitantly expensive approach that yields trivial information, particularly for exceptional children (see Choate et al., 1995; Choate & Evans, 1992; Poteet, Choate, & Stewart, 1993). Thus, although standardized testing is extremely valuable in assessing learning disabilities, other assessment strategies must be considered as well.

*Teacher-Made Tests* **Teacher-made tests** may include a variety of procedures devised by a classroom teacher or other professional to assess specific skills. Such testing has the advantages of flexibility and low cost and offers the possibility of deriving data with direct relevance to classroom instruction in that the tests measure small increments of knowledge or skill and thus indicate how close the student has come to mastering the material being taught. The disadvantages of teacher-made tests are that there are no norms, aside from comparisons to the student's classmates, and the tests can be so poorly constructed or administered that they are misleading (Taylor, 1997). The skillful teacher knows when and how to probe students' understanding and how to use these informal measurements in planning the next step in instruction. Informal teacher-made testing is indispensable in assessing students with learning disabilities. These students' progress in the curriculum must be monitored more frequently and more accurately than that of typical learners.

*Curriculum-Based Assessment* **Curriculum-based assessment (CBA)** or **curriculum-based measurement (CBM)** is a way of addressing the mismatch between what is taught and what is tested by sampling the student's performance very frequently. Performance is sampled at least twice weekly, usually more often, in the

Council for Exceptional Children

**CEC Knowledge Check**
List two types of valuable information that standardized tests can yield. These tests are considered to be biased. Give two reasons why.
CC8K4, CC8S2, LD8S1

**teacher-made tests** a variety of procedures devised by a classroom teacher or other professional to assess specific skills

**curriculum-based assessment (CBA),** or **curriculum-based measurement (CBM)** an approach to assessment based on the assumption that learning problems and progress are best measured directly, as performance in the curriculum, rather than indirectly, as test performance related to underlying processes; includes systematic, frequent, brief samples of the student's performance in the curriculum being taught

## Norm-Referenced Tests

Norm-referenced tests allow us to measure how a student performed on a test compared to other students. The normative group used for comparison may be any specified collection of students (e.g., other students in the school or district, the state, or the nation). The normative group's scores have a *range* (highest and lowest score), *mode* (the most frequent score), *median* (the score in the middle of the range, with half the scores higher and half lower), and *mean* (the average score, calculated by adding all the scores and dividing by the number of scores).

These basic statistical components can be used to describe how a student's test score compares to that of others in any defined comparison group for which scores are available. *Percentile rank*—what percentage of the normative group scored the same or lower on the test—is another useful and easily understood comparison. For example, if a student's score is at the 77th percentile, we know that 77% of the individuals in the normative sample scored the same as or lower than this student (and, of course, 23% scored higher); if the student's percentile is 48, then 48% scored the same or lower and 52% scored higher. *Standard scores* are additional statistics depicting how a student performed in comparison to the *normative group.* The normative group is the group that is assumed to be a representative sample and is used to establish a typical or normal distribution of scores, including a normal range, mean, and percentiles.

## Criterion-Referenced Tests

Criterion-referenced tests are designed to measure the extent to which students have mastered specific skills. The test items are administered under standard conditions, and there are objective criteria for scoring, but students' scores are compared to a standard expectation (e.g., at least 90% correct) rather than to a comparison group's performance. The standard expectations or criteria were undoubtedly derived from an analysis of what most students of comparable age were able to learn, but the idea of criterion-referenced testing is to compare the student's performance only to the criterion itself, not to the performances of others.

## Nonreferenced Tests

Some tests with standardized administration and objective scoring do not use a normative group or criterion for comparison, but instead focus on the problem-solving strategies used by students in approaching problems. The assumption behind these *nonreferenced tests* is that it is important to find out how the student formulates answers to problems, not to compare the student to a group or expected level of performance. For example, if a student is asked to solve the problem $x - 27 = 53$, then we may assess how the student attacks the problem and thereby obtain a better understanding of what he or she needs to learn, if anything, in order to solve similar problems efficiently.

Council for
Exceptional
Children

**CEC Knowledge Check**
What are the primary uses and limitations of each type of test described?   CC8K4

Council for
Exceptional
Children

**CEC Knowledge Check**
What are the advantages and disadvantages of teacher-made tests vs. CBA/CBM?
LD4S6, CC8K4, CC8S2, CC8S8, CC8S1

curriculum materials that are being used for daily instruction in reading, math, or other curriculum areas (Choate et al., 1995; Deno & Fuchs, 1987; Howell & Morehead, 1987; Lovitt, 1991). For example, three days per week a student might be asked to read orally for two minutes from a story being used in reading instruction, and the teacher might record the number of words read correctly per minute and the number and types of errors made. As samples of the student's performance are collected on subsequent days, the information is entered systematically in a table and also plotted on a graph to reveal the student's progress (in this example, progress in oral reading fluency). The student's performance in the curriculum is tracked, and decisions about changing instructional materials or procedures are based on the extent to which the student reaches the performance goals.

The core methods of CBA—frequent systematic performance sampling, results recorded systematically and plotted on a graph, and both quantitative and qualitative results used to guide teaching procedures—can be applied to a wide variety of curricular areas and performances. For example, CBA is not limited to oral reading fluency, but can also be applied to reading comprehension, as indicated by reactions to what is read, perhaps in the form of story retelling (Tindal & Marston, 1990). In fact, a wide variety of language, math, and social skills has been assessed using CBA (Colvin et al., 1993; Walker, Colvin, & Ramsey, 1995).

***Behavioral Assessment*** The essential features of CBA—repeated measurement under controlled conditions, direct measurement of desired outcomes, and decisions based on quantitative and qualitative data—are also the essential features of **behavioral assessment** (see Alberto & Troutman, 2003; Kerr & Nelson, 1998; Lovitt, 1991). Behavioral assessment is often thought to apply primarily to emotional or behavioral problems, but this method encompasses much more (Colvin et al., 1993; Walker et al., 1995). The specific behaviors measured may be academic or social. However, in both CBA and behavioral assessment, precise specification of the desired outcome is important, direct and frequent measurement of the desired performance is continued across time, and decisions about teaching the student academic or social skills are made on the basis of the data.

Behavioral assessment is particularly important, because students' individualized education programs (IEPs) must now by law include plans for managing behavior problems if the student exhibits serious inappropriate behavior (Yell & Shriner, 1997). The IEP must include positive behavioral interventions, strategies, and supports to address such difficulties. Teachers must have a proactive behavior intervention plan based on a **functional behavioral assessment,** and such assessment should delineate the inappropriate behavior, the expected behavior, and the positive and negative consequences that will be applied to help the student learn to behave appropriately. (See Alberto & Troutman, 2003; Kauffman, Mostert, Trent, & Hallahan, 1998; Kerr & Nelson, 1998; Walker, 1995; Walker et al., 1995, for further discussion of behavior management.)

***Interactive Assessment*** Standardized tests administered according to the instructions in the test manual provide a static measure of the student's ability. This measure is fixed by what the student has learned up to the time of testing. A relatively new way of testing, one that bridges standardized and teacher-made tests, is interactive assessment. Feuerstein (1979) introduced this way of testing, which he called dynamic assessment. Feuerstein's methods have been modified and elaborated by others (e.g., Budoff, 1987; Campione & Brown, 1987; Carlson & Wiedl, 1992).

**Interactive assessment** is a way of assessing how the student uses cues, prompts, and instruction to learn during testing (Haywood, 1992; Palincsar, Brown, & Campione, 1991). (See Figure 3.2 on page 84.) This method attempts to assess the potential of the student to learn with specific instruction; the intention is to use the information gained through this assessment for prescribing more effective instruction (Palincsar et al., 1991).

The interactive assessment of intelligence or learning potential has been criticized as lacking reliability and validity as well as implications for remedial methods (see Frisby & Braden, 1992; Laughon, 1990). One of the reasons reliability of measurement is difficult to achieve with interactive assessment is that the prompting

**behavioral assessment** direct, frequent observation and recording of specific target behaviors

**functional behavioral assessment** procedures designed to find out why a student exhibits problem behavior, including assessment of the antecedents and consequences of behavior and the apparent purpose of the problem behavior

Council for Exceptional Children

**CEC Knowledge Check**
A functional behavioral assessment (FBA) plan is part of an IEP when a student exhibits what? What are the three essential parts of an FBA? CC5K2

**interactive assessment** a way of assessing how the student uses cues, prompts, and instruction to learn during testing

## FIGURE 3.2  Example of Interactive Assessment

In the following vignettes, Palincsar and colleagues (1991) illustrate the difference between static and interactive, or dynamic, assessment. First, they describe how an examiner might respond in a static assessment.

> The child is seated with an examiner and presented a page that has five rows of letters, with eight letters in each row. At the end of each row of letters are four blank lines. The examiner tells the child that she is to look at the letters in each row and then figure out what letters belong in the blank spaces. The task is structured in such a way that, with each problem, the relationship among the letters is increasingly more complicated. The child, with furrowed brow, examines the first row of letters (GWHWIWJW _ _ _ _) pointing to each letter. After a few moments, she smiles, and proceeds to fill in the blank spaces (KWLW). She moves on to the second problem (PZUFQZFV _ _ _ _). She puzzles over it, looks to the examiner who shrugs her shoulders and gently urges "just try your best." (p. 75)

Because this is a typical "by-the-book" static examination, the examiner gives no assistance. The child writes four seemingly random letters in the blanks for each of the remaining problems, spending less time pondering her answers as she proceeds.

This scenario is of the same problem, but the examiner uses an interactive assessment procedure.

> After a few unsuccessful minutes, the examiner asks the child, "Is this problem like any other that you have seen before?" The child responds, "I thought it was like this one but it doesn't work." The examiner urges the child to "read the letters in the problem out loud. . . . Did you hear a pattern in the letters?" The prompt failing, the examiner continues with "Are there any letters written more than once in the problem? Which ones? Does this give you any ideas about how to continue?" With this prompt, there is a smile of recognition and the child successfully completes the problem. When she is presented with the third problem, a problem identical in nature to the second, she is heard to say, "Oh, I know how to do this one. . . . Which letters are here more than one time?" The session continues with the examiner presenting problems either similar to the one presented previously, or differing in degree of difficulty. With each problem, the examiner provides, as needed, a series of prompts facilitating the child's successful completion of the problem. (pp. 75–76)

### A Note of Caution

The interactive assessment of intelligence or learning potential has been criticized as lacking reliability and validity as well as implications for remedial methods (see Frisby & Braden, 1992; Laughon, 1990). One of the reasons reliability of measurement is difficult to achieve with interactive assessment is that the prompting procedures cannot be standardized. The approach requires that the prompts be tailored to each child, so it is difficult to obtain results that can be duplicated at another time or by another examiner. Validity is particularly difficult to achieve when the tasks given in the assessment are substantially different from those the student is given in the curriculum. That is, it is difficult to show that what is being measured is a cognitive skill that applies to other tasks. Although the idea of interactive assessment is quite appealing, it has proven to be extremely complex to implement in ways that are useful to teachers or psychologists, who are expected to assess students with tools that are reliable and valid (Taylor, 1997).

---

**Council for Exceptional Children**

**CEC Knowledge Check**

Will interactive assessment data improve in usefulness over time? Explain.
CC5S6

procedures cannot be standardized. The approach requires that the prompts be tailored to each child, so it is difficult to obtain results that can be duplicated at another time or by another examiner. Validity is particularly difficult to achieve when the tasks given in the assessment are substantially different from those the student is given in the curriculum. That is, it is difficult to show that what is being measured is a cognitive skill that applies to other tasks. Although the idea of interactive assessment is quite appealing, it has proven to be extremely complex to implement in ways that are useful to teachers or psychologists, who are expected to assess students with tools that are reliable and valid (Taylor, 1997).

*Authentic Assessment* Traditional testing, whether standardized or teacher-made, has been severely criticized since the late 1980s, and reformers have called for assessment techniques that better reflect education's emphasis on critical thinking and problem solving (Wiggins, 1993). **Authentic assessment** is thought to give a more "real," or authentic, useful picture of what the student can and cannot do. The emphasis is on examination of what the student has produced as a completed piece of work, not on fragments of performance (as in CBA) or test items taken out of context. Although the idea of authenticity of assessment is inherently appealing, the meaning of "authentic" in assessment procedures is anything but clear (Terwilliger, 1997).

**authentic assessments** assessments emphasizing an examination of what the student has produced as a completed piece of work

To some educators, typical test scores lack authenticity, failing to represent the real abilities of the student and not accurately representing what the student can do or, more important, is expected to do in real life. Interactive assessment procedures may be somewhat more authentic in that they demonstrate what the student can do in a situation more closely approximating real life, in which the individual is likely to get appropriate help from a teacher, peer, parent, or supervisor in learning new tasks. Teacher-made tests can be more authentic if they consist of samples of tasks the student has been taught, are administered under typical instructional conditions, or address real-life problems. However, alternative assessment practices are considered necessary if measurement of student abilities is to be most meaningful.

Alternatives to typical assessment procedures may take a wide range of forms and are described by a variety of labels, including authentic assessment (Poteet et al., 1993; Taylor, 1997; Wiggins, 1993; Worthen, 1993). Performance assessment (a wide variety of samples of student work) and **portfolio assessment** (collecting samples of students' best work over time) are two examples of authentic assessments.

**portfolio assessment** the collection of samples of student's best work over time

The idea of portfolio or performance assessment may initially seem simple. On closer examination, such assessment becomes much more complex. How does the teacher decide just what to include, how and to whom to present it, and how to evaluate it? Evaluating the products of a portfolio or performance assessment requires developing a scoring system for various aspects of the products in it. If the evaluation of such portfolio items is to be reliable and valid, the teacher must not only be able to specify the criteria for scoring, but also communicate those criteria effectively to students, parents, and other teachers.

Council for Exceptional Children

**CEC Knowledge Check**
What types of assessment instruments would be used to evaluate labeling of learning disability? Defend your answer.
LD1K5, CC8K2, CC8K3, CC8K4

### Requirements for Evaluation Procedures

IDEA does not identify what specific strategies are to be used in the determination of a learning disability but it does outline requirements for the evaluation procedure. These requirements include:

1. using a variety of assessment tools and strategies to gather relevant functional, developmental, and academic information, including information provided by the parent;
2. not using any single procedure, measure, or assessment as the sole criterion for determining whether a child is a child with a disability or determining an appropriate educational program for the child; and

3. using technically sound instruments that may assess the relative contribution of cognitive and behavioral factors, in addition to physical or developmental factors. (IDEA, S.1248, 2003)

In addition, the LEA must guarantee that the tests and other measures are not discriminatory on a racial or cultural basis; are provided and administered to the extent practicable "in the language and form most likely to yield accurate information on what the child knows and can do academically, developmentally, and functionally"; are used for purposes for which the assessments or measures are valid and reliable; are administered by trained and knowledgeable personnel; and are administered in accordance with any instructions provided by the producer of such tests (IDEA, S.1248, 2003).

### A Special Note about the Teacher's Role and Confidentiality

The classroom teacher is the most critical member of the team that completes a student's educational evaluation. This evaluation cannot be handled solely by a psychologist or other person designated to do testing and observations. Although formal testing and structured observations may be necessary to assess a student's eligibility, the teacher needs to provide data on the student's performance and behavior in the classroom. The teacher should be able to answer such questions as the following:

1. Is the student academically lagging behind peers? If so, by how much is the student delayed? What evidence is there of this delay (e.g., work samples, test scores, curriculum-based assessment)? What are the student's instructional levels in the subjects you teach?
2. Does the student perform much better in some curriculum areas than in others? How even or uneven is the student's performance across the curriculum and across time (i.e., day to day and week to week)? How does classroom performance compare to what you would expect from standardized test results?
3. What is the student's record of completing in-class and homework assignments correctly and on time?
4. Does the student exhibit problem behavior in school? If so, how often, in what circumstances, and with what consequences does it occur?
5. To what extent does the student exhibit discrepancies in ability to learn through listening and speaking compared to reading and writing? That is, what evidence do you see that the student has particular problems related to language in its oral and written forms?
6. What support services has the student received (e.g., speech-language therapy)? What evidence do you see that these have been beneficial?
7. What instructional or behavior management strategies have you tried with the student, for how long, and with what results? What support and guidance in using these strategies have you received from other professional personnel (e.g., principal, special education teacher, school psychologist)?

Council for
Exceptional
Children

**CEC Knowledge Check**
Who is the most critical member of the student's evaluation team in terms of collecting, creating, and maintaining confidential records?
CC8K2, CC8S10

Clearly, assessment for special education entails amassing a lot of information about the student. Questions then arise about who should have access to the information and how differences of opinion about it should be resolved. School personnel must keep test results and other records about the student confidential. No one but teachers and other professionals who work with the student should have access to this information without parental permission. It is illegal and unethical to share information from the assessment with others who are not directly involved with the student's education. However, parents must, by law, be informed of the results of the assessment in language they can understand and must be allowed to see their child's records if they so request. If the parents and school personnel do not agree that the assessment has been adequate, the parents have a right to have their child evaluated somewhere else and present the results to the school. Then, if the parents and school cannot reach an agreement about the assessment, they may ask for mediation by a third party. By law, either the parents or the school system may request a due process hearing, which is much like a court proceeding. If the hearing fails, either party may file a formal legal suit to resolve the issue.

Jamal's evaluation consisted of a variety of assessments across skill domains. In the eligibility meeting, each person tried to make clear to Mrs. Smith the types of information collected about Jamal.

Council for Exceptional Children

**CEC Knowledge Check**
Who has the right to agree or disagree with assessment findings and ask for mediation, a hearing, or a legal suit? CC1K6

Now that we've introduced ourselves, Mrs. Smith, I'd like to begin our meeting by letting you know exactly what types of information we will be sharing with you to help us all understand Jamal. I evaluated Jamal's achievement using both standardized and informal measures, including the *Woodcock-Johnson Psychoeducational Battery—III* (WJ—III), which evaluates achievement across language arts and math domains. I also administered the *Boehm Test of Basic Concepts* and the *Comprehensive Test of Phonological Processing,* targeting specific areas of difficulty mentioned by Jamal's teacher. Finally, I collected an informal writing sample and completed an error analysis and holistic evaluation.

*Clinton Brown, special educator*

Jamal

Mrs. Smith, I collected data related to Jamal's intelligence, social relations, and participation in the classroom environment. I administered a standardized, norm-referenced test to measure intelligence, the *Wechsler Intelligence Scale for Children—III* (WISC-III), and completed a classroom observation to assess social relations and classroom context.

*Maria Rivera, school psychologist*

Council for
Exceptional
Children

> As you may remember, Mrs. Smith, I met with you to gather information about Jamal's developmental, health, and school history, as well as his adaptive behaviors and family information.
>
> *Marcie Chan, school social worker*

## Eligibility Decision

Once all of the evaluation components are completed, the team meets to review the assessment data and to answer two questions: (1) Is this a student with a disability? and (2) Does this student need special education services? The team consists of qualified professionals, particularly those who conducted the assessments, and the parents. The team cannot determine that the student is a student with a disability if the determining factor is "lack of scientifically-based instruction in reading, lack of instruction in mathematics, or limited English proficiency" (IDEA, S.1248, 2003, p. 7).

The team must explain the results of the evaluation in language that the parents understand and provide the parents with copies of the evaluation documentation. If a student is determined not to be eligible for special education services, the team can make suggestions for other forms of assistance. If the student is determined eligible for special education services, the process moves to the development of an individualized education program (IEP). Development of an IEP can occur at the same meeting but often it is done at a subsequent meeting of the IEP team. In Jamal's case, the team had a difficult decision to make.

Jamal

> As we review all of the information gathered, I want you to know I concluded that Jamal is a capable learner with a strong vocabulary and large store of incidental knowledge. I noted deficits in memory of repetition of digits and abstract assembly of objects, as well as the fact that Jamal has some "issues" with his mother and misses his father. During the classroom observation, I noted that Jamal was disruptive and attempted to recruit other students to join him. These behavioral issues may have been affecting his learning and should be evaluated more thoroughly. I do not see, from my current data, that Jamal has a learning disability.
>
> *Maria Rivera, school psychologist*

> I conducted the educational evaluation and determined that Jamal had some weaknesses in the areas of oral language, reading, and written language. Specifically, Jamal has difficulties decoding words, spelling, and comprehending text that does not include picture clues. I concluded that Jamal is not achieving as would be expected for his world knowledge and intelligence.
>
> *Clinton Brown, special educator*

For more detail about the deliberations, review the conversation in the Case Connections boxes on pages 91–93.

> I think we should try more prereferral strategies, including behavioral assessments, and collect more curriculum-based data before declaring Jamal eligible for services, even though a discrepancy exists between his ability (measured by IQ; WISC—III) and his achievement in reading, written, and spoken language (measured by the WJ—III and informal measures). Jamal has been evaluated by a speech pathologist in the past. Perhaps we also need to get more detailed information about his spoken language skills.
>
> *Maria Rivera, school psychologist*

> I'm afraid we need to catch Jamal early and get him some help or he'll get too far behind.
>
> *Irene Smith, Jamal's mother*

> Why don't we defer our decision and collect a little bit more information about what's going on in the classroom with Jamal? I'll collect more behavioral data and curriculum-based data, and Ms. Hamilton can try more strategies aimed at helping Jamal. I think having Jamal reassessed by a speech-language pathologist is also a good idea. That will really help us generate information for instruction.
>
> *Clinton Brown, special educator*

(See Figure 3.3 A and B, page 90, for examples of the curriculum-based data collected over the 30-day deferment period. The special educator collected approximately three weeks of oral reading fluency and correct letter sequence data on Jamal after the team deferred decision on his eligibility. As you can see from both graphs, Jamal is lagging behind his peers in both absolute terms (i.e., number of words read) and in growth rate (i.e., the two trendlines have different slopes). From these data, it is clear that Jamal is having difficulty in both areas when compared to his class peers.)

> [Jamal's Eligibility Meeting Reconvened] Mrs. Smith, we are meeting again to share the new data we've collected about Jamal. Now that we've collected more data, we can make decisions about his needs. The behavioral data indicated that Jamal did no more talking out than many of his peers. The curriculum-based information indicated that Jamal was behind his peers in reading in both absolute terms (i.e., number of words read correctly) and in his learning rate (i.e., the two trendlines had markedly different slopes).
>
> *Clinton Brown, special educator*

 Jamal

 Council for Exceptional Children

**CEC Knowledge Check**
Before reading further, do you believe that Jamal's mother is being included as an active participant through effective communication? Why, or why not? CC10S4, CC10S10

 Council for Exceptional Children

**CEC Knowledge Check**
Do you believe it was in Jamal's best interest to conduct the additional assessments after the first meeting? Or should they have been done before? Explain. CC8S7, CC9S3, CC9S12

 Jamal

**trendline** the line indicating the general direction of data change

**learning rate** the pace at which a student is learning (e.g., John learns three new words a day)

FIGURE 3.3    Jamal's Curriculum-Based Measures Visual Display. The
special educator collected approximately 3 weeks of oral reading fluency and
correct letter sequence data on Jamal after the team deferred decision on his
eligibility. As you can see from both graphs, Jamal is lagging behind his peers in
both absolute terms (i.e., number of words read) and in growth rate (i.e., the red
and green trendlines have different slopes). From this data, it is clear that Jamal is
having difficulty in both areas when compared to his class peers.

## A. Jamal's Reading Fluency

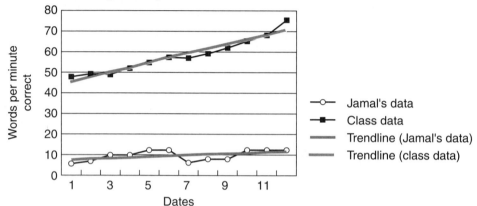

## B. Jamal's Correct Letter Sequence

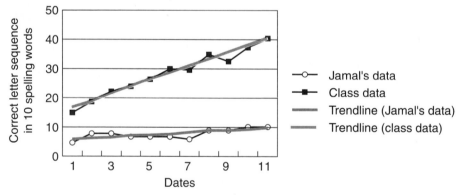

Hi, Mrs. Smith. I'm Jannette Jones, the speech-language pathologist.
I worked with Jamal to try to determine how he was performing in
the area of spoken language skills.

   In terms of Jamal's auditory processing skills, tests indicate
he has well-developed auditory discrimination skills—he can distinguish between the different sounds used in English. However, he has

# Jamal's Initial Eligibility Meeting

Excerpts from Jamal's evaluation data:

## WISC—III Scores

Verbal IQ 109
Performance IQ 99
Full-scale IQ 105

## Classroom Observation:

During the observation, the teacher interacted with Jamal very little. The class was rehearsing their part in the holiday pageant for the next day. The situation was unsettled. Jamal seemed to have a problem with following directions. He had a conflict about the authority of the teacher. She treated it gently, so he got away with challenging her. The other children seemed to follow his lead. One time he scowled at the authority figure (teacher) and turned back to his peers to propose that they do something wrong.

## WJ—III scores

| | Grade Score | Age Score | Standard Score By Grade | By Age |
|---|---|---|---|---|
| Reading | 0.9 | 5–10 | 80 | 90 |
| Mathematics | 1.4 | 6–7 | 95 | 105 |
| Written language | 1.0 | 6–0 | 87 | 92 |
| Oral language | 0.8 | 5–5 | 78 | 80 |
| Knowledge | 3.2 | 8–6 | 123 | 126 |

## Comprehensive Test of Phonological Processing

Phonological awareness 75
Phonological memory 80
Rapid naming 90

The team considering Jamal's evaluation data met on two separate occasions before making a final decision. In the initial meeting, members determined that more data needed to be collected about Jamal's performance in several areas. Here are excerpts from the original eligibility discussion.

*School psychologist:* I realize there is a significant discrepancy between Jamal's full-scale IQ score and his performance on achievement tests given by the special educator in the areas of reading and oral language. However, I'm worried about his performance in the classroom. I don't think we have enough data to

*(continued)*

make a decision today. I want to know if Jamal has any issues of attention deficit hyperactivity disorder or of behavior problems that could be impacting his learning. I also want to know more about his reading and spoken language skills.

*Special educator:* At this point, we do not have the number of times that Jamal talks out or acts out in class. It is an area of concern at times but not nearly as much of a concern as his reading and spoken language performance.

*School psychologist:* What do we know about his performance in those areas when compared to his peers in the classroom? What types of interventions have you been using, Ms. Hamilton?

*Ms. Hamilton:* I have tried giving Jamal extra time to read and also giving him some individual attention in the classroom during reading instruction.

*School psychologist:* Are there other strategies or interventions that could be tried before we say Jamal has a learning disability? In my assessment, he did not show the discrepancies that you all are describing.

*Mrs. Smith:* I just want my son to get some help with his reading. I've been listening to all of the reports that say if you don't catch kids early then they may fall behind. Can we do something to help Jamal now?

*Special educator:* I think it's important to know exactly how we could help Jamal without just labeling him and putting him in a program. We need more data for the IEP about what his specific needs are and how he is performing in relation to his peers.

*Ms. Hamilton:* We wouldn't be here if he wasn't performing poorly in relation to his peers. But I am more than happy to try some alternate strategies if I can get some help in doing that. I'm not trying to push him into special education. I just want to make sure he receives some help.

*School psychologist:* I realize that Jamal may appear to be struggling. I still think he is quite a bright young man. Before we make a decision, I think we need to try a few more instructional strategies, collect data about Jamal in the classroom, and get more information about the behavioral component. A speech-language assessment would be appropriate also.

*Mrs. Smith:* I'm willing to go along with this as long as we set a date in the near future to meet again and make a decision. My son needs some help.

*School psychologist:* That won't be a problem. We all want to get Jamal some help so we are not going to waste time here. Let's reconvene in about three weeks to see what more we know about Jamal.

**Council for Exceptional Children**

**CEC Knowledge Check**
Why do you think the special educator wanted to collect more data before making a decision?
CC8S1

# Jamal's Eligibility Meeting Reconvened

Excerpts from the subsequent eligibility meeting:

*School psychologist:* I want to thank everyone for meeting to discuss Jamal again today. In our initial meeting, we decided that we would collect more data on Jamal's behavior and his reading skill as it compares to other students in his classroom. Over the past month, Mrs. Smith, the special educator, Jamal's teacher, and I have collected more information to help us all make the decision about whether Jamal is a student with a learning disability. We also have a report from the speech pathologist.

*Mrs. Smith:* I'm anxious to hear what you found.

*School psychologist:* I asked Ms. Hamilton to keep track of the number of times that Jamal talked out of turn or was disciplined in the classroom for inappropriate behavior. This was to rule out the behavior issues I saw in my initial classroom observation. In reviewing the information that Ms. Hamilton gave me, it appears the behavioral issues are minimal—Jamal acted out no more than other students in the classroom. So we can cross that out as a possible cause of any learning problems.

*Special educator:* I worked with Ms. Hamilton to provide Jamal with more time to complete reading tasks. I work in her classroom as a co-teacher during reading, so I was able to help him a bit, do some repeated readings with him, and give him more supervised time to read. I also taught the class some reading strategies and did some choral reading with groups. While doing these things, I asked that Jamal read to me from the classroom text for one minute every other day or so. I recorded the number of words he read and also the number of words read by other students in the class. Here is a chart that gives you a display about his oral reading. [Special educator shows Mrs. Smith the chart. See Figure 3.3.]

*Special educator:* As you can see, Jamal's oral reading fluency is below the rest of the class and it doesn't appear to be improving, even with the strategies we tried.

*Speech-language pathologist:* Many of Jamal's reading problems could stem from his difficulty manipulating the sounds of spoken language at the syllable and phoneme level. In my assessment of Jamal, it was quite clear that he struggles when asked to do tasks that require breaking words down. This is definitely an area of need for instruction for Jamal.

*Mrs. Smith:* It looks like he's way below the others in the classroom! I didn't realize he was having such trouble.

*Ms. Hamilton:* Neither did I. I think we now know the extent of the problem and can act on it.

difficulty with rapid repetition of isolated sounds. I said, "/h/ /h/ /m/ /h/ /h/ /f/ /h/ /h/ /r/" and he couldn't repeat them.

When I assessed Jamal's ability to manipulate sounds or phonemes, he began to struggle. These are the skills that are so important in reading. For example, Jamal had difficulty segmenting words into their distinct sounds. He could say *cat* but could not break the word into /c/ /a/ /t/. Jamal's lower level of performance on this skill and others, such as blending, may be causing some of his difficulties in reading.

*Jannette Jones, speech-language pathologist*

With this evidence and the standardized test data, I think we can all agree that Jamal is a student with a learning disability who needs special education services.

*Maria Rivera, school psychologist*

Thank goodness—now he can get some help.

*Irene Smith, Jamal's mother*

## What Is an Alternative Eligibility Process?

The most recent reauthorization of IDEA allows LEAs to use a process of determining if a student responds to scientific, research-based instruction to determine eligibility for special education services as a student with learning disabilities rather than requiring the LEA to document a severe discrepancy between ability and achievement (IDEA, S.1248, 2003). This process is being called *response-to-treatment* or *response-to-intervention*. The process has been implemented in a few school districts around the country, with varying rates of success.

### How Does Response-to-Treatment Work?

There are several ways in which researchers and schools have begun to implement response-to-treatment processes (Fuchs, Mock, Morgan, & Young, 2003). Many of these experimental sites have used the process at the younger elementary grade levels (e.g., first and second grade; Speece, Case, & Molloy, 2003) and on a small scale (e.g., experimental schools or districts). In general, a response-to-treatment process includes several stages of data collection and intervention. First, students who are not achieving at the level of their peers are identified, and they receive some form of intervention. This intervention may be additional instructional strategies in the general education classroom or some form of remedial instruction. Again, data are collected on these students, and those who still do not respond to instruction (i.e., those who do not improve their skills with the intervention) may receive another level of more intense intervention. This may be in the form of more intensive instruction or individual tutoring. If students then do not respond by improving their skills, they are referred for special education services (Vaughn & Fuchs, 2003). In most cases, the data collected through the process and the information contained in the student's school records provide enough information for the eligibility decision. Therefore, the student does not have to go through additional evaluation procedures for an eligibility decision to be made. The variations in this approach include differing instructional interventions, differing numbers of levels of intervention before special education, and differing ways in which students are determined to be "nonresponders" to instruction.

## Issues around the Response-to-Treatment Process

The response-to-treatment alternative eligibility process is relatively new, with little research to indicate whether it alleviates the problems identified in the discrepancy model of determining eligibility (Fuchs et al., 2003). There are at least four potential advantages of the response-to-treatment alternative: "(1) identification of students using a risk rather than a deficit model, (2) early identification and instruction of students with learning disabilities, (3) reduction of identification bias, and (4) a strong focus on student outcomes" (Vaughn & Fuchs, 2003, p. 140). These potential advantages directly address shortcomings alleged in the discrepancy model. However, there are also six potential questions that may cause problems with the model (Vaughn & Fuchs, 2003).

Council for
Exceptional
Children

CEC Knowledge Check
What are the advantages in the response-to-treatment labeling process? LD1K5

One question is whether learning disabilities are "real" in this model. In the LEAs that have implemented a response-to-treatment model, once a student failed to respond to instruction, they were determined eligible for special education services and served in a noncategorical fashion (Fuchs et al., 2003). This has the potential to focus teachers on the individual needs of each student but also to make it more difficult to deliver specific instructional services to students with learning disabilities and not other disabilities.

Another question is whether there are validated intervention models and measures to ensure that the instruction that students receive is the quality instruction that would improve their achievement. A related question is whether there are adequately trained personnel to implement these interventions and collect data. The major premise behind the response-to-treatment model is that the instructional variables are taken out of the picture—students receive the best instruction available. So, if they do not respond to this instruction, a specific disability must exist in the child. Is it possible to guarantee that teachers know and are able to implement the level of quality instruction to ensure an eligibility committee that a disability exists? At present, this would be hard to prove. Still another question is whether inadequate response-to-instruction is a defensible endpoint in the identification process (Vaughn & Fuchs, 2003). How does the eligibility committee determine whether the lack of response is due to a learning disability or whether it is due to mental retardation or another disability? Will the special education instruction provided produce better outcomes for the student?

A further question is how intensive does the instruction have to be to determine a learning disability? In one study of the response-to-treatment approach, the intensive instruction was defined as strategies delivered in a general education classroom. In another, the intensive instruction included hours of individual tutoring (Fuchs et al., 2003). These two models would identify different students as those with disabilities. A final issue is when would due process be initiated? IDEA guarantees many rights and protections, including timelines that force schools to act within a reasonable time standard. These are not guaranteed under a response-to-treatment alternative. What is even more of an issue is that the models rely on data collected at different points in time. Therefore, an LEA that uses a model that collects data on a weekly basis may be able to determine that a child is a nonresponder in a shorter period of time than an LEA that collects data on interventions on a monthly basis.

One of the most powerful questions about this model is how an LEA decides what a nonresponder is. Should a cutoff point on a standardized test be used? Should a **dual discrepancy,** both a significant difference in the rate of progress and in the level of skill ability, be used to identify nonresponders? In recent research, different tests and cutoff points identified different groups of children as having learning disabilities (Fuchs, 2003). This is an issue with the discrepancy model also. It is one of the difficulties inherent in the identification of learning disabilities. (For more on the issues of identification, see the Multicultural Considerations box on page 97.) In sum, though there are many problems with the traditional or IQ-discrepancy model of eligibility that has been the hallmark of learning disabilities since P.L. 94-142, there are also problems with the alternatives. More research is necessary to determine if the response-to-treatment alternative is truly viable on a large scale.

**dual discrepancy**   a student's performance on an academic measure (e.g., reading fluency) is significantly different than that of peers, in both level of achievement and rate of progress

Council for Exceptional Children

**CEC Knowledge Check**
The response-to-treatment approach carries a number of unresolved issues. Which is most critical? Why? Is there is a potential solution? LD1K5, CC8K2

## What Is the Individualized Education Program?

An IEP is a written agreement between the student's parents and the school about what the student needs and what will be done to address those needs. It is, in effect, a contract about services to be provided for the student. The IEP must have the parents' approval. It must be written within 30 calendar days after the student has been found eligible for special education services. A new IEP can be written each year, but LEAs may also offer a three-year IEP to students who have reached the age of 18 (IDEA, S.1248, 2003). The IEP cannot be changed without parental approval.

The IEP team develops the program. This team includes the parents of the child, a general education teacher who teaches the child, a special education teacher, an LEA representative, an individual who can interpret the instructional implications of the evaluation results (may be one of the members described previously), other members who have special knowledge of the child (at the discretion of the parents or LEA), and, if appropriate, the child (IDEA, S.1248, 2003). These members can meet face-to-face or through other means, such as conference telephone call, as long as all can participate.

The IEP must be written before the decision is made about the least restrictive environment for the student (see Bateman, 1996; Yell, 1998). A good program

## Overrepresentation and Learning Disabilities: A Changing Concern

The overrepresentation of minority students in special education is a concern to many (e.g, Patton, 1998; Reschly, 2002). It has not always been an issue in the field of learning disabilities. In the 1999–2000 school year, the percentage of students identified with a learning disability from the American Indian, Asian/Pacific Islander, Hispanic, and white racial/ethnic groups closely matched the percentage of those groups in the student population. Blacks represented approximately 18% of the learning disabilities population and approximately 14% of the school population (U.S. Department of Education, 2001). According to the 23rd Annual Report to Congress, the discrepancies in minority representation appear to be greatest in the categories of mental retardation and developmental delay. Evidently, a learning disability is not viewed with the same stigma as mental retardation (MMR). However, following litigation about overrepresentation of minorities in mental retardation, there has been an increase in the number of students identified with learning disabilities (Reschly, 2002). It is probable that reluctance to identify minority students as mentally retarded has led to labeling many of them learning disabled—a less pejorative classification. Much of the controversy comes from the eligibility process.

Some have criticized the traditional eligibility process for the disproportionate representation of minority students in special education and in learning disabilities specifically (e.g., Patton, 1998). One of the major concerns, drawn from the difficulties with MMR identification, is the use of IQ tests in the identification of students with learning disabilities. For example, Patton (1998) states, "Given the ambiguity and subjectivity embedded in the mild disabilities categories, teacher judgments in the referral process combined with the inherent biases of the assessment process contribute to the disproportionate referral and special education placement of African American students" (p. 27).

The National Research Council examined the problem of overrepresentation of minority students in special education and issued a report in 2002. The committee found that "The higher representation of minority students occurs in the high-incidence categories of mild mental retardation (MMR), emotional disturbance (ED), and to a lesser extent learning disabilities (LD), categories in which the problem is often identified first in the school context and the disability diagnosis is typically given without confirmation of an organic cause" (p. 1). In addition, the committee made two other important findings: (1) that a disproportionately high number of minority students lived in poverty and were poorly prepared for school entry and (2) that the urban schools that many minority students attend lacked resources and adequately trained teachers to help students make up for lost ground. These difficulties often lead to students being identified as having a disability and needing special education services once they fail in school. The committee went on to say, "The subjectivity of the referral process allows for students with significant learning problems to be overlooked for referral, and the conceptual and procedural shortcomings of the assessment process for learning disabilities and emotional disturbance give little confidence that student need has been appropriately identified. Importantly, current procedures result in placements later in the educational process than is most effective or efficient" (National Research Council, 2002, p. 4).

Recommendations to combat the problem include an alternative eligibility process similar to the response-to-treatment approach described in this chapter. Proponents suggest that this process is less reliant on controversial IQ tests, more able to "catch" students early, and less racially biased. Much research must be done to determine if this, in fact, is the case. The National Research Council report includes a proposal similar to the response-to-treatment approach but concludes, "Early efforts to identify and intervene with children at risk for later failure will help all children who need additional supports. But we would expect a disproportionately large number of those students to be from disadvantaged backgrounds" (2002, p. 5). It will be important for research to determine whether it is race or poverty that affects the identification of minority students for special education services and whether an alternative eligibility process is truly more racially blind.

**Council** for
**Exceptional**
**Children**

**CEC Knowledge Check**
Is it poverty or race or some other factor(s)? Is response-to-treatment the solution to finding an answer?
LD1K5

Council for
Exceptional
Children

**CEC Knowledge Check**

An IEP must be written within how many days after eligibility? Name four people who must attend the IEP meeting. When is the LRE determined? Who must approve the IEP?
CC1K4, CC1K6, CC7S3, CC8S6, CC10K2

cannot be written on the basis of standardized test information alone. Performance data from teacher-made tests related to the curriculum as well as observations, interviews, and other nonstandardized assessment strategies are indispensable for writing adequate instructional goals and objectives and specifying the instructional services to be provided. These data are also important in making decisions about where services will be provided.

## Components of the Individualized Education Program

The IEP includes components related to every aspect of the student's education, from annual goals to transition and behavioral plans. In fact, IDEA states that the IEP team must consider the strengths of the child, the concerns of the parents, the results of the initial (or most recent) evaluation, and the academic, developmental, and functional needs of the child (IDEA, S.1248, 2003). Therefore, it is important that the data collected for determining the eligibility of a student address all aspects of a student's learning and behavioral needs so that they can be used in IEP development.

### Present Level of Performance and Goals

The IEP must include a statement of the student's present levels of academic achievement and functional performance (IDEA, S.1248, 2003). The IEP team develops this statement of performance from the evaluation data available, whether through initial evaluation or from documented progress throughout the IEP review term, usually one year. This statement must include how the disability affects the student's progress in the general curriculum or, if the student is a preschooler, how the disability affects participation in appropriate activities.

Council for
Exceptional
Children

**CEC Knowledge Check**

What data besides standardized test scores are used to design an IEP?
CC5S6, CC8S1, CC8S2

The IEP must also include a statement of measurable annual goals (IDEA, S.1248, 2003) that meet the student's needs to progress in the general curriculum, as well as to meet the other educational needs of the student that result from the child's disability. In other words, the IEP must contain goals toward which the student and teachers will work that will help the student progress in the general curriculum. This does not mean that standards or goals from the state-mandated general curriculum be included in the IEP. Rather, it means that measurable goals must be included that will help the student achieve in the state-mandated curriculum. For example, if a student is having difficulty reading, the IEP should address annual goals for the specific reading skill development necessary for this child, not include the general curriculum goals for that grade level for all students.

The annual goals for the IEP must be measurable, because the team must include a description of how the student's performance toward these goals will be measured and reported. This progress monitoring is a high priority in IDEA. The IEP team may include curriculum-based assessments, authentic assessments, contextual assessments, teacher-made tests, or behavioral assessments as means to monitor a student's progress toward goals. Parents must receive a report of the student's progress at least as frequently as report cards are issued to all students (IDEA, S.1248, 2003).

Jamal's team developed a present level of performance statement that includes data relevant to comparing Jamal with his peers and to developing instruction.

> Jamal obtained an 80 standard score on the WJ—III Reading composite. This corresponded to a 0.9 grade score and a 5 years 10 months age score. In the Reading Fluency subtest, Jamal responded to 7 sentences with 3 errors. As of March 3, Jamal read 29 words per minute correctly in a first-grade text. He is reading at a rate that is below his classroom peers and has difficulty completing assignments that require reading.
>
> *IEP team*

Jamal

Council for
Exceptional
Children

**CEC Knowledge Check**

Do you believe this to be an appropriate present level of performance for Jamal? Defend your answer. CC8S6, CC8S7

The team also developed annual goals for Jamal. Here is one example.

> Jamal will read 70 words per minute in connected first-grade text with no more than 3 errors.
>
> *IEP team*

This annual goal addresses an area of Jamal's weakness (i.e., oral reading fluency) and describes how the goal will be measured (i.e., by reading for one minute in connected first-grade text). The data will be entered into the visual display already created for eligibility determination and provided to the parent on a schedule similar to the report card schedule.

### Statement of Services

> I am so happy that Jamal will be receiving resource room help every day. He needed something extra to help him learn.
>
> *Irene Smith, Jamal's mother*

Council for
Exceptional
Children

**CEC Knowledge Check**

Do you think Jamal needs any related services or assistive technologies in his educational program? If so, what and why? CC5S3, CC7S9

The IEP must also include a statement of the special education and related services, as well as supplementary aids and services, that will be provided for the student. It should also include a statement of the program modifications or supports for school personnel that will be provided. The IEP team must note the services that are necessary for the student to advance toward the annual goals of the IEP, to be involved and progress in the general curriculum, to participate in extracurricular activities, and to be educated with other students with or without learning disabilities. Under IDEA, the IEP must also include a statement of explanation about the extent to which a student will not participate with students without disabilities in the general classroom, a switch from the explanation of how a student would participate with such peers. We come back to the issue of service delivery in the next section.

### Participation in State- and Districtwide Assessments

As the press for higher educational standards has increased emphasis on standardized testing and other statewide or systemwide evaluations, concern for including students with disabilities has grown (McDonnell, McLaughlin, & Morison, 1997).

**CEC Knowledge Check**

What other assessment accommodations might Jamal need? (Refer to the Case Connections boxes, pages 91–93.) CC8K5, CC8S4

The concern is that students with disabilities be included in assessments that will allow them to demonstrate their competence and give them access to later education and employment (Yell & Shriner, 1997).

Whenever possible, students with disabilities must be included in the general or typical testing or other assessment procedures used by the school district or state to monitor all students' performance. In fact, the IEP must include any individual accommodations that are necessary for students to participate in state- and districtwide assessments. If the IEP team determines that the student will participate in alternate assessments, the IEP must include a statement as to why the student cannot participate in the regular assessment and why the alternate assessment is appropriate for the child.

Jamal

It would seem appropriate for Jamal to participate in all standard district- and statewide assessments because he spends most of his time in the general education classroom and curriculum. I would recommend that he receive the accommodations of testing in a small group, redirection by the teacher (for when he was off task), and writing with a scribe.

*Clinton Brown, special educator*

### Transition Plan

**transition** a change in status from the role primarily as student to the role of emergent adult in the community

At the age of 14, the IEP must include **transition** goals and services. These should be appropriate measurable postsecondary goals based upon age-appropriate transition assessments (IDEA, S.1248, 2003). The IEP team may include transition services provided by other agencies in the IEP, as long as a representative of that agency participates in the development of the goals and services. Other agencies may include departments of rehabilitative services, outreach programs, summer programs, or social services. Finally, once the student is within one year of reaching the state's age of majority, the IEP must include a statement that the student has been informed of the rights that transfer at the age of majority. These rights include the transfer of parental rights to the student, meaning the student is then the one to give informed consent and participate as the "parent" member of the IEP team.

### Other Components

The IEP may also include components for special situations. For example, if behavior impedes the student's learning or that of others, the IEP must include strategies and positive behavioral interventions and supports to address the behavior. We deal with this component in greater detail in Chapter 7. If a student has limited English proficiency, the IEP must address the language needs of the student.

### Review of the IEP

The IEP team is required to review the IEP on an annual basis. It may also review and revise the IEP if the student is not making progress toward the annual goals or if new information is provided through a reevaluation or other means. With the reauthorization of IDEA, parents may also opt for three-year IEPs. The IEP team may also revise the IEP if the student's needs change for some reason, such as behavioral issues or greater-than-anticipated progress. At its discretion, the IEP team may decide to revise the IEP if other matters of concern arise. As described before, the parent is an integral part of the IEP team and must be consulted and give approval for IEP changes before they are made.

**CEC Knowledge Check**
Currently, how often is the IEP rewritten?
LD1K3

## Special Education Service Delivery

After the development of instructional goals, the IEP team must determine the **least restrictive environment (LRE)** in which the student will receive special education services. Given that special instruction and related services are to be provided, a model must be constructed for how they are to be delivered to students. A service delivery model is a plan for bringing students, teachers, and instructional methods and materials together—a model of the physical and interpersonal environment required to foster effective teaching and learning. Many models of service delivery have been constructed. Each has certain advantages and disadvantages. None is without merit for some students, and none is without fault if applied universally. Six such models are briefly described, along with a summary of possible advantages and disadvantages of each, in Table 3.1 (pages 102–103).

**least restrictive environment (LRE)** the least restrictive or most "normal" place in which appropriate education, and the greatest access to the general education curriculum that is compatible with the student's needs and goals, can be offered

We can speak of possible advantages and disadvantages of each service delivery model only in the abstract because different individuals perceive and respond to any given environment in very different ways (Gallagher, 1993; Kauffman, 1995). Furthermore, a service delivery model offers only potential advantages and disadvantages; poor implementation can undermine the benefits of any model, and adroit implementation can minimize drawbacks. All six of these models have existed in some form for decades, and it is possible to find many variations and combinations of them in practice.

The order in which these models are presented in Table 3.1 might be considered a ranking from less to more restrictive. Because the LRE provision of IDEA emphasizes removing students with disabilities from the ordinary school environment only as necessary to meet their needs for special education, we begin with the model that involves removing students from their general classrooms as little as possible. Many people associate removal with restrictiveness—the longer the student is in the special education placement, the more restrictive the environment. However, what makes an environment more or less restrictive is open to debate (Kauffman, 1995). Least restrictive must be interpreted in the light of what the student learns in the classroom and school environment (Bateman, 1996).

**CEC Knowledge Check**
Is the general classroom always the least restrictive environment? Explain.
CC5K1

### *What Are Some Issues in Service Delivery?*

The variety of plans or models for delivering special education and related services has led to much controversy about legal, philosophical, and research issues. These issues are interdependent and overlapping. One set of legal and philosophical issues centers on teaching students in inclusive settings, usually interpreted to mean in general classrooms with little or no pullout. Another set of issues has to do with maintaining the full continuum of alternative placements so that there are service delivery

**TABLE 3.1** Service Delivery Options

| SERVICE DELIVERY OPTION | DESCRIPTION | ADVANTAGES | DISADVANTAGES |
|---|---|---|---|
| Collaborative consultation in the general education classroom | Special educators serve as consultants to general education teachers, collaborating with them in planning and implementing instructional accommodations in regular classrooms. | 1. The distinctions between general and special education among students and teachers are blurred.<br>2. There is the opportunity for preventive work with students not identified as having disabilities.<br>3. The stigma of being identified as receiving special education is minimized.<br>4. General education teachers can learn how to approach instructional and management problems and make successful accommodations for learners with special needs. | 1. The special educator's work is spread over a number of classrooms, which prevents intensive, sustained work with individual students.<br>2. Both general and special education teachers can feel that the services they provide are insufficient to meet their students' needs. |
| Co-teaching in the general education classroom | General and special educator team up to teach a class together. | 1. Special and general education can be fully integrated, both for students and teachers.<br>2. Students with disabilities are not labeled as obviously as in pullout models.<br>3. Teachers need not be identified by the students as "special" or "regular." | 1. Both teachers can fall into stereotyped roles with students and with each other so that they are actually on very different tracks that are parallel only in the sense that the teachers share physical space.<br>2. It is possible for students with learning disabilities to play highly predictable roles in the class and to be stigmatized by their differences in academic performance or behavior. |
| Special education resource room | The special education teacher takes students into the special class for instruction only in specific areas in which they have difficulties, perhaps for as little as 30 minutes several times a week, perhaps as much as half of each school day. | 1. Students can spend the majority of their time in the regular classroom with nondisabled peers.<br>2. Special, intensive instruction in one or more specifically targeted areas of the curriculum can be provided with minimum disruption of the students' school experience.<br>3. The articulation between general and special education can be improved. | 1. There is difficulty in coordinating students' and teachers' schedules to avoid disrupting students' general education and in coordinating general and special teachers' schedules so that there is time for consultation.<br>2. With a heavy caseload, the resource teacher can find it virtually impossible to offer adequately intensive and sustained instruction to students in the resource room as well as sufficient consultation with students' regular classroom teachers.<br>3. Students who receive services in resource rooms may be stigmatized by leaving their regular classes and attending a special class, even if for only a relatively brief time. |

TABLE 3.1 Continued

| SERVICE DELIVERY OPTION | DESCRIPTION | ADVANTAGES | DISADVANTAGES |
|---|---|---|---|
| Self-contained special education classroom | A dozen or fewer students are enrolled, with a special education teacher and a paraprofessional staffing the classroom. The purpose of such a class is to provide an environment in which intensive instruction can be offered to individuals and small groups. | 1. There is the opportunity for intensive, individualized, and small-group instruction.<br>2. Students may need to make fewer transitions from one class and teacher to another than they would were they placed in regular classes. | 1. There can be a stigma attached to attending a different class.<br>2. Students can have added difficulty in making friends with students in regular classes.<br>3. Students can experience difficulty in making the transition back to regular classes.<br>4. Curriculum is not aligned with that of the regular class, making a student's integration into the mainstream of the school more difficult. |
| Special day school | A special day school is designed to serve a special student clientele during the entire school day but not before or after school hours. | Major potential advantages of special day schools include those described for residential schools in the next section, except that the day school does not have any direct control over the student's environment during non-school hours. | Major potential disadvantages are also those of the residential school, except that contact with the home and transition back to the regular neighborhood school may be easier. |
| Residential school | Students live in dormitories or other residential units, at least during the school week if not seven days a week, and attend a special school on the campus. | 1. A highly structured environment can be provided 24 hours a day.<br>2. Work can take place on a student's self-control, work habits, and social relationships; this is hard to duplicate when educators have little or no control over what happens outside the school building and before or after the school day.<br>3. Special education and related services are highly concentrated and continuously available.<br>4. The staff are mutually supportive and are in constant close communication about the student's needs and progress.<br>5. Students can benefit from being in a community in which all the other students share many of the same problems. | 1. There is a high per pupil cost.<br>2. There may be a long distance from the student's home to the school.<br>3. Residential schools are "artificial" environments in that they are quite different from the typical home and neighborhood school.<br>4. Some students may feel stigmatized by attending a special residential school, and some may gravitate toward the worst peer models in the school.<br>5. There is limited opportunity to spend time with students who do not have learning disabilities.<br>6. Residential schools are often small, and academic and extracurricular options may be limited, especially in the upper grades. |

options. Research can inform decision makers about these issues, but research has not answered all the important questions about service delivery and policy decisions.

### Teaching Students in Inclusive Settings

Teaching in inclusive settings is often different from what is portrayed in the literature by proponents of the full inclusion of all students with disabilities (e.g., see the cases "Yours, Mine or Ours" [pp. 170–174] and "What's Inclusion Got to Do with It?" [pp. 164–169] in Kauffman, Mostert, Trent, & Hallahan, 1998). Much of the literature on teaching in inclusive settings describes working with students who have severe physical disabilities and/or mental retardation, and these descriptions do not fit the typical situation confronting a teacher of a student with learning disabilities (cf. Bassett et al., 1996; Deno, Foegen, Robinson, & Espin, 1996; Manset & Semmel, 1997).

Teachers in inclusive settings often find that they do not have enough time for planning. Special education teachers often find that they are expected to work with too many teachers and that their time in any one class or with a particular child is too short. Sometimes special education teachers are relegated to the role of teacher's aide or find that the instruction they believe the student with learning disabilities should have is not what the general education teacher wants them to give (e.g., Weiss & Lloyd, 2003). Pulling students aside for special instruction in the general classroom can be more stigmatizing than teaching them in a separate classroom. Resources of time, personnel, training, and materials are often inadequate, and in the absence of the needed supports, teachers often are ineffective. In short, there are many potential problems in teaching in inclusive settings, and research strongly suggests that poorly implemented or inappropriate inclusion frustrates teachers and shortchanges students (Deno et al., 1996; Weiss & Lloyd, 2003; Zigmond & Baker, 1996).

Nevertheless, when inclusion is properly implemented for students for whom it is appropriate, teaching in inclusive settings can be highly rewarding for teachers and beneficial to students. The key is planning carefully, allocating adequate resources to support inclusion, and understanding that inclusion in general education is neither best for all students nor necessarily best done for the entire school day. Working out the specifics of co-teaching and other inclusionary models requires careful attention to the details of what is going to be taught, what specific roles each teacher will play, what materials will be used, and how teaching and learning will be evaluated. We address many of these issues in Chapter 15. Teaching in inclusive settings can be successful and highly rewarding. However, success will not occur automatically, and many educators argue for alternatives to inclusion.

### Maintaining a Continuum of Alternative Placements

The idea of a full array of placement options in special education has been under serious attack since the mid 1980s. The alternative—**full inclusion**—has been proposed as a way of serving all students effectively. However, the presumption that a single model of service delivery can effectively meet the needs of all students inevitably dilutes the focus on individuals that is the hallmark of special education. "Because of its wholesale nature, the concept of inclusion contradicts the individualization that is central to a 'special' education" (Manset & Semmel, 1997, p. 176).

Council for
Exceptional
Children

**CEC Knowledge Check**
Why is inclusion sometimes not beneficial? What needs to occur to improve implementation? CC9S2, CC9S5

**full inclusion** delivering all special and general education services to students with disabilities in the general education classroom

Overenthusiasm for inclusion may bring what Zigmond and Baker (1996) call "too much of a good thing."

> Based on our research, we cannot support elimination of a **continuum of services** for students with LD. Inclusion is good; full inclusion may be too much of a good thing.
>
> Scheduling and excessive case loads have prevented special education teachers from accomplishing their intended purposes. Nevertheless, for students with LD, there are skills and strategies that need to be acquired if instruction in the mainstream is to be meaningful and productive, and these skills and strategies must be taught explicitly and intensively. Providing a venue and the resources for delivering this instruction is not only our moral obligation to students with LD, it is also our obligation under the law. (p. 33)

Zigmond and Baker (1996) and Marston (1996) note that proponents of full inclusion recommend the drastic reduction, if not the complete elimination, of all models but those keeping students with disabilities in general classrooms on a full-time basis. However, research does not support such drastic measures, and many leaders now note the necessity of maintaining the full continuum of placement options that has characterized special education and that is required by IDEA. Marston (1996) concludes:

> The movement toward full inclusion of special education students in general education settings has brought special education to a crossroads and stirred considerable debate on its future direction. Proponents of full inclusion argue that the needs of students with disabilities are best met in the general education setting. For these supporters, the direction to take is to reduce, if not eliminate, special education as a service delivery model. Some critics of full inclusion argue for a different direction, one that returns the special education focus to unique instructional settings such as the resource room. (p. 129)
>
> What is needed in special education is not a retreat from the basic principles that support a continuum of services for students with disabilities, but rather a renewed commitment to the thoughtful deployment of these ideas. Serious attention to the least restrictive environment, including a shared philosophy and commitment by general and special educators, will insure that a variety of learning opportunities across educational settings will exist for all students. (p. 131)

## What Is the Effectiveness of Service Delivery Models?

For those who want to make decisions about service delivery issues based on reliable evidence about outcomes for students, research is critical. Consequently, there has been great interest in finding out which service delivery model produces the best outcomes. Research to date does not provide evidence that any one service delivery model meets the needs of all students, particularly all students with learning disabilities (Deno et al., 1996; Manset & Semmel, 1997; Marston, 1996; Zigmond & Baker, 1996). The research most often cited as evidence that inclusive models are successful was done with students having severe physical and/or cognitive disabilities, not students with learning disabilities.

The legal, philosophical, and research issues discussed here suggest that we should be cautious about promoting a particular service delivery model or saying

**continuum of services,** or **continuum alternative placements**   the full range of alternative placements or educational environments, ranging from full-time placement in regular classes, with supplementary aids and services, through resource room programs, special self-contained classes, special day and residential schools, and programs provided in hospitals or through home-based instruction

**Council** for **Exceptional Children**

**CEC Knowledge Check**

Does research support full inclusion for all students with learning disabilities? LD9S2

that research has provided much guidance for selecting service delivery models. Therefore, our first concern should be improving instruction wherever it is offered; we should be more concerned about the integrity of the services delivered than about the location in which they occur (Crockett & Kauffman, 1999; Kauffman, 1994). Our second concern should be finding out where instruction of a given type can be delivered most effectively (Kauffman & Lloyd, 1995; Kauffman, Lloyd, Astuto, & Hallahan, 1995). Our third concern should be helping students understand that no shame or stigma is attached to receiving the special instruction one needs, being taught by a specialist, or going to a special place to receive that instruction (Bateman, 1994; Hallahan & Kauffman, 1994).

After completing the eligibility process, the team determined that Jamal was eligible for special education services as a student with a learning disability. He received services in both the general education classroom and the resource room. We have reviewed his evaluations, present levels of performance, and annual goals. Throughout the text, we will consider Jamal's performance and his educational needs in the relevant chapters to follow. We have included all of the evaluation data and the IEP for Jamal in the Companion Website for this book (www.ablongman.com/hallahanLD3e). Please refer to this information as you progress through the text.

In addition, information related to Shannon's eligibility for special education services (e.g., her present levels of performance, strategies attempted) is included in subsequent chapters. Shannon was identified early and has received special education services for some time. Her complete file is also available on the Website.

**Council** for **Exceptional Children**

**CEC Content Standards**

1. Foundations
4. Instructional Strategies
7. Instructional Planning
8. Assessment

## PORTFOLIO-BUILDING ACTIVITY

### Demonstrating Mastery of the CEC Standards

The essentials you have now added to your knowledge base from Chapter 3 can be used to design an Action/Decision Flowchart that will be useful in helping you determine what steps to take in assisting a student who exhibits learning disability characteristics. See the Companion Website (www.ablongman.com/hallahanLD3e) for specific directions on how to create your flowchart and for an example. You can use these questions to guide your thinking:

- How do evolving laws and policies influence assessment planning and implementation?

- What are the functions of school systems in the structure of special education? How does this knowledge influence your personal philosophy of special education?

- How are student assessment results used to promote positive learning results, adapt/modify learning environments, and incorporate appropriate learning technologies, while taking into consideration general and special education curricula and cultural/linguistic factors?

- What are the ethical principles of measurement and assessment related to screening, referral, eligibility, program planning, instruction, and placement for individuals with learning disabilities?

# SUMMARY

**What laws govern the delivery of special education?**

- The Individuals with Disabilities Education Act (IDEA) outlines special education processes and services. Students are guaranteed a free appropriate public education through IDEA.
- How is special education defined?
  - Special education is specially designed instruction, at no cost to the parents, to meet the unique needs of a child with a disability.
  - Special education is different from general education in the training and support teachers receive, class or group size and composition, degree of individualization and teacher direction, accuracy and scope of pupil assessment, precision of implementation of instructional strategies, closeness of monitoring of instructional progress, and empirical validation of teaching practices.

**How is learning disability defined in IDEA?**

- There are differences in the conceptual definition and how it is operationalized.
- The definition is often operationalized using a severe discrepancy between ability and achievement of a student.
- There is a traditional eligibility process and an alternative eligibility process. The traditional process is based on assessment data gathered by a team. The alternative eligibility process is based on a student's response to increasingly intensive instructional intervention.

**What is the traditional eligibility process?**

- Teachers implement prereferral strategies to help students before they refer them for special education evaluation.

- The process includes referral for evaluation, evaluation, and determination of eligibility as a student with a disability who needs special education.
- There are a variety of domains of assessment and strategies of assessment used in determining eligibility.

**What is an alternative eligibility process?**

- The response-to-treatment, or response-to-intervention, model provides levels of increasing instructional intensity to students who are not progressing in the curriculum. If students respond to the instruction, they do not continue into higher levels of intensive instruction. If students do not respond to instruction at lower levels, the intensity is increased and may include special education services.
- There are a number of potential advantages in the response-to-treatment model, including identification of students at risk and early identification. There are also disadvantages, including whether the model views a learning disability as "real."

**What is an individualized education program?**

- An individualized education program is an agreement between parents and the school about services that will be provided to a student with a disability.
- An IEP includes statements about a student's present level of performance, goals for achievement, transition plans, participation in state- and districtwide assessments, and related services.
- An IEP also includes statements about where special education services will be delivered.
- There is much controversy over the concept of full inclusion of students with disabilities but IDEA guarantees a student a continuum of alternative placements to serve his or her individual needs.

## REFLECTIONS ON THE CASES

1. Do you agree with the school psychologist's and special educator's request for more data in the initial eligibility meeting? Why, or why not?

2. What seems to be the major issue in the team's decision to defer a decision until more data are collected?

3. Review the case materials related to Jamal. In what areas does he seem to have the most difficulty, according to test results?

4. What would have happened differently if the school Jamal attended used a response-to-treatment approach to identification?

Council for
Exceptional
Children

See Companion Website for detailed correlations between chapter content and Council for Exceptional Children Standards; **www.ablongman.com/ hallahanLD3e**

**CEC Knowledge and Skills Discussed in This Chapter**

**1** The cultural perspectives and environmental factors that influence families, schools, and communities, along with the collaborative relationships fostering respect and beneficial communication.

**2** Identification of roles and responsibilities in creating a learning environment that maintains confidentiality yet assists families and others in assessment and educational planning for individuals with exceptional needs.

**3** Communicating effectively with families of individuals with exceptional learning needs, taking into consideration personal cultural biases as well as culturally responsive factors necessary to promote collaboration in the education planning process.

**4** Ethical accountability in terms of encouraging self-advocacy/independence; support of appropriate services; and identifying services, networks, and organizations to provide life-span support for individuals with learning disabilities.

# Parents and Families

4

I've heard some teachers and other professionals talk about parents and families in such negative terms. They blame them for students' problems, they claim parents don't care, and they dread speaking with them. I can't relate to such statements. I see immense value in working closely with families. With information from Mrs. Smith, for example, I've been better able to identify strategies to address Jamal's reading needs. She has even bolstered my efforts by implementing reinforcement activities at home.

*Ms. Hamilton, Jamal's first-grade teacher*

Historically, parents of children with learning disabilities have played a critical role in advocating for services for their children. In fact, parents have probably influenced the area of learning disabilities more than any other area of special education. It was largely through the efforts of a parent group known as the Association for Children with Learning Disabilities (now known as the Learning Disabilities Association [LDA] of America) in the 1960s that the category of learning disabilities was created. Although teachers and administrators tended to view the academic difficulties of some students as due to laziness or obstinacy, parents argued long and vociferously that their children had bona fide learning problems that needed special attention. Their efforts have paid off in funding and legislation for learning disabilities programs.

## How Have Professionals' Views of Parents Changed?

Professionals' views of the role of parents of children with disabilities have changed dramatically. At one time, it was common for professionals to discount or ignore the concerns of parents regarding their children's development or, worse, automatically blame parents for their children's learning and social problems. The neurological organization theory of the late 1950s and 1960s is an example of how parents were sometimes blamed for the learning problems of their children. This theory held that external manipulation of the limbs of children with learning disabilities would remediate supposedly damaged pathways of the brain and hence improve these children's reading ability (Delacato, 1959). Not only did research fail to demonstrate the effectiveness of this treatment approach, but the program was soundly criticized for placing undue stress on parents to carry out the treatment regimen strictly (Robbins

& Glass, 1969). In 1968, several professional and parent organizations adopted an official statement listing concerns about this approach, including the following:

1. Promotional methods . . . appear to put parents in a position where they cannot refuse such treatment without calling into question their adequacy and motivation as parents;
2. The regimens prescribed are so demanding and inflexible . . . that they may lead to neglect of other family members' needs;
3. It is asserted that if therapy is not carried out as rigidly prescribed, the child's potential will be damaged, and that anything less than 100% effort is useless. (quoted in Hallahan & Cruickshank, 1973, p. 94)

Because of its popularity, this treatment program was much publicized for its allegedly questionable treatment of parents; however, one could make the case that its view of parents was not that atypical for the time. Many professionals, including teachers, viewed parents with little respect, focusing on the negative rather than the positive contributions they could make toward their children's development.

Today, however, the knowledgeable professional understands that parents can play a critical role in helping meet the needs of children with disabilities. Although there are still far too many instances in which teachers ignore or blame parents and although there are undoubtedly some parents who are detrimental to their children's progress, teachers and parents are increasingly working together for the benefit of students with learning disabilities. There have been at least two reasons for this shift toward a more positive working relationship: the recognition of reciprocal effects and the passage of federal laws giving parents opportunities for more involvement.

## Reciprocal Effects

Evidence has accumulated that parents can not only influence the development of their children, but also the reverse can occur—children can exert effects on their parents. This concept is referred to as **reciprocal effects,** the notion that causation between child and adult behavior can go in either direction (Bell & Harper, 1977). Researchers, for example, have shown that some babies, especially those with disabilities, are born with difficult temperaments, which can influence how their parents respond to them (Brooks-Gunn & Lewis, 1984; Mahoney & Robenalt, 1986). For example, Mrs. Smith recounts:

> I've been amazed by the differences between my daughter, Patricia, and my son, Jamal. Patricia was a perfect baby. I remember my initial concerns about having kids . . . overwhelming responsibilities . . . sleepless nights, but when I had Patricia, I thought, "This is a breeze." That changed when Jamal was born. I did things the same way, but he didn't react like Patricia. He cried more and required much more attention. I was more nervous with him than I had been with Patricia.
>
> *Irene Smith, Jamal and Patricia's mother*

Council for Exceptional Children

**CEC Knowledge Check**
How has the role of parents/families of children with disabilities changed over time in terms of involvement in the educational process? CC1K7

**reciprocal effects** the idea that causation between child and adult behavior can go in either direction

Research on reciprocal effects has made professionals more aware that parents are not necessarily to blame for their children's behavioral and learning problems. These findings have also helped teachers gain a better understanding of why some parents of children with learning disabilities sometimes act differently than other parents. That is, it is not difficult to imagine how living with a child with learning disabilities might put parents under stress.

## Passage of Federal Laws

A second reason professionals are now working more closely with parents is that Congress has passed laws stipulating opportunities for more parental involvement. The Individuals with Disabilities Education Act stipulates that parents be given opportunities to participate in meetings involving identification, evaluation, and educational placement of their child. In accordance with the law, parents should also play an integral role in the development of their child's **individualized education program (IEP).** In the case of children under three years of age, schools must involve parents in the design of an **individualized family service plan (IFSP),** which specifies services for the child as well as the family. See Table 4.1 (page 112) for a list of some of the IDEA provisions involving parents.

Research and legislation have thus created a greater appreciation of the importance of being able to work constructively with families of students with disabilities. To ignore parents is to miss out on a potentially powerful source of support for teachers.

## What Treatment Models Are Used with Families?

Recognizing the potentially positive influence parents of children with disabilities can have on the treatment of their children, professionals are more likely than they once were to involve parents as much as possible in the treatment process. It is no longer as common as it once was for professionals to view themselves as the sole source of expertise and parents as the recipients of that expertise. Today, most authorities advocate **family-centered models** of treatment.

> *Family-centeredness* characterizes beliefs and practices that treat families with dignity and respect; individualized, flexible, and responsive practices; information sharing so that families can make informed decisions; family choice regarding any number of aspects of program practices and intervention options; parent-professional collaboration and partnerships as a context for family-program relations; and the provision and mobilization of resources and supports necessary for families to care for and rear their children in ways that produce optimal child, parent, and family outcomes. (Dunst, 2002, p. 139)

Today's approaches to working with families are also characterized by attention to social systems. Bronfenbrenner (1979), a renowned child development and family

Council for Exceptional Children

**CEC Knowledge Check**
What are two important reasons for supporting family involvement in educational planning for a child with learning disablilities?
CC2K4

**individualized education program (IEP)** IDEA requires an IEP to be drawn up by the educational team for each exceptional child; the IEP must include a statement of present educational performance, instructional goals, educational services to be provided, and criteria and procedures for determining that the instructional objectives are being met

**individualized family service plan (IFSP)** a plan mandated by P.L. 99-457 to provide services for young children with disabilities (under three years of age) and their families; drawn up by professionals and parents; similar to an IEP for older children

**family-centered model** treatment model that places the family in control of decision making

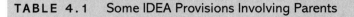

## TABLE 4.1   Some IDEA Provisions Involving Parents

Schools must

- obtain parental permission before conducting evaluations
- provide notice to parents describing evaluation procedures
- use a variety of assessment tools and strategies in conducting evaluations, including information provided by the parent

Parents have a right to

- participate in the development of an individualized family service plan (a plan to provide services for young children with disabilities and their families)
- participate in determining their child's eligibility for special education
- request an assessment to determine whether their child continues to qualify for special education services
- participate in the development of their child's individualized education program
- participate in the consideration of intervention strategies and supports for their child if the child's behavior impedes the child's learning or the learning of others
- participate in the development, review, and modification of their child's behavioral intervention plan if such a plan is deemed necessary
- participate in decisions involving the educational placement of their child
- participate in any manifestation determination review[a] involving their child and to request a hearing if they disagree with the outcome of the review
- examine all records pertaining to their child

---

[a]This procedure is conducted in some cases when a student's behavior is subject to disciplinary action by the school; the IEP team and other qualified personnel determine whether a relationship exists between the student's disability and his or her behavior. If it is determined that no relationship exists, the relevant disciplinary procedures applicable to students without disabilities may be applied to the student.

*Source:*  From "Working with Families" by D. P. Hallahan and E. A. Martinez, 2002, in J. M. Kauffman, M. Mostert, S. C. Trent, and D. P. Hallahan (Eds.), *Managing Classroom Behavior: A Reflective Case-Based Approach* 3rd ed. (pp. 124–140), Boston: Allyn and Bacon. Copyright © 2002 by Pearson Education. Reprinted by permission of the publisher.

**Council for Exceptional Children**

**CEC Knowledge Check**
Federal law upholds the rights of parents to be actively involved in all stages of a child's special education. In implementation, where do you think problems might occur? Why? CC10K1, CC10S1

**social systems approach**
the view that an individual's behavior can best be understood in the context in which it occurs, a significant part of which concerns the family

theorist, was one of the first to promote a **social systems approach** to understanding behavior. His model posits that an individual's behavior can be best understood by considering the context in which it occurs, a significant part of which is the family. Bronfenbrenner stressed that the family, in turn, is influenced by other social systems, such as the extended family (e.g., grandparents), friends, and professionals. The philosophy that there is a reciprocal relationship between the family and society has had an impact on how the field views the role of the family in the educational process.

Several practitioners and researchers have developed models that take into account the fact that individuals fit within families and families fit within a broader social context. Two such models are the family systems approach of the Turnbulls (Turnbull & Turnbull, 2001) and the social support systems approach of Dunst and colleagues (Dunst, Trivette, & Jodry, 1997). These frameworks are helpful in understanding the role of families in the educational process.

## Family Systems Approach

The **family systems model** consists of four interrelated components: family characteristics, family interaction, family functions, and family life cycle.

### Family Characteristics

Descriptive information on the family is referred to as **family characteristics.** These include characteristics of the family (e.g., size, cultural background, socioeconomic status, and geographic location), personal characteristics (e.g., type and severity of the exceptionality, family health, and coping styles), and special conditions (e.g., poverty, substance abuse, and parents with disabilities).

These family characteristics are important considerations for teachers when working with students with learning disabilities. In Jamal's case, for example, some circumstances can make it difficult for the family to offer support. As Jamal's mother indicates:

> I am certainly interested in my son's education, but I'm a single mother and, because I'm a nurse, I work long hours, and my work schedule changes from week to week. Fortunately, I have a good relationship with Jamal's teacher, and I've made it clear to her that I want to help my son. I may not be able to attend every conference, but I always make an effort to be there. Also, I'm more than willing to help Jamal at home, but I don't always know what to do.
>
> *Irene Smith, Jamal's mother*

Teachers must recognize the fact that parents are living under more stress than ever, and competing issues (e.g., job constraints, time pressures, child care, transportation problems) can impede their ability to return phone calls or attend conferences (Spinelli, 1999). As a result, teachers should understand that parents may be distracted and seem uninterested or otherwise nonsupportive of their children's education when, in fact, they are doing the best they can to cope. See the Current Trends and Issues box on page 114 for some recent findings regarding family involvement as it pertains to students with learning disabilities.

### Family Interaction

As Turnbull and Turnbull (2001) indicate, "The family consists of the sum of its members' mutual and reciprocal interactions" (p. 110). To fully understand a child, teachers must understand the child's family. Interaction among family members varies according to the subsystems within each family (e.g., marital partner interactions, parent-child interactions, sibling interactions, and extended family interactions) and the families' cultural beliefs (e.g., overprotection versus appropriate nurturance, passivity versus responsiveness). These interactions can range from facilitative to dysfunctional. Cohesion and adaptability determine the quality of family interaction.

**family systems model** a social systems approach that focuses on family characteristics, family interaction, family functions, and family life cycle in explaining individuals' behavior

**family characteristics** descriptive information on the family, including size, cultural background, socioeconomic status, geographic location, type and severity of the exceptionality, family health, coping style, and special conditions

 Jamal

 Council for Exceptional Children

**CEC Knowledge Check**
What are some of the competing demands/stresses on families that affect teacher-parent/guardian interaction and also affect the education of students with learning disabilities? CC2K3

CURRENT
TRENDS
&
ISSUES

## Family Involvement

Should teachers expect parents and families to be involved in the schooling of students with learning disabilities? This question cannot be answered unequivocally. Some families are highly involved. For others, participation is more passive, and for some, participation is low or nonexistent. What are parents' perceptions of IEP-related activities? To what degree are school experiences a topic of conversation at home? What kind of at-home support do parents provide? Until recently, "no national data have described the extent to which families of elementary and middle-school students receiving special education participate in activities at their children's schools or create home environments that promote student learning" (U.S. Department of Education, 2001, p. III-8).

Results of the Special Education Elementary Longitudinal Study (SEELS), involving families of 13,500 elementary and middle-school students with varying disabilities, provide insight into these important issues. Following are some of the SEELS findings with respect to students with learning disabilities:

### IEP-Related Activities

- A large majority (i.e., 88%) of elementary and middle-school students with learning disabilities had an adult family member attend their IEP meeting during the preceding school year.
- Approximately 65% of parents reported collaborating with school staff on the development of IEP goals; however, 33% indicated that school staff primarily developed the goals.
- A large majority of parents (i.e., almost 90%) agreed or strongly agreed that the IEP goals were challenging and appropriate.
- A large majority of parents (i.e., 91.5%) reported that their children's special education services were either "somewhat" or "highly" individualized.

### At-Home Support

- Fully 90% of parents of students with learning disabilities reported that they "regularly" talked with their children about school experiences (e.g., projects, homework assignments, field trips).
- Almost 84% of students with learning disabilities had help with homework from a family member three or more times per week.
- Almost 64% of respondents reported that someone read to their child three or more times per week.
- Over 90% of students with learning disabilities reportedly had household rules about completing homework and chores and bedtime on school nights.
- Almost 47% of students with learning disabilities reportedly had household rules about acceptable grades.
- Almost 62% of students with learning disabilities in elementary and middle schools reportedly had computers at home.

Council for Exceptional Children

CEC Knowledge Check
Do you think these percentages are acceptable levels, given the regulations of federal law? Why, or why not? What should be the response of an educator? CC10K2

*Source:* From "Family Involvement in the Education of Elementary and Middle School Students Receiving Special Education," in U.S. Department of Education, *Twenty-Third Annual Report to Congress on the Implementation of the Individuals with Disabilities Education Act* (Section III: Programs and Services), 2001b (pp. 7–34), Washington, DC: U.S. Government Printing Office.

---

**cohesion**  the degree to which individual family members are free to act independently

**Cohesion** refers to the degree to which individual family members are free to act independently. Parents of children with learning disabilities often struggle with how much freedom to give their children. Research has shown that parents of children with learning disabilities have a tendency to be overprotective (Green, 1992). Although parents may want to encourage independence in their children, they are also aware that these children require more than the usual amount of supervision. For example, the parents of a young child who has difficulties with directions (a relatively common characteristic of children with learning disabilities) may wrestle with whether they should allow the child to go alone to visit friends in the neighborhood. Similarly, the parents of a teenager who is highly distractible, impulsive, and has poor coordination may debate whether to let their adolescent obtain a driver's license.

**Adaptability** refers to the degree to which families are able to change their modes of interaction when they encounter unusual or stressful situations. Some family members can be very rigid, which makes it difficult for them to adjust to the variable behavior often displayed by children with learning disabilities. Some family members may be so unpredictable or chaotic in their responses that it increases their children's problem behavior. Maintaining the proper amount of adaptability can be very difficult when dealing with children with learning disabilities. It is important that parents be able to "roll with the punches" while maintaining a degree of firmness that communicates appropriate expectations for behavior.

> **adaptability** the degree to which families are able to change their modes of interaction when they encounter unusual or stressful situations

### Family Functions

The many activities in which families engage to meet their everyday needs are considered **family functions.** Families must do a wide variety of things to meet their economic, medical, social, and educational needs. All of these competing demands on the family can make it difficult for parents to be as involved in the education of their children as some teachers would like. Parents of children with learning disabilities tend to be relatively passive participants in IEP meetings (Valle & Aponte, 2002). Teachers need to keep in mind that there may be other reasons why some parents are less than totally engaged in their child's education. Minimal parental involvement may indicate apathy or it may signify that the family is overwhelmed in meeting its other living demands.

> **family functions** activities in which families engage to meet their everyday needs

### Family Life Cycle

The impact that a child with a disability has on the family varies according to the stage of the **family life cycle.** In the early childhood years, for example, there may be little impact on parents of children with learning disabilities, because these children are usually not identified as having problems until they enter school. The early elementary years, however, are typically a time of much unrest. Usually, at this time, parents and siblings are learning to adjust to the child's disability, and parents are faced with myriad decisions pertaining to diagnosis and treatment. Adolescence is a period of turmoil for many families, as teenagers strive to find their own identities. For families of children with learning disabilities, adolescence can be even more challenging. Issues pertaining to such things as dating, planning for postsecondary education or work, and interactions with peers are all likely to be more problematic for teenagers with learning disabilities. As we discuss in Chapter 6, most adults with learning disabilities will struggle to some degree with their problems throughout their lives.

> **family life cycle** the varying stages a family or individual goes through depending on age and stage of development

Council for Exceptional Children

**CEC Knowledge Check**
What family issues may interfere with these families' ability to participate fully with a school? CC10K3

## Social Support Systems Approach

The **social support systems model** stresses the importance of informal rather than formal sources of support for families. This model proposes that families turn to

> **social support systems model** a social systems approach that stresses the importance of informal sources of support (i.e., family, friends, neighbors, social clubs, churches)

friends, neighbors, social clubs, and extended family members for support, rather than relying solely on professionals for help (Dunst et al., 1997). Although Dunst and colleagues probably had in mind families who have children with relatively severe disabilities, this model can also apply to families of children with learning disabilities. These parents may not need respite care, but they will benefit from having someone with whom they can share their concerns and worries. If their child has been recently diagnosed, they can learn from other friends or acquaintances who have children with learning disabilities.

When families do not have their own sources of informal support, a social systems approach can help establish support connections. Putting families in contact with the local chapter of the Learning Disabilities Association (at www.ldanatl. org/), for example, can help them get in touch with other parents for support as well as valuable information on child-rearing approaches and educational options.

Council for Exceptional Children

**CEC Knowledge Check**
Where can families of children with learning disabilities find social support?
LD10K2

## What Are Some Current Trends in American Family Life?

With each passing year, diversity becomes more and more a hallmark of the population of the United States. For teachers, this means that they must be more diligent than ever in understanding their students' surroundings and the **microcultures** to which they belong. These factors can have a profound influence on families and how they respond to having a child with a learning disability. Three important, interrelated areas of diversity that teachers need to be aware of are the family unit; race, ethnicity, and language; and socioeconomic status.

**microcultures** smaller groups (e.g., disability, ethnic group, gender, race, region, religion, social class) within a larger cultural group having unique values, style, language, dialect, ways of communicating nonverbally, and so forth

### The Family Unit

Societal changes marked the latter half of the 20th century (Gersten, Irvin, & Keating, 2002). It is no longer possible to describe the typical family in the United States as consisting of a mother and father, with only the father working outside the home. In 1950, 78% of households contained married couples; by 2000, married couples accounted for 52% of households. Since 1950, the number of single-parent families has increased (Hobbs & Stoops, 2002). There have also been some increases in other nontraditional families (e.g., gay and lesbian couples who have adopted or given birth using surrogates). A variety of factors have contributed to these changes, including women having fewer children, individuals waiting longer to marry, and increased mobility of the population (Hobbs & Stoops, 2002).

### Race, Ethnicity, and Language

In 1900, approximately one out of eight Americans was of a race other than white; in 2000, the ratio was one out of four. This increase in diversity is due to a number of factors, especially the influx of immigrants (primarily from Asia and Latin America). From 1980 to 2000, the Asian and Pacific Islander population tripled, accounting for 3.8% of the total U.S. population by the close of the 20th century. During the same time period, the Hispanic population more than doubled. By 2000, Hispanics represented 12.5% of the U.S. population, almost twice the 1980 proportion of 6.4% (Hobbs & Stoops, 2002). In schools in and around large cities, it is not unusual to find any of a dozen different languages that represent a student's primary language.

Teachers must make concerted efforts to recognize and value family diversity (see the Multicultural Considerations box on page 118). When teachers neglect to consider issues related to diversity, they may come across as disrespectful and patronizing, as one mother of a child with a learning disability recounts: "Is it that maybe some of us don't have the education so they [professionals] look down on us? Is it our race? I don't know if it's because I'm Hispanic. I don't know if it's because of the way that I speak" (Valle & Aponte, 2002, p. 473). Teachers who value family diversity respect and consider family structure and roles, values, decision-making styles, communication styles, language, and background knowledge that may differ from their own.

**Council for Exceptional Children**

**CEC Knowledge Check**

Why is it so important for educators to recognize and value family diversity? CC3K3, CC3K4

## Socioeconomic Status

Teachers are involved with increasing numbers of families in poverty. Almost 17% of all children under 18 are poor—in 2001, a family of three with an income below $14,630 was considered poor (Children's Defense Fund, 2003). According to the U.S. Census Bureau (2002), the nation's poverty rate was 11.7% (i.e., 32.9 million people) in 2001. Poverty is related to the factors of family unit and ethnic diversity in that poverty is disproportionately represented in single-parent families and some ethnic minority groups. For example, for non-Hispanic whites, the poverty rate was 7.8%; for African Americans, the poverty rate was 22.7%; for Hispanics, 21.4%; and for Asians and Pacific Islanders, 10.2% (U. S. Census Bureau, 2002).

Because it involves environmental risks, such as poor health care and inadequate nutrition, poverty not only places children at greater risk of having a disability, but also affects how families are able to cope with a child with a disability. Severely strained financial and psychological resources may impede a family's ability to work with school personnel.

**Council for Exceptional Children**

**CEC Knowledge Check**

What cultural conditions stereotype individuals with learning disabilities and their families? How do these stereotpyes impact education of these students? CC5K9, CC5S1

## What Is the Family's Role?

Families are an amazingly complicated phenomenon to study. So-called normal families display a variety of intricate interactions, both positive and negative. Most of us have strong reactions to and memories about our families. We can recall vividly good as well as bad times in our families. And it is not uncommon to receive very different interpretations of family dynamics from different members of the same family. Families that contain a member with learning disabilities are even more complicated. Just the extra time required to parent a child with learning disabilities can alter how parents and siblings interact with the child who has learning disabilities as well as with nondisabled family members.

# Valuing Diversity

Today, more than ever, teachers can expect to encounter diversity in their classrooms. As a result, they must examine their own cultural expectations and identify any biases that might have a negative effect on their interactions with diverse families (O'Shea & Lancaster, 2001). Teachers can take deliberate steps to show that they value family diversity. O'Shea and Lancaster (2001) offer several ideas:

- Teachers can learn as much as they can about their students' diverse families by talking with parents and other staff, reading books, attending in-service sessions, and viewing films on diversity.
- Family structures, values, and child-rearing practices vary greatly. Teachers can use cultural differences as strengths rather than working at cross-purposes.
- Instead of lumping all groups together, effective teachers recognize that many differences exist within groups of Hispanics, whites, African Americans, or Asian individuals. Lessons reflect this philosophy.
- Each country, each region, and most important, each individual has unique ways of interpreting individual cultural experiences. Teachers recognizing the uniqueness of interpretation experiences plan lessons accordingly.
- Effective teachers actively seek to weed out the stereotypes and prejudices that have been acquired through the teachers' own cultural roots. They try to approach people individually and openly in all home-school encounters.
- Teachers can support families' cultural pluralism by recognizing students' contemporary cultures, cultural pride, and identity.

- Teachers can discuss the negative effects of prejudice and discrimination during lessons.
- Planning ways to include families of linguistically/culturally diverse students in classroom activities can recognize students' use of their native language while encouraging family members to participate in school activities.
- Teachers can plan how to involve minority parents formally and informally in their children's education by asking how and when they want to be involved.
- Adjusting instructional approaches and activities to accommodate cultural backgrounds can help teachers to adjust cultural differences and bring schools and families together.
- Teachers can familiarize themselves with different cultural, language-based, and religious practices, such as fasting or holiday celebrations, that might affect students' school attendance and participation. They can also learn to correctly pronounce students' names in the proper order and how to address students' parents.
- Effective teachers realize the importance of never feeling that they have to apologize for their own culture or ethnicity. As human beings, they recognize that all people have something special to contribute.
- Teachers seek actively to learn about family differences and are sensitive to unique differences. They seek opportunities for students to share information about their home life during social studies, geography, and other classes. (p. 66)

Council for Exceptional Children

**CEC Knowledge Check**
Cultural differences in classrooms will increase over time. Do some teachers have personal cultural bias? Do these affect teaching? Do you believe this is a problem that must be addressed and overcome? If so, how? CC6K2, CC6K3, CC9K1

*Source:* From "Families of Students from Diverse Backgrounds" by D. J. O'Shea and P. L. Lancaster, 2001, in D. J. O'Shea, L. J. O'Shea, R. Algozzine, and D. J. Hammitte (Eds.), *Families and Teachers of Individuals with Disabilities: Collaborative Orientations and Responsive Practices* (pp. 51–76), Boston: Allyn and Bacon. Copyright © 2001 by Pearson Education. Reprinted by permission of the publisher.

## Family Adjustment

For many years, the customary way of viewing parental reactions was to consider them in terms of stage theory—the notion that parents, on learning that their child has a disability, go through a set sequence of emotional reactions over a period of time. Much of the impetus for a stage theory approach comes from work done on reactions people have to the death of a loved one. A typical sequence of reactions, based on interviews of parents of infants with serious physical disabilities, is shock and disruption, denial, sadness, anxiety and fear, anger, and adaptation (Drotar, Baskiewicz, Irvin, Kennell, & Klaus, 1975). Although such a theoretical framework has been more popular when considering children with more serious disabilities, some professionals have used this model in working with parents of children with learning disabilities.

More recently, many researchers have rejected the idea of a fixed sequence of stages through which all parents of students with disabilities pass (Hammitte & Nelson, 2001). Some parents do not experience some of these stages; of those who do, not all experience them in the same order (Friend & Cook, 2003). Further, "within the same family, some members may have strong coping capabilities and others may need much more support because their own capabilities have not yet been developed fully" (Turnbull & Turnbull, 2001, p. 99).

### Parental Guilt

Of the many emotions parents feel when they first learn that their child has a disability, perhaps the most common is guilt. This reaction may occur because the causes of most disabilities are unknown (see Chapter 2). Some parents respond to this uncertainty about cause by blaming themselves for their child's disability.

Results of **familiality studies** and **heritability studies** indicate that learning disabilities can be inherited. There are, however, no quick and easy tests to determine that a child has inherited a learning disability from one or both parents. For some parents, the possibility that their child's learning disability may have been inherited can arouse feelings of guilt; for others, a genetic or biological explanation may help alleviate guilt and even help explain some of their own problems.

### Parental Stress

Raising any child can be stressful. Although helping children to negotiate the many pitfalls of childhood, adolescence, and even adulthood can be very rewarding, the responsibility for the well-being of a child in a society that is undergoing as many changes as ours can be overwhelming. Influences on children of the media, violence, and drugs, to mention a few, make the responsibilities of being a parent complex and difficult.

There is abundant evidence that being the parent of a child with learning disabilities increases the chances of experiencing stress (Dyson, 1996; Green, 1992; Lardieri, Blacher, & Swanson, 2000; Margalit & Almougy, 1991; Margalit, Raviv, & Ankonina, 1992). Although the deficits of learning disabilities are often not as conspicuous as those of children with physical or psychological disabilities, the very fact that students with learning disabilities do function within or close to the mainstream may create some very difficult decisions for parents and students, especially during adolescence. In particular, parents of adolescents with learning disabilities are likely to have difficulty deciding how much freedom and independence to allow

**familiality studies** a method of determining the degree to which a given condition is inherited; consider the prevalence of the condition in relatives of the person with the condition

**heritability studies** a method of determining the degree to which a condition is inherited; a comparison of the prevalence of a condition in identical twins versus fraternal twins

Council for Exceptional Children

**CEC Knowledge Check**

Parents and families of a child with learning disabilities often experience many emotions and reactions. How can these be barriers to the school partnership process?  CC10K3

their children (Morrison & Zetlin, 1992). For example, deciding when the child is ready to assume the responsibility of driving a car is often more difficult for parents of children with learning disabilities.

Another complicating factor is that many parents of children with learning disabilities exhibit external attributions; that is, they view themselves as being powerless to help their children cope with their problems (Green, 1992). How much their attributions are caused by their children's problems, or vice versa, is open to speculation, but the end result is that some of these parents either become dependent and give up trying to direct their children's lives or become overly rigid and controlling (Margalit & Almougy, 1991; Margalit et al., 1992; Michaels & Lewandowski, 1990).

Adding to the plight of some children with learning disabilities and their families is a higher prevalence of family instability and disruption. Researchers have found that children with learning disabilities are more likely than those without such disabilities to experience parental divorce, change of schools, or parental or sibling death or illness (Lorsbach & Frymier, 1992). There is speculation about whether such factors are causal. That is, does a child with a learning disability make the family more susceptible to some of these disruptions, or do some of these traumas contribute to the child's learning disability? Regardless of whether there is a causal connection and in which direction it is manifest, family instability makes it difficult for some families to cope with a child who has a learning disability.

### Sibling Reactions

Research on whether siblings of children with learning disabilities experience more problems in adjustment is mixed. Some siblings have trouble adjusting, some adjust well, and some report that they actually benefit from the experience (Dyson, 1996; Seligman & Darling, 1989; Senapati & Hayes, 1988). Others experience the same positive and negative dynamics found in all sibling relationships (Lardieri et al., 2000), as Jamal's sister indicates:

Jamal

> Jamal has a learning disability because he has trouble reading. Sometimes, he needs contracts and special rewards, but that doesn't bother me. To me, he's just my brother, Jamal. Sometimes, I like him, and sometimes, I don't. We can get along and play games, and I usually like looking out for him since I'm older. Other times, I think he's annoying and I want him to leave me alone.
>
> *Patricia Smith, Jamal's sister*

Generally speaking, however, brothers and sisters of children with disabilities are at a greater risk of having problems in their relationships with their siblings than are siblings of children without disabilities. Resentment can build, for example, because the child with a learning disability receives more attention from parents. It is often difficult for parents to provide an equal amount of care and attention to the child with a learning disability and to the other children in the family. Furthermore, some of the same social problems children with learning disabilities have with their peers (see Chapter 7) are likely to play a role in interactions with siblings. Poor impulse control, difficulties in reading social cues, and so forth can make for volatile sibling relationships.

### Family Reaction

Although a number of problems can confront families of children with learning disabilities, the majority of families adapt very well. Some parents experience having a child with a disability as actually having some positive benefits. They say they have become more concerned about social issues and more tolerant of differences in other people. Some report that their families and marriages have been brought closer together because of their child's disability; they think that the common purpose of rallying behind their child has resulted in greater family cohesiveness. Although there is no definitive research on this, anecdotal evidence suggests that many special education teachers chose their profession because they had a sibling with a disability.

Professionals working with children with learning disabilities and their families must keep in mind that there is no universal set of reactions experienced by these families. Most families adjust well, some experience minor difficulties, and a few experience enough turmoil and stress to be considered dysfunctional.

## Family Values and Attitudes toward Learning

Parents and families play a significant role in determining the social, intellectual, and physical well-being of their children. Parents can exert influence on their children through interactions with them as well as through attitudes. For example, parents can challenge their children intellectually and expose them to a variety of learning experiences, or they can subtly discourage their intellectual development through their attitudes toward school and learning.

A good example of how important families are to the academic achievement of their children is that of the Southeast Asian boat children who have immigrated to the United States. Despite severe economic disadvantages, many of these children do exceedingly well in school. In particular, Indochinese families that maintain their traditional values, which include an emphasis on achievement and learning, outperform their American peers of the same economic status. However, if Indochinese families allow their children to become acculturated to certain American values (e.g., pursuing material possessions and entertainment), the achievement of these children is lower, being closer to that of their American peers (Caplan, Choy, & Whitmore, 1992).

Regardless of the cultural group to which one belongs, children whose parents value education are at an advantage. And for the child with learning disabilities, it is even more important that the family instill a positive attitude toward learning and school.

Council for
Exceptional
Children

**CEC Knowledge Check**
What factors contribute to a family's reaction to a child's learning disability? What is your ethical responsibility to working with these families in a collaborative partnership?
LD9K1, CC10S3

## Parents and Homework

Ask parents of children with learning disabilities what their greatest areas of concern regarding schooling for their children are, and they are very likely to put homework at the top of the list. Ask teachers whether this concern is valid, and they are very likely to concur. Several researchers have documented that parents and teachers view homework as a major stumbling block for students with learning disabilities (Bryan, Nelson, & Mathur, 1995; Bryan & Sullivan-Burstein, 1997; Epstein, Munk, Bursuck, Polloway, & Jayanthi, 1999). Homework can cause a great deal of stress in families of these students, as is revealed in this parent's statement: "Homework has dominated and ruined our lives for the past eight years" (Baumgartner, Bryan, Donahue, & Nelson, 1993, p. 182). Unfortunately, this negative perception of homework starts in the early primary grades (Bryan et al., 1995).

Given that students with learning disabilities have academic problems, they understandably will have difficulties with homework. Their cognitive and metacognitive difficulties, such as poor memory and organizational skills, can cause them problems with homework (see Chapter 8). For example, these students are more likely than students without learning disabilities to forget to bring their homework home or to take their completed homework to school, and they are more likely to lose their homework. In sum, there are few aspects of homework that do not pose major problems for students with learning disabilities.

**Council for Exceptional Children**

**CEC Knowledge Check**

What do parents say is one of the greatest problems they have with their child who has a learning disability? CC10K3

### What Teachers Can Do

To combat difficulties associated with completing homework,

> students with LD need to learn skills related to listening for and accurately recording an assignment, planning how much time should be scheduled to complete it and when to complete it, identifying what materials are needed and taking them home, setting attainable goals related to the homework, recruiting help when needed, monitoring where they are with regard to task completion, and rewarding themselves for sticking to the plan and completing the task. (Hughes, Ruhl, Schumaker, & Deschler, 2002, p. 2)

One promising means for accomplishing this is teaching assignment-completion strategies such as the PROJECT Strategy, which has been taught to middle-school students with learning disabilities (see Figure 4.1).

First, students prepare their forms by noting events (e.g., tests, project due dates, athletic games/events, holidays, birthdays) on monthly calendars and, then, on a weekly study schedule, so time can be planned accordingly. Second, students record assignments on sheets, such as the one depicted in Figure 4.1, and ask questions about any confusing elements of the assignment. Third, students organize their day's assignments. Fourth, students "jump to it" to combat task avoidance. Fifth, students engage in the work, noting problems and recruiting help as needed. Sixth, students check and evaluate the quality of their work. Finally, students make arrangements (e.g., place the work in a backpack by the door) for turning in the assignment (Hughes et al., 2002).

FIGURE 4.1    PROJECT Strategy Steps and an Assignment Sheet Example

**PROJECT Strategy Steps**

Prepare your form.

Record and ask.

Organize.

    Break the assignment into parts.

    Estimate the number of study sessions.

    Schedule the sessions.

    Take your materials home.

Jump to it.

Engage in the work.

Check your work.

Turn in your work.

**Assignment Sheet Example**

| Subject | (Read) Book | Partner John |
|---|---|---|
| Eng. | Answer | Phone 583-8888 |
| | (Write) Report – 2 pgs. | |
| | Other | |

A
B
C
D
E

# of parts 5

Due 4/18

# of study sessions 10

Done 4/17

*Source:* From "Effects of Instruction in an Assignment Completion Strategy on the Homework Performance of Students with Learning Disabilities in General Education Classes" by C. A. Hughes, K. L. Ruhl, J. B. Schumaker, and D. D. Deschler, 2002, *Learning Disabilities Research and Practice, 17,* 1–18. Copyright 2002 by Blackwell Publishing. Reprinted by permission.

In addition to teaching assignment-completion strategies, there are at least four ways that teachers can increase the chances of making homework a successful experience for students with learning disabilities. First, teachers, especially in elementary school, should not assign homework that emphasizes the acquisition of new information (Cooper, 1989). In the case of students with learning disabilities, it is probably even more important that the homework not require students to perform skills they have not already been taught in school. Instead, the homework should focus on proficiency and maintenance of skills already within the student's repertoire (Polloway, Foley, & Epstein, 1992).

Second, teachers need to be careful that students with learning disabilities understand their assignments. Because these students have problems listening and copying directions accurately, they often misunderstand assignments or forget them. Teachers should therefore be explicit in their assignments. Some suggestions for making sure students understand their assignments are (1) encourage students to ask questions, (2) specify resources and how much help they can get, (3) choose students to review the directions for the class, and (4) allow students to begin homework in class under the teacher's guidance (Salend & Schliff, 1989; Sawyer, Nelson, Jayanthi, Bursuck, & Epstein, 1996).

Third, teachers should set up a system whereby they can efficiently monitor students' homework. One popular method is for each student to have an assignment book wherein (1) the teacher initials the assignment before the student leaves school to make sure the information was written down correctly, (2) the parent signs the assignment after the student has completed it, and (3) the teacher checks it the next day at the start of class (Epstein, Polloway, Foley, & Patton, 1993). Teachers should also provide positive consequences for homework completion (Hughes et al., 2002).

Finally, some research suggests that involving parents in the homework process can be beneficial (Rosenberg, 1989). How much involvement is helpful will vary with the particular parents. It is a good idea, however, that teachers at least make parents aware of homework policies and seek their feedback regarding their views on homework. Communicating with parents about homework is important, because as the following quote suggests, parents are often frustrated by what they perceive to be a lack of sympathy for their plight: "Sure, I'd like to get involved, but when? There's just not enough time. I can't come home to conferences during school hours! And then the teacher makes me feel like a bad parent" (Baumgartner et al., 1993, p. 182).

### What Parents Can Do

By definition, homework is done primarily at home; therefore, it is logical that parents can be influential in reducing homework problems. In addition to contingencies that most parents use with their children regarding homework (e.g., allowing the child a privilege or special reward—TV, visits with friends, etc.—if homework is finished), parents of students with learning disabilities also need to be particularly attentive to organizational factors. As already noted, it is not just academic work that may be difficult for many students with learning disabilities. These students also need help in planning and organizing their work time. Parents can help them decide on the best time and place for their homework and assist them in choosing a quiet, distraction-free area for studying.

**Council for Exceptional Children**

**CEC Knowledge Check**

List what teachers can do to help students with learning disabilities become successful in their homework.
CC10K3

**Council for Exceptional Children**

**CEC Knowledge Check**

What can you do to assist parents in helping students with learning disabilities succeed with homework?
CC10S2

## What Students Can Do

Students need to take an active role in managing their own homework routine. No amount of teacher or parent involvement will be enough if the student does not have the desire to do well on homework assignments. Unfortunately, students with learning disabilities are renowned for their poor study habits. For example, when researchers interviewed students about their homework practices, those with learning disabilities differed on several questions pertaining to attention, motivation, and study skills (Gajria & Salend, 1995). Table 4.2 lists those questions on which students with learning disabilities differed from their nondisabled peers.

Finally, parents should give careful thought to who, if anyone, will give the child direct help with homework. Depending on the particular family, a sibling, parent, or family friend might be designated as the helper. But for many students, learning disabled or not, family members and close friends are not good choices as helpers. Disagreements, arguments, and so forth that are likely to arise over other matters can interfere with the homework session. For parents who can afford it, tutors are often an excellent alternative.

Council for
Exceptional
Children

**CEC Knowledge Check**
What is the best course of action for some students with learning disablilities who are seeking help with their homework?
CC10S4

| TABLE 4.2 | Items Regarding Homework on Which Students with Learning Disabilities Differ from Nondisabled Peers |
| --- | --- |

- After working for 30 minutes on my homework, I lose interest and quit or take a long break.
- I get easily distracted when I am doing my homework.
- It takes me a long time to begin my homework.
- I feel unsure about which homework assignment to do first.
- It takes me a very long time to do my homework, so I get tired and cannot finish my work.
- I must be reminded to start my homework.
- I need someone to do my homework with me.
- I feel teachers are unfair and give too much homework.
- I go to school without completing my homework.
- I complain about homework.
- I forget to bring my homework assignments back to class.
- I have problems completing extralong assignments such as projects and lab reports because I do not divide the work into smaller parts and work on it a little at a time.
- When I do not understand an assignment or find it too hard, I stop working on it.
- I start my homework with subjects I like and then find no time or feel too tired to complete the assignment in other subjects.
- I have difficulty estimating the time needed to complete my homework, so my homework is incomplete.
- After I finish my homework, I do not check to see that I have completed all my assignments.

*Source:* Adapted from "Homework Practices of Students with and without Learning Disabilities: A Comparison" by M. Gajria and S. J. Salend, 1995. *Journal of Learning Disabilities, 28*(5), p. 294. Copyright 1995 by PRO-ED, Inc. Reprinted by permission.

## Parents as Advocates

Even though IDEA protects the rights of students with disabilities to receive a free, appropriate education, there are times when schools or other community agencies are not completely responsive to these students' needs. Even the best schools are not perfect, and given the myriad learning and social problems presented by most students with learning disabilities, it is understandable that there are times when it will be helpful to have someone speak on the student's behalf. At some point, most parents of students with learning disabilities find it necessary to advocate for their children to ensure that they receive the best education possible.

Some parents may not be able to assume the role of advocate because of the time commitment this entails. As one manual for parents of children with learning disabilities states:

> If you decide to undertake the role of advocate for your child, it should be with the realization that this is not a skill you will learn and then use for a year or two. Parents of LD children need to acknowledge that they will be the person (actually the only person) who has the overall picture of the child's disability, not only at a single point in time but throughout the years. You will find yourself playing the role of facilitator, coordinator, and overseer—no matter how good your child's school program and no matter how competent the professionals working with your child. It's much better to undertake the job realizing that it's a long-term commitment that will demand the best of your skills and energy than to approach the situation with the idea that your responsibilities will be to find the right school and the right teacher, and, that done, you will be able to relax while others take over. (Learning Disabilities Council, 2002, pp. 20–21)

The Learning Disabilities Council (2002) manual for parents also recommends that parents or guardians keep a file containing information pertaining to the student's academic, health, and work experiences (see Table 4.3). This information can be used by the parent, and later by the child, to advocate for services and provisions.

As children with learning disabilities mature, they must become more and more comfortable with being their own advocates, especially after they finish secondary school. For example, it is helpful for students who attend college to know how to talk about their disability and the accommodations they need with their advisor, the staff from the office providing assistance to students with disabilities, and individual instructors.

**Council for Exceptional Children**

**CEC Knowledge Check**

Why is it important to teach parents and students advocacy and independence skills? CC5S8, CC5S9

## How Can Communication Be Enhanced between the Family and Professionals?

Implicit in much of what has been said thus far is the maxim that good communication between professionals and parents is the key to successful programming for students with learning disabilities. Unfortunately, communication between parents and professionals does not always go well. That is understandable, given that

## TABLE 4.3   Maintaining a Filing System: A Guide for Parents

1. Secure a complete and entire copy of your child's cumulative and confidential file from the school system and from all agencies that have ever evaluated or worked with your child.
2. Obtain a large three-ring notebook and tab dividers.
3. Using the tab dividers, organize your notebook into the following sections:
    a. *Telephone calls.* Record significant telephone conversations with teachers and other professionals. Be sure to include the date, time, name of the person with whom you spoke, the reason for the conversation, and any important points to remember, including any follow-up steps to be taken.
    b. *Meetings.* Keep a short written summary of each meeting you have with teachers and other professionals.
    c. *Correspondence.* Record all documents and correspondence received, as well as copies of letters you have written about your child.
    d. *Reports of tests; notes about test results.* These include medical test reports, significant birth and developmental history, visual exams, auditory evaluations, etc. These include psychological and educational test reports as well as any notes you have made during conferences where your child's evaluations were interpreted.
    e. *Official special education documents.* Include referral, child study, eligibility, IEP, and all other official documents pertaining to your child's special education process and program.
    f. *Report cards.* This includes official school and interim report cards as well as written comments from all teachers, camp counselors, Sunday school teachers, tutors, etc.
    g. *Samples of your child's classwork.* Keep dated samples of your child's school papers, collected over a period of time, in a separate notebook. Make a note of the subject for which the work was completed.
4. Other suggestions:
    a. Maintain a Table of Contents—list each document with information about the date, evaluator or author, description of the type of document, and a brief summary or explanation.
    b. Date each item in your notebook in the lower right-hand corner in pencil. Do this even if the date appears elsewhere on the document. This date will be used to keep and to locate all documents in chronological order. In case of documents that span a period of time, such as report cards and telephone logs, use date of the last entry.
    c. Keep your notebook organized and up-to-date. Whenever you receive a new report, file it immediately.
    d. As you come across helpful written material about learning disabilities, make a copy of the material, three-hole punch it, and file it in your notebook.
    e. Refer to your notebook often. Take it with you whenever you meet with a professional about your child.

**Council for Exceptional Children**

**CEC Knowledge Check**
Why do you think an educator should assist a parent in setting up a record-keeping system? Do parents need to know why it is valuable? Why?
CC8S10, CC10S1, CC10S4

---

*Source:* Adapted from *Understanding Learning Disabilities: A Parent Guide and Workbook,* 3rd ed. (pp. 73–76) by M. L. Trusdell and J. W. Horowitz (Eds.), 2002, Richmond, VA: Learning Disabilities Council. (Address inquiries to York Press, Inc., P.O. Box 504, Timonium, MD 21094.) Copyright © 2002 by the Learning Disabilities Council. All inquiries should be addressed to York Press, Inc., P.O. Box 504, Timonium, MD 21094, www.yorkpress.com or 1-800-962-2763. Reprinted by permission.

# School-Home Communication

Jamal's mother, Irene Smith, and his teacher, Alice Hamilton, agree that maintaining close contact is key to Jamal experiencing success in school. However, they have both become frustrated with their attempts to communicate, as they continually find themselves playing "phone tag." As a nurse, Irene works odd hours and is difficult to contact. Thus, both have decided that their primary mode of communication will be via e-mail. In this way, their communication is more convenient yet remains personal. It also has the added benefit of providing written documentation of their contacts. Following are excerpts from some of their exchanges:

From: Irene Smith
To: Alice Hamilton
Re: school-home note

Alice,
I've thought a lot about what you said with respect to giving Jamal some responsibility in his schooling. As you mentioned, you and I could certainly keep track of everything Jamal has to do, but it's important to get him to do some of that himself. I know my initial reaction was, "He's only in first grade!" However, I think you're right about starting him on the road to self-advocacy. Asking him to be responsible for bringing notes home is a good way to do that. How often should I expect to see one?

Thank you.
Irene

From: Alice Hamilton
To: Irene Smith
Re: Re: school-home note

Irene,
Glad to hear you want to try the school-home notes. I'll send one home every day for a while, then we'll do it once a week. It'll be a good way to track Jamal's progress and reinforce him based on that progress. And we'll be giving him some responsibility.

Thanks.
Alice

From: Irene Smith
To: Alice Hamilton
Re: thank you

Alice,
Jamal was so happy today. He said he's learning how to sound out words! Thank you so much for everything you're doing with him.
I greatly appreciate it.

Irene

From: Alice Hamilton
To: Irene Smith
Re: Re: thank you

Thank you, Irene. You deserve a lot of credit, too. I can tell that the reinforcement activities you've been doing at home with him are helping.
Thanks.
Alice

From: Alice Hamilton
To: Irene Smith
Re: IEP

Irene,
Jamal's IEP meeting is coming up. I'd like to schedule a convenient time for you to come in. How do the next couple of weeks look for you? Also, I'll want your input as we draft Jamal's IEP. I've attached an IEP planning form that I'd like you to fill out. Please let me know if you have any questions or want to discuss things over the phone.
Thank you.
Alice

From: Irene Smith
To: Alice Hamilton
Re: Re: IEP

Thank you for the information, Alice. I'll try to fill out the form in the next few days. I think I can meet after school one day, but I have to check my schedule again.

I do have some concerns, but I'm also feeling overwhelmed by this whole process. Even after taking part in Jamal's eligibility, I'm not sure I really understand what all this means. Will Jamal always be in special education? What about college?

Anyway, for now, I want to make sure that he continues to get the kind of instruction that will be most beneficial to him. The phonics activities seem to be working. I want that to continue.

I look forward to meeting with you.

Irene

parents of students with learning disabilities are often under stress and that teachers are often frustrated by the enigma of a child with complex learning and behavioral problems. Furthermore, except for parent-teacher days or nights, which occur once or twice per year, and periodic IEP meetings, which are attended by several people and are quite formal, schools do not usually have established mechanisms for parents and teachers to meet. Unless the parent or teacher initiates contact, there is little opportunity for the two to discuss the student's progress.

The ability to work with parents can often be one of the last skills that teachers develop. Because many beginning teachers are not yet parents themselves, they may not readily empathize with the parental point of view. The sooner both teachers and parents recognize that they need each other, however, the better off the student with learning disabilities will be. Each has something to offer the other that will ultimately benefit the student. Because parents spend considerably more time with the child, they are a source of information for the teacher on the child's behavior and interests. Likewise, teachers can keep parents apprised of the student's progress in class.

Most teachers learn to work with parents reasonably well. Some become truly adept at communicating with parents, knowing that understanding and communicating with parents helps enhance their teaching. These teachers often devise creative ways to communicate with parents. Some, for example, have Web-sites that inform parents about class assignments. Others send home periodic newsletters. Many now communicate with parents via e-mail, as in the case of Jamal's mother and his first-grade teacher (see the Case Connections box on pages 128–129). In the remaining sections of this chapter, we discuss parent-teacher conferences and the IEP planning form as well as school-home note programs.

## Parent-Teacher Conferences

Teachers can use parent-teacher conferences to serve at least four general purposes: (1) to impart information to the parents about the student's academic and social behavior; (2) to gather information from parents regarding such things as the student's interests, hobbies, and homework; (3) to plan for the student's educational program; and (4) to solve problems the student may be having in school (Schulz, 1987).

Some recommend that, if possible, the conference be combined with a letter and a telephone call (Hallahan & Martinez, 2002). The teacher uses the phone call to indicate that a conference would be a good idea and follows up with a letter reminding the parents of the time and place of the meeting. We also recommend that professionals take an active role in helping parents prepare for conferences and meetings. Teachers should alert parents about discussions that will likely take place during the conference. In preparation for IEP meetings, for example, teachers can assist parents by providing them with an IEP planning form (see Figure 4.2). Teachers should also provide parents with additional resources to which they may

**Council for Exceptional Children**

**CEC Knowledge Check**

Why is it so important to foster a partnership with parents?
CC10S3

**Council for Exceptional Children**

**CEC Knowledge Check**

Prior to a parent meeting, what should the teacher do to encourage a parent to be an active participant?
CC10S4

**FIGURE 4.2** IEP Planning Form

Child's name: _____  Date: _____

*This form provides a guideline for your imput at the IEP meeting. Plan to share this information at the meeting or with your child's special education teacher prior to the meeting. You may wish to submit the completed form or use it as a basis for discussion.*

My child's strengths are:

_____

_____

_____

My child needs the most help with:

_____

_____

_____

At this time, the most important goal(s) for my child for the next year are:

_____

_____

_____

Effective rewards for my child are:

_____

_____

_____

Homework considerations:

_____

_____

Other information about my child the school should know:

_____

_____

_____

*Source:* From *IEP—An Overview* by J. Bamuel, 2000. Copyright © 2000 by Schwab Learning. Retrieved February 25, 2003, from http://www.schwablearning.org/articles.asp?r=73. Reprinted by permission.

## TODAY'S TECHNOLOGY FOR LEARNING DISABILITIES

### Resources on the World Wide Web

Parents and families can access a variety of potential resources via the World Wide Web. Some, which may be of particular interest to parents and families of children with learning disabilities, are listed here:

**The Alliance—www.taalliance.org/index.htm**

The Alliance (The Technical Assistance Alliance for Parent Centers) is funded by the U.S. Department of Education, Office of Special Education Programs, to serve as the coordinating office for the Technical Assistance to Parent Projects. The Alliance focuses on providing technical assistance for developing and funding Parent Training and Information Projects and Community Parent Resource Centers under the Individuals with Disabilities Education Act (IDEA).

**Children and Adults with Attention Deficit/Hyperactivity Disorder (CHADD)— www.chadd.org/**

Through collaborative leadership, advocacy, research, education, and support, CHADD provides science-based, evidence-based information about ADHD to parents, educators, professionals, the media, and the general public.

**Coordinated Campaign for Learning Disabilities— www.aboutld.org/about_ccld.html**

CCLD is supported by the Emily Hall Tremaine Foundation, which funds innovative projects that foster the success of individuals with learning disabilities. The foundation works to increase public awareness of learning disabilities and provides practical information and resources.

**Council for Learning Disabilities (CLD)— www.cldinternational.org**

CLD promotes effective teaching and research. It establishes standards of excellence and promotes innovative strategies for research and practice through interdisciplinary collegiality, collaboration, and advocacy.

**Family Education Network— familyeducation.com/home/**

The FEN's mission is to be an online consumer network of the world's best learning and information resources, personalized to help parents, teachers, and students of all ages take control of their learning and make it part of their everyday lives.

**Family Village— www.familyvillage.wisc.edu/index.htmlx**

Family Village integrates information, resources, and communication opportunities for persons with cognitive and other disabilities, for their families, and for those that provide them services and support.

**International Dyslexia Association (IDA)— www.interdys.org/index.jsp**

IDA is dedicated to helping individuals with dyslexia, their families, and the communities that support them. It strives to provide the most comprehensive forum for parents, educators, and researchers to share their experiences, methods, and knowledge.

Council for Exceptional Children

**CEC Knowledge Check**
How can you use this information to support parent(s) of students with learning disabilities across their life span? LD10K2

turn for help. See the Today's Technology box above for an explanation of resources available on the World Wide Web.

Planning is crucial in conducting a successful conference. Planning involves not only gathering pertinent information prior to the meeting, but also preparing for the meeting itself as well as for postconference activities. Table 4.4 (page 134) presents some guidelines for effective parent-teacher conferences.

Parent-teacher conferences often require a great deal of sensitivity and tact on the teacher's part. This is particularly true if the reason for the conference is the

**Learning Disabilities Association of America (LDA)—www.ldanatl.org/**

LDA is dedicated to identifying causes and promoting prevention of learning disabilities and to enhancing the quality of life for all individuals with learning disabilities and their families by encouraging effective identification and intervention, fostering research, and protecting their rights under the law.

**LDOnline—www.ldonline.org/**

This site contains information on learning disabilities for parents, teachers, and other professionals.

**National Clearinghouse for English Language Acquisition and Language Instruction Educational Programs (NCELA)—www.ncela.gwu.edu/index.htm**

NCELA is funded by the U.S. Department of Education's Office of English Language Acquisition, Language Enhancement, and Academic Achievement for Limited English Proficient Students to collect, analyze, and disseminate information relating to the effective education of linguistically and culturally diverse learners in the United States.

**National Association for the Education of African American Children with Learning Disabilities (NAEAACLD)—www.charityadvantage.com/aacld/HomePage.asp**

NAEAACLD increases awareness and promotes an understanding of the specific issues facing African American children. The organization's mission is to link information and resources provided by an established network of individuals and organizations experienced in minority research and special education with parents, educators, and others responsible for providing a quality education for all students.

**National Center for Learning Disabilities—www.ncld.org/**

The National Center for Learning Disabilities offers information, resources, and referral services; develops and supports educational programs; promotes public awareness; and advocates for more effective policies and legislation to help individuals with learning disabilities.

**Schwab Learning—www.schwablearning.org/index.asp**

Schwab Learning provides information, resources, links to publications pages, and support to parents of children with learning differences.

**TeachingLD—www.teachingld.org**

TeachingLD is a service of the Division for Learning Disabilities (DLD) of the Council for Exceptional Children. The purpose of TeachingLD is to provide trustworthy and up-to-date resources about teaching students with learning disabilities.

*Note:* Web addresses are known to change. The addresses listed here were current when this book went to press.

---

child's misbehavior or poor academic progress. Following are some questions teachers can ask themselves to ensure tact in their meetings with parents:

- Am I able to avoid blaming parents? One of the least helpful things a teacher can do is lay the blame on parents for the misbehavior of their children. Parents will already be on the defensive because you have called them to have this meeting. Weigh your words carefully so as not to give the impression that you think they are the culprits. Even if you are convinced that they are the cause of their children's

## TABLE 4.4  Guidelines for Parent-Teacher Meetings and Conferences

Lay the foundation
- Review the student's cumulative records.
- Familiarize yourself with the student and family's culture.
- Consult with other professionals about the student.
- Establish rapport with the parents and keep them informed.
- Collect information to document the student's academic progress and behavior.
- Share positive comments about the student with parents.
- Invite the parents to observe or volunteer in your classroom.

Before the meeting
- Discuss the goals of the meeting with the parents and solicit their input.
- Involve the student, as appropriate.
- Schedule a mutually convenient day and time for the meeting.
- Provide written notice prior to the meeting.

During the meeting
- Welcome the parents and speak informally with them before beginning.
- Reiterate the goals of the meeting.
- Begin with a discussion of the student's strengths.
- Support your points with specific examples and documentation.
- Encourage the parents to ask questions.
- Encourage parents to share insights.
- Ask open-ended questions.
- Avoid jargon.
- Practice active listening (e.g., show interest, paraphrase comments, avoid making judgments, etc.).
- Review the main points of the meeting and determine a course of action.
- Provide additional resources (e.g., support groups, family resource centers, Websites).

After the meeting
- Document the results of the meeting.
- Share results with colleagues who work with the student.
- Follow up with the parents as needed to discuss changes.

*Source:* From "Working with Families" by D. P. Hallahan and E. A. Martinez, 2002, in J. M. Kauffman, M. Mostert, S. C. Trent, and D. P. Hallahan (Eds.), *Managing Classroom Behavior: A Reflective Case-Based Approach,* 3rd ed. (pp. 124–140), Boston: Allyn and Bacon. Copyright © 2002 by Pearson Education. Reprinted by permission of the publisher.

**Council for Exceptional Children**

**CEC Knowledge Check**

Why is it important for educators to conduct collaborative conferences with students with exceptional learning needs and their families?
CC10S5

problems, you should avoid accusations. If they are at fault, it is better to let them arrive at that judgment on their own.
- Am I willing to admit when I'm wrong? Some teachers, especially those who are relatively inexperienced, feel that it is a sign of weakness to acknowledge to parents

that they have made mistakes. We don't think you need to see the meeting as an opportunity to reveal your shortcomings, but if you have doubts about how you have handled the student it is a good idea to concede this point.

- Am I willing to admit when I don't know the answer to parents' questions? Again, be careful not to fall into the trap of feeling that you need to have answers to every question posed by the parents. Confident teachers are more than willing to say that they are not all-knowing. In fact, teachers should view the parent-teacher conference as an opportunity to learn more about the child from the parents.
- Can I accept the family as it is? Some teachers view parent-teacher conferences as quasi therapy sessions in which they should try to influence family dynamics. Your focus should be on what the student is doing in your classroom. To be sure, you will want to talk about how the child behaves at home, and you may want to suggest that parents carry out certain procedures in the home to back up what you are doing at school, but you should not see yourself as a family therapist.
- Am I attuned to cultural differences between myself and the parents? It is important that you respect the cultural backgrounds of parents and not misinterpret their behavior or offend them because their customs vary from yours.
- Can I find something positive to say about the child and something positive about the parent that I can support? It is very important that you try to find something positive and supportive to say about the child and the parent in every parent contact. Sometimes this may be difficult. Nevertheless, if all the parent receives is negative information, you are not likely to get very far in resolving the problem. (Hallahan & Martinez, 2002, pp. 133–134)

## School-Home Note Programs

If parents are willing, a **school-home note program** can be an excellent way for teachers to involve parents in the child's educational program. This can also benefit teachers, because it gives them another means of reinforcing appropriate social and academic behavior. Sometimes referred to as home contingency programs, school-home note programs involve the teacher in evaluating the student's behavior and the parents in providing the reinforcement at home. Based on a brief report filled out and signed by the teacher, the parents deliver a reinforcement that has already been negotiated with the child. Program particulars are usually decided by the teacher in consultation with the parents and sometimes with the student.

Considerable research has been conducted on the use of school-home note programs (e.g., Kelley & McCain, 1995; McCain & Kelley, 1994). Most researchers suggest that the school-home note program be implemented in the beginning on a daily basis and later adjusted to a once-per-week accounting. The use of punishment is discouraged, because some parents can become too punitive. In addition, the target behaviors must be clearly defined; the student, teacher, and parent must all be committed to the program and understand their respective roles; and the note should be minimally instrusive (Kelley, 1990). Figure 4.3 (page 136) is an example of a school-home note.

As we have discussed in this chapter, parents and families can play a critical role in helping meet the needs of students with learning disabilities. Teachers

**CEC Knowledge Check**
What are a few collaboration strategies that teachers overlook yet are important to consider?
CC10K1

**CEC Knowledge Check**
Why should you as a teacher be culturally responsive to parents in your communication and collaboration with them?
CC10K4

**school-home note program** a system of communication between teacher and parent in which the teacher evaluates the child's behavior at school on a simple form that goes home to the parent, and the parent then reinforces the child

**CEC Knowledge Check**
Describe one effective method that can increase communication with parents and encourage them to become active partners in the educational process.
CC10S4, CC10S10

FIGURE 4.3    A School-Home Note

**Teacher Completes**

Today, in _____*reading*_____    I rated _____*Jamal's*_____ behaviors as follows (using a 1 to 5 pt. scale [1 = lowest, 5 = highest]):

|  | Rating | Points Earned |
|---|---|---|
| 1. *attention* | 5 | 10 |
| 2. *blending/segmenting* | 3 | 6 |
| 3. *accuracy* | 2 | 4 |

TOTAL POINTS = _20_

Teacher Comments:

*Overall, Jamal had a good day. Accuracy should improve; he was learning new sounds today.*

Signature and date: *Alice Hamilton    3/11/02*

**Parent Completes**

I gave the following reward(s): _____*1/2 hour of television*_____

Parent Comments:

*It was really good to see the "5" in attention, and the blending/segmenting is improving.*

Signature and date: *Irene Smith    3/11/02*

**Teacher Completes**

Signature and date: *Alice Hamilton    3/12/02*

*Source:* Adapted from "Home-School Collaboration: Evaluating Effectiveness of a School-Home Note Program for Children with Attention Deficit-Hyperactivity Disorder" by E. Cotton, 1998, unpublished doctoral dissertation, University of Virginia. Reprinted by permission.

should understand that parents may be distracted and seem uninterested or otherwise nonsupportive of their child's education when, in fact, they are doing the best they can to cope. Teachers can help parents and families deal with issues such as homework and encourage parents to be advocates for their children. Finally, teachers should view parents as allies and remain in contact with them via telephone, e-mail, conferences, and/or school-home notes.

## Demonstrating Mastery of the CEC Standards

Referencing the knowledge you have gained in Chapter 4, you can now put the final additions to your Personal Philosophy of Special Education. Include in your final version your understanding of the following topics:

- Define what you believe to be effective models of collaboration that will foster respectful and beneficial communication, given cultural perspectives and environmental characteristics/effects.

- Identify the roles and responsibilities of educators and families in the assessment and educational planning process that supports a nonbiased environment and maintains a system of confidential information.

- Discuss how to effectively communicate, in a culturally responsive manner, with families and individuals whom you are seeking to become active participants in the educational planning process, while at the same time examining the characteristics of your own culture and language that may affect biases.

- Describe the special educator's ethical responsibility to encourage self-advocacy and independence for individuals with learning disabilities, as well as to provide information about appropriate support services throughout their life span.

**Council for Exceptional Children**

**CEC Content Standards**
5. Learning Environments and Social Interactions
8. Assessment
9. Professional and Ethical Practice
10. Collaboration

# SUMMARY

**How have professionals' views of parents changed?**

- At one time, professionals viewed parents of children with disabilities negatively. They often blamed them for the problems their children had.
- Professionals now view parents more positively. This is the result of two factors:
  - Research has demonstrated the principle of reciprocal effects—that is, parents not only influence children's development, but also children have effects on parents.
  - Congress has passed laws stipulating that parents be given more opportunities for involvement.

**What treatment models do professionals use with parents?**

Today's methods of working with parents often are characterized as family-centered and stressing social systems. Two such approaches are:
- the Turnbulls' family systems model, which includes the following components:
  - family characteristics
  - family interaction
  - family functions
  - family life cycle
- Dunst's social support systems model, which stresses informal sources of support

**What are some current trends in American family life today?**

Microcultures are becoming more and more diverse with respect to:
- the family unit
- race, ethnicity, and language
- socioeconomic status

**What is the family's role?**

- At one time, a stage theory, similar to that used with people who experience the death of a loved one, was used to explain family reaction to having a child with a disability. The typical stages were shock and disruption, denial, sadness, anxiety and fear, anger, and adaptation.

- Two reactions that parents often have are:
  - guilt
  - stress
- Siblings can also experience stress.
- Most families adjust well, some experience minor difficulties, and a few experience enough stress to be considered dysfunctional.
- How do family values and attitudes toward learning affect students?
  - Children whose parents value education are at an advantage.
  - For the child with learning disabilities, it is even more important that the family instill a positive attitude toward learning and school.
- Homework is a major problem area for many students with learning disabilities and their families.
  - Teachers can help by teaching assignment-completion strategies. They can also help by
    assigning homework that does not require acquisition of new skills
    making sure that the students understand their assignments
    setting up a system so that they can monitor students' homework and provide positive consequences for completion
    attempting to involve parents
  - Parents can help by:
    providing contingencies to get their children to finish homework

helping students plan and organize their work time
organizing homework time
carefully considering who will give direct help to the student
  - Students can help by attempting to allocate their time efficiently.
- Parents can be effective as advocates for their child (e.g., by keeping a file containing information pertaining to the student's academic, health, and work experiences).

## How can communication be enhanced between the family and professionals?

Two common methods of parent-teacher communication are:

- parent-teacher conferences—meetings for imparting information about students' academic and social behaviors; gathering information about students' interests, hobbies, and homework; planning for students' educational programs; and solving problems students are having in school.
  - Conferences should be carefully planned.
  - Teachers should provide parents with additional resources.
- school-home note programs—a system of communication between teacher and parent in which the teacher evaluates the child's behavior at school on a simple form that goes home to the parent, and the parent then reinforces the child.

## REFLECTIONS ON THE CASES

1. Do you think the relationship between Ms. Hamilton and Mrs. Smith is typical of most teacher-parent relationships? Why or why not?

2. What are some keys to the connection established between Ms. Hamilton and Mrs. Smith?

3. Describe at least three ways Jamal has likely benefited from the teacher-parent relationship.

## Focus On ▸ Parents and Families

### *Do Now* Activities for Communicating with Home

## Home-School Communication Systems

### ● *What is it?*

The purpose of any home-school communication system is to connect school-based goals with home support or connect home-based goals with the school. Communication can take the form of a contract, a note-home program, a regular e-mail update, or a student-managed chart signed by both parent and teacher. Students whose rules and expectations flow seamlessly from school to home recognize the shared value and importance their teachers and parents place on the identified behaviors. Home-school communications systems should be clear and easy to manage and should directly address the identified behaviors of concern. In addition, the system should be evaluated periodically to determine its effectiveness.

Teachers and parents who attempt to implement cumbersome, time-consuming communication systems become frustrated, and the system loses its power due to inconsistent implementation. The need for a simple, standard system is underscored by the fact that students with learning disabilities experience difficulty with organization and poor memory. These characteristics can make the delivery of notes to and from school challenging. Optimal home-school communication systems highlight target behaviors, send notes on a regular basis, and have specific consequences and rewards tied to the behavior.

### ● *How to implement it*

Teachers should work with the family to identify the best system based on (1) behavioral or academic goals, (2) student characteristics, and (3) time considerations and/or constraints. Rhode, Jenson, and Reavis (1992) recommend the following steps for implementing a home-school communication program:

1. Design or select a simple chart, note, or contract. (See samples on pages 140–141.)
2. Decide the target behaviors. Limit to fewer than five.
3. Gain parental feedback on identifying positive or mild negative consequences (e.g., extra time with friends/loss of time with friends, additional privileges/loss of privileges, such as TV, phone, or computer). It is important to convince parents to accept no excuses for missing communication.
4. Decide when the program will begin. Moving the frequency of communication from daily to weekly to fading out is a recommended strategy.
5. Implement the communication program. Share communication with the student and provide specific feedback to the student on which behaviors were on target and what can be done for improvement.
7. Call the parent on a regular basis during the first few weeks of the program to troubleshoot and provide support.
8. After four to six weeks of implementation, arrange for another parent-teacher conference to review the student's progress.

● *What to do if . . .*

- *the student fails to bring the communication home on a regular basis . . .*
  Failure to bring a form home should result in a loss of privilege or mild consequence.
- *the student changes notes or markings on the chart . . .*
  The teacher or parent should treat the situation as a lost note. Loss of privileges or consequence should be administered.
- *the parent does not follow through with consequences at home . . .*
  The teacher can provide specific suggestions or support by providing potential reinforcers (stickers or games) for the parent to use. Alternatively, the teacher can also ask if the parent would like the teacher to provide the reward or consequence at school.

## Sample Home-School Communications

**Contract**

Date _____

I, _____ , promise to _____
      (student name)                                              (state behavior—e.g., turn in completed homework on time)

If I meet this goal, I will _____
                                               (state positive consequence)

If I do not meet this goal, I will _____
                                                   (state loss of privileges or mild negative consequences)

This contract will start _____ and end _____ .

_____
Student signature

_____
Parent signature

Check if met goal:

☐ Monday    ☐ Tuesday    ☐ Wednesday    ☐ Thursday    ☐ Friday

**Weekly Note Home**

This week _____ was rated by the teacher: _____

☐ Needs improvement    ☐ Working on success    ☐ Great!

An example of this was: _____
_____

To improve _____ will: _____
_____

Teacher: _____    Date: _____

Parent: _____    Date: _____

**Daily Note Home**

| Time of Day | Used appropriate language | Kept hands and feet to self | Followed teacher request immediately | Spoke in a calm voice to teachers and peers |
|---|---|---|---|---|
| Morning meeting | | | | |
| Reading | | | | |
| Social studies | | | | |
| Lunch | | | | |
| Math | | | | |
| Science | | | | |
| Specials (P. E., Art, Music) | | | | |
| Recess | | | | |
| Daily Total  Note: √ indicates "yes"; — indicates "no." | | | | |

Teacher comments and initials:

_____

Parent comments and initials:

_____

## Additional Resources

Rhode, G., Jenson, W. R., & Neville, M. H. (2002). *The tough kid parent book: Why me?* Longmount, CA: Sopris West.

Rhode, G., Jenson, W. R., & Reavis, H. K. (2000). *The tough kid toolbox.* Longmount, CA: Sopris West.

*Source:* Kristin L. Sayeski

## How Can Learning Disabilities Be Prevented?
- Addressing Risk Factors in Infancy and Early Childhood
- Distinguishing Disabilities from Cultural Differences and Normal Variations

## How Are Learning Disabilities Identified in Infancy and Early Childhood?
- Two Approaches to Early Identification
- Promises and Pitfalls of Early Identification

## How Is Early Childhood Intervention Provided?
- Popular Early Intervention Programs
- Legal Requirements of Early Intervention
- Evaluating Early Childhood Program Quality

## What Are Some Trends in Early Childhood Special Education?
- Inclusive Education
- Developmentally Appropriate Practices (DAP)
- Education for Transition
- Family-Based Education
- Assessment
- Self-Determination
- Technology

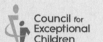

**Council for Exceptional Children**

See Companion Website for detailed correlations between chapter content and Council for Exceptional Children Standards; **www.ablongman.com/ hallahanLD3e**

### CEC Knowledge and Skills Discussed in This Chapter

**1** The legislative provisions and ethical principles regarding education and assessment of individuals with learning disabilities, including the necessity of upholding high standards of competence and integrity in professional practice.

**2** An understanding of the effects of cultural and linguistic differences on development that can impact coexisting conditions and often contribute to factors of learning disability misidentification in young children.

**3** The issues of cultural characteristics from a variety of perspectives and how using languages as well as behaviors across cultures can facilitate families as active participants in the program-planning process.

**4** Assessment procedures that address family concerns, including the collection of relevant background information to identify young children who may be at risk for learning disabilities.

**5** Appropriate research-supported methodologies in the areas of prevention, social skills, technology/communication assistance, self-assessment, problem solving, self-advocacy, and reading, including the needs of phonological awareness for preschool children.

# Prevention and Intervention in Early Childhood

5

When her special ed teacher showed us how much trouble she was having in reading and math, we really wondered why they hadn't done something earlier.

*Daniel Ireland, Shannon's father*

Yes, I noticed that Jamal was having some difficulty with word sounds, writing, and following directions, but I didn't want to jump the gun and see a problem if there really wasn't one. A lot of kids have difficulty in kindergarten. It's a terrible thing to label a young child.

*Rhonda Lastiri, Jamal's kindergarten teacher*

If we could prevent most disabilities, we could avoid most of the personal disadvantages and social costs that go with having them. Most people agree that if a child's disability cannot be prevented, then intervention should be started as soon as it is detected. In fact, if we detect a disability in its earliest stages and begin effective intervention at once, then we may be able to avoid a variety of complications, and the ultimate outcome for the child may be much better (Walker & Shinn, 2002).

Prevention and early intervention are closely linked in concept and in practice (Kamps & Tankersley, 1996; Kauffman, 1999, 2003, 2004). Others have noted, "Waiting to identify students who will experience reading disabilities is a costly mistake that contributes to the persistence of reading problems" (Speece, Mills, Ritchey, & Hillman, 2002, p. 223; see also Graham & Harris, 2002; Schwartz, Garfinkle, & Davis, 2002; Simmons, Kame'enui, Good, Harn, Cole, & Braun, 2002).

# How Can Learning Disabilities Be Prevented?

Prevention is usually described as primary, secondary, or tertiary, depending on when and why preventive action is taken. The prevention of learning disabilities may involve all three types.

**primary prevention** prevention that precludes the emergence of a problem, usually applied to an entire population without regard to specific need

**Primary prevention** means keeping the disability from occurring in the first place. Primary prevention in learning disabilities might involve reducing the chances of brain injury, improving teachers' skills in instruction and behavior management, or teaching parents child-rearing skills. For primary prevention to work, the strategy must be aimed at reducing or eliminating the cause(s) of learning disabilities or protecting against causal factors.

Jamal

For example, it was too late to do primary prevention of the difficulties noticed in kindergarten by Jamal's teacher. After problems emerge, it is too late for primary prevention.

We caution that even if primary prevention is implemented—including good instruction—learning disabilities will occur. Primary prevention may reduce the number of children who have learning disabilities or lessen the severity of the disabilities, but it will not eliminate learning disabilities (the same statement can be made regarding primary prevention of any type of disability; see Kauffman, 1999, 2003). Thus, primary prevention is important in keeping the prevalence of learning disabilities as low as possible. However, it is a mistake to assume that it will reduce the prevalence to zero.

**secondary prevention** taking action to correct a problem after it occurs, or at least keeping it from getting worse

**Secondary prevention** means correcting the disability after it occurs, or at least keeping it from getting worse. Remedial instruction is a secondary preventive strategy. In fact, most of the interventions for learning disabilities involve secondary prevention, because the child's learning problems have been noticed and the aim is to correct the problems or prevent them from getting worse. If a special education teacher works not only with students already identified as having learning disabilities but also with others who are struggling academically but have not yet been identified, the teacher may be practicing secondary prevention, both with labeled students and those not labeled as having learning disabilities.

Jamal

Shannon

Jamal's kindergarten teacher could have done secondary prevention for the problems she detected. She would not have had to label him as having learning disabilities, but she would have had to label him or his problems as something needing intervention—noting, perhaps, "child in need of special instruction" (CINOSI) or something similar. It is impossible to practice secondary prevention without a word (label) designating the need for special attention or instruction (Kauffman, 1999, 2003, 2004). Although math disabilities are currently Shannon's major problem, she was first identified as having a learning disability in reading. However, she was not identified with this disability in reading until she was about 7½ years old. Any preventive action taken at that time had to be secondary or tertiary simply because she already had serious problems in reading.

**tertiary prevention** taking action to keep the effects of a problem or disability from spreading to other areas of functioning

**Tertiary prevention** means keeping the effects of the problem or disability from spreading to other areas of functioning. When remedial interventions are initiated long after a learning disability has developed, the primary goal may be tertiary prevention. For example, if a student has had learning disabilities in reading

CASE
CONNECTIONS

Shannon

## Shannon's Science Teacher Sees the Value of Previewing

Shannon's science teacher, David Hightower, became aware of Shannon's learning disabilities through conversations with Martin Schein, her special education teacher. He understood that he needed to have a way of averting the problems that Shannon would experience with new science concepts, so he developed a plan to go over the concepts with Shannon on an individual basis before the concepts were introduced in class to the rest of the students.

Mr. Hightower's classroom routine was to introduce a concept, then give his class a reading or seatwork assignment while he circulated around the class, helping students individually. He always worked with Shannon during this time. At first, he tried helping Shannon with concepts the class had previously studied. This was an after-the-fact response to Shannon's "not getting it," as he came to understand. At the suggestion of Mr. Schein, Mr. Hightower changed his routine slightly so as to work with Shannon on the next concept to be introduced to the class. This was a proactive, anticipatory approach that precluded the difficulties Shannon would have had as new concepts were introduced. In essence, Mr. Hightower gave Shannon a preview, a little practice session in advance of what the class was to learn.

Although Mr. Hightower's adjustment or accommodation did not fully compensate for Shannon's learning disability, it did help her do better than she would have done otherwise. "Previewing" the concepts with Shannon meant that she would be more likely to be able to give correct answers in class, which bolstered her confidence and led to less anxiety and embarrassment on her part.

Council for Exceptional Children

**CEC Knowledge Check**
What preventative intervention method did Shannon's science teacher use? LD4S1

that have existed since the early grades and these have not been corrected, tertiary prevention at the high school level may involve teaching the student skills that will prevent failure in finding and holding a job.

If Jamal's teachers in the primary grades address his problems effectively so that additional problems of academic failure or misbehavior do not develop, then they are practicing tertiary prevention. To the extent that teachers can provide services to avoid future problems for Shannon, they are practicing tertiary prevention.

Of course, it is possible to practice secondary and tertiary prevention at the same time and in essentially the same way. Secondary prevention addresses existing problems. Tertiary prevention addresses complications or the development of additional problems. The Case Connections box above illustrates how Shannon's science teacher implemented a combination of secondary and tertiary prevention. This teacher knew of Shannon's problem with new concepts and also knew that failure to address it would lead to problems of low self-esteem and anxiety.

Jamal

Shannon

Council for Exceptional Children

**CEC Knowledge Check**
What are the three intervention methods? Why, or why not, would these be effective for Jamal and Shannon? LD4S1

## Addressing Risk Factors in Infancy and Early Childhood

Children at risk of learning disabilities are not likely to be identified before they experience academic failure. That is, given their present behavior, learning characteristics, or life circumstances, young children who appear likely to fail academically do not typically receive special attention. But trying to identify risk factors raises many questions that are not easy to answer, such as:

- What should we look for in preschool children's characteristics or life circumstance that puts them at risk for learning disabilities?
- Precisely what behavioral, emotional, or learning characteristics are reliable precursors of learning disabilities?
- Is the child actually at risk for developmental problems, or does the child merely exhibit behavior different from that expected in school owing to the circumstances or culture in which the child has been reared?

As we noted in Chapter 1, learning disabilities are of many types and have a wide variety of possible and suspected causes. Moreover, they may coexist with a wide range of other disabilities. The risk of learning disabilities varies along multiple dimensions. That is, the factors giving rise to risk of learning disabilities are those that increase risk for a wide variety of other disabilities as well. For example, risk for disabilities of any type is heightened if the child is reared in poverty, experiences abuse or neglect, is malnourished, has a very low birthweight, inherits genetic markers for the disability, is exposed to substances that cause birth defects, or is not nurtured and taught specific skills necessary for normal cognitive, social, and physical development. Adverse conditions that may put children at high risk for learning disabilities include:

- poverty, poor nutrition, and exposure to environmental conditions likely to cause disease and disability
- teenage mother, particularly mothers in their early or middle teens
- mothers receiving inadequate prenatal care and poor nutrition during pregnancy or using substances that can harm the fetus
- environmental hazards, including both chemical and social dangers
- abuse, neglect, and an environment in which violence and substance abuse are pervasive
- cuts in social programs that widen the gap between the needs of children and families and the availability of social services

Unfortunately, many children are born and reared under adverse conditions. Such conditions predictably result in more children being identified as having disabilities of all types, including learning disabilities.

Learning disabilities also vary tremendously in severity and pervasiveness. Their hallmark is intraindividual differences, and individuals with specific learning disabilities have extraordinary differences between their abilities in some areas (e.g., skill in sports or mechanical abilities) and in others (e.g., reading or math). These individuals vary not only in the type and severity of disabilities, but also in their vulnerability to specific causal factors and their resilience or ability to resist potential causes. This means that although children at extremely high risk may be easily identified, those at relatively low to moderate risk may be difficult or impossible to pick out reliably.

Moreover, learning disabilities are developmental disorders persisting over the life span. The implication is that changes in risk may occur over time. Children and youths may go through periods during which they are especially vulnerable and others during which they are relatively immune to the development of learning disabilities (Keogh & Sears, 1991).

Thus, the factors that increase risk for learning disabilities are particularly difficult to assess because (1) the possible causes of learning disabilities are multiple and complex and overlap with the causes of other disabilities, (2) learning disabilities vary enormously in severity and may affect a wide range of areas of abilities, and (3) vulnerability to various causal factors may change with age. However, if learning disabilities are to be prevented, risk factors must be evaluated carefully and action must be taken to reduce the risk.

## Distinguishing Disabilities from Cultural Differences and Normal Variations

Cultural difference may be mistaken for developmental delay. Different cultures prepare children to accomplish developmental tasks in different ways and at different times. Children from low-income homes may not be prepared to meet the expectations that most middle-class schools have for students, yet these children may not be at risk for developmental failure. It is important to distinguish between developmental and cultural differences so that the assessment, prevention, and remediation of disabilities are not misguided and children are not inappropriately placed in special education (Hallahan & Kauffman, 2003).

Educators must be particularly careful in assessing the abilities of children who are **culturally and linguistically diverse (CLD),** because language differences and their implications for learning can be mistaken for learning disabilities. Language differences are particularly important to understand; language is the basis for reading and other forms of communication in schools (van Keulen, Weddington, & DeBose, 1998). Some children are not provided with many opportunities for language learning because their parents do not read to them and they seldom observe reading and writing in their homes. These children may have normal cognitive skills, and their primary need may be simply a heightened level of exposure to literacy.

Other children come from homes in which there is a high degree of literacy but not in English, so the teacher who does not speak their language may underestimate their language competence. Still others may have learned a variation of English that they seldom or never have seen in print and that is not typically used by teachers. Teachers not aware of such differences and their meanings may mistakenly believe that such a child has a learning disability.

Failure of teachers and others to differentiate between difference and disability may account for the misidentification of students for special education and the

Council for Exceptional Children

**CEC Knowledge Check**
Can the label of learning disability be separated from the conditions that put children at risk for learning disabilities? Do educators need to separate these variables before labeling a child?
LD3K1

Council for Exceptional Children

**CEC Knowledge Check**
What are the important background factors to be aware of in the labeling assessment process?
CC8S1

**culturally and linguistically diverse (CLD)** (or cultural and linguistic diversity) students or others from cultures or having a native language other than the dominant group (i.e., in the United States, individuals who are not Caucasian or native English speakers)

**CEC Knowledge Check**
Might children be labeled as learning disabled because of a cultural language difference?
CC6K2, CC6K3

overrepresentation of minority students in special programs. Thus, teachers must be familiar with multicultural issues in special education (Hallahan & Kauffman, 2003). Familiarity with multicultural issues and understanding that many differences are not disabilities should not, however, lead teachers to neglect the referral of CLD students for evaluation when difference signifies a disability. Ortiz (1997) cautions that the neglect of CLD students with disabilities is just as serious as mistaking cultural differences for disabilities.

> Patterns of underrepresentation pose problems as serious as those associated with overrepresentation but are more difficult to explain, as underrepresented students are an invisible population. A possible explanation is that teachers do not refer CLD students to special education because they inaccurately attribute their academic difficulties to differences of language and culture. In some cases, school districts discourage referrals because (a) they do not have personnel with the expertise to assess CLD students; (b) they fear they will not be able to defend assessment procedures; and/or (c) if students qualify for services, schools lack personnel who can address disability-related needs in linguistically and culturally appropriate ways. It is not uncommon, for example, for districts to prohibit referrals of LEP [limited English proficiency] students until these students have been in school for at least 2 years. Presumably, such policies are intended to give students time to adjust to the school culture and acquire English, thus increasing the likelihood of accurate diagnoses if they are eventually referred. . . . Such policies, though well-intentioned, not only violate the right of CLD students to an appropriate education, but also can have long-term negative effects because the lack of access to early intervention and specialized services can prevent students from realizing their social and academic potential. (p. 322)

**CEC Knowledge Check**
Why must educators be aware of developmental vs. cultural differences in assessing students who might or might not have LD?
CC6K1, CC8S6

One implication of the discussion here is that teachers must be keenly aware of both cultural and linguistic differences that are not disabilities and the distinguishing features of disabilities. Another implication is that teachers must be more understanding and accepting of the cultural diversity of the families of young children and work more closely with families.

Besides cultural differences, it is important to recognize that there is considerable variation in young children's development of particular skills. Although we may know the approximate age at which children typically learn particular skills (e.g., letter sounds, writing their name), we know that some learn these skills much earlier and some much later than is typical. However, both the early learners and the "late bloomers" may develop normally. And some young children have temperaments that are difficult for teachers, especially if the teacher has a different temperament (Keogh, 2003). A **temperament** is a behavioral style of responding to people and situations, such as being slow to warm up or respond, impulsive in responding, or wary of new situations and tasks. Thus, variability in normal development complicates the identification of early difficulties in learning. Consequently, we must always try to judge whether the child will continue to lag behind age mates or whether the child will catch up and not have a learning disability.

**temperament** a behavioral style, present from birth, of responding to people and situations

# How Are Learning Disabilities Identified in Infancy and Early Childhood?

The more severe the child's disability, the easier and earlier it can be identified. Few learning disabilities are severely disabling to children younger than five years old, and therefore their detection before the child enters school is quite difficult (Satz & Fletcher, 1988; Vaughn, Bos, & Schumm, 1997).

Some of the children who will be identified in school as having learning disabilities are slower than average in reaching early developmental milestones in motor, language, and social skills. However, they are not so limited in cognitive skills as to be thought to have mental retardation. For example, they may be slower than most children in learning to walk, dress themselves, and use the toilet. They may begin saying words and using sentences at a later age than most children or have particular difficulty making themselves understood. Or by the age of 3 or 4 years, they may have begun exhibiting an unusually persistent pattern of aggressive behavior, tantrums, hyperactivity, and refusal to follow adults' directions. These children may be identified early if their parents seek help from a clinic or other community social service because they are concerned about their child's slow development or difficult behavior. If the parents are not concerned about the child's development, the problem may be detected by a preschool teacher.

Preschool programs that provide prekindergarten education for 3- to 5-year-olds may identify disabilities, including emerging learning disabilities. The identification procedures used in clinics and preschools may involve a variety of standardized tests or developmental scales that compare a child's skills to a norm. However, many standardized instruments, particularly intelligence tests, have substantial limitations in assessing preschoolers. Careful observation of the child in a variety of contexts by experienced teachers and assessment of preacademic skills are more appropriate procedures for identifying the early stages of learning disabilities. Nevertheless, an important caution about reliance on teacher observation is that the teacher must be sensitive to the ways in which biological factors or home and community factors have shaped the child's behavior (Keogh, 2003). For example, in Jamal's case, it is not really clear what his early difficulties indicated. An open question is, "At what point could Jamal's learning disabilities have been predicted reliably?" In spite of her father's expressed wish that Shannon's reading difficulties had been identified earlier, the same question applies: "At what point could Shannon's learning disabilities have been predicted reliably?"

Most of the young children later identified as having learning disabilities may appear to be developing quite similarly to their age peers unless we look closely at the specific skills that are the most immediate precursors of academic problems. For example, research is increasingly indicating that key aspects of reading problems involve difficulties in understanding how sounds and words are put together to make sense. Children who have trouble in understanding and using language when they are in kindergarten and first grade, for example, typically have problems learning to read and are likely to be clearly identified as poor readers by the third grade (see Speece et al., 2002).

Council for Exceptional Children

**CEC Knowledge Check**
Are typical language development milestones for children relevant information for teachers of special education? If so, why? Or why not? LD6K1

Jamal

Shannon

## Two Approaches to Early Identification

Our discussion to this point suggests that recognizing children who later will be identified as having specific learning disabilities in the early grades or before they enter school is extraordinarily difficult. Given this, it is not surprising that there is some debate as to how to approach early identification. Educators attempting to do this may take a generic or a specific approach.

### Generic Approach

Many early childhood educators propose a generic approach to early identification. That is, they recognize that children may be at risk because of developmental lags that might indicate any of a variety of disabilities, including mental retardation, learning disabilities, or emotional or behavioral disorders. These early childhood educators therefore suggest that we identify preschoolers whose characteristics suggest disability in the general case. The general case includes slow development in motor skills, language, and learning the skills associated with reading and other areas of the school curriculum. These skills might include, for example, developmentally and culturally relevant skills in manipulating objects precisely, describing objects, carrying on a conversation, naming shapes and colors, associating sounds with letters, being able to reproduce sounds, counting, paying attention to a given task for an appropriate amount of time, following adults' commands, and making appropriate social approaches and responses to others.

The generic approach to early identification is not concerned with differentiating learning disabilities from other disabilities. Therefore, it directs attention to a wide variety of developmental milestones. Skills required for successful academic and social learning in school are the focus, regardless of the disability category into which the child might eventually be placed. Some schools choose not to use specific labels such as "learning disability" during the primary grades. Instead, they may use a more generic designation such as "**developmentally delayed**" to cover all types of identified disabilities for children below fourth grade.

**developmentally delayed**
a general term used to refer to a variety of disabilities of young children

A major advantage of a generic approach is that if relatively small lags in these skills result in early identification, then most children with learning disabilities will be included. A major disadvantage is that it can result in a high number of false identifications. For example, if relatively small lags result in early identification, then the percentage of false identifications will be high. However, if only large lags in development result in early identification, then the percentage of children with true disabilities who are not identified will be high.

### Specific Approach

The younger the child, the greater the benefit of a generic approach, because there is no real measure for learning disabilities prior to school. However, as children approach school age, enter kindergarten, and proceed through the grades, a more specific approach to identifying learning disabilities becomes more desirable. A specific disability label (e.g., "learning disability" or "reading disability") might be used. Moreover, specific skills, such as language or reading, may be identified as the basis for identifying the child as having a disability and as targets for remediation.

From kindergarten on, it is possible to begin focusing more specifically on reading-related skills, which are most often the central problem in learning disabilities. These skills involve segmenting words into individual phonemes or blending individual phonemes into words and are often referred to as **phonemic awareness.** By the time a child is in the third grade, a reading disability is usually obvious to the teacher, the child, and parents. It is manifested in test scores, the child's everyday classroom performance, and the observations of experienced teachers. The key question regarding early identification is this: Can we identify in kindergarten the children who will, without intervention, have reading disabilities by third grade? The findings of reading research suggest that we may be able to do this (cf. Speece et al., 2002; Vaughn et al., 1997). In fact, "Without early intervention, children who experience reading problems in the first and second grades most likely will continue to have these reading problems over time" (Speece et al., 2002, p. 223).

In both the cases of Jamal and Shannon, an issue is, specifically, at what point or at what age they should have been considered to have a learning disability. The people assessing their problems and needs no doubt had to debate whether to use a more general or a more specific label for the problems they saw.

## Promises and Pitfalls of Early Identification

Early identification of learning disabilities seems intuitively a promising practice. The common wisdom is that it will be followed by early intervention, which will lead to effective secondary and tertiary prevention. The pitfalls of early identification are not so obvious, and only after careful reflection have many people seen the possible downside of efforts to catch learning disabilities in their very earliest stages. The federal No Child Left Behind Act (U.S. Department of Education, 2002a) seems to be aimed at preventing failure, and the President's Commission on Excellence in Special Education, appointed by President George W. Bush, suggested in 2002 that special education should be focused on prevention, not intervention after a child has failed (see www.ed.gov/inits/commissionsboards/whspecialeducation/index.html). But averting failure requires anticipation of it, and the question really becomes how much failure a child should experience before intervention (Kauffman, 1999, 2003, 2004). If we are intent on prevention, then we also must be willing to risk more cases of false identification.

The earliest stages of learning disabilities are not so easy to recognize as one might think. Furthermore, the early identification procedures available today are far from perfect (Speece et al., 2003). Ideally, identification of a child as having a learning disability will not only be accurate (i.e., there will be no misdiagnoses), but will also lead to effective programming to address the disability. If the identification is accurate and appropriate intervention is promptly provided, then we might expect overwhelmingly positive consequences. The only possible negative consequences of accurate early identification followed immediately by effective intervention are the potential stigma and anxiety created by the identification of any disability, and these are clearly outweighed by the advantages of early and effective help in coping with learning problems. Given that we can accurately identify children who have learning disabilities and provide effective intervention, we should do so as early as possible.

**phonemic awareness**
skills or awareness of sound-symbol correspondence related to reading, especially those involving segmenting words into individual phonemes or blending individual phonemes into words

Council for Exceptional Children

**CEC Knowledge Check**
Why is it so difficult to diagnose children with possible learning disabilities before kindergarten and first grade? LD3K2

Council for Exceptional Children

**CEC Knowledge Check**
What are the limitations of assessments in identifying young children with special needs? CC8K4

Council for Exceptional Children

**CEC Knowledge Check**
Why is it important to identify students with special needs at an early age? CC9S2

Over three decades ago, Keogh and Becker (1973) warned of the dangers of early misidentification and of early identification that is not followed promptly by effective intervention. That caution is reiterated by Speece et al. (2002). Misidentification may carry with it not only the stigma and anxiety of disability, but also the costs of any intervention provided. Accurate early identification without prompt and effective intervention is likely to make the problems worse for both child and family. Major issues in early identification thus involve accuracy (avoiding errors) and the availability of early intervention (Speece et al., 2002).

Haring et al. (1992) questioned the wisdom of identifying preschoolers as having learning disabilities. They suggested that a learning disability is defined specifically by lack of academic progress in school; therefore, one cannot define learning disabilities in preschool children. Furthermore, they noted that special services to preschool children with disabilities do not require categorical labels and can be channeled through more generic labels such as "developmentally disabled" or "at risk." Labels associated with specific disabilities, Haring et al. (1992) maintain, create lowered expectations for children that may follow them throughout their school careers. Whether more generic labels are more or less problematic than more specific ones we do not know. How to provide special services to children with special needs without any label at all—except primary prevention that is given equally to all children, regardless of identified problems—is a puzzle not likely to be solved (Kauffman & Hallahan, 1993; Kauffman, 1999, 2003).

What purpose would have been served by identifying Jamal's problems or Shannon's much earlier if no special services were provided? It seems likely to us that identification of a problem, regardless of the child's age, carries with it the obligation of services to address it.

**Council for Exceptional Children**

**CEC Knowledge Check**
What factors must be considered when assessing and identifying preschool children with special needs? Do the disadvantages of identification outweigh the advantages? LD8K2

Jamal

Shannon

## How Is Early Childhood Intervention Provided?

Special education and early childhood education are separate entities, yet they are intertwined. We cannot fully understand one without considering the other. To a large extent, both special and general early education aim to provide high-quality educational experiences for young children. They may both be derived from the disciplines of child development and education, but the specific instructional techniques used may be somewhat different. Special education tends to offer greater direction and more explicit instruction in specific skills.

The best-known early intervention programs straddle the line between general and special education. Most of the students for whom they are designed have not been identified as having disabilities, although they are at risk for later identification if they do not receive effective instruction. Thus, these programs are focused on primary and secondary prevention. That is, they are intended to prevent learning disabilities from emerging and to correct learning problems that have been perceived.

### Popular Early Intervention Programs

Three early intervention programs are particularly well known nationally. All are designed to provide prevention and early intervention for young children who are at high risk for school failure (Vaughn et al., 1997).

## Project Head Start

Perhaps the most visible historical link between general and special early childhood education is Project Head Start. In the 1960s, the federal government launched Head Start with the intention of addressing the needs of preschool children from low-income families for educational experiences prior to their entry into kindergarten (Zigler & Styfco, 2000). Head Start remains one of the most popular government social programs, and its basic premise—that early educational intervention can prevent school failure and related developmental problems—remains the foundation for other early childhood education programs serving children at risk.

Although Head Start is not focused on children with disabilities, these children may be identified and served in the context of Head Start classrooms. However, federal legislation separate from Head Start now requires early intervention programs for preschoolers with disabilities, and these children may be served in a variety of environments. Most often today they are served in the context of integrated preschools attended by both normally developing and developmentally delayed children. Often, these programs are concerned with the emergence of a variety of difficulties, including emotional and behavioral disorders, attention problems, hyperactivity, and learning disabilities (see Redden, Forness, Ramey, Ramey, & Brezausek, 2002; Redden, Forness, Ramey, Ramey, Brezausek, & Kavale, in press; Serna, Lambros, Neilsen, & Forness, 2002; Sinclair, 1993).

## Reading Recovery

Reading Recovery is a program imported from New Zealand (Clay, 1985; Pinnel, 1990). It requires special teacher training in how to provide individual tutoring for low-achieving first-graders. The tutoring sessions last for 30 minutes, and a typical session involves the following:

1. child rereading a familiar book
2. teacher analyzing the reading by keeping a running record
3. letter identification activities, if necessary
4. child writing a story, with emphasis on hearing the sounds of words
5. putting together a cut-up story
6. child becoming acquainted with and reading a new book (Vaughn et al., 1997, p. 320)

The success of Reading Recovery depends not only on having a well-trained teacher who knows how to assess reading skills and teach those the child needs, but also on having enough such teachers to provide individual sessions with all the students who need them. Although Reading Recovery has strong proponents, others caution that it is expensive and largely unproven (go to www.TeachingLD.org and click on Reading Recovery).

## Success for All

Success for All (SFA) is a program designed at the Center for Research on Effective Schooling for Disadvantaged Students at Johns Hopkins University in Baltimore (Slavin, Madden, Dolan, & Wasik, 1994). It focuses on children in kindergarten through third grade who are at risk of school failure. SFA combines emphasis on reading in the general class curriculum with tutoring, small-group instruction, and work with families to try to ensure that every child learns to read. During reading instruction, which is scheduled for 90 minutes, the pupils leave their general grade-level class for instruction in smaller, more homogeneous groups. These groups are comprised of 10 to 20 children who are all reading at about the same level, although their general classrooms might range from grades 1 to 3. The primary components of the program are:

1. a family support team (including a social worker and a parent liaison)
2. reading tutoring for students with particular problems for as long as necessary
3. an innovative curriculum that integrates reading and writing instruction in meaningful contexts
4. regrouping of students across grades for reading instruction (Vaughn et al., 1997, p. 321)

All popular early intervention programs focus on teaching young children in small groups or individual tutoring. There appears to be no substitute for intensive, focused, and skillful teacher attention. The fact that a program is popular and widely used across the nation does not necessarily mean it is highly effective. Further research on the effects of early intervention programs on children's learning and school success will tell which approach is most effective and efficient. However, researchers have shown that small-group or individualized tutoring are hallmarks of effective reading instruction (Vaughn & Linan-Thompson, in press).

Not all services for young children with learning disabilities are part of a popular program. Both Jamal and Shannon received services tailored to their needs that were not part of Head Start, Reading Recovery, or Success for All. The services they received involved assessment to pinpoint their instructional needs and special instruction to address their academic deficits.

## Legal Requirements of Early Intervention

The federal role in early childhood education, particularly for young children with or at risk of disabilities, has gradually increased over the years (Bailey, 2000; Gallagher, 2000; Smith, 2000; Zigler & Styfco, 2000). Federal laws now require that all preschool children, including infants and toddlers, receive free and appropriate services if they have disabilities (Huefner, 2000; Yell, 1998). These laws are the Individuals with Disabilities Education Act (IDEA) and other laws enacted primarily to address severe disabilities of preschool-age children. The 1997 amendments of IDEA extended the law to cover infants and toddlers. As we have already noted, however, most children with learning disabilities are not identified until they are in school; the pitfalls of earlier identification of learning disabilities are great.

IDEA allows special education teachers to work with general education students who do not have identified disabilities as long as the needs of those with identified disabilities are being met. This opens additional possibilities for prevention in the form of early intervention—additional help before a learning problem becomes

**Council for Exceptional Children**

**CEC Knowledge Check**

For young children with learning disabilities in the area of reading, what are the essential elements of a research-validated reading method? LD4S8

Jamal

Shannon

a learning disability. If children are identified as needing special services due to a disability during their preschool years, federal laws require a plan for working with the child's family. Specifically, the families of infants and toddlers must be involved in developing an individualized family service plan (IFSP), which is similar to the individualized education program (IEP) required for school-age children under IDEA. An IFSP must include:

- present levels of the child's cognitive, physical, language and speech, psychosocial, and self-help development
- family resources, priorities, and concerns relating to the child's development
- major expected outcomes for the child and family, including criteria, procedures, and time lines for assessing progress
- specific early intervention services necessary to meet the child's and the family's needs, including frequency, intensity, location, and method of delivery
- projected dates for initiating and ending the services
- name of the case manager
- steps needed to ensure a smooth transition from the early intervention program into a preschool program

IFSPs, like IEPs, are not easy to implement well. However, they do provide a structure for ensuring that families are involved and that the child's needs are addressed. Federal mandates to provide early intervention programs for children with disabilities are perceived as among the least burdensome or wasteful and most cost-effective social programs of government. Research data will likely provide increasing support for this perception.

## Evaluating Early Childhood Program Quality

An early intervention program is not necessarily of high quality just because it meets the legal requirements. A high-quality program goes beyond the law to provide a nurturing and effective learning environment for the child. A good program makes certain that young children are acquiring both the academic skills and the social skills that they will need to be successful in school (see Speece et al., 2002; Vaughn et al., 2003).

Katz (1994) provides an overview on program quality from the perspectives of the preschool children served, parents, staff, and community and suggests some of the questions each participant in early childhood programs might ask in evaluating program quality. For example, the following are questions we might expect children to ask—if they could—about their program. (Affirmative answers would indicate high program quality.)

- Do I usually feel that I belong to the group and am not just part of the crowd?
- Do I usually feel accepted, understood, and protected by the adults rather than scolded or neglected by them?
- Am I usually accepted by some of my peers rather than ignored or rejected by them?

Council for Exceptional Children

**CEC Knowledge Check**
Given the requirements of an IFSP, who would be essential team members in the program planning process? How would you get each individual involved? CC10K2, CC10S4

Council for Exceptional Children

**CEC Knowledge Check**
What has been the significant impact of federal legislation on families of young children with special needs? LD1K3

- Am I usually addressed seriously and respectfully rather than being treated as someone who is "precious" or "cute"?
- Am I usually glad to be here rather than reluctant to come and eager to leave?
- Do I find most of the activities engaging, absorbing, and challenging rather than just amusing, fun, entertaining, or exciting?
- Do I find most of the experiences interesting rather than frivolous or boring?
- Do I find most of the activities meaningful rather than mindless or trivial?
- Do I find most of my experiences satisfying rather than frustrating or confusing? (Katz, 1994, p. 201)

**Council for Exceptional Children**

**CEC Knowledge Check**

Why might it be important to self-assess the quality of early child special education programs?
CC8K2, CC9S9

Certainly, these questions are relevant to both general and special education programs, in both the higher grades and preschool. One final question posed by Katz (1994) seems essential in judging program quality, particularly for students with disabilities: Am I acquiring the specific skills necessary for my satisfactory progress through school? The Effective Practices box on page 157 will help teachers meet the expectation of high-quality programming for young children.

## What Are Some Trends in Early Childhood Special Education?

There may be overwhelming public support for early intervention programs, but there is also controversy among early childhood educators regarding the most effective practices. These controversies encompass both general and special early education and concern contemporary trends in educating young children. Seven trends in the early twenty-first century in early childhood special education include:

1. inclusion of young children with disabilities in preschools serving normally developing youngsters
2. practices described as developmentally appropriate
3. transition of children from home to preschool and preschool to kindergarten
4. family involvement in the education of young children and family-based education
5. new approaches to the assessment of young children
6. self-determination of young children with disabilities
7. technology in early childhood special education

### Inclusive Education

In early childhood special education, considerable controversy has been generated by the inclusive schools movement, which promotes the full inclusion of children with severe disabilities in classes with nondisabled pupils (Jakubecy, Mock, & Kauffman, 2003; Kauffman & Landrum, in press; Mock & Kauffman, 2002, in press). However, even in early childhood special education, "in some context[s] and for some children, inclusive programs may not be the answer" (Odom, 2000, p. 25).

Most of the controversy about this trend involves children who may have a variety of developmental problems and labels, some of whom might at some time

## Effective Practices

**FOR LEARNING DISABILITIES**

## Spotting the Early Indications of Reading Problems

Teachers of young children want to know the most important signs indicating that a child is at risk of reading failure or social difficulties. That is, teachers want to know the most reliable or trustworthy indicators for identifying children who are likely to experience reading failure or social problems later. Knowing these indicators will help reduce the incorrect identification of children who are likely to be unsuccessful. And it will also help avoid failing to identify those children who need help.

Unfortunately, there is no single measure or combination of measures or tests that will accurately identify every case. In any event, a combination of indicators is better than one single test. It is not a good practice to teach only the skills that will allow a child to score well on particular measures (e.g., teaching a child only to say letter names). Here are some indicators that Speece and her colleagues (2002) found best in identifying kindergartners at risk of reading failure. These should help teachers provide a balanced early literacy program that includes a broad range of prerequisite reading skills.

1. Kindergarten children may be at high risk of reading failure if they:
   - have little or no phonemic awareness (can't add, delete, or substitute sounds in words)
   - cannot name letters of the alphabet and say the sounds they typically make

- cannot name letters of the alphabet fluently (i.e., name all the letters of the alphabet within a minute or so)
- cannot sound out nonsense CVC (consonant, vowel, consonant) words, like *tav*

2. Young children may be at risk of social difficulties if they exhibit one or more of the following characteristics (taking into consideration the child's culture and social experience):
   - do not play with others appropriately (e.g., do not know how to share)
   - do not seem to understand the reciprocity of positive responses involved in friendship
   - show aggression toward or intimidation of peers
   - fail to respond to peers' social initiatives and remain loners in a group
   - fail to make appropriate social responses to adults (e.g., do not respond when spoken to, avoid eye contact)
   - do not seem to understand differences in emotions or predictable emotional responses to social situations

Vaughn and her colleagues (2003) discuss appropriate social skills interventions for young children, including direct instruction, guided practice, reinforcement, modeling, role-playing, prompting, and play activities.

*Sources:* From "Initial Evidence That Letter Fluency Tasks Are Valid Indicators of Early Reading Skill" by D. L. Speece, C. Mills, K. D. Ritchey, and E. Hillman, 2003, *Journal of Special Education, 36,* 223–233; "Social Skills Interventions for Young Children with Disabilities: A Synthesis of Group Design Studies" by S. Vaughn, A. Kim, C. V. M. Sloan, M. T. Hughes, B. Elbaum, and D. Sridhar, 2003, *Remedial and Special Education, 24,* 2–15. Copyright 2003 by PRO-ED, Inc. Reprinted by permission.

be said to have a learning disability. However, relatively few studies involve only children categorized specifically as having learning disabilities (Manset & Semmel, 1997).

Virtually all early childhood educators suggest that children with mild disabilities and those considered at risk for school failure should be included in programs designed to serve a diverse group of learners. The controversy surrounding integration of children likely to be identified as having learning disabilities tends to be centered on the relationship between general and special early childhood education.

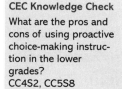

Council for Exceptional Children

**CEC Knowledge Check**
What are the pros and cons of using proactive choice-making instruction in the lower grades?
CC4S2, CC5S8

The extent to which practices in one are appropriate for children served by the other and the extent to which children at risk of school failure need special services that are not an integral part of general early childhood education programs are matters of controversy. Some research suggests that inclusive classrooms for young children produce better outcomes than do special classes, but particularly for children with milder disabilities and especially when the program for young children is a full-day as opposed to a half-day program (e.g., Holahan & Costenbader, 2000; see also Brown, Odom, & Conroy, 2001; Odom, 2000; Soodak, Erwin, Winton, Brotherson, Turnbull, Hanson, & Brault, 2002, for further discussion of inclusive education for young children).

## Developmentally Appropriate Practices (DAP)

Among the similarities and differences between general and special early childhood education, perhaps the most hotly debated issue is what has become known as **developmentally appropriate practice (DAP).** The features of DAP were introduced in the late 1980s in a publication of the National Association for the Education of Young Children (Bredekamp, 1987). DAP involves providing an educational program that is appropriate for the child's age and individual needs, given knowledge of child development. This program takes into consideration the child's progression through developmental stages and emphasizes avoidance of pushing children's achievement beyond their current developmental levels. Another way of describing DAP is that it is based on the assumption that learning must be child centered and child directed, that teachers should do relatively little to direct children or teach specific skills.

> **developmentally appropriate practice (DAP)** an educational program that is appropriate for the child's age and individual needs

DAP is controversial in early childhood special education because the mission of special educators has been to speed up the rate at which children with disabilities develop important skills. Moreover, special educators typically have emphasized the need for teachers to direct learning by explicitly teaching the skills important to overcoming or compensating for learning disabilities.

More than a decade ago, one group of early childhood special educators noted, "While DAP has focused primarily on preventing attempts to artificially accelerate the progress of children who are developing normally, the explicit mission of [early childhood special education] is to produce outcomes that would not occur in the absence of intervention or teaching" (Carta, Schwartz, Atwater, & McConnell, 1991, p. 4). Thus, the differences between early education programs designed for normally developing children based on a DAP philosophy and the basic premises of special education programs for preschool children with disabilities make integrating general and special early education difficult.

DAP may well be a beginning point for many young children with disabilities. However, some special educators have noted that "although DAP might be necessary, without further individualized intervention it may not be sufficient for promoting some young children's emerging peer-related social competence" (Brown et al., 2001, p. 165; see also Odom, 2000). It is extremely likely that the same could be said for some young children's emerging literacy or other skills necessary for success in school. Further research will be necessary to reveal the extent to which DAP and

**Council for Exceptional Children**

**CEC Knowledge Check**

Which practice—inclusion or DAP—has stronger research support?
LD4S1

early childhood special education are compatible, particularly for the acquisition of all of the skills necessary for academic success.

## Education for Transition

A major trend in early childhood special education is to plan for the transition of young children from home to school and from preschool to kindergarten. Much of the thinking about transition is based on child development literature indicating the importance of transitions in cognitive and social characteristics that occur at certain ages (Rosenkoetter, Whaley, Hains, & Pierce, 2001).

Furthermore, as children move from families to preschools and from preschools to kindergarten and on to first grade, they must become more self-directed and less dependent on adults. The child who does not exhibit these expected behaviors in kindergarten is likely to be at risk of failure in later grades.

## Family-Based Education

Family involvement in special education is usually highly desirable. Particularly strong emphasis is placed on families in early childhood education for children with disabilities. So much of early education is grounded in the home that family participation is required for effective early intervention. The language experiences—being talked to and read to and observing others using written and oral language—provided by the family environment are critical to children's early learning (Hart, 2000; Hart & Risley, 1995). Nevertheless, lack of empathy with caregivers and an oversimplified view of a family-centered approach can result in problems (Bruder, 2000). Two aspects of families are points of critical concern and controversy: cultural diversity and diversity of family structure.

Cultural diversity is important because of the variety found in families' language and literacy traditions, views of disability, assumptions about learning, and ways of relating to school personnel. Inviting and encouraging parent participation in special education will be effective only if teachers accept and understand the reality of cultural differences (Linan-Thompson & Jean, 1997; van Keulen et al., 1998). Effective communication with families is the key to their involvement (Barrera & Corso, 2002). The Multicultural Considerations box on page 160 illustrates one of the considerations necessary in serving children from diverse families.

The structure and composition of families vary tremendously, and traditional assumptions about the strengths and weaknesses of diverse families may need to be revised (Hanson & Carta, 1996; Unger, Jones, Park, & Tressell, 2001). The very definition of *family* has become controversial due to the frequent dissolution of family units by divorce and the changing, multicultural groupings that constitute families. Teachers must learn to set aside stereotypes of family constitution and strength or weakness and work with families, regardless of their structure.

Families differ tremendously in what they need and what they can do. The structure and economic conditions of the family may have huge effects on how much involvement is acceptable and feasible. The effects of family-based education

Council for Exceptional Children

CEC Knowledge Check

Why is it important to understand the cultural diversity of families with children who might have special needs? CC3K4

## Relationships among Culture, Language, and Reading

Black children who come from print-rich environments where the parents model and reinforce emerging literacy skills will likely enter first grade equal to their White counterparts having had the same or similar experiences. The primary differences will most likely be in the language spoken by Black children and the written language in print. This means that Black children may bring different assumptions about the world to the printed page, so teachers must be aware that Black children's interactions with text may be different from White mainstream American English speaking children. These differences are often caused by not having written word–spoken word correspondence, and these differences are what most teachers do not understand. Typically, Black children's spoken home language is not represented in conventional storybooks or textbooks. Therefore, learning to read for some Black children involves making meaning of the letters, words, and sentence structure, as well as the identification of words. On the other hand, White children typically have congruence in the language they speak at home with the written words found in conventional print. This lack of congruence for African American children is where culture and language variation makes a difference in language, speech, and learning. These are also areas where teachers need knowledge and understanding of cultural differences to prevent the promotion of misconceptions about Black children as individuals and false perceptions about their abilities to learn.

### Questions to Ponder

What are some of the different assumptions about the world that black children and white children may bring to the printed page?

How might the lack of congruence between African American children's oral language and the print they read be addressed most effectively?

How might issues similar to those described here for African American children arise for children who speak Spanish or another language other than standard American English at home?

*Source:* From *Speech, Language, Learning, and the African American Child* (pp. 231–232) by J. E. van Keulen, G. T. Weddington, and C. E. DeBose, 1998, Boston: Allyn and Bacon. Copyright © 1988 by Pearson Education. Reprinted by permission of the publisher.

Council for
Exceptional
Children

**CEC Knowledge Check**
What are some of the major concerns of families of children with potential learning disabilities?
CC10K3

may be greatest for families experiencing the greatest economic disadvantage (Wagner, Spiker, & Linn, 2002).

## Assessment

Educational assessment, including that of special education, is undergoing substantial changes. Standardized testing, the traditional approach, is being deemphasized in favor of alternative procedures. The alternatives to standardized testing include performance testing, portfolio assessment, and curriculum-based assessment. In early childhood special education, too, a similar shift in thinking about assessment is occurring. Educators of young children with disabilities are increasingly concerned about how assessment information matches up with classroom activities and goals (e.g., Wolery, Brashers, & Neitzel, 2002).

The trends in assessment are clearly away from testing and toward performance criteria directly related to the preschool curriculum. However, controversy continues about the role specific types of tests (e.g., IQ tests, developmental scales) should play in diagnosis and evaluation and about the relative value of various alternative procedures such as portfolios and teacher observation (McMaster, Fuchs, Fuchs, & Copton, 2002; Taylor, 1997). Most early childhood educators believe that it is important in any assessment strategy to emphasize the strengths of the child, not just areas in which improvement is needed (e.g., Campbell, Milbourne, & Silverman, 2001; see also McConnell, 2000).

**Council** for
**Exceptional**
**Children**

**CEC Knowledge Check**
Name alternatives to standardized testing that can be used in educational assessments. LD8K3

## Self-Determination

Self-determination is a trend in thinking about all people with disabilities. The term **self-determination** usually has been used with reference to adults with severe disabilities. "Self-determination refers to making one's own decision about important aspects of one's life—for example, where to work and live, with whom to become friends, and what education to pursue" (Hallahan & Kauffman, 2003, p. 43). However, many special educators now recognize that self-determination is something that should be part of the school's curriculum (Browder, Wood, Test, Karvonen, & Algozzine, 2001).

**self-determination**
making decisions about important aspects of one's own life, such as where to work and live, with whom to become friends, and what education to pursue

Self-determination is now seen by some as beginning in the early elementary years of schooling. It is also seen as something that applies not just to individuals with severe disabilities, but to young children with relatively mild disabilities, including such problems as learning disabilities and speech impairments. In fact, of the 50 young children participating in one study of self-determination, 21 were labeled as having a learning disability (Palmer & Wehmeyer, 2003). The students ranged in age from 5 to 9 years. The Current Trends and Issues box on page 162 shows the kinds of questions these students were presented and the educational supports provided to help them. Other parts of the self-determination curriculum for these students included taking action (asking themselves "What is my plan?") and adjusting the goal or plan (asking themselves "What have I learned?").

In another study, researchers found that students did better at self-management when they directed their own activities (setting goals, assigning work, recording and evaluating performance) than when the teacher directed their activities (Mithaug & Mithaug, 2003). We also discussed self-determination in Chapter 2.

**Council** for
**Exceptional**
**Children**

**CEC Knowledge Check**
How can educators help encourage independence in students with special needs? CC5S8, CC5S9

## Technology

Ordinarily, we think of assistive technology as being particularly important for individuals who have sensory impairments, need alternative or augmented communication, or do not have the ability to accomplish typical physical activities (see Hallahan & Kauffman, 2003). However, appropriate technology can also be very valuable to young children with mild disabilities.

Technology in early childhood special education involves not only the use of technology by children but also resources for teachers and trainers of personnel. Many children learn to use computers at a very early age, and computer-assisted instruction shows promise as a special education intervention (Forness, Kavale,

CURRENT
TRENDS
&
ISSUES

## Self-Determination Includes Young Students with Learning Disabilities

From an early age, children with learning disabilities need to be involved in self-determination. They need to be involved in choosing their life course to the greatest extent possible. This requires that teachers help students think about what they are learning and why, what they know, what they need to know, and so on. Following are examples of the kind of self-questioning students need to be taught.

### Problem for Student to Solve: What Is My Goal?

**Educational Supports**

**Student question 1: What do I want to learn?**

*Teacher Objectives*

- Enable students to identify specific strengths and instructional needs.
- Enable students to communicate preferences, interests, beliefs, and values.
- Teach students to prioritize needs.

Student self-assessment of interests, abilities, and instructional needs

**Student question 2: What do I about it now?**

*Teacher Objectives*

- Enable students to identify their current status in relation to the instructional need.
- Assist students to gather information about opportunities and barriers in their environments.

Awareness training
Choice-making instruction

**Student question 3: What must change for me to learn what I don't know?**

*Teacher Objective*

- Enable students to decide if action will be focused toward capacity building, modifying the environment, or both.
- Support students to choose a need to address from a prioritized list.

Problem-solving instruction
Decision-making instruction

**Student question 4: What can I do to make this happen?**

*Teacher Objective*

- Teach students to state a goal and identify criteria for achieving that goal.

Goal-setting instruction

*Source:* From "Promoting Self-Determination in Early Elementary School: Teaching Self-Regulated Problem-Solving and Goal-Setting Skills" by S. B. Palmer and M. L. Wehmeyer, 2003, *Remedial and Special Education, 24,* 115–126, figure 1. Copyright 2003 by PRO-ED, Inc. Reprinted by permission.

Council for Exceptional Children

**CEC Knowledge Check**

What are the top four essential preskills for reading and social skills that might be early indicators of school failure? Provide a rationale.
LD3K2, CC5K5

---

**computer-assisted instruction (CAI)** instruction in which a computer is used to present tasks or perform other functions usually performed by a person

Blum, & Lloyd, 1997). **Computer-assisted instruction (CAI),** in which the computer is used to present instructional tasks, is an option that can be used with good results for teaching preacademic or basic academic skills. One example is provided in the Today's Technology box on page 163. It is important to note that instruction can be *assisted* by a computer, but it is not feasible merely to turn instruction over to a computer or rely on computer technology to provide all instruction.

## Using Computers for Programming Time Delay

Hitchcock and Noonan (2000) compared teacher-assisted instruction (TAI) and computer-assisted instruction (CAI) for five preschoolers who had "early childhood learning impairment" (ECLI). ECLI is a broad category of disability indicating significant delays in cognitive, language, or adaptive behavior skills (remember the discussion in this chapter of the "generic" approach to identification of disabilities in early childhood).

The children were learning to identify shapes, colors, numbers, and letters. The instruction in both teacher-assisted and computer-assisted versions included a procedure called constant time delay (CTD). CTD has been used successfully in teaching children with disabilities. It involves a brief delay (usually just a few seconds) after a task is presented and the use of a prompt that is very likely to result in the child giving a correct answer. The reason for the delay is to give the child time to look at the task and consider the answer. The reason for the prompt is to minimize errors.

Hitchcock and Noonan summarized the following implications of their study for teachers:

1. Computer software (used with constant time delay) is an effective tool to reinforce learning of academic skills during guided practice. The software used in this study [Intellipics 2.1] was programmable and varied.
2. Constant time delay is an effective instructional method with both the computer software and the classroom manipulatives.

3. Computer software can be used as a tool to promote generalization of skills and reinforce maintenance through additional practice.
4. Computers are motivating. The children in this study enjoyed the interaction and control they had with the computer and responded with delight when they could activate items on the screen with the mouse or keyboard.
5. Computers promote teacher and student interaction, allowing the teacher to encourage, prompt, or point to items in the display. The computer requires more teacher assistance at the beginning, when students are learning new academic skills or learning how to access programs. This time decreases as students' proficiency and confidence increase.
6. Computers create opportunities for practice. This medium is effective with students who are resistant to traditional practice or adult interaction. It is nonthreatening and allows the student control.
7. The computer is an excellent means of modifying or adapting instruction to promote inclusion in general education settings. It can be programmed to meet individual student learning needs (e.g., circle, triangle, square, rectangle versus oval, diamond, hexagon, cylinder). Preservice and inservice teachers should be trained to use computer technology as a tool to promote students' learning and self-reliance.

*Source:* From "Computer-Assisted Instruction of Early Academic Skills" by C. H. Hitchcock and J. J. Noonan, 2000, *Topics in Early Childhood Special Education, 20,* 145–158. Copyright 2000 by PRO-ED, Inc. Reprinted by permission.

Council for Exceptional Children

**CEC Knowledge Check**
Will long-term outcomes for children in schools without technology be different than for those who have access to technology? CC9S2

Besides the computer or computer-assisted programs that children may use to help them learn academic or preacademic skills (e.g., the programs marketed under the trade name "Leap Pad"), teachers of young children with disabilities should be aware of World Wide Web resources for early intervention. Hains, Belland, Conceicao-Runlee, Santos, and Rothenberg (2000) provide a listing of such resources, including online journals devoted to early childhood issues. One online journal, *Contemporary Issues in Early Childhood,* has devoted a special issue to technology (Yelland & Siraj-Blatchford, 2002).

Council for Exceptional Children

**CEC Knowledge Check**
How might you use a computer to teach the reading preskill of rhyming to a preschool student? CC7K4

PORTFOLIO-BUILDING ACTIVITY

## Demonstrating Mastery of the CEC Standards

Applying the information you have learned in Chapter 5, you can now craft a visual representation of the needs, cultural issues, and educational issues for a young African American student with a learning disability. The activity should be in the form of a web or a semantic map. As a teacher, you can use this visual aid in helping others to understand the interactions between cultural issues and educational needs. This will assist individuals to advocate for themselves in a more informed manner. See the Companion Website (www.ablongman.com/hallahanLD3e) for specific directions on how to create your semantic map and an example to follow. Questions to think about as you progress:

**Council for Exceptional Children**

**CEC Content Standards**

3. Individual Learning Differences
4. Instructional Strategies
5. Learning Environments and Social Interactions
9. Professional and Ethical Practice
10. Collaboration

- How do primary language, culture, and familial background interact with an individual's exceptional condition to affect academic and social options?

- What instructional strategies promote positive learning results and enhance the learning of problem solving, self-advocacy, and self-independence for young children?

- What is needed to actively create learning environments for individuals with learning disabilities that foster cultural understanding and positive social interactions where diversity is valued?

- How can special educators demonstrate a commitment to understanding diverse cultures and language, and be sensitive to the many aspects of diversity?

- In what ways will it be vital for special educators to understand collaboration when working with families in culturally responsive ways for young children who are at risk of being labeled learning disabled?

# SUMMARY

**How can learning disabilities be prevented?**

- Prevention of learning disabilities may be:
  - primary—keeping the disability from occurring at all
  - secondary—correcting a problem or keeping it from getting worse
  - tertiary—keeping the problem from spreading to other areas of functioning
- Addressing risk factors for learning disabilities in infancy and early childhood requires identifying and removing the conditions that increase the chances that a child will develop a disability. These factors are multiple and complex and vary greatly from individual to individual and with the age of the child.
- Distinguishing disabilities from cultural differences of young children requires knowledge of the cultural and linguistic diversity of families. Sensitivity to cultural differences should reduce both the overrepresentation of minority children in special education and the underidentification of children with disabilities from culturally and linguistically diverse groups.

**How are learning disabilities identified in infancy and early childhood?**

- Two approaches to early identification are:
  - a generic approach—specific disability labels are not assigned to children's difficulties, but instead a very general designation (e.g., "developmentally delayed") is used to indicate problems that may indicate a variety of disabilities.

- a specific approach, meaning that specific labels (e.g., "learning disability," "reading disability") are used, and specific skill areas are targets for remediation.
- Promises and pitfalls of early identification include the promise of prevention and the pitfall of misidentification.

### How is early childhood intervention provided?

- Popular early intervention programs include:
  - Project Head Start, a preschool program for disadvantaged youngsters, began in the 1960s and now frequently includes preschoolers with disabilities.
  - Reading Recovery, a reading tutorial program imported from New Zealand, has questionable research support.
  - Success for All, a program designed for disadvantaged primary-grade children, involves special reading instruction in small, homogeneous groups plus tutoring for individual children.
- The legal requirements of early intervention include the Individuals with Disabilities Education Act and other federal laws. Preschoolers with disabilities must have an individualized family service plan detailing what services they will be provided and how their families will be involved.
- Guidelines for evaluating early childhood program quality include questions relevant to both general and special education, including the type and intensity of instruction offered, the way the child feels about the program, and family and community involvement.

### What are some trends and controversies in early childhood education?

Contemporary issues and trends include:
- greater inclusion of young children with disabilities in preschools serving normally developing youngsters
- the widespread acceptance of practices described as developmentally appropriate, although there is controversy about the extent to which such practices, which do not focus on accelerating the child's acquisition of specific skills, are appropriate for children with disabilities
- new approaches to the assessment of young children, including alternate assessment that relies less on standardized testing and accommodates cultural and linguistic diversity
- emphasis on transition of children from home to preschool and preschool to kindergarten so that the child is more likely to experience success in the primary grades
- emphasis on family involvement in the education of young children and family-based education, with recognition of the need to adapt to cultural and linguistic diversity and diversity of family structure

## REFLECTIONS ON THE CASES

1. What would have been the advantages and disadvantages of identifying Shannon's or Jamal's learning disabilities at an earlier age?

2. If Shannon or Jamal had received one of the most popular early intervention programs, which one do you think would have been most appropriate? Why?

3. Which of the trends in early childhood special education do you think would be (or would have been) most important for Shannon and Jamal? Why?

## What Are Learning Disability Outcomes across the Life Span?
- Higher Dropout Rates
- Higher Underemployment
- Greater Dependency on Others

## What Transition Programs and Services Are Available?
- Federal Initiatives
- Interagency Collaboration and Service Delivery
- Social Skills and Self-Advocacy Training
- Parental Involvement
- Vocational Training and College Preparation

## How Are Students with Learning Disabilities Prepared for College?
- Programming Goals for College Preparation

## How Can Students with Learning Disabilities Succeed in College?
- Guidelines for Choosing a College
- Predictors of Success in College
- Instructional Accommodations

## How Can Students with Learning Disabilities Prepare for the Work World?
- Programming Goals for Vocational Training
- School-Business Partnerships

## How Can Employers Encourage Success for Adults with Learning Disabilities?
- Workplace Accommodations

## How Can Employees with Learning Disabilities Succeed in the Workplace?
- Choose a Job That Is a Good Match
- Use Personal Contacts to Find a Job
- Become a Self-Advocate
- Develop Compensatory Strategies
- Take Advantage of Technology
- Gain Control over One's Life

Council for
Exceptional
Children

See Companion Website
for detailed correlations
between chapter content
and Council for Excep-
tional Children Standards;
**www.ablongman.com/
hallahanLD3e**

### CEC Knowledge and Skills Discussed in This Chapter

1. Definitions and laws regarding transition and why a protective mandate is needed.
2. Transition services, which include active collaboration with the student, educators, related services, families, community, employers, and postsecondary personnel and involve
   academic, social, self-advocacy, and life skills in creating an individualized program.
3. Successful postsecondary transition, which requires appropriate assessment, role
   planning, self-advocacy, educational choices, and accommodation needs.
4. Transition to employment or vocational training, which is multifaceted but must have the goal
   of developing the highest quality-of-life potential for the student with learning disabilities.
5. Potential cultural responsiveness to transition services and postsecondary expectations.

# Transition Programming in Adolescence and Adulthood

# 6

Our hope is that she can go to college, at least the community college.

*Kerrie Ireland, Shannon's mother*

A once-ignored population, adults with learning disabilities are coming into their own. More and more researchers are turning their attention to issues pertaining to this group. Whereas professionals used to believe that children with learning disabilities outgrew their problems during adolescence, we now recognize that many adults are in need of special programming. And more and more adults are taking an active role in the recognition and treatment of their problems.

This interest in adults with learning disabilities has spawned a variety of programs designed to enhance the transition of adolescents into adulthood. **Transition** has been defined as:

> a change in status from behaving primarily as a student to assuming emergent adult roles in the community. These roles include employment, participating in post-secondary education, maintaining a home, becoming appropriately involved in the community, and experiencing satisfactory personal and social relationships. The process of enhancing transition involves the participation and coordination of school programs, adult agency services, and natural supports within the community. The foundations for transition should be laid during the elementary and middle school years, guided by the broad concept of career development. Transition planning should begin no later than age 14, and students should be encouraged, to the full extent of their capabilities, to assume a minimum amount of responsibility for such planning. (Halpern, 1994, p. 117)

This definition stresses the need for a comprehensive array of services and does not focus solely on employment. This broad conceptualization is in keeping with the attitude of many in the field who consider transition from a quality-of-life perspective,

**transition** a change in status from behaving primarily as a student to assuming emergent adult roles in the community

**Council** for **Exceptional Children**

**CEC Knowledge Check**
Do you agree with this definition? Create your own definition of *transition.*
CC1S1, LD1K5

which includes such things as independence, happiness, and contentment (Halpern, 1993; Scanlon & Mellard, 2002; Szymanski, 1994).

## What Are Learning Disability Outcomes across the Life Span?

Two general types of evidence lead us to the conclusion that learning disabilities usually persist into adulthood: research on characteristics and research on outcomes. A body of research, largely conducted in the 1970s and 1980s, focused on the characteristics of secondary students and adults. It shows that the same academic and social problems manifested in childhood are likely to continue into adulthood (Kavale, 1988). Even intensive programming at the elementary and secondary levels will not "cure" most learning disabilities, especially those that are relatively severe. The disabilities may change their form slightly as older persons with learning disabilities learn to cope with their problems, but for the most part, to have a learning disability is to have a lifelong condition.

The second type of evidence suggesting the intractability of learning disabilities focused on outcomes related to major phases in life. Researchers have found that learning disabilities are associated with higher rates of dropping out of secondary school, underemployment, and greater dependency on others.

### Higher Dropout Rates

In recent years, dropout rates for students with disabilities have declined from 34.5% in 1993–1994 to 28.9% in 1998–1999 (U.S. Department of Education, 2001). Despite this encouraging trend for students with any kind of disability, students with learning disabilities are still far more likely than their nondisabled peers to drop out of school. In 1998–1999, 63.3% of students age 14 and older with learning disabilities graduated with a standard diploma, while 27.1% dropped out (U.S. Department of Education, 2001a). That figure is significantly higher than the overall national dropout rate of approximately 11% (National Center for Education Statistics, 2001c).

### Higher Underemployment

The findings of several large-scale studies have been relatively consistent in showing that the employment rates of persons with learning disabilities are similar to those of the general population. However, because individuals with learning disabilities are less likely to attend postsecondary school, their long-run earning potential is likely to be significantly less than that of individuals who complete postsecondary education (Goldstein, Murray, & Edgar, 1998; Murray, Goldstein, Nourse, & Edgar, 2000). There are some indications that the employment status for women with learning disabilities may be lower, but that may be because some of them have chosen to stay home with their children (Murray et al., 1997; Murray et al., 2000).

Whereas the best available data suggest that, except for the possible exception of females, unemployment rates for adults with learning disabilities are generally not critically high, there is abundant evidence that underemployment is a major problem. **Underemployment** is the condition in which individuals hold jobs that are below their level of skills or training. For example, data from the National Longitudinal Transition Study (NLTS) survey of students with learning disabilities out of school three to five years indicate that only 45% earned more than $6 per hour. The types of jobs held by young adults with learning disabilities tend to require low-level skills; many are part-time service, fast-food, or laborer positions (Gajar, 1992; Shapiro & Rich, 1999; Tomblin, 1999 [as cited in Wehman, 2001]).

**underemployment** the condition in which individuals hold jobs that are below their level of skills or training

## Greater Dependency on Others

Although few data exist on the residential status of adults with learning disabilities, those available suggest that a disproportionate number live with their parents or relatives. For example, researchers have found that within a few years after high school, about 75% of individuals with learning disabilities are living with relatives (Haring, Lovett, & Smith, 1990; Sitlington & Frank, 1999). And researchers using the NLTS data found that only 44% of persons with learning disabilities were living independently three to five years after high school, compared to 60% of the general population (Blackorby & Wagner, 1996).

**Council for Exceptional Children**

**CEC Knowledge Check**
What are the long-term effects of having a learning disability? Statistically, what do most students with learning disabilities have to look forward to in their lives? CC3K1

# What Transition Programs and Services Are Available?

Results from outcome studies of adults with learning disabilities as well as adults with other types of disabilities (e.g., mental retardation, emotional or behavioral disorders) have done much to convince policy makers that major initiatives need to be directed toward transition programming. There have been a series of federal government initiatives to strengthen educational programming for secondary-school students with disabilities to enable them to make a more successful transition to adulthood.

## Federal Initiatives

**Council for Exceptional Children**

**CEC Knowledge Check**
Why is IDEA the most important legislation passed by Congress, relative to transition? CC1K2

Prior to the passage of P.L. 94-142 in 1975, public school programming for students with disabilities beyond elementary-school age was minimal. This law mandated that students with disabilities receive an appropriate education until graduation from high school or until 21 years of age. In the mid-1980s, the federal government announced the "transition initiative" (Will, 1984). Based on this call for action, Congress passed several pieces of legislation, the most important of which was IDEA (P.L. 101-476, passed in 1990 and amended in 1997 as P.L. 105-17), which mandates that schools provide transition services for all students with disabilities.

In order to ensure proper and timely planning for the implementation of transition services, the law requires that a transition plan be integrated into each student's individualized education program (IEP). IDEA requires the IEP to contain the following:

1. beginning at age 14 and updated annually, a statement of the transition service needs of the child under the applicable components of the child's IEP that focuses on the child's courses of study (such as participation in advanced-placement courses or a vocational education program)
2. beginning at age 16 (or younger, if determined appropriate by the IEP Team), a statement of needed transition services for the child, including, when appropriate, a statement of the interagency responsibilities or any needed linkages. (IDEA Amendments of 1997, Sec. 614(d)(I)(A)vii, p. 55)

By mandating that the transition plan be part of a student's IEP, Congress has underscored the importance of each student's need for a unique transition experience. With the wide variety of employment and postsecondary experiences, as well as the many living opportunities available, individualization becomes increasingly important as the student with learning disabilities progresses through secondary school. As Shapiro and Rich (1999) state, "transition programming must not only be comprehensive but individualized, based on personal needs, interests, and preferences" (p. 142). The needs of many will change as they progress through secondary school. Adolescence is a time of rapid physical and emotional alterations. Students at this age frequently modify their vocational and educational aspirations, as the following quote indicates:

Shannon

> I've wanted to be a teacher since I was in second grade, but when I met my friend, Ashleigh, and found out that her father writes for the newspaper, I thought I wanted to do that. Maybe it would be more fun to be a reporter on TV . . . I'm not sure . . . I would love to work with famous people.
>
> *Shannon*

See the Case Connections box on page 171 for excerpts from Shannon's transition plan.

## Interagency Collaboration and Service Delivery

Implicit in current conceptualizations of transition services is the idea of a coordinated set of services. This coordination

> helps ensure that transition outcomes, service needs, and expectations for how they will be provided are communicated among and agreed to by key participants. . . . It also guards against duplication of services and, therefore, the more unfortunate

# Excerpts from Shannon's Transition Plan

A few days before her individualized education program (IEP) meeting, Shannon sat down with her case manager to complete her transition plan. After some discussion, they settled on several points. Shannon was told that she would be responsible for presenting her transition plan at her IEP meeting. Following are excerpts from Shannon's transition plan:

**Student Career Information**

*Interests:*

> *sports, music, art, watching TV, creative writing*

*Strengths/Capabilities:*

> *kind, good sense of humor, written expression*

*Goal(s):*

> *— go to college*
> *— pursue a career in the entertainment field*

**Activity-Based Goals**

*Career: I will*

> *— investigate college and university programs for students with learning disabilities*
> *— investigate career opportunities*

*Self-advocacy: I will*

> *— ask for help when I need it*
> *— check with teachers periodically to make sure all assignments have been turned in*
> *— bring up grades in science and math*

*Interpersonal/Social: I will*

> *— establish/maintain positive relationships with family, friends, and teachers*
> *— seek appropriate ways to express anger*

*Independent Living: I will*

> *— take responsibility for all school assignments*
> *— complete responsibilities at home (e.g., keep room clean, laundry)*

Council for
Exceptional
Children

**CEC Knowledge Check**

Why is the self-assessment process the first thing that needs to be addressed and completed in the transition planning process? LD8K1

Council for
Exceptional
Children

**CEC Knowledge Check**

Why are goals so important in the transition planning process? Can a successful transition occur without well-defined goals? CC7S3

occurrence of students who "fall through the cracks" and fail to access needed services. (DeStefano & Wermuth, 1992, p. 540)

For example, vocational rehabilitation personnel might be involved for those headed toward employment, as might college representatives for those headed toward college. Although it may not always be practical for college personnel to participate in IEP meetings, some have noted that if a student plans to attend a college nearby, it can be beneficial for the college learning disabilities specialist to become involved as early as possible in the transition process (Aune & Johnson, 1992). This gives the specialist an opportunity to inform the student and the family of the college's services and expectations while learning more about the student's interests.

## Social Skills and Self-Advocacy Training

One of the most persistent problem areas for students with learning disabilities is that of social skills. (See more on social skills in Chapter 7.) Because social skills deficits can have profound effects on adults' functioning at work and in college, many authorities point to the need for social skills training as a part of transition programming. Unfortunately, social skills are not easily trained, and many adults with learning disabilities continue to face problems in interacting with friends and colleagues. One of the problems in training social skills for transition is that although identifying the social skills necessary to function in school is difficult, doing so may be even more difficult in the workplace. Among other things, there is a wider variety of work settings, rules of the workplace may be less well defined, and feedback for poor performance may be more subtle (Mellard & Hazel, 1992).

Social skills are also extremely important for successful transition to college. Students with or without disabilities who are able to interact with other students and faculty are in a better position to be successful in college. It may be even more necessary that students with learning disabilities display good social skills. For example, being able to act as their own advocates serves college students with learning disabilities well, and being able to talk with professors about their learning disabilities in order to receive accommodations requires a great deal of social poise and tact. Because learning disabilities are "invisible" and poorly understood by so many, an articulate spokesperson is often needed to explain their ramifications. Students who are either too aggressive or too timid may have great difficulty talking with professors about their learning disabilities. Shannon's mother has some concerns:

**Council for Exceptional Children**

**CEC Knowledge Check**

Other than the college LD specialist, who else might be part of a transition team? Why? CC10K1, CC10K2, CC10S5, CC10S6

**Council for Exceptional Children**

**CEC Knowledge Check**

Other than work and education, what other settings might involve social skills? CC7S7, CC7S14, CC5K5

Shannon

> I want my daughter to attend college, but I'm worried. I've been so involved in her schooling. I make sure she gets her homework done . . . I remind her about upcoming tests. Have I done too much? Will someone be there for her in college? Should she be able to do it on her own? What about her social skills? Will she be able to control her anger? How will she come across to her peers and professors?
>
> *Kerrie Ireland, Shannon's mother*

CURRENT
TRENDS
&
ISSUES

## Improving Transition Services for Students with Learning Disabilities

The IDEA (Individuals with Disabilities Education Act) stresses the importance of transition plans and services for secondary-school students. However, "progress in creating comprehensive and responsive secondary education and transition services has . . . been slow and inconsistent across states and school districts nationwide" (Johnson, Stodden, Emanuel, Luecking, & Mack, 2002, p. 520). To the same extent, there is general consensus (e.g., Cummings, Maddux, & Casey, 2000; Janiga & Costenbader, 2002; Thompson, Fulk, & Piercy, 2000) that students with learning disabilities are not receiving adequate transition services. We address three critical issues here:

Issue 1: Many students with learning disabilities are not actively involved in transition planning (Brinckerhoff, McGuire, & Shaw, 2002; Hitchings et al., 2001).

- Transition planning only works when students are actively involved in decision making (Shapiro & Rich, 1999).
- Students (and parents) should be taught requisite skills and knowledge in order to participate in a meaningful manner (Thompson et al., 2000).

Issue 2: Many students with learning disabilities have inadequate self-advocacy skills (Janiga & Costenbader, 2002).

- Students must have an understanding of what accommodations they will need at the postsecondary level and how they can access those accommodations and other supports (Mull, Sitlington, & Alper, 2001).

- Students must be able to "describe their disability, understand its significance in day-to-day activities, and understand their rights and responsibilities as persons with a disability" (Scanlon & Mellard, 2002, p. 255).

Issue 3: Some special educators and support staff may not fully understand the postsecondary needs of students with learning disabilities (Janiga & Costenbader, 2002).

- Special educators and counselors should consider creating "multi-year plans that incorporate academic preparation and career activities, including self-advocacy and disability awareness skills" (Hitchings et al., 2001, p. 15).
- Teachers must be familiar with the demands of postsecondary education in order to help their students acquire the skills needed to be successful (Mull et al., 2001).

### Council for Exceptional Children

**CEC Knowledge Check**
Why must self-advocacy skills be taught to students soon after they are identified? Why is it important for parents to be involved in the transition process? CC4S6, CC1K6, CC5S8, CC5S9, CC9S3

**CEC Knowledge Check**
What is your responsibility for learning as much as possible about the transition process and the demands placed on students in postsecondary education? What is your responsibility for talking with and educating local business leaders about issues, characteristics, and employment opportunities for students with learning disabilities? LD9K1, LD10K2

Many authorities have pointed out that secondary-school students need to take the initiative in developing their transition programming. (See the Current Trends and Issues Box above.) Being actively involved in their own transition planning does not come easily for some students. Some authorities (e.g., Scanlon & Mellard, 2002) think it is important that **self-advocacy** be a part of transition training in high school, and there is some evidence that self-advocacy can be taught (Durlak, Rose, & Bursuck, 1994; Lock & Layton, 2001). According to Skinner (1998), "Students become self-advocates when they (a) demonstrate understanding of their disability, (b) are aware of their legal rights, and (c) demonstrate competence in communicating rights and needs to those in positions of authority" (p. 279). One team of researchers taught students

**self-advocacy** the ability to act as one's own advocate in explaining learning disabilities and the accommodations they necessitate; this is important for individuals with learning disabilities in order for them to succeed, especially in adulthood

## MULTICULTURAL CONSIDERATIONS

# Parent Involvement in Transition Planning

What do we know about cultural issues as they relate to transition? Unfortunately, "information regarding the cultural aspects of transition planning is scarce" (Geenen, Powers, & Lopez-Vasquez, 2001, p. 266). In their study, Geenen et al. (2001) surveyed 308 African American, Hispanic American, Native American, and European American parents of students with disabilities to gain insight into their involvement in transition-related activities. They also surveyed 52 professionals (i.e., special education teachers, transition specialists, and school counselors) to investigate their views with respect to parent involvement in transition. The researchers found that culturally and linguistically diverse (CLD) parents generally described themselves as actively involved in transition-related activities. Professionals, on the other hand, described CLD parent involvement as low. To what factor(s) is this discrepancy attributed? The researchers discuss several possibilities including the following:

- Educators may "have limited awareness of family activities, beliefs, and values within other spheres of

life, such as community, extended family, and religion. Therefore, the view professionals have of CLD parent participation may be based upon only one context (i.e., school)" (p. 279).
- Parents may face "racism, discrimination, insensitivity, and cultural unresponsiveness" (p. 279).

One or more of these factors may be related to the aforementioned discrepancy, but the true explanation for the inconsistent views in this study is unknown. Further research in this area is certainly warranted. In the meantime, professionals should remain ever cognizant of their own beliefs and behaviors as they strive to foster positive relationships with CLD parents during the transition process.

**Council for Exceptional Children**

**CEC Knowledge Check**
Why must professionals build relationships with the parents of their identified students? What is the ultimate goal for these students? CC1K8, CC2K3, CC3K4, CC3K5, CC8S6, CC9K1

---

**Council for Exceptional Children**

**CEC Knowledge Check**
What do students with learning disabilities generally experience after learning self-advocacy skills? CC7S14, CC5S9

with learning disabilities to state the nature of their disability and its impact on academic and social functioning and to identify accommodations and strategies for implementing them with their general education teachers (Durlak et al., 1994). Another team of researchers successfully implemented a self-awareness and self-advocacy program for persons with learning disabilities who had graduated from high school and were enrolled in college in a nondegree program focused on achieving independence (Roffman, Herzog, & Wershba-Gershon, 1994).

## Parental Involvement

The role of parents can be crucial to many aspects of educational programming for students with learning disabilities. As a result, the importance of professionals seeking to establish and maintain positive relationships with parents and families cannot be overstated. (See the Multicultural Considerations box above.) As students enter transition programming, parents begin to grapple with issues pertaining to their child's emerging sexuality, vocational choices, and dependency. It is at this time that many parents begin to face the prospect that their child's learning disability is a lifelong condition that may require relatively constant emotional and financial support.

Some strategies that professionals have recommended for increasing parental participation in transition programming are to encourage parents to (1) begin precareer development activities with their children by assigning them chores and paying them a small allowance, (2) honor their children's choices in order to increase their independence, and (3) develop informal sources of support such as friends, relatives, and community organizations (Brotherson, Berdine, & Sartini, 1993). In addition, students with learning disabilities who achieve successfully are often supported by their parents. One thing that parents can do is help them find areas in which they can excel in order to compensate for the areas in school in which they perform poorly. By finding an area in which they can develop talent and succeed, children with learning disabilities may begin to think that they could do better in school if they worked harder (Reis, Neu, & McGuire, 1997). According to Shapiro and Rich (1999), parents should "provide support and guidance, nurturing and mentoring. They can help identify cognitive strengths, encourage involvement in extracurricular activities, stimulate career exploration, provide a good study environment, and foster independence" (pp. 132–133).

### Vocational Training and College Preparation

Although transition plans are individualized, by the time students near graduation, they should have already been pointed toward either employment or postsecondary schooling. The need to decide how much a particular student's transition program should be oriented toward one or the other is one of the biggest challenges facing students, parents, and teachers.

Some think that many students with learning disabilities do not live up to their academic potential because they are routed into a non-college-bound track from which they are unable to escape. These authorities assert that there are diminished expectations for students with learning disabilities that result in an unchallenging curriculum. One team of researchers, for example, found that secondary-school learning disabilities classrooms exhibited an "environmental press against academic content" (Zigmond & Miller, 1992, p. 25).

But some think that an overemphasis on academics can leave some students with learning disabilities ill prepared for the workplace. They maintain that many students with learning disabilities have such severe problems that it is unrealistic to expect them to succeed in college. Investigators have found that vocational training has a certain degree of "holding power" by helping to keep students in school rather than dropping out. Furthermore, students who do not attend college but participate in vocational training end up with higher-paying jobs than those who do not receive vocational training (Evers, 1996).

In some cases, students, parents, and teachers agree from the start about the direction the student is headed—college or work. The advantage to determining direction early is that it allows for a longer period of appropriately focused instruction; however, one needs to be cautious not to start the student off on a sequence of courses that are a waste of time.

## How Are Students with Learning Disabilities Prepared for College?

As described by Zigmond (1990), the college-bound model of programming for secondary-school students with learning disabilities should include five features:

Council for Exceptional Children

**CEC Knowledge Check**
Should students with learning disabilities be challenged academically, or should they be educated in a vocational program?
CC2K2, CC3K1, CC3K2

Council for Exceptional Children

**CEC Knowledge Check**
What can parents do to help their child with learning disabilities achieve success in transition?
CC10S3, CC10K3, CC10K2

1. LD students are assigned to mainstream classes for math, content subjects required for graduation, and elective courses. . . .
2. One special education teacher is assigned as a support or consulting teacher to work with mainstream teachers in whose classes LD students are placed. . . .
3. Additional special education teachers are responsible for yearly English/reading courses, one survival skills class, and a supervised study hall, which LD students are scheduled to take each year of high school. . . .
4. From the start of ninth grade, LD students interact regularly with a counselor for transition planning. . . .
5. Courses required for graduation are spaced evenly throughout the four years to reduce academic pressures, particularly in ninth grade. (pp. 16–17)

**CEC Knowledge Check**

Do you think this is a good strategy? Why would this work or not work?
CC4S6, CC7S7

An advantage of this model is that it stresses the strengths of special education teachers by not requiring them to teach in all content areas. Many secondary special education teachers are not prepared to teach a variety of subjects, such as social studies, science, and math. Instead, this model requires them to teach only English/reading courses and survival skills (e.g., behavior control and study and organizational skills) and to consult with general education teachers on how to modify their instruction to accommodate students with learning disabilities.

## Programming Goals for College Preparation

An important aspect of preparing for college is taking courses that meet the entrance requirements. In Zigmond's model, for instance, there are several electives that need to be chosen carefully. It is usually better for students to take college prep classes, even though they will probably obtain a lower grade, than to take mostly general education classes. In fact, "if students do not select certain college prep courses such as algebra I or chemistry during the freshman or sophomore years in high school, they may find themselves woefully underprepared for the rigors of a college curriculum" (Brinckerhoff et al., 2002, p. 46).

**CEC Knowledge Check**

Why is it so important that students with learning disabilities learn organizational, time management, and study skills?
CC4S6

Another key aspect of transition programming for students with learning disabilities who are headed for college is to provide them with organizational, time-management, and study skills. These students are notorious for their deficiencies in these skills, which most college-bound students have in their repertoires. Zigmond's model also emphasizes classes devoted to these important skills.

## How Can Students with Learning Disabilities Succeed in College?

More students with learning disabilities than ever before are attending college (Shapiro & Rich, 1999; Westby, 2000). Kavale and Forness (as cited in Janiga & Costenbader, 2002) report that between 1985 and 1996, the number of full-time first-year college students who reported having a learning disability more than doubled. Some of the increase in students with learning disabilities attending college is undoubtedly due to legislation prohibiting discrimination against persons with disabilities. At one time, college was out of the question for many students with learning disabilities. Beginning in the mid-1970s, however, federal law prohibited institutions of higher education from discriminating against students with disabilities. Section 504 of the Rehabilitation Act of 1973 mandates that "no otherwise qualified handicapped individual . . . shall, solely by reason of his/her handicap, be excluded from participation in, be denied the benefits of, or be subject to discrimination under any program or activity receiving financial assistance."

Applying the phrase "otherwise qualified" in individual cases is not always easy. It is clear, however, that the courts have interpreted it not to mean the lowering of admissions standards. The Supreme Court, in *Southeastern Community College v. Davis* (1979), ruled that a nursing program could deny admission to a student who was hearing impaired and unable to understand speech because, being unable to hear patients, she might put them in danger. What the law did mean was that decisions should be based on actual abilities rather than prejudicial assumptions (Brinckerhoff, Shaw, & McGuire, 1992). In addition, colleges are to make adjustments in requirements for courses, but these accommodations are not expected to alter the essential aspects of the curriculum (Westby, 2000).

Immediately following the passage of Section 504, colleges and universities did not suddenly throw open their doors to students with disabilities. Over time, as the courts have helped to define the parameters of the law and public opinion about persons with disabilities has improved, many colleges and universities have become more comfortable with the idea of admitting and accommodating students with disabilities, including learning disabilities. Some have centers devoted to services for students with learning disabilities (Westby, 2000). Others have a full-time faculty or staff person who specializes in learning disabilities. This coordinator may have a variety of support staff who provide a number of services, including monitoring academic progress, tutoring, and acting as a liaison to the faculty (Brinckerhoff et al., 2002). In fact, some institutions of higher education have gained reputations as good places for students with learning disabilities to attend because of the level of support offered.

## Guidelines for Choosing a College

Choosing a college is difficult for any student. Reputation, academic rigor, location, types of majors offered, extracurricular activities, and cost are just some of the many variables that parents and students consider. In the case of students with learning disabilities, the choice can be even more difficult. They and their parents will also want to consider the level of support offered for those with learning disabilities. See Table 6.1 (page 178) for a list of questions students should consider before applying to a college.

Secondary-school teachers and counselors now recommend that students with learning disabilities who are likely to be college bound begin to seek information on different colleges early in their secondary schooling. In fact, some advocate that one of the transition goals on the IEP be that students be able to research various colleges' entrance requirements, curricula, and learning disabilities services (Blaylock & Patton, 1996).

Council for
Exceptional
Children

**CEC Knowledge Check**

Should students with learning disabilities be provided this information, or should they be taught to find this information themselves? Should you share this responsibility with the school media specialist/librarian? How important are information and search skills to students with learning disabilities? CC7S1

## TABLE 6.1    Questions to Ask before Applying to a College

### College/University Requirements

- What, if any, entrance exams must students with learning disabilities take? Can any of these exams be waived?
- Is the untimed Scholastic Aptitude Test (SAT) acceptable?
- Is a minimum score required on any of these tests? If so, what is it?
- What, if any, minimum academic standing must the student have achieved in high school?
- Are there specific course requirements (e.g., foreign language) for admission? If so, can any of these requirements be waived? If not, can other courses be substituted (e.g., sign language or a computer language for a foreign language)?
- Is admission limited to certain fields of study?
- What are the specific requirements for program completion? Can any of these requirements be waived?
- Can a student take a reduced course load?
- Must the student complete the program in a specified length of time?

### Special Services and Accommodations

- Can the student tape record classes?
- Are oral examinations possible?
- What kinds of tutorial services are available? How long does each session last? How frequently are the sessions held?
- Are tutors specifically trained to work with students with learning disabilities?
- Is there a program that addresses remediation of basic skills, such as reading, spelling, etc.?
- Is a support group available specifically for students with learning disabilities?
- What kinds of special counseling (e.g., career counseling) are available?
- Is there a learning center or learning lab on campus?
- Would these special services involve any extra expense?
- What is the name and contact information of the director/coordinator of services for students with learning disabilities?

### Experience of Students with Learning Disabilities

- Has the college/university accepted students with learning disabilities in the past?
- Have the students been successful?
- Are there any current or former students with learning disabilities with whom I may speak about their experiences?

*Source:* Adapted from *Understanding Learning Disabilities: A Parent Guide and Workbook,* 3rd ed. (pp. 127–129) by Learning Disabilities Council, 2002, Timonium, MD: York Press. Copyright 2002 by York Press. Reprinted by permission.

One issue students need to address when considering colleges is whether they should attend a two-year or a four-year institution. This decision depends on several factors. Many students value two-year colleges because they more often "have open admissions policies; smaller class ratios; comparatively low tuition fees; academic and personal counseling; and a wide range of vocational, remedial, and developmental courses" (Brinckerhoff, 1996, p. 127). Some students, especially those whose disabilities are less severe, are able to handle the less structured setting of a four-year college.

## Predictors of Success in College

Most college admissions officers will tell you that predicting how well a particular student will do in college is nearly impossible. Some who have excelled in high school have not been able to do the same in college. Some who barely scraped by in high school suddenly find their niche in college. College and university officials have developed a relatively uniform set of criteria based on predictive studies involving large numbers of applicants. These criteria, such as high school grade-point average (GPA) and SAT scores, are often used because they are the best predictors available, but they are far from perfect.

Selecting which students with learning disabilities are likely to succeed in college is even riskier. We do not yet have a well-established research base on which to make these kinds of predictions with much accuracy, and using traditional criteria is problematic. Students with learning disabilities may not "test well" on standardized tests such as the SAT, even though they are entitled to accommodations, and their GPAs may be difficult to interpret because the courses and accommodations they received may vary considerably, depending on the high schools they attended.

The little research that has been done on predicting college success for students with learning disabilities suggests that admissions officers should look at factors pertaining to performance in high school rather than at admissions tests such as the SAT or the ACT. One team of researchers found that, although far from perfect, such things as high school GPA and number of mainstream English courses completed with a grade of C or better were better predictors than standardized test scores (Vogel & Adelman, 1992). Some indicators such as

> strong grade point averages in college preparatory courses, well-developed reading and mathematical skills, above average intelligence, and extracurricular involvement in high school correlate highly with success in college. Indeed, college admissions counselors, often working with support services coordinators, tend to look at these factors when determining whether to accept a student with a learning disability. (Shapiro & Rich, 1999, p. 128)

Demands placed on students differ from high school to college, but colleges require a great deal more student independence than secondary school. For example, there is considerably less classroom instruction in college, the implication being that students will spend more time outside of class reading and studying on their own. Many students have problems adjusting to the decreased structure in college. Students with learning disabilities may have an even more difficult time because they are prone to have problems in independence and their high school programs may have been even more structured than those of most students (Brinckerhoff et al.,

**Council for Exceptional Children**

**CEC Knowledge Check**
Why are standardized test scores not a good predictor of success in college?
CC8K4, LD8S1

**Council for Exceptional Children**

**CEC Knowledge Check**
Why are high school data a more reliable indicator of success in college for these students? What part does motivation and working independently have in a college program?
CC8S1, CC5S9

1992). These observations have led many college admissions officers to point to motivation and the ability to work independently as important attributes to consider in selecting students with learning disabilities (Spillane, McGuire, & Norlander, 1992). Shannon wonders what it will be like in college:

Shannon

> My parents really want me to go to college, and I guess I do, too, but I think it will be really hard for me. I've heard that sometimes your grade is based on only two tests! What if I don't do well on the first one? How am I going to make myself study ahead of time? I have a tendency to wait until the last minute.
>
> *Shannon*

## Instructional Accommodations

As noted, Section 504 of the Rehabilitation Act requires that colleges make reasonable adjustments for students with disabilities in order that they not be discriminated against on the basis of their disabilities. These adjustments can take three general forms: "adaptations in the manner in which specific courses are conducted, the use of auxiliary equipment, and modifications in academic requirements" (Brinckerhoff et al., 1992, p. 421). The following are some examples of relatively common accommodations for students with learning disabilities:

- adjustments in course requirements and evaluation
    giving extra time on tests
    allowing students to take exams in a distraction-free room
    allowing students to take exams in a different format (e.g., substituting an oral exam for a written one)
- modifications in program requirements
    waiving or substituting certain requirements (e.g., a foreign language)
    allowing students to take a lighter academic load
- auxiliary aids
    providing tape recordings of textbooks
    providing access to a Kurzweil Reading Machine (a computer that scans text and converts it into auditory output)
    recruiting and assigning volunteer note-takers for lectures

**Council for Exceptional Children**

**CEC Knowledge Check**

How can you create a safe and equitable learning environment for students with learning disabilities? CC5S1, CC5S3

Although the intent of the law and subsequent litigation is fairly clear relative to modification of course requirements, program requirements, and evaluation of students, it is less obvious with regard to individual instructors' approaches to instruction. One can make a strong case that, especially with regard to lectures and discussion courses, some of the same pedagogical strategies that make for good instruction for many students without learning disabilities are of particular benefit to those with them. Starting lectures with a review of past material, providing advance organizers, and using an overhead projector or computerized graphic displays to emphasize main points are just a few of the techniques that help most students, especially those with learning disabilities, attend to and retain information presented in lectures. As yet, however, the law has not been used to dictate that instructors use such techniques.

Institutions of higher education vary widely in how they handle implementation of accommodations for students with disabilities. Although Section 504 has been in effect since the 1970s, the process of interpreting the law through litigation continues. Many universities have adopted policy advisory committees to help university administrators educate faculty about accommodations and resolve disputes when they arise. The notion of academic freedom is ingrained deeply into the consciousness of many faculty, and some are immediately suspicious of anything they think will impinge on it. Policy advisory boards, some of whose members are faculty, can do much to alleviate tension concerning appropriate accommodations.

Some have also pointed out that providing accommodations can help faculty better understand their own programs. Determining what are appropriate accommodations and what are essential components of a program takes more than a cursory review of program requirements:

> Defining the essential requirements of academic programs and courses is, in some respects, a Herculean task. Faculty and academic departments are being asked to define and come to consensus on the core of their disciplines. Often, faculty are faced with this task in response to an immediate request for accommodation by a student currently enrolled in a course. On a short-term basis, faculty must apply their best professional judgment in defining the essential elements of a course or program. However, determining essential requirements should ultimately be viewed as an ongoing dialogue for professional examination, perhaps extending beyond individual faculty members and departments to a topic to be addressed within the fields or disciplines. (Scott, 1994, p. 408)

Council for
Exceptional
Children

**CEC Knowledge Check**
Why do you think many college faculty have a hard time making accommodations for students with learning disabilities?
CC5K4, CC9S4

## How Can Students with Learning Disabilities Prepare for the Work World?

As described by Zigmond (1990), the programming model for non-college-bound secondary-school students should include five features:

1. All basic skills are taught by a special educator and instruction in basic skills is linked to transition planning. . . .
2. Required "content" subjects are taught by special educators. . . .
3. Vocational education is provided in the mainstream and coordinated with transition planning provided with special education. . . .
4. All ninth-grade students with learning disabilities will take a required course on **survival skills** [bold added] taught by a special educator. . . .
5. Students' schedules would reflect a light academic load in ninth grade to ensure successful completion of the first year of high school. (pp. 18–19)

**survival skills** strategies required for daily living (e.g., budgeting, managing time, prioritizing tasks, etc.)

One problem with this model, conceded by Zigmond, is that it requires special education teachers to teach in content areas in which they might not be completely

**CEC Knowledge Check**

Zigmond identifies five strategies for successful transition to the work world. What others would you include? Why would you include them?

CC4S6

proficient, although the level of the content would be lower than that typically taught in these subjects.

An important advantage of this model is that it provides two classes of vocational education for each of four years.

## Programming Goals for Vocational Training

More and more authorities are moving toward a developmental approach to vocational programming. This assumes that an individual's career development occurs well into adulthood. Most developmental models of career development include three stages: career awareness, career exploration, and career experiences (Morningstar, 1997). Students' individualized transition plans

> should include a vocational component that covers systematic vocational assessment, career exploration, job training, and vocational counseling to help set realistic goals. Vocational training needs to be diverse enough to reflect the range of occupational roles held by individuals who have learning disabilities. (Shapiro & Rich, 1999, p. 142)

Researchers have suggested several student-centered objectives for vocational preparation:

- Develop and implement assessment procedures which identify functional skills and interests related to current and future employment and training opportunities in the community. . . .
- Provide necessary support services to ensure access to mainstream vocational classes. . . .
- Provide at least four work experiences, six to eight weeks each, in identified areas of interest and skill for students between the ages of 15 and 18. . . .
- Assist the student in locating and securing employment prior to graduation. . . .
- Provide supervision and follow-up services to students in full-time or part-time employment until graduation (or the student's twenty-second birthday). . . .
- Develop individual transition plans with appropriate adult services agencies (i.e., vocational rehabilitation, community college, state employment service, or mental health) for students who need continued services following graduation. (Brody-Hasazi, Salembier, & Finck, 1983, pp. 207–208)

**CEC Knowledge Check**

What kind of supports do students with learning disabilities need after they leave high school?

LD4S1, CC5S3, CC5S7

## School-Business Partnerships

Most vocational specialists promote the idea that non-college-bound students with disabilities have a great deal to gain from on-the-job experiences with employers in the community. It is often difficult to arrange consistent work experiences for students, however. That is one of the reasons some have advocated formal school-business partnerships that facilitate the placement of students in real jobs while they are still in school (Tilson, Luecking, & Donovan, 1994). In addition to providing useful job training for students, such arrangements can help businesses prepare well-trained personnel for their workforce (Goldberger & Kazis, 1996).

Apprenticeship experiences for secondary-school students in general education are commonplace in some European countries, such as Germany. They have not been widely adopted in the United States because of the reluctance to identify students too early for non-college-bound "tracks." In the case of students with disabilities, the issue of tracking students too early into a vocational orientation is no less real. But many see this potential problem outweighed by the advantages of building relationships with businesses so that students can have ready access to training in meaningful job settings.

Council for Exceptional Children

**CEC Knowledge Check**
Who makes the decision for students with learning disabilities to "track" into a college or work apprenticeship program?
CC9S2, CC9S3, CC9S5, LD9K1

## How Can Employers Encourage Success for Adults with Learning Disabilities?

Recent changes in the workplace are making the employment picture look less optimistic for adults with learning disabilities. Although generally seen as improvements necessary to make American business more competitive worldwide, many of these changes have worked to the disadvantage of adults with learning disabilities.

Brown and Gerber (1994) have identified four trends in the workplace that have created more problems for adults with learning disabilities. First, teamwork is replacing a more bureaucratic, hierarchical structure. Unfortunately, because they often have difficulties in social interactions (e.g., reading social cues), workers with learning disabilities may be perceived as unfriendly and uncooperative.

Second, although some technology has made the workplace more accessible to adults with learning disabilities, technology has also placed more cognitive demands on the worker. And technological innovations are introduced at such a rapid pace that workers with learning disabilities have difficulties keeping up with these advances, thus putting them at a disadvantage to their nondisabled peers.

Third, there is an increased emphasis on credentials and passing standardized tests for certain jobs. Many jobs that used to require only a high school diploma now require a college degree. Furthermore, some jobs (e.g., truck driver and plumber) now require passage of a licensing exam.

Fourth, in order to compete in the global economy, American businesses have placed a greater emphasis on productivity. Corporations are restructuring and reducing their work force, which means that greater demands are being placed on workers. Those employees who require less supervision and are more efficient in carrying out their assignments are more likely to be kept in the work force and to advance in their careers.

> In keeping with all of these changes in the workplace, it is important to keep in mind that the proverbial bottom line for businesses is profit: While they acknowledge that good corporate citizens hire persons with all kinds of disabilities, they also take the

Council for Exceptional Children

**CEC Knowledge Check**
What are the major issues and trends that create roadblocks to success for students with learning disabilities? CC3K2, LD1K2

position that they are not running a social service agency. . . . [T]hey are looking for those who have mastered basic skills as well as other skills that will make them successful employees (i.e., social skills). (Gerber, 1992, p. 331)

## Workplace Accommodations

Although employers are generally not interested in "running a social service agency," federal law requires that they make accommodations for workers with disabilities in the job application process and the job itself (so that the employee can perform the job's essential functions) and also make adjustments that allow the worker to enjoy privileges enjoyed by other workers. Specifically, the Americans with Disabilities Act (ADA) of 1990 defines accommodations in the following way:

> Reasonable accommodation means (i) modifications or adjustments to a job application process that enable a qualified applicant with a disability to be considered for the position such qualified applicant desires; or (ii) modifications or adjustments to work environment, or to the manner or circumstances under which the position held or desired is customarily performed, that enable a qualified individual with a disability to perform the essential functions of that position; or (iii) modifications or adjustments that enable a covered entity's employee with a disability to enjoy benefits and privileges of employment as are enjoyed by its other similarly situated employees without disabilities. (*Federal Register,* July 26, 1991, pp. 35735–35736)

There are two keys to making accommodations: Employers need to know the functional limitations associated with a particular disability, and they need to understand the job's requirements (Jacobs & Hendricks, 1992). Employers often, but not always, have a grasp of the latter, but they usually need help in comprehending the former. Transition specialists can help explain the characteristics of the disability and specify the job requirements, if need be. Employers need to gain a fuller understanding of all disabilities, including learning disabilities. The Committee on Employment of People with Disabilities (Brown, Gerber, & Dowdy, 1990) identified widespread ignorance about learning disabilities as the major impediment to furthering the employment success of adults with learning disabilities.

Council for Exceptional Children

**CEC Knowledge Check**
What has been the impact of the ADA for students with learning disabilities who are looking for jobs? LD1K3

As more and more employers comply with federal laws and hire and accommodate workers with learning disabilities, attitudes toward these employees may improve. A better strategy, however, is for professionals involved in transition programming to take active roles in promoting a realistic portrayal of what adults with learning disabilities can do on the job, given appropriate support and accommodations. In addition, investigators need to continue developing and testing transition models and accommodation strategies.

Ironically, in some cases, employers may need to take a more active role in making accommodations for employees with learning disabilities than they would for employees who have more severe disabilities, such as mental retardation. This is because workers with mental retardation are often provided more support under a

**supported employment model,** which uses job coaches to integrate workers with mental retardation into competitive employment situations. This has become very popular, but it is rarely used with workers who have learning disabilities because the prevailing professional opinion is that the latter group is not disabled enough to need that much support. Some professionals disagree.

**supported employment model** a method that uses job coaches to integrate workers into competitive employment situations

Most accommodations that have been recommended by transition specialists have addressed the first two types of accommodations—those having to do with applying for a job and those dealing with enabling the worker to perform essential job functions. Here are some examples of accommodations for the latter:

- reading problems
  Consider verbal rather than written instructions.
  Assign a coworker who is responsible for letting them know about important information contained in memos.
- listening and distractibility problems
  Assign them to quiet work space.
  Use short, simple sentences; enunciate clearly; and repeat instructions when necessary.
  Provide them with a written copy of important instructions.
  Demonstrate exactly what needs to be done, rather than merely describing the task.
- organizational problems
  Encourage them to use a daily checklist to keep track of their duties/assignments.
  Encourage them to use an appointment calendar.
  Provide them a three-ring binder to keep track of important written materials.
- social problems
  Be patient if they misinterpret social interactions.
  Make all communications direct, without sarcasm, hints, or hidden messages they might misinterpret. (Luecking, Tilson, & Willner, 1991)

Council for Exceptional Children

**CEC Knowledge Check**
What kinds of support are needed from employers for students with learning disabilities to have a greater chance for success? What attitudes must employers exhibit?
CC5S2, CC5S3, CC5S7, CC10S6, CC10S8

## How Can Employees with Learning Disabilities Succeed in the Workplace?

Transition specialists have identified a number of ways that adults with learning disabilities can enhance their chances of successfully obtaining and holding jobs (Adelman & Vogel, 1993; Gerber, 1992; Gerber, Ginsberg, & Reiff, 1992; Siegel & Gaylord-Ross, 1991). One way of looking at these strategies is that the more one is able to use them, the less one will need to rely on employer accommodations. Some of the most frequently cited methods are the following:

- Choose a job that is a good match.
- Use personal contacts to find a job.
- Become a self-advocate.
- Develop compensatory strategies.
- Take advantage of technology.
- Gain control over one's life.

## Choose a Job That Is a Good Match

Adults with learning disabilities must be realistic about what jobs suit them. They need to realize that some jobs will be more difficult because of their particular disabilities. An individual who has severe problems with math, for example, should not expect to pursue engineering as a profession. Adults with learning disabilities need to consider jobs that utilize their strengths. A person with excellent social skills, for example, might consider a job that requires meeting the public, such as sales. Shannon seems to understand this:

Shannon

> My parents and teachers have always said that if I work hard and don't give up, I can pretty much do anything. They've also said, though, that I should use my strengths. For me, math is not a strength. You won't see me in a job that involves lots of math . . . I wouldn't be good at it, and I wouldn't like it!
>
> *Shannon*

**CEC Knowledge Check**

Do most students with learning disabilities recognize their limitations? How would you help students who do not realize their limitations? CC5S2

The ability to choose an appropriate job or profession requires a thorough understanding of one's disability and its impact on cognitive and social functioning. Special education teachers, transition specialists, and career counselors can work together to offer assistance in identifying jobs that bring out a person's strengths and minimize weaknesses.

## Use Personal Contacts to Find a Job

**CEC Knowledge Check**

Do students who have few or no friends have less of a chance for a successful transition? CC5S7

Several researchers have found that adults with learning disabilities often obtain employment by relying on personal contacts (Adelman & Vogel, 1993). Although job skills will ultimately determine whether the worker with learning disabilities is able to perform the job, being able to prove that one has the ability to do the job is often difficult, especially in a tight job market. Getting one's foot in the door can make all the difference in securing a job. Thus, networks developed through family or friends can be helpful to adults with learning disabilities, and they should be encouraged to cultivate such contacts.

## Become a Self-Advocate

Although having others who can serve as advocates is helpful, this should not be done at the expense of being a self-advocate. Adults with learning disabilities who are able to speak for themselves are at a distinct advantage in obtaining and holding jobs. Given the fact that many employers do not have a good understanding of learning disabilities, sometimes confusing them with mental retardation or other disabilities, they often must rely on these workers themselves to explain their disabilities (Gerber, 1992).

Even though adults with learning disabilities are potentially in the best position to explain their strengths and weaknesses, they are not always skilled in doing so. Not only does self-advocacy mean being aware of how one's learning disability affects one specifically, it also requires social skills in order to communicate effectively with the employer.

Evidence indicates that many persons with learning disabilities are reluctant to disclose them during the application process or after they are hired for fear of discrimination (Greenbaum, Graham, & Scales, 1996; Witte, Philips, & Kakela, 1998). Even the most skilled communicator should be extremely cautious when approaching the issue of self-disclosure. Although workers with learning disabilities are protected by the Americans with Disabilities Act,

> in the downsizing and restructuring efforts of business and industry in the early 1990s, persons with learning disabilities who are already employed should be aware of the risks of self-disclosure. . . .
>
> While ADA provides for reasonable accommodation and other protections in the workplace, individuals with learning disabilities should carefully plan how they wish to self-disclose and think through the implications of their action. (Gerber, 1992, p. 331)

## Develop Compensatory Strategies

Adults with learning disabilities who are successful in work often employ strategies to compensate for their disabilities. Two of the most common involve taking extra time to complete work and rechecking work several times for possible errors (Adelman & Vogel, 1990). **Compensatory strategies** may also involve relying on others for certain aspects of work as well as putting out extraordinary effort oneself, as shown by the following case of a highly successful lawyer with learning disabilities:

> The severe reading difficulties posed problems early on in his law practice. He found trial law to be particularly stressful. He related, "I would be anxious that I'd have to read a document with people around, and I knew I couldn't do it. So I was *always* overprepared." As his law practice and businesses have become more established, he has learned to compensate for his weaknesses in reading by hiring a highly competent staff. Associates and assistants do most of his law and business reading. He explained, "To this day, now that I'm out of trial practice, I have a lady in particular who has been with me for seventeen years and who in effect is my reading eye. If I have to read under pressure, I go off to my office and deal with it."
>
> During the developing years of his practice and business, [he] used to read everything in order to keep up. . . . "When things got better financially and I didn't have to depend on law, I threw my reading material away." Now he has a CPA who tells him what he needs to know. However, when he needs to do his own reading and

Council for Exceptional Children

**CEC Knowledge Check**
What is the balance between self-advocacy and self-disclosure? How much self-disclosure should be made to an employer or future employer? CC5S8

**compensatory strategies** strategies, such as taking more time and rechecking work, that allow individuals to compensate for their disabilities

Council for Exceptional Children

**CEC Knowledge Check**
Is this lawyer typical of adults with learning disabilities? Why is it important to teach students to monitor for oral or written errors? Why should students learn self-checking strategies? LD6K7, CC9S5

TODAY'S
TECHNOLOGY

FOR LEARNING
DISABILITIES

## Assistive Technology and Postsecondary Education

As more and more students with learning disabilities pursue post-secondary education, ways to help them compensate for their difficulties become even more critical. Recent "advances in computer-based technology and the recognition of the instructional accessibility capabilities of assistive technologies have prompted an array of adaptation solutions for students with learning disabilities" (Bryant, Bryant, & Rieth, 2002, p. 399). Following are examples of assistive technology available today:

### Speech Synthesis

Speech synthesis systems (e.g., Kurzweil 3000) may be used to review material written by others, including software tutorials, help systems, letters, reports, online data bases, and information banks and systems. These systems read essentially anything on a computer screen, providing it is DOS-based. Some organizations, including Recording for the Blind and Dyslexic and the American Printing House for the Blind, produce "books on disk" that make it possible for people with learning disabilities to listen to text by means of a speech synthesis system.

### OCR/Speech Synthesis Systems

An optical character recognition (OCR) system might be thought of as a "reading machine." OCR systems provide a means of inputting print (e.g., a page in a book, a letter) into a computer and hearing the print "read" by the computer.

### Variable Speech Control Tape Recorders

Tape recorders can be used as playback units for listening to books on audiotape, which may help students with reading difficulties circumvent their disability by listening to prerecorded text (of books, journals, and newspapers). Prerecorded text is available from a number of sources, including the Library of Congress, Recording for the Blind and Dyslexic, and several private companies.

### Outlining and Brainstorming Programs

Outlining programs (now included in many standard word-processing programs) may help some people generate and organize their ideas; outlining is a good tool to use during the prewriting stage of writing development. These programs enable the user to construct information electronically so that it can be placed in appropriate categories and order.

### Word Prediction

Word prediction software supports word-processing programs by "predicting" the word a user is entering into the computer. Predictions are based on syntax and spelling, as well as frequency, redundancy, and recency of words. Some programs also "learn" the user's word preferences.

### Proofreading Programs

These software programs (now included within some word processors) are useful for the proofing stage of writing because they scan word-processing documents and alert users to probable errors in punctuation, grammar, word usage, structure, spelling, style, and capitalization.

research, he knows how to outline and pull out important information (a skill he used in law school). He has self-tailored organizational skills that he developed for himself, and they work well for him. (Gerber & Reiff, 1991, pp. 49–50)

## Take Advantage of Technology

**assistive technology**
technology, especially computer software, that helps persons with learning disabilities learn or perform their jobs

There is a variety of technological products that can assist employees who have learning disabilities. Much of this **assistive technology** has been in the form of computer software, including that for problems in written language, reading, and organization and memory. See the Today's Technology box above for a description of some assistive technology available today.

### Speech or Voice Recognition

Speech recognition systems (e.g., Dragon Speak) are an example of an alternate input device. They operate in conjunction with personal computers (and specific laptops) and consist of speech recognition hardware (internal board), software, headphones, and a microphone. Speech recognition systems enable the user to operate the computer by speaking to it.

### Speech Synthesis and Screen Reading

Speech synthesis refers to a synthetic or computerized voice output system usually consisting of an internal board or external hardware device. In conjunction with "screen-reading" software, a speech synthesizer will read back text displayed on a computer screen so that the user can hear as well as see what is displayed. Text can be read back a letter, word, line, sentence, paragraph, or "screen" at a time.

### Talking Calculators

A talking calculator can be used to help with basic calculation difficulties. A talking calculator is simply a calculator with a speech synthesizer. When number, symbol, or operation keys are pressed, they are "vocalized" or "spoken" by a built-in speech synthesizer. In that way, the user receives simultaneous auditory feedback in order to check the accuracy of visual-motor operations.

Once a calculation has been made, the number can be read back via the synthesizer.

### Personal Data Managers

The use of personal data managers can compensate for difficulties in remembering, organizing, and managing personal information, whether it is a question of remembering important dates or deadlines; prioritizing activities; scheduling appointments; or recording and accessing names, addresses, and phone numbers. Personal data managers are available as software programs as well as self-contained hand-held units and allow the user to easily store and retrieve vast amounts of personal information.

### Electronic Reference Materials

Electronic reference materials provide students with a way to access resources such as dictionaries, thesauruses, almanacs, and encyclopedias via computer. These materials can be transferred to a word-processing program to assist students with writing papers or completing other course requirements.

**CEC Knowledge Check**

Is assistive technology only to be used in the transition process and in postsecondary education? What should be asked when advocating the use of any assistive technology? Should assistive technology be used for at-risk students? All students? Why?
CC7K4, CC7S9

*Source:* Adapted from "The Use of Assistive Technology in Postsecondary Education" by B. R. Bryant, D. P. Bryant, and H. J. Rieth, 2002, in L. C. Brinckerhoff, J. M. McGuire, and S. F. Shaw, (Eds.), *Postsecondary Education and Transition for Students with Learning Disabilities,* 2nd ed., (pp. 389–429). Austin, TX: PRO-ED. Copyright 2002 by PRO-ED, Inc. Reprinted with permission.

There is a downside to the infusion of so much technology into the marketplace: Consumers often have a difficult time sorting out the various products, as Shannon's mother indicates:

Shannon

> I've been involved in this process long enough to know about accommodations and services for students with learning disabilities, but I can't keep up with things. There's so much out there now. I'm not sure what Shannon will need or what would best help her compensate for her difficulties.
>
> *Kerrie Ireland, Shannon's mother*

The following are some guidelines for selecting assistive devices:

1. Products should be selected that are directly tied to the functions that need to be performed. . . .
2. Whenever possible, assistive technologies need to be identified that are appropriate across contexts . . . home, workplace, school, and social settings.
3. An effort should be made to identify technologies that are compatible with one another. . . .
4. In consideration of the various contexts in which adults with LD function, products should be identified that can be easily transported.
5. Assistive technology products should be intuitive and straightforward to learn and operate. . . .
6. Technologies should be reliable. . . .
7. Products should be selected that provide clearly written and easy-to-understand documentation. . . .
8. If possible, products should be supported with hot lines (1-800 numbers) linked to readily available company representatives and support service centers.
9. Products should be selected that are easy to install and set up.
10. An attempt should be made to identify technologies with a high "benefit/cost ratio," that is, a high potential for compensation relative to cost. . . .
11. Standard technologies should be chosen whenever possible. "Standard technology" refers to technology that is commercially available from a number of sources, is widely used in a variety of settings, and is designed for the general population. (Raskind, 1993, p. 193)

## Gain Control over One's Life

Perhaps the single most important thing that adults with learning disabilities can do to ensure employment success is to gain control of their lives—not only of the physical environment, but also psychological and emotional control of their lives: "A major attribute for personal success among highly successful adults with learning disabilities is a strong sense of control over career-related events and a conscious decision to take charge of one's life" (Hitchings et al., 2001, p. 9). Extensive interviews with highly successful adults with learning disabilities have revealed that "control was the fuel that fired their success" (Gerber et al., 1992, p. 479).

Researchers have found that a major way for adults with learning disabilities to achieve success is through reframing (Reiff, Gerber, & Ginsberg, 1997; Shapiro & Rich, 1999). **Reframing** is the recognition that the disability itself is not the biggest problem; one must accept the weakness caused by the disability while finding ways to shore them up and exploit one's strengths. Reframing consists of four stages. First, one needs to recognize the disability. Knowing that one is different from others is important. Second, one needs to accept the disability in the sense of recognizing that one can still be a worthwhile person with something to offer. Third, one needs to understand the disability and the limitations it imposes. Fourth, one needs

Council for
Exceptional
Children

**CEC Knowledge Check**
How is assistive technology chosen? Is it appropriate to select an assistive technology in the IEP meeting? Should you suggest an assistive technology that has yet to be tested? Is "high" technology always better than "low" technology?
CC6K4, CC7K4, CC7S9

**reframing**  reordering perceptions of a situation so that one can see the positives to take action to achieve realistic goals of achievement. The following excerpt from a highly successful practicing dentist with learning disabilities who is also a clinical professor in New York University's College of Dentistry provides a good description of some of the components of reframing:

> Needless energy is wasted on what I call the "Why me?" syndrome. Why do I have this problem? Why must I face so many difficulties presented by this problem? In my position, as director of the Learning Disability Program for students in a professional school, I have found that those students who have the "Why me?" syndrome usually fare the worst because they waste so much energy. Those who say, "OK, this is what I have, now I understand some of my problems, how do I deal with it in the future" fare the best. They accept their status, and this creates understanding and hope. Desire and motivation alone are not always enough to create success. The research corroborates that reframing or acceptance of the problem is a necessary ingredient. (Reiff et al., 1997, p. 129)

**CEC Knowledge Check**
How can you, as a professional, help students to reframe and take control of their lives and learning? What examples and attitudes do your students see in you? Do you recognize your own limitations and model for students how to take control of life? Do you complain with other teachers about things that cannot be changed? Or do you search for opportunities to change the things you do not like in a positive way?
CC1K4, CC4S5, LD5S1, CC5S8, CC7S14, CC9K2, CC9S7, CC9S11

## PORTFOLIO-BUILDING ACTIVITY

### Demonstrating Mastery of the CEC Standards

Chapter 6 asks the question: What are the relative strengths and weaknesses of Shannon's Individualized Transition Plan (ITP)? You can attempt to answer this question by engaging in the following activity:

- Search the Internet, including the Companion Website (Table of Transition Assessment/Planning; www.ablongman.com/hallahanLD3e) for information on transition assessment/planning information.

- Use the information from your search and from Shannon's transition plan to create what you believe to be an appropriate (1) transition assessment plan, and from that, (2) the components to be addressed in Shannon's ITP, and (3) who the individuals in attendance at the transition planning meeting should be. Questions to think about as you progress:

- What multiple types of assessments, formal and informal, will be needed to provide useful information in designing a transition plan?

- How does the transition plan, from the assessment through implementation, include individuals with exceptionalities, families, and personnel from other appropriate agencies?

- What are the laws and policies regarding the assessment and planning processes of the transition plan that are specifically related to culturally responsive collaboration?

**CEC Content Standards**
7. Instructional Planning
8. Assessment
10. Collaboration

# SUMMARY

**What are learning disability outcomes across the life span?**

- higher dropout rates
- higher underemployment
- greater dependency on others

**What transition programs and services are available?**

- In the mid-1980s, the federal government announced a "transition initiative."
- Legislation (IDEA of 1990 and amended in 1997) mandates that schools provide transition services and that a transition plan be included in the IEP.
- Interagency collaboration is essential to ensure that service needs are communicated between high school program representatives and representatives at receiving agencies, including vocational rehabilitation facilities and colleges.
- Many young adults with learning disabilities have problems with social skills, and these are important. Training to overcome these problems is not easy, for one reason, because of the difficulty identifying the social demands of various workplace or postsecondary education settings. One social skill that is particularly important and that appears to be teachable is self-advocacy—that is, the ability to describe specific needs resulting from the disability.
- It is also crucial that transition programs include parent involvement, because parents often play an important role in the lifelong treatment of learning disabilities.
- Transition programming needs to take into account how much the student should be prepared for work through vocational training versus how much the student should be prepared for college.

**How are students with learning disabilities prepared for college?**

- In a college-bound model of secondary instruction, students are mainstreamed for math, content subjects, and elective courses; special educators consult with mainstream teachers and are responsible for English/reading and study skills classes. An advantage of this model is that special education teachers, who may not be proficient in every subject, are not required to teach all content areas.

- Key aspects of programming for college-bound students are to:
  - have students take as many courses as possible in mainstreamed settings
  - teach students organizational, time-management, and study skills

**How can students with learning disabilities succeed in college?**

- There has been a dramatic increase in the number of students with learning disabilities attending college. Between 1985 and 1996, the number of full-time first-year college students who reported having a learning disability more than doubled.
- One reason for this increase can be attributed to Section 504 of the Rehabilitation Act of 1973, which prohibits institutions of higher learning from discriminating against disabled students.
- There are a number of factors to consider in choosing an appropriate college, including the amount of support provided for students with learning disabilities.
- Students need to seek information on possible colleges as early as possible in their secondary schooling.
- Many students opt to attend two-year colleges because of their open admissions policies, smaller class sizes, lower tuition fees, and a variety of counseling services and vocational, remedial, and developmental courses.
- In predicting college success, college and university officials tend to rely on a relatively uniform set of criteria, such as high school GPA and SAT scores, based on predictive studies involving large numbers of applicants. However, students with learning disabilities may have difficulty with standardized tests such as the SAT, and their GPAs may be difficult to interpret because courses and accommodations vary widely, depending on high schools attended. Admissions officers should consider the following as predictors of college success for students with learning disabilities:
  - high school GPA
  - the number of mainstream English courses completed with a grade of C or better
  - motivation
  - ability to work independently
- Accommodations often used for college students with learning disabilities are:

- adjustments in course requirements and evaluation
- modifications in program requirements
- auxiliary aids

## How can students with learning disabilities prepare for the work world?

- In a non-college-bound model of secondary instruction, the special educator is responsible for most of the instruction, and students are mainstreamed in vocational education classes and take a light academic load.
- Key aspects of vocational programming include:
  - assessment procedures focused on functional skills related to future employment
  - support services to ensure access to mainstream vocational classes
  - at least four work experiences, six to eight weeks each
  - assistance in locating and securing employment
  - individual transition plans with appropriate adult service agencies
- Many professionals advocate school-business partnerships to help vocational programming for students with learning disabilities.

## How can employers encourage success for adults with learning disabilities?

- Four trends in the workplace have created problems for those with learning disabilities:
  - emphasis on teamwork
  - technology is sometimes placing excessive cognitive demands on the worker
  - increased emphasis on credentials and the passing of standardized tests
  - emphasis on productivity
- The Americans with Disabilities Act requires employers to make accommodations for workers with disabilities. To do this, employers need to know
  - the functional limitations associated with particular disabilities
  - the job task requirements
- Supported employment, often used with workers who are mentally retarded, has been suggested as a possible model for those who have learning disabilities.

## How can employees with learning disabilities succeed in the workplace?

Employees with learning disabilities can optimize their chances of success in the workplace by:
- choosing a job that is a good match
- using personal contacts to find a job
- becoming a self-advocate
- developing compensatory strategies
- taking advantage of technology
- gaining control over one's life
  - using the technique of reframing—recognizing that the disability itself is not the biggest problem
  - accepting one's weaknesses and exploiting one's strengths

## REFLECTIONS ON THE CASES

1. How would you advise Shannon with respect to whether or not she should attend college?

2. What are the relative strengths and weaknesses of Shannon's transition plan as it is written?

3. What accommodations do you think Shannon would need in college? What accommodations would she need in the workplace?

## What Is the Link between Learning Disabilities and Social, Emotional, and Behavioral Problems?

- Social Competence
- Conduct Problems
- Other Social, Emotional, and Behavioral Problems

## What Are the Major Causes of Social, Emotional, and Behavioral Problems?

- Schooling as a Possible Cause

## How Should We Access the Characteristics of Social, Emotional, and Behavioral Problems?

- Screening

- Prereferral Interventions
- Social, Emotional, and Behavioral Problems in IEP Development
- Functional Behavioral Assessment and Behavior Intervention Plans
- Other Possible Legal Aspects of Dealing with Behavior

## What Are the Main Educational Methods Used for Social, Emotional, and Behavioral Problems?

- Modifying the Learning Environment for Proactive Management
- Teaching Desired Behavior
- Discouraging Undesired Behavior

 Council for Exceptional Children

See Companion Website for detailed correlations between chapter content and Council for Exceptional Children Standards; **www.ablongman.com/ hallahanLD3e**

### CEC Knowledge and Skills Discussed in This Chapter

1. Social, emotional, and behavioral characteristics of individuals with learning disabilities, which can potentially be related to effects of the cultural environment.

2. Importance of understanding one's own personal cultural biases in order to reflect on practice, foster collaborative relationships, demonstrate cultural sensitivity, and serve as a model for individuals with exceptional needs.

3. Awareness of the laws, policies, and ethical principles related to assessment, particularly with respect to the referral and monitoring process in special education.

4. Usage of assessment findings in developing an instructional plan that sets realistic behavioral expectations, incorporates crisis prevention, appreciates cultural heritage, and employs effective management strategies in the least restrictive environment.

# Social, Emotional, and Behavioral Problems

7

Sometimes I just feel like I don't have any friends. I really want to be friends with someone, but other kids just don't seem to want to be my friend.

*Shannon*

Many children and youths with learning disabilities are well adjusted, emotionally healthy, popular with their schoolmates, and liked by their teachers. However, a significant portion of those with learning disabilities do have problems in getting along with others, making and keeping friends, and feeling good about themselves (Sridhar & Vaughn, 2001). Some are openly hostile toward others, including peers and adults. Others are shy and withdrawn. Some vacillate between the extremes of open hostility and withdrawal. Many, like Shannon, have poor self-concepts, are shy in social circumstances, and feel socially rejected or lonely (Margalit & Al-Yagon, 2002).

It is often clear to teachers that students with learning disabilities have social, emotional, and behavioral problems. Teachers themselves may be the targets of hostility or notice that a student with learning disabilities is noncompliant with their rules and requests. Sometimes teachers notice that a student is exceptionally quiet, withdrawn, or friendless. Shannon's teachers noticed that she had extreme difficulty in making and keeping friends. It is clear that Shannon wants friends; she simply doesn't know how to make them. Her shyness and lack of social skills get in the way of her ability to relate well to her peers. She does not really present a problem for teachers, but her teachers are concerned about her lack of peer relationships.

Shannon

## What Is the Link between Learning Disabilities and Social, Emotional, and Behavioral Problems?

An informed guess is that the majority of students with learning disabilities exhibit behavior problems in school. Perhaps as many as 30% of students with learning disabilities could also be formally diagnosed with another disability—that is, they could have ADHD, depression, or another disorder as well as a learning disability. Shannon shows some of the signs of depression: dawdling, daydreaming, few friends.

The assumption that students with learning disabilities may have social, emotional, or behavioral problems is based in part on decades of child development research showing that children typically exhibit behavior problems at home or at school—or in both environments—at some time during their development (Kauffman, 2005). More important are two additional facts: First, emotional and behavioral disorders are frequently accompanied by serious academic difficulties (Forness & Kavale, 1997; Kauffman, 2005). Second, numerous studies of students with learning disabilities have shown that many of them exhibit behavior problems in school, have problems in socialization with their peers, or have emotional or behavioral disorders (see Forness & Kavale, 1997; Haager & Vaughn, 1997; Kavale & Forness, 1997; Pearl & Bay, 1999; Sridhar & Vaughn, 2001; Wong & Donahue, 2002).

In short, many students with learning disabilities are likely to present behavior management problems more demanding than those presented by typical students. Teachers of students with learning disabilities should be equipped with skills for managing the social, emotional, and behavioral problems or disorders that a significant percentage of their students will exhibit. However, *not all individuals with learning disabilities exhibit social or behavioral problems.* In fact, the social domain is an area of strength for some students with learning disabilities. For example, one adult with severe reading disabilities said, "I could talk my way out of anything. I couldn't read in high school but I always managed to do 'OK' because I could get the teachers to believe anything I told them" (Haager & Vaughn, 1997, p. 130). In the case of Jamal, he has many friends and is not seen as a behavior problem by his teachers. However, he has some problems in academic learning that could result in his developing behavior problems in future years. Inability to perform academically as expected is often a prelude to acting-out behavior.

For a variety of reasons, many educators are unwilling to identify emotional or behavioral problems in their beginning stages and take preventive action (see Kauffman, 1999, 2004, 2005). Such problems seem, in a sense, to "sneak up" on people because their early identification takes a practiced eye, knowledge of the child, recognition of the subtle signs that trouble lies ahead, and willingness to take the risk of being wrongly concerned. Most emotional and behavioral problems are allowed to become severe and protracted before they are addressed. We discuss the prevention of emotional and behavioral problems in addition to prevention of academic failure in the Current Trends and Issues box on page 197.

Jamal

Council for
Exceptional
Children

**CEC Knowledge Check**

Why do learning disabilities often result in social problems? Why do these social problems then create behavior problems?
LD2K3, CC1S1

## Social Competence

We can think of social competence as having four components, all of which are important to being liked, accepted, and self-confident: (1) effective use of social skills, (2) absence of maladaptive behavior, (3) positive relations with others, and (4) accurate, age-appropriate social cognition (Haager & Vaughn, 1997). Social competence is not just having good social skills. Neither is it merely the absence of maladaptive behavior. Social competence is a complex concept consisting of the combination of all these four elements.

## What Prevents Us from Practicing Prevention?

Among the current issues in learning and behavior problems in school is how to practice prevention, which is often assumed to mean early identification and early intervention. Prevention is usually lauded in principle, but it is often not practiced. Following are some of the reasons prevention may not be practiced:

1. *It requires labeling.* Many educators resist labeling a problem, which means that it cannot be addressed effectively simply because it cannot be named and talked about without a label.
2. *It requires anticipating failure.* Many educators believe that anticipating something makes it happen and are loath to predict failure, preferring to deal with problems after the fact.
3. *It requires greater concern about missing problems than about false identification.* Many educators prefer absolute certainty that a problem exists before addressing it. Their fear of being wrong in identifying a child as having problems keeps them from acting.

4. *It requires rejection of a "new paradigm."* Many educators seem to assume that science does not apply to education and that schools will change so that singling out those with special problems is not necessary.
5. *It requires concluding that special education is effective.* Many educators believe special education is ineffective, which keeps them from identifying students who need it.
6. *It requires serving more students.* Many educators feel that the special education category is already too large and includes too many students. But prevention involves serving more students, at least initially.
7. *It requires spending more money now to save money later.* Many educators feel that special education already consumes an exorbitant proportion of the education budget. But spending more money on early intervention is required if money is to be saved on services that will otherwise be needed later.

Many students with learning disabilities are not high in social competence. They may have lower social status and fewer friends than students without learning disabilities (see Hallahan & Mercer, 2002; Wong & Donahue, 2002). They may be ignored or socially rejected by their peers. Their difficulty in social relationships may be due to deficits in social skills. They may not be able to "read" social situations as skillfully as most youngsters and, as a consequence, not understand how others are trying to influence them, what others want them to do, or how others perceive them (Petti, Voelker, Shore, & Hayman-Abello, 2003). They may lack social tact in approaching others, making evaluative social comments, or offering or receiving criticism or praise. They may not have skills in resisting negative peer pressure and may choose the wrong peer models to imitate. They may exhibit behavior that others find highly irritating or unacceptable (i.e., maladaptive behavior) yet be unaware that others are upset with them. Sometimes they may know that what they are doing is socially inappropriate but not know what is appropriate or be unable to behave as expected. As a result, they may have few friends but be unable to figure out why or how to make and keep them, as in the case of Shannon (see Sridhar & Vaughn, 2001; Pearl, 2002).

Teachers need to be concerned about the self-perceptions or self-concepts of students with learning disabilities. They often have a low opinion of themselves or their abilities, because they typically have both academic and social problems. It is important to consider self-concept in several areas: academic, social, and general self-esteem (see Cosden, Brown, & Elliott, 2002).

When it comes to academic self-concept, students with learning disabilities tend to perceive themselves in more negative terms than do students without learning disabilities and to attribute their academic failure to things they cannot change. Socially, too, students with learning disabilities tend to see themselves as less competent and less accepted than their normally achieving peers. However, two points are important: First, not all students with learning disabilities have lowered academic and social self-concepts. Second, some students maintain a normal degree of general self-esteem although their academic and social self-perceptions are lower than normal.

The self-concept of students with learning disabilities is a more varied and complex issue than is often realized. The peers with whom they compare themselves and the specific comparisons they make may shape their self-perceptions. For example, if a student has a high athletic ability and focuses on comparisons in this area, the student may have a good self-concept in spite of academic limitations.

Some have voiced concerns about the presumed negative effect on students' self-esteem of receiving special education in a separate setting (i.e., being taught in a resource room or self-contained class). Contrary to popular belief, research suggests that receiving education in a separate setting has a positive effect, if any, on self-esteem (Pearl & Bay, 1999). Students with learning disabilities may be encouraged to see themselves more positively when they compare themselves to others who are academically more like them than when they compare themselves to normally achieving students in the regular classroom (Coleman, McHam, & Minnett, 1992; Coleman & Minnett, 1992).

Exactly why most students with learning disabilities experience more problems of social adjustment than typical students is not known for certain. Perhaps their low social status and problems of social adjustment are shaped by their low academic achievement, lack of social understanding, inappropriate behavior, deficient social motivation, inability to resist peer pressure and undesirable social environments (e.g., negative peer or teacher bias, parent or teacher rejection, social gravitation toward poorly adjusted peers), or some combination of these (Pearl & Bay, 1999; Wong & Donahue, 2002).

## Conduct Problems

Conduct problems are overt antisocial behavior, such as aggression, tantrums, and disruption, and covert antisocial behavior, such as lying and stealing. All conduct problems involve noncompliance—not obeying adults or meeting normal social demands. Children with serious conduct problems are at high risk for developing lifelong patterns of social maladjustment, particularly when they experience low academic achievement as well (Kauffman, 2005). Thus, students with learning disabilities who show conduct problems need particularly effective intervention for academic and behavioral difficulties (MacMillan & Siperstein, 2002).

Conduct problems are not necessarily indications of delinquency. However, many children and youths who have conduct problems become involved with the

Council for Exceptional Children

**CEC Knowledge Check**

What are some of the negative impacts of having students with learning disabilities in the general education classroom? In a self-contained class or resource room? How do you decide which setting is best for an identified student? CC1K6, CC1S1

juvenile justice system—that is, they become juvenile delinquents. Youths with learning disabilities constitute a high percentage of the population of youths in correctional institutions.

The conduct problems of students with learning disabilities may be due in part to deficient social skills in understanding expectations, social roles, and consequences. Whatever the causes, conduct problems make children and youths more likely to fail academically and socially and to become involved with the law. Conduct problems carry the most severe social consequences of any type of maladaptive behavior that students may exhibit and are among the most difficult to change (Kauffman, 2005).

Council for
Exceptional
Children

**CEC Knowledge Check**
Create a list of student behaviors that will prompt you to intervene or advocate for those students. CC1K5, LD2K3

### Other Social, Emotional, and Behavioral Problems

Persons with learning disabilities frequently have anxiety and depression (Forness & Kavale, 1997; Kavale & Forness, 1997). They may be sad, discouraged, and hopeless. These problems may in part result from academic and social failure but may also contribute to failure in these arenas. As is the case with most social, emotional, and behavioral problems, there is a reciprocal relationship between them and achievement. Academic failure contributes to social, emotional, or behavioral problems, which in turn makes academic failure more likely.

## What Are the Major Causes of Social, Emotional, and Behavioral Problems?

When someone's behavior is problematic, we ask questions such as:

"What makes him behave that way?"
"What on earth could she have been thinking that would lead her to do that?"

Popular notions about the causes of problem behavior usually contain elements of truth, but they are simplistic. Oversimplifications ascribe nearly all the fault to a single factor. In explaining behavior problems, most people are prone to sweeping statements like the following:

"It's the parents' fault because of the way they raised her."
"The school and those teachers are really to blame for the way they handled him."
"It's a neurological thing that she just can't control."
"In today's culture, with all the bad models and nobody setting limits, how could you expect him to behave?"

We know that a variety of factors can contribute to the growth and development of problem behavior, and in typical cases, there is good reason to believe that several of these are involved. A youngster's misbehavior may be partly biological in origin, partly attributable to the family's child-rearing practices, partly due to mismanagement at school, and partly a function of cultural influences (see Kauffman, 2005). All possible causes of learning disabilities are potential causes of emotional and behavioral problems. Moreover, some of the characteristics of learning disabilities—problems of memory and communication, for example—may contribute to problems of social competence.

## Schooling as a Possible Cause

The possible causes most pertinent to teachers are the ones involving schooling. In fact, most of what we know about the social problems of students with learning disabilities is related to the school context (Haager & Vaughn, 1997; Wong & Donahue, 2002). Teachers cannot do very much directly about biological, family, or cultural factors, but they can do a lot to ensure that the student's experience at school does not contribute to misbehavior (see Kauffman, 2005; Kauffman, Mostert et al., 2002; Kerr & Nelson, 2002; Walker, 1995; Walker, Ramsey, & Gresham, 2004). Teachers should consider ways in which their own behavior, their classroom, and their school might contribute to a student's misbehavior. They can then work to make sure that the school environment is not a source of the problem. For example, here are six school-related issues that teachers should consider (Kauffman, 2005; Kauffman, Mostert et al., 2002).

1. *Instruction.* A sound instructional program is the first defense against social, emotional, or behavioral problems in school. A good instructional program is characterized by the following:

- *Clarity* of the task (the student knows exactly what to do)
- *Level* that is right for the student (the student can respond correctly most of the time)
- *Opportunities* to respond frequently (lots of chances to give answers)
- *Consequences* for responding that are overwhelmingly positive (lots of positive reinforcement for correct responses)
- *Sequential* presentation of tasks (tasks are sequenced to help the student get the big idea)
- *Relevance* to the student's life (the student sees the advantage in learning the tasks)
- *Application* to everyday circumstances (applications to everyday problem solving)
- *Monitoring* of results (frequent measurement of student performance to track progress)

Council for Exceptional Children

**CEC Knowledge Check**
Rank these eight characteristics from most important to least important. How can you ensure that your list is implemented in your classroom?
CC4S5, CC9S10, CC9S11, CC1S1

Effective instruction offered at the student's level is critically important as a way of preventing the student's feelings of threat, failure, resentment, and defeat. We should not expect students to behave well if they are not being taught well. Often students do not see the relevance of the skills they are being taught in school. If they see what they are being asked to do as a waste of their time, they are likely to behave inappropriately in protest or out of boredom or frustration. One of the teacher's tasks is to teach skills that are important to students' lives and to find ways of making "uninteresting" skills worth students' time to learn, sometimes by modifying teaching methods or learning activities, sometimes by offering meaningful rewards for learning.

Moreover, if students have deficits in social skills or social cognition, then the instructional program must include effective instruction in these areas.

2. *Expectations.* Expectations that are too high for a student's ability lead to constant feelings of failure; expectations that are too low lead to boredom and lack of progress. A good teacher adjusts expectations to fit the student's level of ability so that improvement is always both possible and challenging. Unless an appropriate level of expectations is set for the individual, the teacher will set the student up for failure. Getting the expectations just right is no small task, but this fundamental task, if not accomplished, is virtually certain to induce misbehavior.

3. *Tolerance.* A school environment that is conducive to appropriate behavior must allow students sufficient freedom to demonstrate their individuality. Teachers who demand strict uniformity and regimentation and who are unable to tolerate and encourage appropriate differences among their students are likely to increase the tendency of some to exhibit troublesome behavior. However, the teacher who will tolerate anything and everything is surely headed for trouble, too. Finding the balance between conformity to necessary rules and tolerance for acceptable difference is a key to building a school and classroom environment conducive to appropriate behavior. Particularly important is the difference between culturally based, appropriate behavior and behavior that is inappropriate, regardless of the student's culture.

4. *Reinforcement.* In many classes, students with problems are ignored when they are behaving well and given lots of attention (usually in the form of criticism and reminders or threats) when they misbehave. This arrangement is certain to perpetuate the student's behavioral difficulties because students are getting reinforcement (e.g., the reward of attention) for the wrong thing. Expert **positive reinforcement** (reward) is typically given frequently, immediately, interestingly, and contingent on desired behavior. To be used expertly, reinforcement must be combined with other behavior management strategies for maximum effect (see Rhode, Jenson, & Reavis, 1992; Walker et al., 2004). These other strategies include effective instruction, knowing when and how to ignore misbehavior, using nonviolent **punishment,** and talking with students in ways that enhance their self-confidence and self-control.

5. *Consistency.* One of the most significant features of a good school experience for any student, but especially one who exhibits emotional or behavioral problems, is a high degree of structure. Structure means that instructions are clear to the student, the teacher holds firm expectations that the student will follow instructions, and the consequences for behavior are consistent. When the student is being managed consistently, the classroom routine and the consequences for behavior are highly predictable. Inconsistent management is one factor that is almost certain to increase any student's tendency to misbehave.

6. *Models.* Children and adolescents, not to mention adults, are great imitators. If the teacher's behavior is a desirable model for students, then appropriate conduct may be encouraged. Students also imitate their classmates, but just having classmates whose behavior is desirable is not sufficient to ensure that they will be imitated. If it were, then how do we account for some students' misbehavior in classes in which most of their peers are well behaved? Appropriate peer models are found not only in regular classes, but also in special classes. The best models often are not those who are perfect, but those who share many of the characteristics of the student having difficulty. The most effective models are usually those who are only somewhat better

Council for Exceptional Children

**CEC Knowledge Check**
How do you balance the need for challenge vs. maintaining self-esteem? If misbehavior occurs, would this indicate that expectations be adjusted? CC5S2

**CEC Knowledge Check**
What is the balance between freedom and strict uniformity? How do you determine culturally appropriate behavior from behavior that is inappropriate? List culturally appropriate behaviors. List behaviors that would be inappropriate for anyone from any culture. CC5K8, CC5S5

**CEC Knowledge Check**
If you saw or heard a fellow teacher destroying the self-esteem or confidence of a student, what would you do? Why? CC9S1, CC9S2, CC9S11, CC10S3

**positive reinforcement** presentation of a positive reinforcer (reward) contingent upon a behavior, which increases the probability that the behavior will be repeated

**punishment** consequences that reduce future probability of a behavior; may be response cost (removal of a valued object or commodity) or aversive conditioning (presentation of an aversive stimulus such as a slap or an electric shock)

**Council for Exceptional Children**

**CEC Knowledge Check**

Is it ever appropriate for teachers to exhibit behaviors that they want students to stop? Why is it important for teachers to exhibit the behaviors they want to see in students?
CC1K1, CC5K4, CC9K2

**Council for Exceptional Children**

**CEC Knowledge Check**

If you are teaching, what are some of the modifications to the learning environment you have made to help manage behaviors? If you are not teaching, make a list of the modifications to the learning environment you would make.
CC5S5, CC5S10, CC5S11

**internalizing behavior** behavior problems that do not involve acting out against others; internal states such as depression and anxiety

**nonverbal learning disabilities** learning disabilities that do not involve academic learning, usually social in nature

**externalizing behavior** acting-out behavior, such as aggression, antisocial behavior, tantrums, etc.

than the student who is experiencing problems. The teacher must choose models carefully, call attention to the behavior to be imitated, and reward imitation if these models are to be effective. (Hallenbeck & Kauffman, 1995)

We know that many factors, both physical and interpersonal, can contribute to causing students' social, emotional, and behavioral problems. Possible causes include biological, family, cultural, and school factors. Teachers have an obligation to be aware of all of these possible factors but a special responsibility to make sure that the student's experience in the classroom and at school does not contribute to these problems.

## How Should We Assess the Characteristics of Social, Emotional, and Behavioral Problems?

Learning disabilities may coexist with or predispose children and youths to a wide variety of social, emotional, or behavioral problems. In the contemporary language of special education, there is no attempt to distinguish among social, emotional, and behavioral problems because all are indicated by the individual's inappropriate behavior (cf. Forness & Kavale, 1997; Kauffman, 2005). When distinctions among types of problems are made, they are more often between internalizing and externalizing behavior. **Internalizing behavior** is characterized by anxiety and social withdrawal, which are often taken as indications of emotional (affective) problems. For example, internalizing behavior often indicates depression. Recall that in Chapter 2 we discussed **nonverbal learning disabilities.** Children with nonverbal learning disabilities may be particularly prone to internalizing problems (Petti et al., 2003). **Externalizing behavior** is characterized by acting out or antisocial behavior. For example, fighting, tantrums, property destruction, and hyperactivity are externalizing behaviors. A given individual may exhibit either or both types of maladaptive behavior.

The dividing line between emotional or behavioral problems and emotional or behavioral disorders is not precise. The difference between problem and disorder is primarily a matter of judgment of severity. Disorder indicates a problem so severe that it becomes a critical concern and interferes significantly with the individual's everyday functioning (cf. Forness & Kavale, 1997; Kauffman, 2005). Put another way, all disorders are problems, but not all problems are disorders. Our discussion of problems includes those serious enough to be considered disorders.

The assessment of students' emotional or behavioral problems, like that of problems in various academic areas, should identify those students who need special help, guide the planning of programs to address their problems, and provide the basis for monitoring progress toward specific goals. An adequate assessment does not focus exclusively on the student's behavior. Rather, it includes consideration of the student's social and physical environments and the student's thoughts and feelings about these circumstances. Assessment should be solution centered—that is, it should not merely be descriptive of what is, but also should be a process that leads to interventions. It should be based on the most accessible and reliable sources of information, not on speculation that cannot be confirmed, and should yield a picture not only of the student, but also of the context in which the behavior is causing concern (Haager & Vaughn, 1997).

An important principle of the assessment of social competence and emotional or behavioral problems is that information must be obtained from multiple sources. All aspects of assessment should include multiple perspectives and should never rely entirely on one person's judgment. The multiple sources of information should include the student, parent(s), and peers, in addition to the teacher. Moreover, a complete assessment will include social skills, maladaptive behavior, interpersonal relationships, and social cognition.

The full range of assessment strategies includes screening for possible problems, prereferral strategies, and evaluation. Assessment should guide writing individualized education programs (IEPs) and behavior intervention plans (BIPs) (Kauffman, 2005).

The Individuals with Disabilities Education Act (IDEA) dictates that the IEP must include plans for dealing with problem behavior if behavior problems become evident in the student's assessment. In addition, IDEA makes special provisions for disciplining students with disabilities.

## Screening

Systematic screening for social, emotional, or behavioral problems is relatively uncommon in American public schools, primarily because it would likely turn up many more problems than school personnel could address effectively. However, a variety of screening instruments and strategies is available. Most of these are behavior rating scales that have been normed on a comparison population. Some are appropriate for screening entire school populations. Many would be useful for screening students already identified as having academic learning disabilities to determine whether they may have emotional or behavioral problems as well.

Screening is a process of eliminating or confirming the suspicion that a student may have a problem. Ideally, it requires a series of steps in which the criteria for selecting students are successively narrowed so that in the end only those students who actually have problems have been identified. The instrument conforming most closely to the ideal screening process in the elementary grades is the *Systematic Screening for Behavior Disorders,* or SSBD (Walker & Severson, 1990; see also Feil, Severson, & Walker, 2002). It assesses both adaptive and maladaptive behavior. The SSBD is a multiple-gating process designed to ensure not only that just those students who actually have problems are identified, but also that equal attention is given to internalizing and externalizing problems.

Screening should not depend entirely on one individual's opinions, one measure of behavior, or student behavior in one setting. It should represent the convergence of data from a variety of sources and situations indicating that the student needs further study. A major concern is that cultural difference or nondeviant personal idiosyncrasies might be mistaken for emotional or behavioral problems. In fact, bias in screening and identification could result in the overidentification or underidentification of students based on ethnic, gender, or individual differences.

Council for Exceptional Children

**CEC Knowledge Check**
Why is it important to get a multifaceted perspective before making intervention plans? LD2K3, CC7S4, LD8K1, CC10S2

Council for Exceptional Children

**CEC Knowledge Check**
When would screening for behavior become a gender or ethnic issue? If all of your identified students with behavior problems were males of color, would this always indicate racial bias? Why, or why not? If your identified students with behavior problems were 50% male and 50% female, would this indicate to you a gender bias? Why? CC1K5, CC8S1, CC8S2, CC8S5, CC8S6, CC9K1

Thus, screening, as well as other aspects of identification, must take into account cultural differences while not mistaking problems for mere differences in culture.

## Prereferral Interventions

Critics of special education have sometimes charged that teachers refer students too quickly, typically for minor behavioral rather than for serious behavioral or academic reasons. However, research has not shown this to be the case (e.g., Lloyd, Kauffman, Landrum, & Roe, 1991). In the vast majority of cases, a teacher refers a student out of concern for the student's lack of academic progress or for academic problems combined with inattentive or disruptive classroom behavior. Teachers do not see the problems for which they refer students as minor. They are asking for help.

However, before referring a student out of concern for social, emotional, or behavioral problems, a teacher should document that effective behavior management strategies have been used and have not achieved the desired result. These prereferral behavior management strategies consist of the kinds of positive, problem-solving efforts described later in this chapter and in sources such as Alberto and Troutman (2003), Kauffman, Mostert et al. (2002), Kerr and Nelson (2002), Walker (1995), and Walker et al. (2004).

## Social, Emotional, and Behavioral Problems in IEP Development

Given confirmation that a student has a social, emotional, or behavioral problem in addition to a learning disability, teachers must plan a program designed to change the student's behavior. The plan must be based on information from multiple sources and be included in the IEP. Bateman and Linden (1998) provide an example of including problem behavior in an IEP. (See Figure 7.1, part of an IEP for Curt.)

## Functional Behavioral Assessment and Behavior Intervention Plans

The purpose of a **functional behavioral assessment (FBA)** is finding the specific purposes or goals of a student's behavior. If the goal or purpose—the function—of a behavior is found, then the student may be taught to achieve essentially the same goal but with different and more acceptable behavior (Alberto & Troutman, 2003; Cullinan, 2002; Kerr & Nelson, 2002; O'Neill, Horner, Albin, Sprague, Storey, & Newton, 1997). Although the concept of functional assessment is as old as behavioral psychology, the current trend toward widespread implementation in schools began in the 1990s.

An emphasis on functional assessment has several advantages: First, it is consistent with attention to academic and social skills curricula. Also, it more specifically focuses on the environmental events that trigger undesirable social behavior and what the student obtains as a consequence of behaving in a given way. Further, it is consistent with an instructional approach to behavior management known as **precorrection,** in which the goal is to find ways of altering circumstances to teach a

Council for Exceptional Children

**CEC Knowledge Check**
When a teacher refers a student to you for social, emotional, or behavioral problems, how do you find how well the teacher has tried to implement effective behavior management strategies? How far should you press this question before accepting the student for screening? LD1K4, CC8K3

**functional behavioral assessment (FBA)** procedures designed to find out why a student exhibits problem behavior, including assessment of the antecedents and consequences of behavior and the apparent purpose of the problem behavior

**precorrection** the strategy of anticipating and avoiding misbehavior by identifying and modifying the context in which it is likely to occur; using proactive procedures to teach desired behavior rather than focusing on correction of misbehavior

**FIGURE 7.1** Individualized Education Program

Student: ___Curt___   Age: ___15___   Grade: ___9___   Date: _10/12/94_

| Unique Characteristics/ Needs | Special Education, Related Services, Modifications | (begin duration) | Present Levels, Objectives, Annual Goals (Objectives to include procedure, criteria, schedule) |
|---|---|---|---|
| Social Needs:<br>• To learn anger management skills, especially regarding swearing<br>• To learn to comply with requests<br><br>Present Level: Lashes out violently when not able to complete work, uses profane language, and refuses to follow further directions from adults | 1. Teacher and/or counselor consult with behavior specialists regarding techniques and programs for teaching social skills, especially anger management.<br>2. Provide anger management training for Curt.<br>3. Establish a peer group which involves role playing, etc. so Curt can see positive role models and practice newly learned anger management skills.<br>4. Develop a behavior plan for Curt which gives him responsibility for charting his own behavior.<br>5. Provide a teacher or some other adult mentor to spend time with Curt (could be talking, game play, physical activity).<br>6. Provide training for the mentor regarding Curt's needs/goals. | 30 min., 3 × week<br><br>30 min., 2 × week<br><br><br><br><br>30 min., 2 × week | Goal: During the last quarter of the academic year, Curt will have 2 or fewer detentions for any reason.<br>Objective 1: At the end of the 1st quarter, Curt will have had 10 or fewer detentions.<br>Objective 2: At the end of 2nd quarter, Curt will have had 7 or fewer detentions.<br>Objective 3: At the end of 3rd quarter, Curt will have had 4 or fewer detentions.<br>Goal: Curt will manage his behavior and language in a reasonably acceptable manner as reported by faculty/peers.<br>Objective 1: At 2 weeks, asked at end of class if Curt's behavior language was acceptable or not, 3 out of 5 teachers will say "acceptable."<br>Objective 2: At 6 weeks, asked same question, 4 out of 6 teachers will say "acceptable."<br>Objective 3: At 12 weeks. 6 out of 6 will say "acceptable." |

Adaptations to regular program:
- In all classes, Curt should be near front of class
- Curt should be called on often to keep him involved and on task
- All teachers should help Curt with study skills as trained by spelling/ language specialist and resource room teacher
- Teachers should monitor Curt's work closely in the beginning weeks/months of his program

*Source:* From *Better IEPs,* 2nd ed. (p. 89) by B. D. Bateman, 1996, Longmont, CO: Sopris West. Copyright 1996 by Barbara D. Bateman. Reprinted by permission.

**CEC Knowledge Check**

What is the main goal of a functional behavioral assessment? CC7S4

**behavior intervention plan (BIP)** a proactive plan designed to avert problems, not to merely react to behavior once it has occurred

Council for Exceptional Children

**CEC Knowledge Check**

What behavior motivation goal should teachers try to instill in all students? What part does intrinsic motivation play in this process? CC7S14

**manifestation determination**
a determination of whether a student's misbehavior is or is not a manifestation of his or her disability

**interim alternative educational setting (IAS)** a setting other than the regular school in which a student with disabilities may be placed temporarily for disciplinary purposes

Council for Exceptional Children

**CEC Knowledge Check**

Why would the IAES usually be the method of last resort in providing education services to students with behavior problems? CC1K2, CC5S2, CC5S11

desired behavior (see Kauffman, Mostert et al., 2002; Walker et al., 2004). Functional assessment may reveal, for example, that a student misbehaves out of frustration, boredom, or overstimulation. It may uncover the fact that misbehavior is maintained because of the attention it garners or because it allows the student to avoid difficult tasks or unpleasant demands. Although it is a highly useful tool in teaching, conducting a functional assessment and basing teaching procedure on it requires careful training, especially in the case of students whose behavioral problems are severe or long-standing (see Alberto & Troutman, 2003; Cullinan, 2002; Kerr & Nelson, 2002; Walker et al., 2004).

Federal and state regulations may require a **behavior intervention plan (BIP)** for students whose behavior is of concern. The plan must be proactive—designed to avert problems, not merely react to behavior once it has occurred. "The behavior intervention plan for each student should delineate expected behaviors, inappropriate behaviors, and positive and negative consequences. The disciplinary process that will be followed, including intervention techniques, should be outlined in the plan. The plan also should include procedures for dealing with behavioral crises" (Yell & Shriner, 1997, p. 12). Figure 7.2 shows a behavior intervention plan that might be included in an IEP, using a format suggested by Yell (1998).

Behavior intervention plans are, like functional behavioral assessment, consistent with the proactive teaching plans known as precorrection (see Kauffman, Mostert et al., 2002; Walker et al., 2004). The focus of the plan needs to be on helping the student learn appropriate behavior through positive strategies rather than punishment.

## Other Possible Legal Aspects of Dealing with Behavior

Teachers may be called to participate in a **manifestation determination,** a procedure designed to determine whether a student's behavior is or is not a manifestation of disability. The rules for making the decision are set by federal and state regulations. However, regardless of the rules and procedures followed, the objective is to decide whether the student should be disciplined as a student without a disability or whether alternative disciplinary procedures should be followed because the behavior problem is actually a part of the student's disability. The manifestation determination is a controversial issue in special education. Some argue that it is necessary; others, that it is a way of allowing students with disabilities to avoid responsibility for their behavior (see Dupre, 2000; Katsiyannis & Maag, 2001).

Depending on federal and state regulations, a student with a disability may be placed in an **interim alternative educational setting (IAES).** An IAES is an alternative setting chosen by the IEP team that will allow the student to continue participating in the general education curriculum and continue to receive the services described in the IEP. The student must be able to continue working toward IEP goals and objectives, including those related to the behavior that resulted in placement in the IAES. IAES may include alternative schools, instruction at home ("homebound instruction"), and other special settings (see Huefner, 2000).

**FIGURE 7.2** Sample Behavior Intervention Plan for IEP

**Student:** Patrick Milton Wills        **Date:** March 17, 2004

**Teacher(s):** Patricia Pullen

**Parent(s):** Judith & John Wills

**Administrator(s):** Rebecca Dailey, principal

**Other(s):** Ron Reeve, school psychologist

**Problem behaviors:** Patrick violates other students' personal space and property by touching, grabbing, or using others' possessions without their permission. He also annoys other students by aggressively touching them. Inappropriate touching of others or their possessions occurs on average about 5 times per day.

**Antecedents of problem behaviors:** These problems occur throughout the day in a variety of settings, but are particularly likely when students are making a transition from one activity to another and when Patrick is excluded from an activity in which he wants to participate.

**Positive procedures to redirect behaviors:** Ms. Pullen will explain to Patrick that he sometimes touches others and their possessions inappropriately and needs to learn alternative ways of relating to his peers. She will also explain and demonstrate alternative, expected behaviors (e.g., keeping hands to self, touching your own possessions, requesting permission, avoiding touching by using self-talk). She will make a plan with Patrick about how she will remind him prior to transitions and other times to exhibit the expected behavior.

**Intervention plan (reinforcers and consequences):** Ms. Pullen will offer frequent praise and encouragement for Patrick's appropriate behavior. Patrick will chart his behavior daily, based on a log kept by Ms. Pullen, and take his parents a daily report of his behavior. Mr. & Mrs. Wills will offer praise for improvement and a small tangible reward for each week in which there is improvement over the previous week or fewer than 3 incidents per week reported by Ms. Pullen. Mr. & Mrs. Wills agree not to provide criticism or other negative consequences for poor reports.

**Procedures to teach positive replacement behaviors:** Mr. Reeve will give Patrick instruction in how to obtain permission to touch others' belongings, how to refrain from inappropriate touching, and how to obtain peer attention in appropriate ways. The instruction in these social skills will involve modeling, role playing, and rehearsal. Mr. Reeve will keep Ms. Pullen informed of the instruction Patrick has been given, and Ms. Pullen will encourage Patrick to use these strategies by giving him prompts and praise for demonstrating them.

**Method of evaluation:** Ms. Pullen will keep a log of Patrick's inappropriate touching, recording the date, time, and activity during which each incident occurs. At the end of each school day, Patrick will be given a copy of the day's log to take home to his parents. He will also plot the number of inappropriate touching incidents for the day on a graph to be kept by Ms. Pullen.

**Goal and criteria for success:** Patrick will touch other students and their property only with their permission and in an appropriate manner as judged by the teacher's observation of students' reactions. Successful intervention will reduce recorded incidents of inappropriate touching to 2 or fewer per week for 6 weeks.

# What Are the Main Educational Methods Used for Social, Emotional, and Behavioral Problems?

The focus of behavior management in special education has changed. Whereas the emphasis was once on reacting to misbehavior, it is now on planning proactive programs intended to avoid problems. Proactive plans can be much more effective and efficient than reactive techniques. The idea of precorrection—a strategy for anticipating misbehavior and avoiding it by teaching desired behavior—is extremely useful to classroom teachers (Kauffman, Mostert et al., 2002; Walker et al., 2004).

Nevertheless, not all behavior problems can be predicted or avoided. Teachers still need strategies for dealing reactively when problems occur. Teachers must be prepared to deal with ordinary misbehavior and the kind of rule infraction that invokes special discipline considerations. A crucial point in planning programs of behavioral change, whether proactive or reactive, is that *it is unacceptable to focus on eliminating inappropriate behavior without also teaching desirable behavior.* The teacher's first line of attack on social, emotional, or behavioral problems is to ensure competent academic instruction. The second is to teach the social skills needed for good functioning in society and to reinforce (reward) appropriate behavior exhibited by the student. The third is to decrease or eliminate the student's socially inappropriate behavior.

Our focus on competent instruction and positive reinforcement for desirable behavior should not be taken as an indication that teachers should never intervene to stop undesirable behavior. Actually, unless a teacher steps in to stop certain types of misbehavior, this behavior will escalate (Kauffman, Bantz, & McCullough, 2002). Stopping misbehavior, even if it involves nonviolent punishment, can be critically important (see Kauffman, Mostert et al., 2002; Kerr & Nelson, 2002; Lerman & Vorndran, 2002; Walker, 1995; Walker et al., 2004). The teacher must also be able to distinguish between behavior that is culturally different from the teacher's yet is nonetheless acceptable and behavior that is out of bounds, regardless of culture. What are the boundaries of acceptable behavior, and what should adults do when children cross the line? The answers are not always easy ones, and teachers may find themselves wondering where to draw the line and how to do it. The Multicultural Considerations box on page 209 provides one illustration.

Our emphasis in this chapter on managing behavior should not be taken as an indication of unconcern for students' self-esteem or emotional lives. How students feel about themselves and about school is very important. However, the surest way to help them feel better about school and themselves is to help them achieve academic success and behave in a socially acceptable, if not socially skillful, manner. Focusing on effective instruction and being sensitive to students' feelings is the most effective way to improve students' self-perceptions.

## Modifying the Learning Environment for Proactive Management

Proactive management means avoiding behavior problems. Increasingly, research suggests that the best single proactive strategy for avoiding behavior problems in

## When and How to Respond to Troublesome Behavior

In an editorial opinion article titled "What Would You Have Done?" (*Washington Post,* January 3, 2003, p. A19), the experiences on the Washington, DC, subway (the Metro) of Shannon Fitzsimmons are described.

One afternoon on the way home, she encounters 6 or 7 youths, one a girl, who range in age from about 10 to about 13. They use coarse and foul language with one another, and boarding passengers have to step over the kids' legs, which they do not remove from the aisle.

Fitzsimmons has been a teacher in middle and high schools, so she's not put off by generic "gangster" demeanor. Still, she realizes that these kids are just skirting the range of acceptable behavior. Adults are not smiling at the kids, and some move away from them.

New passengers are eyeing a boy sitting in front of Fitzsimmons. He is drawing on the seat (nothing nice; actually, he's vandalizing the seat, although the subway car is full of adults at rush hour). She asks him what he's doing. He calls her a bitch and asks what it looks like he's doing. He's about 11 years old, and he's staring hard at her. She tells him he can't do that (draw on the seat). Nobody else says anything. He calls her a bitch again and threatens to rob her, and tells her—repeatedly—to "shut the _____ up." He continues to threaten her, but no other adult gets involved. Fitzsimmons ends by asking what we would have done under similar circumstances.

Fitzsimmons has been a teacher. Many teachers are confronted by similar circumstances. Such confrontations take place in both urban and nonurban schools and communities. What should teachers and other adults do?

We are tempted always to think of ethnic differences as defining multicultural issues. But Fitzsimmons does not mention her own ethnicity or that of the children. Actually, the multicultural issues in the circumstance she describes have a lot more to do with generational issues, class differences, and community standards than with ethnic identity. Children and youths of every ethnicity ride subways in major cities. Some children of every ethnic group are contemptuous of and intimidate adults of every ethnicity, and they do so in a variety of public and private places, including schools.

The question is, what should Fitzsimmons (or any other adult) have done, regardless of her ethnicity or that of the youngsters? What were her options? What were the options of the observing adults? Should such behavior of children and youths be accepted or tolerated? If so, under what conditions? If not, what should be done to stop them? What are the long-term implications for the children involved and for a community when no one intervenes to stop such behavior? How should teachers respond to such behavior in school, regardless of whether it is their classroom, the hallway, the lunch room, the playground, or any other place?

school is effective academic instruction, in which students give frequent correct responses and have a low error rate (cf. Kauffman, Mostert et al., 2002; Walker et al., 2004). Students who experience frequent success on the tasks they are given have fewer reasons to resist instruction and avoid academic work through misbehavior.

However, many students with learning disabilities, even with effective academic instruction, exhibit predictable misbehavior in particular contexts. Therefore, teachers still need to have proactive plans for dealing with behavior problems that can be anticipated. Sometimes the teacher has learned through observation that a particular context is a rough spot in which the student is likely to make a mistake. The teacher might be compared to an athletic coach who can anticipate that a player is likely to make a particular mistake (Colvin, 1992). The teacher needs to adopt a good coaching model—to anticipate behavioral mistakes in various classroom contexts and offer effective coaching in how to avoid them. Knowing where a student is likely to have trouble understanding or performing and teaching the

**Council for Exceptional Children**

**CEC Knowledge Check**
How would you have responded in Shannon's place? What responsibility do cultural communities have to "police their own"?
CC2K3, CC5S5, CC5S10, CC5S11, CC5K6, CC5S2, CC6K3, CC7S7

Council for
Exceptional
Children

**CEC Knowledge Check**
Why should the teacher
never assume the stu-
dent knows what behav-
iors are expected?
CC4S5, CC5K2

student how to avoid the predictable errors is an approach used by teachers who are skillful in all types of instruction (Walker et al., 2004).

The most effective approach is to assume that the expected, desirable behavior needs to be taught. Precorrection focuses on teaching students to do what is expected. Social competence is acquired through learning particular behavioral skills and knowing when and how to demonstrate them. Teaching these skills can be approached using the same basic principles expert teachers use for helping students learn any other type of performance—not only in athletics, for example, but also in music, drama, or reading.

The precorrection checklist and plan devised by Colvin, Sugai, and Patching (1993) provides a convenient format for organizing an approach for proactive behavior management (see also Kauffman, Mostert et al., 2002; Walker et al., 2004). The following outline can provide a way of thinking about how to anticipate and prevent behavioral mistakes:

1. *Evaluate the context*—the setting, circumstances, or situation in which a predictable misbehavior occurs. Through observation, the teacher learns that, in a given context (e.g., the class is making a transition from one activity to another), a behavioral mistake (e.g., failure to follow instructions) is highly likely on the part of a student. Identifying the context of predictable misbehavior is critically important. The basic idea is to see recurrent patterns in misbehavior so that the context can be modified to avert them.

2. *State the expected behavior*—what the teacher wants the student to do instead of making the behavioral mistake. This step is essential, because precorrection involves teaching students what to do, not simply what to avoid.

3. *Modify the context* in a way that will reduce the likelihood that the student will make a behavioral mistake. The modification can be very simple and straightforward, but small changes can often be critical in helping students learn to behave as desired. The context modification might be a change in location of the student or the teacher, a change in the teacher's behavior, a change in the way the assignment is presented, and so on. Whatever the change, it must be calculated to lower the probability that the student will exhibit the predictable misbehavior and increase the chances that the student will do what is expected.

4. *Involve the student in rehearsal*—either practice runs through the expected behavior or cognitive rehearsal in which the student describes the expected behavior. Rehearsal, or trying the behavior out before the expected performance, is basic to learning all skills, including those required for behaving as expected in school. Rehearsal should occur just before the performance is expected so that it is fresh in the student's mind.

5. *Reinforce correct performance* of the expected behavior. Reinforcement refers to a rewarding consequence, which may be social or tangible. To ensure high motivation to perform the expected behavior, the teacher must ensure that doing what is expected results in some highly satisfying consequence—a privilege or "perk" beyond the ordinary. However simple or ordinary the task or expectation may seem

to someone else, strong reinforcement typically results in faster and more permanent learning whenever a person is learning to do something new or not customary.

6. *Use prompts or signals* that the student understands to mean "remember" or "do it now." Like strong reinforcement, prompts are typically necessary to help students acquire a new skill. At first, if students do not have a special prompt, they may miss the typical cue and forget to apply what they know. As they become accustomed to performing as expected, they will begin reading more subtle cues or prompting themselves.

7. *Establish a monitoring plan* to help judge whether the student is acquiring the expected behavior. Effective monitoring involves systematic, direct observation and recording so that progress, or lack of it, is not a matter of guesswork. It is a reliable check on the effectiveness of the plan. The precorrection strategy may be applied to one student at a time, to small groups, to individuals within groups, or to an entire class.

Precorrection is an example of a technology of instruction. Technology refers not only to gadgets that may be useful in teaching, but also to application of specific instructional or behavior management techniques. Doing the right thing at the right time—applying a technique with precision—is a technology that is often overlooked, because when people hear "technology," they tend to think of something electronic or mechanical (computers or other machines). *Teaching is not merely technological; it is an art and a science. However, there is a technology of teaching.* The Today's Technology box on page 212 provides a completed precorrection checklist and plan. Precorrection is, in a sense, like computer software—a plan for anticipating and responding to behavior. However, in the case of precorrection, the technology is a set of practices addressing student behavior that the teacher must implement with consistency and precision. Precorrection, like Direct Instruction, might be considered a human technology or software for the mind. Such technology is more adaptable and immediately adjustable than a computer program. It runs on actual intelligence, not artificial intelligence—on neurons, not microchips.

The precorrection plan fits with the requirements of IDEA for a behavior intervention plan. It is proactive; states what is expected; details the positive behavioral interventions, strategies, and supports that will be used; and includes an evaluation component (the monitoring plan). The precorrection plan could also be written to specify procedures for disciplinary action or management of behavioral crises.

Council for
Exceptional
Children

**CEC Knowledge Check**
Why must the student be involved in the behavior modification process? What is accomplished by this involvement? CC10K1, CC10S7

## Teaching Desired Behavior

Precorrection is a general, proactive plan for teaching expected behavior. However, the effective implementation of such a plan depends on careful attention to the details of a variety of teaching tactics, many of which have long been used by master teachers. Many of these practices are seemingly simple. As is true in any area of art

# The Teaching Technology of Precorrection

## A Completed Precorrection Plan

Teacher: ___Pat Puller___          Student: ___Jimmy Ott (6th grade)___          Date: ___Oct. 11, 2002___

1. Context [where and when; situation, circumstances, or conditions in which predictable behavior occurs]
   *Upon entering the classroom in the morning, when at least one other student is in the room*

   a. Predictable behavior [the error or misbehavior that you can anticipate in the context]
   *Jimmy describes his deviant behavior or deviant intentions (e.g., how he drank or did drugs or got into a fight or stole something or is going to "take someone out")*

2. Expected behavior [what you want the student to do instead of the predictable behavior]
   *Jimmy will talk about appropriate topics when he enters the class*

3. Context modification [how you can change the situation, circumstances, or conditions to make the predictable behavior less likely and the expected behavior more likely to occur]
   *Meet Jimmy at the door and immediately ask a question demanding appropriate talk as an answer*

4. Behavior rehearsal [practice; dry run; try out; drill]
   *Practice with Jimmy coming into class and responding to my question, then talking about appropriate topics*

5. Strong reinforcement [special reward for doing the expected behavior]
   *Praise for appropriate talk on coming into the classroom, plus 5 min. to talk with his choice of me, principal, cook, or custodian if no inappropriate talk before first period assignment is given (principal, cook, and custodian agreed and trained in how to handle conversation)*

6. Prompts [gestures or other signals indicating "remember; do it now"]
   *Hand signal to Jimmy when I first see him in the morning, worked out in advance to indicate "appropriate talk"*

7. Monitoring plan [record of performance; indicator of success that you can show someone]
   *Jimmy and I to record daily successful school entry talk*

*Source:* From *Managing Classroom Behavior: A Reflective Case-Based Approach,* 3rd ed. by J. M. Kauffman, M. P. Mostert, S. C. Trent, and D. P. Hallahan, 2002, Boston: Allyn & Bacon, p. 63 (figure 3.1). Copyright 2002 by Pearson Education. Reprinted by permission of the publisher.

or science, the difference between a master and a less-skilled performer is often found in the details of execution—doing the seemingly simple things with extraordinary finesse.

## Early Intervention

Research of the past several decades has led to increasing emphasis on early intervention (Kauffman, 2004; Strain & Timm, 2001; Walker, Ramsey, & Gresham, 2004). Early intervention does not mean merely intervention beginning when the child is young. It also means intervening before misconduct has become a more serious problem.

Teachers tend to wait until misbehavior goes through its earliest stages and has become intolerable before attempting to address it. Misbehavior tends to proceed through a predictable cycle, from a state of calm to a crisis state. It is much more effective to take action at the earliest indications of problem behavior to prevent misconduct from developing further (Kauffman et al., 2002; Smith & Churchill, 2002; Walker et al., 2004). In using an early intervention strategy, the teacher makes a special effort to give students attention when they are calm, compliant, and on task.

**Council for Exceptional Children**

**CEC Knowledge Check**
If early intervention in behavioral problems is so effective, why do early intervention efforts meet resistance from many in education? CC1S1, CC9S3

## Instructions

In approaching behavioral problems, it is easy to overlook the most obvious and simplest of intervention strategies—telling students what you want them to do. Besides good instruction (teaching), providing instructions is perhaps the most overlooked skill in behavior management. Research suggests that teachers and parents often make serious errors in the way they give instructions to children and youths, mishandling in the most mundane ways the simplest instructional interactions (Kauffman, Mostert et al., 2002).

Giving good instructions and following them up with appropriate monitoring and consequences is not as simple as it might seem. Teachers must give their directions simply and clearly, in a firm but polite and nonangry voice, and when the student is paying attention. Too many instructions at a time will confuse students. To be effective, the teacher must monitor the student's compliance, give the student a reasonable amount of time to obey, and follow through with consequences. Students need recognition and social praise for following instructions and mild negative consequences for failing to comply (see Walker et al., 2004).

## Models

Showing students how to behave—providing observable examples or models—is often a highly effective instructional strategy. Teachers should set good examples by their own behavior, but in addition, they should use peer models. However, a review of the research on modeling and regular classroom environments suggests that if peer models are to be effective, the teacher must make sure that students see and understand exactly what they are to imitate and that they receive reinforcement for imitation (Hallenbeck & Kauffman, 1995). Moreover, the modeled performance must be something the student can do. Students are more likely to imitate models they see as like themselves. Modeling alone is likely to be effective only for students who are already highly motivated. Strong positive reinforcement for imitating desirable models will be required for most students with emotional or behavioral problems.

### Choices

A simple but frequently overlooked technique of managing emotional or behavioral problems is giving students choices. All of us are likely to be more compliant with authority when we have the power to make choices that are important to us. Conversely, we often behave badly when we feel "boxed in," perceiving that we have no alternatives. The alert teacher finds ways to give students meaningful choices about classroom tasks. Master teachers understand that they must structure options for students in order to prevent catastrophic consequences; however, the options also must foster interest and personal responsibility (Jolivette, Wehby, Canale, & Massey, 2001; Kern, Bambara, & Fogt, 2002).

Constructing alternatives is a simple strategy that can be used very creatively and often successfully to manage problem behavior. These options may seem trivial to some teachers, but to students, they may be significant. The choices may be as simple as which assignment or problem to do first, which assignment from an array of acceptable alternatives to choose, or even what color paper or pen to use or where to sit for a particular activity. Also, students might be allowed to choose one of two or more tangible rewards or special activities when they have earned it or to pick a friend with whom to work. The Effective Practices box on page 215 illustrates how one teacher used choice of academic assignments to deal with the undesirable behavior of a student with ADHD in a general classroom.

Research shows that for some students with emotional or behavioral problems, choices increase achievement and decrease problem behavior (Powell & Nelson, 1997). However, being given a choice of activity may be more effective in reducing behavior problems for students whose primary motivation is to escape from academic demands (they want to get out of doing a task) than for students who are motivated primarily by getting attention from others (Romaniuk, Miltenberger, Conyers, Jenner, Jurgens, & Ringenberg, 2002).

### Positive Reinforcement

The staple of effective behavior management is positive reinforcement—supplying effective reinforcing consequences for the behavior one wishes to encourage (Alberto & Troutman, 2003; Kauffman, Mostert et al., 2002; Kerr & Nelson, 2002; Rhode et al., 1992; Walker et al., 2004). Positive reinforcement is elegantly simple in concept (i.e., reward the behavior you want), but teachers must make astute choices about what and how to reinforce and must practice the procedure so they can use it with finesse and maximum effect. Finding words, activities, or tangible things that are effective reinforcers for individual students who are "tough kids" may present a real challenge (Rhode et al., 1992; Walker, 1995). Giving the right amount or magnitude of reinforcers and making them accessible only for desired behavior are critical.

Positive reinforcement is likely to be most effective when it includes variety and choice of reinforcers. Other variables that determine how effective reinforcement

Council for Exceptional Children

**CEC Knowledge Check**
What is the best way that teachers can help students advance toward self-control and self-advocacy? How does allowing students to explore, identify, and rationalize their choices affect their intrinsic motivation? CC4S5, CC5S8, CC5S9, CC7S14

# Using Choices to Reduce Undesirable Behavior

The following case example in which choices are used to reduce undesirable behavior is related by Powell and Nelson (1997):

> Evan was a 7-year-old boy who had been diagnosed with ADHD. . . . Prior to this study, his teacher described the majority of his behaviors as undesirable. . . . Evan had poor peer relations and did not understand second-grade work.
>
> This study was conducted in Evan's classroom. Observations were taken during language arts instruction between 1:30 and 2:00 P.M., when Evan's undesirable behaviors were reported to be the most severe. . . . For Evan, undesirable behavior included noncompliance, being away from his desk, disturbing others, staring off, and not doing work. . . .
>
> For both the choice and no-choice conditions, Evan's classroom assignments were given by the teacher. During data collection in the baseline no-choice phases, Evan was directed to work on the same assignment as the rest of the class. During the choice phases, the teacher presented Evan with three different language arts assignments taken from the class curriculum, and he chose one to complete. The assignment choices were identical in length and difficulty. They varied in content (e.g., spelling lists, silent reading assignments, grammar and punctuation exercises, etc.) because they were taken from the language arts assignments the class was completing. In addition, the assignment choices varied, and Evan was not given the same choice of assignments twice. . . .
>
> Compared to no-choice conditions, Evan's levels of undesirable behaviors decreased during choice conditions. . . . [See Figure A.]
>
> These results suggest that choice procedures may be helpful to educators in managing the behaviors of students in general education classrooms.

## Questions to Ponder

What do you think were the most serious of Evan's behavior problems?

What additional interventions, besides choices, might Evan's teacher have considered?

What might Evan's teacher have done to increase the chances that Evan would imitate the appropriate peer models in his class?

**FIGURE A** Percentage of Intervals Rated as Containing Undesirable Behaviors across Conditions

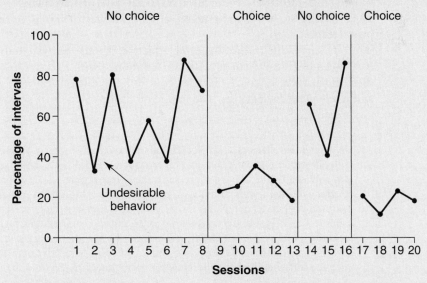

*Source:* From "Effects of Choosing Academic Assignments on a Student with Attention Deficit Hyperactivity Disorder" by S. Powell and B. Nelson, 1997, *Journal of Applied Behavior Analysis, 30,* pp. 181–183. Copyright 1997 by Journal of Applied Behavior Analysis. Reprinted by permission.

**Council** for
**Exceptional**
**Children**

**CEC Knowledge Check**
Are these behavior inter-
vention strategies also
appropriate for use with
any student exhibiting
behavior problems?
Why?
CC4S5, CC5K2, CC5K3,
CC5S10, CC5S11

will be include immediacy and frequency of the reinforcement, enthusiasm of the teacher, description of the behavior being reinforced, anticipation of receiving reinforcement, and eye contact with the teacher (Rhode et al., 1992). Furthermore, the effort required to obtain the reinforcer, the quality of the reinforcer, and the availability of other competing reinforcers will likely alter the effectiveness of positive reinforcement.

### Social Skills

A notion first popularized in the 1980s is that social skills can be readily assessed and taught through explicit training. Although social skills and social competence are notoriously difficult to define, programs to teach such skills have been designed to improve students' perceptions and understanding of social interactions through modeling the skill to be learned, shaping approximations of the skill through verbal cues and reinforcement, and providing rehearsal or guided practice. In other words, effective social skills training requires the masterful use of all the teaching procedures discussed to this point. Social skills may be taught directly or through books in which the social skills of characters are analyzed and the perspectives of various characters are considered (e.g., Cartledge & Kiarie, 2001; Lo, Loe, & Cartledge, 2002).

Intuitively, social skills training seems to offer great promise, because the majority of students with learning disabilities have serious problems of social competence. However, analyses of research on social skills training offer only scant evidence that it has been an effective strategy (Kavale & Forness, 1995; Sridhar & Vaughn, 2001). The results of these programs may be disappointing because the social skills training has been too brief, been given to students who are already socially skilled, or did not follow a well-designed and field-tested curriculum. The training may too often have focused on social skills deficits themselves, rather than on correcting the low achievement that may have resulted in poor self-esteem and peer rejection.

If social skills training is to be effective, it must be systematic, prolonged, based on a field-tested curriculum, and combined with effective instruction to address the academic failure that may contribute to low self-esteem, peer rejection, and inadequate social skills. The implications for teachers of young children can be summarized:

> When educators implement social skills interventions, it is recommended that they provide modeling and prompting of appropriate social skills as well as opportunities for children to practice the social skills they are learning. . . . For some children, especially children with disabilities, providing opportunities to practice social skills without explicit teaching may not be enough to improve their social skills. For these children, teachers should consider (a) providing explicit modeling on not only what a specific social skill is but also how it is used, (b) systematically prompting children's use of appropriate social behaviors, and (c) providing extensive opportunities to practice the social skills that children learn. (Vaughn, Kim, Sloan, Hughes, Elbaum, & Sridhar, 2003, p. 13)

## Discouraging Undesired Behavior

This point cannot be overemphasized: *Correcting behavior problems requires that procedures for teaching desired behavior already be in place.* Traditional discipline has tended to emphasize punitive procedures for misbehavior rather than positive procedures for teaching and correction. Yet positive procedures designed to instruct and strengthen desired behavior are more effective in the long run and create a classroom climate in which students are more likely to learn. Hence, teachers should use the most positive procedures possible and be very cautious in the use of procedures designed to discourage unwanted behavior—particularly, the procedures that constitute punishment (Lerman & Vorndran, 2002).

*Punishment* has a technical definition in behavioral psychology that is often misunderstood by the general public and can easily be misused or abused (see Kauffman, 2005; Rhode et al., 1992; Walker et al., 2004). Punishment is any consequence that reduces the future probability of a particular behavior (Alberto & Troutman, 2003). Punishment is, in fact, a natural phenomenon that happens with or without human planning. It behooves teachers to learn how to use punishment effectively and humanely (Vollmer, 2002). Used skillfully and humanely, it is a legitimate if not indispensable tool in the classroom. Not all misbehavior can be anticipated, and proactive behavior intervention plans do not prevent all misconduct. Therefore, teachers must have additional humane and effective procedures for discouraging students' misbehavior.

The consequences that educators intend to be punishing (e.g., shouting, criticizing, lecturing, or sending a student out of the classroom) often are not. In fact, such intended punishing consequences are often highly rewarding for obstreperous students. Effective punishment need not cause pain or embarrassment. In fact, corporal punishment and strategies that rely on embarrassment or humiliation place educators at risk of legal sanctions and cannot be justified on ethical grounds. Used properly and as a secondary strategy to supplement positive strategies for teaching expected behavior, some forms of nonviolent punishment are appropriate and legally and morally defensible. However, strategies other than punishment (some of which we have already discussed) may discourage misbehavior, and these are always preferable when punishment is not required to resolve a problem.

### Response Cost

The most effective and defensible type of punishment involves withdrawing a privilege or reward contingent on a particular unacceptable behavior. This type of punishment is known as **response cost,** because the unacceptable response "costs" a privilege or reward. It is, in effect, a "fine" levied for inappropriate behavior. For example, suppose that a student who frequently disturbs others in the class finds it highly reinforcing to sit with his friends rather than next to the teacher at lunch. This student might be given five points (perhaps represented as symbols on an index card) at the beginning of the day, with the understanding that if he still has two or more points at lunchtime, he will be allowed to sit with his friends at lunch.

**response cost**
punishment technique consisting of taking away a valued object or commodity contingent on a behavior; a fine; making an inappropriate response "cost" something to the misbehaving child

## Ms. Hamilton Uses Response Cost with Jamal

Jamal's first-grade teacher, Ms. Hamilton, wrote reports of her problems and successes. One of her reports read, in part, as follows:

I found a response cost procedure effective in helping Jamal follow directions. First, I kept some daily records to determine the extent of the problem and help me find a reasonable expectation for Jamal. By keeping track, I found out that I usually gave Jamal (either him individually or the group he was in) 10 to 12 directions per day. I also found that Jamal sometimes followed my instructions, but he didn't on average 6 times per day (his failure to do what I asked ranged from 3 to 8 times). I explained to Jamal that following my instructions or directions about what to do was really important. I even role-played following instructions for Jamal to make sure he understood what following directions meant. Then I explained that I was going to tape a piece of paper to his desk each morning that would have 6 happy faces on it. If he followed my direction to do something, that was good. However, if he did not follow a direction, I would just mark one of the happy faces with an *X*. If at the end of the day he had at least one happy face left that was not marked out, then he could lead his bus line. However, if he had none left, then he would have to be last in line. As he got better at following directions, I gradually lowered the number of happy faces he started the day with to 2, but I still marked one out each time he failed to follow an instruction. I never started with less than 2. I didn't want him to get the idea that I expected absolute perfection, so he could always lose one and still have one left for his reward.

**Council for Exceptional Children**

**CEC Knowledge Check**

What other kinds of punishment can be used to achieve the desired behavioral results? CC5S10

The teacher will mark off one point each time he disturbs another student. An unacceptable behavior (disturbing others) costs him a point; if he loses more than three of his five points, he loses a special privilege.

Response cost, like positive reinforcement, is a simple idea that requires careful implementation if it is to work well. If managed well, the withdrawal of rewards and privileges is less likely than other punishment procedures to produce aggression and lead to legal liabilities. The wise teacher consults and follows detailed guides for using such procedures (e.g., Alberto & Troutman, 2003; Kerr & Nelson, 2002; Rhode et al., 1992; Walker, 1995; Walker et al., 2004).

You may recall that one of Jamal's problems was that he often did not follow directions. The Case Connections box above is an example of how Jamal's teacher used response cost effectively.

Jamal

### Positive Reinforcement of Alternative Behavior

The preferred tactic for discouraging undesirable behavior is reinforcing competing or incompatible behavior—replacing undesirable behavior with expected behavior by using positive reinforcement rather than punishment (Kauffman, Mostert et al., 2002; Kerr & Nelson, 2002; Walker et al., 2004). Choosing the particular behaviors to reinforce is a key issue. Competing behaviors are those that are difficult to do simultaneously. Incompatible behaviors are those that are impossible to do at the same time. Misbehavior can sometimes be successfully discouraged simply by offering reinforcement for expected behavior that makes misbehavior more difficult or impossible. For example, reinforcing attention to and completion of seat work makes out-of-seat behavior less likely; doing seat work and being out of the seat are competing behaviors. Reinforcing in-seat behavior tends to decrease out-of-seat behavior because in-seat and out-of-seat behaviors are incompatible; they cannot be done at the same time. The suggestion is simply this: Focus first on using positive reinforcement for appropriate behavior as a means of correcting behavior problems, and then give thought to reinforcing specific behaviors that make concurrent misbehavior more difficult or impossible.

Another way to use positive reinforcement to decrease behavior problems is to make reinforcement contingent on the problem behavior not occurring at all or occurring less than a stated number of times for a specific period. For example, earning a rewarding consequence might depend on a student's not talking out or talking out less than three times during a 20-minute lesson. Rewarding the omission or reduced level of undesirable behavior is a strategy that can be used very effectively with many types of classroom behaviors. As with other strategies, however, reinforcement requires careful attention to detail and understanding of the behavior principles on which it is based (Alberto & Troutman, 2003; Kerr & Nelson, 2002).

## PORTFOLIO-BUILDING ACTIVITY

### Demonstrating Mastery of the CEC Standards

**Council for Exceptional Children**

**CEC Content Standards**
5. Learning Environments and Social Interactions
8. Assessment

Use the information on Jamal in the Case Connections box to create a proactive behavior management plan that you can use in your classroom. Write your document in narrative format, with headings.

- What specific behavior problem is Jamal having that needs to be changed?
- What desired behavior does the teacher want to instate for Jamal?
- What type of education method is being used to manage the behavior problem?
- What are the specific components of the method Jamal's teacher is using as they are mentioned in Chapter 7?
- Is this the most effective method for the teacher to use with Jamal? Defend your answer.

Pick another behavior management method and describe in detail the implementation steps you would use in planning a proactive program for Jamal. Defend your choice of the method. Questions to think about as you progress:

- What needs to be done to create a learning environment for individuals with learning disabilities that fosters cultural understanding yet promotes emotional well-being, active engagement, and positive social interactions?

- What are the tools educators can use to encourage student personal empowerment and independence?

- How can you use direct motivational and instructional interventions to teach students with learning disabilities to respond effectively to current expectations?

- Why is it important to regularly monitor the progress of students with learning disabilities in making ongoing educational decisions?

# SUMMARY

## What is the link between learning disabilities and social, emotional, and behavioral problems?

- Not all students with learning disabilities have social, emotional, or behavioral problems. However, the full range of other emotional and behavioral problems may accompany learning disabilities. A majority of students with learning disabilities present behavior management problems for teachers.

- Problems of social competence include difficulties in using social skills effectively, avoiding maladaptive behavior, developing positive relations with others, and acquiring age-appropriate social cognition. Such problems may have a negative influence on the self-concepts of students with learning disabilities. However, the issue of self-concept is complex, and low achievement may be the primary factor responsible for lowered self-concepts of students with learning disabilities.

- Conduct problems include overt antisocial behavior—such as aggression, tantrums, noncompliance, disruption—and covert antisocial behavior—such as lying and stealing. These problems are common among students with learning disabilities, who are overrepresented among youths detained by the juvenile justice system.

- Other emotional or behavioral problems, such as anxiety and depression, may accompany learning disabilities.

## What are the major causes of social, emotional, and behavioral problems?

- All potential causes of learning disabilities are potential causes of emotional or behavioral problems, including biological, family, cultural, and school factors. Teachers should be particularly concerned about causes related to schooling, including inadequate instructional programs, inappropriate expectations, insensitivity to students' individuality, reinforcement of undesirable behavior, inconsistency in behavior management, and inappropriate models.

**Council for Exceptional Children**

**CEC Knowledge Check**
Because learning disabilities and behavioral problems are closely linked, does having a problem in one area create a concern about the other area? CC1K2, CC1K4

## How should we address the characteristics of social, emotional, and behavioral problems?

- Like academic assessment, the assessment of emotional or behavioral problems should guide intervention. IDEA now requires that the behavior problems of students with disabilities be assessed in ways that will help in writing IEPs.

- Systematic screening is often not done because of the number of problems that would likely be detected.

However, a useful multiple-gating procedure (the SSBD) is available for screening students for internalizing and externalizing problems. A major concern in screening, and in all other aspects of assessment, is cultural sensitivity.

- Prereferral strategies provide useful information regardless of whether the student is later found to be eligible for special education.

- A functional behavioral assessment (FBA) is required for addressing behavior problems. The FBA is designed to identify the reasons for the student's behavior (its function or goal) and suggest alternative ways the student might achieve the same goal with more appropriate behavior.

- IDEA also requires that all students with disabilities who have behavior problems have a behavioral assessment and a behavior intervention plan (BIP) included in their IEP. The behavior intervention plan must delineate expected behaviors, inappropriate behaviors, positive and negative consequences, disciplinary procedures, and procedures for handling behavioral crises.

- There are other possible legal aspects of dealing with behavior problems, including the manifestation determination—deciding whether the behavior is or is not a manifestation of the student's disability.

### What are the main educational methods used for social, emotional, and behavioral problems?

- The focus of intervention should be on proactive plans for teaching appropriate behavior, not reaction to misconduct. IDEA requires proactive behavior intervention plans as well as plans for dealing with discipline and behavioral crises.

- Modifying the learning environment for proactive management is a key concept. Precorrection is a proactive teaching plan that appears to be consistent with IDEA requirements. It is a way of anticipating predictable misbehavior in particular contexts and devising a strategy for teaching expected behavior. Precorrection involves describing the context of misbehavior, stating the expected behavior, modifying the context, planning rehearsal of the expected behavior, arranging strong reinforcement for exhibiting the expected behavior, arranging prompts or cues to perform the expected behavior, and devising a monitoring plan.

- Teaching appropriate behavior requires early intervention and effective use of instructions, models, choices, positive reinforcement, and instruction in social skills.

- Effective strategies for discouraging undesired behavior are important, because not all misbehavior can be anticipated and proactive behavior intervention does not prevent all misconduct. Punishment has a technical definition—a consequence that reduces the likelihood of a particular behavior. Though punishment can be abused and some forms (e.g., corporal punishment) cannot be defended, certain forms of nonviolent punishment are defensible.
  - Response cost punishment means withdrawing rewards or privileges contingent on particular misbehaviors.
  - Positive reinforcement of alternative behavior is preferred to punishment and may involve rewarding specific competing or incompatible behaviors or giving rewards for omitting particular misbehaviors.

## REFLECTIONS ON THE CASES

1. What skills do you think Shannon needs to be taught if she is to become socially competent and have the friends she wants?

2. If you were going to plan early intervention for Jamal to capitalize on his strengths and avoid behavior problems, what would you suggest?

3. If you were advising the teachers of Shannon and Jamal on behavior management, what strategies would you stress for each?

## How Can We Explain Learning and Memory?

- Information-Processing Theory

## What Do We Know about the Learning and Memory of Students with Learning Disabilities?

- Learning Styles
- Cognitive Styles
- Memory Abilities
- Metacognitive or Executive Control Abilities
- Motivation

## How Can Learning, Memory, and Motivation Needs Be Addressed?

- Self-Instruction
- Self-Monitoring of Academic Performance
- Self-Determination
- Mnemonic Strategies
- Attribution Training
- Cognitive Strategies
- General Teaching Practices to Activate Learning and Memory

Council for Exceptional Children

See Companion Website for detailed correlations between chapter content and Council for Exceptional Children Standards; **www.ablongman.com/ hallahanLD3e**

### CEC Knowledge and Skills Discussed in This Chapter

1. The educational, cognitive, social, and emotional implications of auditory and information-processing learning disability characteristics.

2. Research-supported instructional approaches and technologies used to address deficits in academic and nonacademic skills across environments.

3. Selection and adaptation of specialized procedures used to promote self-advocacy, cognitive problem solving, and self-esteem and to address cognitive processing in the academic content areas of mathematics, reading/vocabulary, and test-taking.

4. Assisting students with learning disabilities to learn how they can use their own errors to guide their learning growth and locus of control.

5. Cultural perspectives that impact interactions with students and families positively and negatively.

# Cognition, Metacognition, and Memory in Students with Learning Disabilities

**8**

I know I won't make it in algebra—there's just too much to learn. Even now in math, I sometimes just give up because there is no way that I can remember all the facts *and* how to do the problem. It doesn't really matter if I study or not.

*Shannon*

The overall goal of most parents and teachers is to help children become self-regulated learners. Self-regulated learners are those who

> show initiative and independence in learning. Their motivation to learn is clearly reflected in the commitment of effort in learning. More important, such effort is sustained and unwavering despite possible setbacks and distractions from task completion. Their focus and determination in learning indicate a will to reach academic success. Upon successful task completion, self-regulated learners give themselves due reinforcement (a pat on the back), and through appropriate attributions of success of academic goal attainment, they increase their own sense of self-efficacy. (Wong, 1996, p. 120)

Defined in this way, self-regulation includes many aspects, including cognition, metacognition, and motivation. In this chapter, we describe the information-processing theory, which includes these components in memory and learning, the difficulties that students with learning disabilities have in these areas, and instructional strategies that have been successful in meeting the challenges of these students. (Chapter 9 includes a discussion of attention.)

# How Can We Explain Learning and Memory?

**cognition**   the ability to think and solve problems

**metacognition**   the ability to think about thinking

**attention**   ability to concentrate

**motivation**   desire to engage in and sustain effort for tasks

Learning and memory include **cognition** (our ability to think), **metacognition** (our ability to think about thinking), **attention** (our ability to concentrate), and **motivation** (our desire to engage in all three). In many ways, all four are interconnected: A person who has a problem with one is likely to have problems with one or more of the others. In addition, educational methods developed for each of these areas are frequently similar. It is important to understand how these components interact so that learning takes place.

## Information-Processing Theory

**information-processing theory**   theory of how information is learned or remembered in the brain, including components of sensory register, short-term memory, working memory, and long-term memory

**sensory register**   component of the memory system in which information is received and held for very short periods of time

Learning and memory are complex and there are many theories about them. One of the current dominant theories is called the **information-processing theory** (Slavin, 2003), which describes several components of a learning or memory system. It is important to keep in mind that these components work in concert and are not isolated or separate entities within the brain. In this theory, incoming information enters the **sensory register** from each of the senses (e.g., eyes, ears). If nothing happens to the information, it is lost. If attention is given to the information, then it moves to the short-term memory. For example, a student may concentrate (or not) on a teacher's directions while at the same time hear the pencil sharpener run, smell the perfume of the girl next to him, and feel how hard the chair is on which he is sitting. It is the teacher's hope that her instructions are the bit of information that moves to short-term memory. The sensory register holds information for a fraction of a second before moving it on or losing it.

### Short-Term Memory

**short-term memory**   the ability to remember information over a few seconds to a minute or two at most

Next, information moves to **short-term memory,** which holds information for a short time before it is either discarded or passed to working memory for processing. Short-term memory is, in essence, a holding tank where information can be rehearsed (repeated) but otherwise not processed. The capacity of short-term memory can be assessed by asking individuals to repeat a series of numbers or letters that increase with each trial (e.g., 1, 3, 5; 1, 3, 5, 7). Short-term memory sorts information into that to be processed and that to be discarded from the sensory register.

### Working Memory

**working memory**   the ability to keep a small amount of information in mind while carrying out further mental operations

**chunking**   breaking memory tasks into several smaller tasks

**clustering**   grouping information to be remembered based on categories

**rehearsing**   repeating information over and over in order to remember it

In **working memory,** the brain actively processes the information it receives (hence the term *working*) while simultaneously performing another cognitive task. For example, working memory may try to connect the incoming information with information that is already in long-term memory storage, or it may choose another strategy to organize the information for storage, such as **chunking** (breaking it into tasks), **clustering** (grouping it into categories), or **rehearsing** (repeating it). Information in working memory may be lost due to interference (other information comes in that crowds it out), displacement (other information comes in that supersedes it), or decay (information is not processed). Working memory capacity varies but is small in comparison to long-term memory capacity, so information is held there for short periods of time.

## Long-Term Memory

The final storage step for information is **long-term memory.** We store information in long-term memory for long periods of time, and there is virtually infinite capacity within it. Long-term memory stores information in a variety of ways. **Episodic memory** includes images of experiences we have had, and these memories are organized by space and time. **Semantic memory** "contains the facts and generalized information that we know; concepts, principles, or rules and how to use them; and our problem-solving skills and learning strategies" (Slavin, 2003, p. 179). These memories are organized in interconnected series, or networks, called **schemata.** These schemata help a student fit new knowledge into what is already known. Finally, **procedural memory** stores information about how to do things that are relatively automatic, such as driving a car or riding a bike, and these memories are organized in a series of stimulus-response pairings (Slavin, 2003).

## Executive Control or Metacognitive Processes

An **executive control** oversees the information-processing system and is often viewed as part of working memory. This executive control has three main functions: **task analysis, strategy** control (selection and revision), and **strategy monitoring** (Borkowski & Burke, 1996). In other words, it focuses and maintains attention, chooses problem-solving activities, applies strategies, monitors success or failure, and activates motivation. It is in this center that the decisions about how to remember or to learn take place—the metacognitive component of learning.

## Motivation

Motivation is the "internal process that activates, guides, and maintains behavior over time" (Slavin, 2003, p. 329). Many authorities have noted the close link between metacognition and motivation. As some have put it:

> The absence of vivid, dynamic, and functional possible selves may inhibit the emergence of executive processing, especially in challenging, demanding situations (i.e., a failure to aspire to a college career may not only restrict the choice of college preparatory courses but also produce less reflective, deliberate decision-making activities in many academically related areas). Hence, an immature developmental connection between the emerging self and executive systems likely prolongs or exacerbates academic difficulties for students who are underachievers or have learning impairments. (Borkowski & Burke, 1996, p. 240)

Motivation affects strategy use and monitoring, but even researchers specializing in this are not quite sure how (Meltzer & Montague, 2001). The components of motivation that lead to appropriate executive functioning seem to be positive

---

**long-term memory** the components of memory in which large amounts of information can be stored for long periods of time

**episodic memory** a part of long-term memory that stores images of our personal experiences

**semantic memory** a part of long-term memory that stores facts and general knowledge

Council for Exceptional Children

**CEC Knowledge Check**
If a student with a learning disability has an information-processing deficit, what might this look like in terms of short- and long-term memory skills? LD3K3

**schemata** mental networks of related concepts that influence understanding of new information

**procedural memory** a part of long-term memory that stores information about how to do things

**executive control** a component of information processing that analyzes a task, chooses a strategy to attack a task, and revises and monitors the strategy

**task analysis** determining the necessary steps and prerequisites to complete a task

**strategy** approach to a task

**strategy monitoring** reflection on whether or not an approach to a task is successful

**self-esteem** the value each of us places on our own characteristics, abilities, and behaviors

**locus of control** the degree to which one views oneself as being controlled by internal or external forces

Shannon

**attributional beliefs** how people explain the causes of their own successes and failures

**CEC Knowledge Check**
What are some long-term educational implications for students with learning disabilities, given the information on metacognition and motivation? CC2K2, CC3K1

**self-esteem,** an internal **locus of control,** and effort-related **attributional beliefs.** In other words, for effective executive functioning, students need to believe that they can accomplish a task, that they are in control of the outcomes, and that their effort will result in positive outcomes. Figure 8.1 shows Borkowski's theory of the interrelationship of metacognition and motivation (Borkowski & Burke, 1996).

Before we begin our discussion of the characteristics of students with learning disabilities, let's take a look at Shannon's opening quote.

> I know I won't make it in algebra—there's just too much to learn. Even now in math, I sometimes just give up because there is no way that I can remember all the facts *and* how to do the problem. It doesn't really matter if I study or not.
>
> *Shannon*

From the quote, we can guess that Shannon is having difficulties in the areas of metacognition, memory, and motivation. Her statement "There is no way that I can remember all the facts" indicates that she has a difficult time storing and retrieving facts from long-term memory. She also has a difficult time retrieving the algorithms from long-term memory. Both of these problems may be due to a lack of strategies available in working memory to transfer the information to long-term memory, inadequate practice of strategies to get the information into long-term memory, or a lack of understanding about what to use when. These problems may also stem from her executive control choosing ineffective strategies and not monitoring success or failure. Whatever the case, Shannon's motivation for math is declining, as evidenced by her statement "It doesn't really matter if I study or not." (For more information about her areas of strengths and weaknesses, see the Case Connections box on pages 228–229.)

## What Do We Know about the Learning and Memory of Students with Learning Disabilities?

Researchers have studied the learning and memory characteristics of students with learning disabilities with interest because of the disparity between what we think they can learn and what they actually are learning in school. This research has led to many advances in instruction, such as the teaching of cognitive learning strategies, but also to some false starts, such as learning styles. It is important to remember that though we can describe characteristics of a general population of students with learning disabilities, the performance of individuals with learning disabilities will vary based on their individual strengths and weaknesses and on task demands.

FIGURE 8.1    The Interrelationship of Metacognition and Motivation

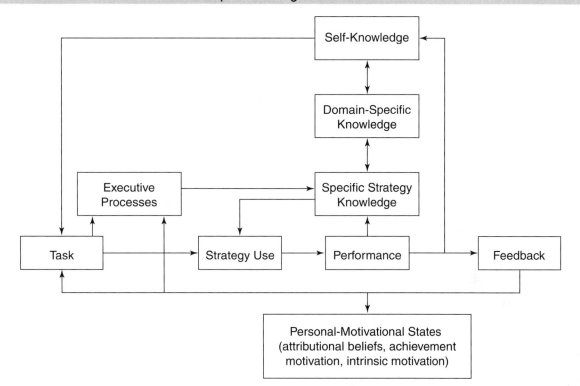

*Source:* Adapted from "Theories, Models, and Measurements of Executive Functioning: An Information Processing Perspective" (p. 240), by J. G. Borkowski and J. E. Burke, 1996, in G. R. Lyon and N. A. Krasnegor (Eds.), *Attention, Memory, and Executive Function,* Baltimore, MD: Paul H. Brookes Publishing Co. Copyright 1996 by Paul H. Brookes. Reprinted by permission.

## Learning Styles

The language test that had the greatest influence on the field of learning disabilities is the *Illinois Test of Psycholinguistic Abilities,* or ITPA (Kirk, McCarthy, & Kirk, 1968; see also Kirk, 1976). There is also a recent revision of the test (Hammill, Mather, & Roberts, 2001). The ITPA was designed to allow clinicians to assess specific processes presumed to be associated with school success. The history of the instrument (Kirk, 1969, 1976) reveals that its purpose was to enable identification of a student's deficit areas and then adjust instruction to meet that student's individual needs. The presumption underlying this approach is that individuals have unique strengths and weaknesses that can be identified by examining performance on tasks that tap specific skills.

Performance on just one subtest rarely formed the basis for diagnoses and prescriptions. Most students showed general patterns of strengths and weaknesses. For

## Shannon's Metacognition and Memory: Strengths and Weaknesses

Shannon's evaluation data indicate that she has both strengths and weaknesses in areas of metacognition and memory. Let's take a look at some examples from her reports.

**Teacher Reports**

Shannon is currently an eighth grader at Bishop Memorial Middle School. She receives one period of resource assistance from a special educator daily and one period of collaborative math daily, wherein the special education teacher works in the general education classroom with the math teacher. Her academic grades are English language arts A-, social studies A, earth science D, and math D. Her science grade is low because Shannon did not do well on tests. Her teacher reports that she has problems grasping new concepts and applying learned facts to new situations. Although she pays attention in class during direct instruction, she is very unengaged when involved in cooperative learning activities. Her math teacher reports that basic math facts and sequential operations are weak, but basic concepts and problem solving are a relative strength. She is attentive some of the time and somewhat disorganized but turns assignments in on time in math. Shannon's social studies teacher reports that she actively participates in class discussions and seems eager to learn more about the subject matter. Her English teacher reports that she likes creative writing and expressing her opinions about what she has read but still has some problems with some mechanics in writing. Her special education teacher reinforces whatever skills the language arts teacher is trying to teach. In resource, Shannon uses her time wisely; however, sometimes she complains because she wants to use the class as a study hall instead of a time to get extra drill and practice in her weak areas. Left on her own, though, she seems to forget what she is doing and dawdles and daydreams. Classroom observations reveal that Shannon sometimes experiences anxiety when taking a test. For example, when given a science test, she missed several ques-

example, some generally scored better on subtests assessing the visual-motor channel; others scored better on subtests assessing the auditory-vocal channel. The former might be called "visual learners," and the latter, "auditory learners."

**learning styles**
orientations for approaching learning tasks and processing information in certain ways

Today people readily recognize these terms; they are called **learning styles.** But in the 1960s and 1970s, the ITPA offered the first carefully developed means of determining learning styles. According to the learning styles model, different learners should get different kinds of instruction. If learners scored better on the visual-motor subtests, they should receive instruction that plays to their strengths, not their weaknesses (e.g., using a sight or visual approach to reading). If learners

tions on the first try. After experiencing some success, she was able to go back and correct some of her mistakes.

### Test Results

*Reading.* Shannon missed one easy comprehension question because she answered impulsively. She seemed to apply excellent strategies to help her pick out relative information and answer comprehension questions even when she did not understand every word she was reading.

*Math.* On the word problem subtest, Shannon missed two easy questions because she did not pay attention to detail. Shannon was asked the question "Six children were playing in a park that has 8 swings. If only 2 children are swinging, how many swings are empty?" Shannon responded "Three," because the picture accompanying the question shows three empty swings. She was asked the question "Bob bought a new shirt for $6. The store gave him a $2 belt free. How much did he have to pay for his things?" Shannon responded, "Four." Shannon missed several questions dealing with memorization of basic information.

### Recommendations

Shannon needs instruction in study skills. She needs help learning strategies and techniques to help her memorize facts for tests.

Shannon's IEP gives examples of goals and objectives that are geared toward improvement of her metacognitive and memory weaknesses.

*Math.* Given multiplication facts with factors of 11 or less, Shannon will give the answer verbally or in written form to each fact within 10 seconds.

Given ten examples, Shannon will solve multistep word problems using any operations.

*Written Language.* Shannon will revise and edit all written work.

*Spelling.* Shannon will recognize and correct misspellings from own writings.

Council for Exceptional Children

CEC Knowledge Check
What do you consider to be Shannon's three most important concerns? Why? What techniques might you use to help Shannon?
LD3K3, CC4S3, LD4S1

---

scored better on the auditory-vocal subtests, they should receive instruction that plays to their strengths (e.g., using a sound-based or phonics approach to reading). This idea of learning best through a certain modality was applied to students with learning disabilities.

The ITPA received substantial criticism (Engelmann, 1967; Hallahan & Cruickshank, 1973; Mann, 1971; Mann & Phillips, 1967; Sedlak & Weiner, 1973; Waugh, 1975; Ysseldyke & Salvia, 1974). People questioned the psychometric adequacy of the instrument (e.g., whether the subtests actually measured what they purported to measure). They also questioned the effectiveness of providing remedial exercises for

Council for
Exceptional
Children

**CEC Knowledge Check**

Is there a sustained body of research proving that teaching according to "learning styles" is a validated practice for students with learning disabilities?
CC4S3, LD4S1

deficits in specific areas (patch-up teaching) and basing instruction on learning styles (e.g., teaching reading only using sight).

The idea of ITPA learning styles has appeared again as various learning styles inventories (e.g., Barsch & Creson, 1980; Dunn, Dunn, & Price, 1976). These models have also received substantial criticism (e.g., Kavale & Forness, 1987; Knapp, 2003; Snider, 1992). Basically, "those who advocate the use of learning styles believe that a student's unique way of processing information can be identified and matched to a particular teaching method and/or classroom environment to enhance learning" (Snider, 1992, p. 6). Even though anecdotal accounts report student gains, a review of research done on the Dunn model indicates that students gained very little on standardized and curriculum-based assessments when taught to their learning style (Kavale and Forness, 1987). Though the term *learning style* is often used in schools, there is little evidence that learning styles can be assessed adequately or used effectively for instruction.

## Cognitive Styles

**cognitive styles** the particular approaches individuals use in problem solving (e.g., impulsive or reflective)

In the 1960s, there was rapid growth in an area of study that came to be called **cognitive styles**—ways of approaching problem-solving tasks. The two cognitive styles that have received the most attention, first in populations without learning disabilities and then in populations with learning disabilities, were the dimensions of field independence–field dependence and reflectivity-impulsivity.

### Field Independence versus Field Dependence

**field independence–field dependence** the degree to which people are influenced by their environment when asked to make decisions on perceptual tasks

The concept of **field independence–field dependence** refers to how much individuals are influenced by their physical surroundings when asked to make decisions on perceptual tasks. Persons who are heavily influenced by their environment are considered field dependent. Their perceptions are less accurate because they can be "thrown off" by misleading information in their environment. Individuals who are able to focus on the most essential perceptual data without being influenced by inessential details are referred to as field independent. Their perceptions tend to be more accurate than those of persons who are field dependent.

Researchers have used several methods to assess field independence. In the most elaborate one, the person is seated on a chair within a small room. Both the chair and the room can be tilted by the experimenter and the person in the chair. After both the chair and room are tilted so that neither is in a vertical position, the individual is requested to "right" the chair to the true vertical. Those who are able to ignore cues from the room and place the chair in a position close to true vertical are categorized as field independent. Those who cannot are classified as field dependent. Children become more field independent with age (Witkin, Goodenough, & Karp, 1967). Children who have learning disabilities are generally more field dependent than their nondisabled peers (Blackman & Goldstein, 1982).

**reflectivity-impulsivity** the degree to which a person takes time to reflect on alternatives before making a choice

### Reflectivity versus Impulsivity

The idea of **reflectivity-impulsivity** refers to whether a person takes time to reflect on various alternatives before making a choice on difficult but solvable tasks. Most studies of reflectivity-impulsivity have used a visual-perceptual matching task. The child is presented with line drawings of familiar figures (e.g., car, teddy bear, etc.) one at a time and is asked to pick one exactly like it from several figures (Kagan, Rosman, Day, Albert, & Phillips, 1964). Two things are recorded: (1) response time, or how long it takes the child to make the first choice, and (2) errors, or how many incorrect choices the child makes before getting the correct answer. Reflective children respond more slowly and make fewer errors, whereas impulsive children respond quickly but make many errors.

Researchers have generally found the reflectivity-impulsivity dimension to be developmentally sensitive, with children becoming more reflective with age. Students with learning disabilities are more apt to be impulsive than are their nondisabled peers (Blackman & Goldstein, 1982).

Cognitive style research was immediately appealing to special education practitioners. Teachers and school psychologists could easily associate laboratory researchers' findings with their own experiences with students with learning disabilities. Teachers are the first to acknowledge that many of these students do not seem to think before they respond but instead blurt out the first thing that comes into their heads. More educationally oriented researchers made several efforts to train students with learning disabilities to be more reflective. Generally, they found that they could make students more reflective on the perceptual matching task but that this behavior did not carry over to the classroom (Epstein, Hallahan, & Kauffman, 1975).

Even though training did not lead to educational benefits, this early research on cognitive styles has had a substantial impact on how we now view persons with learning disabilities and also on educational programming for them. These studies also laid the groundwork for later work on cognitive and metacognitive training (discussed later in this chapter) by showing that students with learning disabilities do approach problem-solving tasks in a different manner than nondisabled students and that attempting to train them to think in a more "normal" manner is not likely to be successful if the training is based on laboratory tasks rather than on classroom behavior. (See the Multicultural Considerations box on pages 232–233 for a discussion of differences between teachers and their students.)

**Council for Exceptional Children**

**CEC Knowledge Check**
If cognitive and metacognitive training for students with learning disabilities is to be successful, what is an essential component? CC4S2, CC4S3

## Memory Abilities

Much recent research on cognition in students with learning disabilities has focused on memory abilities. Like the work on cognitive styles, the study of memory processes of students with learning disabilities has gained impetus from the fact that teachers see it as relevant to the everyday functioning of these students. Teachers are quick to agree that many students with learning disabilities display significant difficulties with memory. "In one ear and out the other" is a commonly heard phrase when teachers discuss these students.

There are numerous research studies demonstrating that persons with learning disabilities have problems with various types of memory tasks (Beale & Tippett, 1992; Hulme & Snowling, 1992; Swanson & Sachse-Lee, 2001). We briefly explore work on short-term memory, working memory, and executive functioning.

MULTICULTURAL
CONSIDERATIONS

## What Are General and Special Education Teachers' Perceptions of Teaching Strategies for Multicultural Students?

There is much discussion in education about the racial and ethnic differences between teachers in public schools and the students they teach. For example, in the 1996 school year, 74% of the teachers in the United States were women, and 91% were white. In the 1999 school year, 62% of the students in the United States were white, 17% were black, and 16% were Hispanic (National Center for Education Statistics, 2001a, b). Also in the 1999–2000 school year, approximately 82% of all teachers in the United States taught students with IEPs, and 41% of all teachers taught students with limited English proficiency (LEP). Of those teachers, only 31% had received training for eight hours or more in teaching students with IEPs in the last three years, and 12% had received training for LEP (National Center for Education Statistics, 2002). A survey of 403 general and special educators in Kansas (Utley, Delquadri, Obiako, & Mims, 2000) provided more evidence of the difference between the students in the classroom and the teachers who teach them and also provided information about the training needs of these teachers.

The researchers chose 47 school districts with less than 10% of their population identified as multicultural

and 47 school districts with over 10% of their population identified as multicultural. Surveys were sent to principals, who then distributed them to elementary, middle, and high school teachers. The surveys included questions about professional development, cultural knowledge, linguistic foundation, and teaching strategies.

### What Did the Researchers Learn about the Teacher Sample?

Of the 403 respondents, 83% were female, and 93% were Caucasian/Northern European. Seventy-five percent of the teachers taught at least one multicultural student with or without disabilities.

### What Type of Training Did the Teachers Have in Multicultural Education?

Thirty-seven percent of the teachers had no training at all. Those who did receive training identified district and regional workshops as their sources (25%). Only 7% of those who received training received it in their undergraduate education program and 11% in their graduate programs. Reading of professional journals was the most

### Short-Term Memory

Short-term memory tasks can vary in several ways. For example, they can require the retention of auditory or visual information. In a typical auditory short-term memory task, the tester says a series of five to seven digits. After each set of digits, the individual is to repeat as many of the numbers as possible in the correct order. In a typical visual short-term memory task, the person is shown several groups of five to seven pictures. After each set, the person is to say the names of as many pictures as possible in the correct order. Although researchers have found that students with learning disabilities have some problems with visual short-term memory (e.g., Hallahan, Kauffman, & Ball, 1973; Tarver, Hallahan, Kauffman, & Ball, 1976), most research has focused on auditory short-term memory. The evidence that students with learning disabilities perform less well than their nondisabled peers on auditory short-term memory tasks is overwhelming (Hulme & Snowling, 1992).

often cited source of information about multicultural issues (52%).

## How Would Cultural Knowledge Help the Teacher?

Forty percent of the teachers reported that understanding a student's cultural background would help them better understand the student's behavioral and learning styles; 38% said it would help them better assess students; and 37% said it would help them better understand student expectations. Teachers also noted that having more knowledge of a student's cultural heritage would help them increase motivation and facilitate peer interactions.

## What Teaching Strategies Are Most Useful?

Teachers identified the following teaching strategies as the most useful in working with students from culturally and linguistically diverse backgrounds:

1. teacher-student discussion
2. cooperative learning
3. peer tutoring
4. using prompts and cues to elicit active responses
5. preparing students for instruction through discussion
6. directly relating classroom activities to academic objectives
7. providing practice
8. maximizing time in direct instruction activities
9. presenting many examples of new concepts
10. minimizing time in noninstructional transitional activities

## What Does This Mean?

Although this is only one survey, it does correspond to the current literature on multicultural education, particularly as it interacts with special education. It is one of many sources of evidence indicating that (1) the majority of teachers have students in their classrooms from cultures different than their own, (2) many teachers do not receive training in multicultural education issues, (3) teachers are eager for knowledge in this area, and (4) teachers are trying to meet the needs of these students using strategies that may also be effective for students with learning disabilities. There is a continued need for research on effective interventions and effective teacher training to meet the needs of students with learning disabilities who are from culturally and linguistically diverse backgrounds.

Council for Exceptional Children

**CEC Knowledge Check**
In your opinion, are the methodologies presented in this chapter effective across cultures? Or are there cultural differences that would block the teacher's ability to implement with all students? Discuss your reasons.
CC3K4, CC3K5

## *Working Memory*

There is evidence that working memory and executive functioning problems are even more important than short-term memory problems in the reading and math difficulties of students with learning disabilities (Swanson & Ashbaker, 2000; Swanson & Sachse-Lee, 2001; Swanson, 1999, 1994).

In one study of word recognition and reading comprehension, researchers used tasks to assess the **phonological, orthographic,** and **semantic processing** of 40 students with learning disabilities and 40 skilled readers (Swanson & Ashbaker, 2000). In addition, the researchers assessed working memory using tasks such as sentence span (a series of sentences is presented, students are asked comprehension questions about the sentences, and then asked to recall the last word in each sentence), visual-spatial span (identifying whether dots exist in cells in a matrix), and a counting task (counting dots with other items in the picture). Finally, the researchers also assessed metacognitive or executive functioning skill with a questionnaire, a

**phonological processing** processing or understanding spoken-language units

**orthographic processing** processing or understanding written language

**semantic processing** processing or understanding the meaning of written or spoken language

task that requires students to identify inconsistencies in pictures, and a task that requires students to answer inferential questions after listening to or reading a story. In all tasks, the students with learning disabilities performed significantly below the skilled readers. The researchers concluded that working memory abilities predicted how well each group would do on reading comprehension tasks and that students with learning disabilities had difficulty processing information in word recognition and reading comprehension tasks.

In a similar study, researchers investigated the impact of phonological processing, verbal working memory, and visual-spatial working memory in students with learning disabilities in math (Swanson & Sachse-Lee, 2001). The authors concluded that students with learning disabilities have problems with both working memory and with the executive functioning that integrates the long-term and working memory ability to choose and use algorithms.

The description of the memory performance of students with learning disabilities fits Shannon's case. She has difficulty with the storage and retrieval of facts and algorithms. She also has a difficult time choosing strategies to integrate new and previous knowledge. These difficulties cause her to take longer than others in completing math tasks. As Mr. Taylor, Shannon's math teacher, says:

> Shannon has a difficult time working her math problems. It takes her twice as long as the other students to remember the facts and how to do the problem. Sometimes, we'll be working on problem 6 and Shannon is still struggling with 1.
>
> *Winn Taylor, Shannon's math teacher*

## Metacognitive or Executive Control Abilities

Metacognition has two components: (1) an awareness of what is needed in the way of strategies, skills, or resources to perform a task, and (2) an ability to regulate one's performance by monitoring it and making adjustments if one starts to make errors in performance (Borkowski & Burke, 1996). Students with learning disabilities can be deficient in many metacognitive areas. We discuss three: metamemory, metalistening, and metacomprehension in reading.

One of the first studies of the metacognitive abilities of students with learning disabilities (Torgesen, 1979) compared these students' abilities with those of nondisabled students to answer such questions as "If you wanted to phone a friend and someone told you the phone number, would it make any difference if you called right away after you heard the number or if you got a drink of water first? Why? What would you do if you wanted to try to remember a phone number?" These questions assess **metamemory** skills—the ability to think about memory strategies. Students with learning disabilities have more difficulty than their nondisabled peers in answering these metamemory questions. For example, in answer to the last question, most students in both groups said they would write the number

**Council** for **Exceptional Children**

**CEC Knowledge Check**
Given Shannon's concerns in eighth-grade math, what do you think an appropriate modification might be? Defend your answer.
CC4S3, LD4S5

Shannon

**metamemory** strategies for thinking about and remembering major points of material

down. When asked what they would do if they did not have a pencil and paper, nondisabled students were almost twice as likely to reply that they would use verbal rehearsal as a strategy.

Teachers often describe students with learning disabilities as looking as though they understand what you are telling them, although their subsequent behavior reveals that they have not understood a word you've said. This anecdotal observation was corroborated by a study that involved **metalistening**—the ability to conceptualize the listening process (Kotsonis & Patterson, 1980). In this study, children were told they were going to play a game that involved several rules. An adult presented one rule at a time, asking the children after each rule presentation if they thought they now had enough information to play the game. Students with learning disabilities were much more likely than their nondisabled peers to voice a readiness to play, even though, by objective standards, they had not yet heard enough information to play the game appropriately.

The concept of **metacomprehension**—the ability to think about how one understands—has helped special educators better understand the reading comprehension problems of students with learning disabilities (e.g., Anderson, 1980; Baker & Anderson, 1982; Bos & Filip, 1982; Forrest & Waller, 1981; Gardill & Jitendra, 1999; Jitendra, Hoppes, & Xin, 2000; Paris & Myers, 1981; Raben, Darch, & Eaves, 1999; Swanson, 1999; Wong, 1982). This research has shown that many students with learning disabilities lack the following metacomprehension strategies:

1. *Clarifying the purposes of reading.* Before efficient readers even begin to read, they have a mind-set about the general purpose of their reading. For instance, their approach to reading to obtain the gist of a news article is different from their approach to reading to gain information from a textbook on which they will be tested. Students with learning disabilities are not adept at adjusting their reading styles to fit the difficulty level of the material and tend to approach all reading passages with the same degree of concentration and effort.

2. *Focusing attention on important parts of passages.* Students with learning disabilities have difficulties in picking out the main idea of a paragraph. Good readers spend more time and effort focusing on the major ideas contained in the paragraphs they read.

3. *Monitoring one's level of comprehension.* Efficient readers know when they are not understanding what they are reading. Knowing when you are and are not understanding something is an important metacomprehension skill.

4. *Rereading and scanning ahead.* When good readers do note that they are having problems comprehending, they often use a couple of basic metacomprehension strategies that students with learning disabilities do not readily use. They stop and reread portions of the passage and/or scan ahead for information that will help them understand what they are reading.

5. *Consulting external sources.* When good readers encounter a word they do not know, they are more likely than poor readers to turn to external sources such as a dictionary or an encyclopedia for help.

**metalistening** strategies for thinking about and remembering major points of material as one listens

**metacomprehension** strategies for thinking about and remembering major points of material as one reads

Council for Exceptional Children

**CEC Knowledge Check**
What are the implications for a student with learning disabilities who has trouble with metamemory? Metalistening? Metacomprehension? CC2K2

Shannon has significant problems with metacognition and executive control functions. As Ms. Regents, her special education resource teacher, says:

Shannon

> Shannon gets very frustrated when working through math word problems or problems that take multiple steps. She makes the decision that she is going to solve the problem in one way and doesn't really check to see if that way will work or not. She just keeps going until she has one number left. One example from yesterday's class was when we were figuring out the volume of cylinders. Each problem included a number that the students didn't need to use to solve the problem. Shannon just took all of the numbers in the problem and multiplied them together. She didn't seem to register that she got all of the problems wrong.
>
> *Darlene Regents, Shannon's resource teacher*

In Shannon's case, she has difficulty choosing appropriate strategies and monitoring these strategies. As Ms. Regents indicates, Shannon has used one strategy before (combine all of the numbers in the problem, to get one number), she is comfortable with it, and continues to use it even though it does not produce the correct answer. Her executive control does not seem to monitor the success of the strategy nor does it "encourage" her to try a new strategy. Her feelings of frustration and failure have convinced her that trying something new will only make the process harder without any guarantee of success.

Council for Exceptional Children

**CEC Knowledge Check**
Do you think Shannon's problems with information processing will affect her socially and emotionally? LD2K3

## Motivation

Given the metacognitive problems of many students with learning disabilities, it is not surprising that so many also have motivational problems. These students appear to let events occur without attempting to take control. Their motivational problems stem from three interrelated areas: external locus of control, negative attributions, and learned helplessness.

### External Locus of Control

Locus of control refers to whether you view yourself as being controlled by internal or external forces. Students with an internal locus of control are able to motivate, organize, and evaluate themselves. Students with an external locus of control wait for others (e.g., teachers, parents, other students) to motivate, organize, and evaluate them. Persons with learning disabilities are more likely than those without disabilities to have an external rather than an internal locus of control (Hallahan, Gajar, Cohen, & Tarver, 1978; McInerney, 1999; Short & Weissberg-Benchell, 1989; Tabassam & Grainger, 2002). For example, when asked a question such as "Suppose you did a better-than-usual job in reading at school. Would it probably happen (1) because you tried harder or (2) because someone helped you?" these students are more likely to choose the second response.

### Negative Attributions

What you think are the causes of your successes and failures are known as **attributions.** Researchers have consistently found that, unlike their nondisabled peers, students with learning disabilities do not take pride in their successes, are prone to minimize those they do have, and tend to accept more readily responsibility for their failures. These negative attributions can lead to damaging effects on academic self-efficacy. In one study of elementary students, authors reported:

> Both the students with learning disabilities and with LD/ADHD demonstrated an overall negative attributional style whereas typically achieving students reported an overall positive attributional style for academic success and failure. Both the students with learning disabilities and with LD/ADHD also reported significantly lower academic self-efficacy beliefs than the normally-achieving group. (Tabassam & Grainger, 2002, p. 149)

**attribution** what one thinks are the causes of successes or failures

### Learned Helplessness

Closely related to locus of control and attributions is the concept of **learned helplessness**—the belief that your efforts will not result in the desired outcomes (Seligman, 1992). Persons with learned helplessness have come to expect failure no matter how hard they try; therefore, they often tend to lose motivation. It is easy to see why students with learning disabilities are frequently referred to as exhibiting learned helplessness, given their propensity for academic failure and their external locus of control and negative attributions.

**learned helplessness** the belief that one's efforts will not result in the desired outcomes

Whether these motivational problems cause academic problems, or vice versa, is not known. It is logical, however, to assume that a vicious cycle is operating. For example, because of difficulties in learning, the student with learning disabilities learns to expect failure and therefore tends to give up when faced with new learning tasks that are the least bit difficult, which results in more failure.

This cycle of failure has led some to refer to students with learning disabilities as **inactive learners** (Hallahan, Kneedler, & Lloyd, 1983; Torgesen, 1977). Many students with learning disabilities do not actively involve themselves in the learning situation. Their cognitive, metacognitive, and motivational problems combine to make them passive in the face of situations that require active task involvement. They are likely to have difficulties working independently and are not likely to be "self-starters."

**inactive learner** a learner who is not engaged in the learning process and who relies on others to determine and direct learning

Council for
Exceptional
Children

**CEC Knowledge Check**
What are the major motivational issues that contribute to "inactive learners"?
CC2K2, LD2K3, CC3K1

As evidenced by the following statement from Mr. Hightower, her science teacher, Shannon has developed a sense of external locus of control, learned helplessness, and negative attributions:

 Shannon

> Shannon seems to think that I *give* her grades, as if it's a random act that I go through and she has no control over the outcome. She doesn't engage with the other students around her during lab time to get feedback or work through problems with them. But she does seem to put effort into her assignments.
>
> *David Hightower, Shannon's science teacher*

We can conclude that Shannon thinks teachers "give" her grades. This is a common example of how students with learning disabilities try to deal with their inability to complete tasks as expected. Shannon also does not engage with other students to get feedback and correct her work. She has developed a sense that no matter what she does, it will not necessarily affect her learning.

## How Can Learning, Memory, and Motivation Needs Be Addressed?

Practitioners and researchers have developed a number of educational techniques to combat the constellation of cognitive, metacognitive, and motivational problems of students with learning disabilities. Several different names have been used to refer to these techniques, including cognitive training, cognitive-behavior modification training, metacognitive training, and cognitive strategy instruction. The differences among the use of these terms is often relatively subtle, and sometimes they are used virtually interchangeably. Depending on which theorist you read, the methods are referred to in slightly different terms. In other words, one person's cognitive training techniques might be another's cognitive-behavior modification techniques, which might be another person's metacognitive training techniques. For purposes of simplicity, in this book, the classification **cognitive training** refers to techniques and methods that address the combination of cognitive and metacognitive problems of students with learning disabilities. Cognitive training involves (1) changing the thought processes of students, (2) providing students with strategies for learning, and (3) teaching students self-initiative.

**cognitive training**
techniques and methods
that address the combina-
tion of cognitive and
metacognitive problems
of students with learning
disabilities

Several specific techniques fall under the rubric of cognitive training, and we discuss some briefly: self-instruction and self-questioning, self-monitoring of academic performance, and mnemonic strategies. We also provide two examples of how these techniques can be combined into comprehensive cognitive strategies. Figure 8.2 lists principal characteristics of cognitive training methods.

### Self-Instruction

**self-instruction**
verbalizing the steps
in a task

One of the first cognitive training methods to be used with students with learning disabilities was **self-instruction,** which involves verbalizing the steps in a task. Meichenbaum was the pioneer in this area, relying heavily on the earlier work of well-known Russian language theorists (Luria 1961; Vygotsky, 1962). The following training sequence, based on that developed by Meichenbaum and Goodman (1971), has served as the prototype for many subsequent self-instruction efforts:

1. The teacher performs the task while verbalizing the following aloud:
   a. questions about the task
   b. self-guiding instructions on how to perform the task
   c. self-evaluation of performance
2. The child performs the task while the teacher instructs aloud.
3. The child performs the task while verbalizing aloud.

## FIGURE 8.2 Principal Characteristics of Cognitive Training Methods

### Eight Principles of Effective Cognitive Training Programs

Many specific techniques fall under the rubric of cognitive training, which can sometimes make it difficult for teachers to know which strategies are most likely to be successful. After examining several effective cognitive training programs, Pressley and colleagues arrived at a list of eight common features (Pressley, Symons, Snyder, & Cariglia-Bull, 1989; Symons, Snyder, Cariglia-Bull, & Pressley, 1989). Teachers can use these as a guide when choosing among cognitive training options.

1. *Teach a few strategies at a time.* Rather than bombarding students with a number of strategies all at once, teach them just a few. In this way, there is a better chance that the students can learn the strategies in a comprehensive, and not a superficial, fashion.
2. *Teach self-monitoring.* It is helpful if students keep track of their own progress. When checking their own work, if they find an error, they should be encouraged to try to correct it on their own.
3. *Teach them when and where to use the strategies.* Many students with learning disabilities have problems with the metacognitive ability of knowing when and where they can use strategies they have been taught. Teachers must give them this information as well as extensive experience in using the strategies in a variety of settings.
4. *Maintain students' motivation.* Students need to know that the strategies work. Teachers can encourage motivation by consistently pointing out the benefits of the strategies, explaining how they work, and charting students' progress.
5. *Teach in context.* Students should learn cognitive techniques as an integrated part of the curriculum. Rather than using cognitive training in an isolated manner, teachers should teach students to employ cognitive strategies during academic lessons.
6. *Don't neglect a nonstrategic knowledge base.* Sometimes those who use cognitive training become such avid proponents of it that they forget the importance of factual knowledge. The more facts children know about history, science, math, English, and so forth, the less they will need to rely on strategies.
7. *Engage in direct teaching.* Because the emphasis in cognitive training is on encouraging students to take more initiative in their own learning, teachers may feel that their involvement is less necessary. However, teachers should continue directly teaching students. Early on, teachers need to be in control of supervising students' use of cognitive strategies. Later, students' reliance on teachers will lessen.
8. *Regard cognitive training as long term.* Because cognitive training often results in immediate improvement, there may be a temptation to view it as a panacea or a quick fix. To maintain improvements and have them generalize to other settings, however, students need extensive practice in applying the strategies they have learned.

**Council for Exceptional Children**

**CEC Knowledge Check**
Why is cognitive training an essential teaching method with students with learning disabilities? CC4S2, CC4S4, CC4S5, LD4S5

---

4. The child performs the task while verbalizing in a whisper.
5. The child performs the task while verbalizing covertly.

An example of using self-instruction and self-questioning with students with learning disabilities involves a seven-step strategy for solving math word problems (Montague, Warger, & Morgan, 2000). The steps for the process are listed in Figure 8.3 (page 240). Within each step are three substeps: say, ask, and check. These substeps guide the student to give specific self-instructions (say), self-questions (ask), and self-monitoring tactics (check). In a large-scale study of seventh- and eighth-graders, students with learning disabilities who were taught the strategy "approximated the performance of the comparison group, average-achieving students

**Council for Exceptional Children**

**CEC Knowledge Check**
Do you think this teaching method will help Shannon? Why, or why not? Does this change your previous answers about her math problems? LD4K4, LD4S12

**FIGURE 8.3**   Math Strategy Steps

## Math Problem Solving

**Read** (for understanding)
Say:      Read the problem. If I don't understand, read it again.
Ask:      Have I read and understood the problem?
Check:   For understanding as I solve the problem.

**Paraphrase** (your own words)
Say:      Underline the important information.
            Put the problem in my own words.
Ask:      Have I underlined the important information?
            What is the question? What am I looking for?
Check:   That the information goes with the question.

**Visualize** (a picture or a diagram)
Say:      Make a drawing or diagram.
Ask:      Does the picture fit the problem?
Check:   The picture against the problem information.

**Hypothesize** (a plan to solve the problem)
Say:      Decide how many steps and operations are needed.
            Write the operations symbols $(+, -, \times, \div)$.
Ask:      If I do . . . , what will I get?
            If I do . . . , then what do I need to do next?
            How many steps are needed?
Check:   That the plan makes sense.

**Estimate** (predict the answer)
Say:      Round the numbers, do the problem in my head, and write the estimate.
Ask:      Did I round up and down?
            Did I write the estimate?
Check:   That I use the important information.

**Compute** (do the arithmetic)
Say:      Do the operations in the right order.
Ask:      How does my answer compare with my estimate?
            Does my answer make sense?
            Are the decimals or money signs in the right places?
Check:   That all the operations were done in the right order.

**Check** (make sure everything is right)
Say:      Check the computation.
Ask:      Have I checked every step?
            Have I checked the computation?
            Is my answer right?
Check:   That everything is right. If not, go back.
            Then ask for help if I need it.

*Source:* From "Solve it! Strategy Instruction to Improve Mathematical Problem Solving," by M. Montague, C. Warger, and T. H. Morgan, 2000, *Learning Disabilities Research and Practice, 15,* 110–116. Copyright 2000 by Lawrence Erlbaum Associates, Inc. Reprinted by permission.

who were not given instruction but had demonstrated problem-solving ability" (Montague, Warger, & Morgan, 2000).

An example of the use of self-instruction with diagrams in science (e.g., components of the heart) involved students using the cover, copy, and compare steps and the following instructions: (1) review the complete diagram, (2) cover the complete diagram, (3) copy the name of the item on the first blank line, (4) compare that item to the complete diagram, (5) if correct, repeat; if incorrect, write the correct response three times. The student then repeated the procedure. Researchers have demonstrated that the copy, cover, and compare steps improved the accuracy of the student's labeling of science diagrams (Smith, Dittmer, & Skinner, 2002).

After a decade of research on his own and with others, Meichenbaum (1981) set forth ten guidelines for the development of self-instruction programs. These are listed in Figure 8.4 and are still appropriate for today's instruction.

Although research has provided teachers with many helpful cognitive training techniques, we should not assume that these are a cure-all. For example, consider what Shannon has said about self-instruction:

My resource teacher has taught me to ask myself questions as I work on writing papers or reading my textbooks. It helps sometimes, especially if I write the questions down and go through them over and over again. The worst part is that it takes me longer to do things that way. So sometimes I get lazy and just don't do it even though I know I probably should.

*Shannon*

Shannon

Council for Exceptional Children

**CEC Knowledge Check**
How do you see external locus of control and learned helplessness manifesting in Shannon's response?
CC2K2, CC3K1

**FIGURE 8.4** Guidelines for Development of Self-Instruction Programs

Ten Guidelines for Developing Self-Instruction Programs

1. Carefully analyze the target behaviors that you want to change.
2. Listen for the strategies that the student is presently using, paying special attention to whether they are inappropriate.
3. Use training tasks that are as close as possible to those you want to change.
4. Collaborate with the student in devising the self-instruction routine rather than imposing the regimen.
5. Be sure that the student has all the skills necessary to use the self-instructions.
6. Give the student feedback about the utility of the self-instructions for performance.
7. Explicitly point out other tasks and settings in which the student can use the self-instructions.
8. Use a variety of trainers, settings, and tasks to increase the chances that the student will learn to use the self-instructions successfully outside the training setting.
9. Anticipate failures and include failure management in the training activities.
10. Train until a reasonable criterion of performance has been reached. Then follow up with "booster" sessions in order to improve the chances that the trained skills will be maintained.

*Source:* Adapted from "Teaching Thinking: A Cognitive Behavioral Approach" by D. Meichenbaum, April 1981, paper presented at the meeting of the Society for Learning Disabilities and Remedial Education, New York. Reprinted by permission of the author.

As can be seen from Shannon's comment, changing the thought processes of students with learning disabilities can be a difficult task. Students are often reluctant to give up the strategies they currently use, even if they are not successful, because they do not feel comfortable with the new strategy, they have not committed the new practice to memory, or the new strategy takes longer than the old one. This is the point at which many teachers give up using self-instruction. However, consistency, continued practice, and generalization to other tasks will help win these students over to the new approach. For more information about student effort and strategy use, see the Current Trends and Issues box on page 243.

## Self-Monitoring of Academic Performance

**self-monitoring of academic performance** keeping track of one's own work and making some type of recording of it

Students employ **self-monitoring of academic performance** by keeping track of their own work and making some type of recording of it. For example, students may record the number of words written in a paragraph or essay or the number of math problems completed in a certain period of time. Although self-monitoring was originally used with students with learning disabilities as a means of monitoring attention, some have also applied it specifically to academic performance. (We discuss the use of self-monitoring of attention for students with ADHD in Chapter 9.) Students have improved their spelling, for example, by being taught to count the number of words they have correctly spelled on spelling lists and recording this number on a graph (Harris, Graham, Reid, McElroy, & Hamby, 1994). This method has led to more words being spelled correctly. Self-monitoring has also resulted in an increase in the length and quality of written stories (Harris et al., 1994). The procedure in this case involved having the students count the number of words in their stories and record this number on a graph.

In another study, students with learning disabilities and ADHD were taught to chart their academic progress in reading comprehension, written expression, and mathematics. All showed gains in academic productivity and accuracy (Shimabukuro, Parker, Jenkins, & Edelen-Smith, 1999). Although self-monitoring of performance can be highly effective, its effectiveness is limited to skills that the student already possesses. In other words, "self-monitoring does not create new behaviors . . . rather, it affects behaviors that are already in the child's repertoire" (Reid, 1996, p. 322). The fact that students with learning disabilities often have problems fluidly executing skills they possess, however, makes self-monitoring a very useful teaching technique.

**Council for Exceptional Children**

**CEC Knowledge Check**
Is self-monitoring an effective tool for teachers to use with students with learning disabilities?
CC4S5, LD4S1

## Self-Determination

**self-determination** making one's own decision about important aspects of one's life

As you recall, in Chapter 5, we discussed the importance that many authorities are now placing on **self-determination.** In the 1990s, researchers in special education put many metacognitive, cognitive, and motivational topics together into the concept of self-determination. Self-determined behavior is "actions that are identified by four essential characteristics: (1) the person acted autonomously, (2) the behavior(s) are self-regulated, (3) the person initiated and responded to the event(s) in a psychologically empowered manner, and (4) the person acted in a self-realizing

## Effort and Strategy Use in Students with Learning Disabilities

Students with learning disabilities have long been thought of as "passive" learners or have been stereotyped as "lazy." Recent research has begun to include the concept of effort in the evaluation of students' use of strategies, and the research results are somewhat surprising.

In a review of strategic learning in students with learning disabilities, Meltzer and Montague (2001) state that "students with learning disabilities exert considerable effort in the learning process and . . . their global self-concepts are positive enough to give them the impetus to expend the effort needed to learn" (p. 116). Their conclusions come from several investigations into student and teacher perceptions of effort and strategy use. The first is by Sawyer (1996, as cited in Meltzer and Montague, 2001) who found "students with learning disabilities who experienced success as a result of their effort felt more personal responsibility for their achievements, expressed a stronger intent to succeed, and were therefore more likely to continue to work hard" (p. 116).

Meltzer and colleagues found similar results in a group of studies done on the project Strategies for Success. In one particular study, researchers compared student and teacher perceptions of effort and strategy use by students with learning disabilities and those without disabilities. In addition, the researchers used the same students to compare the student and teacher perceptions of effort and strategy use in high and average achievers (Meltzer, Katzir-Cohen, Miller, & Roditi, 2001). There were 663 students in grades 4 through 9, and there were 59 general education teachers involved in the study. Using a variety of questionnaires, observations, and rating scales, the researchers found:

1. Students with learning disabilities judged themselves "as hard workers who put forth above-average effort to achieve academically" (p. 90). Students without learning disabilities rated themselves as putting in above-average to superior effort; however, the students with learning disabilities still rated themselves significantly lower than their nondisabled peers. Teachers' ratings of both groups of students were lower than students' ratings.
2. Students rated effort as the greatest determinant of their strategy use. Teachers rated planning as the greatest determinant of strategy use.
3. In a regression analysis across subject areas, "effort was the most important contributor to academic performance" (p. 90).
4. When students were split into high-average achievers and low achievers (based on student academic achievement), high-average achievers rated their effort and strategy use as very high, significantly more so than low achievers. Teachers rated these two groups similarly.

One of the most interesting findings of this study was that teachers rated students with learning disabilities similarly to their peers when grouped in the high-average or low-achieving group. In other words, it seems that the achievement level of the student mattered more in the teacher ratings than did the existence of a learning disability.

Obviously, more research is needed, but this area is one of great interest, particularly to those who observe students with learning disabilities working two to three times longer than their nondisabled peers to accomplish class or homework tasks.

manner" (Wehmeyer, Agran, & Hughes, 1998, p. 7). What does this mean? The following essential characteristics include many of the topics discussed in this chapter:

1. Students are able to make choices.
2. Students are able to make decisions.
3. Students are able to problem solve.
4. Students are able to set goals and evaluate attainment of those goals.

Council for Exceptional Children

**CEC Knowledge Check**
Could teaching these students to be strategic learners have impacted the results of this study? If so, how?    LD4S1

5. Students are independent, take calculated risks, and understand safety.
6. Students engage in self-observation, self-evaluation, and self-reinforcement.
7. Students use self-instruction skills.
8. Students show self-advocacy and leadership skills.
9. Students have an internal locus of control.
10. Students have positive attributions of self-efficacy and efficacy expectations.
11. Students show self-awareness and self-knowledge. (Price, Wolensky, & Mulligan, 2002; Wehmeyer et al., 1998)

These characteristics develop across the life span of students; however, research indicates that teachers must directly teach these skills to students with learning disabilities and must provide practice in using these skills (Malian & Nevin, 2002). Authors have developed and field-tested curricula in self-determination for use in both special and general education classrooms. For example, the Steps to Self-Determination curriculum (Field & Hoffman, 1996) includes four major components: know yourself; value yourself; plan, act, and experience outcomes; and learn. After using the curriculum with students with disabilities, the authors found a significant increase in scores on a self-determination scale, of types of behaviors that are indicators of self-determination, and in responses of students indicating an internal locus of control (Field & Hoffman, 2002).

But helping students develop self-determination skills does not require using an entire curriculum. In one study, student surveys indicated a significant increase in perceptions of their reading abilities after participation in strategy instruction and practice through literature circles (Blum, Lipsett, & Vocom, 2002). Others have found that providing choice in assignments, evaluation of goal setting, and practice in making everyday classroom decisions has also increased the ability of students with learning disabilities to engage in these behaviors on their own (Price et al., 2002). Because self-determination skills are important for successful outcomes, both in school and in the transition from school to workplace or college, it is important for teachers to provide direct instruction and multiple opportunities for students to practice the skills outlined above in the day-to-day routine of the classroom.

**Council for Exceptional Children**

**CEC Knowledge Check**
Should students with learning disabilities be encouraged to participate in determining their own curriculum? CC4S2, CC4S5

## Mnemonic Strategies

Shannon's mother recalls some of the teaching strategies Shannon's teacher used to help aid her memory of facts:

Shannon

> When Shannon was younger, one of her teachers taught her class all of the state capitals by using pictures like a hamster flying the Concorde for Concord, New Hampshire (hamster). We thought, "Oh, no. Even more to remember than just the names of the states and capitals! How will she ever do it?!" Shannon brought home a 100% on her capitals test one day. You should have seen the smile on her face. We were amazed!
>
> *Kerrie Ireland, Shannon's mother*

Teachers can use **mnemonic strategies** to enhance the memory performance of students with learning disabilities. Mnemonic strategies are ways to enhance memory and retrieval skills using visual or acoustic representations. Four such strategies have been used and researched extensively: (1) letter strategies, (2) the keyword method, (3) the pegword method, and (4) reconstructive elaborations. The rationale behind mnemonics is that students with learning disabilities (and others) will remember information better if they can use concrete cues and draw on prior knowledge. For example, many students learn the names of the Great Lakes by using the letter strategy HOMES (Huron, Ontario, Michigan, Erie, and Superior). Another example of a letter strategy is FACE for the musical notes that fall in the spaces on the staff.

In the **keyword method,** "the new word to-be-learned is recoded into a keyword that is concrete, already familiar to the learner, and acoustically similar to the target word. The keyword is then linked to the definition in an interactive picture which shows the keyword and definition 'doing something together'" (Scruggs & Mastropieri, 2000). Figure 8.5 gives the keyword mnemonic for *buncombe* (empty, insincere speech). The keyword for *buncombe* is bun, and the interactive picture is of an audience throwing buns at someone giving an empty, insincere speech. Students are taught to think of the keyword, think of the picture, identify what else is

**mnemonic strategies** strategies to enhance memory and retrieval using visual and acoustic representations of information

**keyword method** a mnemonic strategy that uses an acoustically similar word and picture to help students remember factual information

Council for Exceptional Children

**CEC Knowledge Check**
Create a keyword memory device for the word *viaduct.*
LD4S7

Council for Exceptional Children

**CEC Knowledge Check**
Design a letter-sound correspondence picture for the letter *C.*
LD4S7

---

**FIGURE 8.5**    Mnemonic for Buncombe

*Source:* From *Teaching Students Ways to Remember: Strategies for Learning Mnemonically* (p. 20), by M. A. Mastropieri and T. E. Scruggs, 1991, Cambridge, MA: Brookline Books. Copyright 1991 by Brookline Books, Inc. Reprinted by permission.

in the picture, and respond with the definition. In another example, young children were taught letter-sound correspondence by presenting each letter as an integrated part of a familiar figure (e.g., F is the stem of a flower) (Fulk, Lohman, & Belfiore, 1997).

The **pegword method** uses both the keyword method and a rhyming proxy for numbers (e.g., one is bun, two is shoe, etc.) to remember ordered or numbered information (Scruggs & Mastropieri, 2000). An example of a pegword mnemonic for remembering that the mineral garnet has a hardness level of six is shown in Figure 8.6. The keyword for *garnet* is garden, and the pegword for six is sticks—a garden of sticks. Keywords and pegwords have been used successfully with middle-school students with learning disabilities. For example, Mastropieri, Scruggs, and Whedon (1997) used keywords and pegwords to help students remember the order of the presidents of the United States. Each president was represented by a picture with two elements—one for his name and one for his ranking. For example, for George Washington, the picture showed someone washing (a cue for Washington) buns (a cue for 1). For Franklin Pierce, the picture showed a purse (a cue for Pierce) being stabbed by a fork (a cue for 14).

Mnemonics also include the technique of **reconstructive elaborations** for teaching abstract concepts. Reconstructive elaborations "make unfamiliar content more familiar, nonmeaningful information more meaningful, and abstract information more concrete" (Mastropieri & Scruggs, 1991, p. 45). For example, to teach that *radial symmetry* refers to structurally similar body parts that extend out from the center of organisms, such as starfish, an acoustically similar keyword (*radio cemetery*) was constructed from the unfamiliar term, *radial symmetry*. In the picture, *radio cemetery* was shown in the shape of a star, with radios as headstones, and skeletons dancing to the music from the radios. Each arm of the star is shown to be similar in

**pegword method**
a mnemonic strategy that includes using an acoustically similar word for a number (e.g., one = bun) and a visual representation of that word to aid in memory and retrieval of factual information in lists or specific order

Council for Exceptional Children

**CEC Knowledge Check**
Why do you think the pegword method is effective for students with learning disabilities? LD3K3, LD4S1

**reconstructive elaborations**
a mnemonic strategy that uses visual representations, keywords, and pegwords to enhance memory and retrieval of abstract and/or unfamiliar concepts

**FIGURE 8.6    Mnemonic for Garnet**

*Source:* From *Teaching Students Ways to Remember: Strategies for Learning Mnemonically* (page 39), by M. A. Mastropieri & T. E. Scruggs, 1991, Cambridge, MA: Brookline Books. Copyright 1991 by Brookline Books. Reprinted by permission.

appearance to each other arm to reinforce the concept. (Scruggs & Mastropieri, 1992, p. 222).

In all cases, students are taught both the pictorial representation of the concept and a metacognitive strategy to retrieve the information from memory (i.e., think of the picture, think of what is happening in the picture, recall the definition or concept). In a review of 34 studies of mnemonic instruction conducted at all grade levels, researchers found substantial gains for students taught using mnemonics (Scruggs & Mastropieri, 2000).

## Attribution Training

Authorities have suggested several strategies for working with students who have motivational problems. Figure 8.7 lists several suggestions for teachers to consider.

**Council for Exceptional Children**

**CEC Knowledge Check**
Describe what mnemonic instruction is and what characteristics students with learning disabilities have that make the usage of mnemonics so effective.
CC2K2, LD3K3

---

**FIGURE 8.7     Motivating Students with Learning Disabilities**

Teachers can use the following strategies to try to motivate students with learning disabilities and keep them actively involved:

1. Reduce the amount of external reinforcement and focus on reinforcing student performance. Rather than saying "Good work" or "Excellent job," focus on the behaviors, such as, "You really concentrated and finished this biology assignment. You needed to ask for help, but you got it done. How do you feel about it?"
2. Link students' behaviors to outcomes. "You spent ten minutes working hard on this worksheet, and you finished it."
3. Provide encouragement. Because they have experienced continued failure, many students are discouraged from attempting tasks they are capable of performing.
4. Discuss academic tasks and social activities in which the student experiences success.
5. Discuss your own failures or difficulties and express what you do to cope with these. Be sure to provide examples of when you persist and examples of when you give up.
6. Encourage students to take responsibility for their successes. "You received a B on your biology test. How do you think you got such a good grade?" Encourage students to describe what they did (e.g., how they studied). Discourage students from saying "I was lucky" or "It was an easy test."
7. Encourage students to take responsibility for their failures. For example, in response to the question, "Why do you think you are staying after school?" encourage students to take responsibility for what got them there. "Yes, I am sure Billy's behavior was hard to ignore. I am aware that you did some wrong things to get you here. What did you do?"
8. Structure learning and social activities to reduce failure.
9. Teach students how to learn information and how to demonstrate their control of their learning task.
10. Teach students to use procedures and techniques to monitor their own gains in academic areas.

**Council for Exceptional Children**

**CEC Knowledge Check**
Why is overt instruction in social and academic success necessary for students with learning disabilities?
CC4S5, CC5S9

*Source:* Adapted from *Strategies for Teaching Students with Learning and Behavior Problems,* 3rd ed., by C. S. Bos and S. Vaughn, 1994, Boston: Allyn and Bacon. Copyright © 1994 by Pearson Education. Reprinted by permission of the publisher.

**attribution training**
teaching students to
recognize the relationship
between hard work and
success

Council for
Exceptional
Children

**CEC Knowledge Check**
What is the best method
of reversing external
locus of control to in-
ternal locus of control
in order to increase
motivation?
CC4S5

Many of these techniques fall under the rubric of attribution training (Borkowski, Wehring, & Carr, 1988). **Attribution training** involves attempting to recognize the relationship between hard work and success. Most of this training takes the form of pointing out to students that when they do well, it is due to having tried hard and not giving up. For example, in one study (Fulk, 1996), every time the student got an answer correct on a spelling task, the experimenter said, "Why do you think you spelled that word correctly? Right, you tried hard, used the study strategy, and spelled the word correctly." After an incorrect spelling, the experimenter reminded the student to try hard and to use the study strategy.

In another example, researchers taught students a reading comprehension strategy in four conditions: (1) strategy only, (2) strategy instruction plus goal-setting, (3) strategy instruction plus self-instruction, and (4) strategy instruction plus self-instruction and goal-setting. Within the goal-setting conditions, students were taught to set and monitor goals for reading as well as to say attributions. All students improved on reading comprehension measures following strategy instruction. Unfortunately, students in the goal-setting condition did not improve over the students without goal-setting instruction (Johnson, Graham, & Harris, 1997).

As compelling as the arguments for the use of attribution training appear, research on its effectiveness has been mixed (Fulk, 1996). There is enough positive evidence to indicate that teachers should definitely consider using it with students who have motivational problems. But an external locus of control, learned helplessness, and negative attributions can become deeply entrenched in students with learning disabilities and are highly resistant to change in some cases. The best way to get students to turn this attitude around is to make sure they experience academic success (Meltzer & Montague, 2001).

## Cognitive Strategies

Comprehensive cognitive strategies are designed to teach students how to approach and complete various learning tasks in an efficient and effective manner. These strategies include self-instruction, self-monitoring, mnemonic strategies, and attribution training. In essence, students are taught ways to reproduce the strategies of more expert learners. In cognitive strategy instruction, students are taught when to use the strategy, how to use the strategy, and how to determine if they were successful. The strategies are general enough to apply in many situations (e.g, how to take a test) but not so general as to be difficult to use (e.g., draw a picture to solve a problem). The Effective Practices box on page 249 describes the steps necessary to teach cognitive strategies to students. We provide two examples of cognitive strategies that may be applied to any content area: **test-taking strategies** and **content textbook strategies.** Effective cognitive strategies for specific content areas (e.g., mathematics, written expression) are included in each content chapter of this book.

**test-taking strategy** an
approach to taking a test
that reduces anxiety and
helps students show what
they know of the content

**content textbook strategy**
an approach to completing
reading tasks successfully
in content area textbooks

### Test-Taking

Students with learning disabilities often have difficulty showing what they know on tests. Researchers at the University of Kansas developed and validated a strategy for

## Learning Strategies Research

In 20 years of research and instruction, Don Deshler, Jean Schumaker, and colleagues at the University of Kansas have developed an eight-stage instructional sequence for the teaching of cognitive strategies. The Strategic Instruction Model (SIM) has gained national prominence as an efficient and research-validated approach to teaching students strategic thinking skills. The stages are appropriate for teaching any cognitive strategy, and they rely on the following instructional principles (Ellis, & Lenz, 1996):

1. Teach prerequisite skills before strategy instruction begins.
2. Teach strategies regularly and intensively.
3. Emphasize personal effort.
4. Require mastery of the strategy.
5. Integrate instruction with strategy learning.
6. Emphasize covert processing.
7. Emphasize generalization of the strategy in the broadest sense.

Keeping these principles in mind—and keeping in mind that it will take repeated instruction, practice, and cuing for students with learning disabilities to use new cognitive learning strategies—the teacher should follow these steps in teaching (Deshler, Ellis, & Lenz, 1996):

**CEC Knowledge Check**
How can feedback be used to improve internal locus of control?
LD4S6, LD5S1

1. *Pretest and make commitments.* The teacher assesses the student's current abilities related to the strategy, discusses the results with the student, and gains a commitment from the student to learn the strategy.

2. *Describe.* The teacher gives students a detailed description of the strategy and describes its use.
3. *Model.* The teacher models not only the steps of the strategy but "thinks aloud" through it so that students will see the thought processes that go in to make it successful.
4. *Verbal practice.* Students practice describing the strategy, its use, and its purpose as well as committing the steps to memory. (It is important to have the steps memorized so that the strategy can become more automatic.)
5. *Controlled practice and feedback.* Students practice the strategy with material on which they can be successful (not necessarily grade-level materials). This gives them the chance to experience success and to understand how to apply the strategy without the demands of difficult content material.
6. *Advanced practice and feedback.* Students apply the strategy to grade-level material in a controlled environment, with appropriate help from the teacher.
7. *Posttest and commitment to generalize.* The teacher administers a posttest to verify that students have mastered the strategy and gains commitment from them to try the strategy in new situations.
8. *Generalization.* Students try the strategy in situations outside of the classroom where they learned the strategy. At this stage, students may need to adapt the strategy to fit real-world demands.

**CEC Knowledge Check**
Why are covert processing and emphasis on generalization to other settings critical to these students' success?
CC4S4, CC4S5, LD7K2

students taking an objective test (Hughes, 1996). The strategy uses the first-letter mnemonic PIRATES to help students remember the steps to the strategy. Within each step, students are taught to give self-instructions or to self-question. For example, step 1 is **P**repare to succeed. Within this step, students are taught to "Put your name and PIRATES on the test. Allot time and order to sections. Say affirmations. Start within 2 minutes." Step 2 is **I**nspect the instructions. Students are taught to

**Council for Exceptional Children**

**CEC Knowledge Check**
What are the design features of this strategy that contribute to its effectiveness (i.e., mnemonic)?
CC4S5, LD4K1

"Read instructions carefully. Underline what to do and where to respond. Notice special requirements." Step 3 is **R**ead (each question), remember (the information), and reduce (the obviously incorrect answer choices). Step 4 is **A**nswer or abandon (the question). In step 5, students are to **T**urn back and try to answer questions that they left abandoned. In step 6, they **E**stimate (guess answers), and in step 7, students are to **S**urvey the test to make sure that they have answered every question and that they have answered the questions as intended. The PIRATES strategy has been used successfully with adolescents with learning disabilities (Hughes, Ruhl, Deshler, & Schumaker, 1993; Hughes & Schumaker, 1991).

### Content Textbook Strategies

Various strategies have been developed to help students gain information from textbooks. Many of these strategies direct student attention to bold print, headings and subheadings, and text structure or teach summarization skills (e.g., Boyle, 1996; Ellis, 1996; Englert & Mariage, 1991; Schumaker, Deshler, Alley, Warner, & Denton, 1984). The following is an example of a content textbook strategy (Rooney, 1998):

1. Identify the first subtitle in the text selection.
2. Read material between the main title of the text selection and the first subtitle.
3. Read the subtitle and the section under the subtitle. While reading, write the names of people and places, important numbers, and terms on separate index cards.
4. Return to the subtitle and turn it into the best test question possible. Write the question on one side of an index card and the answer on the back.
5. Repeat these steps for the entire text selection.
6. Study the cards by looking at them one by one. For the detail cards, ask the question, "How is this related to the material?" For the main idea cards, try to answer the question from memory.

This example includes a consistent sequence of strategy steps, self-instructions, and self-questions. It also provides students with concrete reference materials that they can use to study at a later date, giving them a sense of control over how to study and how much effort they put into the task.

Although cognitive strategies can be powerful, we caution that it can sometimes be difficult to get students to learn them and to use them correctly. For example, Ms. Cartwright, Shannon's language arts teacher, comments:

**Shannon**

> I require my students to use checklists in my language arts class for all of the writing projects they do. The checklists include all of the steps of the writing process and certain items that each student should check before turning in a rough draft. For example: Did I include a topic sentence in each paragraph? or Did I state my main ideas for the essay in the first paragraph? When I used these checklists with Shannon, I thought it helped her to be more consistent. But

they were far from being a panacea. Her rough drafts and final copies were still pretty similar.

*Jill Cartwright, Shannon's language arts teacher*

Even though Shannon had a checklist of the steps necessary to complete in writing a paper, she was still not able to master completely how to revise initial drafts. Teachers must be consistent in many aspects of their teaching of cognitive strategies: the wording of each step, the choice of when to use a certain strategy, the monitoring of successful use of the strategy, and the generalization of the strategy to other situations. Most important, teachers must evaluate whether students have the prerequisite skills necessary to use the strategy correctly. In Shannon's case, she may not have had the necessary revision skills to be able to complete that part of the strategy.

## General Teaching Practices to Activate Learning and Memory

For students with learning disabilities who have memory, learning, and motivation problems, it is very important that teacher instruction help them develop efficient and effective strategies to gain knowledge. In addition to the examples of effective teaching techniques given in this chapter, there are also teacher behaviors that can help students with learning disabilities better develop their learning capacities. (These are also discussed in Chapter 15.) These behaviors include the following:

1. Provide **advance organizers.** (Helps students understand the task and the task demands so they are better able to develop their own means of task analysis in their executive control.)
2. Activate or provide background knowledge. (Helps students learn to search their long-term memory to integrate new information with that already known.)
3. Organize material coherently and make the organization explicit to the student. (Helps students to develop or modify schemata on a topic in their long-term memory to aid in storage and retrieval.)
4. Provide continuous feedback and **distributed practice.** (Helps students develop strategies to attack new knowledge, monitor their strategy use, and develop an understanding of where to place their effort and how that effort contributes to their learning.)
5. Engage in dialogue that allows students to understand how you (an expert learner) learn. (Provides a means for students to learn new strategies to incorporate into their working memory.)
6. Set and communicate appropriate expectations. (Helps students develop their sense of academic self-efficacy.)
7. Engage students in active learning. (Allows students to use their working memory and executive function to manipulate new knowledge for storage and retrieval.)

**advance organizer** activities and techniques that orient students to the material before reading or class presentation

**distributed practice** technique in which items to be learned are repeated at intervals over a period of time

Council for Exceptional Children

**CEC Knowledge Check**
How do these teacher behaviors help a student move information from short- to long-term memory and then retrieve it?
LD4K4, LD4S1, LD4S5

## Assistive Technology Evaluation Guide: The ABCDs of Students with Learning Disabilities

Assistive technology garners much attention these days in the discussion of students with learning disabilities. LDOnline (www.ldonline.org) provides a wealth of information about this topic, including a thorough evaluation guide for teachers and parents (see Figure A). The site provides a no-nonsense approach to determining what types of assistive technology (no-tech, low-tech, or high-tech) may be right for students in writing, reading, math, studying/organizing, and listening. The evaluation begins with the ABCDs:

A. What difficulties is the student experiencing in the school environment for which assistive technology intervention is needed?

1. What are the student's strengths and weaknesses?
2. What educational task(s) is the student unable to perform because of the student's disability, and will the use of assistive technology help the student accomplish task(s) more independently and within the least restrictive environment?
3. Will the use of assistive technology enable the student to compensate for difficulties in various settings?

B. What strategies, materials, equipment, and technology tools has the student already used to address the concerns?

C. What new or additional assistive technology or accommodations should be tried?

1. What is the student's prior experience with technology, and does the student want to use the assistive technology device and/or service recommended?
2. Will the student be involved in the decision-making process to determine the most appropriate assistive technology device and/or service?
3. Is the teacher comfortable with the assistive technology? If not, will training and support be available?

D. What will the criteria be for determining whether or not the student's needs are being met while using assistive technology?

1. What plan will be in place to integrate the technology effectively?
2. What will the time frame be for evaluating the potential success of using assistive technology?
3. Who will be responsible for determining if the criteria are being met?
4. Are the assistive technology devices and/or services being utilized? If not, explain why.
5. Does the use of assistive technology enable the student to meet IEP goals?

The evaluation guide also provides a sampling of strategies, materials, equipment, and technology tools to consider when answering these questions. (The entire evaluation guide can be retrieved from www.ldonline.org/ld_indepth/technology/evaluation.pdf)

---

**FIGURE A**   Assistive Technology Evaluation Guide for Students with Learning Disabilities

|         | NO-TECH    | LOW-TECH              | HIGH-TECH                              |
|---------|------------|-----------------------|----------------------------------------|
| Writing | Dictionary | Slant board<br>Keyguard | Word processor<br>Word prediction software |

---

Finally, assistive technology devices should always be considered in planning instructional programs for students with learning disabilities. There is a wide variety of devices available to help students organize (e.g., personal digital assistants),

Council for
Exceptional
Children

**CEC Knowledge Check**

Look at Shannon's information in the Case Connections box (pages 228–229). What assistive technology would you recommend? How would it be used? Why? CC7S9

| | | | |
|---|---|---|---|
| | | Alternate keyboard<br>Electronic spell checker without auditory output<br>Electronic spell checker with auditory output<br>Tape recorders for note-taking<br>Pencil grip<br>Rubber stamp<br>Adapter paper (bold line, raised line, different spacing) | Voice recognition software (computer software programs that recognize your voice)<br>Talking word processor<br>Multimedia software for expression of ideas<br>Laptop computer<br>Abbreviation expansion programs (macros)<br>Semantic organizers |
| Reading | | Changes in text size<br>Changes in spacing<br>Changes in background color<br>Reading pen<br>Reading window | Optical character recognition (OCR) software/speech synthesizer (using a scanner, takes written text and turns it into spoken language via speech synthesizer)<br>Electric books<br>Screen readers<br>Books on tape |
| Math | Graph paper<br>Calculation chart<br>Turn paper sideways | Modified paper (enlarged, raised line)<br>Calculator<br>MathLine<br>Talking watches<br>Calculator on computer | Software with template for math computation<br>Hand-held talking calculator<br>Electronic math worksheet |
| Studying/<br>Organizing | Aids for organizing materials (color-coded folders, index tabs)<br>Highlight text with markers or highlight tape<br>Index cards | Appointment book<br>Beeper/buzzer<br>Graphic organizer worksheets | Software for organization of ideas<br>Variable-speech-control tape recorders<br>Electronic organizer (e.g., Palm Pilot) |
| Listening | | Pressure-sensitive paper for user to tear off copies of notes to share with a student who has difficulty listening and taking notes | FM amplification device<br>Laptop computer for note-taking<br>Compact word processor for note-taking<br>Variable-speech-control tape recorder |

brainstorm (e.g., webbing software), and revise (e.g., grammar and spell-check devices). For information on how to choose the right assistive technology devices, see the Today's Technology box above.

**Council for Exceptional Children**

**CEC Content Standards**

2. Development and Characteristics of Learners
3. Individual Learning Differences
8. Assessment
9. Professional and Ethical Practice

## PORTFOLIO-BUILDING ACTIVITY

## Demonstrating Mastery of the CEC Standards

After reading Chapter 8, create a diagram that represents incoming information (sensory register) and all the things that can happen to this information as it moves through the process of working memory. Make this into a working document that you can share with your students so they will understand (1) how their brains work, (2) what they need to do so they can perform at their best, and (3) what they need from their teachers so they can learn optimally. See the Companion Website (www.ablongman.com/hallahanLD3e) for (1) specific directions on how to create your diagram, and (2) an example to follow. Questions to think about as you progress:

- How do information-processing conditions interact with abilities and behaviors of individuals with learning disabilities?

- What aspects of how an individual can learn, organize, store, and retrieve information provide the foundation on which special educators individualize meaningful and challenging instruction?

- What supports and adaptations might be required for individuals with learning disabilities in order to access the general curriculum?

- In what ways can communicating interweave understanding of culture along with an influence on language interaction and exceptionalities with sensitivity to aspects of diversity?

# SUMMARY

**How can we explain learning and memory?**

- Information-processing theory is currently the most prominent theory of learning in learning disabilities. The information-processing system includes short-term memory, working memory, long-term memory, executive control, and motivation.

**What do we know about the learning and memory of students with learning disabilities?**

- Much research has been done on the learning and memory of students with learning disabilities. One area that has proven ineffective is the study of learning styles. Early research focused on cognitive styles such as field independence versus field dependence and reflectivity versus impulsivity. Current research has focused on the difference between students with learning disabilities and their nondisabled peers in the areas of short-term and working memory.

**Council for Exceptional Children**

**CEC Knowledge Check**

In your opinion, what is one of Shannon's major learning-related problems? LD3K3

- Students with learning disabilities often lack appropriate metacognitive or executive control abilities and therefore cannot apply their skills and knowledge effectively.
- Students with learning disabilities may show motivation difficulties, including external locus of control, negative attributions, and learned helplessness.

**How can learning, memory, and motivation needs be addressed?**

- Self-instruction teaches students to guide their own actions in completing tasks.

- Self-monitoring of academic performance teaches students to keep track of and monitor their academic performance in order to understand their strengths and weaknesses.
- Self-determination is the ability to use skills to problem solve and make decisions. Often, self-determination skills must be directly taught to students with learning disabilities.
- Mnemonic strategies provide aids in the storage and retrieval of information and concepts from long-term memory.
- Attribution training helps students credit their performance to appropriate outlets, including hard work, studying, and use of strategies, instead of to luck or "the teacher doesn't like me."

- Cognitive strategies combine self-instruction, mnemonic strategies, and attribution training to help students with learning disabilities approach tasks such as test-taking and textbook reading successfully.

Council for Exceptional Children

**CEC Knowledge Check**

If you were Shannon's teacher, what would be the first method you would use in your classroom? Why? LD4S1

- General teaching practices to activate learning and memory include providing advance organizers, activating background knowledge, providing distributed practice, engaging students in dialogue, and setting appropriate expectations.

## REFLECTIONS ON THE CASES

1. How do you think Shannon's motivation is affected by her academic struggles in mathematics?
2. What are Shannon's major areas of difficulty in cognition, metacognition, and memory?
3. Which practices described in this chapter would help Shannon? Why?

## *Focus On* Memory and Cognition

### *Do Now* Activities for Organizing and Remembering Information

## Organizing and Retaining Information through Note-Taking Strategies

### ● *What are they?*

Note-taking strategies refer to any process designed to assist students in identifying main ideas, concepts, or themes from text, lecture, or other information source. Different note-taking strategies serve differing purposes. Teaching students specific strategies for particular tasks will help students store and retain the information longer. Additionally, the strategies will increase student independence and self-sufficiency.

Understanding how people process information can illuminate why effective note-taking strategies facilitate memory. Below is a graphic representation of information processing that shows how information is received, processed, and stored. (For more detailed information, refer back to the section on information-processing theory in Chapter 8.) Note-taking strategies force students to (1) attend to key external stimuli (short-term memory), (2) actively engage information in working memory by making decisions about what to write or where to place key concepts, and (3) connect new information received to prior knowledge, information, or concepts stored in their long-term memory.

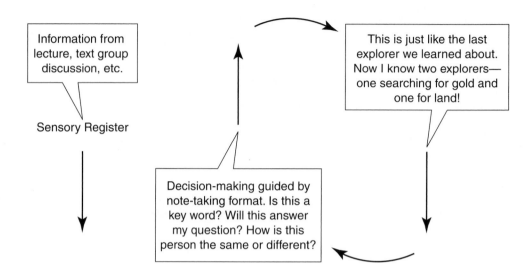

For students with learning disabilities, note-taking strategies can address memory deficits through careful organization, attention, and rehearsal.

● *How to implement them*

In the chart, three different note-taking strategies are described.

| NOTE-TAKING STRATEGY | DESCRIPTION | STEPS TO FOLLOW |
|---|---|---|
| Cornell system | The Cornell system for note-taking was designed to support students in identifying main points, key terms, and people by creating a graphic organizer for gathering and sorting information. | 1. Divide the top two-thirds of the paper into two sections by drawing a line down the center of the paper. Leave the bottom third open.<br><br>2. In the right-hand space, write notes from lecture or text. Skip a line between topics or ideas.<br><br>3. In the left-hand space, write down main ideas and key people or terms. |

| NOTE-TAKING STRATEGY | DESCRIPTION | STEPS TO FOLLOW |
|---|---|---|
| | | 4. In the bottom section, write several sentences of summary.<br>5. Read the notes after you have written them for a quick review and then later for studying. |
| Post-it notes | Post-it note-taking is a great strategy for note-taking from a textbook. Post-it notes can be placed directly on the text for studying pur-poses or sorted for further organization. | 1. Decide on the purpose of the Post-it notes. Post-its can be used for defining terms, asking questions of the text, or writing summary statements. Teachers can also generate a generic list of questions students can respond to at key points. For example, students can be directed to answer the following questions at the end of each section: (1) What was the big idea for this sec-tion? (2) Who or what was involved? (3) What do you predict will happen next?<br>2. Model using the Post-its on several occasions prior to having students use the notes independently.<br>3. Practice sorting the notes in a variety of ways—collecting all the predictions or making a chart of all the key terms, etc. |
| Pattern notes | Pattern notes are a non-linear system for note-taking. Pattern notes can look like concept maps or diagrams. Lines or arrows between topics connect the material and concepts. Pattern notes are particularly useful for processing information from linear notes or when preparing for writing about a theme. Pattern notes encourage students to connect disparate parts of the text to main concepts or themes. | 1. Decide on the main idea or topic. This should be the center of your map.<br>2. Build the map around the center topic and then con-nect the supporting statements, concepts, or topics by drawing lines to the main idea.<br>3. Because pattern notes are more abstract and require higher levels of thinking (analysis, synthesis, evalua-tion), it is important to model pattern notes with familiar material when teaching the strategy.<br>4. Research suggests that pattern notes are more mean-ingful if students create their own maps and can justify the connections.<br><br>Post-it — Note-Taking Strategies — Pattern / Cornell |

## ● *Additional Resources*

Dodge, J. (1994). *The study skills handbook.* New York, NY: Scholastic.

Strichart, S. S., & Mangrum, C. T. 11 (2002). *Teaching study skills and strategies to students with LD, ADD, or special needs.* Boston: Allyn & Bacon.

*Source:* Kristin L. Sayeski

Council for Exceptional Children

See Companion Website for detailed correlations between chapter content and Council for Exceptional Children Standards; **www.ablongman.com/ hallahanLD3e**

**CEC Knowledge and Skills Discussed in This Chapter**

① The historical foundations and major contributors in the field of ADHD, as related to learning disabilities.

② Issues of definition and classification, including cultural diversity, along with characteristic similarities and differences.

③ Understanding of how learning environment modifications can be used on a continuum from least to most intensive in order to manage behaviors and learning.

④ The importance of practicing within one's skill limit and advocating for research-supported appropriate interventions.

# Attention Deficit Hyperactivity Disorder

Sometimes, Shannon's so lost in her own thoughts that it seems like she's daydreaming. And then other times, if she's working in a group at one side of the room and somebody says something about a planet—or just says some word that sounds like a planet's name—she'll pick up on that and forget about the lesson.

*Julie Robinson, Shannon's sixth-grade teacher*

Researchers have documented that many students with learning disabilities have attention problems. Using a variety of laboratory tasks, as well as behavioral observations in classrooms, they have shown that students with learning disabilities often have difficulty with many aspects of attention (Hallahan & Reeve, 1980; Pelham, 1981). In addition to problems of sustaining their attention or sticking to academic work once they begin it, they also often have problems with distractibility and selective attention. As we see from the excerpt above, Ms. Robinson was all too aware of Shannon's tendency to "tune out" as well as her distractibility. And Shannon's distractibility also led to her problems in selective attention. **Selective attention** is the ability to focus on the relevant features of a task without being distracted by its irrelevant aspects. Over the years, many of Shannon's teachers have commented on how much difficulty she has focusing her attention. For example, her fourth-grade special education teacher remarked that although Shannon might have problems finishing a worksheet on time, she would have no trouble recalling the number of stray pencil marks on the page. Also, transitions to new assignments have always been difficult for Shannon, because she has trouble recognizing what information is relevant.

> Shannon

**selective attention** the ability to focus on relevant features of a task without being distracted by irrelevant aspects

## What Are the Links between Learning Disabilities and Attention Problems?

Shannon was formally diagnosed as having attention deficit hyperactivity disorder (ADHD). The fact that Shannon has both learning disabilities and ADHD does not make her all that unusual. In fact, learning disabilities and ADHD often go hand in hand. Girls with ADHD, in particular, tend to have poorer academic achievement than do boys with ADHD (Gershon, 2002). Estimates vary, but a conservative estimate is that about 20% of students identified as having learning disabilities could also be diagnosed as having ADHD (Riccio, Gonzalez, & Hynd, 1994). Still other students, like Jamal, have symptoms of inattention and poor impulse control that are not severe enough to warrant a diagnosis of ADHD but still interfere significantly with academic and social functioning.

 Jamal

There are at least three reasons that there is much overlap between learning disabilities and ADHD, as follows:

1. The learning disability may precede the attention problems. Students may develop inattentive behaviors because of being frustrated by repeated failures.
2. The attention problems may precede the learning disability. Inattention may result in the student failing to process important academic instruction, thus causing the student to fall behind.
3. The attention problems and learning disabilities may be separate conditions that co-occur.

Council for
Exceptional
Children

**CEC Knowledge Check**
What are the three overlaps between learning disabilities and ADHD?
CC2K5

It is very difficult to tell which of the three scenarios, or combination of scenarios, applies for individuals who have both learning disabilities and ADHD.

As we discuss later, heredity figures in as a cause of ADHD, just as it does for learning disabilities. This has led researchers to explore whether there is a genetic link between learning disabilities and ADHD. Thus far, the evidence favors the conclusion that different genes are involved in the two conditions (Barkley, 2000).

Given that problems of attention, impulse control, and hyperactivity occur so frequently in students with learning disabilities, teachers need to be familiar with educational methods aimed at students with ADHD. Teachers likely will need to use these techniques for many students, whether or not they have an official diagnosis of ADHD. For this reason, we have devoted this chapter solely to a discussion of ADHD. We begin with a brief history of how professionals came to recognize ADHD as a condition warranting diagnosis and remediation.

## What Are the Historical Origins of ADHD?

The most striking thing you find when considering the development of the category of ADHD is that a variety of labels have been used to refer to this condition. This maze of terminology reflects the fact that researchers and practitioners have struggled to determine what exactly is the core symptom. Is it hyperactivity? Is it inattention? Is it some combination of the two? Or, as many now believe, is the primary cause a problem with self-control? Interestingly, George F. Still, the first to bring the condition we now call ADHD to the attention of the scientific community, focused on the issue of self-control.

### Early Observations of ADHD Symptoms

In 1902, George F. Still delivered a series of lectures to the Royal College of Physicians of London in which he described a number of cases of children with a common set of behaviors (Still, 1902). In addition to displaying disobedience, inattention, and hyperactivity, these children also showed an inability to refrain from engaging in impulsive, inappropriate behavior (Still, 1902).

Other characteristics were similar to what has been identified as ADHD:

1. He believed that many of the children had mild brain pathology.
2. Many of the children had normal intelligence.
3. A greater percentage of the cases were boys than girls.
4. He speculated that there was a hereditary basis to the condition.
5. Many of the children also had other symptoms, such as depression and tics.

## The Strauss Syndrome

Following an outbreak in 1917 of **encephalitis,** an infection of the brain, a number of children in the United States were left with a variety of behavioral problems. Chief among the symptoms exhibited by these affected children were inattention, impulsivity, and hyperactivity. Through several reports in the medical literature, many physicians and educators thus became aware of the significant effects brain damage could have on cognitive and behavioral functioning.

In the 1930s and 1940s, Heinz Werner and Alfred Strauss, who worked at a residential institution for children with mental retardation, noticed that many of the children exhibited the same behaviors as those attributable to brain injury. These researchers conducted a series of experiments in which they compared the performance of supposedly brain-injured children with mental retardation to that of non-brain-injured children with mental retardation on a variety of figure-background tasks (Strauss & Werner, 1942; Werner & Strauss, 1939, 1940, 1941). For example, each child was shown slides of familiar objects (e.g., sailboat, hat, iron, cup) embedded in backgrounds (e.g., wavy lines) at very fast exposure times, such as half a second. (See Figure 9.1.) When asked what they had seen, the children in

**encephalitis** an inflammation of the brain; can affect the child's mental development adversely

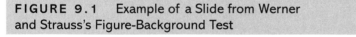

**FIGURE 9.1**  Example of a Slide from Werner and Strauss's Figure-Background Test

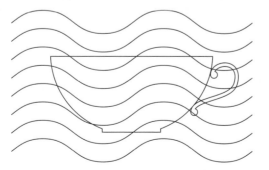

*Source:* From *Psychopathology and Education of the Brain-Injured Child* (p. 47), by A. A. Strauss and L. E. Lehtinen, 1947, New York: Grune & Stratton. Copyright 1947 by Grune & Stratton. Reprinted by permission.

the brain-injured group were more likely to refer to the background and less likely to recall the figure correctly. Werner and Strauss saw this as indicative of their distractibility.

Werner and Strauss's work was deservedly criticized on the grounds that the diagnostic classification of their children as brain-injured was faulty; however, they did find a subgroup of students with mental retardation, brain-injured or not, who were highly distractible. Their work brought attention to the particularly devastating consequences that distractibility and hyperactivity can have on children's functioning. Children with high levels of distractibility and hyperactivity soon came to be referred to as exhibiting the **Strauss syndrome.**

## The Bridge from Mental Retardation to Normal Intelligence

More than a decade after Werner and Strauss's work, William Cruickshank replicated their findings. But instead of looking at students who were mentally retarded, he tested the figure-background abilities of students with cerebral palsy who were of near-normal, normal, or above-normal intelligence (Cruickshank, Bice, & Wallen, 1957). Unlike the children studied by Werner and Strauss, there was little doubt that the students studied by Cruickshank were brain injured. **Cerebral palsy,** a relatively easy condition to diagnose in young children, is characterized by problems in movement and results from damage to the motor areas of the brain.

The finding of distractibility in students with cerebral palsy who were not mentally retarded served as a conceptual bridge between persons with mental retardation and those of average intelligence. Thus, by showing that a person can have normal intelligence and yet display inattention and hyperactivity, this research paved the way for linking attention problems with learning disabilities, which, by definition, can occur in students of average or above-average intelligence.

Bolstered by the results of his study of students with cerebral palsy, Cruickshank went on to set up educational programs for children who today would be referred to as having learning disabilities and/or ADHD. These were students whose intelligence levels were above those of persons with mental retardation but who exhibited academic achievement problems and high levels of inattention and hyperactivity. (Cruickshank's educational approach is discussed later in this chapter.) At the time, many of these children were referred to as having minimal brain injury.

## Minimal Brain Injury and the Hyperactive Child Syndrome

Two other labels that emerged in the 1950s and 1960s were minimal brain injury and the hyperactive child syndrome. **Minimal brain injury (MBI)** was used to refer to children who did not have abnormal neurological exams but who exhibited behaviors—such as inattention, hyperactivity, and impulsivity—that were similar to behaviors displayed by individuals with documented brain injury. The popularity of the MBI label, however, was short lived. Professionals objected to the qualifier "minimal," because it belied the substantial problems that these children experi-

**Strauss syndrome**  behaviors of distractibility, forced responsiveness to stimuli, and hyperactivity; based on the work of Alfred Strauss and Heinz Werner with children with mental retardation

**cerebral palsy**  a condition characterized by paralysis, weakness, incoordination, and/or other motor dysfunction; caused by damage to the brain before it has matured

**minimal brain injury (MBI)**  a term used to describe a child who shows behavioral but not neurological signs of brain injury; the term is not as popular as it once was, primarily because of its lack of diagnostic utility (i.e., some children who learn normally show signs indicative of minimal brain injury)

enced. In addition, they objected to the inference that the brains of these children had actual tissue damage, because there was insufficient neurological evidence that this was the case.

In his authoritative text on ADHD, Barkley (1998) refers to the 1960s as the "Golden Age of Hyperactivity." It was during this period that the notion of a **hyperactive child syndrome** arose and began to replace the MBI label. Authorities preferred this new designation because it focused on observable behavior rather than the unreliable diagnosis of subtle brain injury.

A syndrome implies a common group of behaviors. In the case of the hyperactive child syndrome, these behaviors were such things as hyperactivity, inattention, impulsivity, academic learning problems, and poor peer relationships. Although all of these behavioral characteristics were considered important, for the most part, researchers and practitioners focused on hyperactivity. By the 1980s, however, researchers began to point to inattention as the major deficit exhibited by these children. Today, as you will see below, some authorities are pointing to problems in behavioral inhibition as the key characteristic of ADHD.

## What Is Today's Definition of ADHD?

Today, most professionals rely on the American Psychiatric Association's (APA's) *Diagnostic and Statistical Manual of Mental Disorders* (DSM) for diagnosing children with ADHD. The current DSM recognizes three types of ADHD, depending on how much the individual displays attention versus hyperactivity-impulsivity problems: (1) ADHD, Predominantly Inattentive Type; (2) ADHD, Predominantly Hyperactive-Impulsive Type; and (3) ADHD, Combined Type (American Psychiatric Association, 2000). (See Table 9.1, pages 264–265.)

The characteristics associated with inattention are more closely linked to learning disabilities than those associated with hyperactivity-impulsivity. In other words, children with the Combined Type and those with the Predominantly Inattentive Type are more likely to have academic problems than are those with the Predominantly Hyperactive-Impulsive Type (Wilens, Biederman, & Spencer, 2002).

Shannon fits the typical profile in that she is both learning disabled and has been diagnosed with ADHD, Predominantly Inattentive Type. As part of the diagnostic workup that was done on Shannon, Maria Rodriguez, a child psychiatrist, showed Shannon's parents a checklist based on the DSM criteria in Table 9.1 and asked them whether they thought any of the DSM criteria applied to Shannon. Both parents agreed that several items were very applicable. Specifically, they concurred that Shannon often

- failed to attend to details and made careless mistakes on schoolwork
- seemed as though she was not listening when spoken to
- did not follow through on work in school and/or at home
- was disorganized in her work
- avoided work that required continuous attention
- lost things

**hyperactive child syndrome** a term used to refer to children who exhibit inattention, impulsivity, and/or hyperactivity; popular in the 1960s and 1970s

**Council for Exceptional Children**

**CEC Knowledge Check**
Who were the early pioneers in studying the causes and remedies for ADHD?
LD1K1

**Council for Exceptional Children**

**CEC Knowledge Check**
Name and describe the differences among these three types of ADHD.
CC1K5

Shannon

**A.** Either (1) or (2):

(1) six (or more) of the following symptoms of *inattention* have persisted for at least 6 months to a degree that is maladaptive and inconsistent with developmental level:

*Inattention*
(a) often fails to give close attention to details or makes careless mistakes in schoolwork, work, or other activities
(b) often has difficulty sustaining attention in tasks or play activities
(c) often does not seem to listen when spoken to directly
(d) often does not follow through on instructions and fails to finish schoolwork, chores, or duties in the workplace (not due to oppositional behavior or failure to understand instructions)
(e) often has difficulty organizing tasks and activities
(f) often avoids, dislikes, or is reluctant to engage in tasks that require sustained mental effort (such as schoolwork or homework)
(g) often loses things necessary for tasks or activities (e.g., toys, school assignments, pencils, books, or tools)
(h) is often easily distracted by extraneous stimuli
(i) is often forgetful in daily activities

(2) six (or more) of the following symptoms of hyperactivity-impulsivity have persisted for at least 6 months to a degree that is maladaptive and inconsistent with developmental level:

*Hyperactivity*
(a) often fidgets with hands or feet or squirms in seat
(b) often leaves seat in classroom or in other situations in which remaining seated is expected
(c) often runs about or climbs excessively in situations in which it is inappropriate (in adolescents or adults, may be limited to subjective feelings of restlessness)
(d) often has difficulty playing or engaging in leisure activities quietly
(e) is often "on the go" or often acts as if "driven by a motor"
(f) often talks excessively

*Impulsivity*
(g) often blurts out answers before questions have been completed
(h) often has difficulty awaiting turn
(i) often interrupts or intrudes on others (e.g., butts into conversations or games)

**B.** Some hyperactive-impulsive or inattentive symptoms that caused impairment were present before age 7 years
**C.** Some impairment from the symptoms is present in two or more settings (e.g., at school [or work] and at home).
**D.** There must be clear evidence of clinically significant impairment in social, academic, or occupational functioning.
**E.** The symptoms do not occur exclusively during the course of a Pervasive Developmental Disorder, Schizophrenia, or other Psychotic Disorder and are not better accounted for by another mental disorder (e.g., Mood Disorder, Anxiety Disorder, Dissociative Disorder, or a Personality Disorder).

**TABLE 9.1** Continued

Code based on type

314.01 Attention-Deficit/Hyperactivity Disorder, Combined Type: if both Criteria A1 and A2 are met for the past 6 months

314.00 Attention-Deficit/Hyperactivity Disorder, Predominantly Inattentive Type: if Criterion A1 is met but Criterion A2 is not met for the past 6 months

314.01 Attention-Deficit/Hyperactivity Disorder, Predominantly Hyperactive-Impulsive Type: If Criterion A2 is met but Criterion A1 is not met for the past 6 months

*Coding note:* For individuals (especially adolescents and adults) who currently have symptoms that no longer meet full criteria, "In Partial Remission" should be specified

*Source:* From *Diagnostic and Statistical Manual of Mental Disorders,* 4th ed., text rev. (pp. 92–93) by American Psychiatric Association, 2000, Washington, DC. Copyright 2000 American Psychiatric Association. Reprinted by permission.

- forgot things and/or activities
- talked seemingly nonstop
- interrupted conversations

Dr. Rodriguez pointed out that the first seven items the parents checked suggested that Shannon had ADHD, Predominantly Inattentive Type. She also told them that the psychiatric profession (as indicated by the DSM) recommended a diagnosis of this type if the person had six or more of the nine inattentive criteria on the checklist. However, Dr. Rodriguez told the Irelands two other important things. First, she wanted Shannon's teacher also to complete the checklist, because the DSM dictated that ADHD should be present in at least two settings. Second, she noted that even though Shannon didn't appear to meet the standard for having the predominantly hyperactive-impulsive type of ADHD, the Irelands had checked two criteria from this type—talking nonstop and interrupting conversations. These behaviors should be targets for change, especially if Shannon's teachers also observed them.

## What Is the Prevalence of ADHD?

It is generally accepted that ADHD is the most common reason for children being referred to child guidance clinics. Studies indicate that between 3 to 5% of school-age children have been diagnosed with ADHD in the United States (National Institutes of Health, 1998). The most common subtype of ADHD is the Combined Type, accounting for about 50 to 75% of all persons with ADHD. The second most common type is the inattentive type (20 to 30%), followed by the hyperactive-impulsive type (fewer than 15%) (Wilens et al., 2002).

Some critics, mostly writing in the popular press, have claimed that ADHD is almost exclusively a U.S. condition. They state that it has become almost fashionable to claim that one has ADHD as a way of excusing low achievement. However, similar proportions of ADHD are found in the populations of many other countries, including Australia, New Zealand, Germany, Japan, and Brazil (Kanbayashi, Nakata, Fujii, Kita, & Wada, 1994; Wilens et al., 2002).

The diagnosis of ADHD is more prevalent for males than for females. Estimates vary, but we can be pretty certain that about 3 to 4 times more boys are identified as ADHD than girls (Barkley, 1998). What is not certain is whether this is due to the overidentification of boys or the underidentification of girls. Evidence that the latter might be true comes from statistics showing that the gap in prevalence of ADHD in boys and girls is narrowing (Robison, Skaer, Sclar, & Galin, 2002). In other words, it is quite possible that professionals have been slow to recognize ADHD in girls. We can speculate that this is because girls are more likely to exhibit the inattentive type of ADHD. In contrast to hyperactivity and impulsivity, which are more prevalent in boys, inattentive behaviors are less likely to bother teachers and parents.

This is probably what happened in the case of Shannon. Although she was diagnosed with learning disabilities in third grade, she was not referred and identified as having ADHD until fifth grade. As Shannon's mother says:

Shannon

> All the signs—the inattentiveness, the lack of focus, the disorganization—were there since well before the time she was diagnosed. I don't know. Maybe it was because she already had learning disabilities. Maybe we thought that was what was causing all the attention problems. Or maybe it's because she didn't really cause anyone, the teachers, I mean, any real trouble. She was polite and acted kind of shy. She wasn't one to make waves.
>
> *Kerrie Ireland, Shannon's mother*

Much more research is needed before we can reach firm conclusions regarding the true prevalence of ADHD, generally, and any gender differences in the prevalence of ADHD, specifically. For now, our best scientific evidence leads us to these conclusions:

1. There are undoubtedly cases of children being diagnosed as ADHD who should not be. We know of too many cases of sloppy diagnostic practices to ignore the fact that some misdiagnosis takes place.
2. There are undoubtedly cases of children who should be diagnosed as ADHD but who are not. We know of too many cases of parents and teachers who excuse a boy's hyperactivity and impulsivity with the old adage, "Oh, he's just being a boy." Likewise, we know of too many cases of children, often girls, whose inattentive type of ADHD does not gain the notice of parents and teachers because these children are compliant and quiet.
3. There is undoubtedly some referral bias operating that accounts for some of the difference in the prevalence of the diagnosis of ADHD in males and fe-

males. On the other hand, many other childhood illnesses or physical conditions (e.g., autism, cerebral palsy, stuttering, learning disabilities) are more prevalent in males than females, and virtually no conditions are more prevalent in females than males. Therefore, it is highly probable that there are constitutional differences that account for some of the higher prevalence of ADHD in males.

**CEC Knowledge Check**

Do you think there is gender bias in identifying students with ADHD? LD9K1

## How Is ADHD Assessed?

Authorities recommend that a diagnosis of ADHD should include three elements: (1) a medical examination, (2) a clinical interview or history, and (3) the administration of teacher and parent rating scales (Barkley, 1998). In the case of older children or adults, the psychiatrist or psychologist may also administer a self-report type of rating scale.

### Medical Exam

The medical exam can help rule out any physical reasons for the inattentive and/or hyperactive-impulsive behavior, such as thyroid problems or brain tumors. The physician can determine whether the child's behavioral problems are due to a seizure disorder, such as epilepsy. Environmental factors, such as lead poisoning, can also be considered.

The physician can also determine whether the patient has other conditions that would make it unwise to prescribe certain medications to help control the inattention or hyperactivity. For example, high blood pressure, cardiac problems, or asthma might influence what kind of medication the doctor would prescribe for the child. And if the child has tics, the physician might be more careful in using certain medications, because there is suggestive evidence that commonly used medications for ADHD might make the tics worsen. **Tics** are repetitive motor movements that are sometimes accompanied by multiple vocal grunts or outbursts. Severe tics are one of the major symptoms of someone who has **Tourette's syndrome.** There is a high incidence of ADHD in individuals diagnosed with Tourette's syndrome.

**tics** stereotyped, repetitive motor movements

**Tourette's syndrome** a neurological disorder beginning in childhood (about three times more prevalent in boys than in girls) in which stereotyped, repetitive motor movements (tics) are accompanied by multiple vocal outbursts that may include grunting noises or socially inappropriate words or statements (e.g., swearing)

### Clinical Interview

The clinical interview, or history of the child and parent(s), is important because it can be used to gather information on the child, the parents, and any siblings. The clinician can obtain a picture of the dynamics of the family and the major symptoms that all the family members see as most problematic.

Even though the interview is important, we need to recognize that it is somewhat subjective. For example, some children with ADHD can appear very attentive when in a structured and novel setting. In fact, researchers have discovered what has been referred to as a **doctor's office effect,** whereby children can be focused in the physician's office but just the opposite at home and school (Cantwell, 1979; Sleator & Ullman, 1981).

**doctor's office effect** the observation that children with ADHD often do not exhibit their symptoms when seen by a clinician in a brief office visit

## Rating Scales

Because of the subjectivity of the clinical interview and the existence of such things as the doctor's office effect, professionals often use rating scales to obtain more objective, behavioral data. See the Case Connections box on page 269.

Jamal

As noted in the Case Connections box, Jamal's pediatrician used rating scales to help determine that Jamal was not ADHD. The rating scale he used, the *Conners' Teacher Rating Scale–Revised* (S) (Conners, 1997), is one of the most commonly used standardized rating scales. As we noted earlier, Shannon's psychiatrist, Dr. Rodriguez, used an informal checklist, or rating form, based on the DSM criteria, to help in the diagnosis of Shannon's ADHD. But Dr. Rodriguez also requested that Shannon's teacher fill out one portion of the *Conners'* scale. (Recall that, according to the DSM, symptoms of ADHD should be observed in at least two settings.) The ratings on this scale were in agreement with those of the parents. Her teacher rated her as highly inattentive but not very hyperactive on this 28-item rating scale. (There is a longer version of this rating scale that contains 59 items.)

Shannon

Council for
Exceptional
Children

**CEC Knowledge Check**

What are the three methods of assessing ADHD?
CC8K3

## Using Technology to Assess ADHD

Although medical exams, clinical interviews, and rating scales will probably always be a necessary part of the identification of students with ADHD, researchers are turning to technology to find additional methods of assessing ADHD. For example, there are several commercial computerized versions of continuous performance tests (CPTs). CPTs vary somewhat. A typical one projects stimuli (e.g., $X$s and $O$s) one at a time on a screen rapidly (about one per second), and the individual is instructed to push a button every time a particular stimulus (e.g., $X$) appears or a particular sequence (e.g., $O$ followed by an $X$) appears. The computer keeps track of the number of correct responses, failures to respond to a correct stimulus (omission errors), and incorrect responses or responses to the wrong stimulus (commission errors).

It has now become relatively common for clinicians to use a computerized CPT to help evaluate children for ADHD. There are other technologies that hold potential for helping identify ADHD that are much more experimental. See the Today's Technology box on pages 270–271 for an example.

Council for
Exceptional
Children

**CEC Knowledge Check**

How do you plan to keep informed about the use of technology in assessing ADHD?
CC8S3

## Issues Related to Identification for Special Education Services

The overlap between learning disabilities and ADHD has created considerable controversy in the field. (See the Current Trends and Issues box on pages 272–273.) This controversy has made it difficult to keep track of how many students with ADHD are served in special education. Furthermore, it makes it difficult to keep track of such things as the gender and ethnicity of students identified as ADHD and receiving special education. This is unfortunate, because some have claimed that African American boys are disproportionately identified as ADHD. (See the Multicultural Considerations box on page 274.)

# The Doctor's Office Effect

Following the recommendation of the school psychologist, Jamal's mother had Jamal see a pediatrician to assess whether he had ADHD. When making the appointment, Mrs. Smith was asked why she needed to have Jamal assessed. She explained that the school psychologist had suggested the visit: "She said he answered questions impulsively, fidgeted, and was nervous."

Jamal's pediatrician, Dr. Synder, talked with Jamal and administered some informal tests of motor skills in his office. He also requested that Jamal's mother and teacher each complete a brief rating scale about hyperactive behavior. Based on his assessment, he sent this letter to Mrs. Smith.

> Dear Mrs. Smith,
> Thank you for bringing Jamal in for evaluation of possible attention deficit hyperactivity disorder. I am glad you and Hereford School are working together to ensure that Jamal obtains a good education and is successful in school.
>
> Jamal presented as a healthy, alert, inquisitive young man. He is within normal ranges for height and weight and has no apparent developmental motoric delays. He uses language well and appears to be happy and to be well adjusted.
>
> To evaluate the possibility of ADHD, I interviewed Jamal, administered tests for subtle neurological problems, and obtained ratings of his behavior. Based on these tests and my observations, I do not believe that he has a level or degree of problem consistent with the DSM criteria for ADHD. There were no anomalies in my assessments of his neurological functioning. He didn't display any inattention, impulsivity, or hyperactivity in my office. But as I told you when you visited, there's always the possibility of what we call a "doctor's office effect." That's why I also asked you and his teacher to fill out the rating scales. The scores on the *Conners' Teacher Rating Scale* that you and Jamal's teacher completed did not indicate that he has ADHD. Your ratings of his impulsivity and hyperactivity were a little bit on the high side but not high enough to fall into the clinical range. Plus, the teacher's ratings were well below the cutoff for ADHD.
>
> I do not consider a diagnosis of ADHD to be correct for Jamal. He is a young boy with lots of energy who sometimes blurts out answers. He may need other help, but medical management for these issues is not indicated at this time.
>
> Sincerely,
> George Synder, M.D.

In a handwritten sticky note on the letter, Dr. Synder added a personal comment, because he knew Mrs. Smith from her nursing background: "Irene, Jamal's doing well. He's not hyperactive. Work with his teacher on his reading and don't worry about his adjustment."

TODAY'S
TECHNOLOGY

FOR LEARNING
DISABILITIES

## ERICA: A Potential Tool for Identifying Students with ADHD?

The Eye-gaze Response Interface Aid (ERICA) was invented by University of Virginia systems engineering professor Tom Hutchinson. (See Figure A.) Although Hutchinson's original purpose for ERICA was to help individuals with severe physical disabilities communicate by using their eyes, this device has also stimulated research in a variety of areas. One such area currently being pursued by Professor Rick Brigham, also of the University of Virginia, is the potential that ERICA might hold for the identification of students with ADHD and/or learning disabilities. We interviewed Brigham about his work with ERICA.

**FIGURE A**

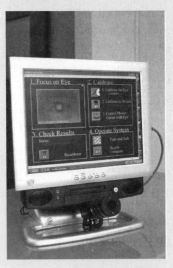

*Source:* Courtesy of Eye Response Technologies (www.eyeresponse.com). Reprinted by permission.

### Briefly, how does ERICA work?

You can use ERICA to track where a user is looking on a computer monitor. ERICA consists of a camera and an infrared light emitting diode (LED) that reflects off the eye of the user. The LED and camera are housed in a compartment sitting just in front of the computer monitor. The effects of the infrared light hitting the eye are measured in such a way that it is possible to tell exactly where the user is looking on the screen and for how long.

### Tell us about your work using ERICA.

A few years ago, I was introduced to Tom Hutchinson, the inventor of ERICA. At first, I was a little skeptical of becoming involved with eye-movement research because it had such a bad reputation from the old days in reading, but I was interested in how people could use visual displays, like maps and charts, to understand information and aid in its recall. ERICA seemed like a way to get a good look at how people processed those kinds of displays. We started looking at differences among students with and without disabilities like LD when reading Websites for information and just continued from there.

### You mentioned problems with the older eye-movement studies. What was wrong with them?

Well, in a nutshell, people now believe that cognitive processes control your attention. In the old eye-movement research, they had it backward. Some researchers noticed that people who read poorly had unusual eye movements. Earlier eye-movement studies suggested that training the eyes to move smoothly and evenly would alter the individual's reading abilities. It doesn't work that way. We now believe that except for extreme cases, eye movements are affected by reading ability, rather than vice versa.

## What Are the Causes of ADHD?

The causal factors we discussed in Chapter 2 pertaining to learning disabilities, generally, are the same ones authorities point to with respect to ADHD. Neurological factors and heredity, in particular, are suspected in many cases of ADHD.

**Have you seen any differences among groups of children in the eye-movement studies?**

Yes, for her dissertation, Rosa Olmeda devised a very nice study comparing the performance of students with and without ADHD when they were viewing a Web page containing science content. She reasoned that kids with ADHD often show increased attention in novel situations but soon become accustomed to the routine and demonstrate decrements in performance. This observation is the basis for the sustained vigilance tasks that are sometimes used in ADHD identification.

Rosa figured that having kids read materials like they would find in school should result in less of an initial focus and a faster deterioration of performance than interacting with a device in an office or conference room. She had the kids read the page and then examined the eye movements. What she found was by examining the eye movement patterns without knowing anything else about the individual, she could identify all of the kids without ADHD and was 95% accurate in identifying the kids with ADHD.

**Wouldn't reading ability give you the same ability?**

I don't think so. First Rosa matched the reading performance of her ADHD and non-ADHD sample, so there really were no differences there. She also matched her groups on IQ measures. Second, the differences in performance were actually somewhat subtle. Just like in the sustained vigilance tasks, initial attention indicators were better than average but not by much in this task. However, by the time that the students had read three short paragraphs (in this case, about weather), the differences became fairly clear. Whereas typical readers read each sentence with about the same level of attention across the entire task, the kids with ADHD began skipping words and sometimes even entire sentences about halfway

through the second paragraph. Many of them omitted the third short paragraph altogether or only looked at one or two words of the 35-word paragraph. Once you know what you are looking for in this data, it jumps right out at you. You can see it in the display of the eye movements on the computer screen. The first paragraph looks like one would expect, with eye fixations on nearly every word and movements mostly left to right, with returns from right to left landing on about the right place for the next line. By the end, there are substantially fewer fixations and far more erratic patterns of eye movement in the ADHD group.

**Do you think that this method can be used to identify kids with ADHD?**

Probably, but we have not yet conducted sufficient research to suggest that it is ready for day-to-day use. For one thing, the equipment, although it is improving rapidly, still takes a little practice to use reliably. Hutchinson and one of his colleagues, Chris Lankford, have made remarkable improvements on both the hardware and the software since we conducted our study last year; these developments should make it easier to use. So far, we have detected this pattern in middle-school kids with ADHD. We still need to make sure that it will appear in younger children. There is a pretty good chance that it will, but we want to prove it before we ask people to use it.

**What else could you do with the eye-movement data?**

For students with ADHD, we think that it stands to reason that eye-gaze data could be a useful indicator of treatment effects for medications. If the medications used enable the students to deploy their abilities, small changes in behavior like the ones ERICA picks up will be noticeable long before changes in grades and social interactions take place.

*Source:* Courtesy of the Eye Response Technologies (www.eyeresponse.com). Reprinted by permission.

## Neurological Factors

With the development of neuroimaging techniques has come the discovery of areas of the brain that are likely to be affected in individuals with ADHD. Using techniques such as MRIs, for example, researchers have pointed to the prefrontal and

# CURRENT TRENDS & ISSUES

## How Many Students with ADHD Are Served in Special Education?

Because ADHD is such a prevalent condition, one would think that it would be relatively easy to find out how many students with ADHD receive special education services. Federal law, after all, requires that schools report how many students with a given disability have been identified for special education services. However, when Public Law 94-142 (the Education for All Handicapped Children Act) was passed in 1975, ADHD was not included as one of the separate categories of special education. This was due in part to two interrelated factors: (1) the research on this condition was still in its infancy, and (2) the advocacy base for children with ADHD was not yet well developed. For example, . . . the major advocacy organization for people with ADHD, CHADD (Children and Adults with Attention Deficit Disorder) was not founded until 1987.

By the time of the reauthorization of the law as the Individuals with Disabilities Education Act (IDEA) in 1990, however, there was substantial research on ADHD, and CHADD's membership was well on its way to its present level of 22,000 members. CHADD lobbied hard for ADHD to be considered a separate category, arguing that children with ADHD were being denied services because they could qualify for special education only if they also had another disability, such as learning disabilities or emotional disturbance. Their lobbying was unsuccessful. However, the U.S. Depart-

ment of Education in 1991 determined that students with ADHD would be eligible for special education under the category "other health impaired" (OHI) "in instances where the ADD is a chronic or acute health problem that results in limited alertness, which adversely affects educational performance." And students with ADHD can also qualify for accommodation under another law (Section 504).

Many professionals are still disappointed with the decision not to include ADHD as a separate category because they say that using the OHI category is too roundabout a means of identification, and Section 504 is not completely satisfactory because it does not require an individualized education program (IEP). . . .

However, the growth of the OHI category since 1991 suggests that more and more students with ADHD are being identified as OHI (see Figure A). Although numbers in the OHI category have [quadrupled] in ten years, the [0.40] percent reported for [1999–2000] is still well below the prevalence estimates of 3 to 5 percent. Many authorities think that fewer than half of students with ADHD are receiving special education services. As long as ADHD is not recognized as a separate category of special education, however, it will be virtually impossible to know exactly how many school-age children with ADHD are receiving special education services. (Hallahan & Kauffman, 2003, p. 191)

---

**Council for Exceptional Children**

**CEC Knowledge Check**

Even though PET-scans show that individuals with ADHD have reduced blood flow in critical cognitive areas of the brain, would an individual with similar PET-scan patterns necessarily have ADHD? Why?

LD2K2

frontal lobes, basal ganglia, and cerebellum as being structurally smaller in individuals with ADHD (Castellanos, 2001; Castellanos et al., 2002; Filipek et al., 1997; Hynd et al., 1993; Teicher et al., 2000). In addition, PET-scans suggest reduced blood flow in the frontal lobes and basal ganglia in persons with ADHD (Lou, Henriksen, & Bruhn, 1984; Lou, Henriksen, Bruhn, Borner, & Nielsen, 1989).

The **prefrontal** and **frontal lobes** are located in the front of the brain. (See Figure 9.2, page 274.) The former, in particular, are involved in the ability to control one's behavior, or executive functions. (We discuss executive functions more fully later.) The **basal ganglia,** responsible for motor movement, consist of several parts, with the **caudate** and the **globus pallidus** being the structures that tend to be smaller

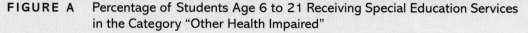

**FIGURE A** Percentage of Students Age 6 to 21 Receiving Special Education Services in the Category "Other Health Impaired"

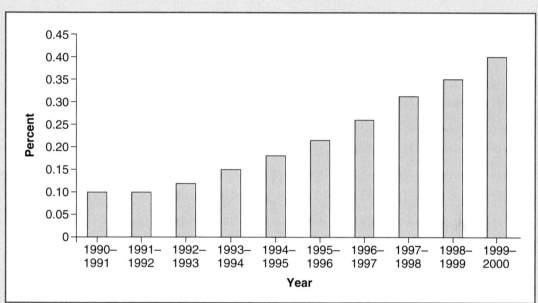

*Source:* From *Fourteenth, Fifteenth, Sixteenth, Seventeenth, Eighteenth, Nineteenth, Twentieth, Twenty-First, Twenty-Second, and Twenty-Third Annual Reports to Congress on the Implementation of the Individuals with Disabilities Education Act* by U.S. Department of Education, 1992, 1993, 1994, 1995, 1996, 1997, 1998, 1999, 2000, Washington, DC: Author.

*Source:* From *Exceptional Learners: Introduction to Special Education*, 9th ed., by D. P. Hallahan and J. M. Kauffman, 2003, Boston: Allyn and Bacon. Copyright © 2003 by Pearson Education. Reprinted by permission of the publisher.

in persons with ADHD. The **cerebellum** is also responsible for the coordination and control of motor behavior. Research has suggested that the more cognitive aspects of ADHD, for example the inattention and disorganization, are related to impairments in the prefrontal and frontal cortex, whereas the hyperactivity aspect of ADHD is related to impairments in the basal ganglia and/or cerebellum (Solanto, 2002).

There has also been considerable research on the particular neurotransmitters implicated in ADHD. **Neurotransmitters** are chemicals that enable electrical impulses to travel from one neuron to another. **Dopamine** and **norepinephrine** are two of the most likely neurotransmitters that are out of balance in persons with ADHD (Barkley, 2000; Solanto, 2002).

**prefrontal lobes** two lobes located in the very front of the frontal lobes; responsible for executive functions; site of abnormal development in people with ADHD

**frontal lobes** two lobes located in the front of the brain; responsible for executive functions; site of abnormal development in people with ADHD

## Ethnicity and ADHD

Many practitioners and researchers suspect that African American children, especially African American boys, are more likely to be identified as ADHD than are white children. However, large-scale, epidemiological studies have not been done to confirm if this is true.

Even though we do not have good comparative data on whether there are ethnic differences in actual identification as ADHD, we do know that there are differences in how teachers rate African American versus white children with respect to inattentive and hyperactivity behaviors. Researchers have found that African American boys are rated as having the most severe symptoms of ADHD, white girls as having the least severe symptoms, and African American girls and white boys are in the middle and indistinguishable from one another (Reid et al., 2000). Another related finding is that African American boys are 2.5 times more likely to screen positive for ADHD than white boys, and African American girls are 3.5 times more likely to screen positive than are white

girls (Reid, Casat, Norton, Anastopoulos, & Temple, 2001).

What we do not know for sure is whether these differences are due to actual differences in behavior or to rater bias. There is suggestive evidence that rater bias may be operating. Researchers found that white teachers were more likely than African American teachers to rate African American students as high inattentive and hyperactive (Reid et al., 2001). But even if the differences in behavior between African American and white children are real, there remains the issue of whether, as a society, we should tolerate higher levels of inattention and hyperactivity in African American children before identifying them as ADHD.

Council for Exceptional Children

**CEC Knowledge Check**
Why would there be different standards of behavior for different cultures? Is this effective management of racial bias, or does it justify not providing services to individuals who may truly need assistance or services? Why?
CC1K5

---

**FIGURE 9.2**   Areas of the Brain Identified by Some Researchers as Abnormal in Persons with ADHD

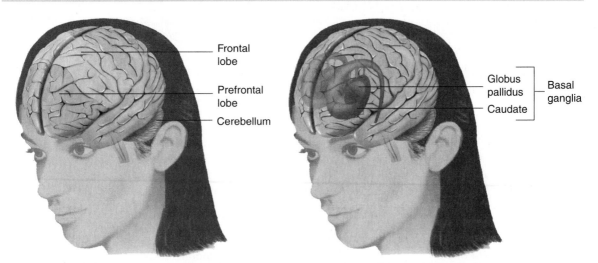

*Source:* From *Exceptional Learners: Introduction to Special Education,* 9th ed., by D. P. Hallahan and J. M. Kauffman, 2003, Boston: Allyn and Bacon. Copyright © 2003 by Pearson Education. Reprinted by permission of the publisher.

## Hereditary Factors

There is strong evidence for a hereditary basis to ADHD. For example, research has suggested that if a child has ADHD, the odds of a sibling also having ADHD are about 32% (Barkley, 1998). Also, the parents of a child with ADHD are two to eight times more likely to have ADHD than are the parents of non-ADHD children (Faraone & Doyle, 2001).

Studies of identical (from the same egg) versus fraternal (from two eggs) twins also indicate that ADHD can be inherited. When an identical twin and a fraternal twin each has ADHD, the second identical twin is much more likely to have ADHD than the second fraternal twin (Gillis, Gilger, Pennington, & DeFries, 1992; Sherman, Iacono, & McGue, 1997; Stevenson, 1992).

In the case of Shannon, there is some evidence that her ADHD was inherited from her father. Interestingly, Mr. Ireland was not formally diagnosed with ADHD until after Shannon was referred for evaluation. Because we have become better aware of ADHD as a serious condition in the past 20 or 30 years, many adults with ADHD were not diagnosed with the condition as children. Thus, Mr. Ireland's description of the following scenario is not uncommon:

> We were sitting with Shannon's psychiatrist, Dr. Rodriguez. She was asking us all these questions about Shannon's behavior, like did she have trouble focusing on homework, was she disorganized, was she forgetful? And then she had us fill out this checklist of behaviors. The more we talked about Shannon, the more I came to realize that I had always had pretty much the very same problems. It was like a light-bulb went off in my head.
>
> *Daniel Ireland, Shannon's father*

## Factors That *Don't* Cause ADHD

Over the years, a number of myths have developed concerning causes of ADHD. As one prominent ADHD expert has put it, "Some of these were originally founded in sound hypotheses but have since been disproved. Others are sheer falsehoods; there is not now and never has been any scientific support for them" (Barkley, 2000, p. 75). Chief among these unsubstantiated claims are food additives, sugar, and bad parenting.

Back in the 1970s, Benjamin Feingold, a pediatric allergist, introduced the theory that certain food additives caused hyperactivity in children (Feingold, 1975). Specifically, he claimed that such things as artificial food coloring, preservatives, and salicylates, which occur naturally in many foods, should be eliminated from the diets of children with ADHD. The Feingold diet is highly restrictive, because so many foods contain not only additives but relatively high levels of salicylates (e.g., olives, honey, avocados, cherries, grapefruit, apples, broccoli, and cucumbers, to name a few).

Although there are still proponents of the Feingold diet, research has long ago disproved it as of benefit for most children with ADHD (Kavale & Forness, 1983).

**basal ganglia** a set of structures within the brain that includes the caudate, globus pallidus, and putamen, with the first two being abnormal in people with ADHD; generally responsible for the coordination and control of movement

**caudate** a structure in the basal ganglia of the brain; site of abnormal development in persons with ADHD

**globus pallidus** a structure in the basal ganglia of the brain; site of abnormal development in persons with ADHD

 Shannon

**cerebellum** an organ at the base of the brain responsible for coordination and movement; site of abnormal development in persons with ADHD

**neurotransmitters** chemicals involved in sending messages between neurons in the brain

**dopamine** a neurotransmitter, the levels of which may be abnormal in persons with ADHD

**norepinephrine** a neurotransmitter, the levels of which may be abnormal in persons with ADHD

Sugar, too, has been implicated as a culprit in causing hyperactivity. However, careful research has demonstrated that sugar does not cause high levels of motor activity in most children (Wolraich, Wilson, & White, 1996). Where the mistaken notion that sugar causes hyperactivity may have gotten its start is from the frequent observation that children are hyperactive in situations where sweets are served. Parents and teachers often remark that young children's birthday parties are an occasion for high levels of motor activity and distractibility. They often point to the sugar in the cake or cookies as causing this hyperactivity when it's more likely that the unstructured and stimulating nature of the situation are the causes.

Although research has clearly shown that food products, whether it be food additives, salicylates, or sugar, are not causes of ADHD, we should be open to the possibility that some individuals may have a relatively small reaction to foods because of food allergies. However, the evidence is overwhelming that such reactions are, at most, extremely rare.

It is common for parents of children with ADHD to be targeted as the reason for their child's condition. Many people believe that overly lenient parenting and/or disorganized and dysfunctional family dynamics account for children's ADHD. This seems especially true of children with ADHD, Predominantly Hyperactive-Impulsive Type. Shannon's mother has not experienced this, but the following quote from the mother of a child with ADHD, Predominantly Hyperactive-Impulsive Type, is instructive.

**Council for Exceptional Children**

**CEC Knowledge Check**
Even though reactions to food are rare, how would you identify a reaction to food? How much is a "relatively small reaction"?
LD2K1

> I don't know what it is about some people. I guess I can kind of understand it. Before we had Michael, I think I was guilty of the same thing. Whenever I saw a kid who was out of control in the supermarket, I'd immediately jump to the conclusion that his parents must be at fault. I just know that some folks, including some teachers, think we must have some kind of terribly disorganized family life or that we don't discipline him when he misbehaves. I wouldn't want to wish having a child with Michael's problems on anyone. But I do think it's usually parents who happen to be blessed with near-perfect children who think this way. If they were to have a child with ADHD, I think they'd quickly change their tune.
>
> *Sharon Irving, mother of a child with*
> *Predominantly Hyperactive-Impulsive Type ADHD*

Some have observed that many parents of children with ADHD exhibit ADHD symptoms themselves. However, this may be explained by the fact, which we have already discussed, that ADHD is highly heritable (Barkley, 2000). One team of researchers (Biederman, Faraone, & Monuteaux, 2002), for example, compared the behavior of over 1,000 offspring from three groups of parents: (1) parents who currently displayed ADHD, (2) parents who had previously displayed ADHD but not longer did so, and (3) parents without ADHD. Children of parents with

ADHD were much more likely to have ADHD. However, children's risk of having ADHD did not differ between parents who had persistent ADHD and those who did not have active ADHD symptoms during the child's lifetime. One interpretation of these results is that a child's being exposed to ADHD behavior in the parent does not put the child at as great a risk for having ADHD as does the fact of being genetically linked to a parent with ADHD.

In summarizing the research on parenting and ADHD, one authority has concluded:

> All of this evidence makes it highly unlikely that any purely social cause, such as "bad parenting" or a disruptive, stressful home life, creates ADHD in the children of such families. Instead, the research suggests that children with ADHD can create stress for their parents and cause some disruption of family life. In cases where poor parenting and disruptive family life have some influence on children, it seems to be one of contributing to aggressive and defiant child behavior, not to ADHD. (Barkley, 2000, p. 81)

# What Are the Behavioral Characteristics of Persons with ADHD?

As we noted earlier, most authorities point to impairment in behavioral inhibition as the main characteristic of persons with ADHD. **Behavioral inhibition** is composed of three elements—the ability to

1. delay a response
2. interrupt an ongoing response, if one detects that the response is not appropriate because of sudden changes in the demands of the task
3. protect a response from distracting or competing stimuli (Lawrence et al., 2002).

Problems with behavioral inhibition, thus, can lead to a number of difficulties that interfere with performance, such as being able to wait one's turn, to delay immediate gratification in order to work for longer-term goals, to stop pursuing a faulty line of performance in order to switch to a new strategy, or to resist distraction in order to meet one's goals. See the Effective Practices box on page 278 for strategies one can use to address the problems these individuals often have with task switching.

## Barkley's Model of ADHD: Behavioral Inhibition and Time Awareness and Management

Russell Barkley (1997, 1998, 2000a, b) has been instrumental in conceptualizing ADHD as primarily a problem in behavioral inhibition, which then leads to a

**behavioral inhibition** the ability to stop an intended response, to stop an ongoing response, to guard an ongoing response from interruption, and to refrain from responding immediately; allows executive functions to occur; delayed or impaired in those with ADHD

Council for Exceptional Children

**CEC Knowledge Check**
What are the three elements of behavioral inhibition? What is the educator's goal in regard to these elements? LD2K3

## Effective Practices

### FOR LEARNING DISABILITIES

Council for Exceptional Children

**CEC Knowledge Check**

Would this be the main reason for scheduling large blocks of time for students with ADHD? CC5K1

## Task-Switching: Preparing Students with ADHD for Change

### What the Research Says

Many researchers contend that the primary deficit of students with attention deficit hyperactivity disorder (ADHD) is deficient behavioral inhibition. In other words, once students with ADHD begin a task, it is difficult for them to mentally switch to a new activity. Researchers hypothesize that the deficit in executive controls needed to "inhibit" the current activity and "start up" the next makes it difficult for students with ADHD compared to students without ADHD.

### Research Study

A group of researchers examined the task-switching ability of students with and without ADHD (Cepeda, Cepeda, & Kramer, 2000). Results from this study indicate that clear performance deficits exist for unmedicated students with ADHD in the first trial after a "task-switch," even when the tasks were considered compatible, such as both tasks involving numbers. All students with ADHD, unmedicated or medicated, had higher "switch costs"—increased response time—when the new task was incompatible with the old task (e.g., switching from a number-identification task to a word-identification task). This type of switch requires the inhibition of thinking about numbers and the preparation for thinking about letters and sounds. The findings suggest that differences do exist between students with and without ADHD in the ability to efficiently and effectively task-switch.

### Applying the Research to Teaching

Studies such as the one presented here indicate the need to support students with ADHD as they transition from one activity to another. Cognitive support for such transitions can include:

- allowing for time between asking a student to do or say something and expecting the response (i.e., increasing wait time)
- avoiding overloading a student's working memory (Barkley, Murphy, & Kwasnik, 1996) by limiting the number of steps or sequence of procedures a student must keep in working memory or by providing a visual for students to refer to
- creating routinized procedures for daily transitions
- preparing students for the type of response that will be required when asking a question
- dividing instruction into consistent, predictable sequences throughout the day

*Source:* From "Boxed Feature: Task Switching" by K. L. Sayeski in *Exceptional Learners: Introduction to Special Education* (p. 197) by D. P. Hallahan and J. M. Kauffman, 2003, Boston: Allyn and Bacon. Copyright © 2003 by Pearson Education. Reprinted by permission of the publisher.

**executive functions**
the ability to regulate one's behavior through working memory, inner speech, control of emotions and arousal levels, and analysis of problems and communication of problem solutions to others; delayed or impaired in those with ADHD

faulty sense of time awareness and management. And for Barkley, it is the deficit in time awareness and management that is the most detrimental for persons with ADHD:

> Understanding time and how we organize our own behavior within and toward it is a major key to the mystery of understanding ADHD. . . . I now believe that the *awareness of themselves across time is the ultimate yet nearly invisible disability afflicting those with ADHD.* (Barkley, 2000a, p. 30)

Barkley notes that persons with ADHD have difficulties with executive functions. **Executive functions** involve a number of self-directed behaviors, such as working memory, inner speech, and self-regulation of emotions. **Working memory,** which we discussed in Chapter 8, is the ability to hold things in mind while also engaging in other cognitive tasks. Problems in working memory can affect the ability of the person with ADHD to have hindsight and foresight (Barkley, 2000a). Hindsight enables us to learn from prior experiences, which we can then apply when formulating plans for new experiences. Foresight allows us to "see" ahead and anticipate events, so that they may guide our behavior. Together, hindsight and foresight create

**working memory** the ability to remember information while also performing other cognitive operations

> a window on time (past, present, and future) of which the individual is aware. The temporal opening of that window probably increases across development, at least up to age 30 years. This might suggest that across child and adolescent development, the individual comes to organize and direct behavior toward events that lie increasingly distant in the future. (Barkley, 2000a, p. 21)

Inner speech, another executive function, develops in young children and helps them regulate their behavior. **Inner speech** is the inner "voice" we use to "talk" to ourselves when faced with difficult problems. This speech may start out as talking out loud and then become internalized over time. Very young children, for example, often talk aloud when playing or concentrating on tasks. For most of us, this speech has become internalized by the teenage years, even though as adults we may find ourselves talking out loud when faced with very complex problems. For those with ADHD, however, the almost seamless border between inner speech and thought fails to occur naturally, and this interferes, among other things, with their ability to follow rules or instructions.

**inner speech** an executive function; internal language used to regulate one's behavior; delayed or impaired in those with ADHD

Self-regulation of emotions also presents problems for many students with ADHD. They often overreact to emotionally charged situations. For example, Shannon's parents and teachers have commented on her inability to modulate her emotions. Shannon's mother, for example, recounts:

Shannon

Shannon's always had a problem with either very positive or very negative news. Her father and I have learned that we can't just "surprise" her with good news. For example, last month when we were out to dinner at a nice restaurant, I wanted to tell her that I had just found out that afternoon that her best friend, Marcia, was inviting her over for a sleep-over the upcoming weekend. I knew I couldn't tell her while we were eating because she would likely explode with joy and embarrass us all. So I waited until we were in the car on the way home. And, of course, we all got to be the recipients of her ear-splitting shouts of glee.

And she also overreacts to bad news. Shannon's temper can really flare up if she thinks you've wronged her in any way.

*Kerrie Ireland, Shannon's mother*

Barkley hypothesizes that such problems in regulating emotions contribute to motivational problems for individuals with ADHD. They are unable to channel their emotions to help them persist in the pursuit of future goals. And having learning disabilities in combination with ADHD makes it even more difficult to maintain motivation in the face of failure. As one adult with ADHD and learning disabilities has put it:

> I can see how easy it is for someone with LD and ADHD to give up. It hurts so much to try hard every day, sometimes relearning what you learned the day before because you forgot it all, and comparing yourself to others and realizing you are different! If you fail, then you don't have to push on. Others can feel sorry for you—take care of you; it's easier, at least it seems so. But what happens when we give up is that we try to find other avenues to make up for what we lost. Often, those avenues are devastatingly more painful than struggling to get what we need to be independent. Giving up our independence, giving up our dream, is like dying. The key is not to give up but to be realistic, to be optimistic, and to find the support one needs. Then, apply the hard work. Though it may take a lifetime, it is time well spent. (Crawford, 2002, pp. 139–140)

## What Educational Methods Are Used with Students with ADHD?

There are several educational approaches for attention problems. Classroom interventions can be categorized under five general headings: stimulus reduction, structure, functional behavioral assessment, contingency-based self-management, and self-monitoring of attention. These approaches should not be viewed as competing; professionals often recommend a combination of them, as well as medication.

### Stimulus Reduction

As noted earlier in the chapter, Cruickshank, expanding on the prior work of Werner and Strauss, made educational recommendations for hyperactive and inattentive students. Believing that being distracted by extraneous stimulation was the major problem for hyperactive children, Cruickshank developed a program that emphasizes the reduction of inessential stimuli and the enhancement of stimuli essential for learning. In addition, his program is highly structured—that is, highly teacher directed (Cruickshank, Bentzen, Ratzeburg, & Tannhauser, 1961).

Cruickshank recommended placing students who are distractible in a classroom that is as devoid as possible of extraneous environmental stimuli. Recommended classroom modifications include soundproofed walls and ceilings, carpeting, enclosed bookcases and cupboards, limited use of colorful bulletin boards, and cubicles and three-sided work areas. To contrast with the blandness of those aspects of the environment not involved in the teaching activity itself, the material directly necessary for instruction should be designed to draw the student's attention to it. For example, in the early stages of reading, the teacher would present the child with only a few words per page, and these would be in bold colors. This modification differs from the more common reading text in which a page of print usually contains many words plus miscellaneous pictures.

Russell Barkley, too, advocates the use of highly salient cues in the environment of the student with ADHD. Noting that students with ADHD are deficient in executive functions, which are largely internal operations, he recommends externalizing these for the student. For example, he says the goal is to "beat the environment at its own game," by minimizing distractors and highlighting cues and prompts for performance, such as classroom rules (Barkley, 2000).

## Structure

Cruickshank reasoned that because students who are distractible are so much at the mercy of their impulses, their educational program should be heavily structured. He proposed that these students, being unable to provide their own structure, may become disoriented in a classroom that promotes the idea of having students make their own decisions. Thus, Cruickshank and colleagues (1961) advocated that the teacher maintain a tightly prescribed schedule of educational activities for the students so that they would have very little opportunity to engage in nonproductive behaviors.

Even today, the notion of a highly structured classroom is still the heart-and-soul of many educators' recommendations for students with ADHD:

> *All* children, and particularly, those with ADHD, benefit from clear, predictable, uncomplicated routine and structure. It helps if the day is divided into broad units of time and if this pattern is repeated daily. Within each block of lesson time there should be a similar breaking down of tasks and activities into subtasks/activities. . . . An important goal should be to create a simple overarching daily routine that the student will eventually learn by heart. The number of tasks should be kept small and tight timelines should be avoided. Complexities of timetabling and working structures merely confuse students with ADHD, because a major difficulty that goes with this condition is a poorly developed ability to differentiate between and organize different bits of information. This clearly makes the formal curriculum difficult to manage, without having to struggle with the organizational arrangements that surround the curriculum. Once a workable daily timetable has been established this should be publicly displayed and/or taped to the student's desk or inside his or her homework diary. (Cooper, 1999, p. 146)

## Functional Behavioral Assessment

Authorities advocate the use of functional behavioral assessment for many kinds of behavioral and learning problems, including those associated with ADHD (DuPaul, Eckert, & McGoey, 1997). **Functional behavioral assessment (FBA)** centers on the purpose that behaviors serve for individuals. Using it, the teacher tries to determine which events trigger target behaviors (e.g., inattention) and which factors

Council for
Exceptional
Children

**CEC Knowledge Check**
How will you decide the proper balance between decorating with colorful educational props and removing as many distractions as possible? Could you position students for less distractibility? CC5S5

**functional behavioral assessment (FBA)** evaluation that consists of finding out the consequences (purposes), antecedents (what triggers the behavior), and setting events (contextual factors) that maintain inappropriate behaviors; this information can help teachers plan educationally for students

maintain them (Horner, 1994; Kratochwill & McGivern, 1996). For example, many students with both learning disabilities and ADHD may use their propensity to be inattentive to avoid work. And some may use it because they have learned that it elicits attention from adults or peers.

After the FBA, the teacher can develop an intervention that changes the factors triggering and/or maintaining the undesirable behavior. Several studies have found FBA effective in reducing inattentive behavior in students with ADHD. For example, in one study,

the intervention for one student involved altering the nature of the task (i.e., requiring assignments to be completed on a computer rather than in writing) because this student's off-task behavior appeared to be motivated by escape from written tasks. Alternatively, the intervention for a second student involved providing peer attention contingent on the display of on-task behavior given that this student's off-task activities appeared to be an attempt to gain peer attention. In both cases, the interventions were effective. (DuPaul et al., 1997, p. 376)

## Contingency-Based Self-Management

**Contingency-based self-management** involves individuals keeping track of their own behavior and then receiving consequences based on the behavior. For all students, especially those with ADHD, it is highly recommended that the consequences be positive rewards rather than punishment whenever possible (Davies & Witte, 2000; Shapiro, DuPaul, & Bradley-Klug, 1998).

Elementary or secondary teachers can use a combination of FBA and contingency-based self-management techniques to increase appropriate behavior of students with ADHD (DuPaul, Eckert, & McGoey, 1997; Ervin, DuPaul, Kern, & Friman, 1998; Shapiro et al., 1998). In one study at the secondary level, for instance, a combination of FBA and contingency-based self-management increased the on-task behavior of two adolescents with ADHD. For one of the students, interviews with the teacher and observations in the classroom (FBA phase) revealed that the boy's disruptive behavior was a function of gaining peer attention (Ervin et al., 1998). Therefore, the researchers set up a contingency-based self-management phase whereby the student evaluated his own on-task behavior on a five-point scale (0 = unacceptable to 5 = excellent) at the end of each math class. The teacher also rated his behavior, and the student was awarded points based on how closely the ratings matched. During writing class, the teacher awarded negative or positive points to members of the class depending on whether or not they responded to attention-seeking behaviors from any member of the class. In both classes, students could turn in the points for privileges.

## Self-Monitoring of Attention

Self-monitoring is another self-management technique highly recommended for students with ADHD (Reis, 2002). **Self-monitoring** involves two components: (1) self-evaluation and (2) self-recording of performance. Although teachers have

**CEC Knowledge Check**
Do you think that treating students differently (perceived preferential treatment) could cause other negative behaviors, particularly if gender or racial differences were involved?
CC5S11

**contingency-based self-management**
educational techniques that involve having students keep track of their own behavior, for which they then receive consequences (e.g., reinforcement)

**CEC Knowledge Check**
Even though extrinsic motivation can and does improve behavior, how and when should students start building self-control?
CC5K7

**self-monitoring** a self-management technique in which students monitor their own behavior, such as attention to task, and then record it on a sheet

used it successfully when academic performance is the target of the monitoring, here we focus on its use when attention is the focus. Although self-monitoring can be coupled with some kind of contingency-based procedures, it has often been used successfully without the use of external reinforcement. Some have speculated that self-monitoring of attention is successful because it helps students become more aware of and in control of their attention (Hallahan & Hudson, 2002).

Self-monitoring involves students asking themselves the question "Was I paying attention?" and recording a "yes" or "no" on a score sheet every time they hear a tone on a tape recorder. (The time between tones varies randomly.) The following is a set of sample instructions:

**CEC Knowledge Check**
What are the five general categories of classroom interventions for students with ADHD? CC4S3, LD4S1, CC5S5

> "Johnny, you know how paying attention to your work has been a problem for you. You've heard teachers tell you, 'Pay attention,' 'Get to work,' 'What are you supposed to be doing?' and things like that. Well, today we're going to start something that will help you help yourself pay attention better. First we need to make sure that you know what paying attention means. This is what I mean by paying attention." (Teacher models immediate and sustained attention to task.) "And this is what I mean by not paying attention." (Teacher models inattentive behaviors such as glancing around and playing with objects.) "Now you tell me if I was paying attention." (Teacher models attentive and inattentive behaviors and requires the student to categorize them.)
>
> "Okay, now let me show you what we're going to do. While you're working, this tape recorder will be turned on. Every once in a while, you'll hear a little sound like this." (Teacher plays tone on tape.) "And when you hear that tone quietly ask yourself, 'Was I paying attention?' If you answer 'yes,' put a check in this box. If you answer 'no,' put a check in this box. Then go right back to work. When you hear the sound again, ask the question, answer it, mark your answer, and go back to work. Now, let me show you how it works." (Teacher models the entire procedure.)
>
> "Now, Johnny, I bet you can do this. You've shown me how to do it. Tell me what you're going to do every time you hear a tone. . . . Correct! Ask yourself, 'Was I paying attention?' Let's try it. I'll start the tape and you work on these papers." (Teacher observes student's implementation of the entire procedure, praises its correct use, and gradually withdraws his or her presence.) (Hallahan & Hudson, 2002, pp. 8–9)

Research has demonstrated the effectiveness of self-monitoring of attention in increasing on-task behavior and academic productivity. This technique has been used with students ranging from the elementary (Hallahan, Lloyd, Kosiewicz, Kauffman, & Graves, 1979; Harris et al., 1994; Mathes & Bender, 1997) to the secondary grades (Prater, Joy, Chilman, Temple, & Miller, 1991).

Researchers have also found that adding the component of having students graph the results of their assessments is beneficial (DiGangi, Maag, & Rutherford, 1991). When Shannon was in sixth grade, Mr. Martens, her special education teacher, recommended that Ms. Robinson, Shannon's regular education teacher, have Shannon self-monitor her attention while doing math seat work. Ms. Robinson also had Shannon graph her on-task behavior and the number of math problems solved correctly each day. (The teacher gave her an answer sheet at the end of

FIGURE 9.3    An Example of One of Shannon's Self-Monitoring Sheets

## Was I Paying Attention?

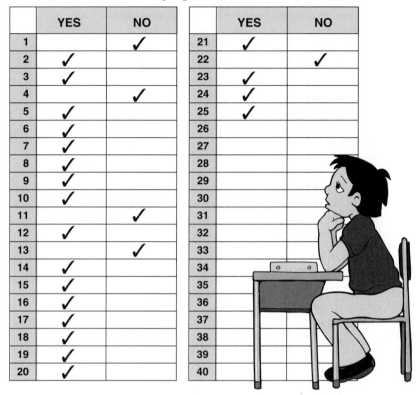

| | YES | NO | | | YES | NO |
|---|---|---|---|---|---|---|
| 1 | | ✓ | | 21 | ✓ | |
| 2 | ✓ | | | 22 | | ✓ |
| 3 | ✓ | | | 23 | ✓ | |
| 4 | | ✓ | | 24 | ✓ | |
| 5 | ✓ | | | 25 | ✓ | |
| 6 | ✓ | | | 26 | | |
| 7 | ✓ | | | 27 | | |
| 8 | ✓ | | | 28 | | |
| 9 | ✓ | | | 29 | | |
| 10 | ✓ | | | 30 | | |
| 11 | | ✓ | | 31 | | |
| 12 | ✓ | | | 32 | | |
| 13 | | ✓ | | 33 | | |
| 14 | ✓ | | | 34 | | |
| 15 | ✓ | | | 35 | | |
| 16 | ✓ | | | 36 | | |
| 17 | ✓ | | | 37 | | |
| 18 | ✓ | | | 38 | | |
| 19 | ✓ | | | 39 | | |
| 20 | ✓ | | | 40 | | |

each session so she could correct her own work.) Figure 9.3 is an example of one of Shannon's self-monitoring sheets. Figure 9.4 depicts her graphic assessment of her own on-task behavior and academic productivity over a one-month span.

Here is what Shannon's teacher had to say about using self-monitoring:

Shannon

> At first, I was skeptical that it would work. Shannon had been having extreme difficulty getting her worksheets done. And math worksheets can be important, because they allow students to practice what they've been taught. It's a way for them to make "automatic" skills that they are just learning. I'd never ask a student to do a worksheet on problems that are too difficult or too easy. Like so many students with learning disabilities and ADHD, Shannon was fine as long as I was there sitting with her. But the second I'd leave, she'd be off task.

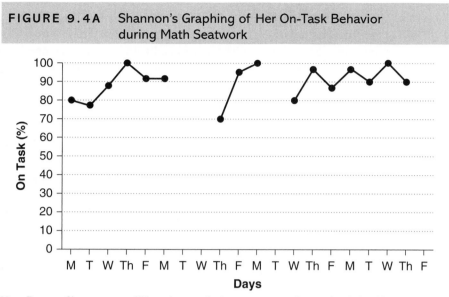

**FIGURE 9.4A** Shannon's Graphing of Her On-Task Behavior during Math Seatwork

*Note:* Because Shannon was still learning to calculate percentages, her teacher helped her convert her scores to percentages. Breaks in the line indicate when Shannon was absent.

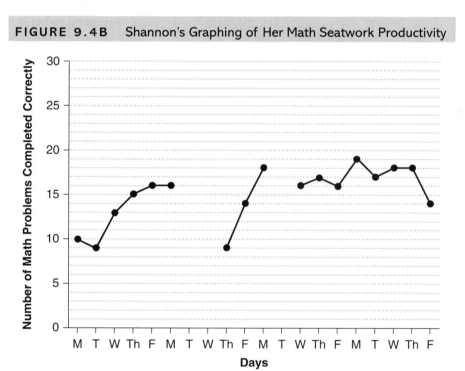

**FIGURE 9.4B** Shannon's Graphing of Her Math Seatwork Productivity

*Note:* The seatwork was for 20 minutes in each day and involved math computation at approximately a fifth-grade level. (Shannon was in sixth grade at the time.) Breaks in the line indicate when Shannon was absent.

Council for
Exceptional
Children

**CEC Knowledge Check**

Explain how self-monitoring is philosophically the opposite of extrinsic motivation.
CC1K1

> But almost from day 1, the self-monitoring procedure worked. And after she used it for about a month, I weaned her off of it. First, I took away the tape recorder with the tones. I told her to every once in awhile, whenever she thought about it, to ask herself, "Was I paying attention?" then, to record her behavior. Next, I removed the sheet and told her to ask herself the question and then just say to herself, "Yes. Good job" or "No, I better get back on task."
>
> *Julie Robinson, Shannon's sixth-grade teacher*

Self-monitoring and other self-management methods can be very useful for teachers working with students with ADHD. See the Focus on ADHD feature on pages 291–293 for more information on how to implement self-management techniques.

## What Is the Role of Medication for Persons with ADHD?

Medication has become the most common method of treating children with ADHD. And the use of medication for adults with ADHD is also on the rise. Psychostimulants are by far the most frequently used type of medication for persons with ADHD. **Psychostimulants** stimulate or activate neurological functioning; the most common type of psychostimulant used for ADHD is **Ritalin,** or methylphenidate. Although it may seem counterintuitive that stimulants would be used for persons who exhibit inattention and/or hyperactivity, what actually happens is that Ritalin stimulates those parts of the brain responsible for inhibition. Ritalin helps in the release of the neurotransmitter dopamine, thus enabling the brain's executive functions to operate more normally (Solanto, 2002).

For most persons, it takes about one hour for Ritalin to take effect, with the optimal effect occurring at about two hours and the effects wearing off after about four hours. However, the effects can vary from one person to another, so it is important that the physician, teacher, parents, and child work together to arrive at the proper dose and timing of the medication.

Another psychostimulant that is gaining in popularity is **Adderall.** Researchers have found Adderall to be at least as effective as Ritalin, and its effects are longer lasting, meaning that it does not have to be administered as often (Faraone, Pliszka, Olvera, Skolnik, & Biederman, 2001; Manos, Short, & Findling, 1999; Pliszka, Browne, Olvera, & Wynne, 2000).

**psychostimulants** medications that activate dopamine levels in the frontal and prefrontal areas of the brain that control behavioral inhibition and executive functions; used to treat persons with ADHD

**Ritalin** the most commonly prescribed psychostimulant for ADHD; generic name is methylphenidate

**Adderall** a psychostimulant prescribed for ADHD

Council for
Exceptional
Children

**CEC Knowledge Check**

Do you have an ethical right or responsibility to tell the parents of a student with ADHD that Ritalin is needed? Why or why not?
CC9S3, CC9S7

### Side Effects

Side effects are relatively common with psychostimulants. However, most side effects are not serious and can be dealt with without too much trouble. The most common side effects are insomnia and diminished appetite. These can usually be controlled if one is careful with respect to when the doses are administered (e.g., not too close to mealtimes or bed times). Less common side effects are abdominal pain, headaches, and irritability. There is also speculative evidence that in a very small number of cases, Ritalin may heighten one's susceptibility to have tics or increase their intensity in those already having a tic disorder, such as Tourette's syndrome.

**CEC Knowledge Check**
Why is it important for you to pay attention to the possible side effects of students taking psychostimulants? CC2K7

## Negative Publicity Regarding Ritalin

Ritalin has had more than its share of negative publicity in the popular media. For example, several critics of its use have appeared on high-profile TV shows, such as "Oprah," "Geraldo," and "20/20." Many of the critics have claimed that parents and teachers are too intolerant of behavioral deviations and turn to drugs to make children more docile and compliant. Many have also claimed that prescribing Ritalin for children in the early years somehow teaches them or encourages them to turn to illicit drugs, such as marijuana or cocaine, in the teenage years. Although there is a higher incidence of illicit drug use among teenagers with ADHD, there is no evidence that this is the result of using Ritalin (Barkley, 1998). In fact, there is some evidence suggesting that just the opposite is true—those who take Ritalin are less likely to abuse other drugs later (Biederman, Wilens, Mick, Spencer, & Faraone, 1999).

## Research on the Effectiveness of Medication

Over the past twenty to thirty years, there have been dozens, if not hundreds, of studies on the effectiveness of psychostimulants for ADHD. The results have been overwhelmingly positive with respect to their effectiveness for improving inhibition and executive functions. For example, in one large-scale, 14-month study, funded by the National Institute of Mental Health, medication was found to be more effective than behavior management. However, what was most effective was when medication was combined with behavior management techniques (Pelham, 1981; Swanson & Sachse-Lee, 2001).

Even though psychostimulants can be highly effective for many persons with ADHD, there are some for whom the medication does not appear to be effective. Research is not conclusive, but perhaps as many as 30 percent do not respond favorably to the drug (Spencer et al., 1996).

## Cautions Regarding Ritalin

Even though Ritalin is so highly effective, there are many very important cautions regarding its use:

- Ritalin should not be prescribed at the first sign of a behavioral problem. Only after careful analysis of the student's behavior and environment should Ritalin be considered.
- Although research has demonstrated the effectiveness of Ritalin on behavioral inhibition and executive functions, the results for academic outcomes have not been as dramatic. Although important academic measures, such as

work completed or accuracy on assignments, have improved substantially, the impact on achievement tests has been much less (Forness et al., 1999). Thus, teachers should not assume that Ritalin will take care of all the academic problems these students face.

- Parents, teachers, and physicians should monitor dosage levels closely so that the dose used is effective but not too strong. Proper dosage levels vary considerably (Hale et al., 1998).

- Teachers and parents should not lead children to believe that the medication serves as a substitute for self-responsibility and self-initiative.

- Teachers and parents should not view the medication as a panacea; they, too, must take responsibility and initiative in working with the child.

- Parents and teachers should keep in mind that psychostimulants are a controlled substance. There is the potential for siblings, peers, or the child himself or herself to attempt to "experiment" with it. (Hallahan & Kauffman, 2003, pp. 212–213)

**Strattera** a nonstimulant prescribed for ADHD; acts on stabilizing the level of norepinephrine

In addition to psychostimulants, a nonstimulant medication has come onto the market relatively recently. **Strattera,** which can be administered once per day, affects levels of norepinephrine. It is too early to say how Strattera will compare with the psychostimulants, such as Ritalin, with respect to effectiveness.

Council for Exceptional Children

CEC Content Standards
3. Individual Learning Differences
4. Instructional Strategies
5. Learning Environments and Social Interactions

## PORTFOLIO-BUILDING ACTIVITY

## Demonstrating Mastery of the CEC Standards

This chapter describes characteristics that Shannon exhibits relative to ADHD and learning disabilities. Use this information, along with what you have learned about educational methods, to design a series of educational recommendations for Shannon that include both extrinsic and intrinsic motivation. Make sure your document (1) has recommendations that link to Shannon's needs, (2) uses research-validated practices, and (3) details how each recommendation can be implemented. Be specific in addressing only one or two behaviors you want to increase, yet do not be so narrow that you cannot apply your ideas to another student. See the Companion Website (www.ablongman.com/hallahanLD3e) for an example to follow that has been created for Jamal. Questions to think about as you progress:

- How does the exceptionality of an ADHD condition affect the behaviors and abilities of an individual to learn, and in what ways does this impact the roles and responsibilities of educators?

- What are the evidence-based practices that will promote self-management and positive learning results for students with ADHD and learning disabilities?

- How do educators shape learning environments in order to encourage personal empowerment and effective responding for students with ADHD and learning disabilities?

# SUMMARY

### What are the links between learning disabilities and attention problems?

- A conservative estimate is that about 20% of students with learning disabilities are also diagnosed as ADHD.
- Some students with learning disabilities who are not formally identified as ADHD also have attention problems that affect their learning.
- The learning disability may precede the attention problems, the attention problems may precede the learning disability, or the attention problems and learning disabilities may be separate conditions that co-occur.

### What are the historical origins of ADHD?

- In 1902, Dr. George F. Still delivered a series of lectures in London in which he described children who had characteristics similar to children who are today labeled as ADHD: many had mild brain pathology, appeared to have inherited the condition, had other symptoms (such as tics and depression), and were boys.
- An outbreak of encephalitis in 1917 left many children with symptoms of inattention, impulsivity, and hyperactivity.
- In the 1930s and 1940s, Heinz Werner and Alfred Strauss found that children with mental retardation, whom they believed to be brain injured, demonstrated distractibility (based on their performance on figure-background tasks) and hyperactivity; these children were referred to as exhibiting the Strauss syndrome.
- In the 1950s, William Cruickshank, using the figure-background tasks of Werner and Strauss, found distractibility in children with cerebral palsy who were of normal intelligence.
- In the 1950s and 1960s, the term *minimal brain injury* was used to refer to children with behavioral (inattention, impulsivity, hyperactivity) but not neurological signs of brain injury. The term fell out of favor because the problems of these children were not minimal and there was little evidence of actual brain injury.
- In the 1960s, the term *hyperactive child syndrome* replaced *minimal brain injury* in referring to these children.
- By the 1980s, professionals saw inattention rather than hyperactivity as the behavioral characteristic that most affected learning.
- Today, many practitioners and researchers believe that behavioral inhibition is the most important symptom of ADHD.

### What is today's definition of ADHD?

- Today, most professionals rely on the American Psychiatric Association's (APA's) *Diagnostic and Statistical Manual of Mental Disorders* (DSM) for diagnosing children with ADHD.
- The current DSM recognizes three types of ADHD: ADHD, Predominantly Inattentive Type; ADHD, Predominantly Hyperactive-Impulsive Type; and ADHD, Combined Type.

### What is the prevalence of ADHD?

- Studies indicate that 3 to 5% of school-age children are diagnosed with ADHD in the United States.
- The rank order of subtypes, from most to least prevalent, is: Combined Type, Inattentive Type, Hyperactive-Impulsive Type.
- Boys outnumber girls about 3 or 4 to 1.
- Some children may be misdiagnosed as ADHD; however, some children who should be diagnosed with ADHD may be overlooked. Boys' ADHD behavior is sometimes excused as "gender appropriate," and girls, who are more likely to be in the inattentive subtype, are sometimes overlooked because their behavior doesn't attract teacher attention.

### How is ADHD assessed?

- Authorities recommend that a diagnosis of ADHD should include a medical examination, a clinical interview or history, and the administration of teacher and parent rating scales.
- Technology is beginning to be used to assess ADHD. For example, computerized versions of continuous performance tests (CPTs) are now available.
- Until the early 1990s, the only way children with ADHD could qualify for special education services was if they also had a learning disability; now, they can receive services under the other health impaired category.

### What are the causes of ADHD?

- Neurological factors are suspected in many cases of ADHD, and research indicates that the most likely sites of dysfunction are in the prefrontal and frontal lobes, the basal ganglia, and the cerebellum.
- The neurotransmitters most likely affected are dopamine and norepinephrine.

- There is strong evidence that hereditary factors are at play in many cases of ADHD.
- Despite some reports in popular media, factors that are *unlikely* to cause ADHD are food allergies, sugar, and poor parenting.

## What are the behavioral characteristics of ADHD?

- Most authorities believe that a problem with behavioral inhibition is the major characteristic of individuals with ADHD. Behavioral inhibition involves the ability to delay a response, to interrupt an ongoing response when needed, and to protect an ongoing response from disruption.
- According to Barkley's model of ADHD, behavioral inhibition leads to problems in time awareness and management.
- ADHD results in problems in executive functioning (e.g., working memory, which influences hindsight and foresight), inner speech, and self-regulation of emotions.

## What educational methods are used with students with ADHD?

- Stimulus reduction, first recommended by Cruickshank, is sometimes used for distractible students; it involves decreasing extraneous stimuli and enhancing relevant stimuli.
- A highly structured learning environment is important for students with ADHD.
- Functional behavioral assessment, which focuses on determining the consequences (purposes), antecedents (what triggers the behavior), and setting events (contextual factors) that maintain inappropriate behaviors, is highly recommended for students with ADHD.
- Contingency-based self-management (having students keep track of their own behavior and then receive consequences based on the behavior) can be used in combination with functional behavioral assessment.
- Self-monitoring (involving the student in self-evaluation and self-recording) can help students with ADHD attend better and produce better academic work; students can focus on monitoring their own attention-to-task or academic output.

## What is the role of medication for persons with ADHD?

- Researchers have found the psychostimulant Ritalin, which activates parts of the brain responsible for behavioral inhibition, to be highly effective in increasing attention and decreasing impulsivity and hyperactivity.
- Outcomes for students with ADHD are best when psychostimulants are used in combination with behavior management techniques.
- Medication should not be used at the first sign of a behavioral problem, and teachers and parents should
  - not assume that all the student's problems will be solved with medication
  - monitor dosage levels carefully
  - not lead children to believe they can substitute medication for self-responsibility and initiative
  - keep in mind that psychostimulants are a controlled substance, with potential for abuse

## REFLECTIONS ON THE CASES

1. Jamal is not formally identified as having ADHD, but he has significant attention and impulse control problems that sometimes interfere with learning. What kinds of strategies might a teacher use with Jamal? Would these be the same or different than those used with Shannon, who has the predominantly inattentive type of ADHD?

2. Several educational methods can be used for students with ADHD: stimulus reduction, structure, functional behavioral assessment, contingency-based self-management, and self-monitoring of attention. We have discussed how Shannon used self-monitoring of attention successfully. Pick one of the other methods and describe how you would use it to help Shannon.

3. In the chapter, no information is presented with respect to whether Shannon is on medication. Given her behavioral characteristics, do you think medication might be indicated for Shannon?

## Focus On ADHD

### *Do Now* Activities for Self-Management

## Self-Management

### ● *What is it?*

Self-management is a systematic process used to teach students to manage their own behavior. For students with ADHD, self-management techniques can assist them in addressing inattentiveness and/or impulsivity—two characteristics of the disorder.

Self-management systems can be divided into three categories: (1) self-monitoring, (2) self-evaluation, and (3) self-reinforcement. For a self-monitoring system, students check whether or not they are meeting their goals. For example, if a goal is to be "on task" (defined as either listening to the teacher or peer, doing assigned work, or asking a relevant question), the student would ask at a set interval or signal, "Am I on task?" Self-evaluation involves a student assessing whether or not the goal has been achieved by the end of an assigned period. For self-evaluation, a student might ask, "Did I complete all of my assignments today?" Finally, the student provides positive self-reinforcement: "I was on time and had my materials for all of my classes today, so I will get five minutes of computer time." Typically, students will move through these self-monitoring systems in a developmental manner: (1) self-monitoring to become aware of the behavior, (2) self-evaluation to determine level of success in comparison to the determined goal, and (3) self-reinforcement for meeting the goals that were set.

### ● *How to implement it*

In order for students to use self-management techniques successfully, teachers need to follow a teaching process similar to those employed when teaching an academic skill or concept. First, teachers should model the steps of the system and then provide students with ample opportunities to learn and practice the strategy on their own. Students should be given positive and corrective feedback during the process.

King-Sears and Carpenter (1997) have identified the following steps for implementing a self-management system with students:

- **Select the behavior for self-management**
  - Select behaviors that are important to student success academically and/or socially (e.g., staying on task, completing homework, working cooperatively in groups).
  - Define the behavior in specific, observable terms (e.g., complete work neatly and with at least 80% accuracy, work cooperatively during partner work time by observing turn-taking rules and listening to your partner). (*Note:* Behaviors should be easy to define, count, evaluate, observe, and record.)

- **Determine the mastery criteria**
  - Consider the student's current level of performing the task (e.g., on task 50% of the time). Conduct four to five observations to determine the student's current level.
  - Determine what level of proficiency is demonstrated by peers and what would be an acceptable initial goal for the student.

- **Choose the self-management component**
  - Self-monitoring (e.g., "Am I on task?")
  - Self-evaluation (e.g., "Did I reach my goal today?")
  - Self-reinforcement (e.g., "I met my goal and choose to use crayons during recess.")

- **Develop the self-management component**
  - Develop performance goals by describing the behaviors in enough detail that others can understand and correctly record the data.
  - Determine when and how often to collect data on the behavior.
  - Develop a simple system to record data. Two sample recording systems are:

**Behavior Checklist**

| Did I? | Reading | Math | Science |
|---|---|---|---|
| Have my homework? | ✓ | X | ✓ |
| Have needed materials? | ✓ | ✓ | ✓ |
| Write homework in my assignment book? | ✓ | ✓ | ✓ |
| Follow all directions when given? | X | X | ✓ |
| TOTAL | 3 | 2 | 4 |

**Frequency Chart**

| Time | | Behaviors | |
| | Working hard? | Keeping hands to self? | In my assigned area? |
|---|---|---|---|
| 9:00 | ✓ | ✓ | ✓ |
| 9:15 | ✓ | ✓ | X |
| 9:30 | X | ✓ | ✓ |
| TOTAL | 2 | 3 | 2 |

- **Teach the student to use self-management**
  - Introduce the behavior by providing the student with examples and nonexamples; the student should demonstrate understanding.
  - Discuss why the behavior is important to the student's school success.
  - Discuss the criteria for success.
  - Discuss when self-management will be used.
  - Provide guided practice and role-playing.
  - Provide ample opportunities for the student to practice recording under your direct supervision. Provide ample reinforcement as the student is learning the monitoring system, even though the student may not be implementing it 100% correctly.
  - Provide independent practice.

- **Evaluate the student's performance**
  - Assess performance of the behavior and determine success.
  - Assess maintenance of self-management in other settings.

## Additional Resource

Agran, M., King-Sears, M., Wehmeyer, M. L., & Copeland, S. R. (2003). *Student-directed learning teachers' guides to inclusive practices.* Baltimore, MD: Brookes.

*Source:* Kristin L. Sayeski

## What Conceptual Models and Educational Approaches Have Been Described?

- Medical Model
- Diagnostic-Remedial Model
- Behavioral Model
- Cognitive Model
- Constructivist Model

## Why Is It Important for Teachers to Know What Research Says about Effective Practices?

- Research Syntheses: Meta-Analysis and Effect Size
- Cautions about Research Syntheses

## How Are Educational Approaches Different, and How Are They Similar?

- How Approaches Differ
- How Approaches Are Similar

Council for Exceptional Children

See Companion Website for detailed correlations between chapter content and Council for Exceptional Children Standards; **www.ablongman.com/ hallahanLD3e**

### CEC Knowledge and Skills Discussed in This Chapter

1. Models of theory and instruction in the field of learning disabilities, which are governed by research findings and practical methodology.

2. The value of using student assessment information in making collaborative and informed instructional decisions.

3. The importance of reflection in exercising sound judgment as a practicing, nonbiased educational professional.

# Educational Approaches

I'm not so interested in all the theories. I care about if it works.

*Pete Martens, Jamal's special education teacher*

In learning disabilities, a **conceptual model** is a set of assumptions about the nature of the problem. An **educational approach** is what the model suggests we should do about the problem. The conceptual model provides the basic assumptions or ideas about how students learn; the educational approach is the way these ideas are put into practice in instruction. Theory must be related to practice. If it is not, then it is a useless theory. Actually, theory should be derived from practice. A theory should be not just philosophical speculation but a way of conceptualizing why teachers should do what they do. A conceptual model is a theory—a way of thinking about problems and their resolution. Each model and its associated educational approach has implications for teaching students with learning disabilities.

Conceptual models are useful for several reasons:

- They provide general guidelines from which educational approaches or more specific practices can be deduced.
- They help clarify similarities and differences between educational approaches.
- They promote conceptually integrated descriptions of learning disabilities and approaches to teaching students with learning disabilities.
- They encourage research on educational approaches.

However, conceptual models also have drawbacks. Some are very loosely related to teaching practices. They tend to emphasize differences and mask similarities among instructional approaches. Also, the advocates of a given conceptual model may ignore certain evidence or facts in favor of poorly tested ideas.

In spite of these problems, conceptual models offer enough benefits to make them worthy of study because they guide the way teachers teach. Bear in mind that these models are valuable in understanding educational approaches to learning

**conceptual model**  a set of assumptions about the nature of the problem of learning disabilities

**educational approach** what a particular conceptual model suggests should be done about the problem of learning disabilities

Council for Exceptional Children

**CEC Knowledge Check**
If theory is derived from practice, how do you explain the process of your education? Are you not learning theory so that you can practice? Explain. CC1S1

**Council for Exceptional Children**

**CEC Knowledge Check**
What is the relative importance of conceptual models vs. assessment and intervention models?
CC1S1

disabilities, but there are sometimes no sharp boundaries among them. Many of the differences among conceptual models are of greater theoretical than practical importance. Indeed, advocates of different models may claim that the same assessment and intervention practices are consistent, at least in part, with very different conceptual models.

Our discussion begins with conceptual models, because they are the basis for educational approaches. Our discussion includes both old, or "classic," references and more recent ones. We believe it is important to know that no conceptual model or related educational approach is really new, in that all have long histories of development. Understanding the history of any current conceptual model requires understanding that its invention has been a long process (see Hirsch, 1996).

## What Conceptual Models and Educational Approaches Have Been Described?

**Council for Exceptional Children**

**CEC Knowledge Check**
Why must the special educational professional avoid focusing on only one conceptual model?
CC1S1

When learning disability was first recognized as a separate area of special education, authorities in the field generally discussed three conceptual models: medical, diagnostic-remedial, and behavioral (Bateman, 1965). More recently, cognitive and constructivist models have been added. These five models differ in their assumption about the nature of the problem of learning disabilities, the educational approach they support, and the implications for teaching. We briefly review the basics of each model. Table 10.1 outlines basic features of the five models.

**TABLE 10.1** Five Conceptual Models and Associated Educational Approaches

| CONCEPTUAL MODEL | CENTRAL ASSUMPTION ABOUT THE PROBLEM | MAJOR FEATURE OF EDUCATIONAL APPROACH | IMPLICATIONS FOR TEACHING STUDENTS WITH LEARNING DISABILITIES |
|---|---|---|---|
| Medical | Problem is in physiology | Medicating or other therapies that make teaching more effective | Collaborate with medical personnel |
| Diagnostic-remedial | Problem is in process or achievement | Testing to identify problems | Use test results to pinpoint problems and plan remediation |
| Behavioral | Problem is in inadequate teaching | Manipulating tasks and consequences | Use task analysis and applied behavior analysis |
| Cognitive | Problem is in thinking | Teaching students strategies for solving problems | Teach metacognitive and mnemonic strategies |
| Constructivist | Problem is in construction of knowledge | Using authentic and social events | Take direction from student or student's life |

CURRENT
TRENDS
&
ISSUES

## Questionable Ideas about Teaching in Special Education

Heward (2003) lists 10 ideas about teaching that he considers faulty and believes impede the effectiveness of special education.

1. Structured curricula impede true learning.
2. Teaching discrete skills trivializes education.
3. Drill and practice limits student's deep understanding and dulls their creativity.
4. Teachers do not need to (and/or cannot, should not) measure student performance.
5. Students must be internally motivated to really learn.
6. Building students' self-esteem is a teacher's primary goal.
7. Teaching students with disabilities requires unending patience.
8. Every child learns differently.
9. Eclecticism is good.
10. A good teacher is a creative teacher. (p. 188).

What do you think about the ideas Heward lists? What evidence can you bring to bear to support your thinking? What conceptual model do you (or could you) associate with each of these ideas? What conceptual model do you assume Heward is promoting?

*Source:* From "Ten Faulty Notions about Teaching and Learning That Hinder the Effectiveness of Special Education" by W. L. Heward, 2003, *Journal of Special Education, 36,* 186–205. Copyright 1997 by PRO-ED, Inc. Reprinted by permission.

Conceptual models are controversial because of the way they influence teaching practices. Some have challenged popular ideas about teaching and learning. The proponents of one model are likely to suggest that the proponents of a different model have made faulty assumptions (e.g., Bialostok, 1997; Engelmann & Carnine, 1982; Goodman, 1992; Heward, 2003; Rosenshine & Stevens, 1986; Tarver, 1994). You might ponder the ideas listed in the Current Trends and Issues box above and consider how each is connected to a conceptual model and to evidence that is or is not faulty.

## Medical Model

The basic idea behind a **medical model** is that the problem is physiological and the solution is a medical treatment, such as medication. Brain dysfunction has usually been the suspected cause of learning disabilities, and procedures to address or compensate for the neurological problem have historically been the centerpiece of thinking within a medical model. However, recent thinking about the medical model has portrayed medical interventions as supplementary to, not a substitute for, instructional programs.

Medical approaches to disorders focus on finding the etiology (physiological cause) of a problem and correcting it. For example, if we know that a particular learning or behavior problem is caused by an imbalance in blood chemistry, then a physician might prescribe a medication that would correct that imbalance. Learning disabilities have usually been presumed to be neurological problems, which could have many different ultimate causes (genetics, for example).

**medical model** the assumption that the problem of learning disabilities is primarily physiological and that the solution is a medical treatment, such as medication

Medical models based on causes usually emphasize many of the factors presented in Chapter 2. Concerns about neurological, genetic, and biochemical factors are paramount. Problems such as anoxia (inadequate supply of oxygen during birth), hemispheric asymmetry (an imbalance of the left and right halves of the brain), and exposure to lead are seen as particularly important. Assessment practices emphasize medical and neurological examinations, and interventions often include medications.

The medical approach to learning disabilities still has advocates, and future research into the physiological causes of learning disabilities will probably be helpful. However, medical causes alone offer little direction for the practice of special education. Teachers should strive to be informed about causes of learning disabilities so that they can help students and parents understand them, but they should not expect knowing the causes of learning disabilities to help them design effective educational programs for students with disabilities.

One view, articulated long ago, is that the medical model is simply a scientific model (Kauffman & Hallahan, 1974). However, in the early twenty-first century, the term *medical model* has taken on a new meaning. Forness and Kavale (2001) have noted that what they call the **new medical model** is not merely scientific but also acknowledges the role of contemporary medicine in the treatment of many learning and behavioral disorders. New techniques of brain imaging and recent findings on the value of medications must be combined with educational programs to have maximum effect on children's learning and behavior. The intention of the new medical model described by Forness and Kavale is not to replace educational programming but to supplement it. Their contention is that pediatric medicine—including medication (psychopharmacology) and diagnostic techniques—can be a significant addition to educational programming.

**new medical model**
acknowledgment of the role of contemporary medicine in the treatment of many learning and behavioral disorders

### Implications for Teachers

A medical model implies that teachers should not try to address learning disabilities alone. They, along with parents, need to collaborate with physicians to find out what neurological factors might be involved or might be addressed with medication. Medication will not make children learn, but it might make them more teachable. However, it is a mistake to assume that medication necessarily will make a student more teachable. Sometimes medication is not given in the best dosage or has side effects that either make no difference or make teaching even more difficult. Teachers and parents need physicians to diagnose and prescribe medication when appropriate. Physicians need teachers and parents to give them accurate feedback on the student's academic learning and social behavior so that the right medication in the right dosage can be prescribed (given that any medication is appropriate).

Council for
Exceptional
Children

**CEC Knowledge Check**
How can you improve your communication skills with stakeholders? CC8S7

**diagnostic-remedial model**
the assumption in learning disabilities that certain psychological processes (e.g., visual memory) or areas of learning (e.g., reading) have gone awry

## Diagnostic-Remedial Model

The central idea in a **diagnostic-remedial model** of learning disabilities is that certain psychological processes (e.g., visual memory) or areas of learning (e.g., reading) have gone awry. Testing will reveal which processes or areas of academic performance are faulty, and remedial programs will address the faulty processes or learning. If basic processing problems have been diagnosed and remediated, then the child will be able to learn more normally. If deficits in a basic academic area are revealed by standardized testing, then remedial instruction focuses on the skill in which the child is deficient—or on an area that testing reveals is a relative strength.

The diagnostic-remedial model has typically focused on particular academic areas such as reading (Jorgenson, 2002) or severe and multiple disabilities (Snell, 2003). Diagnosticians and teachers often focus on identifying problems in underlying psychological processes, such as auditory memory, which they assume can be remediated. For example, if a student has difficulty with reading, the diagnostician might assess whether the student also has difficulties with auditory memory (remembering things heard), constancy of form (knowing that the identity of an object does not change when it is shown in a different size or orientation), visual closure (recognizing an object after seeing only part of it), or any of many similar areas. If the student has difficulty with these, teachers then try to remediate them or design instruction that avoids using the weak areas.

Perhaps the most crucial aspect of the diagnostic-remedial model is standardized testing to assess the student's achievement in specific areas. Regardless of why a student has difficulty in reading, it is important to know as accurately as possible how well the student reads. Regardless of why a student has difficulty in math, it is important to know what mathematical concepts a student has learned and what kinds of problems the student can solve. In any area of learning, knowing what the student knows and does not know and how the student's learning compares to the learning of other students is important.

The diagnostic-remedial model has two important legacies for the future of learning disabilities. First, it offers hope that careful testing will reveal a student's specific learning disabilities. Testing to diagnose and plan remediation continues to be an important and controversial idea in learning disabilities as well as in other categories of special education. The emphasis on diagnosis—determining the nature of a condition—is still evident in the extensive use of tests to identify learning disabilities. Second, it focuses on information processing—the procedures involved in thinking. This focus foreshadowed much of the later emphasis on cognition in learning disabilities (see Swanson, 2002; Torgesen, 2002).

### Implications for Teachers

Standardized test scores can be helpful in understanding what a student has learned (and not learned) compared to other students. Students with learning disabilities are usually behind others in specific academic skills and have areas of relative strength compared to others. Thus, it is unwise to reject or ignore the results of standardized testing (Kauffman, 2002). Tests can help teachers narrow the field of possibilities when it comes to identifying a student's needs and strengths. They help teachers bring things into focus more quickly. Wise teachers understand both the promises and the pitfalls of testing. Test scores are not the end of evaluation for instruction, and they can be quite inaccurate. Testing that supposedly reveals problems in underlying processes rather than the academic skills themselves (e.g., visual processing

**Council for Exceptional Children**

**CEC Knowledge Check**

Why is it important to have knowledge of what the student knows or doesn't know in specific academic areas? CC8S5

rather than reading itself) is particularly unreliable, and attempting to remediate the underlying processes rather than the academic skills themselves is likely to make little difference in a student's academic achievement (Forness & Kavale, 1994; Kavale & Forness, 1987b).

## Behavioral Model

**behavioral model**
the assumption that behavior is a response to situations and consequences

The most basic idea in a **behavioral model** is that learning disabilities reflect inadequate teaching. Academic behavior (responses to academic tasks), like social behavior, is assumed to be a response to situations and consequences. Behaviorists are likely to put it this way: Behavior is a function of its consequences (i.e., behavior is shaped and maintained by its consequences). In a more general sense, the behavioral approach assumes that behavior, both academic and social, is learned from environmental feedback. Therefore, the way to change behavior or remediate a learning deficit is to change the specifics of the tasks a student is presented and the environmental feedback on the student's responses to those tasks (specifically, the consequences of behavior).

The focus of behavioral views is not so much on the learner as on the environment surrounding the learner, particularly the tasks to be learned. A behavioral approach to learning disabilities does not emphasize biophysical causes of problems or indirect remediation (e.g., working on underlying psychological processes). Behaviorists stress explicit remediation of the most obvious problems of students with learning disabilities: academic and social-behavioral deficits. Two major strategies of a behavioral approach to learning disabilities are *applied behavior analysis* (ABA and an associated procedure known as task analysis) and Direct Instruction (DI).

### Applied Behavior Analysis

**applied behavior analysis (ABA)** systematic analysis of the observable behavior of individual learners or groups in which a relationship is demonstrated between the behavior and environmental events such as consequences or other signals

**Applied behavior analysis (ABA)** for learning disabilities focuses on the systematic analysis of the observable behavior of individual learners (Alberto & Troutman, 2003; Lovitt, 1975, 1978, 1991, 1995). It is applied in that it is implemented in real-life cases. It is behavior analysis in that is an experimental test of what works—an analysis of effects of an intervention on behavior.

Teachers use ABA to measure the effects of changes in tasks and consequences on how well students acquire academic skills. Important student behaviors that teachers have measured have included the number of words read correctly, questions answered correctly, arithmetic problems completed correctly, and words written correctly. For example, researchers found long ago that students make many fewer reversal errors (mistakenly writing a *b* for *d*) when teachers systematically provide rewards for correctly written letters (e.g., Smith & Lovitt, 1973).

Although many of the important teaching procedures behavior analysts examine depend on reinforcement and punishment, behaviorally oriented researchers do not simply reward correct responses with small candies and punish mistakes by yelling "No!" They employ far more complex social consequences and self-instructional techniques (see Alberto & Troutman, 2003; Shapiro, Durnan, Post, & Levinson, 2002). For example, applied behavior analysts have identified ways to improve students' completion of homework assignments (Olympia, Sheridan, Jenson, & Andrews, 1994), examined ways that different teaching procedures affect students' spelling skills (Birnie-Selwyn & Guerin, 1997; Gettinger, 1993), and evaluated procedures to teach self-control to children with deficits in academic behavior and attention (e.g., Neef, Bicard, & Endo, 2001).

Applied behavior analyses have revealed many important practices for teachers of students with learning disabilities. Although these techniques are important, perhaps the greatest contributions of ABA are its emphasis on empirical verification of outcomes and its recommendation that teachers measure pupil performance.

However, another important aspect of ABA is **task analysis.** Task analysis refers to specifying the components required to complete an action. It means identifying and sequencing all of the component subtasks required to do something, such as add two-digit numbers or thank someone for assistance in a socially appropriate manner.

Task analysis has obvious applications in motor skills. However, one of the most important aspects of a behavioral approach to learning disabilities is the analysis of cognitive tasks (thinking something through). Cognitive tasks or operations can also be conceptualized as a series of steps. In performing a task analysis, one describes the competencies students must have if they are to use a given strategy to solve a kind of problem.

The purpose of task analyses is to turn the steps in a cognitive process inside out—to make the usually covert parts of a strategy overt (Alberto & Troutman, 2003). Even though they may not realize it, people perform a complicated series of steps to complete simple tasks such as reading words or adding numbers. Although they may think they are reading a word as a unit, skillful readers are automatically converting the letters into sounds and, aided by their expectations about how those sounds might make sense, are deriving the word's pronunciation. Students with learning disabilities may not have these subskills and must be taught them. Similarly, people who are skilled at arithmetic computation may think they automatically know the sum of a pair of numbers (e.g., 3 and 4), but they are likely to use counting systems to derive the actual sum. Task analysis specifies the steps through which naive learners go in acquiring facility with reading words, computing sums, writing essays, deducing relative returns on investments, and so forth. Students with learning disabilities may need to be taught these subskills explicitly.

Task analysis forms a foundation not only for behavioral interventions, but also for teaching associated with cognitive theories. Advocates who design cognitive-behavioral treatments, for example, identify the steps that students will learn to use when completing tasks. Task analyses describe cognitive strategies. Promoting students' use of cognitive strategies is a foundational concept in learning disabilities today.

## Direct Instruction

**Direct Instruction (DI)** is a set of programs that can be purchased, whereas generic **direct instruction (di)** is a less carefully designed and tested but nonetheless useful set of instructional practices. DI and di share many features based on behavioral psychology. Both are teacher controlled and use small groups. Both present lessons

Council for
Exceptional
Children

**CEC Knowledge Check**
If you use ABA, why should you verify a baseline of data before applying a behavior intervention program? CC5S5

**task analysis** specifying the components required to complete an action; listing and sequencing the subtasks required to perform a larger task

**Direct Instruction (DI)** a set of programs that can be purchased; the program includes materials and scripts for teaching that have been field tested and found effective

**direct instruction (di)** compared to DI, a less carefully designed and tested but nonetheless useful set of instructional practices, including direct teacher control of instruction, small groups, small steps and frequent questions asked of the group by the teacher, extensive practice, and clear teacher feedback

in small steps and include frequent questions asked of the group by the teacher, extensive practice to make sure concepts are learned, and clear teacher feedback so that students know whether their answers are right or wrong. However, the materials known as Direct Instruction (DI) differ from the general approach called direct instruction (di) in one very specific way (see Table 10.2).

Direct Instruction programs have been designed and tested over a period of years, and the typical teacher does not have the time or resources to do such careful evaluation. DI is the foremost example of instruction based on behavioral task analysis. It incorporates teacher actions that have regularly been associated with effective instruction (Brophy & Good, 1986; Engelmann, 1997; Rosenshine & Stevens, 1986; Sindelar, Lane, Pullen, & Hudson, 2002). DI materials are designed for the teacher and tested to make sure that they are effective and efficient. They are like other products (e.g., drugs, cars, airplanes, computers) that have been tested to make sure they work before they are mass marketed.

DI does not refer to a teacher simply lecturing and students sitting passively in rows of desks. DI assumes, as does any behavioral approach, that students learn from their actions. Good teaching means helping students learn most effectively by guiding their actions and giving appropriate feedback on their responses.

Typically, the teacher, in presenting a DI lesson, works with small groups of students, presents examples according to a script, and asks questions that have specific answers (often as many as 10 to 12 questions per minute). The students answer in unison, and the teacher provides praise or corrective feedback, depending on the accuracy of the students' answers. These aspects of the DI approach represent the teacher behaviors that most observers see when they watch a lesson (see Figure 10.1). When watching any one lesson, however, an observer may not see the sequencing based on the logical analysis that discriminates DI from di.

The emphasis of Direct Instruction (DI) on logical analysis of concepts and operations is unique (Engelmann, 1997; Engelmann & Carnine, 1982; Simmons, Kame'enui, Good, Harn, Cole, & Braun, 2002). According to this view, effective

Council for
Exceptional
Children

**CEC Knowledge Check**
Why is the educational presentation sequence important? CC5K3

---

**TABLE 10.2**  Shared and Distinguishing Features of Approaches Using Direct Instruction

| direct instruction | Direct Instruction |
|---|---|
| Structured, teacher-led lessons | Structured, teacher-led lessons |
| Small-group instruction | Small-group instruction |
| Lessons presented in small steps | Lessons presented in small steps |
| Frequent questions | Frequent questions |
| Extensive practice | Extensive practice |
| Feedback, reinforcement, and correction | Feedback, reinforcement, and correction |
| | Lessons designed according to *Theory of Instruction* (Engelmann & Carnine, 1982) |

---

FIGURE 10.1    Thinking Operations

Exercise 1—Analogies

*Task A*

The first Thinking Operation today is Analogies.

1. We're going to make up an analogy that tells how animals move. What is the analogy going to tell? (Signal.) *How animals move.* (Repeat until firm.)
2. The animals we're going to use in the analogy are a hawk and a whale. Which animals? (Signal.) *A hawk and a whale.*
3. Name the first animal. (Signal.) *A hawk.* Yes, a hawk. How does that animal move? (Signal.) *It flies.* Yes, it flies.
4. So, here's the first part of the analogy. A hawk is to flying. What's the first part of the analogy? (Signal.) *A hawk is to flying.* Yes, a hawk is to flying. (Repeat until firm.)
5. The first part of the analogy told how an animal moves. So, the next part of the analogy must tell how another animal moves.
6. You told how a hawk moves. Now you're going to tell about a whale. What animal? (Signal.) *A whale.* How does that animal move? (Signal.) *It swims.* Yes, it swims.
7. So, here's the second part of the analogy. A whale is to swimming. What's the second part of the analogy? (Signal.) *A whale is to swimming.* Yes, a whale is to swimming.
8. (Repeat steps 2–7 until firm.)
9. Now we're going to say the whole analogy. First, we're going to tell how a hawk moves and then we're going to tell how a whale moves. Say the analogy with me. (Signal.) (Respond with the students.) A hawk is to flying as a whale is to swimming. (Repeat until the students are responding with you.)
10. All by yourselves. Say that analogy. (Signal.) *A hawk is to flying as a whale is to swimming.* (Repeat until firm.)
11. That analogy tells how those animals move. What does that analogy tell? (Signal.) *How those animals move.*
12. (Repeat steps 10 and 11 until firm.)

*Individual Test*

(Call on individual students to do step 10 or 11.)

Exercise 12—Analogies: Opposites

Now we're going to do some more Analogies.

1. Here's an analogy about words. Old is to young as asleep is to . . . (Pause 2 seconds.) Get ready. (Signal.) *Awake.* Everybody, say the analogy. (Signal.) *Old is to young as asleep is to awake.* (Repeat until firm.)
2. What are old and asleep? (Signal.) *Words.* (To correct students who say "Opposites"):
   a. Old and asleep are words.
   b. (Repeat step 2.)
   Old is to young as asleep is to awake. That analogy tells something about those words. (Pause.) What does that analogy tell about those words? (Signal.) *What opposites those words have.* (Repeat until firm.)
3. Say the analogy. (Signal.) *Old is to young as asleep is to awake.* (Repeat until firm.)
4. And what does that analogy tell about those words? (Signal.) *What opposites those words have.*
5. (Repeat steps 3 and 4 until firm.)

*continued*

## FIGURE 10.1    Continued

Exercise 13—Analogies

(Note: Praise all reasonable responses in this exercise, but have the group repeat the responses specified in the exercise.)

1. Everybody, what class are a towel and a plate in? (Signal.) *Objects.*
2. Finish this analogy. A towel is to rectangular as a plate is to . . . (Pause 2 seconds.) Get ready. (Signal.) *Round.*
3. Everybody, say that analogy. (Signal.) *A towel is to rectangular as a plate is to round.* (Repeat until firm.)
4. The analogy tells something about those objects. (Pause.) What does that analogy tell about those objects? (Signal.) *What shape those objects are.*
5. (Repeat steps 3 and 4 until firm.)
6. A towel is to cloth as a plate is to . . . (Pause 2 seconds.) Get ready (Signal.) *Plastic.*
7. Everybody, say that analogy. (Signal.) *A towel is to cloth as a plate is to plastic.* (Repeat until firm.)
8. The analogy tells something about those objects. (Pause.) What does that analogy tell about those objects? (Signal.) *What material those objects are made of.*
9. (Repeat steps 7 and 8 until firm.)

*Note:* The scripts come from two different lessons. The second would normally be taught about a month after the first.

*Source:* From *Thinking Basics: Corrective Reading Comprehension A* (pp. 121, 251) by S. Engelmann, P. Haddox, S. Hanner, and J. Osborn, 1978, Chicago: Science Research Associates. Copyright 1978 by Science Research Associates. Reprinted by permission of the McGraw-Hill Companies.

**CEC Knowledge Check**

When using DI methods, is it important to avoid skipping steps? Why? LD4K2, LD4S2

teaching requires that teachers show many different examples of a concept or operation and present them in a way that rules out misinterpretation. To ensure that students are, in fact, acquiring the concepts, teachers must require them to respond in ways that demonstrate they are learning. In short, DI is characterized by control of the details of instruction, teaching component skills, teaching students to solve problems on their own, and teaching complex skills.

***Controlling the Details of Instruction***  Advocates of DI stress the importance of controlling the details of instruction. The interactions between teachers and students are structured by having lessons presented according to scripts. Authors of DI programs develop these scripts so that they can specify the examples to use and the order in which to present them. As they develop the scripts, the authors test them repeatedly in the field to be sure they do not misteach the students.

**CEC Knowledge Check**

Why do you need to check the phonological awareness of your students with learning disabilities? LD3K2

***Teaching Component Skills***  A DI approach teaches students the component skills in a strategy. In the decoding example from Figure 10.2, the strategy would be described verbally in this way: "Start at left and move right, say sounds for letters, and blend the sounds into a word." Students would not have to state the strategy orally, however. Instead, they would simply learn to use it by practicing with it repeatedly with different examples (words, in this case). Having built up the ability to

**FIGURE 10.2** Illustrative Task Analyses for Academic Strategies

These examples show the rudiments of task analyses. They are not complete analyses; much more detail would be needed to carry them to the level of instruction. But they do provide a level of detail illustrating how tasks can be analyzed logically.

What would the student have to know how to do or have been previously taught to do? These are the questions basic to a task analysis. To answer them, there must be a given task (a group of items that are similar in certain ways) and a system or strategy that students can use to solve the task. This strategy is then analyzed to identify the necessary skills.

### Task Analysis: Decoding Simple Words

*The task:* Given written words composed of regularly pronounced consonant-vowel-consonant strings, the student says the words.

*The strategy:* Start at the left of the word and say the sound for each letter in the order shown, sliding from one letter sound to the next. If needed, say the word at a normal speech rate.

*The task analysis:* The student will have to know how to:

- *Start here and go that way* ◯————————▶
  This would not necessarily include knowing left and right (gee and haw, port and starboard); more simply, when reading, one begins at the circle and moves in the direction of the arrow.

- *Say sounds for letters*
  This illustrates the sound-symbol, or phoneme-grapheme, relationship (sometimes also called the alphabetic principle) that undergirds the correspondence between spoken and printed English. The student does not need to know the letter names or even how to map all of the 44 sounds of English to letters. He or she simply needs to know, for instance, that when one sees the letter m, one says "mmmm" and that when one sees the letter i one says "iiiii."

- *Blend the sounds*
  Blending actually consists of two skills: (1) sliding from one sound to the next without stopping between

them and (2) converting the stretched-out pronunciation of words to their normal speech equivalents.

### Task Analysis: Multiplying Binomials

*The task:* Given a binomial expression, the student writes the expanded expression.

*The strategy:* Multiply the first number in the first set of parentheses by the first number in the second set of parentheses; multiply the first number in the first set of parentheses by the last number in the second set of parentheses; multiply the last number in the first set of parentheses by the first number in the second set of parentheses; multiply the last number in the first set of parentheses by the last number in the second set of parentheses. (Note: This is the FOIL strategy: multiply the *f*irst, *o*utside, *i*nside, and *l*ast expressions.)

*The task analysis:* The student will have to know how to:

- *Identify the first, outside, inside, and last parts of the expressions*
  Because it is useful to use the mnemonic of FOIL here, it is important that the student knows the labels for these parts of the algebraic expressions.

- *Multiply numbers, including combinations of known and unknown variables*
  This competency presupposes that the student knows how to multiply known numbers (e.g., to write 6 when shown $2 * 3$) and unknown numbers (e.g., to write $9x^2$ when shown $3x * 3x$). Furthermore, the student must know how to handle multiplying that involves positive and negative numbers and two unknowns (e.g., that $-2y * 17x = -34yx$).

- *Reduce complex equations to simpler forms*
  Sometimes, applying the strategy results in an expression that has parts that can be combined. The student must know how to determine whether an expression has parts that can be combined and know how to combine them (e.g., to add like parts).

Council for
Exceptional
Children

**CEC Knowledge Check**
Does task analysis break tasks down too far, just right, not enough? Explain.
CC4S2, LD4K4

read words, students would later apply these simple skills (e.g., spelling conventions that produce "long" vowel sounds) to read even more complex words. Throughout the development of facility with the decoding strategy, students would have opportunities to use it in reading brief passages of text.

***Teaching Students to Solve Problems on Their Own*** A critical goal of DI is to teach students how to solve problems on their own. Teachers or those who write instructional materials cannot identify and teach each and every problem that a student might ever encounter; students will simply see more words than they can be taught, have more ideas than they can write, and come upon more arithmetic problems than they can learn in a few years. So instruction must provide them with generalized skills. DI teachers accomplish generalization by teaching students strategies for solving problems. Students learn these strategies by practicing them with carefully selected and sequenced tasks while the teacher provides systematic guidance and feedback.

***Teaching Complex Skills*** To teach complex skills, DI follows the task-analytic practice of breaking the skill into component parts, teaching the parts separately, and then teaching students how to use the parts to perform the larger skill. In this sense, DI follows what is often called a bottom-up approach—competent performance is built from smaller parts. The task analyses in Figure 10.2 illustrate how component skills in decoding simple words or multiplying binomials can be identified. Figure 10.2 shows three scripts for teaching students the structure and use of analogies.

In teaching students to use DI, the teacher helps students learn how to:

- perform component skills (e.g., letter sounds and blending in reading)
- use the strategies with simple examples
- practice with the strategies on more difficult and diverse examples
- apply the strategies in more realistic and complex situations

Researchers have conducted many studies of DI instructional programming principles. Their studies have involved both nondisabled and atypical learners, including students with learning disabilities. The research has revealed that students learn faster and generalize better when details of instruction, such as the choice of examples and the order in which they are introduced, are controlled carefully (Engelmann, 1997). Overall, the DI methods have consistently shown substantial benefits in academic learning (Adams & Engelmann, 1996; Becker & Gersten, 2001).

Many of the same factors that can be found in DI methods are present in other methods, too. Teaching strategic behavior, for example, is present in both task-analytic and cognitive approaches. Cognitive approaches are having substantial influence on learning disabilities today.

### Implications for Teachers

A behavioral approach gives teachers useful tools to work with. These tools may be used poorly or well. The tools will be more helpful if the best one is selected for the job and if it is used properly and skillfully. Sometimes, teachers are expected, in effect, to make their own tools (curriculum or specific instructional procedures) based on particular principles (e.g., to perform a task analysis for a particular computation skill or to decide just how to implement reinforcement or punishment with a particular student). However, some tools have been made by others and tested to see that they work (e.g., Direct Instruction materials). Ignoring the behavioral model is very risky for teachers simply because the best available evidence supports the instructional and behavior management procedures that this model suggests. And ignoring DI means failing to use tested materials and methods.

## Cognitive Model

The fundamental idea behind a **cognitive model** is that we must understand how people process information—specifically, how they think when they learn and remember (see Chapter 8). Today's cognitive models emphasize specific functions, particularly those related to memory (e.g., rehearsal), thinking (e.g., metacognition), and specific skills (e.g., the role of phonological awareness in reading competence; see Chapter 12; see also Bisanz, Ho, Kachan, Rasmussen, & Sherman, 2003; Jenkins & O'Connor, 2002).

Proponents of a cognitive model base their ideas on cognitive psychology. A basic premise underlying cognitive theory is that learners actively manipulate mental processes such as memory and attention to integrate prior experiences with current information. Attention and memory are ways of processing information during learning. Combining previously acquired information with observations about a current problem leads to understanding of the new information. In processing information, students probably use executive function or metacognitive processes (see Chapter 8)—reflective consideration of their own approaches to solving problems.

### Information Processing

Studies of how students with learning disabilities process information have advanced greatly since the 1960s and 1970s, when pioneers in learning disabilities first studied this matter. Early work in learning disabilities focused on understanding relationships among sensory systems. Emphasis on sensory systems led to instructional recommendations about adapting instruction to the student's modality preferences or learning style, an idea that has found little support in research (Kavale & Forness, 1987; Snider, 1992). "Style" is difficult to define and measure in learning, although it has frequently been suggested as important in meeting the needs of diverse students, including cultural diversity (See the Multicultural Considerations box on page 308.)

Contemporary studies indicate that many students with learning disabilities have problems with memory, particularly in using strategies regularly used by their nondisabled peers. These strategies include rehearsal (repeating things to be remembered, as one would do to remember a phone number), organization (sorting things to be remembered according to similar features, such as remembering what one needs from the grocery by remembering that one needs things to make a dinner of salad, French bread, and chili beans), and **mnemonics** (remembering that the order for multiplying binomials is FOIL—multiply the **f**irst terms, the **o**utside terms, the **i**nside terms, and then the **l**ast terms).

**CEC Knowledge Check**
Could you be sued for "malpractice" if you did not use methods and models supported by research?
CC9S2

**cognitive model** the assumption that one must understand how people process information, specifically, how they think when they learn and remember

**CEC Knowledge Check**
If learning styles help meet the needs of culturally diverse students, shouldn't this be a good reason to use this approach?
CC3K5

**mnemonics** aids to memory; ways of remembering

## What Is Multiculturalism in Instruction?

Some educators see multicultural education as consisting primarily of altering teaching to match the culturally based "styles" of learning of students. Others conceptualize multicultural education as teaching so that students learn regardless of their cultural identity; the assumption is that students all learn the same way, regardless of their cultural heritage.

Teachers are faced with difficult issues and choices about multicultural education. They must decide what is in the long-term best interests of their students—teaching to their "style," which may mean teaching in a way that does not prepare them for the world of work, or using a single method, which may mean ignoring other "styles" of learning. Teachers must also decide whether learning styles actually exist or can be reliably identified. If styles exist, are they based on particular cultures, or do they cut across cultural identities?

Questions that you will face as a teacher include these:

1. What conceptualization of multicultural education is most helpful to students?
2. How do you know that your teaching has embodied the most helpful conceptualization of multiculturalism?
3. How would you explain your ideas about which of the theories or conceptual models of learning disabilities we have presented is most compatible with multiculturalism in its best sense?
4. If a student fails to learn what you hope, what role does the student's cultural heritage—and yours—play in the student's failure?

**Council for Exceptional Children**

**CEC Knowledge Check**

What is your definition of multiculturalism? CC9K1

---

### Metacognition or Executive Process

**metacognition** thinking about thinking; awareness of one's own thought processes

**Metacognition** is closely related to cognition: In simple terms, cognition refers to thinking, and metacognition refers to thinking about thinking. Metacognition is often assumed to play a crucial role in learning disabilities. Some speak of executive processes, which are hard to define precisely but generally refer to self-direction and self-control (see Chapter 8).

### Cognitive-Behavior Modification

The cognitive-behavioral approach adds features of cognition to the behavioral model. It is an outgrowth of a larger movement in psychology that emphasizes the empirical base of behavioral approaches to work on such problems as hyperactivity, social isolation, schizophrenia, and other areas. But advocates of cognitive-behavioral approaches to learning disabilities also accept certain features of behaviorism's nemesis—**mentalism,** the idea that thoughts and feelings determine people's behaviors. Advocates of an integrated cognitive and behavioral approach, often called **cognitive-behavior modification (CBM),** also stress the role of metacognition (e.g., Meichenbaum, 1977). This means that teachers of students with learning disabilities need to consider how their students think about things—and how aware students are of their own thinking.

**mentalism** the idea that thoughts and feelings determine people's behaviors

**cognitive-behavior modification (CBM)** behavior modification with emphasis on the influence of self-talk or inner language as a means of guiding overt behavior

CBM strategies include strong emphasis on the influence of self-talk or inner language (what students say to themselves or think) as a means of guiding overt behavior. In teaching students with learning disabilities, therefore, teachers using this approach help students become self-aware and use their own language to guide their behavior (Halpern & Donaghey, 2003).

### Instruction in Mnemonics

One of the foremost contemporary examples of cognitive psychology in education is mnemonics (ways of remembering), which we discussed in Chapter 8 (see also Scruggs & Mastropieri, 2000). A cognitive model emphasizes people's thinking and their thinking about their own thinking, including how they learn to remember information. Mnemonics is thus just one aspect of cognitive-behavior modification, but a particularly useful one for teachers of students with learning disabilities (Forness, Kavale, Blum, & Lloyd, 1997).

Learning disabilities do not occur only inside an individual's head. They also have to do with solving real-life problems. Learning disabilities often interfere with everyday problem solving. The anchored instruction described in the Today's Technology box on page 310 illustrates how a cognitive model can be applied with the help of technology (see Rieth et al., 2003). **Anchored instruction** is designed to get students involved in solving realistic or real-life problems rather than simply memorizing information for a test. Its name implies that there is an anchor in solving actual problems (Vye, 2003).

### Implications for Teachers

Understanding how students perceive and think about things is very important in teaching. Helping students see the big picture or big idea and helping them learn strategies for remembering are often critical to success with students who have learning disabilities. Teaching self-awareness, self-talk, and self-control are part of good instruction, which also helps students solve everyday, real-life problems. These practices are not fundamentally in conflict with medical, diagnostic-prescriptive, or behavioral approaches.

## Constructivist Model

A **constructivist model** is built on the idea that students must construct their own knowledge. This model has become a very popular way of viewing all student learning and is often used as the basis for teaching and teacher education.

Some theorists concerned with learning disabilities emphasize the subjective and contextual influences on learning. They argue that individuals with or without disabilities create or construct their own perspectives of the world. Constructivists also argue that educational tasks must be authentic (i.e., intrinsic and real-life) and socially mediated (i.e., learned in social interactions with others). Therefore, the key to working with students who have learning disabilities is to get them to construct their own knowledge in authentic social situations.

Constructivism is based primarily on the idea that understanding something requires perceiving it as a whole—**holism.** In fact, some theorists recommend holistic education, arguing that material analyzed into its constituent parts is meaningless,

**Council** for **Exceptional Children**

**CEC Knowledge Check**
Solving practical, real-life problems is the aim of special education. Explain how and why theory leads to practicality. CC1S1

**anchored instruction** instruction designed to get students involved in solving realistic or real-life problems rather than simply memorizing information for a test

**constructivist model** the assumption that students must construct their own knowledge

**holism** the assumption that something must be perceived or learned as a whole and cannot be reduced to component parts without its becoming meaningless

**TODAY'S TECHNOLOGY**

**FOR LEARNING DISABILITIES**

## Anchored Instruction with Technology

Anchored instruction is teaching designed to get students involved in solving realistic or real-life problems rather than to have them simply memorize information for a test. It is a way of using curriculum and instruction to help students learn important content while attempting to understand and solve authentic problems—that is, to get students to think about things more productively. Anchored instruction helps students learn to remember information and later apply it to solving problems (Vye, 2003; see also Cognition and Technology Group at Vanderbilt, 1997). The "anchor" may be a video or other presentation that provides background information to students who do not read well. This is a technological approach to teaching that is particularly helpful for students with learning disabilities who are included in general education classes.

Rieth and his colleagues (2003) used anchored instruction in a ninth-grade class that included students with learning disabilities. The technology hardware included a commercial videodisc of the movie *To Kill a Mockingbird,* computers (equipped with a scanner and printer), and a projector. The software included word-processing, photo management, and presentation programs, and the students had access to the Internet. The teaching included many higher-order questions about the setting, circumstances, incidents, and people depicted in the movie. Although a variety of positive outcomes were described by Rieth and his colleagues, one of the most telling was the description by the teacher of

how students with learning disabilities responded to the technology:

> I was amazed. Even the kids who were like me—the very technophobic—got in there and did it. Even if it was only word processing, they did it. Kids were teaching each other. Everybody got a chance to develop some piece of their small-group research presentation. For example, some students were responsible for selecting the background and highlighting. By the time they finished their research presentations, even the most wary developed a comfort level so that if in any other class they are asked to [use technology], they [will be] less intimidated and more confident. They may not know how to do something but they can figure it out. They know enough to ask others or ask a peer to help them out. They don't have to know everything. I don't do a lot of group projects because strong students run away with it while others just sit back. This project demanded kids work together and rely on each other's strengths to move along. Nobody could do it all themselves and that is what I liked about this project so much. . . . When one couldn't do it, another would step up and help, instruct, suggest. A lot of interdependence. . . . It was nice to see. (p. 180)

**Council for Exceptional Children**

**CEC Knowledge Check**
With knowledge and technology expanding so quickly, why is it important to teach students how to find answers effectively? CC5K3

*Source:* From "An Analysis of the Impact of Anchored Instruction on Teaching and Learning Activities in Two Ninth-Grade Language Arts Classes" by H. J. Rieth, D. P. Bryant, C. K. Kinzer, L. K. Colburn, S. Hur, P. Hartman, and H. S. Choi, 2003, *Remedial and Special Education, 24,* 173–184. Copyright 2003 by PRO-ED, Inc. Reprinted by permission.

hence the term *holism* (see Heshusius, 1989, 1994, 2004; Iano, 1986, 2004; Lamon, 2003; Poplin, 1988a, b; Reid, Hresko, & Swanson, 1996).

One of the most important, if not the essential, concepts underlying the constructivist view is a rejection of behaviorism and the refusal to analyze the separate components of tasks. Constructivist, or holistic, theory defines learning in opposition to such reduction. Behavioral approaches are considered by constructivists to be reductionistic—falsely representing the whole as an assembly of parts. Constructivists suggest that "the task of schools is to help students develop new meanings in response to new experiences rather than to learn the meanings others have created. This change in the very definition of learning reveals principles of learning that beg consideration in designing classroom instruction" (Poplin, 1988a, p. 401).

A central tenet of constructivism is that the student is more than a repository for information. Constructivists try to "portray the student as a thinker, a creator, and a constructor" (Brooks & Brooks, 1993, p. 126). Consequently, many constructivist educators recommend the following:

- complex, challenging learning environments and authentic tasks
- social negotiation and shared responsibility as a part of learning
- multiple representations of content
- understanding that knowledge is constructed
- student-centered instruction (Hoy, 2003, p. 679)

We elaborate further on two of these—authentic tasks and the social nature of learning—because they are the most obvious ways in which the constructivist model differs from others.

### Authentic Tasks and Experiences

Constructivism puts strong emphasis on intrinsic goals for learners. This aspect of constructivism is closely akin to the project method of teaching popular among educators since the early 1900s (see Hirsch, 1996). The project method, sometimes called the unit method, requires teachers to develop integrated sets of activities.

According to constructivists, teachers must require students to solve real-world problems and, at the same time, lead students to understand fundamental principles (primary concepts). For example, a constructivist science lesson might challenge small groups of students to determine what materials were used to build otherwise identical miniature boats. The teacher would encourage the students to explain (perhaps in writing and illustration) why boats constructed of one material float and those constructed of another material sink. One of the crucial tasks for the teacher would be to lead the students to measuring the level of water in a container before and after the objects were placed into it. If the students offer an explanation incompatible with hydrostatics (Archimedes' principle about density), then the teacher would encourage the students to test their explanation. Such a science lesson should be both entertaining and informative. With careful guidance, students should discover the principle of density. And many authorities say that it would probably be harder for students with learning disabilities to discover this principle than it would be for students without disabilities.

Actually, most students are not capable of discovering on their own all or even most of the principles that have been found by great scientists. This is one of the reasons some people have noted that "we do not have to find out everything for ourselves *from scratch*" (Shattuck, 1999, p. 114, italics in original). Learning vicariously from other people's writing is important. And it may be particularly important for students with learning disabilities.

Council for
Exceptional
Children

**CEC Knowledge Check**

Is there enough time for students to learn everything by self-discovery? What of importance may be left out?
CC7S12

## Socially Mediated Learning

Learning situations should be based on social interactions, according to constructivist theory. Cognitive learning is tightly bound to the social situations in which it occurs. Part of the rationale for this emphasis is that most students will wind up living and working in social situations. Special educators should be preparing their students—even those destined for college and graduate school after K–12 education—for the world of work. Job situations usually require people to work collaboratively with coworkers and clients. Therefore, schools should provide opportunities to solve problems in social situations, as will be demanded in the world of work (see Hoy, 2003; Lamon, 2003).

Constructivists suggest that students should learn by participating in social situations, particularly situations in which they are required to communicate clearly with their peers. Students should learn the natural consequences of their behavior. If they miscommunicate, they should learn from their peers that they need to restate or clarify their messages. Given that many students with learning disabilities have difficulty communicating clearly, the idea of clear communication is obviously important.

The emphasis on social aspects of constructivism makes it an appealing means of promoting inclusion. Many goals associated with inclusion have to do with promoting social relationships between students with disabilities and their nondisabled peers. Those who embrace constructivism believe that students should participate in classrooms that are communities of learners, where social interactions serve as catalysts for learning and where students must learn to deal with the diverse range of human differences.

Some advocates of constructivism reject empirical research or suggest approaches to instruction that are seen by others as unhelpful (such as Heward, 2003; Heward & Silvestri, 2003; Sasso, 2001). In some ways, constructivism seems to be a rejection of the very evidence of effectiveness that would make it appealing to educators with a scientific orientation. It rejects scientific evidence favoring alternative views (see Sasso, 2001).

**Council for Exceptional Children**

**CEC Knowledge Check**
How do you justify using proven practices and methods and rejecting those that are not as successful?
CC1K1, CC9S5

Shannon

Jamal

## Implications for Teachers

A constructivist model undoubtedly contains some ideas that are or can be substantiated by research, such as the idea that students always connect new ideas to ones they already have and that they will learn more if what they are being taught makes sense to them. These ideas are compatible with other (especially behavioral and cognitive) conceptual models. However, some of the favored ideas of a constructivist model (e.g., that teaching must be student centered or authentic) are not supported by careful scientific inquiry. Teachers should be aware that not every conceptual model is equally valid or helpful and that some educational methods have been supported by nothing more than philosophy or ideology.

Both Shannon's teachers and Jamal's were obviously guided by multiple conceptual models, even if they gravitated toward one. The Case Connections box on pages 313 illustrates how Jamal's special education teacher thought about instruction.

CASE
CONNECTIONS

Jamal

## Using Conceptual Models to Guide Education

Mr. Brown, Jamal's special education teacher, made the following comments about his approach to teaching:

> Well, of course I paid attention to the test scores. They helped me understand what Jamal had mastered and where he had the most trouble. These diagnostics were really important. They helped me know what content to focus on and to know how to state his present level of performance when I worked on his IEP.

> But I had to really think about how he thought about things to know how to teach him better. I had to try to look at things through his eyes and imagine how he'd see things. True, he sometimes had ideas that I thought were a little odd, but you can't correct odd ideas unless you understand that a student has them. So trying to figure out his strategy for solving problems—and knowing when he actually didn't have a strategy at all—was an important part of my teaching.

> Overall, though, I had the most success with him when I was very structured and very direct. He and I both liked the predictability of the scripted DI lessons, and he really made the greatest progress in reading when I used those instructional procedures with him. He needed rules and clear expectations and recognition for following instructions. Call it "behavior modification" or whatever you like, but it was very clear to me that Jamal learned more and was happier when I used the principles I learned as "behavioral psychology."

## Why Is It Important for Teachers to Know What Research Says about Effective Practices?

Teaching practices should be validated by systematic research of their effectiveness. The results of research should be made available so that teachers and parents can choose those practices that benefit students the most. Without an understanding of what research says about educational approaches, teachers are left with an inadequate basis for teaching. They are likely to fall into malpractice, which includes choosing instructional methods on the basis of something other than what the evidence shows is most effective. The Effective Practices box on page 314 provides some general suggestions about effective instruction that are grounded in empirical research.

Council for
Exceptional
Children

**CEC Knowledge Check**
Does research complete the circle of theory and practice? How has it influenced the development of theories and models?
CC7K1, LD9S2

## What Instructional Practices Are Best?

What is good teaching? The answer may vary with the conceptual model one embraces. Kauffman, Mostert, Trent, and Hallahan (2002) suggest that good teaching (best instructional practice) is characterized by the following (and they provide a mnemonic, consisting of the first letters of each point—CLOCS-RAM) for remembering the points.

1. *Clarity*—The student must know exactly what to do (i.e., have no doubt about what is expected).
2. *Level*—The student must be able to do the task with a high degree of accuracy (i.e., be able to get *at least* 80% correct), but the task must be challenging (i.e., the student should not easily get 100% correct repeatedly).
3. *Opportunities*—The student must have frequent opportunities to respond (i.e., be actively engaged in the task a high percentage of the time).
4. *Consequences*—The student must receive a meaningful reward for correct performance (i.e., the consequences of correct performance must be frequent and perceived as desirable by the student).
5. *Sequence*—The tasks must be presented in logical sequence so that the student gets the big idea (i.e., steps must be presented and learned in order that the knowledge or skill is built on a logical progression or

framework of ideas, which is a systematic curriculum).
6. *Relevance*—The task must be relevant to the student's life and, if possible, the student understands how and why it is useful (i.e., the teacher attempts to help the student see why the task is important in the culture).
7. *Application*—The teacher helps the student learn how to learn and remember by teaching memory and learning strategies and applying knowledge and skills to everyday problems (i.e., teaches generalizations, not just isolated skills, and honors the student's culture).
8. *Monitoring*—The teacher continuously monitors student progress (i.e., records and charts progress and always knows and can show what the student has mastered and the student's place or level in a curriculum or sequence of tasks).

You might evaluate your own teaching to see how it corresponds to these characteristics.

Council for
Exceptional
Children

**CEC Knowledge Check**
What happens to students with learning disabilities if a teacher is not effective in one or more of these eight points?
CC7S6, CC8S8

*Source:* From *Managing Classroom Behavior: A Reflective Case-Based Approach,* 3rd ed. (p. 7), by J. M. Kauffman, M. P. Mostert, S. C. Trent, and D. P. Hallahan, 2002, Boston: Allyn and Bacon. Copyright © 2002 by Pearson Education. Reprinted by permission of the publisher.

Some of the people working in learning disabilities emphasize empirical research (Heward, 2003). We think that this is entirely appropriate and that there is no justification for using a practice that is simply preferred over a practice that is supported by empirical evidence. Colleagues of ours have put it this way:

> Approaches to teaching beginning reading provide a good example [of rejection of empirical evidence]. It would seem practicable to select the teaching method that produces the lowest rate of reading failure among students in general, which happens to involve phonics. In spite of the accumulated empirical evidence on this issue, schools continue to invest in a variety of less effective approaches to teach children beginning reading. The social and human costs of this failure are reflected in the 4 out of 10 be-

ginning readers who need structured assistance and teaching to master the complexities of reading (Lyon, 2002). This is analogous to a surgeon choosing to perform a procedure that has a 19% mortality rate over one that has a 10% rate because (1) it is easier to do, (2) the surgeon is trained in it, and (3) the surgeon simply likes it better. Given the stakes involved, it is not possible for medical personnel to operate in this manner, yet such a practice continues in many of our schools today. It is likely that this practice is driven by such factors as educators not being trained in more effective intervention or instructional methods or being invested in philosophical approaches that are counter to more effective approaches and that account for their rejection. (Walker, Ramsey, & Gresham, 2004, p. 52).

Many of the practices recommended for learning disabilities have been evaluated. An evaluation of a practice often compares the experimental practice and some other practice. Students are usually divided into two groups; one receives the experimental practice, and the other receives a different one (i.e., a control condition). Researchers compare the outcomes for the two groups and, using statistical techniques, determine whether one group on average had better outcomes than the other group. This is the same basic research strategy that is used in all scientific research.

## Research Syntheses: Meta-Analysis and Effect Size

Because any one study may yield inaccurate results, researchers usually combine the results of many studies. One important way to combine studies is to conduct a meta-analysis (see Cooper & Hedges, 1994; Rumrill & Cook, 2001). A **meta-analysis** combines the results of many studies by determining the extent to which the experimental practice reliably produced better outcomes.

If an experimental practice consistently produces superior outcomes, then the average score of the experimental group will consistently be higher than that of the control group. This produces a positive **effect size.** If the differences favoring the experimental practice are substantial, then the average effect size will be large. There are no exact rules about how large an effect size must be to be considered important, but there are some general guidelines (Forness & Kavale, 1994; Forness et al., 1997). In general, we might assume that if an effect size is

- less than 0.30, the experimental practice is not very powerful
- greater than 0.30 but less than 0.70, the experimental practice makes a modest difference in outcomes
- greater than 0.70, the experimental practice is consistently producing substantial benefits

Researchers have determined effect sizes for many of the practices that have been recommended in learning disabilities. Figure 10.3 (page 316) shows the average effect sizes for several practices that have been studied extensively in the field. The figure summarizes hundreds of studies. Most of these practices are discussed in other chapters, so we only describe them briefly here. The lowest four practices shown in the chart produced effects of little or no clear benefit. These were

**meta-analysis** a statistical procedure combining the results of many studies by determining the extent to which the experimental practice reliably produced better outcomes

**effect size** a number indicating the effects, positive or negative, of an experimental treatment or teaching procedure; a negative effect size indicates that the experimental condition has worse outcomes than the standard to which it is being compared; a positive effect size indicates that the experimental condition is better than the standard to which it is being compared; the larger the number, the stronger the relationship

FIGURE 10.3   Effects of Various Practices in Learning Disabilities

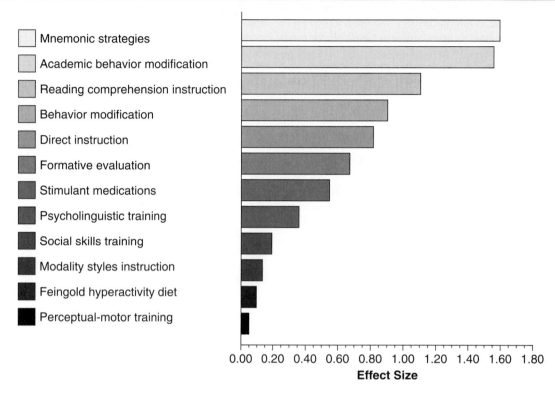

perceptual-motor training, Feingold dietary therapy, modality or learning styles instruction, and social skills training.

The next two practices, going up from the bottom of the chart (Figure 10.3), produced more substantial benefits. They are psycholinguistic training and stimulant medication. However, these benefits are not so large that they should merit a stampede of support.

The benefits of the remaining practices shown in Figure 10.3 are substantial. The research included in the meta-analyses suggests that teachers should incorporate these into instruction for students with learning disabilities: formative evaluation, Direct Instruction, behavior modification (social behaviors are the target), instruction in reading comprehension, academic behavior modification (academic skills are the target), and mnemonic (memory) strategies.

Many other practices in special education and related services have also been evaluated (see Forness et al., 1997). Some practices have not. Thus, the meta-analyses discussed here do not provide a comprehensive comparison of all methods. For example, few practices associated with the constructivist approach are specific enough to be testable. Also, many advocates of constructivism downplay the importance of empirically testing practices, saying that students—especially those with learning disabilities—are too different from each other for average scores to have any meaning.

## Cautions about Research Syntheses

Teachers should regard the results of meta-analyses with some caution. If many studies compared a relatively weak practice to some other very bad practice, then the weak practice would produce much better outcomes and therefore have a larger average effect size. Also, one practice may be consistently compared to controls on broad measures that are reliable and valid, but another may be compared on measures that have lower reliability and validity. The overall effect sizes will not show which used the broad, reliable measures.

In spite of cautions, meta-analyses tell teachers and parents which practices appear to have the best chances of benefiting students with learning disabilities. In that way, they should help guide contemporary practices in learning disabilities.

The IEP for Shannon reveals much about the instruction her teacher thought was most likely to be effective for her in middle school. Mr. Taylor, her math teacher, made the following comment:

**Council** for **Exceptional Children**

**CEC Knowledge Check**
Is meta-analysis a way to pinpoint whether one particular study was effective? Explain.
CC9S11

 Shannon

> A combination of cognitive strategies and Direct Instruction is necessary for Shannon. It's true that she needs to be taught an explicit routine for solving problems. But if she doesn't understand overall what we're doing, then it doesn't make sense for her. I have to teach her how to think about things and how to remember things, too. One kind of instruction isn't much help without the other.
>
> *Winn Taylor, Shannon's math teacher*

# How Are Educational Approaches Different, and How Are They Similar?

Arguments about the appropriateness of contemporary educational approaches to learning disabilities abound. Because no one model or approach has a corner on explanatory power, it is helpful to compare them on important matters. However, it is not only worthwhile to analyze the ways in which these models differ, but also to examine the features that they share.

## How Approaches Differ

Tarver (1986) contrasted models that correspond to those here labeled cognitive, behavioral, and constructivist. Although she omitted some aspects of the cognitive model, her comparison of these models is helpful. She focused on how the models differ along four dimensions: specific versus general emphases, bottom-up versus top-down programming, more structured versus less structured teaching, and effectiveness versus ineffectiveness.

### Specific versus General Emphases

Whereas some models emphasize broader and more general strategies, others emphasize task-specific strategies. Broader strategies emphasize solving real-life problems, but specific strategies focus on acquiring narrower skills, such as **decoding** or computing. Advocates of both cognitive-behavioral and DI approaches seek to help students learn broad strategies by teaching more specific strategies. Following these approaches, teachers would teach students the more fundamental skills, such as planning an essay, and then have them use the skills to solve the higher-order problems encountered in content area studies. Similarly, to help students with attention problems, advocates of these models would alter the environment by changing the features of instruction or teaching the students a self-management strategy for maintaining attention.

**decoding**   being able to sound out words; figuring out the words in reading

Advocates of a constructivist approach to teaching make clear that they reject explicit teaching of learning strategies. They contend that students will acquire the needed strategies when they require them. For example, when students are asked to write up the findings of an experiment, they will need to produce a well-constructed essay. From a combination of this need and social interactions with people who read their essays, they will gradually acquire facility in communicating.

### Bottom-Up versus Top-Down Programming

Models also differ in whether teaching should proceed from the general to the specific or from the specific to the general. Working from the general to the specific is often called "top-down" programming, because it emphasizes deducing the parts from the whole. Working from the specific to the general is called "bottom-up" programming, because it stresses acquiring the parts and from them inferring the whole.

The constructivist model emphasizes top-down programming: Get the meaning first and do not worry about the details of decoding. The DI approach is expressly built on bottom-up programming: Teach decoding skills early and systematically integrate them with comprehension (meaning-getting) strategies. As Tarver (1986) put it:

> The [constructivists] express a primary concern for the whole of reading; they do not attempt to specify the parts that constitute the whole. In contrast, DI curriculum developers begin with an analysis of the whole knowledge system known as reading; this analysis produces many parts which are then sequenced and recombined to reconstitute the whole. (p. 371)

Although Tarver (1986) did not describe the position of the cognitive model on the question of top-down versus bottom-up programming, advocates of cognitive approaches emphasize some combination of the two. Given the evidence from cognitive psychology that reading competence requires mastery of decoding (Juel, 1991), cognitive theorists are obliged to promote teaching of the components of reading, a bottom-up emphasis. However, there is also likely to be an emphasis on top-down features: When reading text, students should be prompted to think about their prior knowledge of the topic.

## More Structured versus Less Structured Teaching

When used in the context of teaching, structure usually refers to the consistency or predictability of classroom routines. In general, advocates of constructivism support less structured, more child-centered instruction, and advocates of DI approaches favor highly organized, teacher-directed instruction (Heward, 2003; Tarver, 1986). One way to conceptualize this difference is to imagine people standing outside a classroom door and being told, "This is the 27th day of remedial instruction in fractions." How well could those people predict what would be happening in the classroom?

- If the observers knew the teacher was using *Mastering Fractions* (Systems Impact, 1986) and were familiar with the program, they would probably be able to say not only how the room would be structured but what kinds of tasks the teacher was presenting.
- If the observers knew that the teacher was following a constructivist approach, they might guess that the teacher would be engaged in any of a variety of activities (measuring for baking, listening to a passage about dividing food among people, manipulating objects of various physical proportions, etc.).

Cognitive approaches emphasize student-directed learning more than DI approaches. However, their stress on drawing strategies from research-based practices separates cognitive approaches from constructivist approaches; using research-based practices is inconsistent with the constructivist notion that student-developed strategies are preferable outcomes.

## Effectiveness versus Ineffectiveness

Presumably, advocates for students with learning disabilities would recommend practices that have produced evidence of effectiveness. But what research demonstrates effectiveness? Differing perspectives about research methods cloud this comparison of the major models.

Constructivist approaches differ from cognitive and behavioral (DI) approaches in whether effectiveness can be demonstrated by research (see Heward, 2003). From a constructivist perspective, learning is too idiosyncratic for any general findings to be useful. Students—especially those with learning disabilities—differ too much for any results from traditional research methods to apply to them; teachers must find their own personally satisfying approaches for each individual student.

In evaluating the research evidence, Tarver (1986) gave greater credence to findings based on traditional research methods. She based her judgments of the effectiveness of practices on research using quantitative methods—that is, methods in which the outcomes of different practices are compared statistically on explicit measures (e.g., achievement tests). "Research to date provides strong support for DI, equivocal support for some CBM [cognitive-behavior modification] programs

Council for
Exceptional
Children

**CEC Knowledge Check**
Do you believe the constructivist approach can be effective for students with learning disabilities? When would you use features of this model?
CC4S3

**CEC Knowledge Check**

What would you do
if a general education
teacher were using con-
structive methods in a
class that had a signifi-
cant number of stu-
dents with learning
disabilities?
LD4S1, CC9S2, CC10S6

and little or no support for the [constructivist] approach" (p. 373). Since Tarver prepared her analysis, other evidence supporting the cognitive model has emerged.
Tarver (1994) acknowledged the evidence supporting these other models; however,
she argued that the good outcomes reported in those studies cannot result from the
cognitive model's inherent strength but from its newfound emphasis on features of
instruction that have been the focus of DI for many years. For illustration she noted
that Engelmann (1967, 1969) had emphasized phonological segmentation and
blending long before these skills became popular in contemporary cognitive models
of reading.

Tarver's (1986) analysis points to important ways to understand the differences
among models. These differences are also stressed by people with diverse views (e.g.,
Heshusius, 1989; Heward, 2003; Poplin, 1988b). Despite the clear emphasis on differences among the models that is evident in many discussions of them, there are important similarities that can guide people concerned with learning disabilities.

## How Approaches Are Similar

Many of the apparent differences in conceptual models and their associated educational approaches are only word deep—the models are actually different only in the
choice of words used to describe a given practice. For example, in referring to remarkably similar ideas, advocates of one approach might use the label "cognitive
strategies" to refer to what advocates of another approach might call "covert operations" (see deBettencourt, 1987). Furthermore, among the activities and practices
used under the auspices of the various models, there are substantial similarities
(Dixon & Carnine, 1994).

Shared ideas in different approaches are important because they indicate
growing consensus about how to teach students with learning disabilities. Contemporary conceptual models agree that at least the following are legitimate purposes of instruction:

- to incorporate *direct assessment* of performance
- to promote acquisition of useful cognitive *strategies*
- to provide extensive opportunities for students to *practice* using those strategies
  in useful situations

### Direct Assessment of Student Learning

In their paper advocating constructivist approaches to assessment, Meltzer and
Reid (1994) comment favorably on using curriculum-based assessment, a behaviorally based method in which brief samples of students' performance in the curriculum are taken frequently (see also Crawford & Tindal, 2002). Across all
approaches, then, there are shared emphases on assessment. All of the approaches
we discuss stress the following:

- evaluating students' performance frequently while they are learning, rather
  than waiting until they are supposed to have finished learning

- assessing students' performance on the actual tasks of concern, not on psychological instruments of related areas
- examining students' performance under differing conditions, rather than examining only under testlike conditions
- linking the results of assessment directly to the provision of instruction

### Teaching Students How to Use Strategies

Another commonality among contemporary approaches is teaching students how to use strategies in solving problems. True, the approaches differ in the ways described by Tarver (1986), but none expects students simply to learn isolated facts. Not only do advocates of the various approaches use a similar word—*strategies*—in referring to this idea, but the idea is remarkably similar. From the cognitive model's interest in memory and attention strategies to the task-analytic model's emphasis on cognitive operations, each model stresses the importance of students learning systems of actions that lead to solutions of problems.

All of the approaches we discuss stress that students benefit from applying strategies to real-life problems. Stripped of their specific terminology, these approaches recommend that students practice strategies under conditions in which they are likely to be valuable. They all agree that students' practice must be embedded in realistic situations.

The treatment of learning disabilities in this book is consistent with the idea that strategy deficits and strategy instruction play a major role in learning disabilities. Indeed, the concern with strategies will probably be one of the most enduring and substantial contributions of the field of learning disabilities to general education.

## PORTFOLIO-BUILDING ACTIVITY

Council for
Exceptional
Children

### Demonstrating Mastery of the CEC Standards

Develop a Direct Instruction Lesson Plan, using the information you have learned in this chapter. Remember, a Direct Instruction Lesson must represent (1) task analysis (see Figure 10.2, page 305) and (2) frequent questions (see Figure 10.1, page 303). Make sure your Direct Instruction Lesson follows the guidelines found in Table 10.2 (page 302). Search the Internet, and also see the Companion Website (www.ablongman.com/hallahanLD3e) for (1) specific directions on how to create your lesson, and (2) an example to follow. Questions to think about as you progress:

**CEC Content Standards**
  4. Instructional
     Strategies
  7. Instructional
     Planning
  8. Assessment
 10. Collaboration

- What are the components of Direct Instruction that research has indicated are necessary to promote positive learning results for individuals with learning disabilities?

- In what ways can Direct Instruction include explicit modeling and efficient guided practice to ensure acquisition and fluency?

- How does the information gathered during a Direct Instruction lesson contribute to the ongoing analysis of the student's learning progress?

# SUMMARY

## Why should we understand conceptual models of learning disabilities?

- They provide general guidelines for more specific practices.
- They help clarify similarities and differences between instructional approaches.
- They promote conceptually integrated descriptions of learning disabilities.
- They encourage research.

## What conceptual models have been described?

- The medical model is based on the idea that the problem is physiological and the solution is a medical treatment, such as medication. A newer medical model sees medical interventions as supplementary to, not a substitute for, instructional programs. A primary implication for teachers is that teachers must collaborate with physicians to address learning disabilities.
- The diagnostic-remedial model is based on the idea that certain psychological processes or areas of learning have gone awry, that testing will reveal which processes or areas of academic performance are faulty, and remedial programs will address the faulty processes or learning. A primary implication for teachers is that they must understand the value and appropriate uses of standardized tests.
- The behavioral model is based on the idea that behavior, including academic behavior (responses to academic tasks), is influenced by consequences. Applied behavior analysis, task analysis, and Direct Instruction are all part of a behavioral model. Direct Instruction refers to a scripted, tested program of instruction. A primary implication for teachers is that they must use the tools provided by a behavioral approach properly and skillfully.
- The cognitive model is based on the idea that we must understand how people learn and remember. A cognitive model includes information processing, metacognition, cognitive-behavior modification, and mnemonic strategies. A primary implication for teachers is that they must be adept at helping students learn self-awareness, self-talk, and self-control.
- The constructivist model is based on the idea that students must construct their own knowledge. A constructivist approach emphasizes teaching that is said to be holistic, authentic, and socially mediated. A primary implication for teachers is that they must be aware that not every conceptual model is equally valid or helpful

and that some educational methods have been supported by nothing more than philosophy or ideology.

## Why is it important for teachers to know what research says about effective practices?

- Teachers need to know what research says so that they can select the most effective instructional methods.
- Syntheses of research findings are important. A meta-analysis is a statistical way of summarizing the results of numerous studies. An effect size is an indication of the size of the effect that a specific instructional procedure had compared to an experimental control procedure. Effect sizes of less than about 0.30 are generally taken as an indication that the procedure being tested against a control group is not very powerful.
- Among the instructional procedures with the largest effect sizes (indicating substantial power in instruction of students with learning disabilities) are formative evaluation, Direct Instruction, behavior modification (when social behaviors are the target), instruction in reading comprehension, academic behavior modification (when academic skills are the target), and mnemonic (memory) strategies.

## How are educational approaches different, and how are they similar?

- Educational models differ in their emphasis on several points:
  - The behavioral approaches place greater emphasis on specific rather than general strategies, in contrast to the cognitive and constructivist models.
  - The cognitive and constructivist approaches stress bottom-up programming less than they do top-down programming; this contrasts with the behavioral views.
  - The behavioral and cognitive models are generally more structured, whereas the constructivist approaches are less structured.
  - The behavioral and cognitive approaches emphasize use of practices with documented effectiveness.
- Despite these differences, contemporary models share an emphasis on
  - direct assessment—evaluating students' performances frequently, on actual tasks, under varying conditions, and linking assessment directly to instruction.
  - strategies—understanding how students solve problems and teaching them to approach tasks systematically.

## REFLECTIONS ON THE CASES

1. What model(s) do you think guided the teachers working with Shannon and Jamal?

2. What would you say to Jamal's special education teacher, who said she is interested only in what works, not in conceptual models?

3. To what extent do you believe the teachers of Jamal and Shannon found what works in practice?

4. What do you believe is the best indicator of what works: personal experience or research?

What Is Language?

Are Language Problems Common in Learning Disabilities?

What Are the Elements of Spoken Language and Characteristics of Students with Learning Disabilities in Spoken Language?

- Receptive Language
- Expressive Language
- Difficulties of Students with Learning Disabilities in Receptive and Expressive Language
- Phonology
- Syntax
- Morphology
- Semantics
- Pragmatics
- Metalinguistic Awareness

How Are Spoken Language Abilities Assessed?

- Standardized Assessment
- Informal Language Assessment Methods
- Methods of Monitoring Progress

How Can Spoken Language Problems Be Addressed?

- General Principles and Accommodations
- Semantic Feature Analysis
- Keyword Mnemonics
- Teaching in Context and Conversation
- Phonemic Awareness
- Statement Repetition

Council for Exceptional Children

See Companion Website for detailed correlations between chapter content and Council for Exceptional Children Standards; www.ablongman.com/hallahanLD3e

**CEC Knowledge and Skills Discussed in This Chapter**

1. Language, as part of the ability to understand and communicate, is part of the identification process in the learning disability label.

2. The effects of cultural diversity can influence language characteristics developed in typical and atypical human growth.

3. Language assessments and results interpretations, both formal and informal, which are individualized for appropriateness, nonbiased accuracy, and instructional usefulness.

4. Systematic language instructional methods and resources, which are needed to facilitate appropriate educational services for individuals with learning disabilities.

5. The special education professional's responsibility to address the language concerns of children in special education classrooms who represent families from diverse cultures.

# Students Who Experience Difficulties with Spoken Language

11

Jannette, his speech-language pathologist, has really pushed him along, and Jamal really has learned a lot about phonological matters already, but he has a long way to go yet.

*Clinton Brown, Jamal's special education teacher*

$S$poken language—often considered a capability unique to humans—is the primary way that most of us communicate. We listen to what others say. We tell others what we have to say. We write to tell others what we have to say. We read what others have to say. Without language skills, we could not enjoy a stand-up comic's routine, listen to a play, explain an answer, or understand the lyrics for a song. Much of what happens in schools either is transmitted in spoken language or, as in the case of reading and writing, requires an understanding of it. **Communication** is the process participants use to exchange information and ideas, needs, and desires.

Communication requires language. **Language** is "a socially shared code or conventional system for representing concepts through the use of arbitrary symbols and rule-governed combinations of those symbols" (Owens, 2001). Communication can involve listening, speaking, reading, or writing or a combination of these. Much of academic learning is based on language. For Garton and Pratt (1998), "the mastery of *spoken language* and reading and writing" define the concept of literacy (p. 1, emphasis added). In this chapter, we examine spoken language as a means of communication and its interconnectedness with reading and writing.

## What Is Language?

Language is extremely complex. It is made up of various modes (e.g., spoken or written) and linguistic elements. The linguistic elements are called paralinguistic, metalinguistic, and nonlinguistic elements. **Paralinguistic elements** are such things as intonation, stress or emphasis, speed of delivery, and pauses that add emotion or

**communication** the process participants use to exchange information and ideas, needs, and desires

**language** a socially shared code or conventional system for representing concepts through the use of arbitrary symbols and rule-governed combinations of those symbols

**paralinguistic elements** elements of communication such as intonation, stress or emphasis, speed of delivery, and pauses that add emotion or attitude to what is being said

Council for Exceptional Children

CEC Knowledge Check
After reading these definitions, develop your own definition of *language*.
LD1K5

**nonlinguistic elements**
elements of communication, often referred to as "body language" (e.g., facial expressions, posture, and eye contact)

**metalinguistic elements**
elements of communication that include thinking and talking about language, as well as the analysis of language

Council for Exceptional Children

**CEC Knowledge Check**

Given the cultural difficulties among whites, African Americans, Latin Americans, and others, what can parents or guardians do to influence language development? CC6K1

Council for Exceptional Children

**CEC Knowledge Check**

What do you need to learn to be an effective professional, considering that language problems are the largest subgroup of learning disabilities? CC9S1

attitude to what is being said. **Nonlinguistic elements** are those often referred to as "body language"—for example, facial expressions, posture, and eye contact. **Metalinguistic elements** include the thinking and talking about language as well as the analysis of language. Competence in communication requires a level of skill in each of these areas, as well as in producing speech and understanding language, that varies with age and development (Owens, 2001).

Because spoken language is such a complex topic, we deal with the aspects that are of most difficulty for students with learning disabilities. Therefore, we do not cover every language topic nor do we provide an in-depth description of language development. (For more information in this area, see Owens, 2001.) Speech or articulation disorders will be dealt with briefly. Clearly, when students have problems using or understanding spoken language, they are likely to struggle in school. Moreover, when not remedied, problems with spoken language can have debilitating effects on a person's life. Language deficits not only affect one's fundamental ability to communicate on a day-to-day basis, but also impede the acquisition of language skills such as reading and writing. They even influence—often negatively—performance in other areas such as in negotiating social interactions and in learning foreign languages (see the Current Trends and Issues box on page 327).

## Are Language Problems Common in Learning Disabilities?

Language problems are common in persons with learning disabilities, and this fact has been known throughout the history of the field. Influential figures such as Orton (1937), Kirk (1976), Strauss and Kephart (1955), and Johnson and Myklebust (1967) emphasized the importance of language in their work (see also Chapter 1). Unfortunately, the emphasis at the time was on perceptual processes, and it took a long time for many in the field of learning disabilities to realize the importance of language problems (Hallahan & Cruickshank, 1973).

The neglect of language skills in the early development of learning disabilities was unfortunate for many reasons. First, because of the basic importance of language in everyday life, students' language difficulties should be a foremost target for remediation. Second, the need for language skills in virtually all areas of academic achievement means that these skills are crucial to success in school, perhaps more so than are perceptual processes. Third, estimates of the prevalence of disorders of spoken language among students with learning disabilities reveal that they are among the most common problems experienced by these students and that these problems have not been readily addressed.

Most definitions of *learning disability* today specifically emphasize language deficits (see Chapter 1). When discussing learning disabilities, authorities often note the special emphasis on language in these definitions:

> A sizable body of research now indicates that, as a group, LD children are less skilled than normal achievers on a wide variety of phonological, semantic, syntactic, and

**CURRENT TRENDS & ISSUES**

# Foreign Language Learning and College Requirements: Where Are We?

Learning a foreign language often strikes fear in the hearts of students with language-learning disabilities, their parents, and teachers. For many, the struggle to become proficient in English makes them dread the idea of having to start all over again in another language so that they can meet high school or college graduation requirements. The issue of whether foreign language requirements discriminate against some students with learning disabilities or attention deficit hyperactivity disorder came to a head with a lawsuit filed by students against Boston University (BU) (*Guckenberger v. Boston University,* 1997).

The lawsuit against BU revolved around the concept of whether BU had violated federal law in its response to requests for accommodations made by students with learning disabilities. One of the subissues of that lawsuit was whether BU discriminated against students with learning disabilities by its "refusal to continue allowing course substitutions in lieu of foreign language requirements for students with documented learning disabilities" (Wolinsky & Whelan, 1999, p. 286). Following the trial and actions on the part of BU, Federal Judge Patti Saris ruled that "although a university does not have to modify its degree requirements to provide course substitutions for students with learning disabilities, it must engage in a rational decision-making process to demonstrate that providing course substitutions creates a fundamental alteration to its degree requirement" (Elswitt, Geetter, & Goldberg, 1999, p. 301).

The lawsuit against BU brought many issues in learning disabilities and language learning to the forefront. Procedures for determining learning disabilities at the college level and for determining who should receive foreign language course substitutions or waivers were called into question. In the early 1990s, many thought that students with learning disabilities who had difficulties with native language acquisition would also experience foreign-language-learning difficulties. Initial case study and anecdotal evidence backed up this hypothesis (Sparks, Philips, & Javorsky, 2002). However, it is not clear how this is playing out at the university level.

In a series of recent studies (Sparks et al., 2002; Sparks & Javorsky, 1999; Sparks, Philips, Ganschow, & Javorsky, 1999a, b), Sparks and colleagues compared students with learning disabilities who had received foreign-language-requirement waivers or substitutions and those who had not at two colleges over the past ten years on variables such as IQ, academic achievement, performance on the *Modern Language Aptitude Test* (MLAT), grade-point averages, and attempts at foreign language courses. They found that there were very few differences between these two groups of students on these measures. In addition, other researchers have found that some of the measures used to predict foreign language course performance (e.g., MLAT) do not have adequate predictive validity and that modified courses and support services can make it possible for some students with learning disabilities to succeed in foreign language courses (Shaw, 1999).

What does this mean for the student with a language-learning disability who wants to graduate from college? First, policies on foreign language requirements vary both across colleges and across degree programs within colleges. Second, the processes and requirements for documentation when requesting substitutions or waivers vary tremendously across colleges. Third, the resources available to help students with learning disabilities in their foreign language requirements (e.g., tutoring, modified instruction) differ across colleges. Fourth, it is very difficult to know exactly what kinds of accommodations, modifications, or substitutions students will need in a college environment before they attempt foreign language courses. And, finally, much more research needs to be done on the appropriate accommodations for students with language-learning disabilities in the college environment.

Council for Exceptional Children

**CEC Knowledge Check**
What are the goals of education? What technology should be allowed to accomplish these goals? Are the answers to these questions different for the general population vs. students with special needs?
CC1K4, CC1K9, CC1S1, LD1K2, CC2K3

communicative tasks. Furthermore, efforts to delineate subgroups of LD children have found that the largest single subgroup can be characterized as language-impaired and usually constitutes over half of the LD sample. (Bryan, Bay, Lopez-Reyna, & Donahue, 1991, p. 119)

**phonemic awareness** the ability to blend sounds, segment the sounds of words, rhyme, and in other ways manipulate the sounds of spoken words

The definition of *learning disability* in IDEA clearly states that language is important—"In general—The term 'specific learning disability' means a disorder in one or more of the basic psychological processes involved in *understanding or in using language, spoken or written*" (IDEA S. 1248, Sec 602(29)(A), 2003, emphasis added). Today, there is renewed concern with language problems, particularly young children's skills in **phonemic awareness,** or the manipulation of the sounds in language. Many children who have difficulty developing certain early language skills later experience substantial difficulty in acquiring reading and writing skills (Lyon, 1999; National Reading Panel, 2000). To understand these problems, one must understand the relationship of speech, language, and communication as well as the components of language and how these language components develop normally.

As can be seen, language is complex and involves a number of modes and elements. Such complexity is underscored by the comments of Ms. Jones, Jamal's speech-language pathologist:

Jamal

> In my observation, Jamal has no trouble using language and body language to interact with his peers when he is the initiator. In fact, he's often a leader in group activities in which he knows quite a bit about the topic. It's in the finer details, syntax and phonemic awareness, that he has some difficulty.
>
> *Jannette Jones, Jamal's speech-language pathologist*

## What Are the Elements of Spoken Language and the Characteristics of Students with Learning Disabilities in Spoken Language?

**speech** the physical production of sounds for communication

Many people use the terms *speech, language,* and *communication* interchangeably. This is unfortunate, because it can lead to confusion. For our purposes, **speech** is the physical production of sounds for communication. *Language* is a socially shared code with rules used to represent concepts. *Communication* is the process of encoding, transmitting, and decoding language to exchange ideas. It is important to keep these terms distinct when discussing language development and language difficulties.

Language can be divided into two major categories: receptive and expressive. It can be further subdivided into major elements: phonology, syntax, morphology, semantics, pragmatics, and metalinguistic elements. We describe each briefly and the problems students with learning disabilities may have with them. It is vital for teachers and others to understand the different elements so that they can identify specific areas of strength and weakness in a student's performance.

## Receptive Language

The first division in language is that of receptive and expressive language. **Receptive language** refers to the listener's behavior. In other words, how skilled is the listener in understanding what is heard? Except for those who communicate using sign language, people receive most language by hearing it. When receiving language, people not only hear it, but also must comprehend it. Comprehension of language is based on many complex and related skills. The process involves attending to the speaker and the speaker's delivery of language, hearing the specific sounds, identifying how the sounds go together, recognizing and understanding these groupings (e.g., words, sentences), and comprehending the message. Difficulties in any of these areas could mean a breakdown in communication.

**receptive language** the listener's behavior

## Expressive Language

**Expressive language** refers to the production of language. Expressing ideas in language requires using many language abilities. When people express themselves, they not only use their ability to make sounds, but also make certain sounds in a specific order in order to create words, order the words to make phrases and sentences, and so forth. As is true with receptive language, expressive language can be broken into many parts, but the parts are actually closely connected.

**expressive language** the production of language

## Difficulties of Students with Learning Disabilities in Receptive and Expressive Language

Council for Exceptional Children

**CEC Knowledge Check**

Is this a formal assessment stage, or just the gathering of relevant facts?
CC8S1

With a student who is having difficulty with language, one of the first questions that can be asked is, "Does this student have problems primarily with receptive or expressive language?" By studying the language skills of students with learning disabilities, researchers have found that though some students have difficulty with both, most difficulties exist in the area of expressive, not receptive, language (Hessler & Kitchen, 1980; Noel, 1980; Semel & Wiig, 1975; Wong & Roadhouse, 1978).

Children who have difficulty expressing themselves may have several different problems. One is called dysnomia. Children who have **dysnomia,** which is also known as a "word-finding problem," often seem to talk in fits and starts; they may stumble over words, rephrase what they are saying, or substitute the word *thing* for words they cannot remember at the moment (Kail & Leonard, 1986). Of course, most people do this sometimes; it only is recognized as a problem when it occurs especially frequently. A student with dysnomia might say, "Well, we had to take the, the . . . big car . . . door in the back . . . uhm . . . the van. So, anyway, we went to . . . to, you know, groceries . . . that place where you get food and, you know, and we were, uhm, you know, looking for . . . shopping! . . . shopping for things, you know, food and stuff and my mom wanted to, uhm, get, uhm, some . . . you put 'em on your legs . . ."

Dysarthia and apraxia are other expressive language problems. Both are difficulties with articulation—that is, the production of speech sounds. Students with **dysarthia** slur their speech and sound hoarse. Students with **apraxia** seem to be

**dysnomia** a word-finding problem; individuals with dysnomia often seem to talk in fits and starts, stumble over words, rephrase what they are saying, or substitute the word *thing* for words they cannot remember at the moment

**dysarthia** a disorder which includes slurred speech and sounding hoarse

**apraxia** a disorder in which persons seem to be trying very hard to speak, talk slowly, and have greatest difficulty with starting to say words

Council for
Exceptional
Children

**CEC Knowledge Check**
Since many of these students can understand instructions but have problems verbalizing, how should their feedback to instruction be structured?
CC6S1

**phonology**   the study of the sound system of language

**phoneme**   the smallest unit of sound

Council for
Exceptional
Children

**CEC Knowledge Check**
Since students with learning disabilities are often deficient in phonemics, how important is it to teach these basic skills?
LD3K2

**babbling**   long strings of sound that children begin to produce at approximately four months of age

trying very hard to speak, talk slowly, and have greatest difficulty with starting to say words (Caplan, 1992).

## Phonology

### What Is It?

**Phonology** refers to the study of the sound system of language. Although we communicate with gestures or body language, most of our communication is based on the sounds we make when using expressive language (e.g., speaking) or the sounds we hear via receptive language. People can make many different sounds, but only some of them are used in each language. For example, English does not use clicks as a part of speech, but some African languages do. Infants learn the unique sounds of their language from their environment. Although they can make all the sounds used in all languages when they are very young, they gradually stop making the sounds that are not used in the language they hear regularly in their environment.

A **phoneme** is the smallest unit of sound. As people talk, they exhale slightly and move the muscles in their mouths and throats to shape the escaping air and form phonemes. In English, there are 44 phonemes. Some of the sounds are not obvious, and, unfortunately, too few teachers are taught how the sound system of English works (Moats, 2000). For example, the word *sin* has three phonemes—/s/, /i/, and /n/. But the words *sing, thin,* and *thing* also have three—/s/, /i/, and /ng/; /th/, /i/, and /n/; and /th/, /i/, and /ng/.

Phonological skills play an important role in acquisition of higher-order skills. For instance, facility with phonology influences children's reading, which we discuss in Chapter 12 (e.g., Hulme, 2002; Schatschneider, Carlson, Francis, Foorman, & Fletcher, 2002).

### How Does It Develop?

In infants, phonological development includes the child's understanding of different combinations or patterns of sounds that convey differences in meaning, the development of the physical mechanisms for articulation, and the development of the auditory perception of differences in sound (Garton & Pratt, 1998). At birth, the infant cries. Starting with the birth cry, the infant engages in crying as a response to discomfort.

From about 3 to 6 months of age, infants engage in **babbling.** Authorities consider this stage as crucial for the later development of speech, because it causes changes in the infant's environment (Eisenson, 1972; Owens, 2001; Sachs, 1989). It is important for children to learn that they can affect the environment by making noises. Infants learn this when adults, particularly parents, attend to and reinforce babbling.

Gradually, infants and young children learn to discriminate sounds they hear on the basis of their distinctive features (Menn & Stoel-Gammon, 2001). The first actual speech sounds children use are those that are highly discriminable. The reason children's first words often are *mama* and *papa* or *dada* is because these words are composed of easily discriminable speech sounds (Menyuk, 1972) and are most likely to be reinforced and shaped by attention and other social interactions with parents, siblings, and others.

Children's development in phonology moves from words to multiple words to sentences and beyond. Early words are limited in their syllables and phonemes.

> In this progression, the child frequently generalizes from one word to another. Thus, phonological development occurs with changes in the pronunciation of individual words. Some changes result in improved identification of structures and sounds, others in new skills of production, and still others in the application of new phonological rules governing production. (Owens, 2001, p. 271)

By age 6, children can identify syllables and master rules for pluralization. By age 7, they are able to recognize unacceptable sound sequences, and by age 8, they are able to produce all American English sounds and blends.

## Problems with Phonology

Some problems with phonology involve production of speech and are referred to as articulation problems. Mastery of articulation requires the development of control over the muscles used in speaking but does not necessarily imply difficulties with understanding spoken language. Dysarthia and apraxia are examples of problems with the production of phonemes.

Students can also have problems with the reception of phonemes. This is referred to as **auditory discrimination.** One test of auditory discrimination would be to show a child pictures of a rake and a lake and then tell the child to touch the picture of a lake; in this way, one could tell whether the child hears the sounds correctly. Studies demonstrate that performance on various auditory discrimination tasks is related to reading achievement in some children with language impairments (e.g., McArthur & Hogben, 2001; Waber et al., 2001). According to Ms. Hamilton, Jamal's first-grade teacher, he often experiences problems with auditory discrimination.

**auditory discrimination** refers to an individual's skill in telling the difference between sounds

Jamal

Jamal is very worried that I think he's got learning problems. At times, I will speak directly to Jamal at my desk or at his desk during an activity. It is apparent to me that he has confused some of the direction words and is therefore going in the wrong direction. For example, yesterday, he remained in his seat as we prepared to go to the music room. When I asked him why, he got very angry with me and said I'd told him to wait for the music teacher, not walk to the music teacher. This generally occurs when I say things quickly and the classroom is noisy.

*Ms. Hamilton, Jamal's first-grade teacher*

According to the speech-language pathologist who evaluated Jamal:

> Jamal has a couple of areas of weakness in phonology and phonemic awareness. First of all, he has difficulty following multistep directions. For example, if his mother asks Jamal to clean off the counters, feed the dog, and take out the trash, Jamal may only complete cleaning off the counters or he may jumble all of the tasks. Second, Jamal has difficulty processing at the individual sound or even syllable level. For example, if you ask him to say the word *cat* slowly, pronouncing all of the sounds individually, he will not be able to do it.
>
> *Jannette Jones, Jamal's speech-language pathologist*

## Syntax

### What Is It?

**syntax** the patterns or rules people use to put words together into sentences

**Syntax** refers to the patterns or rules people use to put words together into sentences. It is roughly equivalent to grammar, but not grammar of the sort that is taught in schools. Syntax rules are not something that someone creates and others memorize; instead, these rules are understood implicitly by those who speak the language. In this sense, syntax refers to the way in which words can be arranged to create meaningful sentences.

People have an underlying understanding of language that gives them the ability to use different sentence structures to say the same things or very similar structures to say things with different meanings. For example, compare these two sentences:

> Kids are faster than kittens.
> Kids are not faster than kittens.

The syntax of these sentences differs in only one word, *not*. That difference, however, completely reverses the meaning of the sentence.

Understanding the syntactic structure of our language allows us to comprehend some parts of a message even when we do not know the words in it. For example, most adult speakers of English could answer the questions in Table 11.1 because they know enough about the syntax (and other aspects) of English to realize that exact word meanings are not required to deduce many of the ideas expressed by a speaker.

### How Does It Develop?

Before the age of 3 or 4 years, children often use one-word utterances to stand for entire sentences. Then they begin to string words together in rudimentary sentences that omit nonessential words such as articles. For example, a child may say "All gone shoe" in place of the sentence "The shoe is not here." Generally, by age 3 or 4,

| TABLE 11.1 | How General Knowledge of Language Helps People Understand Messages |
| --- | --- |

Council for Exceptional Children

Given this passage:

> Before the flangbong, the smarmly gribbles were very murggy. So, they went to the libenstar and libensed their smarmly zwibucks. Then the gribbles went to their yibode counsiber's nebber and libensed themselves. Once they were all flarkly and foebush, the gribbles borrowed their counsiber's marbork and went happily to the flangbong.

See if you can answer these questions.

1. Who was very murggy?
2. What did the gribbles do to their zwibucks? When did they do it?
3. What did the gribbles do to themselves? Where did they do it?
4. Whose marbork did the gribbles borrow?
5. Why do you think the gribbles wanted to be flarkly and foebush?

CEC Knowledge Check
How does this exercise help you see that background definitions and meanings of words are necessary for understanding? CC2K3

they have mastered the sentence forms of subject-verb-object and subject-linking verb-complement. Development then begins within the sentence elements and at the sentence level.

In preschool children, noun phrase development occurs with the addition of articles and modifiers, the use of pronouns, the use of postnoun modifiers, the addition of relative clauses, and the use of several noun phrases in succession (Owens, 2001). In school-age children, noun phrases begin to include better choices of subject and object pronouns, the use of reflexives, and pronouns carried across sentences.

Verbs are also among the single-word phrases that children use. Children then develop the use of –ing verbs and some infinitive forms (such as *gonna, wanna, hafta*). Auxiliary verbs show up first in the negative form (*can't, won't, don't*). In the preschool and school stages of development, children speak of the here and now. All conversation relates to that reference point. As children develop, they speak of the past and the future. Children learn verb tenses and adverbs as they progress through school.

Children develop the basic understanding of sentence types (declarative, interrogative, imperative, and negative) early on, but knowledge of the complexity of each type develops slowly. Passive sentences are particularly difficult and not understood correctly until about the age of 5. Production occurs even later (Tager-Flusberg, 2001). Combining sentences and adding clauses (e.g., "I'm playing baseball with someone *whom you know*") are higher levels of syntactic development that occur progressively throughout the school years.

Council for Exceptional Children

CEC Knowledge Check
Why is it important to be read to in the early developing years? CC2K1, CC2K4

### Problems with Syntax

Many students with learning disabilities experience problems with syntax. For example, when the syntax of a sentence makes it ambiguous, those with learning disabilities are less likely to realize that it can be interpreted in more than one way (Wiig, Semel, & Abele, 1981).

Council for
Exceptional
Children

**CEC Knowledge Check**

If this is true, what value would you place on interventions and strategies to help grammar and sentence structure? CC2K1

Some problems with syntax remain even after many years of schooling. For example, adolescents with learning disabilities may have difficulty understanding what a pronoun refers to (Fayne, 1981) and are more likely to produce grammatically incorrect sentences. In addition, although their sentences become longer and more complex as they grow older, children and adolescents with learning disabilities still seem to use sentences that are simpler than those others use, and they continue to make more grammatical errors (Scott & Windsor, 2000).

## Morphology

### What Is It?

**morphology** the system of rules used to construct words and word forms from basic units of meaning that involves the structure of basic meaning

**morpheme** the smallest unit of meaning in a language

Children learn not only the phonology and syntax of their language, but also how to change parts of words in ways that change meaning. For example, they learn that by adding an ending to most nouns, they can indicate more than one of that thing (e.g., *girl* + *s* = more than one girl). **Morphology** is the intraword rule system that affects the meanings of words.

For example, a **morpheme** is the smallest unit of meaning in a language. In the foregoing example of *girls,* there are two morphemes, one for the concept of "juvenile female" and one for the concept of "more than one," or "plural." Morphology is important not only in its own right but because it also provides important cues in reading and spelling.

Council for
Exceptional
Children

**CEC Knowledge Check**

What role and impact can families have on morphology and phoneme development? What can families do to increase awareness and correct usage? CC2K4

### How Does It Develop?

Children develop morphological rules at a young age, but the period of greatest acquisition is from ages 4 to 7 (Owens, 2001). Morphological development is related to cognitive development and the complexity of the morphemes. One example of a morphological rule is the addition of a letter to the end of a word to indicate that it is plural. Of course, some words do not follow the usual rules. The word *fish* may be both the singular and the plural form; the plural of *man* does not require the addition of a phoneme, but the change of one (the /a/ becomes an /e/ to make *men*). Initially, children often mistakenly apply general rules to all examples and only later learn the exceptions. For example, in making plurals, a young child might say "three mans" but later learn to say "three men."

### Problems with Morphology

Many students with language problems have difficulty with certain morphemes that indicate tense. Although their peers may have advanced to the level of adults, young children with difficulties continue to make mistakes with tasks such as adding an *–ed* to all past-tense verbs—for example, *runned* instead of *ran* (Rice & Wexler, 1996; Windsor, Scott, & Street, 2000).

As illustrated in Figure 11.1, the difficulties of students with learning disabilities often are particularly striking (Vogel, 1977; Wiig, Semel, & Crouse, 1973). These students have great difficulty:

- when the plural of a word requires adding a complex ending, such as *box, boxes*

This dog has spots. He is spotty. But this dog has even more spots. He is_____.

This boy can shake things. Here he is shaking. He does it every day. Every day he_____.

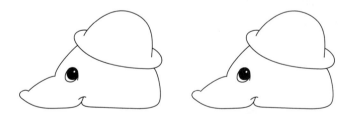

These are lags. They have hats. Whose hats are they? They are the_____.

*Source:* From *Introduction to Learning Disabilities,* 2nd ed. (p. 182) by D. P. Hallahan, J. M. Kauffman, and J. W. Lloyd, 1985, Boston: Allyn and Bacon. Copyright © 1985 by Pearson Education. Reprinted by permission of the publisher.

- when they must give the third-person singular possessive (*his, hers*)
- when they must create the adjective form of a word (particularly comparative terms such as *smart, smarter, smartest*)

## Semantics

### What Is It?

semantics  the study of the meanings of words and words in groups, particularly sentences

Like morphology, **semantics** deals with meaning. Semantics involves the study of the meanings of words and words in groups, particularly sentences. An example of semantics is understanding the meaning of the word *speech* in the following sentences:

> The President's speech gave the country confidence.
> The child's speech is difficult to understand.

In each sentence, *speech* can refer to one's speaking ability or to the delivery of a formal presentation or address. The listener is able to discern the intended meaning by using contextual clues.

### How Does It Develop?

lexicon  individual dictionary of each person

A child's initial **lexicon,** the words the child is able to use appropriately, includes words of one or two syllables, usually of the consonant-vowel or consonant-vowel-consonant-vowel type. These words are, generally, nouns that name objects in the environment at a general level of specificity (e.g., *mommy, doggie, juice*). The use of words is slow at first, and the child continues to use sounds that are close to but not quite words. By 18 months, children have a lexicon of approximately 50 words (Owens, 2001). The characteristics of adults' speech and the environment have an impact on a child's developing semantic knowledge (Pan & Gleason, 2001).

Council for Exceptional Children

Children experience an explosion of new words during the preschool period, learning up to five new words per day between the ages of 18 months and 6 years (Owens, 2001). Initially, each word is seen as unique and in contrast to other words. Slowly, children begin to identify commonalities in terms (e.g., *ran* and *pan, book* and *look*). Children gain new information from both linguistic and nonlinguistic contexts (e.g., listening and watching) and progress to understanding of physical relations, temporal relations (e.g., *next, then, later*), and locational prepositions (e.g., *behind, on, under*). In the school-age and adult stages, individuals continue to add words to their lexicon but develop more abstract understandings of these terms. This overall growth may be related to growth in cognitive processing (Garton & Pratt, 1998; Pan & Gleason, 2001).

**CEC Knowledge Check**

If children grow up exposed to nontraditional terminologies, will they have more problems in school? Is this a "second language" issue? CC2K3, CC3K5, CC6K1, CC6K2

### Problems with Semantics

Vocabulary is an area of difficulty for many students with learning disabilities. In fact, research indicates the following:

- Large vocabulary differences exist between diverse learners and average achievers in terms of the number of words known and depth of word knowledge.
- Vocabulary differences between diverse learners and average achievers are apparent early and increase over time.
- Vocabulary knowledge of diverse learners needs to be addressed strategically and comprehensively if debilitating educational effects are to be avoided. (Kame'enui & Carnine, 1998, p. 34).

In addition, students with language impairments have more difficulty than their normally achieving peers in using words to label pictures (McGregor, Newman, Reilly, & Capone, 2002) and acquire significantly fewer new words per year than average achievers (White, Graves, & Slater, 1990).

Many students with language disabilities have at least some problems with semantics. They may have difficulties understanding sentences in which an ambiguous word is used; for example, they may not realize that the sentence "He was drawing a gun" can have two different meanings (Wiig et al., 1981). Adolescents who have learning disabilities take longer and make more errors than their normally achieving peers when asked to name antonyms (e.g., told *brother,* they were to say *sister*) and make more errors when trying to define common words such as *robin, bridge,* and *opinion* (Wiig & Semel, 1975).

Jamal does not seem to have a poorly developed lexicon, as evidenced by what his speech-language pathologist reports:

> Jamal has a well-developed vocabulary for his age. When asked to tell me what words like *remember* and *animal* mean, he gave me definitions that were more than superficial. For example, Jamal told me that animals could be both domesticated and wild.
>
> *Jannette Jones, Jamal's speech-language pathologist*

Jamal

## Pragmatics

### What Is It?

**Pragmatics** refers to the way in which language is used in social situations (Thompson, 1997). People alter how they speak, depending on whom they are speaking to, why they are speaking, and other factors. For example, most of us talk differently when conversing with our friends than we do when speaking in a class or visiting with our parents at a restaurant.

Most children use shorter and simpler sentences when talking to someone clearly younger than themselves than when talking to someone nearly the same age or older (Shatz & Gelman, 1973). Speaking in short, simple sentences might be insulting to some listeners, however. Thus, speakers must take into account the social situation when they speak, changing their language to fit. When people fail to adapt their language to fit social situations, they increase the chances that they will have social problems. As discussed in Chapter 7, social relations are often a problem for many students with learning disabilities.

**pragmatics** the way in which language is used in social situations

Council for Exceptional Children

**CEC Knowledge Check**
Interaction and communication with adults affect language development. Is this a cultural or an economic problem? Can parental education be a remedial factor? CC6K1, CC6K2

### How Does It Develop?

The preschool-age child learns much about pragmatics within the conversational context. By interacting with adults and others, the child begins to understand turn-taking and sticking to a topic, though only for brief periods of time. Also, the child learns to introduce new topics and slowly learns to take the listener's perspective or understanding into account. Young children use conversation to control the environment or another person's behavior or to give information. They then begin to tell stories or narratives that start out on one topic but may change, depending on what they are thinking about at the time.

During school-age and adult development, children refine their use of language. Narratives develop centrality and causality, and an understanding of a specific story grammar develops. Conversational abilities—such as understanding the listener's perspective and introducing and continuing with topics—align with societal expectations. Of course, there is tremendous variability among individuals in development of these skills, and the pragmatic requirements may be different in different cultures, genders, and situations. Research indicates that development is linked to peer acceptance and behavior in schools (Ely, 2001).

### Problems with Pragmatics

Problems with pragmatics represent one of the most important difficulties for students with learning disabilities. For example, students with learning disabilities also have problems providing descriptive information about objects. That is, they have difficulties describing something so that another person can select it from an array of choices. Also, many students with learning disabilities are less accurate in interpreting adult nonverbal cues, such as facial expressions and gestures, than their nondisabled peers and those with verbal learning disabilities (Petti, Voker, Shore, & Hayman-Abello, 2002).

Mistakes in how they use language may lead to social problems for these students (as discussed in Chapter 7). For example, students who have learning disabilities use more competitive statements in their conversations with peers, but normally achieving students make more comments showing consideration (Bryan et al., 1976). Speaking competitively may cause hard feelings and even lead to arguments and fights. Thus, poor spoken language skills may be related to the social problems that students with learning disabilities experience (Camarata, Hughes, & Ruhl, 1988). Students with language impairments aged 10 to 13 reported more negative statements about scholastic competence, social acceptance, and behavior than nondisabled peers (Jerome, Frijiki, Brinton, & James, 2002).

As we have noted throughout this text, not all students with learning disabilities are alike, nor do they all have the same characteristics. Jamal is a good example of this; whereas many students with learning disabilities have problems with pragmatics, he does not, at least according to his speech-language pathologist:

Jamal

> Jamal's understanding of the use of language is also well developed. In my observation of Jamal in the classroom, he joined a group of students already talking about basketball, waited for an opening in the discussion, and added his opinion about Kobe Bryant. The other students engaged with him.
>
> *Jannette Jones, Jamal's speech-language pathologist*

## Metalinguistic Awareness

### What Is It?

**Metalinguistic awareness** refers to our ability to think about language. It involves two components: the ability to analyze our understanding of language and the ability to control attention to select and process specific linguistic information (Bialystok, 1993). Metalinguistic awareness includes phonemic awareness, word awareness, syntactic awareness, and pragmatic awareness. Because of its prominence in recent research and discussion, we examine phonemic awareness as an example.

Phonemic awareness includes "identifying and manipulating larger parts of spoken language, such as words, syllables, and **onsets** and **rimes**—as well as phonemes. It also encompasses awareness of other aspects of sound, such as **rhyming, alliteration,** and **intonation**" (Armbruster, Lehr, & Osborn, 2001, p. 4). Children can show that they have phonemic awareness in spoken language by creating oral rhymes, by identifying and working with onsets (beginnings of words) and rimes (endings of words), by identifying and working with syllables, and by identifying and working with individual phonemes. Research indicates that phonemic awareness is linked to reading competence (Lyon, 1999; National Reading Panel, 2000).

Problems with phonemic awareness are said to exist when children cannot separate words into their parts (sounds). Rhyming, for example, requires that the last sounds of a word be held constant while the first sounds are changed (e.g., *socks* and *clocks*). In another form of phonemic awareness, **phoneme segmentation,** students hear an entire word and say only part of it; for example, a teacher might direct students to say *sand* but to omit the */s/* (leaving *and*). Skill in segmenting words into their constituent sounds is important in early reading achievement.

Problems with sound blending may also reflect children's difficulties with phonology. **Sound blending**—essentially the opposite of phonemic segmentation— is used to collapse separated phonemes into a whole. For example, the sounds */m/, /i/, /s/,* and */t/* can be blended into the word *mist.* Poor readers have weaker sound-blending skills (Adams, 1990; Kass, 1966; Kavale, 1981; Richardson, DiBenedetto, & Bradley, 1977; Richardson, DiBenedetto, Christ, & Press, 1980).

Problems with segmenting, rhyming, and blending may all reflect deficits in **working memory** (see Chapter 8). To complete a segmenting, rhyming, or blending task, students perform a complex series of cognitive operations. As illustrated in Table 11.2 (page 340), they operate on a stream of sounds several times, exchanging information in and out of working memory and then generating the result.

### How Does It Develop?

Again using phonemic awareness as an example, it is quite difficult to determine exactly how metalinguistic skills develop. Phonemic awareness involves both reflection on language and deliberate control of that reflection. It is not difficult to determine when a child can spontaneously reflect on language (e.g., "The cat in the hat—hey, that rhymes!), but it is more difficult to determine how and when this act is deliberate.

Tasks used to assess phonemic awareness—such as phoneme oddity (i.e., in a list of three words, which word ends or begins differently), tapping out sounds (i.e.,

**metalinguistic awareness** thinking about language

**onset** part of a syllable before the vowel

**rime** term for the part of a syllable that includes the vowel and what follows it

**rhyming** requires that the last sounds of a word be held constant while the first sounds are changed

**alliteration** occurrence in phrase or line of speech of two or more words having the same beginning sound

**intonation** pitch level of the voice in speaking

**phoneme segmentation** breaking words into individual phonemes

**sound blending** the collapsing of separated phonemes into a whole

**working memory** the ability to keep a small amount of information in mind while carrying out further mental operations

**TABLE 11.2    A Simple Illustration of How Memory Might Be Used in Creating a Rhyme**

| STEP | OVERT ACTION | COVERT ACTION | REQUIRES WORKING MEMORY? | EXAMPLE |
|------|--------------|---------------|--------------------------|---------|
| 1 | Hear word | | yes | "Think" |
| 2 | | Parse word into parts | yes | "th" + "ing" + "k" |
| 3 | | Chunk parts for rhyming | yes | "th" + "ink" |
| 4 | | Hold rhyming chunk in memory | yes | "ink" |
| 5 | | Consider alternative sounds to prepend to "ink" | yes | Hmmmm . . . does "f" work? How about "k"? How about "p"? |
| 5a | | Combine new sound with "ink" and compare result to dictionary of known words | yes | Sheesh, "fink"? How about "kink"? Uhm, how about "pink"? |
| 5b | | Select new word | yes | Hey, *pink* . . . That's it! |
| 6 | Say word | | yes | "Pink! Teacher. I know. I know! It's pink! |

Council for
Exceptional
Children

**CEC Knowledge Check**
In what ways does this phonemic awareness strategy follow the sequence of learning? CC6S1

making notice of the sounds of the words, not individual letters), and phoneme segmentation (e.g., *cat* is "cuh ah tuh")—involve interconnected skills and are influenced by whether or not the child has received reading instruction (Garton & Pratt, 1998). The general trend of development in phonemic awareness seems to begin with an awareness of rhyme. By becoming aware of words that sound similar, children then begin to develop the ability to identify how they also sound different—meaning that their focus may shift to the beginning of the word. From here on, children begin to develop awareness of phonemes within words. With the onset of reading instruction, teachers draw children's attention to the phonemes in words, and phonemic awareness increases (Garton & Pratt, 1998).

### Problems with Metalinguistic Skills

Again, metalinguistic skills are the thinking about and manipulating of language. Phonemic awareness is included in metalinguistic skills as well as in processing language. According to Kame'enui and Carnine (1998), students with learning problems in language coding differ from their nondisabled peers in

- storing verbal language in memory (Students with learning problems use meaning or semantic codes, whereas nondisabled peers use sound or phonological codes.)
- using verbal information in working memory (Students with learning problems are less efficient in their use of verbal information to aid memory.)
- retrieving information from long-term memory (Students with learning problems "extract information more slowly, less accurately, and in less detail" than average achievers [p. 40].)
- using learning strategies (Students with learning problems may use similar strategies as average achievers but they use them less efficiently.)

In addition, many students with learning disabilities may have difficulties with phonemic awareness, which can lead to difficulties in mastering simple reading tasks (Adams, 1990; Juel, Griffith, & Gough, 1986; Liberman, 1970; Liberman & Shankweiler, 1991; Tarver & Ellsworth, 1981). Research indicates that without specific intervention, these difficulties are stable over time (Wagner et al., 1997). Difficulties with phonemic awareness skills can impact many academic areas, but these difficulties can also be seen outside of school, as evidenced by this quote from Jamal's grandmother.

> Jamal is a bit slower than his sister when playing word games. To pass time, I'll say, "Tell me all the words you can think of that begin with *s* or *h* or *c*," and he and his sister will shout over top of each other. When I say, "Tell me all of the words you can think of that rhyme with *see* or *heat*," Jamal is pretty quiet.
>
> *Alice Lincoln, Jamal's grandmother*

Jamal

Jamal's speech-language pathologist concurs that phonemic awareness is Jamal's greatest area of weakness in oral language:

> He has difficulty in both segmenting and blending at the individual-sound level and at the syllable level. For example, if I say to Jamal, "Combine these sounds—/s/-/a/-/m/—to make a word," he will have trouble doing it. If I say, "What are the sounds in the word hop?" he will have trouble doing it.
>
> *Jannette Jones, Jamal's speech-language pathologist*

## How Are Spoken Language Abilities Assessed?

Skills and deficits in spoken language are assessed by both standardized tests and informal measures. Language assessment should follow two basic premises: "The first is that to implement equitable assessments of language and communication in today's global society, multi-cultural and multi-linguistic factors must be considered. Secondly, the process must embrace multi-dimensional and multi-perspective approaches" (Wiig, 2001, p. 247).

### Standardized Assessments

If a student is suspected of having academic or behavioral difficulties in school that are language based, a speech-language pathologist should be involved in the evaluation of the student's spoken language skills. (See the Effective Practices box on page 342.) Because there are many tests developed to assess the aspects of language skills, the speech-language pathologist can help determine which to use and can administer the tests and interpret the results. The decision about how to assess language performance depends largely on the purposes of the assessment (see Chapter 3).

Effective
Practices

FOR LEARNING
DISABILITIES

## Speech-Language Pathologists

Council for
Exceptional
Children

### Who Are They and What Do They Do?

Students with learning disabilities in spoken language often receive services from speech-language pathologists. Though some speech-language pathologists provide students services within the classroom, students still "go to speech" in other settings. What the speech-language pathologist does is not always easy to discern for teachers, even though what is learned during speech services should be reinforced in the classroom. Therefore, the American Speech-Language-Hearing Association (ASHA), the major professional organization for speech-language pathologists, gives the following information about who speech-language pathologists are and what they do.

### Nature of the Work

Speech-language pathologists are professionals concerned with evaluation, treatment, prevention, and research in human communication and its disorders. They treat speech and language disorders and work with individuals of all ages, from infants to the elderly. They diagnose and evaluate speech problems, such as fluency (e.g., stuttering), articulation, voice disorders, or language problems, such as aphasia and delayed language and related disorders, such as dysphagia (e.g., swallowing difficulties). They design and carry out comprehensive treatment plans to achieve the following:

- help individuals learn correct production of speech sounds
- assist with developing proper control of the vocal and respiratory systems or correct voice production
- assist children and adolescents with language problems, such as understanding and giving directions, answering and asking questions, understanding and

using English grammar, using appropriate social language, and conveying ideas to others
- assist individuals who stutter to increase the amount of fluent speech and to cope with their disorder
- assist individuals who have had strokes or suffered other brain trauma relearn language and speech skills
- help individuals to use augmentative and assistive systems of communication
- counsel individuals with speech-and-language disorders and their families or caregivers to understand their disorder and to communicate more effectively in educational, social, and vocational settings
- advise individuals and the community on how to prevent speech-and-language disorders.

**CEC Knowledge Check**
After reading this list, do you feel that you will be able to refer students with language problems properly? CC5S3

### Educational Requirements

According to ASHA, speech-language pathologists must have a graduate education. They are also required by ASHA to obtain the ASHA Certificate of Clinical Competence (CCC), which involves the completion of a master's degree, a supervised Clinical Fellowship (CF), and a passing score on a national examination. In most states, speech-language pathologists and audiologists also must comply with state regulatory (licensure) standards to practice and/or have state education certification.

The American Speech-Language-Hearing Association (ASHA) represents 96,636 professionals. There are an estimated 42,000 additional individuals who are providing services in the profession.

*Source:* From the ASHA Website http://professional.asha.org/careers/slp.cfm

### Comprehensive Standardized Assessments

Children's general language competence and performance are usually assessed by measuring their IQ. Because intelligence tests rely heavily on language abilities, IQ can be a good indicator of verbal ability. This was thought to be particularly true with such IQ tests as the original *Wechsler Intelligence Scale for Children,* now the WISC-III (Wechsler, 1991), which has subtests designed to assess language performance (e.g., vocabulary).

Recently developed tests of general language ability are shown in Table 11.3. Many of these comprehensive tests, such as the *Test of Language Development–3* (TOLD–3) (Hammill & Newcomer, 1997; Newcomer & Hammill, 1997), have become popular. The TOLD–3, and special versions of it for students of different ages, focus on assessing the major aspects of spoken language, including phonology, syntax, and semantics. Like the TOLD–3, many of the tests shown in Table 11.3 provide not only an overall language ability score but also scores in specialized areas.

### Specific Standardized Assessments

As previously discussed, language includes the areas of phonology, syntax, morphology, semantics, and pragmatics. People who work with students who have learning disabilities may sometimes need to assess students' performance in one or more of these specific aspects of language. The comprehensive tests of language performance may help satisfy this need, but teachers may want to conduct more extensive, specific assessments.

Table 11.4 (page 344) lists some examples of tests of specific areas of language learning. The table does not list tests for each of the aspects of language learning

Council for
Exceptional
Children

**CEC Knowledge Check**
Even though IQ tests can measure verbal ability, does this measure students' intelligence? Should this IQ score be widely used?
CC8K4, LD8S1

**TABLE 11.3**   Selected Comprehensive Tests of Language

| TEST | AGE RANGE | AREAS ASSESSED (SCORES) |
|---|---|---|
| *Test of Adolescent and Adult Language–3* (Hammill, Brown, Larsen, & Wiederholt, 1994) | 12 years, 0 months to 24 years, 11 months | Listening, speaking, reading, spoken language, written language, vocabulary, grammar, receptive language, expressive language, general language |
| *Test for Auditory Comprehension of Language–3* (Carrow-Woolfolk, 1999) | 3 years to 9 years, 11 months | Vocabulary, elaborated phrases and sentences, grammatical morphemes |
| *Test of Language Development–3—Intermediate* (Hammill & Newcomer, 1997) | 8 years, 6 months to 12 years, 11 months | Syntax, semantics, speaking, listening, spoken language, sentence combining, picture vocabulary, word ordering, general, grammatical components |
| *Test of Language Development–3—Primary* (Newcomer & Hammill, 1997) | 4 years to 8 years, 11 months | Phonology, syntax, semantics, speaking, listening, spoken language, organization (optional) |
| *Test of Early Language Development–3* (Hresko, Reid, & Hammill, 1999) | 2 years to 7 years, 11 months | Receptive language, expressive language, spoken language quotient |
| *Clinical Evaluation of Language Fundamentals—III* (Semel, Wiig, & Secord, 1995) | 6 years to 21 years, 11 months | Receptive language, expressive language, total language, word association, listening to paragraphs, rapid-automatic naming |

**TABLE 11.4** Selected Specific Assessments

| TEST | AGE RANGE | AREAS ASSESSED (SCORES) |
|---|---|---|
| **Phonology** | | |
| *Goldman Fristoe Test of Articulation* (Goldman & Fristoe, 2000) | 2 years, 0 months and older | Sounds in words, sounds in sentences, stimulability |
| **Phonemic Awareness** | | |
| *Roswell-Chall Auditory Blending Test* (Roswell & Chall, 1997) | Grades 1–4 | Total score |
| *Test of Phonological Awareness* (Torgesen & Bryant, 1994) | 5 years to 8 years | Total score |
| **Vocabulary** | | |
| *Comprehensive Receptive and Expressive Vocabulary Test* (Wallace & Hammill, 2002) | 4 years to 17 years, 11 months | Receptive vocabulary, expressive vocabulary, total score |
| *Peabody Picture Vocabulary Test–III* (Dunn & Dunn, 1997) | 2 years to 90 years | Total score |

included in the earlier discussion of language features. For additional information on tests of language skills, see works on assessment of learning disabilities (Overton, 2003; Salvia & Ysseldyke, 2001).

Because phonemic awareness is a critical skill in the development of literacy (Armbruster et al., 2001; Lyon, 1999; Moats, 2000), it is the phonological skill of foremost importance in language learning. Young students' phonemic awareness should be assessed routinely as part of literacy screening. Some states have established programs to screen for problems in phonemic awareness among kindergarten and first-grade students (e.g., Invernizzi, Meier, Juel, & Swank, 1997; Swank, Meier, Invernizzi, & Juel, 1997).

## Informal Language Assessment Methods

Much can be learned about a student's language competence in natural contexts. Teachers and other clinicians can collect and analyze at least three different types of student language samples: (1) spontaneous, (2) imitation, and (3) elicited (Salvia & Ysseldyke, 2001). Teachers obtain spontaneous language samples by recording the language a student produces in an unstructured, everyday setting. For an imitation sample, teachers ask students to directly repeat specific words, phrases, or sentences. In an elicited-language sample, the teacher asks the student to look at a picture and either (1) point to the correct object, (2) point to the picture that best describes the sentence stated, (3) name the picture, or (4) describe the picture (Salvia & Ysseldyke, 2001).

To collect language samples, teachers should create a situation in which students can produce their best language performance, because it is important to know how well the student can do. With younger children, the teacher may want to use toys or activities to promote language, but with adolescents, using social situations is probably sufficient. Rather than asking many specific questions, teachers gathering language samples should use strategies that encourage the student to talk. The idea is to obtain a sample of student language that includes about 50 to 100 **utterances** (a segment of speech that expresses a complete thought). Teachers may want to record the sample on video- or audiotape. Here is a short example of Jamal working with Ms. Hamilton, his first-grade teacher, on using words:

**utterance**   complete segment of spoken language

> *Ms. Hamilton:*  Okay, Jamal. I would like you to use the words I give you in a sentence. What is it I want you to do?
> *Jamal:*  You want me to repeat words in a sentence.
> *Ms. Hamilton:*  I want you to use each word in a sentence. Here is the first word: *cat.*
> *Jamal:*  I like cats.
> *Ms. Hamilton:*  *friend.*
> *Jamal:*  I have a friend.
> *Ms. Hamilton:*  *store*
> *Jamal:*  I am going to the store this afternoon. My mom said she would buy me a new pair of shoes. I'm going to get some Air Jordans.
> *Ms. Hamilton:*  *running*
> *Jamal:*  Yesterday, my sister and I was running down the street to get home. We was late for dinner and that makes mom mad!

 Jamal

The most difficult part of using language samples is scoring them. The first step is to transcribe the sample (transferring it to paper or computer disk) and segment it (mark off individual utterances or units of language). Then, the individual utterances must be analyzed. Some important measures for analysis are **mean length of utterance (MOU), type-token ratio,** and **T-unit.** Table 11.5 describes these measures. In addition, the sample can be analyzed for appropriate use of various language features,

**mean length of utterance (MOU)**   average number of morphemes per utterance

**type-token ratio**   the ratio of the number of different words (type) to the total number of words (tokens) in a language sample

**T-units**   a single main clause and the subordinate clauses that accompany it

---

**TABLE 11.5**   Some Common Measures of Expressive Language for Analyzing Language Samples

| MEASURE | DESCRIPTION |
|---|---|
| Mean length of utterance (MLU) | Calculating MLUs requires counting the number of words in the sample and dividing by the number of utterances. How the sample is segmented into utterances will affect the MLU. |
| Type-token ratio | Type refers to the number of different words, and token refers to the total number of words in a writing sample. For example, the sentence "The girl gave the other girl a smile" has eight tokens and six types. In general, as students get older, the type-token ratio increases, indicating that they are using proportionally more different words. |
| T-unit | A T-unit is a single main clause and the subordinate clauses that accompany it. For example, "The movie we saw" is not a T-unit and neither is "we saw about Moby Dick, the white whale." The following are T-units: "I like the movie we saw" and "I like the movie we saw about Moby Dick, the white whale." T-units may be very brief (e.g., "Birds fly") or longer (e.g., "Flying continuously for many months, the swallows eat and mate in midair while circumnavigating the globe"). |

**CEC Knowledge Check**
Why do recent experiences tend to elicit better responses?
CC8S5

Jamal

**curriculum-based assessment (CBA) or curriculum-based measurement (CBM)**
an approach to assessment based on the assumption that learning problems and progress are best measured directly as performance in the curriculum rather than indirectly as test performance related to underlying processes; systematic, frequent, brief samples of the student's performance in the curriculum being taught

such as use of particular morphemes. Other sources provide additional and more detailed information about language samples and learning disabilities (Lidz & Elliott, 2000; Wing, Leekam, Libby, Gould, & Larcombe, 2002). Technology, such as speech-recognition software, may also help teachers assess a student's language competence. For an overview of assistive technology, see the Today's Technology box on page 347. As you can see from the example, Jamal has a few usage errors (*was* instead of *were*), and his responses are short and in a noun-verb-noun format when they are not part of his recent experience. When provided with words that are part of his recent experience, Jamal can think of quite a lot to say.

In addition to rhyming and phoneme segmentation, phonemic awareness includes other skills. Table 11.6 shows examples of different tasks that can be used in informal assessments of phonemic awareness. Evaluations of phonemic awareness should include both isolation of phonemes and phoneme-deletion tasks.

## Methods of Monitoring Progress

Plans for monitoring progress should be developed according to individual needs. For example, monitoring a student's progress in phonemic awareness makes little sense when the primary language problems are in word knowledge. Decisions about which problem areas to monitor should be based on students' evaluation results and subsequent IEP goals.

We can measure progress in some specific spoken-language areas by means similar to those used in **curriculum-based assessment (CBA).** As we discussed in Chapter 3, CBA involves frequently repeated measurement of specific skills. And phonemic awareness and receptive vocabulary are skills that can be monitored using

---

**TABLE 11.6** Tasks Used to Assess Phonemic Awareness

| TASK | EXAMPLE |
| --- | --- |
| 1. Sound-to-word matching | Is there a /f/ in *calf?* |
| 2. Word-to-word matching | Do *pen* and *pipe* begin the same? |
| 3. Recognition or production of rhyme | Does *sun* rhyme with *run?* |
| 4. Isolation of a sound | What is the first sound in *rose?* |
| 5. Phoneme counting | How many sounds do you hear in the word *hot?* |
| 6. Phoneme counting | How many sounds do you hear in the word *cake?* |
| 7. Phoneme blending | Combine these sounds: /c/-/a/-/t/. |
| 8. Phoneme deletion | What word would be left if /t/ were taken away from the middle of *stand?* |
| 9. Specifying deleted phoneme | What sound do you hear in *meat* that is missing in *eat?* |
| 10. Phoneme reversal | Say *os* with the first sound last and the last sound first. |
| 11. Invented spellings | Write the word *monster.* |

Council for
Exceptional
Children

**CEC Knowledge Check**
What is your plan to increase your own questioning skills?
CC9K3

*Source:* From "The Validity and Reliability of Phonemic Awareness Tests" (p. 161) by H. K. Yopp, 1988, *Reading Research Quarterly, 23.* Copyright 1988 by International Reading Association. Reprinted by permission.

## Assistive Technology in Spoken Language

The Individuals with Disabilities Education Act (IDEA) defines assistive technology as "any item, piece of equipment, or product system, whether acquired commercially off the shelf, modified, or customized, that is used to increase, maintain, or improve the functional capabilities of a child with a disability" (SS300.5, *Federal Register,* p. 12421). Therefore, assistive technology for spoken language would be any device or piece of equipment that would help a child with a disability communicate with others. Because many of the language problems that students with learning disabilities experience are related to reading and writing, much of the research has been done on devices that assist students in these areas, such as word processors, text readers, electronic texts, and word-prediction software (MacArthur, Ferretti, Okolo, & Cavalier, 2001). There are few students with learning disabilities who have language impairments severe enough to need augmentative communication devices.

There is some research on the efficacy of computer-assisted instruction in the area of phonological awareness for students with learning disabilities. In most cases, the students receive instruction in phonological analysis skills (i.e., breaking words apart) as opposed to phonological synthesis skills (i.e., putting sounds together), because the latter requires more costly speech-recognition software. In these programs, students hear words and see them on the screen. They may search for certain words or parts of words that may rhyme, for example. The results of this type of instruction are encouraging, though

more research is necessary (Okolo, Cavalier, Ferretti, & MacArthur, 2000).

One of the more interesting areas of recent research is that of speech-recognition software. Speech-recognition software has a variety of uses, including command-and-control operations of various devices (e.g., dialing wireless phones, getting driving directions), dictating text into word-processing programs, and allowing access to documents or environments. Preliminary research has indicated that speech-recognition software may be helpful in building conversation skills in second-language learners and in the assessment of language competence. For students with learning disabilities, preliminary research has shown improvement in writing, word recognition, reading comprehension, and spelling (Venkatagiri, 2002). With the rapidly changing world of technology, there is still much to learn about using technology to assist students with language-learning disabilities.

Council for Exceptional Children

CEC Knowledge Check

Do you think that allowing students with learning disabilities to use technology in their schoolwork is "cheating" or somehow an advantage over non-identified students? Why?
CC6K4, CC7S9

Council for Exceptional Children

CEC Knowledge Check

Why do some consider it fine to use technologies such as spell-checkers, but view use of technology for students with learning disabilities as an unfair advantage?
LD9K1

CBA. For example, teachers might construct lists of simple words and test how many of them students can segment correctly within two minutes. Similarly, to assess pragmatic use of language, teachers might simply observe students during particular activities and count the proportion of socially appropriate statements they make.

Council for Exceptional Children

CEC Knowledge Check

Does CBA actually make the process of monitoring easier and more accurate? How can this help future educational decisions?
CC8S8

## How Can Spoken Language Problems Be Addressed?

Intervention focused on the language problems of students with learning disabilities is influenced by several factors, such as the theoretical conceptions of language and

## Jamal's Phonemic Awareness Skills

Jannette Jones, the speech-language pathologist who assessed Jamal's language functioning, tested many aspects of his phonemic awareness, some using formal assessments such the *Test of Phonological Awareness* and others using informal assessments based on her own knowledge about phonological skills. She comments that she was interested in his skills because he had so many other language skills but seemed to have highly specific problems in phonemic skills.

Council for
Exceptional
Children

**CEC Knowledge Check**

If you were to use only formal assessments in determining phonological deficits, would you be able to correctly identify all problem areas? How do informal assessments help give a complete picture?
CC7S4, CC8K4, CC8S2

I don't want to say that Jamal is one in a million, but he is special. He can talk about so many things, science and sports for example, but he really struggles with his phonological skills. It is really surprising to me. I gave him a whole battery of tests, and he had trouble with a lot of them.

Like most children with problems in phonological processing, he couldn't segment and blend, but unlike other children, he couldn't even do it with syllables. He couldn't even say the syllables in familiar words like *bigger*. Of course, he couldn't do the harder tasks either. If I asked him to substitute sounds in words—if I asked him to say "stop" but to put an "eh" in it instead of an "ahh," he couldn't do it. If I asked him to say "spit" and then say it without the /p/, he couldn't do it. But I wasn't worried so much about these harder tasks. I read an article about how we shouldn't get carried away with phonological skills. We need to focus on the ones that are really important for reading. So I looked mostly at his segmenting and blending skills.

Jannette Jones, Jamal's speech-language pathologist

learning disabilities that teachers adopt (see Chapter 10) and the programs and materials available for teaching. Most of the actual interventions used with children and adolescents who have learning disabilities have not been aligned exclusively with one or another of the basic approaches to language. In fact, the interventions have been based more on clinical and classroom experience than on any theory.

Today in learning disabilities, concern about effectiveness of interventions should overshadow theoretical orientations. Regardless of the theoretical basis of an intervention, if it can be clearly shown that the intervention benefits students, it should be used. This perspective places increased emphasis on teachers collecting data to monitor progress and basing instructional decisions on those data. With the increased emphasis on skills such as phonemic awareness, teachers must remember that the goal of this instruction is to improve spoken and written language. The Case Connections box above describes how this is important in Jamal's case.

Council for
Exceptional
Children

**CEC Knowledge Check**

How important is the collection of intervention data? Baseline data for assessment progress? Use of data to modify the intervention?
CC8S4, CC8S8, CC8S9

Blachman (1997) has done important research in phonemic awareness, and it is her work to which Jannette refers. Blachman wrote that the emphasis on phonemic awareness reminds her of an earlier emphasis on visual-motor competence in the field of learning disabilities. In both cases, the underlying skills (e.g., phonemic awareness) were focused on more than the overall goal (e.g., to read text). In the visual-motor research, children were given some tasks that had a clear connection to handwriting. For example, they were asked to connect dots in general shapes such as Ls. They had also been given some similar tasks that went far beyond handwriting and required geometric drawing skills. The training tasks took the learners too far, wasting their time by having them master oversophisticated skills. Blachman asks whether children have to learn the most sophisticated phonemic awareness skills to be able to learn to read.

> How good do you have to be at phonological awareness activities . . . to get the maximum advantage out of these important insights about the phonological structure of words? The ability to perform more complex manipulations (e.g., deletion and rearrangement of phonemes) is likely the *result* of learning to read and spell and of being able to visualize the orthographic structure as an aid in making complex phonological judgments. . . . When does additional teaching of phoneme awareness per se stop being productive? Do you need to be able to say *stale* without the /t/? My clinical instincts suggest that once children are aware that speech can be segmented and that these segmented units can by represented by letters . . . children should be engaged in reading and spelling instruction that utilizes these insights." (Blachman, 1997, p. 416)

In the following section, we examine some basic effective practices for teaching spoken-language skills. Most of the methods address more than one area of language skill.

## General Principles and Accommodations

Many students with learning disabilities in spoken language receive their instruction in the general education classroom. Therefore, it is important for both general and special educators to be aware of some basic principles and practices in teaching these students. After reviewing the research on spoken-language interventions, Bos and Vaughn (2002, p. 83) identify the following principles for teaching language:

- Teach language in purposeful contexts.
- In most cases, follow the sequence of normal language development.

self-talk verbalizing thoughts while working through a task

parallel talk verbalizing the actions of others as they complete a task

expansion an adult responding in an interpretive way to children's utterances

elaboration repeating and adding additional information to a child's spoken language

Council for Exceptional Children

CEC Knowledge Check
Are these only special education techniques, or is this effective teaching practice for all students? CC6S1, CC6S2

wait time the amount of time between when a teacher pauses after asking a question or giving a direction and when she expects or asks for a response

- Teach comprehension *and* production.
- Use conversations to promote language development.
- Adjust pacing, chunk information, and check for understanding to promote comprehension.
- Increase wait time to promote production.
- Use effective teaching strategies when presenting a new concept or skill.
- Use **self-talk** and **parallel talk** to describe what you and others are doing and thinking.
- Use modeling to demonstrate language.
- Use **expansion** and **elaboration.**
- Use structured language programs to provide intensive practice and feedback.
- Use language as an intrinsic motivator.
- Systematically plan and instruct for generalization.

The ability to follow extended presentation of information and multiple directions may be difficult for students with spoken-language difficulties. If so, teachers can help students by pacing the delivery of information to match students' comprehension and highlighting important information (e.g., "The first reason the United States went to war . . . " or "There are three major points in our discussion today. The first is . . . The second point is . . . "). In addition, teachers can chunk information into smaller conceptual portions, giving students a chance to process what is being said before moving on to the next concept. Giving students the opportunity to dialogue and ask questions about the content also provides the teacher an opportunity to give feedback about and to expand students' attempts to communicate about concepts or topics. In this situation, it may be appropriate to provide students with increased **wait time** when questions are asked or when their participation is required. Finally, it is often effective to have students with spoken-language problems repeat directions or summarize discussion on topics. Many of these instructional strategies are effective for students who are English-language learners with difficulties in spoken language. For more on this topic, see the Multicultural Considerations box on page 351.

In working with students to improve the content of their spoken language, the goal is to help them build better phonological and semantic/syntactic representations. This is best done in a rich context: "When a word is embedded in a rich context of supportive and redundant information, the learner is more likely to acquire its meaning than when the same word is found in a lean context, as, for example, when the word is surrounded by other equally difficult and unfamiliar words" (Baumann & Kame'enui, 1991, as cited in Kame'enui & Carnine, 1998, p. 35). In this sense, new words and concepts should be linked to students' current knowledge and experience. Examples of methods using this concept include semantic feature analysis and keyword mnemonics.

## Semantic Feature Analysis

semantic feature analysis visual organizers that draw students' attention to features and meanings of words that make them unique

**Semantic feature analysis** draws students' attention to features and meanings of words that make them unique, in addition to describing ways in which they relate to known words or concepts. The purpose behind the study of words or terms is to draw

## MULTICULTURAL CONSIDERATIONS

## Teaching English-Language Learners

In a review of the research on teaching English-language learners, Gersten and Baker (2000) found scant empirical evidence for instructional practices that lead to learning outcomes. However, the authors used information that is available from intervention studies using experimental designs; studies describing learning environments; and professional work groups composed of researchers, teachers, administrators, and staff development leaders to derive the following three themes for effective English-language instruction:

1. "We identified five specific instructional variables or principles from our multivocal analysis that, although supported by limited experimental evidence, suggest critical components for instruction: (a) vocabulary as a curricular anchor, (b) visuals to reinforce concepts and vocabulary, (c) cooperative learning and peer tutoring strategies, (d) strategic use of the native language, and (e) modulation of cognitive and language demands" (p. 62).

2. "We argue that both extended discourse about academic topics and briefer responses to specific questions about content are cornerstones of academic growth for English-language learners. Our review of the data sources suggests that discussions of poten-

tially effective instructional practices . . . overemphasize natural language use and do not clearly articulate the important distinctions involved when language use is the major goal and when cognitive or academic growth is paramount" (p. 66).

3. "We encourage researchers and educators to consider language learning and content area learning as distinct educational goals, rather than assuming that increased use of oral language in school will automatically lead to an increase in academic learning. . . . Instruction for English-language learners should work to blend oral language engagement and intellectual (or cognitive) engagement" (p. 71).

In summary, there is much to learn about the teaching of English-language learners in special and general education. With the growing diversity in public schools, teachers must be aware of how their instructional practices impact second-language acquisition.

Council for Exceptional Children

**CEC Knowledge Check**

List the five instructional principles that suggest effective instruction. What are the two additional cornerstones of academic growth for learners of English? CC6S2, LD4S11

---

a link between the known and the unknown. The teacher must identify major terms or words that are necessary for students to understand and then determine how the words or terms fit together—in other words, what is the big idea that links them, and how are they similar and different? Finally, the teacher must develop an adequate list of examples and nonexamples of the understanding of the terms. See Figure 11.2 (page 352) for an example of a semantic feature analysis. The teacher will teach the students how to use this semantic feature analysis (Bos & Anders, 1990; Greenwood, 2002).

### Keyword Mnemonics

Research indicates that the use of mnemonics with students with learning disabilities can be very powerful, particularly in teaching vocabulary (Lloyd, Forness, & Kavale, 1998). **Keyword mnemonic** techniques involve the use of visual imagery and sound to link existing knowledge with unknown concepts or vocabulary and to provide a memory strategy to retrieve the information (Mastropieri & Scruggs,

Council for Exceptional Children

**CEC Knowledge Check**

How can you help students to expand their vocabulary? LD6K4

**keyword mnemonic**
a technique that involves the use of visual imagery and sound to link existing knowledge with unknown concepts and to provide a memory strategy to retrieve the information

FIGURE 11.2 Semantic Feature Analysis of Government Leaders

|  | INHERITS POWERS | GOVERNS BY FORCE | ELECTED | ELECTED BY PEOPLE | ELECTED BY LEGISLATORS |
|---|---|---|---|---|---|
| King or Queen | x |  |  |  |  |
| Dictator |  | x |  |  |  |
| President |  |  | x | x |  |
| Prime Minister |  |  | x | x | x |

☐ Semantic features

☐ Concepts or vocabulary

1998). See Figure 11.3 for an example. In order to develop keyword mnemonics for vocabulary, teachers must follow these steps (Mastropieri & Scruggs, 2002b):

- reconstructing (turning an unfamiliar word or concept into one that is familiar to students—e.g., ranidae = rainy day)
- relating (linking the word or concept, once reconstructed, to the response—e.g., ranidae = frog, keyword = rainy day, relate = frog sitting in rain)
- retrieving (retrieving the information after being taught the steps—e.g., (1) think of keyword, (2) think of interaction, (3) get definition). For more on keyword mnemonics, see Mastropieri and Scruggs (1991).

**FIGURE 11.3    Mnemonic for Ranidae**

*Source:* From *Teaching Students Ways to Remember: Strategies for Learning Mnemonically* (p. 11), by M. A. Mastropieri and T. E. Scruggs, 1991, Cambridge, MA: Brookline Books. Copyright 1991 by Brookline Books. Reprinted by permission.

## Teaching in Context or Conversation

Following the assessment of students with learning disabilities in spoken language, we can identify specific language skills and activities designed to get students to use them. Table 11.7 (page 354) shows an analysis of the components of language that a task-analytic (or behavioral) approach might assess and teach. As the student uses these components, the teacher reinforces accurate usage and corrects mistakes. For example, if a student does not know the usual plural form of *man* (e.g., the student says "mens" rather than "men"), the teacher might model the correct form ("Listen to me say it: men"), provide the student with an opportunity to repeat it correctly ("How do you say it?"), and praise common usage ("That's it! Men. You said it correctly!"). The teacher might then provide other opportunities for practice under different conditions to help the student remember the pronunciation. For example, while showing a picture of adult males, the teacher might say, "Tell me about these people. Are they boys? That's correct; they're not boys. What are they? Yes! They are men." Related morphological forms (e.g., women) would be assessed and taught as necessary.

In another approach, the teacher presents stories (arranged according to level of linguistic difficulty) and asks questions so that students must use various forms of sentences. Using the sentence that a student utters as a base, the teacher employs one of several techniques to encourage a more grammatically acceptable sentence. For example, when a student uses the wrong inflection of a verb in a sentence (e.g., "He eated bananas"), the teacher might do one of the following.

- ask the student to repeat the sentence ("What did you say?") in the hope that the student will then say it correctly.
- repeat the mistaken statement ("He eated bananas?") to encourage the student to make the correction.
- ask the student whether the statement was correct ("Is 'He eated bananas' correct?") to encourage self-correction.

Another method to encourage acquisition of language is expansion. Expansion refers to an adult responding in an interpretive way to children's utterances: The adult expands on what a child says. For example, if the child says, "Doggie gone," the adult might say, "Yes, the doggie is gone." In this way, it is hoped that the child will learn the more grammatically complete form for the idea.

## Phonemic Awareness

Recommendations about teaching phonemic awareness abound (Lyon, 1999; National Reading Panel, 2000). In the simplest form, training activities closely resemble those described previously in tests of phonology (see Table 11.7). For example:

> **Teacher:** Listen to this word: fan. Say that word.
> **Students:** Fan.
> **Teacher:** Now I want you to say that word without saying the *f* sound.
> **Students:** An!
> **Teacher:** That's it! An. You've got it.

Council for
Exceptional
Children

**CEC Knowledge Check**

What conflicts occur for a student who is exposed to incorrect language usage at home and correct language usage at school? CC2K3

Council for
Exceptional
Children

**CEC Knowledge Check**

When teaching students correct language usage, would you ever use nonstandard English in your instruction? Why? LD6K7

**TABLE 11.7** Content Analysis of Language Domains

| 1<br>SYNTAX/MORPHOLOGY | 2<br>SEMANTICS/VOCABULARY | 3<br>PRAGMATICS |
|---|---|---|
| A. Syntax/Morphology | A. Basic | A. One-Way Communication |
| 1. Noun phrase/verb phrase | 1. Body parts | 1. Expresses wants |
| 2. Regular plurals | 2. Clothing | 2. Expresses opinions |
| 3. Subject pronouns | 3. Classroom objectives | 3. Expresses feelings |
| 4. Prepositional phrases | 4. Action verbs | 4. Expresses values |
| 5. Adjectives | 5. Verb tasks | 5. Follows directions |
| 6. Interrogative reversals | 6. Animals and insects | 6. Asks questions |
| 7. Object pronouns | 7. Outdoor words | 7. Narrates event |
| 8. Negatives | 8. Family members | 8. States main idea |
| 9. Verb *be* auxiliary | 9. Home objects | 9. Sequences events |
| 10. Verb *be* copula | 10. Meals | 10. Subordinates details |
| 11. Infinitives | 11. Food and drink | 11. Summarizes |
| 12. Determiners | 12. Colors | 12. Describes |
| 13. Conjunction *and* | 13. Adverbs | 13. Compares and contrasts |
| 14. Possessives | 14. Occupations | 14. Gives instructions |
| 15. Noun-verb agreement | 15. Community | 15. Explains |
| 16. Comparatives | 16. Grooming objects | |
| 17. *Wh* questions | 17. Vehicles | B. Two-Way Communication |
| 18. Past tense | 18. Money | 1. Considers the listener |
| 19. Future aspect | 19. Gender | 2. Formulates messages |
| 20. Irregular plurals | 20. School | 3. Participates in discussions |
| 21. Forms of *do* | 21. Playthings | 4. Uses persuasion |
| 22. Auxiliaries | 22. Containers | 5. Resolves differences |
| 23. Derivational endings | 23. Days of the week | 6. Identifies speaker's biases |
| 24. Reflexive pronouns | 24. Months | 7. Identifies speaker's assumptions |
| 25. Qualifiers | 25. Emotions | 8. Formulates conclusions |
| 26. Conjunctions *and, but, or* | 26. Numbers | |
| 27. Conjunctions | 27. Celebrations and holidays | |
| 28. Indirect and direct objects | 28. Spatial concepts | |
| 29. Adverbs | 29. Quantitative concepts | |
| 30. Infinitives with subject | 30. Temporal concepts | |
| 31. Participles | 31. Shapes | |
| 32. Gerunds | 32. Greetings and polite terms | |
| 33. Passive voice | 33. Opposites | |
| 34. Complex verb forms | 34. Materials | |
| 35. Relative adverb clauses | 35. Music | |
| 36. Relative pronoun clauses | 36. Tools | |
| 37. Complex conjunctions | 37. Categories | |
| | 38. Verbs of the senses | |
| | B. Advanced | |
| | 1. Reading material vocabulary | |
| | 2. Content area vocabulary | |
| | 3. Idioms/figurative language | |
| | 4. Multiple meaning of words | |
| | 5. Influence of context on meaning | |

*Source:* From *Curriculum-Based Evaluation: Teaching and Decision Making,* 2nd ed. (p. 256) by K. W. Howell, S. L. Fox, and M. K. Morehead, 1993, Pacific Grove, CA: Brooks/Cole. Copyright 1993 by Brooks/Cole Publishing Company, a division of Thompson Publishing, Inc. Reprinted by permission.

In a popular variation, teachers give students tiles representing individual sounds and direct them to move one tile for each sound as they say the sounds in a word. (For further examples of phonemic awareness activities, see www.national readingpanel.org; O'Connor, Notari-Syverson, & Vadasy, 1998).

Regardless of the type of activity used, phonemic awareness training tasks can vary in difficulty (Moats, 2000). Teachers can adjust the difficulty of phonemic awareness tasks by varying the following.

- word length (Words with fewer phonemes are easier than longer words to manipulate.)
- size of phonological unit (Segmenting compound words is easier than segmenting syllables, which is easier than segmenting individual phonemes.)
- position in the word of the phonemes to be manipulated (Segmenting the first sounds is easier than segmenting the last sounds in words.)
- characteristics of the phonemes (Continuous sounds such as *s* and *m* are easier to segment than consonant clusters such as the first sounds in *school.*)

Teaching phonemic awareness is very important today. There are at least two cautions teachers should know. First, "How good do you have to be at phonemic awareness activities . . . to get the maximum advantage out of these important insights about the phonemic structure of words? . . . When does additional teaching of phoneme awareness per se stop becoming productive?" (Blachman, 1997, p. 416). Second, although there is considerable evidence that promoting phonemic awareness has beneficial effects on reading and spelling for young students, there is much less evidence about its benefits for students in later elementary or secondary grades. Educators must be careful not to overgeneralize the evidence.

## Statement Repetition

Another prominent problem for many children with learning disabilities is the repetition of sentences. We have known for a long time that students with learning disabilities do poorly on statement-repetition tasks (Hessler & Kitchen, 1980; Hresko, 1979; McNutt & Li, 1980; Vogel, 1974; Wiig & Roach, 1975; Wong & Roadhouse, 1978). Statement repetition forms the basis for many other skills. Some of these skills are quite rudimentary; others are more complicated. The ability to repeat a statement itself is relatively simple; one must say only what one heard. However, statement repetition is fundamental, for without this skill, students cannot hold a statement in memory long enough to think about it, change it, or do much of anything else with it. As evidenced by the following comments of Jamal, statement repetition is not always an easy task:

Jamal

My mother and teacher are always asking me to repeat things to them. "What did I just say?" "What were those directions again, Jamal?" 'What did I just ask you to do?" I don't like it much, but it helps me figure out what they're saying.

*Jamal*

Performance on statement-repetition tasks may be affected by many of the spoken-language skills described elsewhere. For example, pupils with weaker phonemic skills may have to work so hard at pronouncing words that when they try to say a complicated word, they forget the remainder of a sentence they are repeating. When this happens, it is easy to see why a student might simply shrug, sigh, and stop in midsentence. Statement repetition is clearly one of the skills required for successful learning and one in which many students with learning disabilities are deficient.

The following example illustrates how statement repetition might be used while practicing changing sentences to active voice.

> **Teacher:** Say this sentence: The overdue books were lost by the teachers.
> **Students:** The overdue books were lost by the teachers.
> **Teacher:** Now, I want you to say that sentence in the active voice.
> **Students:** The teachers lost the overdue books.
> **Teacher:** That's it! Whoa! Now, wait a minute. Who are you saying lost those books?

**CEC Knowledge Check**

How do you teach students to generalize skills to different settings? CC4S

As evidenced by many of these recommendations, instruction and practice in oral language skills can occur in the classroom context or almost anywhere quite naturally. The focus must be on getting the student to practice and generalize the skill to different settings.

**CEC Content Standards**

2. Development and Characteristics of Learners
4. Instructional Strategies
6. Communication
8. Assessment

## PORTFOLIO-BUILDING ACTIVITY

### Demonstrating Mastery of the CEC Standards

Use the following words to create teaching materials using the keyword mnemonics method to learning vocabulary (see Figure 11.3, page 352): *dahlia, viaduct, mantle, toreador, pomelo, jambeau,* and *hookah.* See the Companion Website (www.ablongman.com/hallahanLD3e) for an example to follow. Questions to think about as you progress:

- How is language impacted in human development for children with learning disabilities when cultural diversity is a factor? Do these issues affect an individual's ability to learn?

- What research-based instructional strategies can be used to promote positive learning results in the area of language deficits for individuals with learning disabilities?

- How can special education professionals enhance language development for individuals with cultural and linguistic differences?

- How can professionals determine what content to be taught and what instruction methodology should be used to teach students with learning disabilities and language area concerns?

# SUMMARY

## What is language?

- Language is a socially shared code or conventional system for representing concepts through the use of arbitrary symbols and rule-governed combinations of those symbols.
- Speech is the physical production of sounds for communication.
- Communication is the process of exchanging information. It is very complex and includes encoding, transmission, decoding, and other linguistic elements.

## Are language problems common in learning disabilities?

- Language problems are included in all definitions of learning disabilities and have been at the heart of the field since its inception. Unfortunately, in early years, much time was spent studying perceptual processes and not language difficulties.

## What are the elements of spoken language and the characteristics of students with learning disabilities in spoken language?

- Receptive language refers to the listener's behavior: both receiving the information and understanding it.
- Expressive language refers to the production of language. In order to express ideas, people must be able to make sounds, place them in a certain order to create words, and put words together in a manner that makes sense.
- Students with learning disabilities show greater evidence of difficulties in expressive language areas.
- Phonology is the study of the sound system of language. A phoneme is the smallest unit of sound. Phonological skills are linked to achievement in reading. Students with learning disabilities often have difficulties in identifying sounds, segmenting and blending sounds, and in auditory discrimination.
- Syntax refers to the patterns or rules people use to put words together into sentences. Students with learning disabilities often have difficulties with sentences that may have ambiguous meanings, pronoun referents, and more complex structures.
- Morphology is the meaning of words, and a morpheme is the smallest unit of meaning in language. Students with learning disabilities have great difficulties with morphology, including endings for verb tenses, possessives, and plurals.

- Semantics is the study of the meanings of words and words in groups, particularly sentences. Vocabulary differences between students with learning disabilities and nondisabled peers are often large and continue to grow without proper instruction.
- Pragmatics is the way in which language is used in social situations. Students with learning disabilities may have difficulty adjusting the complexity of their language for their audience or using enough description for their audience.
- Metalinguistic awareness refers to our ability to think about language and includes such areas as phonemic awareness. Students with learning disabilities who also have reading problems often show difficulties in segmenting and blending sounds, as well as manipulating sounds within words.

## How are spoken language abilities assessed?

- Standardized assessments include tests that cover all systems of language, such as the *Test of Language Development–3*. Standardized assessments may also be focused on a few specific areas of language, such as phonemic awareness.
- Informal language assessment methods include language observation, specific language tasks (e.g., blending and segmenting words into component parts), and language samples.
- Methods of monitoring progress in language development often include curriculum-based assessment. This includes samples of language taken from classroom contexts, dialogue within the classroom, and observation of students engaged in discussion with peers.

## How can spoken-language problems be addressed?

- General principles and accommodations for teaching language include teaching it in purposeful contexts, adjusting pace, chunking information, checking for understanding, and increasing wait time.
- Semantic feature analysis draws students' attention to features and meanings of words that make them unique, thus increasing vocabulary and understanding.
- Keyword mnemonics provide a visual and auditory memory retrieval device for new and unfamiliar vocabulary and concepts. Pictures and familiar words are used to key into new vocabulary and its meaning.

- Teaching in context and conversation allows students to see the immediate impact of language in their classroom environment.
- Improving students' phonemic awareness skills (e.g., segmenting and blending words by phonemes and syllables) by direct instruction increases their chances of being better readers and teaches them to think about language.
- Statement repetition helps students to improve their strategies for retaining auditory information and for checking their understanding of spoken language.

## REFLECTIONS ON THE CASES

1. In what areas of spoken language is the speech pathologist worried about Jamal's present level of performance?
2. How could these areas of weakness impact Jamal's achievement in other academic areas?
3. What are some areas of strength in spoken language for Jamal?
4. Which instructional strategies included in this chapter would use Jamal's strengths to help improve his overall spoken-language abilities?
5. If you had to write an IEP objective for Jamal in the area of spoken language, what would it be?

## *Focus On* Spoken Language

### *Do Now* Activities for Increasing Vocabulary

### Semantic Feature Analysis

#### ● *What is it?*

A semantic feature analysis (SFA) is a strategy used to increase a student's vocabulary. SFA assists students' semantic language by expanding their repertoire of words, connecting vocabulary to concepts, enhancing their ability to comprehend text, and creating a schema for memory. SFA is a recommended strategy for students with learning disabilities because of the limited vocabulary (numbers of words known and depth of word knowledge) of these students (Kame'enui & Carnine, 1998). Students with learning disabilities often experience difficulties in content area classes (e.g., science, social studies) because of their low vocabulary skills. By using words and features that most students are familiar with, the SFA will assist students in building their vocabulary, helping them consider how words and objects relate to each other.

#### ● *How to implement it*

SFA can be used as both before-reading and after-reading activity. When employing an SFA prior to reading a selection, teachers are preteaching critical vocabulary and concepts. When SFA is conducted as an after-reading activity, the analysis serves to crystallize and clarify key terms and concepts.

Pittelman and colleagues (1999) recommend a seven-step process for creating and implementing SFA.

1. **Select a category.**
2. **List words.**
   - List 3 to 4 familiar terms related to the category down the left side of the grid.
3. **List and add features.**
   - Determine the defining features (3 to 4) and list across the top of the grid. (*Note:* the feature must be one in which students can respond, "Yes, this feature is present" or "No, this feature is not present.")
   - Discuss features with your students. (Students may want to add features as well.)
4. **Determine feature possession.**
   a. Guide your students through the matrix to determine if the words on the left possess the features listed.
   b. If a term does possess the feature, students will place a plus sign (+) in the box. If the term does not possess the feature, students will place a minus sign (–) in the box.
   c. If students are unsure, they will place a question mark (?) in the box.
5. **Add more words or features.**
6. **Complete the grid.**
7. **Discuss the grid with your students.**

SFA can be used with students of all ages. Below is an example that could be used with older students (created by Bernie Dodge):

| Terms | Formed by Fire | Changed by Heat and Pressure | Formed by Other Rocks |
|---|---|---|---|
| granite | + | – | – |
| obsidian | + | – | – |
| slate | – | + | – |
| limestone | – | – | + |

● *Additional Resources*

Johnson, D. D., & Pearson, P. D. (1984). *Teaching reading vocabulary.* New York: Holt, Rinehart and Winston.

Lenski, S. D., Wham, M. A., & Johns, J. L. (1999). *Reading and learning strategies for middle and high school students.* Dubuque, IA: Kendall/Hunt.

*Source:* Kristin L. Sayeski

What Is Reading?

What Are the Major Elements of Reading?

What Problems Do Students with Learning Disabilities Have in Reading?

- Problems with Phonology
- Problems with Decoding
- Problems with Fluency
- Problems with Comprehension

How Is Reading Performance Assessed?

- Screening
- Diagnosing Problems and Planning Instruction
- Monitoring Student Progress

How Common Are Reading Problems in Learning Disabilities?

How Can Instruction Help Prevent Reading Disabilities?

- Teaching Phonemic Awareness
- Teaching Phonics
- Teaching Other Aspects of Early Reading
- Putting It All Together

How Can Instruction Help Remediate Learning Disabilities in Reading?

- Historical Approaches
- Contemporary Approaches
- Instructional Tactics

Council for Exceptional Children

See Companion Website for detailed correlations between chapter content and Council for Exceptional Children Standards; **www.ablongman.com/ hallahanLD3e**

**CEC Knowledge and Skills Discussed in This Chapter**

**1** Discussions about the process of reading, including philosophy, performance of specific skills, and legal descriptions.

**2** The heterogeneous nature of language development and reading skill needs of students with learning disabilities.

**3** The administration and interpretation of reading assessments and the nonbiased use of appropriate technologies for designing instruction.

**4** Early intervention for individuals who are at risk for learning disabilities, including procedures for identification and systematic educational interventions.

**5** Research-validated reading interventions, which improve the skills of individuals with learning disabilities when implemented systematically according to need.

**6** Assistive technologies, which are an essential component of reading instruction for students with learning disabilities.

**7** Reflective practices that help educators to guide instruction, uphold standards of competence, engage in professional growth, and cultivate appreciation of diversity.

# Students Who Experience Difficulties with Reading

We figured that we had to teach her a lot really fast so that she could start to catch up. Like they say, she wasn't going to catch up unless she learned faster than she normally would.

*Peter Martens, Shannon's first special education teacher*

Reading is a tool skill. We use tool skills as a means of accomplishing other things. We read novels about romances, cartoons about politics, signs advertising products, cookbooks telling how to make bread, cereal boxes touting the benefits of the cereal, and Web pages about nearly anything. By reading, we learn the order of the planets in our solar system or entertain ourselves with a novel or poem. Students who read well have great advantages in studying not only literature, but also history, science, and even mathematics. Reading is essential for most adult employment and is almost a necessity for obtaining adult privileges, such as getting a driver's license.

Students who have problems in reading are likely to have problems in many other areas of schooling. Children who are behind in kindergarten and first grade are likely to be behind in second and third grade (Juel, 1988). By the second grade, teachers often have recognized children's reading difficulties and have referred them for special education evaluation (Lloyd, Kauffman, Landrum, & Roe, 1991). By the third grade, students with reading problems begin to fall behind their peers in other school subjects. One consequence of falling behind in other areas is that students with reading problems have less access to sources of information than do their peers; thus, as capable readers gain new information from reading, those who read poorly continue to fall behind in other areas, losing ground to their peers in the knowledge and information that provide the working material for intelligence (the *Matthew Effect* discussed in Chapter 1; see Stanovich, 1986). As adults, some people who had severe reading problems in childhood will be successful in life and work, but most will continue to have substantial reading problems (Bruck, 1998).

Not only do reading disabilities put children at risk for referral to special education and for difficulty in other school subjects, but these deficits are related to other problems as well (Baumeister, Campbell, Krueger, & Vohs, 2003; Bryan, 1986; Juel, 1988). Children who have difficulty learning to read often develop negative views of their own competence and lose interest in academics. By the middle of elementary school, poor readers are so averse to reading that they would rather clean their rooms than read. By the time they are adults, individuals with dyslexia report that they have ongoing concerns about their self-worth related to their problems with reading (McNulty, 2003). Reading problems not only persist across the life span, but also they appear across cultures (see the Multicultural Considerations box on page 363).

In this chapter, we begin by explaining how authorities define reading. We then discuss the major elements of reading and the problems that students with reading problems experience. We then describe how teachers and others assess reading problems and review how many students experience reading problems. We conclude the chapter with two sections on teaching reading, one focused on preventing reading problems by using effective teaching procedures in the early years and another focused on how teachers and other clinicians can remediate reading problems in older students.

## What Is Reading?

In one of the first extensive studies of reading, Huey (1908) wrote that to understand reading would constitute a triumph.

> To completely analyze what we do when we read would almost be the acme of a psychologist's achievements, for it would be to describe very many of the most intricate workings of the human mind, as well as to unravel the tangled story of the most remarkable specific performance that civilization has learned in all its history. (p. 6)

Psychology has advanced greatly in its understanding of reading, but it still has not reached the pinnacle of achievement Huey described. Although psychologists have learned a lot, we do not yet know precisely what happens between the brief time the eye sees the printed page and the reader speaks words corresponding to that print (Adams, 1990). In fact, there is not even clear agreement about what reading is and how to define it.

Discussions of reading almost invariably reflect different sides in what has been called "the reading wars." The opponents in this war place relatively more or less emphasis on the mechanical aspects of reading, the conversion of printed squiggles into spoken language (Adams, 1990; Chall, 1967; Snow, Burns, & Griffith, 1998). One view emphasizes the skills needed to convert print into language and is often called the "skills approach." The opposing view emphasizes skills less and places greater emphasis on getting meaning from print using a wide variety of clues (not just phonics, but pictures and other sources of information). The latter view is often called a "meaning-emphasis approach."

## Is Dyslexia a Cultural-Linguistic Phenomenon?

English is so notorious for its irregularity that song writers and scholars poke fun at it. Ira Gershwin wrote about differences in pronunciation of *potato* and *tomato* in his song "Let's Call the Whole Thing Off." George Bernard Shaw is said to have suggested that in English *ghoti* spells fish," using these pronunciations:

*gh* from *laugh*
*o* from *women*
and *ti* from *nation*

Could Jamal's problems with beginning reading stem from differences between the language he uses and the language of schools (Cazden, 2001; Lundberg, 2002)? What if Jamal learned to read using a language that is more consistent than English? Are the problems educators refer to as dyslexia or reading disabilities present regardless of language and culture?

Researchers have examined some questions similar to these by comparing people's reading performance in different languages. Cross-cultural studies of dyslexia often focus on how closely the spoken language corresponds to its printed version. Because languages like Spanish and Italian have fewer irregularities, people should find it easier to learn to read them than to learn to read English.

Studies of reading performance among people who learn to read in Italian and other languages with more regular spelling-to-sound correspondence show that regardless of the regularity of the language, there are still some individuals who have difficulty learning to decode (e.g., Landerl, Wimmer, & Frith, 1997; Paulesu et al., 2001). Furthermore, differences between those who have trouble learning to decode in more regular languages and their peers who read normally are very similar to the differences between people who have trouble with decoding English and their peers who read normally. In fact, similar patterns between those with and without reading problems appear both on assessments of psychological abilities (e.g., working memory) and neurological function (blood flow in specific parts of the brain when reading).

Thus, it appears that we can expect to see reading problems regardless of the language students learn to read. The basic message for people who work with individuals who have reading problems and come from different language backgrounds is this: Schools should use assessment packages that fit different language backgrounds and identify each individual's needs when developing interventions (Smythe & Everatt, 2002). If that sounds like special education, it should. Special education includes using unbiased assessments and developing individual education plans.

Experts have offered many definitions of reading. Often these reflect a great deal about the particular expert's allegiance in the reading wars. For example, experts' perspectives on the connection between the word *reading* and the concept "reading" reflect their loyalties.

Because reading researchers experience reading differently, they identify different features as epitomizing the *reading*-"reading" relation. To illustrate this consider the following definitions:

Reading is the ability to decode written symbols into spoken sounds (Gough, 1972).
Reading is the ability to do well on a standardized reading test (Perfetti, Goldman, & Hogaboam, 1979).
Reading is the ability to complete one's income tax form (Northcutt, 1975).
Reading is the ability to adopt a perspective (Anderson & Pichert, 1978).

Reading is the ability to reduce uncertainty (Smith, 1971).
Reading is the ability to recognize inconsistent information (Markman, 1979).
(Mosenthal & Kamil, 1991, pp. 1017–1018)

The first two definitions emphasize the more mechanical aspects of reading—turning the squiggles on a page into spoken language that then can be comprehended. In contrast, the last two emphasize readers' use of higher-order thinking to extract meaning from print and then to clarify that meaning by matching what the reader expects to find on the page with what is actually there. The differences in definitions of *reading* illustrate a tension between two opposing perspectives on what happens when a person reads. These emphases also correspond to the two primary aspects of reading (which is the topic of the next section) and are reflected in one last definition of reading.

The following definition was proposed by the Partnership for Learning (composed of the U.S. National Institute for Literacy, the National Institute of Child Health and Human Development, and the Department of Education). This definition is more comprehensive than those just listed, incorporating a balance of the mechanical and the higher-order aspects of reading. According to this definition, reading is

*A complex system of deriving meaning from print that requires all of the following:*

- the skills and knowledge to understand how phonemes, or speech sounds, are connected to print;
- the ability to decode unfamiliar words;
- the ability to read fluently;
- sufficient background information and vocabulary to foster reading comprehension;
- the development of appropriate active strategies to construct meaning from print;
- the development and maintenance of a motivation to read. (National Institute for Literacy, 2003; emphasis in original)

Given all of the components included in this last definition of reading, it is easy to see why Huey refers to "many of the most intricate workings of the human mind" (1908, p. 6). Reading involves most of the potential problem areas discussed in Chapter 8 (cognitive strategies and motivation) and Chapter 11 (phonology, semantics, syntax). Thus, it should come as no surprise that, with so many potential pitfalls, learning to read is the most common difficulty experienced by students with learning disabilities and that experts in learning disabilities most often name reading achievement as a critical marker of learning disabilities (Speece & Shekitka, 2002).

**decoding**   the aspects of reading that happen as the reader converts the printed words on the page into more familiar spoken or heard language

**comprehending**   the ability to understand written or oral language

## What Are the Major Elements of Reading?

As implied in the discussion of definitions of reading, there are two major components of reading: decoding and comprehending. **Decoding** is the mechanical aspect of converting print to spoken language or spoken language equivalents. **Comprehending** refs to the higher-order aspects of reading in which one extracts meaning from language.

Just about all authorities on reading agree that the ultimate purpose of reading is for the reader to gain information, knowledge, pleasure, or other higher-order benefits from reading (Snow et al., 1998). How people accomplish these goals is the source of disagreement, however, leading to different theories about the psychology of reading. Do readers accomplish these goals by first getting an idea of the author's message and then figuring out the details? Or do they use the details of print to construct the message gradually?

The conflicting theories about the psychology of reading have an interesting parallel to perspectives on reading instruction.

> At one pole stand those who claim that the reader is a plodder. He literally ploughs through text a letter at a time, building the words and sentences out of the individually identified phone-sized squiggles on the page; he converts the letters to sounds, which are then formed into phonological representations, which in turn contact the previously learned meanings. This plodder view is essentially a speeded-up, smoothed-out version of what the stumbling first-grader seems to do in "sounding out" the words of his primer. . . . Because, on this account, meaning is derived through the systematic combination of minimal elements, the plodder view can be described as a "bottom up" approach. At the opposite extreme stand those romantics who view the reader as an explorer of the printed page. They suppose the fluent reader . . . looks at the printed page as he does at other aspects of the visual world, sampling selectively from among many available cues, developing expectations for words or meanings, seeking confirmation of these guesses and, in general, bringing to bear at all levels his considerable linguistic, intellectual, and perceptual skills. On this view, then, reading is more problem solving than plodding through phonology. Because the reader is here conceived as arriving at the details of the printed message after deriving its meaning, the explorer view can be characterized as a "top down" approach. (Rozin & Gleitman, 1977, p. 59)

These opposing views of reading stress different skills in explaining reading competence. The plodder view clearly depends more on phonology and the mechanics of reading, whereas the explorer view depends more on semantics and syntax—the comprehending element of reading.

For much of the period between 1960 and the 2000, the **whole-language approach,** which recommends a much stronger emphasis on the semantic and syntactic aspects of reading, had great influence in reading. Advocates of this approach recommended that teachers create print-rich environment (classrooms with many books, labels on objects around the room, poems and songs posted on boards, messages printed on chalkboards, etc.) and provide many opportunities to read and write. They recommended embedding phonics instruction in ongoing literacy activities but not encouraging children to depend on decoding, which uses phonological skills (Ruddell, 2002).

Today, most people agree that the primary components of reading are decoding (the "sounding out" that turns the little squiggles on the page into words) and comprehending (the use of one's language skills to understand the products of

Council for Exceptional Children

**CEC Knowledge Check**
Develop your own working definition of *reading*. LD1KS

**whole-language approach**
the philosophy that children can learn to read without specific decoding or phonics instruction if a print-rich environment that includes embedded phonics instruction is created

Council for Exceptional Children

**CEC Knowledge Check**

Does it seem that the answers to theorists' arguments tend to be a blend of both positions? Why is this? CC1S1

decoding). In a widely known description of the elements of reading, Gough and Tunmer (1986) integrated the main elements of reading in this simple formula:

$$R = D \times C$$

where D stands for decoding, and C for spoken language comprehension. We can understand this formula by thinking about how a computer program can "speak" the words in a text aloud and a human listener can comprehend the meaning of the text the machine "reads." Another way to understand it is to recall the story about a sorority member who knew the Greek alphabet and who visited Greece on a summer trip. She got lost in a desolate area, but she found a Greek man who spoke English. Sadly, the man was blind and couldn't read the road signs. The man suggested that if she could read the signs, he could give her directions. Through her knowledge of the Greek alphabet, she was able to turn the Greek signs into spoken language but had no idea what they meant. Because he was blind, the man couldn't read the signs, but he did know the language. She was the decoder, and he was the comprehender. Together they were a whole-language machine!

There is more to reading than these primary elements, however. Both elements include other subelements, and there are other factors as well. For example, the decoding aspect of reading requires that students know about letters, the direction of reading, and how to blend sounds together. Table 12.1 provides a task analysis of

**TABLE 12.1    Task Analysis of Decoding**

| SKILLS NEEDED TO SOUND OUT SIMPLE WORDS | EXAMPLE | EXPLANATION |
|---|---|---|
| Directionality in reading | ⟶ | In sounding out words, one begins at a designated place and moves systematically to the right. |
| Sound-symbol relationships | *a* = /a/ at<br>*b* = /b/ big<br>*c* = /c/ can<br>*d* = /d/ dog<br>*e* = /e/ etch<br>*f* = /f/ fin | In sounding out regularly pronounced words, one converts the squiggles on the page into the sounds (phonemes) for which they stand. The sounds should be as pure as possible (no schwas attached to them; that is "mmm" rather than "muh"). |
| Blending 1 | "sssaaafff" | In sounding out words, one slides from the sound for one symbol into the sound for the next symbol without an interruption between the sounds. |
| Blending 2 | "sssaaafff" = "saf" | In sounding out words, the stretched-out product of producing the sounds must be converted to a normal rate of speech. |
| Automaticity | *mat* = "mat"<br>*fan* = "fan"<br>*saf* = "saf"<br>*mit* = "mit"<br>*sem* = "sem" | In sounding out words, the skills must be combined so smoothly that they can be performed automatically. |

decoding illustrating these requirements. The analysis in Table 12.1 uses simple, consonant-vowel-consonant words to illustrate the needed skills. Students will have to learn more complex concepts and skills to decode more complicated words (i.e., those with different spelling patterns), but the decoding skills in Table 12.1 are the basic building blocks.

Comprehending what one has decoded also includes subelements. For example, to be able to answer questions about who did what in a sentence, students must be able to store the sentence long enough that they can operate on it (see Chapter 11). On a higher level, when students must determine the theme of a story, they must attend to the relevant aspects of what they have read and deemphasize those parts that may be interesting but are not connected to the theme. This requires students to use considerable attention skills and cognitive strategies (Wilder & Williams, 2001; see Chapter 8).

When students do not learn fundamental decoding skills early in their schooling, they often find alternative ways to solve the puzzle of reading. In Jamal's case, he used his considerable knowledge of the world, his sharp memory, and his motivation to succeed. By using these strengths, he was able to convince some people that he really knew how to read.

> You know, I wasn't worried about Jamal early. Then I realized that he was just telling stories that he'd made up about the books in his book tub. He hadn't really read them, you know. He didn't know how to read them. He was so smart that he could guess what they were about. When I asked him to read some of the words on cards or the chalkboard, he couldn't do it. If I went over a story with him once or twice, he understood it just fine, but he couldn't read it. He just sounded like he could read it.
>
> *Alice Hamilton, Jamal's first-grade teacher*

Jamal

Council for Exceptional Children

**CEC Knowledge Check**
If students like Jamal can learn to read reasonably well, how will their coping strategies help them in the future? Do students like Jamal often have as much or more cognitive ability than their peers? CC2K2, CC2K5

## What Problems Do Students with Learning Disabilities Have in Reading?

Early in the history of learning disabilities, some authorities thought that reading problems might be caused by difficulties in visual perception. People noticed that students with reading problems sometimes confused letters and numbers with their mirror opposites (for example, *b* and *d, 3* and *E*) and even a few read words backward (saying "was" for *saw*). **Reversals,** as these mistakes are often called, were considered indicators of dyslexia and learning disability. The idea has penetrated deeply into our society, going beyond the field of learning disabilities itself. Most people have heard someone say, "Oh, it's just my LD showing up" as an explanation for transposing letters or numbers. However, reversals do not differentiate between students with and without reading problems. If one considers the percentage of total errors that are reversal errors (that is, reversal errors divided by total errors), students with reading problems make no higher a percentage than peers who read

**reversals** the confusion of letters and numbers (*b* and *d*, *p* and *q*, 3 and *E* ) and words (e.g., *saw* and *was*) relatively well. Students with reading problems make more errors of all types, and thus they make numerically more reversal errors (e.g., Fischer, Liberman, & Shankweiler, 1978; Holmes & Peper, 1977).

Even though reversals are not a good indicator of reading problems, other factors are good markers. Among those factors are several that echo problems described in Chapter 11 on spoken language problems. Because reading is closely related to spoken language, this should come as no surprise. The decoding aspects of reading draw heavily on children's **phonological awareness,** and the comprehending aspects draw heavily on semantic and syntactic skills. Students may have difficulty with any one or a combination of these skills.

**phonological awareness** the ability to blend sounds, segment the sounds of words, rhyme, and manipulate the sounds of spoken words in other ways

## Problems with Phonology

Since the 1970s, when many psychologists began to study the cognitive aspects of reading seriously, more and more importance has been assigned to children's competence in manipulating the phonemes of our language. One of the most consistent findings in the research on reading problems has been that phonological skills are intimately linked to reading skill (Blachman, 2001; Brady, 1997; Muter, 1998; Perfetti, 1991; Snider, 1995; Wagner & Torgesen, 1987; see also Chapter 11).

Many authorities in reading and learning disabilities (e.g., Chall, 1967; Chall, Roswell, & Blumenthal, 1963; Engelmann, 1967a; Kass, 1966; Myklebust, Bannochie, & Killen, 1971) recognized the importance of phonological skills before the 1970s. The work of cognitive psychologists strengthened the argument that children must gain competence in manipulating the **phonemes** of our language if they are to become capable readers. More recent developments make it clear that deficits in **phonemic awareness**—the understanding that spoken language is composed of **phonemes**—play a central role in the problems of students who have difficulty learning to read (Blachman, 2001; Brady, 1997; Liberman & Shankweiler, 1991).

**phonemic awareness** the ability to segment words into sounds and to blend sounds together into words; differs from phonological awareness in that the activity occurs at the level of the phoneme, not at the level of larger units (e.g., syllables)

**phonemes** the smallest unit of speech; sounds

Cognitive psychologists and reading researchers have stressed the role of phonemic awareness in the development of early reading skills.

> The student must come to realize that words can be broken into syllables and phonemes, and that the phoneme is the unit in the speech stream represented by the symbols in an alphabetic script. To a person with a well-developed phoneme awareness, our alphabetic system appears to be a reasonable way to represent our language. To those with little or no phoneme awareness, the system probably appears arbitrary. (Ball & Blachman, 1988, p. 51)

Despite its importance, the role of phonemic awareness should be kept in perspective. Words are not identified solely by applying phonological rules. Children apparently use analogies between words to derive the pronunciation of some words (Goswami, 1991, 1998). In theory, students read by analogy when they use what they know about some words to determine the pronunciation of others; in practical terms, use of analogies is particularly evident when children read rhyming words. Phonemic awareness and basic decoding skills probably are required to be able to read words in this way (Ehri & Robbins, 1992; Goswami, 1998;

Wood & Farrington-Flint, 2001). Competent readers probably use multiple sources of information—letter features, letters themselves, phonemes, groups of letters, and even words—almost simultaneously when identifying words. Sensible models of word identification (Ehri, 1998; Gough, 1996; Perfetti, 1991; Stanovich, 1980) stress that readers probably use enough of the phonological representation to derive the word's pronunciation and make a connection to its meaning; the context confirms the meaning of the word.

Problems with phonemic awareness are likely to result in problems in learning how to decode. The reason for this is that some of the main forms of phonemic awareness—blending and segmenting—are component skills in decoding (Pullen, 2002). **Segmenting** refers to taking words apart into their individual phonemes; for example, hearing the word *fun* and saying "fffuuunnn." **Blending** refers to the ability to connect sounds for individual phonemes into words—to say "rat" for "rrraaat."

**segmenting** taking words apart into their smaller units (individual phonemes)

**blending** combining individual sounds into words

## Problems with Decoding

The problems that students experience with decoding are obvious to anyone who has listened to students struggle when reading aloud. The experience of listening to a stumbling reader gives rise to many hypotheses about why these readers have difficulty with decoding. As shown in the Effective Practices box on page 370, students make many different mistakes. Some of them seem to be based on the student diligently trying to make sense of the passage. For example, this boy substituted "a better idea" for "another idea," using a phrase that was common in television advertising at the time. Similarly, he worked hard to make the passage fit with the picture, as illustrated by his comment about the absence of an obvious rope. Also, he used some letters—usually the first letter of a word—to cue his reading. Sometimes, though, he read an entire phrase or sentence without error and read it quickly.

**Council for Exceptional Children**

**CEC Knowledge Check**
Must readers understand the specifics of what they read, or is getting the general idea good enough? What skills do adults need in looking over a legal document or in buying a car or a house?
CC9S5, CC9S11

The kinds of mistakes illustrated in the Effective Practices box have led some to argue that children's accuracy in decoding should be of lesser concern than whether they obtain the meaning of a passage (e.g., Goodman, 1986; Goodman & Goodman, 1979). If they can get the ideas, who cares if they read accurately? In the Effective Practices box, the boy probably did not get the ideas in the passage and thus probably would not have been able to answer either specific questions (e.g., "Did the cars stand still?") or more open-ended ones (e.g., "How did assembly lines save Ford money?").

As Table 12.1 shows, decoding requires facility with the direction of reading, grapheme-phoneme associations, blending, and automaticity. When instruction fails to make these component skills clear to students, some students will still deduce how to decode. Students who come to instruction without prior knowledge about these aspects of decoding (perhaps because of attention, cognitive, or language difficulties) will be more likely to have difficulty mastering them. With repeated failure, they will become discouraged and require even clearer, more systematic instruction to acquire decoding skills. As we discuss in a later section, teaching reading right the first time—systematic and intensive instruction in the early grades—can reduce the occurrence of decoding problems for many children.

**Council for Exceptional Children**

**CEC Knowledge Check**
Although many students with reading difficulties intuitively develop a personal coping strategy, most do not. What is your responsibility to help these students?
CC1S1, CC9S11

## How It Sounds to Hear a Student with Learning Disabilities Read

The following example shows what the reading of a fifth-grade student with learning disabilities sounds like. This passage was drawn from an elementary-level social studies textbook. Next to the passage was a picture of factory workers and automobiles with prominent white side-wall tires. While he was reading the passage, the boy repeatedly looked at the picture.

Here is what the student said:

Then Ford had uh other i . . . a better idea. Take the worrrk to the men. He deee. . . . A long rope was hooked onto the car . . . wheels. . . . There's no rope on there. The rope pulled the car . . . auto. . . . The white wheels along . . . pulled the car all along the way. Men stood still. Putting on car parts. Everybody man . . . put on, on, a few parts. Down the assembly line went the car. The assembly line saved . . . time. Cars costed still

less to buh. . . . bull . . . d . . . build. Ford cuts their prices on the Model T again.

Here is the actual passage the student was to read:

Then Ford had another idea. Take the work to the men, he decided. A long rope was hooked onto a car axle and wheels. The rope pulled the axle and wheels along. All along the way, men stood still putting on car parts. Down the assembly line went the car. The assembly line saved more time. Cars cost still less to build. Ford cut the price of the Model T again.

The student needed nearly 90 seconds to read this passage. Calculate the number of words he read per minute, and compare his reading rate with those shown in Table 12.2. Would you say he was reading fluently?

*Source:* From *Introduction to Learning Disabilities,* 2nd ed. (p. 203) by D. P. Hallahan, J. M. Kauffman, and J. W. Lloyd, 1985, Boston: Allyn and Bacon. Copyright © 1985 by Pearson Education. Reprinted by permission of the publisher.

## Problems with Fluency

Decoding requires great skill with the phonological aspects of language. Many difficulties with reading comprehension can be attributed to poor decoding skills. If one does not read accurately, then one will have trouble getting meaning from what one reads. If one does not read effortlessly and smoothly—that is, if one . . . reads . . . haltingly with . . . lots . . . of . . . pauses—then the meaning of a passage may be obscured. Imagine how hard it is for the boy in the Effective Practices box to understand what he reads, given his lack of skills in fluent reading.

When decoding becomes effortless, it is often said to be automatic. The idea of **automaticity** in reading is based on an influential theory advanced by LaBerge and Samuels (1973). According to the theory of automaticity, readers have only so many units of mental attention to devote to reading. If they have not mastered the mechanical aspects of reading, they will have to devote most of their units of attention to decoding and will have few units left over to devote to comprehending. If they are fluent with the mechanical aspects of reading, they will have more units of attention free to devote to understanding what they are reading.

Fluency usually refers to smooth and effortless decoding, reading that sounds like talking. Since the 1960s and 1970s, researchers in learning disabilities have em-

**automaticity**   the ability to perform a task, especially to decode print, effortlessly

phasized reading rate—the number of words students can read aloud correctly in a minute—as an especially important indicator of reading competence (Deno & Mirkin, 1977; Lovitt, 1967). Fluency is more than how fast students read, however. Fluency includes three components: rate, accuracy, and expression. Students must read passages correctly and with expression, emphasizing words, pausing, changing pitch, and so forth (Armbruster, Lehr, & Osborne, 2001; National Reading Panel, 2000). Students' reading fluency not only correlates with their reading comprehension, but even predicts how well they do on high-stakes tests (Buck & Torgesen, no date; Good, Simmons, & Kame'enui, 2001). Fluency is important because it allows the reader to decode automatically, which then leads to greater comprehension.

Fluency in decoding is reflected in rate of reading not just of connected passages but also of letters and other components of decoding (Good, 2003). Given that reading rate is important as an index of fluency and as a predictor of comprehension, teachers need guidelines for assessing it. Table 12.2 describes fluent and dysfluent reading at different age levels (Carnine, Silbert, Kame'enui, & Tarver, 2004; Good, 2003; Lovett, 1987; Shinn, 2003). Normal rates of reading permit adequate comprehension of text. Students who read at delayed levels will experience many problems in comprehending what they are reading. Teachers can use the rates in Table 12.2 as rough guides to ascertain whether a student's reading fluency is low enough to merit further evaluation and remediation.

Council for
Exceptional
Children

CEC Knowledge Check
Why is it important to have a test or way to quantify reading fluency? Without such information, can you make decisions about remediation?
CC8S1, CC8S5

## Problems with Comprehension

Problems with comprehension are almost always the result of problems with either decoding, more general language abilities, or both. When the problems concern deficits in decoding, they usually result from students not reading well enough to connect the ideas with the text—that is, they have problems with accuracy and automaticity in decoding. When the problems concern semantics, they may result

**TABLE 12.2** Normal and Delayed Reading Fluency for Passages of Text

| GRADE | | NORMAL | DELAYED |
|---|---|---|---|
| First grade | Fall-Winter | 20–60 CWPM[a], 1–2 EPM[b] | <10 CWPM, >2 EPM |
| | Spring | 20–100 CWPM, 1–2 EPM | <20 CWPM, >4 EPM |
| Second grade | Fall-Winter | 50–120 CWPM, 1–2 EPM | <30 CWPM, >4 EPM |
| | Spring | 70–140 CWPM, 1–3 EPM | <50 CWPM, >5 EPM |
| Third grade | Fall-Winter | 75–150 CWPM, 1–3 EPM | <50 CWPM, >5 EPM |
| | Spring | 100–170 CWPM, 1–3 EPM | <60 CWPM, >6 EPM |
| Fourth grade and higher | | 150–180 CWPM, 1–3 EPM | <90 CWPM, >6 EPM |

[a]CWPM = Correct words per minute (words per minute read correctly)

[b]EPM = Errors per minute (words per minute read incorrectly)

from students' difficulty with cognitive processing (working memory, comprehension monitoring) or general knowledge (word meanings), not from decoding problems (Perfetti, Marron, & Foltz, 1996). Both cognition (discussed in Chapter 8) and general language abilities (discussed in Chapter 11)—syntax and semantics, especially—are relevant here.

### Syntax

**syntax**  the set of rules that governs how words are put together in combinations and proper order to form sentences

**Syntax** refers to the grammatical structure of language, whether spoken or written (see Chapter 11). Although there are many other aspects of syntax that make differences in our language, one particular aspect—word order—helps illustrate the importance of syntax. The sentence "Jane kissed John" means something different from "John kissed Jane" or from "Jane was kissed by John." The slight differences in the relationships among the words modify the meaning in subtle but important ways. Clearly, if one has difficulty understanding the subtleties of syntax, one might get the wrong idea from the sentences, even if one can read one of these sentences without hesitation.

Some students who have decoding problems sometimes have difficulty with certain aspects of syntax, particularly morphology. Students who read neither accurately nor fluently apparently also have difficulty with the kinds of tasks and make the sorts of errors illustrated in Figure 12.1, especially those tasks that use nonsense words (Lovett, 1987; Rack, Snowling, & Olson, 1992). These findings are essentially consistent with early research showing similar difficulties (e.g., Kass, 1966). It is interesting to speculate that the automatic skills required in giving morphological variations of words may also be required in fluent, accurate decoding.

Council for
Exceptional
Children

**CEC Knowledge Check**
What value do you place on studying lists of words with different consonant beginnings and endings (e.g., *mat, bat, fat, fan,* etc.)?
CC7K1, LD4S8

Problems in understanding the syntax of written sentences may result in problems in reading comprehension (Clay & Imlach, 1971; Pflaum & Bryan, 1981; Resnick, 1970; Stanovich, Cunningham, & Freeman, 1984). When reading, older students make greater use of syntax than do younger readers. Students with reading problems do not use the clusters of words that occur in English to guide their phrasing of what they read, and they make other mistakes that indicate they are not using syntax to help make sense of passages. However, when students with reading problems are compared with their younger peers who have the same level of decoding skills, the older students are just as adept at using semantic and syntactic cues. In fact, they may depend on these aspects of language too much. Thus, their understanding of what they read apparently is not inhibited as much by their problems with syntax as it is by their problems with decoding.

### Semantics

**semantics**  the intent and meaning of words

**Semantics** refers to the meaning of language. Semantic cues are hints that help readers understand the ideas of a passage and also help in decoding. For example, consider the following sentence: "The student turned in her _____." The meaning of the first part of the sentence helps reduce the number of possible words that could complete the sentence. The missing word will probably be a noun, but it probably will not be *pajamas* or *ear,* because those have little to do with students and school. It is not likely to be *grades* or *classroom,* because teachers, not students, turn

FIGURE 12.1   System for Classifying IRI Mistakes

**Error Pattern Checklist: Specific-Level Procedure 4**

Compare each error in the passage to the checklist (ignore errors on proper names). Make a mark next to the category in which the error seems to fit. Identify the strategic categories in which most errors occur and begin additional testing in those areas. Continue to monitor changes in error patterns.

| Error Categories | No. Errors |
|---|---|
| **Mispronunciations** | |
| Errors are substitutions of real words | |
| Errors are not real words | |
| Errors are phonetically similar to stimulus word | |
| | |
| **Insertions** | |
| Insertions are contextually appropriate | |
| Insertions are contextually inappropriate | |
| | |
| **Omissions** | |
| Omission affects passage meaning | |
| Omission does not affect meaning | |
| | |
| **Hesitation** | |
| **Repetition** | |
| Repeats a portion of a target word | |
| Repeats preceding word | |
| Repeats preceding words or phrases | |
| | |
| **Does not attend to punctuation** | |
| Does not pause at punctuation | |
| Pauses at end of line | |
| | |
| **Self-corrects** | |

**Content Error Checklist: Specific-Level Procedure 5**

Compare the words in the passage to the student's errors and categorize errors by content area and content subskill. Make a mark next to the subskill indicated by each error. Do not record more than two errors per word. Identify the content areas in which the most errors occurred and begin additional testing in those areas. Continue to monitor changes in error patterns.

| Content Categories | No. Errors |
|---|---|
| **Words: Errors involving whole words** | |
| Polysyllabic Words | |
| Contractions | |
| Compound Words | |
| Sight Words | |
| Silent Letters | |
| | |
| **Units: Errors involving combined letter units** | |
| Endings (Suffixes) | |
| Clusters | |
| R-controlled Vowels | |
| Vowel Teams | |
| Consonant Digraphs | |
| Consonant Teams | |
| CVC Words | |
| | |
| **Conversions: Errors involving sound modification** | |
| Double Consonant Words | |
| Vowel + e Conversions | |
| | |
| **Sounds: Errors involving individual letters and sounds** | |
| Vowels | |
| Consonants | |
| Sequence | |
| Sounds | |
| Symbols | |

Directions for Using the Error Pattern Checklist

Use the Error Pattern Checklist to categorize all decoding errors made on the passage. Ask yourself what the most probable reading strategy explanation is for each error. Check it off by marking the appropriate category. If more than two errors were made on a word, categorize only the first two.

| Question | Recommendation |
|---|---|
| 1. Are there clear patterns of errors? | If yes, correct the erroneous pattern by targeting it as an instructional objective. |

Directions for Using the Content Error Checklist

Use the Content Error Checklist to categorize all errors made on the passage. Ask yourself what the most probable content explanation is for each error. Decide what content category the error is from and check it off by marking the appropriate category. If more than two errors were made on a word, categorize only the first two.

| Question | Recommendation |
|---|---|
| 1. Are there identifiable problems of content? | If yes, conduct specific-level testing of decoding skills reflected in the errors. |

*Source:* From *MASI-R: Remedial Screening Test* by K. W. Howell, S. H. Zucker, and M. K. Morehead, 1999, Bellingham, WA: H & Z Publications, Western Washington University. Reprinted by permission of the author.

in grades, and almost no one turns in classrooms. A reader would find words such as *paper, books, homework,* and *test* to be sensible possibilities.

Many students with comprehension deficits have inferior performance on other language tasks that draw on their semantic skills (Golinkoff & Rosinski, 1976; Kavale, 1980; Lomax, 1983; Nation, Marshall, & Snowling, 2001; Perfetti &

Hogoboam, 1975; Pflaum & Bryan, 1981). Students with poor comprehension do not differ from their nondisabled peers in reading familiar words, but they are much slower in reading unfamiliar words and are more likely to make mistakes that change the meaning of the passage. When asked to reason aloud while deducing answers to comprehension questions, competent readers use efficient strategies and reach accurate conclusions; students with learning disabilities use inefficient strategies and produce incorrect answers. Students with learning disabilities make more mistakes when naming pictures that have long names, and their mistakes show their problems with phonology. Other students who have less substantial problems with comprehension do not stumble over long names for objects but name them more slowly and make more mistakes than peers who do not have disabilities (especially for names that are infrequent).

One of the important assertions of advocates of the explorer approach (Rozin & Gleitman, 1977) is that children should use context (a combination of syntax and semantics) to guide their reading. According to an often-cited study (Goodman, 1965), children read words in context much better than they do in lists. People have interpreted these results as indicating that the context in the passages must have facilitated the decoding of words. More recent research (e.g., Nicholson, 1991) has revealed that the improvement probably resulted from the research methods. In the original study, children always read the lists first. After they saw the words in the lists, reading them in the passages was easier, so they made fewer mistakes on words in passages. Actually, poor readers probably rely on context to compensate for their

Jamal

deficits in decoding (e.g., Stanovich, 1980, 1986b). Jamal's approach to reading early in first grade illustrates this. He used his verbal skills to cover for problems in decoding.

Even if one can decode words accurately and rapidly, a limited vocabulary can prevent making connections between words and their meanings (Roth, Speece, & Cooper, 2002). Many students with learning disabilities also have minor vocabulary deficits that contribute to their lower scores on comprehension tests (Ackerman, Peters, & Dykman, 1971; Perfetti, 1991; see also Chapter 11). They have difficulty associating printed words with their meanings, a factor that is clearly important in understanding text. Unfortunately, the orthography of words (their spelling), which guides their pronunciation, does not help much in deriving their meaning (unless the reader has a strong background in other languages, especially Latin). "One can learn to pronounce most written words, familiar or not, by learning the rules that relate spelling and sound . . . [but] word meaning must be learned on a case-by-case basis" (Rueckl & Dror, 1994, p. 571). Effective programs can teach students to decode print, but it takes a powerful, sustained effort to overcome the deficits in vocabulary that some students also bring with them to school (Becker, 1977). The implication is plain: Teachers of students with learning disabilities must not only teach decoding competence, they often must also teach vocabulary (and other aspects of reading comprehension).

In addition to vocabulary, other factors also influence students' understanding of what they can decode. General knowledge—what is sometimes called **world knowledge**—affects reading comprehension (Gersten, Fuchs, Williams, &

Council for
Exceptional
Children

**CEC Knowledge Check**
Since we learn language through hearing, does it make sense to immerse students in listening experiences to increase vocabulary? Why? LD4S7

**world knowledge** general knowledge of one's surroundings and the larger world

Baker, 2001; Williams, 1991; Williams, 2003). Students may use their previous experiences of events or situations to guide comprehension. For example, a student who has taken train trips would likely have an easier time understanding a reading assignment about a surly conductor than would a student who has traveled only by car or bus.

Ironically, world knowledge can sometimes interfere with the reading comprehension of students with learning disabilities, especially gist or theme comprehension. **Gist comprehension** is the ability to understand the theme of a narrative. For some students with learning disabilities, background knowledge intrudes too much into their interpretation of what they read. For example, whereas students without learning disabilities might base their interpretations on the information in the passage they have read, some students with learning disabilities might focus on a thematically less important part of the passage because of its similarity to something in their own experiences. Students may read a passage about a child who wears a blue sweater and is supposed to remember to buy cat food on the way home. The child in the story forgets to buy the food and then feels miserable when it is time to feed the family kitten. Although most students would focus on the theme of responsibility for pets, some students with learning disabilities may focus on less relevant parts of the passage. For example, asked to discuss the meaning of the passage, a student with learning disabilities might reply, "Oh, yeah. I had a blue sweater. One day I wore it and it got dirty at school. My mom was mad at me." Students who often make idiosyncratic responses make more mistakes in identifying the themes of passages they read. Students with learning disabilities have specific difficulty getting the main points of the passages and are somewhat more likely to give answers that reflect idiosyncratic information (Gersten et al., 2001; Wilder & Williams, 2001; Williams, 1991, 2003; Williams et al., 2002).

These findings indicate that instruction for students with learning disabilities should be comprehensive and thorough. As developed in other chapters, there are no magic solutions in learning disabilities. Despite the great importance of such factors as phonemic awareness in understanding reading problems, learning disabilities will not be overcome by identifying and remediating one simple or key factor. Teachers must not only teach rudimentary reading skills, but also teach higher-order thinking skills (Carnine & Kame'enui, 1992)

**gist comprehension**
the understanding of the theme of a narrative

**CEC Knowledge Check**
How would you respond to this student? What questions could you ask that would help focus on the important theme?
CC4S5, LD4S5, LD4S11

**CEC Knowledge Check**
Do a Web search on "Bloom's taxonomy" to find out more about higher-order thinking skills.
LD4S5

## How Is Reading Performance Assessed?

Schools identify students as having learning disabilities so that the identified students can receive additional services. To identify these students, schools must screen large numbers of students and then evaluate these individuals more closely to determine eligibility (see Chapter 3). Often screening and eligibility assessments use comprehensive measures of reading performance.

Once pupils have been identified, teachers need to determine specific instructional needs and plan instruction for them. Sometimes the assessments used in determining eligibility can also be used to identify students' unique educational needs.

diagnosis  identifying students' unique educational
needs

progress monitoring
a process of checking frequently on students' actual
performance to determine
if the current educational
program is working

Once these unique educational needs have been determined, teachers can plan individual education programs. The process of identifying unique educational needs is sometimes called **diagnosis.** However, teachers may also need to conduct additional assessments to plan instructional programs.

When programs have been developed for students, teachers need to make sure that students are benefiting from the instructional programs they receive. To do so, teachers must monitor student progress. **Progress monitoring** refers to a process of checking frequently on students' actual performance to determine whether education programs are working.

## Screening

Some school systems develop explicit practices for assessing students' reading competence and then examining more closely those whose reading skills fall below a certain level (say, the 20th percentile). To identify students in this way, schools use screening tests, often general achievement batteries such as the *Iowa Tests of Basic Skills* (Hoover, Dunbar, & Frisbie, 2001). However, individually administered achievement batteries, such as the *Peabody Individual Achievement Test—Revised,* or PIAT (Markwardt, 1989), and the *Woodcock-Johnson-III* (McGrew & Woodcock, 2001), as well as some devoted specifically to diagnosing reading problems, probably are the instruments most commonly used to identify students with reading disabilities.

Although tests may help identify students who need to be assessed more carefully, teachers are often key in screening for referral and initiate nearly 75% of referrals for special education (Lloyd et al., 1991). Teachers' judgments may be imperfect, but more than anyone else, they have experience with a wide range of students and usually with the student in question (Gerber & Semmel, 1984). Furthermore, they are sensitive to subtle variations in student characteristics that may not be evident from standardized testing.

Teachers probably do not base their evaluations on reading performance alone (Cooper & Speece, 1988; Speece & Cooper, 1990), but many of the important clues in identifying reading problems have to do with reading performance. Although some clues are false leads (e.g., reversals of letters' orientation or letter order do not indicate learning disabilities), other clues are particularly important. Students' reading fluency provides probably the most valuable indication of reading competence. In fact, fluency in saying sounds for individual letters is a good predictor of reading performance (Speece, Mills, Ritchey, & Hillman, 2002).

Council for
Exceptional
Children

**CEC Knowledge Check**
How can you rely on a
first-year teacher's referrals? If you are new to
the field of special edu-
cation, how do you gain
the experience men-
tioned in the test? What
clues, tools, and meth-
ods will you use until you
have that experience?
CC4S3, CC9K4, CC9S2

Jamal

Jamal was different from some of the other children—boys, mostly—I've had who had LD. He really struggled when it came to letters. It was as if he spoke in ideas and had no understanding about words and parts of words. I was worried right away in the fall with him.

*Alice Hamilton, Jamal's first-grade teacher*

# Diagnosing Problems and Planning Instruction

Planning reading programs requires that one assess performance. Assessment for program planning often requires using diagnostic tests, informal reading inventories, and clinical teaching.

## Diagnostic Testing

When diagnosing and planning programs, many teachers of students with learning disabilities use tests in hopes of identifying more specific deficits (Overton, 2003). Diagnostic tests of reading performance provide information at a finer grained level than screening tests. For example, a diagnostic test may include subtests of letter recognition, word recognition, reading rate, and comprehension. If a student has especially lower scores on some subtests than on others, he or she is judged to be weaker in those areas, and the special education teacher should prescribe specific remedial activities accordingly.

Diagnosing specific reading problems requires teachers to go beyond simply administering tests. They must interpret the results carefully. Individual diagnostic testing probably yields more useful information than group tests (Lloyd, Cameron, & Lloyd, 1984). Some of the same instruments that may be used for screening also provide diagnostic information. Individually administered achievement batteries, such as the PIAT (Markwardt, 1989), give scores on separate aspects of reading—decoding and comprehending. The *Woodcock-Johnson-III* (McGrew & Woodcock, 2001) provides scores on some of the component skills in reading, including prereading skills, word recognition, and passage comprehension.

Other useful tests for individually assessing students' reading competence are expressly designed as diagnostic instruments. For example, the *Roswell-Chall Diagnostic Test of Word Analysis Skills* (Roswell & Chall, 1978) is designed for use with young children and gives information about skill in reading words and letters as well as assessing decoding and encoding skills, as does the *Woodcock Diagnostic Reading Battery* (Woodcock, 1997). By judiciously employing tests such as these, as well as informal methods, teachers can identify appropriate areas for instruction.

## Informal Reading Inventories

An **informal reading inventory (IRI)** is a series of reading passages or word lists graded in order of difficulty. A student reads from the series of lists or passages, beginning with one the teacher thinks is likely to be easy. If the student reads well at a given level, the teacher gives the next most difficult level. The student continues to progress through increasingly more difficult lists or passages until the student makes many mistakes. However, IRIs are not as trustworthy as more formal measures of reading and therefore must be used carefully.

As the student reads, the teacher monitors performance and the kinds of errors being made (e.g., omitted word, mispronunciation, hesitation). If the IRI is composed of passages, the teacher may ask questions to probe the student's understanding of the material. The teacher records the errors and answers for later scrutiny.

Council for Exceptional Children

**CEC Knowledge Check**
If your school or district does not have any of these diagnostic tests, what can you do? With whom will you talk? How will you communicate your need? CC9S3, CC10S9

**informal reading inventory (IRI)** an assessment tool that includes a series of reading passages and/or word lists graded in order of difficulty

The teacher can classify the mistakes students make in reading during IRIs. Figure 12.1 shows a classification system. Such a system not only provides an informal perspective about a student's strengths and weaknesses, but also can suggest the reasons for some errors. Such information aids in designing instructional interventions to address deficits. For example, if a student makes many mistakes on words involving vowel conversions (e.g., *con → cone, rid → ride*), the teacher might plan specific instructional lessons to help the student read words of this spelling pattern correctly (Deno, 1997; Howell & Davidson, 1997; Howell, Fox, & Morehead, 1993).

### Clinical Teaching

Using some concepts related to IRIs, Lovitt and his colleagues (Eaton & Lovitt, 1972; Haring, Lovitt, Eaton, & Hansen, 1976; Lovitt & Fantasia, 1980; Lovitt & Hansen, 1976a, b) conducted seminal studies about systematically identifying where in a series of reading materials students should begin reading. The methods used by Lovitt and his colleagues are sometimes called clinical (or trial) teaching, because they are based on specific experiences with individual students. Sometimes clinical teaching is used in a pejorative way to refer to "flying by the seat of one's pants." In the work by Lovitt and his colleagues, however, the methods were carefully shaped by applied behavior analysis.

Clinical teaching is surely the most informal method of assessment. In it, one tests students' performance by presenting lessons and observing whether they succeed (Lloyd & Blandford, 1991). Clinical teaching requires a teacher to sequence lessons carefully so each successive lesson is more difficult than the last and easier than the next. If students perform well on one lesson but have trouble with subsequent ones, the teacher knows to begin instruction at the point at which they began having difficulty. Because it is integral to instruction, clinical teaching should be a fundamental part of assessment for instructional planning (Howell & Davidson, 1997; Zigmond & Miller, 1986).

Clinical teaching as an assessment strategy should focus first on a student's most likely problem areas. In decoding, these areas would include phonemic awareness, letter–sound knowledge, single-word decoding (probably of both real and nonsense words), and passage reading. Regarding comprehension, clinical teaching should focus on the extent to which students remember information from what they have read; comprehension can be assessed clinically by having students verbally retell the content of a passage they have read.

## Monitoring Student Progress

The use of simple performance measures to monitor progress in reading has helped reshape assessment. The concepts, which were promoted early in the history of learning disabilities (e.g., Lovitt, 1967), became commonplace in the 1980s and 1990s. Monitoring progress is an important part of reading instruction, because it allows teachers to make changes in reading programs according to individual student needs. If students with learning disabilities are working on new material and

**Council for Exceptional Children**

**CEC Knowledge Check**
Could clinical teaching be less effective than a focused intervention on identified deficiencies, or is it a method to identify those deficiencies? LD4S9

making little progress, it is probably wise to change the instruction they are receiving rather than continue with ineffective teaching practices. If they are repeating material on which they are already fluent, they are wasting their time; teachers should move them ahead (Deno, 1997; Howell & Davidson, 1997). The students of teachers who use curriculum-based assessment (CBA) to monitor progress have higher scores than about two-thirds of the students whose teachers do not use it (Fuchs & Fuchs, 1986b).

As with clinical teaching and informal reading inventories, progress-monitoring systems for assessing students' progress can be constructed using classroom reading materials. They are also sometimes incorporated into instructional programs.

### Reading Program Assessments

In keeping with the popularity of portfolio assessment, some reading instruction programs have incorporated systems for monitoring progress within the reading program. For example, *Heath Literacy* (Alvermann et al., 1995) provides assessment guides to accompany each of the levels of its reading programs; in one section of the manuals, under the heading "Ongoing Assessment," there are directions for portfolio assessments, evaluations of writing, and tests of dictation and writing as well as recommendations for conducting observations, preparing anecdotal records, holding conferences, and administering self-assessments. Traditional reading programs often provide unit tests to be administered at specific times during the school year (e.g., after completing a specific part of the curriculum, at midyear, at the end of the year, etc.). Teachers are advised to set aside entire class periods for testing; test items often resemble the familiar multiple-choice items.

In contrast, the mastery tests that accompany the *Corrective Reading* program (CRP; Engelmann, Hanner, & Johnson, 1999) are scheduled to occur much more frequently (about every five to ten lessons) and are brief and explicitly connected to what students have been learning. Figure 12.2 (page 380) gives an example of a mastery test from CRP. This test would be given as part of a regular lesson, and students would read the words independently. Based on their performance, the teacher would continue to the next lesson or repeat the lesson to address any difficulties. Depending on their performance as a group, students may complete one level of the program in as few as 30 days by skipping unneeded lessons or as many as 70 days by adding extra practice for those who need it. The mastery tests also allow teachers to restructure groups. For example, if one student in a group is performing at a high level, the teacher can move the student to a higher group to facilitate progress.

### Curriculum-Based Measurement

**Curriculum-based measurement (CBM)** has been part of the learning disabilities field since the 1960s. Much of the early impetus for this approach came from work by Lovitt (1967) and Deno (Deno & Mirkin, 1977), which was continued and amplified by others as well as by Lovitt and Deno themselves (e.g., Deno, 1997; Fuchs & Deno, 1991; Lovitt & Fantasia, 1980; Starlin, 1971). Although distinctions can be made among different variants of what might be called direct assessment (Fuchs &

**Council** for **Exceptional Children**

**CEC Knowledge Check**

In monitoring student progress, how important is the organization and maintenance of accurate records? How does good record keeping help your students? CC8S8, CC8S10

**Council** for **Exceptional Children**

**CEC Knowledge Check**

To keep a record of reading fluency, why might you have students read sections of material into a cassette recording? CC8S2, CC8S3, CC8S10

**curriculum-based measurement**
measurement of student performance based on the assumptions of curriculum-based assessment

**FIGURE 12.2** Example of an In-Program Progress-Monitoring Assessment: Mastery Test 4 from *Corrective Reading: Word Attack Basics*

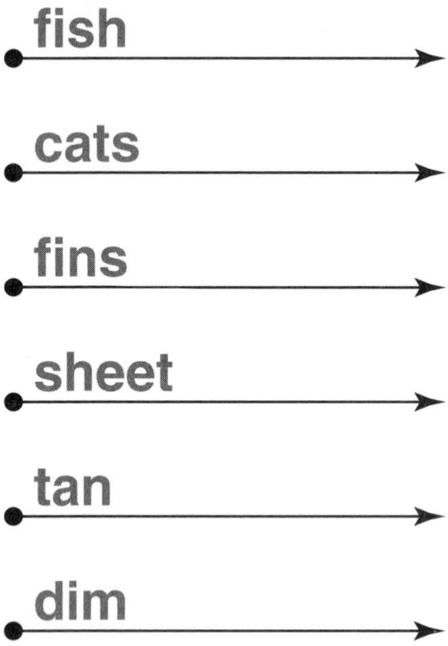

## fish ⟶

## cats ⟶

## fins ⟶

## sheet ⟶

## tan ⟶

## dim ⟶

***Task A*** Word Reading

1. Read these words.
2. (Test item.) Touch the ball of the arrow for **fish.**) Sound it out. (Touch under **f**, **i**, **sh**.) *fffiiishshsh.* (The student should not pause between sounds.)
3. (Test item.) (Touch the ball of the arrow.) Say it fast. (Slash right.) *Fish.*
4. (Repeat steps 2 and 3 for **cats**, **fins**, **sheet**, **tan**, **dim**.)

***Task B*** Word Reading the Fast Way

1. Now you'll read these words the fast way.
2. (Test item.) (Touch the ball of the arrow for **fish**. Pause 4 seconds.) What word? (Slash right.) *Fish.*
3. (Repeat step 2 for **cats**, **fins**, **sheet**, **tan**, **dim**.)

***Evaluating test results***

(If more than 25 percent of the students made more than one error, repeat Lessons 16 and 17. Then test.)

*Source:* From *Corrective Reading* (p. 113) by S. Engelmann, L. Carnine, and G. Johnson, Chicago: SRA/McGraw-Hill. Copyright 1999 by The McGraw-Hill Companies. Reprinted by permission.

Deno, 1991; Howell & Nolet, 2000), CBM and its cousins, applied behavior analysis (Lovitt, 1975) and precision teaching (Starlin, 1971), share the same basic tenets.

To use CBM in reading, teachers have students read aloud several times a week for perhaps 1 or 2 minutes at a time. During their learning of foundational decoding skills, students may read from lists of words, and as they move into work on fluency, they may read from passages of both fiction and nonfiction. Although it is not mandatory, the reading passages for CBM assessments often are taken directly from the school's reading materials (Fuchs & Deno, 1994). Fluency measures of children's reading of pseudo- or nonwords such as *saf, rilp,* and *brop* are sensitive indicators of how well students can decode when reading passages composed of real words (Speece, Mills, Ritchey, & Hillman, 2002).

Assessment procedures such as CBM compare favorably with traditional achievement tests in reading. Not only do CBM reading measures correlate highly with achievement test scores, but they also permit teachers to gather other useful information. CBM measures permit teachers to make their instruction more efficient, thus helping students progress at an optimal pace (Howell et al., 1993, 1997; Howell & Nolet, 2000).

## Overview of Assessment Methods

A national panel of experts on reading assessment examined a wide range of reading assessment instruments and procedures to provide assistance to states that were seeking federal funds under the Reading First program (Kame'enui, 2002). The panel identified many instruments and then rigorously reviewed the usefulness of each of them. The result of their review was a list of acceptable instruments for assessing different aspects of early reading (phonemic awareness, phonics, fluency, vocabulary, and reading comprehension). Table 12.3 provides an overview of the experts' analysis for the areas of screening, diagnosis, and progress monitoring.

**TABLE 12.3** Instruments for Assessing Reading Performance in Kindergarten through Third Grade

| | SCREENING | | | | | DIAGNOSIS | | | | | MONITORING PROGRESS | | | | |
|---|---|---|---|---|---|---|---|---|---|---|---|---|---|---|---|
| | PA | Ph | Fl | Vo | RC | PA | Ph | Fl | Vo | RC | PA | Ph | Fl | Vo | RC |
| CBM Oral Reading Fluency | | | • | | | | | | | | | | • | | |
| Comprehensive Test of Phonological Processing | • | | | | | • | | | | | • | | | | |
| Degrees of Reading Power | | | | | | | | | | • | | | | | • |
| Dynamic Indicators of Basic Early Literacy Skills | • | • | • | | | | | | | | • | • | • | | |
| Early Reading Diagnostic Assessment | | • | | | | • | • | | | • | | | | | |
| Gray Oral Reading Test—IV | | | • | | • | | | • | | • | | | | | |
| Iowa Test of Basic Skills | | | | | | • | | | • | • | | | | | |
| Letter-Sound Fluency | | • | | | | • | | | | | | • | | | |
| Lindamood Auditory Conceptualization Test | | | | | | • | | | | | | | | | |
| Peabody Picture Vocabulary Test—III | | | | • | | | | | • | | | | | | |
| Phonological Awareness Test | • | | | | | • | | | | | | | | | |
| Test of Language Development—Primary—3 | | | | | | | | | • | | | | | | |
| Test of Word Knowledge | | | | | | | | | • | | | | | | |
| Test of Word Reading Efficiency | | • | • | | | | | | | | | • | • | | |
| Texas Primary Reading Inventory | • | • | • | • | • | • | • | • | • | • | • | • | • | • | • |
| Wechsler Individual Achievement Test—II | | | | | | | • | | • | • | | | | | |
| Woodcock Reading Mastery Test—Revised | | • | | | • | | • | | • | • | | | | | |
| Woodcock-Johnson—III—Test of Achievement | | • | | • | • | | • | | • | • | | • | | • | |
| Yopp-Singer Test of Phoneme Segmentation | • | | | | | • | | | | | | | | | |

*Note:* PA = phonemic awareness, Ph = phonics, Fl = fluency, Vo = vocabulary, RC = reading comprehension. Also, instruments may be useful in area indicated at only certain grade levels, not necessary all levels.

# How Common Are Reading Problems in Learning Disabilities?

Some authorities suggest that reading disabilities are quite common, affecting from 15 to 20% or more of children and adolescents (Lyon, 1997; Shaywitz, 2003). Determining exactly how many students have reading disabilities depends on the same variables that influence estimates of the prevalence of learning disabilities, including (1) how the problem is defined, (2) how it is measured, and (3) how samples are selected to study prevalence.

Prior to the changes in IDEA in 2003–2004, many states defined learning disabilities as a discrepancy between ability and achievement (see Chapters 1 and 3). Although authorities have raised questions about the appropriateness of discrepancy between IQ and achievement as the basis for identifying students with learning disabilities (Fletcher et al., 2002; Joshi, Williams, & Wood, 1998; Stanovich, 1991) that are leading to changes in how students are identified, the available evidence about prevalence still comes from studies using discrepancy.

Studies of the prevalence of reading disabilities indicate that between 6.2 and 7.5% of children have reading achievement scores that are substantially lower than their IQs (Lewis, Hitch, & Walker, 1994; Shaywitz, Shaywitz, Fletcher, & Escobar, 1990). Although not all students whose aptitude-achievement discrepancies are this great will be identified as having learning disabilities, many of them will. There are also likely to be other students (e.g., those with arithmetic problems) who would qualify for learning disability services but who do not have highly discrepant scores between ability and reading measures.

Differences in the prevalence of reading disabilities by gender is another matter of concern. In some studies, strict formulas for classifying students as having reading disabilities reveal about equal numbers of boys and girls. However, when one counts the number of children receiving services instead of the results from using the strict research formula, more boys than girls are classified (Shaywitz et al., 1990). The difference between school- and research-identified cases appears to be a consequence of differential referral of boys and girls for services, probably prompted by the boys' behavior (Shaywitz et al., 1990). In other studies, however, research-based formulas reveal that boys outnumber girls about 2 to 1 (Lewis et al., 1994). Because we know that teachers base referral on more than just reading problems (Speece & Cooper, 1990), we can suspect that other factors such as behavior contribute to the differences between prevalence numbers based on teacher referrals and tests.

Another factor affecting prevalence is the interplay of reading disabilities with learning disabilities. There almost surely are some students who would meet the standards for having a reading disability but who might not be identified as having learning disabilities and some who would meet the standards for learning disabilities but not for reading disabilities. Students in the former group might have difficulties that are not severe enough to warrant special education services, and those in the latter group might have disabilities in other areas. That most, but not all, students with learning disabilities have problems with reading reinforces the theme that individuals with learning disabilities form a diverse group.

Council for Exceptional Children

**CEC Knowledge Check**

How can this situation be remedied? Will general education teachers need special education strategies for all learners? What is your role in this process?
LD7K3, CC9S3

Council for Exceptional Children

**CEC Knowledge Check**

Does this mean that more girls should be identified, or fewer boys?
CC7S8, CC9S6

Council for Exceptional Children

**CEC Knowledge Check**

What will happen to these at-risk students? How can they be taught successfully in a general education setting?
LD4S7, CC7K2, LD7K3, LD8K3

# How Can Instruction Help Prevent Reading Disabilities?

The **alphabetic principle** is the critical underlying concept that people must grasp to become competent readers. The alphabetic principle is deceptively simple: Printed words are composed of symbols that represent sounds; the order of the printed words represents the sequence of sounds when people speak. Said another way: "Print is talk written down." Children do not have to learn to recite the alphabetic principle, but they have to learn how to apply it in converting print to spoken language equivalents. Instruction must show them how to apply it consistently and efficiently.

Summarizing across research in many areas (developmental psychology, neuropsychology, linguistics, etc.), eminent authorities have found implications for beginning reading instruction.

> From all these different perspectives, two inescapable conclusions emerge. The first is that mastering the alphabetic principle is essential to becoming proficient in the skill of reading, and the second is that instructional techniques (namely, phonics) that teach this principle directly are more effective than those that do not. This seems to be especially the case for children who are at risk in some way for having difficulty learning to read. (Raynor, Foorman, Perfetti, Peretsky, & Seidenburg, 2001, p. 68)

Many students begin formal schooling already knowing how to read, and others have so much familiarity with English phonology and letters that they rapidly grasp the alphabetic principle. For these students, the quality of instruction probably makes very little difference; they will learn to read no matter what literacy experiences they have in the early grades.

For students who do not have those advantages, the quality of early literacy instruction is critically important. Most students with learning disabilities fall into this group. Their teachers must provide instruction that very plainly shows them the various aspects of the alphabetic principle—segmenting, blending, phoneme-grapheme correspondences, etc. Early instruction must be explicit, provide the scaffolding needed, include adequate practice opportunities, and incorporate other critical aspects of effective instructional design (see Kame'enui, Carnine, Dixon, Simmons, & Coyne, 2002).

Becoming a capable beginning reader requires that students master the various skills discussed in this chapter. As children learn these skills, they progress from identifying a few words as if they were pictures or logos to solving the code and employing the alphabetic principle. Researchers have described this progression in some detail (Ehri & Richardson, 1998; Moats, 1998). One such view is shown in Table 12.4 (page 384). Progressing to the stage of orthographic reading shown in Table 12.4 puts a learner at the threshold of becoming a capable adult reader.

Becoming a capable adult reader requires that people acquire five generalized competencies (Anderson, Hiebert, Wilkenson, & Scott, 1985), the first of which is based on mastery of the alphabetic principle:

1. *Fluency.* Capable readers recognize words readily. They appear to read effortlessly. They can do this because they have practiced *decoding* (turning print into

> **alphabetic principle** the idea that symbols represent sounds and that the order of sounds follows the sequence of letters in a word

Council for Exceptional Children

**CEC Knowledge Check**

For teaching these types of students, what claim to teacher effectiveness in reading can be made? CC2K5, CC5K3

Council for Exceptional Children

**CEC Knowledge Check**

For at-risk students with learning disabilities, would student success validate authentic teacher effectiveness? LD4K2, LD7K3

**TABLE 12.4** Description of Increasing Competence in Early Reading

| STAGE | CHILD'S CHARACTERISTICS | APPROPRIATE ACTIVITIES |
|---|---|---|
| Logographic | Recognizes a few words by special cues (usually visual) such as shape, typeface, or unusual letters | Early- and middle-level phonological awareness tasks such as rhyming and phoneme counting |
| Novice | Uses some phonological awareness skills and letter sounds to cue words, but isn't proficient with sounding out | Advanced phonological awareness activities (segmenting and blending), direct teaching of letter-sound correspondences, and practice with decoding simple words |
| Alphabetic | Able to use known letter-sound combinations and blending to decode simple words readily | Extensive practice with decoding, particularly with words that illustrate common spelling patterns and reading of simple passages |
| Orthographic | Automatic word-reading skills and advancing fluency in reading passages | Work on reading novel words by analogy and extensive practice with texts at the right difficulty level |

*Source:* Adapted from "Teaching Decoding" by L. C. Moats, 1998, *American Educator,* 22(1–2), 42–49, 95. Reprinted by permission.

spoken language) enough that it is *automatic* (requires no conscious work). When readers are fluent decoders, they are free to devote their attention to learning from and enjoying what they read.

2. *World knowledge.* Capable readers use their knowledge of the world to construct the meaning of what they read. They do more than simply extract the meaning from the text; they try to make what they are reading correspond with what they have experienced. Young readers (especially those with disabilities) sometimes construct mistaken representations of what they read; their personal experience may intrude to such a great extent that they read what they think should be on the page, not what is actually there. As readers become more sophisticated, they can suspend their own beliefs and ideas, follow an author's argument, and acquire new world knowledge from the text.

3. *Flexible strategy use.* Capable readers adapt their reading to fit the material they are reading and their understanding of it. When they encounter unfamiliar or difficult words, they slow down and read more carefully. When they realize that they have not been understanding what they have been reading, they employ strategies such as rereading. To help themselves remember what they have read, they use strategies such as paraphrasing and others discussed in Chapter 11.

4. *Motivation.* Capable readers read because of what it gives them. They may gain new knowledge, learn the resolution of a story, or avoid doing some less pleasant task, such as housework. Early in the acquisition of reading skill,

there is little intrinsic reinforcement in reading for children; they may pursue it because they have been told it is fun, but they have not had enough practice with it to find reading easy and inherently interesting. Later, if people read well, reading new information becomes very rewarding.

5. *Continued reading.* Capable readers not only learn fundamental reading skills, but also continue to read. As they do so, they become more and more skillful. Reading becomes a lifelong pursuit.

The major stumbling block in becoming a capable adult reader is developing fluency in decoding. Fluent decoding requires mastery of the alphabetic principle. For students who acquire fluent decoding skills, reading usually is reinforcing enough to provide motivation and continued reading. The limits on their understanding of what they read are imposed by their world knowledge and ability to use strategies flexibly. For students who do not acquire fluent decoding skills, reading is not rewarding, and therefore continuing to read is unlikely. When they are stumbling through a passage, they are not able to apply what they know about the world or use strategies their accomplished peers use.

Council for Exceptional Children

**CEC Knowledge Check**
How can you build success into the early phonological awareness stage to increase motivation at that level? LD3K2, LD4K2

## Teaching Phonemic Awareness

Since nearly the inception of the field, authorities in learning disabilities have recommended teaching what we now call phonemic awareness. Although recent emphasis on them makes the skills of analysis and blending seem new, they were fundamental parts of the instructional practices incorporated into programs for students who have difficulty learning to read (Chall, 1967; Engelmann, 1967b; Williams, 1977, 1980).

As evidence linking poor phonemic awareness to reading disabilities accumulated during the 1970s and 1980s, more and more people began to examine the utility of teaching phonological skills to students. By the early 1990s, it was plain that young children who learned to manipulate the sounds of their spoken language had much lower chances of developing reading disabilities than did their peers who did not learn phonological skills.

There is a wealth of evidence on the benefits of teaching phonological skills to beginning readers. Most studies show the benefits of teaching students segmenting, blending, and similar skills (Ball & Blachman, 1988; Bradley & Bryant, 1983; Byrne & Fielding-Barnsley, 1991, 1993; Content, Kolinski, Morais, & Bertelson, 1986; Cunningham, 1990; Hurford et al., 1994; Lundberg, Frost, & Peterson, 1988; Torgesen, Morgan, & Davis, 1992; Vellutino & Scanlon, 1987; Williams, 1980). But phonemic segmentation training alone is not sufficient. Indeed, improving phonemic segmentation may not improve blending (Slocum, O'Connor, & Jenkins, 1993), so children should be taught both segmentation and blending skills (Pullen, 2002; Torgesen et al., 1992), how to apply the phonological skills they learn (Cunningham, 1990), and how to connect letters with letter sounds (Foorman, Francis, Novy, & Liberman, 1991; National Reading Panel, 2000). Children's facility with phonological tasks also appears to be promoted in part by learning about letters themselves (Wagner, Torgesen, & Rashotte, 1994).

In fact, although phonemic awareness tasks should start as simple spoken-language activities, they should rapidly become associated with letters. Beginning reading programs should be evaluated on the basis of how well they incorporate these features. Combining phonemic awareness training with instruction in letter-sound knowledge provides greater benefits for children's literacy than providing phonemic awareness training alone (National Reading Panel, 2000; Schneider, Roth, & Ennemoser, 2000). Teachers who do not teach phonological skills at all, teach only some of the relevant skills, or do not connect phonology with letters are not likely to prevent learning disabilities. Some research even suggests that children who develop strong phonological skills may be able to compensate for genetic risk for reading problems (Snowling, Gallagher, & Frith, 2003; see Chapter 2).

Once the importance of teaching phonological skills became apparent, many authorities on early reading began to provide guides for teachers showing how to promote the acquisition of phonemic awareness. Teachers need to know how to teach phonemic awareness skills (Moats, 2000; Torgesen & Mathes, 1999). Figure 12.3 lists selected examples of these guides, authored by leading researchers in early literacy. In addition, strong early reading programs incorporate phonemic awareness training.

## Teaching Phonics

The U.S. Congress initiated one of the most ambitious undertakings in the area of reading in 1997 by forming the National Reading Panel (NRP) and charging it with assessing the scientific evidence about teaching reading. The NRP was composed of individuals with extensive knowledge of the research and who did not have a vested interest in any one outcome of the review; members could not be authors of commercial programs or tests that might benefit from the panel's findings. After conducting a series of hearings around the country to learn what teachers, parents, and others considered important, the panel began collecting research articles to review.

The NRP identified thousands of studies about different aspects of reading and then focused more closely on the most scientifically rigorous of them. As one

Council for
Exceptional
Children

**CEC Knowledge Check**
How can you communicate the importance of phonemic awareness techniques to other professionals who may not know of their effectiveness?
LD3K2, LD4S8

---

**FIGURE 12.3**    Examples of Phonemic Awareness Curricula

*Ladders to Literacy: A Kindergarten Activity Book,* by Rolanda E. O'Connor, Angela Notari-Syverson, & Patricia F. Vadasy (1996)

*Ladders to Literacy: A Preschool Activity Book,* by Angela Notari-Syverson, Rollanda E. O'Connor, & Patricia F. Vadasy (1998)

*Phonemic Awareness in Young Children: A Classroom Curriculum,* by Marilyn Jager Adams, Barbara R. Foorman, Ingvar Lunberg, & Terri Beeler (1997)

*Phonological Awareness Assessment and Instruction: A Sound Beginning,* by Holly B. Lane & Paige C. Pullen (2004)

*Phonological Awareness Training for Reading,* by Joseph K. Torgesen & Bradley T. Bryant (1994)

*Road to the Code: A Phonological Awareness Program for Young Children,* by Benita A. Blachman, Eileen Wynne Ball, Rochella Black, & Darlene M. Tangel (2000)

---

part of their study, the NRP focused on methods for teaching phonics, and they analyzed those studies to identify effective instructional methods and practices. They reported on the relative effectiveness of three alternative—analytic phonics, synthetic phonics, and miscellaneous phonics—ways to teach phonics and compared them to the control condition.

- **Miscellaneous phonics**—teaching students to read unfamiliar words by analogy, to spell spoken words so that they will learn how to read them, or embedding phonics instruction in reading of text
- **Analytic phonics**—teaching students to study words they have learned previously and identify letter-sound relations in them; this is done so children do not have to pronounce sounds in isolation
- **Synthetic phonics**—teaching students letters for sounds and how to convert letters and letter combinations into sounds (phonemes) and then blend the sounds to form recognizable words (as illustrated earlier in Table 12.1)

**miscellaneous phonics** reading unfamiliar words by analogy; spelling spoken words, and assimilating phonics knowledge by reading text

**analytic phonics** identifying letter-sound relations of words by examining the spelling patterns of words

**synthetic phonics** converting letters and letter combinations into sounds (phonemes) and blending the sounds to form recognizable words

Figure 12.4 shows the results of the NRP review. On the whole, all three methods of teaching phonics produced better outcomes for children than not teaching phonics (the control). Although differences between the three methods were not as striking, the synthetic methods appeared the strongest. Many experts in learning

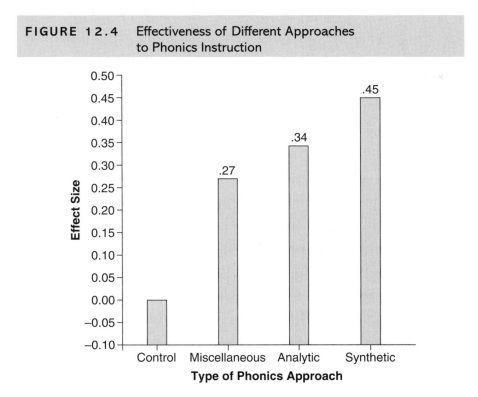

**FIGURE 12.4** Effectiveness of Different Approaches to Phonics Instruction

disabilities advocated synthetic methods of reading instruction, even before the NRP reported its study (Ball & Blachman, 1988; Bateman, 1996; Carnine et al., 2004; Chall, 1967; Engelmann, 1967b; Simmons & Kame'enui, 1998; Williams, 1980).

## Teaching Other Aspects of Early Reading

As is true for the instruction in phonemic awareness and phonics, instruction in fluency, vocabulary, and reading comprehension must be explicit and systematic. There is extensive research on effective instruction in promoting fluency (Chard, Vaughn, & Tyler, 2002; Kuhn & Stahl, 2003), for example, that shows how providing adequate opportunities to practice reading aloud is important. But, equally or even more important, teachers must provide feedback to students about how fluently and accurately they read and must set clear goals and show students how they are progressing toward meeting those goals.

The situation in reading comprehension is similar (Gersten et al., 2001; Williams, 2003). Helping students get the main idea of passages, for example, requires that teachers ensure that their students know the concept of "main idea," correct for some students' tendency to attend to less important aspects of what they are reading, teach verbal paraphrasing, and so forth. For some students, these aspects of reading comprehension seem to come naturally, but for those with learning disabilities, careful instruction is required.

We discuss specific procedures for teaching fluency and comprehension in a later section of this chapter.

## Putting It All Together

Combining sustained, systematic, and explicit teaching of phonemic awareness, phonics, fluency, vocabulary, and reading comprehension can prevent reading problems for many students. Based on their analyses of whether reading instructional programs included these important components, some states (Alabama, Michigan, New Jersey, Massachusetts, Washington, California) recommended commercial reading programs to their schools. The curricula they recommended included *Legacy of Literacy* (published by Houghton Mifflin), *Open Court* (SRA/McGraw-Hill), *Reading Mastery* (SRA/McGraw-Hill), *Success for All, Trophies* (Harcourt), and *Universal Literacy System* (Voyager Learning). Special education teachers who work with young children in their general education classrooms are likely to encounter one of these commercial programs. They will need to know how to identify gaps in the programs and provide additional support for students who struggle with early reading.

Many schools in the United States are adopting a comprehensive approach to reading instruction for young children that provides different levels of support depending on how well students are learning reading skills. These approaches go by a variety of names—tiers, levels, cascades—but all share the characteristics illustrated in the Current Trends and Issues box on pages 390–391. They are aimed at preventing reading problems by providing additional services for students who need more intense levels of instruction to ensure that they acquire fundamental literacy skills. Educational and psychological research is clear about what counts as effec-

**Council for Exceptional Children**

**CEC Knowledge Check**

Does using magazines and materials that interest students help motivate students to look for the main idea? LD4S5, LD4S9

**Council for Exceptional Children**

**CEC Knowledge Check**

Does this sound like a good strategy to help all students, including at-risk students, succeed? CC4S3, LD7K3, LD8K3

tive reading instruction. The challenge is to implement that effective reading instruction broadly, across general education and special education, for millions of students (Denton, Vaughn, & Fetcher, 2003).

## How Can Instruction Help Remediate Learning Disabilities in Reading?

In many cases, early reading instruction fails. Too often, when young children are not learning to read, teachers and parents decide they are "not ready" for reading. The children are passed along while people wait for them to mature. These young children who have been passed along become older children who cannot read, lose ground in content knowledge, develop low self-concepts, and are at risk for dropping out of school. As helpful as early and systematic instruction may be, there are still students who fall behind their peers (Hiebert & Taylor, 2002; Snow et al., 1998).

When students have not acquired reading skills during **developmental reading instruction** (instruction usually provided in general education settings in the primary grades), teachers usually must provide instruction designed to correct or remedy their reading deficits. Instruction designed to correct reading deficits is often called **remedial,** or **corrective, reading.** In this section, we discuss historical approaches and contemporary approaches to remedial reading and briefly describe some effective teaching procedures for remedial reading.

### Historical Approaches

One of the strongest currents in the history of learning disabilities has been an emphasis on sensory modalities. Because of the emphasis on sensory modalities, many methods in learning disabilities were called **multisensory approaches** or identified by the initials for the modalities: **VAKT**—for **visual** (seeing), **auditory** (hearing), **kinesthetic** (body or muscle feeling), and **tactile** (touch). Concern with modalities forms the basis for three historically important approaches to remedial instruction. Each approach is associated with one of the pioneers in learning disabilities: Fernald (1943), Orton (1937), and Kirk (1976).

### *Fernald Approach*

Fernald (1943) is probably the figure most readily associated with multisensory approaches. The rationale for the Fernald Word Learning Approach is that by being taught to use as many senses as possible, the child comes to have additional experiences or cues in learning to read. If the child is weak in any one modality, the other modalities will help convey the information. In practice, Fernald's approach is not confined to reading; it is also used in spelling and writing instruction. It is essentially a language-experience and whole-word approach. Fernald believed that overcoming the emotional problems failing students have with reading would be easier if their reading material was of interest to them. Therefore, stories are written down as suggested by the students, with as much help from the teacher as needed, and then read.

Council for Exceptional Children

**CEC Knowledge Check**
Are we acting in the student's long-term interest to pass them on to the next grade before they are ready? Should social concerns override academic concerns?
CC3K2, LD7K3

**developmental reading instruction** instruction provided in the early years, usually in general education settings in the primary grades

**remedial instruction** instruction designed to correct deficits in basic skills

**corrective reading** instruction that addresses reading deficits; also known as remedial reading

**multisensory approach** a teaching method that emphasizes using visual, auditory, kinesthetic, and tactile senses

**VAKT** teaching methods that emphasize visual-auditory-kinesthetic-tactile modalities; also called multisensory approach

**visual** refers to sight or anything related to sight

**auditory** hearing or processing of sounds and words

**kinesthetic** refers to body or muscle senses

**tactile** refers to sense of touch

## Applying Prevention Concepts to Beginning Reading

Can we prevent reading disabilities? Some educators believe a sensible approach to helping young children avoid reading problems is to provide a comprehensive system of services arrayed in "levels" or "tiers." Three-tiered, or three-level, systems of early reading instruction provide increasingly intense instruction depending on students' needs. As with levels of prevention (see the Current Trends and Issues box on page 38), the tiers of reading instruction are often referred to as primary, secondary, and tertiary, with the primary tier being the least intense and the tertiary level being the most intense. The idea of a three-level system is shown in Figure A, based on a model for prevent-

ing both reading and behavior problems at Juniper Gardens Children's Project (www.jgcp.ku.ed/Grants/CenterforEarly.htm).

- *Primary.* Usually, reading intervention takes place in general education classrooms, employs a core reading program that has strong empirical support, incorporates monitoring of pupil progress, and includes help for teachers in assessing students' performance and implementing effective teaching practices.
- *Secondary.* Instruction at the second level is provided to students who are not succeeding with only primary-

**FIGURE A** Reading-Behavior Linkages

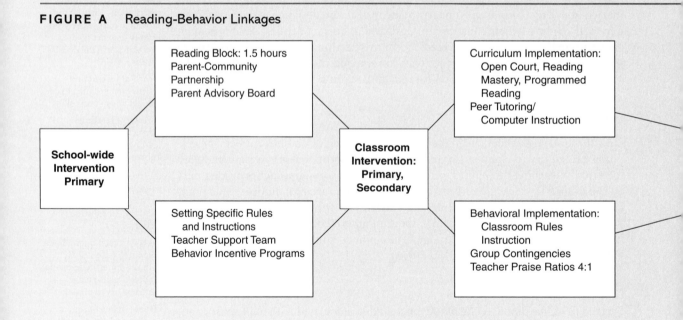

Students also select words they wish to learn and then work on them, repeatedly tracing and saying words until they can write them from memory. Mastered words are kept in a file so students may refer back to them as needed. Fernald was opposed to having students "sound out" words; she emphasized the reading and writing of words as wholes. Although there are strong advocates of the Fernald approach who can provide case studies of its successful use, there is only limited research evidence demonstrating its effectiveness (Thorpe, Lampe, Nash, & Chiang, 1981).

level intervention. Secondary intervention often includes (1) additional time devoted to extra practice with literacy activities, (2) small-group teaching or volunteer or peer tutoring, (3) specific focus on critical skills such as blending, and (4) frequent monitoring of progress. Often, when students make sufficient progress at the secondary level of intervention, these supports are discontinued.

- *Tertiary.* When primary and secondary interventions prove inadequate, as reflected in progress-monitoring data, schools employing a three-tiered model will increase the intensity of intervention even more. Students receiving tertiary services will not only continue to receive primary and secondary services, but will also receive additional small-group instruction with more emphasis on critical decoding skills and with closer progress monitoring.

Compare the Juniper Gardens Children's Project model with one from the reading program at the University of Texas (www.texasreading.org/utcrla/projects/3tier_research.asp). Whereas the Juniper Gardens system aims to prevent both reading and behavior problems, the Texas project focuses exclusively on reading problems. Research conducted at these and other projects will help us learn whether three-tiered systems can, in fact, prevent reading problems.

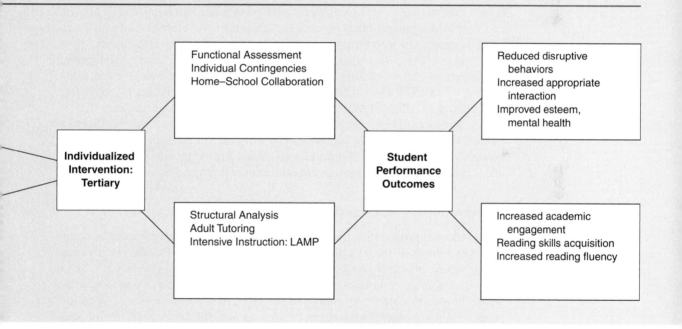

## Hegge-Kirk-Kirk Approach

Although not always considered a multisensory approach, Hegge, Kirk, and Kirk (1970) emphasized use of multiple modalities during reading instruction. The Remedial Reading Drills of the Hegge-Kirk-Kirk approach are designed to help students remember phoneme-grapheme relationships by providing extensive practice and by simplifying the relationships between letters and their sounds (e.g., using only one sound for a letter until it has been thoroughly mastered; see Carnine, 1976). In the program, students are taught to (1) say sounds for individual letters, (2) blend combinations of sounds, (3) write letters for sounds from memory, and (4) practice reading words aloud from prescribed word lists. Practice in reading from connected prose has to be provided by the teacher because the program is limited to reading letters and words in isolation. Revised versions of the materials, *Phonic Remedial Reading Lessons* (Kirk, Kirk, & Minskoff, 1985), appeared in the 1980s.

### Orton-Gillingham Approach

Based on work the authors did with Orton in the 1930s, another multisensory approach to reading has been advocated by Gillingham and Stillman (1965). It is often known as the Orton-Gillingham approach. Gillingham and Stillman made Orton's recommendations into a practical procedure. They created a program designed to remediate not only problems in reading, but also related problems in spelling and handwriting. They recommended that students learn associations between letters and their sounds in all of the modalities required by the reading, spelling, and handwriting tasks. Thus, students are taught to see a letter (visual) and say its sound (auditory), hear a sound (auditory) and write it (kinesthetic), and so forth. After mastering the first ten letter associations, the student begins work on blending letters into words. Spelling and story reading are gradually introduced as the student develops facility with the vocabulary that can be built from the mastered grapheme-phoneme associations.

Studies of the Orton-Gillingham approach reveal improved reading and spelling for elementary school children (e.g., Joshi, Dahlgren, & Boulware-Gooden, 2002; Kline & Kline, 1975; Oakland, Black, Stanford, Nussbaum, & Balise, 1998; Vickery, Reynolds, & Cochran, 1987) and improved spelling for college students (Guyer, Banks, & Guyer, 1993). On average, however, studies of the Orton-Gillingham method show benefits lying somewhere between the comparison and the analytic phonics methods shown in Figure 12.4 (National Reading Panel, 2000). Nevertheless, some of the method's features are consistent with other effective approaches.

## Contemporary Approaches

Shannon

More recent approaches to remedial reading have not necessarily adhered to the theoretical views of the past but have sought to ensure that students rapidly learn the alphabetic principle and then develop fluency and comprehension skills. Shannon was fortunate enough to have received effective remedial reading instruction when she was in elementary school. As a result, in her middle-school years, her progress in some other areas was not delayed. In fact, she developed a love of reading. In the Case Connections box on page 393, Mr. Martens, Shannon's first special education teacher, who helped her learn to read, describes how he taught her.

Part of the reason that Shannon made strong progress was because the special education situation made it possible for her teacher to work with her in small groups. Small-group instruction is a part of many interventions and is probably responsible for some of the benefits these methods demonstrate (Elbaum, Vaughn, Hughes, & Moody, 2000). Although Shannon's instruction took place in small groups, it also incorporated Direct Instruction, strategy training, CBM, and other factors that many consider critical for successful remediation (Lovett, Barron, & Benson, 2003).

# Shannon's Reading Instruction

Shannon Ireland's mother gives "all the credit" to Peter Martens, the special education teacher who taught Shannon when she was first identified as having a learning disability. Martens, who had a master's degree in special education and was in his fifth year of teaching when Shannon was assigned to his class, recollects how he worked with her. Martens's class was a self-contained class for students with severe problems; he was able to structure the entire school day (other than physical education and the related arts) for his students.

> Thanks for the chance to remember Shan. She was one of my stars. She started in my class when she was in third grade, and I had her for two years. Then she switched to an inclusion program in fifth grade and went on another teacher's case load.
>
> We (I include my aid, Jeanne Armstrong, because she worked with Shan, too) did a whole lot of different things in reading with her. We used the Direct Instruction programs, of course, but that wasn't all we did. We had them do timed readings every day and graph their results. We also had a reward system, and the kids could earn extra points by reading books that I had on different shelves. I made the shelves so that they had to be able to read at a certain speed before they could move up to the next shelf and the higher shelves were worth more points.
>
> We figured that we had to teach her a lot really fast so that she could start to catch up. Like they say, she wasn't going to catch up unless she learned faster than she normally would. That's why we combined the DI, CBM, and everything. And she really took off. At first, it was slow going. We had to go all the way back to letter sounds and blending. But by October/November she was really "clicking." I had to move her up to a higher reading group. It was still a remedial group, but she was in with some older kids. By the end of that first year, she really had the basics down and had jumped about two grade levels. By the end of the second year, she was actually a little ahead of grade level in reading, so we figured she was ready for the regular classroom.

**Council for Exceptional Children**

**CEC Knowledge Check**
After reading this description of Shannon, do you think Shannon was intelligent before she started remedial reading? What makes the difference in success or failure for students like Shannon? CC4S3, LD4K2

Success depends on the nature of instruction teachers provide. Although historically important methods are still used in special education today, other methods are more common. Major contenders in remedial reading such as Reading Recovery, Corrective Reading, and computer-assisted instruction illustrate the kinds of interventions in use today.

### Reading Recovery

Reading Recovery (Clay, 1985; Pinnell, 1989) has been among the most popular methods advocated in reading disabilities. This intensive, tutorial approach is designed to help developmental readers who are likely to have difficulty acquiring reading skills. However, concern about the utility of Reading Recovery has decreased its popularity recently. Reading Recovery is based on several valuable practices: (1) screen first-graders early in the school year; (2) select the lowest rank (usually the lowest 20%); (3) deliver intensive instruction to the selected students. Reading Recovery also emphasizes reading of familiar texts and promotes writing of words in ways that encourage discovery of phonological relationships.

After encouraging early studies, more rigorous evaluations of the Reading Recovery program soon became available. For example, in one study, researchers compared the growth of three groups of students. One group received a standard remedial program, one group received regular Reading Recovery, and a third group received a modified version of Reading Recovery. The modified version of the Reading Recovery program was much more explicit than the usual version; it provided practice in phonemic awareness and showed the students symbol-sound relationships. Students in both the regular and the modified Reading Recovery programs improved more than their peers in the control group. However, the students in the Reading Recovery group that also received instruction in phonological skills progressed more rapidly (Iversen & Tunmer, 1993).

Researchers have aggregated numerous studies about Reading Recovery to assess whether it is effective in many studies or just one or two. Generally, they found that although Reading Recovery has short-lived and very special benefits, it provides nowhere near the acceleration required for students who need to catch up with their peers (Chapman, Tunmer, & Prochnow, 2001; Denton & Mathes, 2002; Fawcett, Nicholson, Moss, Nicholson, & Reason, 2001; Grossen, Coulter, & Ruggles, 1996; Heibert, 1994). According to its own standards (whether students can read a specific book), Reading Recovery looks pretty good. When teachers assess its benefits on generalization tasks (reading other books) or sustained benefits (improvements several years later), the results are less encouraging.

### Corrective Reading Program

The DI materials for remedial reading are called the Corrective Reading Program (CRP; Engelmann et al., 1999). Corrective Reading is designed to teach students general-case strategies for attacking and solving types of reading tasks. A sound-it-out strategy is a general-case procedure for decoding; this is based on a task analysis similar to the one provided in Table 12.1 (page 366). Because corrective readers already know some things about the alphabetic code, in Corrective Reading, there is relatively less emphasis on teaching the basics of the strategy (e.g., individual sounds for letters) and more emphasis on teaching use of those skills to increase reading accuracy.

Corrective Reading includes scripted daily lessons designed to teach the component skills needed for fluent, accurate decoding. Students read from carefully structured word lists and then participate in group and individual reading of stories.

Research shows that Corrective Reading improves the reading of pupils with learning disabilities and may be particularly valuable for students who have relatively greater deficits in reading (Adams & Carnine, 2003; Lloyd, Epstein, & Cullinan, 1981; Maggs & Maggs, 1979; Pflaum & Pascarella, 1980; Polloway, Epstein, Polloway, Patton, & Ball, 1986; White, 1988).

### Computer-Assisted Instruction

Despite the potential value of computer-assisted practice in learning, technology has little value in teaching the decoding aspects of reading, because students themselves must turn the written letters into sounds. Given rules, computers can convert print to sound, but when computers do this, students do not get the practice they need to gain proficiency. Also, students will likely rely on the computer's decoding of the words rather than learning how to do it themselves.

Computer technology has not advanced far enough to make sophisticated comparisons between a student's reading of a word and its correct pronunciation. Despite progress in speech-recognition technology, computers cannot decipher subtle differences in pronunciation. Thus, clinical experience and experimental evidence (e.g., Farmer, Klien, & Bryson, 1992) show that computers can have only limited value listening to students read. Computers can, however, be used to improve students' reading of individual words (Cohen, Torgesen, & Torgesen, 1988; Olson, Wise, Ring, & Johnson, 1997; Rashotte & Torgesen, 1985; Torgesen, Waters, Cohen, & Torgesen, 1988; Wise, Ring, & Olson, 2000; Wise & Olson, 1998; Wise, Olson, Ring, & Johnson, 1998).

Although the person in the street probably would say that brain problems cause reading problems, there is mounting evidence that this view may not be true. In at least two studies (Simos et al., 2002; Temple et al., 2003), there is evidence that providing intensive remedial instruction actually changes brain functions. The Today's Technology box on page 396 shows how modern medicine is revealing that teaching changes brains.

## Instructional Tactics

There are many specific techniques teachers can use to help students acquire reading skills. We describe some that have been effective with students with reading problems.

### Fluency Enhancement

When students do not read fluently, their rendition of a passage is choppy, halting, and stumbling. But problems of dysfluent reading also affect other areas. For example, students with reading problems may read material about science at only half the speed of their nondisabled peers (Parmar, Deluca, & Janczak, 1994). When students can read accurately but slowly (see guidelines in Table 12.2, page 371), they will probably benefit from instruction designed to improve fluency.

Students should have opportunities to practice reading fluently, and there are many ways to provide these. One popular method for providing practice is called repeated readings (e.g., National Reading Panel, 2000; Samuels, 1979, 1981; Samuels,

## Do Dyslexic Brains Cause Reading Problems, or Vice Versa?

One of the most common assumptions in learning disabilities is that biological differences cause behavioral differences. People assume that children who have problems with learning probably have those difficulties because of differences in their biological makeup, specifically, differences in their neurological structures or functions. For example, children who have reading problems have those problems because they are "wired differently." However, current technology allows scientists to examine brain functioning and the results of some of these studies challenge this assumption.

Magnetic source imaging (MSI) (functional magnetic resonance imaging—fMRI; see Chapter 9) allows scientists to detect which parts of an individual's brain are active when an individual is performing a particular task. With MSI, researchers can examine what parts of many people's brains are used during, for example, the reading of words. If individuals with dyslexia are using different parts of their brains than individuals who read normally, then there must be an association between the MSI-revealed activities of the brain used by the different groups and the reading performance of those groups. For individuals with dyslexia, MSIs show, for example, that many more areas of the brain are activated than for normally reading individuals. A natural interpretation is that this reflects different biological structure in the brains of people with reading problems.

An alternative interpretation is that instead of the brain making it possible for children to learn from instruction, instruction may program the brain! Studies that describe the functioning of the brain before and after remedial reading intervention show that this possibility, which seemed so improbable in the last millennium, may be accurate (Simos et al., 2002; Temple et al., 2003). These studies show that as children learn to read, the MSI data for their brains become more organized, looking more and more like the brains of normal readers.

Schermer, & Reinking, 1992). Many special education students do not have enough opportunities to practice reading:

> This is not done in training athletes and musicians. Basketball players practice jump shots over and over again; musicians practice short musical selections repeatedly. Their goal is to develop skills to a level of fluid accuracy. With enough practice, they do not have to devote much attention to the mechanics of their skills. With enough practice, readers will not have to devote much attention to the mechanics of decoding. (Samuels, 1981, pp. 23–24)

Several factors affect fluency (Chard et al., 2002; O'Connor et al., 2002). Fluent reading is substantially improved by practice, especially repeated practice with material at the right level of difficulty, and corrective feedback about performance that includes clear standards or criteria. Repeated reading even enhances the benefits of otherwise strong remedial reading instruction for both younger and older students receiving remedial reading (Archer, Gleason, & Vachon, 2003; Harris, Machand-Martella, & Martella, 2000; Steventon & Frederick, 2003).

Research with students who have learning disabilities shows that repeated practice aids both fluency and comprehension, not only for those with severe difficulties, but also for those who experience moderate problems with reading (Bos, 1982; Chard et al., 2002; Kuhn & Stahl, 2003; Mather & Goldstein, 1999; Rashotte & Torgesen, 1985, Sindelar, Monda, & O'Shea, 1990). However, the benefits of repeated reading occur mostly when the same passage is reread; otherwise, repeated reading helps mostly to the extent that there are common words in the practiced passage and in the material read later.

Another way to provide additional practice is to give a preview of the reading materials (e.g., the teacher may lead students in a discussion of the story in a passage they are about to read). Although previews may take different forms, the most widely studied method with students who have reading problems is for someone else to read the passage aloud before the students read it themselves. The previewer is usually an adult, but a peer may read the passage, or it can be tape recorded. Multiple studies show that previewing improves the rate and accuracy of students' reading of passages (Rose, 1984a, b, c; Rose & Sherry, 1984; Rose & Beattie, 1986; Salend & Nowack, 1988).

## Peer-Mediated Instruction

Peer-mediated instruction occurs when one student provides instruction for another student. Peer-mediated instruction has been used extensively in special education and can be used in both reading and other areas of instruction (Fuchs, Fuchs, & Burish, 2000; Greenwood, Delquadri, & Carta, 1988; Maheady, Harper, & Sacca, 1988; Mastropieri et al., 2001). It is sometimes called peer tutoring or classwide peer tutoring (CWPT). Although there are many variations on classwide peer tutoring, most have common features.

> There are four, primary components to the CWPT program: (a) weekly competing teams, (b) a highly structured tutoring procedure, (c) daily point earning and public posting of pupil performance, and (d) direct practice in functional instructional activities. In using CWPT, the teacher's role changes from primary "deliverer" of instruction to facilitator and monitor of peer-teaching activities. (Maheady, Harper, & Mallette, 2003, p. 1)

The tutoring procedures often involve the tutor following an explicit script. The script tells the tutor what questions to ask, what answers to expect, and what to do if the answers are correct or incorrect. For example, a tutor might ask the tutee to say the sounds for individual letters presented on flash cards. If the tutee says the correct sound, the tutor would acknowledge the accuracy of the answer and go to the next card. If the tutee says the wrong sound or does not know the sound, the tutor would supply the correct sound and give the tutee another chance to answer correctly. Obviously, such instruction requires that the tutors know the correct and incorrect answers. Thus, peer tutoring plans must be developed and implemented carefully.

Peer tutoring has been applied to teaching both beginning and remedial reading as well as content areas such as high school science (Mastropieri et al., 2001; Mastropieri, Scruggs, & Graetz, 2003; Mathes, Torgesen, & Allor, 2001; Mathes & Fuchs, 1993). Not only can teachers use peer-mediated strategies with learners of different ages and subject areas, but they can also apply it to teaching different aspects of reading. Researchers have demonstrated peer-mediated instruction in teaching decoding, fluency, and comprehension (Fuchs et al., 2000; Mastropieri, Scruggs, Spencer, & Fontana, 2003; Mathes, Fuchs, Fuchs, Henley, & Sanders, 1994).

Council for Exceptional Children

**CEC Knowledge Check**
Describe how you might use prerecorded audiocassettes or CD ROMs of books for your students. Can reading comprehension be affected by listening comprehension? LD4S11, LD6K2

Council for Exceptional Children

**CEC Knowledge Check**
Does peer tutoring sound like fun? Can students learn when they are having fun? Is peer tutoring a skill you want to develop and use? Why? LD4S6, CC5K5, CC7S7

## Reciprocal Teaching

Reciprocal teaching integrates features of different instructional models, particularly the cognitive and constructivist views of learning disabilities (see Chapter 10). It emphasizes **scaffolded instruction,** an important feature of instruction for students with learning disabilities (Kame'enui & Carnine, 1998). Although it can be conducted in a tutorial format, reciprocal teaching often

**scaffolded instruction** an instructional technique in which the teacher provides assistance as the student is first learning a task but gradually removes help so that the student can do the task independently

> refers to an instructional procedure that takes place in a collaborative learning group and features guided practice in the flexible application of four concrete strategies to the task of text comprehension: questioning, summarizing, clarifying, and predicting. The teacher and group of students take turns leading discussions regarding the content of the text they are jointly attempting to understand. (Palincsar & Klenk, 1992, p. 213)

Council for
Exceptional
Children

**CEC Knowledge Check**
Would you use reciprocal teaching all the time, or periodically with another method such as Direct Instruction? CC3K2, CC5K5, CC7S7

Advocates of reciprocal teaching stress the importance of having instruction occur within a social context, of initially providing supports (prompts or scaffolds) to help students perform activities, and of having students demonstrate their increasing competence by explaining to others how to do things. In teaching reading comprehension, instructors model how to derive ideas from a text, help students do so by asking questions, and have students explain to teachers and peers what they have learned from reading a passage. Reciprocal teaching is also readily applied to composition instruction (Klinger & Vaughn, 1998).

## Comprehension Strategies

Although it is crucial for students to be able to decode the printed word fluently, competent decoding does not ensure adequate comprehension of the material. Thus, teachers must also teach students how to use strategies to comprehend what they read. But strategy training by itself may not be sufficient. Furthermore, students rarely know how to extract themes from what they read. Research on reading comprehension in learning disabilities has led to methods that address these needs, including procedural facilitation, enhanced strategy training, and gist comprehension training (Gersten, Fuchs, Williams, & Barker, 2001).

***Procedural Facilitation*** One method for improving comprehension that has gained substantial currency in the last few decades is the use of procedural facilitation, in which students are taught a strategy or set of procedures for accomplishing a task. A valuable application of procedural facilitation to reading comprehension is called story grammar, which is a general or fairly standard system for organizing the content of what one reads or writes (see discussion in Chapter 13). One would expect to find a story grammar that includes important questions with answers in a passage of prose: Who was involved? Where did the action take place? What happened?

This strategy and others like it have been used successfully with students with learning disabilities (e.g., Carnine & Kinder, 1985; Gardill & Jitendra, 1999; Gurney, Gersten, Dimino, & Carnine, 1990; Mathes et al., 1994; Idol & Croll, 1987). Moreover, the connection between using story grammar for reading comprehension and for written expression makes it a good candidate for inclusion in an integrated language arts program for students with learning disabilities.

***Strategy Training*** Teachers can also teach students general-case strategies for comprehension skills. For example, there are strategies to help students answer questions about the sequence of events in stories they read. Sequence questions require readers to indicate which event happened first, next, and last in the story. Many students have difficulty with this type of task. Teachers can show them how to locate each part of the possible answer in the story and mark it. Then the students can determine the order of those parts and use that order to answer the question (Carnine, Prill, & Armstrong, 1978). Another type of comprehension task has students answer questions that require understanding sentences with clauses. Passive voice clauses often cause confusion; a sentence of this type is "Henry, who was kissed by Joan, ran home crying" (Kame'enui, Carnine, & Maggs, 1980). Students can be taught to restate the original sentence as two separate sentences so they can answer questions about it (e.g., "Who did the kissing? Who was crying?").

Borkowski and his colleagues (e.g., Grotelushchen, Borkowski, & Hale, 1991) maintain that strategy training in itself is insufficient. They agree that teaching students to use strategies is very important, but add that students also must learn to persist in using strategies and to attribute their success to their own efforts (see also Chapter 7). In one study, Borkowski, Wehring, and Carr (1988) had teachers demonstrate the use of strategies with memory tasks so that students learned that using those strategies improved their performance on the memory tasks. Then the teachers taught the students a strategy for summarizing the main ideas and other aspects of what they read. Later, the teachers modeled how to use the strategies even under difficult conditions. When the teachers made mistakes, they reverted to using the strategies, thus illustrating the value of persistence in using the original plan. Throughout the demonstrations and practice sessions, the teachers emphasized positive attributions for success. Students who received the entire package of training had better scores on comprehension measures than those who were taught only the reading comprehension strategy.

Learning strategies instruction is often associated with the work of University of Kansas researchers, who have developed many useful techniques that can be taught to adolescents with learning disabilities (see Deshler, Ellis, & Lenz, 1996; Lenz, 2000). As students move from learning to read into reading to learn, especially in the secondary grades, they must acquire skills that permit them to comprehend what they read in science, social studies, and other content areas. Deshler and colleagues have promoted many strategies to meet this need. Included among them are systems to teach students paraphrasing (read the paragraph; ask yourself questions; restate the main idea), a first-letter strategy for recalling key content (scan the text for key terms; create a mnemonic based on the letters of the terms), and others.

***Gist Comprehension Training*** One of the most challenging things to teach students with learning disabilities is gist comprehension. As discussed earlier in this chapter, Williams (1991) found students with learning disabilities particularly deficient in getting the theme or message from what they read. In subsequent research, Williams evaluated an instructional program for helping students identify and interpret themes. She and her colleagues taught upper-elementary-school-aged students a general strategy for extracting themes from what they read. This strategy encouraged the students to use a series of organizing questions, some of which are similar to those a teacher would use as part of teaching story grammar (e.g., "Who is the main character?") and some of which guided students to evaluate the story situation (e.g., "Was this good or bad?"). Teachers modeled how these organizing questions could lead to the development of statements about what the main character should do and then helped the students generalize these themes to real-life situations. The program Williams and her colleagues provided helped both students with and without learning disabilities gain greater facility in identifying themes, regardless of whether they were compared to uninstructed peers or to peers who received an alternative form of instruction (Williams, 2003; Williams, Brown, Silverstein, & deCani, 1994).

Because teachers hope they can teach students to learn things on their own, preparing students to extract themes from what they read is an important skill. Students with learning disabilities apparently have trouble with this aspect of higher-level comprehension, so procedures for teaching this are still sorely needed. The work of Williams and her colleagues represents important progress in teaching these complex, subtle skills and points the way toward future developments in high-quality instruction.

Effectively addressing the reading problems of students with learning disabilities is a complex and demanding task. It requires the very best instruction that schools can provide. In the last decades of the twentieth century, researchers made great progress in identifying the problems students experience in learning to read and ways to prevent or correct those problems. Although further research will continue to be needed, teachers who are informed about the evidence about effective instructional practices can apply their knowledge to help lessen reading problems and the negative consequences of failing to learn how to read.

**Council for Exceptional Children**

**CEC Knowledge Check**

Do you feel overwhelmed by so many options for intervention? Do you wonder "If the experts can't agree, what hope do I have in choosing the correct strategies"? CC9S2, CC9S11

**Council for Exceptional Children**

**CEC Content Standards**

4. Instructional Strategies
5. Learning Environments and Social Interactions
6. Communication

## PORTFOLIO-BUILDING ACTIVITY

### Demonstrating Mastery of the CEC Standards

Use the information in Chapter 12 to create a reading summative table with the following headings: Method, Skills, Description, Strengths, Concerns, Research. See the Companion Website (www.ablongman.com/hallahanLD3e) for (1) specific directions on how to create your table and (2) an example to follow. Questions to think about as you progress:

- What research-supported instructional interventions can special education teachers use that will enhance reading performance skills for individuals with learning disabilities?

- Of these interventions, which ones emphasize the development, maintenance, and generalization of reading skills across environments?

- How can special education teachers use reading interventions to help general education teachers integrate individuals with learning disabilities into inclusion classrooms?

- Are assistive technologies for reading appropriate for students with learning disabilities to use at all ages and grade levels? If so, why, or why not?

# SUMMARY

## What is reading?

- Reading has been defined in many different ways.
- Reading is a tool for learning content and for entertainment.

## What are the major elements of reading?

- Reading requires mastery of the alphabetic principle.
- Reading requires fluent decoding.
- Reading requires comprehension of content.

## What problems do students with learning disabilities have in reading?

- Students who have difficulty with reading may have problems with the phonology of the English language, decoding of print, fluency in decoding, or comprehending what they have read.
- Students may have difficulty with any one of these aspects of reading or with several of the areas.

## How is reading performance assessed?

- Educators may screen large numbers of students to identify those who need help with reading.
- They may use various instruments to diagnose problems—that is, to pinpoint the areas of difficulty and plan programs to correct those problems.
- Educators should use simple assessments of students' reading performance so that they can monitor progress and make instruction efficient.

## How common are reading problems in learning disabilities?

- The prevalence of reading problems depends on the criteria researchers use to decide whether an individual has or does not have problems.

- About as many as 6 to 8% of school-age children have reading scores that are substantially lower than expected based on their general ability.
- Reading problems are the most common form of learning disabilities, but not all students with learning disabilities have reading problems.

## How can instruction help prevent reading disabilities?

- Instruction can provide appropriate activities for teaching the alphabetic principle, including phonemic awareness, phonics, fluency, and comprehension.
- Instruction that is systematic and explicit has the best record for preventing reading problems.

## How can instruction help remediate learning disabilities in reading?

- Instruction should identify the unique educational needs of students with reading problems, address those needs directly (i.e., explicitly and systematically), and employ tactics that have consistently proven to be effective.
- Historical approaches include the Fernald Word Learning Approach, the Hegge-Kirk-Kirk Remedial Reading Drills, and the Orton-Gillingham approach. These approaches stress the multisensory, or VAKT, view.
- Contemporary approaches include Reading Recovery, the Corrective Reading Program, and computer-aided instruction.
- Instructional tactics include fluency enhancement practice, peer-mediated instruction, reciprocal teaching, and comprehension strategies, which include procedural facilitation, strategy training, and gist comprehension training.

## REFLECTIONS ON THE CASES

1. What was the same about the problems that Jamal and Shannon experienced in reading in the elementary grades? What was different about their early reading?

2. What do you predict will happen to Jamal's knowledge about the world around him if he does not develop fluency in decoding?

3. What did Mr. Martens mean when he talked about Shannon learning "faster than she normally would"?

## *Focus On* Reading

### *Do Now Activities to Promote Comprehension*

## Comprehension Strategies—Industry Standards

● *What are they*

Five basic comprehension strategies proven to increase student understanding of text are predicting, summarizing, retelling, rereading, and questioning (Swanson & De La Paz, 1998). These strategies are particularly valuable for students with learning disabilities in helping address their inefficiency in recognizing semantic cues.

● *How to implement them*

When teaching strategies to students, teach only one strategy at a time. A new strategy should not be introduced until an old one is established. Most strategies will take more than three lessons before students are able to employ the strategy either independently or with less teacher support. When planning to introduce a new strategy, plan for one day of modeling and guiding students through the strategy prior to having them independently practice the strategy.

- **Predicting**

  Prior to reading, activate and assess students' prior knowledge through predicting activities. Students can make predictions based on the story title, a scanning of story pictures, or past experience with the topics, themes, or characters in the story. Predicting sets a purpose for learning and guides comprehension.

  > *Teacher:* Look at the title of our story—"Frog and Toad Are Friends." What do you think this story is going to be about?
  > *Student:* Frogs who can talk!
  > *Student:* Friendship and what it means to be a friend.
  > *Student:* Swamps.
  > *Teacher:* Excellent. Let's read the story to find out if our predictions are correct.

  Predicting activities should be brief and can occur throughout the reading process. (*Note:* Spending a great deal of time on predicting can take away from the momentum of a lesson and detract from focused reading.)

- **Summarizing**

  The goal of summarizing is for students to identify the main idea of a story. Teaching students strategies for summarizing helps them focus on main idea concepts. Two strategies for summarizing are the one-sentence summary and paragraph shrinking.
  - **One-sentence summarizing.** Have students read a paragraph or a short section of a book and then sum up what was read in one sentence. Students can share their summaries with each other and then vote on who did the best job of summarizing in one sentence.
  - **Paragraph shrinking.** Ask students to name the "who" or "what" of the story. Then have students write who or what the paragraph was about in ten words or less. (*Note:* This technique is designed to help students identify the main idea of a paragraph but can also be used for a story.)

- **Retelling**

  Allow opportunities for students to retell stories after they have read them or listened to them. Retellings can be scored for
  - inclusion of main idea,
  - correct chronological sequence, or
  - inclusion of characters, settings, and main events

- **Rereading**

  Teach students a variety of rereading strategies.
  - One strategy is the "look back" strategy. If a student does not know the answer to a question, teach students how to look back in the story to find the answer.
  - Another strategy is reading for fluency. Teach students to reread a sentence or paragraph if they had difficulty with more than two words. Rereading of familiar books also encourages fluency (speed and accuracy when reading)—an important component to comprehension.

- **Questioning**

  Have students ask the following questions when reading a selection of text: who, what, when, where, and how. These words can be printed on cards for a variety of instructional uses. Students reading in small groups can randomly select a card and answer the prompt, or students working in pairs can select a card and prompt their partner to answer the question. Teachers can also use the cards to select questions for students.

### Additional Resources

Dacruz Payne, C., & Browning Schulman, M. (2000). *Guided Reading: Making it work.* New York: Scholastic.

## Story Mapping

### What is it?

Story mapping is a visual organizer used to teach students structural elements of a story. Story maps allow students to relate story events and make connections among critical story elements. A basic map may only include the concepts of beginning, middle, and end, whereas a complex map may include questions about characters, setting, and events (see sample maps below). Teaching students structural elements of a story enables them to anticipate the type of information they should be looking for as they read and strengthens their recall of story events. The goal of story mapping is to have students internalize key features of stories. Students with learning disabilities typically have difficulty with such tasks as identifying characters and themes. The explicit and visual nature of story mapping supports development of these skills with students with learning disabilities.

Story mapping has been shown to be successful in increasing these students' ability to retell stories and remember key story features.

● *How to do it*

Teachers can create their own story maps with headings to match their instructional goals. Appropriate headings can include story structure (e.g., characters, settings, and main events) or questions (e.g., who, what, when, where, and how). In the boxes, students will fill in answers to the prompts or questions. Below are two examples of story maps:

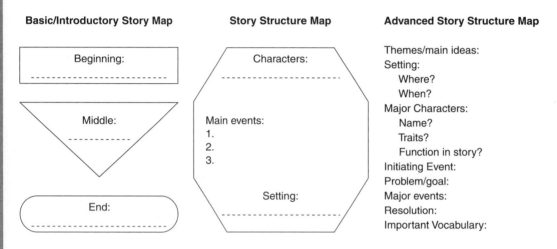

**Basic/Introductory Story Map**

Beginning:

Middle:

End:

**Story Structure Map**

Characters:

Main events:
1.
2.
3.

Setting:

**Advanced Story Structure Map**

Themes/main ideas:
Setting:
 Where?
 When?
Major Characters:
 Name?
 Traits?
 Function in story?
Initiating Event:
Problem/goal:
Major events:
Resolution:
Important Vocabulary:

When introducing story mapping to students, teachers should model how to complete the story map on several occasions prior to having students independently complete a map. Story mapping typically occurs after an initial reading of the story. During the modeling process, teachers should use self-instruction statements (think-alouds). For example:

> *Teacher:* As I reread our story, I am filling in the names of the characters. We just met the main character. What is her name?
> *Students:* Goldilocks.
> *Teacher:* Excellent listening. I am going to list Goldilocks as our first character. As I do that, who can remind us what a character is?
> *Student:* A person in the story.
> *Teacher:* Wonderful definition. Yes, a character is a person in the story and Goldilocks is the first person we found. I will write her name in the section labeled "Characters." Let's see if we find some more . . .

Once students have mastered the structural elements, teachers should fade out the graphic organizer.

● *Additional Resource*

Interactive story map Website at www.readwritethink.org/materials/storymap/
Lesson plan and grading rubric Website at www.education-world.com/a_tsl/archives/ 01-1/lesson0019.shtml

# Letter-Sound Matching

## ● *What is it?*

Letter-sound matching is a fundamental beginning phonics skill. A defining characteristic of students with leaning disabilities is their difficulty with phonics. Explicit, direct instruction of letter-sound correspondences is a critical first step for students learning to read. Carnine, Silbert, and Kame'enui (1996) recommend teaching students letter-sound correspondences in the following order: consonants, short vowels, consonant blends, consonant digraphs (e.g., /sh/, /th/, /wh/, /ck/, /ng/), silent *e,* long vowel/open syllable (e.g., /me/, /I/), vowel teams, and finally, diphthongs (e.g., /oi/, /ow/, /ou/).

## ● *How to do it*

One proven strategy for teaching students letter sounds is the model-lead-test approach. Although the strategy appears simplistic, this can be a powerful strategy. Having students practice the correct sound repeatedly reinforces the connection.

- **Model-lead-test**
  - Point to a letter and say the sound of the letter. (*model*)
  - Point to a letter on a card, chart, or the board. State, "This letter makes the sound /mmmm/. What sound does this letter make?" Signal the students to respond with you. Remember to drag out continuous sounds and stop with stop sounds. (*lead*)
  - Point to the letter. Ask the group or an individual student to say the matching sound as you point to a letter. (*test*)
  - Repeat this process often for each letter. Repetition will reinforce the concept and increase the connection.

  (*Note:* Continuous sounds are *a* (*cat*), *e* (*met*), *f, i* (*fit*), *l, m, n, o* (*cot*), *r, s, u* (*nut*), *v, w, y, z.* Stop sounds are *b, c, d, g, h, j, k, p, q, t, x.* Teaching students to stretch the continuous sounds leads the way for blending—a critical sounding out skill.)

  Games and partner work are other excellent ways to increase the number of exposures (learning opportunities) students will have with a given letter-sound match.

- **Flash cards**
  - Students can work in partners to quiz each other on sounds. It is important that students practice the sounds correctly when working independently from the teacher. To ensure correct practice, the front of the flash card shows the letter, and the back of the flash card shows a representational or key word picture. For example, on the back of the S card there could be a picture of Sam the Snake.
  - Students can track the sounds they got correctly and the sounds they need more practice with by placing the correct and incorrect flash cards in piles as they play.

- **Bingo**
  - Create a variety of student boards that have the letters that you are currently teaching. The "caller" (the teacher or a student) selects a letter from a bowl and makes the sound of that letter.
  - Students cover the corresponding letter/letter combination if they have it on their board.

*Source:* Kristin L. Sayeski

## What Handwriting Problems Do Students Experience?
- Problems with Letter Formation
- Problems with Fluency
- Causes and Effects of Handwriting Problems

## How Is Handwriting Performance Assessed?
- Planning Handwriting Instruction
- Monitoring Handwriting Progress

## What Interventions Can Help with Handwriting Difficulties?
- Teacher Modeling and Student Practice
- Reinforcement
- Self-Instruction Training

## What Spelling Problems Do Students Experience?
- Spelling Errors
- Effects of Spelling Problems

## How Is Spelling Performance Assessed?
- Standardized Assessment
- Planning Spelling Instruction
- Monitoring Progress in Spelling

## What Interventions Help Students' Spelling Difficulties?
- Developmental Interventions
- Remedial Interventions
- Effective Teaching Procedures

## What Composition Problems Do Students Experience?

## How Is Composition Performance Assessed?
- Screening
- Planning Composition Instruction
- Monitoring Progress in Composition

## What Interventions Help Students with Composition Difficulties?
- Developmental Interventions
- Remedial Interventions
- Effective Teaching Procedures

**Council for Exceptional Children**

See Companion Website for detailed correlations between chapter content and Council for Exceptional Children Standards; **www.ablongman.com/ hallahanLD3e**

### CEC Knowledge and Skills Discussed in This Chapter

1. Learning characteristics of students that impact their performance in the area of written language, which includes basic preskills.

2. Instruction decisions in written language, which are based on authentic student assessment findings, including error analysis and scope and sequence of general and special curricula.

3. Written language instruction, which includes methods for creating legible communication, spelling accuracy, and the organization and fluent composition of written products.

4. Students' self-assessment and performance progress monitoring, as well as peer evaluation, which encourage active participation in the learning process.

5. Teaching individuals with learning disabilities how to use written language for successful transitions to independence, including assistive technologies.

# Students Who Experience Difficulties with Writing

# 13

It's not too surprising that he has terrific spelling problems, too. Both the decoding and encoding parts of written language use sounds and phonological awareness.

*Alice Hamilton, Jamal's first-grade teacher*

Council for Exceptional Children

**CEC Knowledge Check**

What font or typeface is used in your writing curriculum and reading materials? Is there a possibility of confusion between New Times Roman *g* and Century Gothic *g*? LD4S11

Students who have difficulties with oral language and reading often also have problems with writing. Just as it is important to be able to express oneself clearly in spoken language and to be able to read written language, one should be able to communicate in writing.

Written expression requires skills in three major areas: handwriting, spelling, and composition. Although expression of thoughts and feelings may be more important than the mechanical aspects of writing, such problems as illegible handwriting, misspellings, grammatical inaccuracies, and poor organization can make it difficult for a reader to understand the meaning of a written piece. Effective writers are skilled enough in these three major areas of written expression to communicate with minimal misunderstanding.

In this chapter, we focus on each major area of written expression: handwriting, spelling, and composition. Dividing written expression into these categories is useful for discussion purposes, but the areas overlap. Emphasizing their common features is one of the values of thinking about language as a whole, integrated group of competencies. This overlap is important to consider when designing and instituting assessment and intervention programs and techniques. Just as teachers need to coordinate their instruction in spelling, reading, and writing, they should also coordinate their instruction in handwriting, spelling, and composition.

## What Handwriting Problems Do Students Experience?

Handwriting has long been an area of interest to those concerned with learning disabilities. Perhaps this is because some individuals with writing disabilities produce

**dysgraphia** a written-language disorder that concerns the mechanical writing skill—may be characterized by poor letter formation; letters that are too large, too small, or inconsistent in size; incorrect use of capital and lower case letters; letters that are crowded and cramped; inconsistent spacing between letters; incorrect alignment; incorrect or inconsistent slant of cursive letters; lack of fluency in writing; and/or slow writing

Council for Exceptional Children

**CEC Knowledge Check**

How many of these nine characteristics would a student need to exhibit for you to initiate further assessment?
CC8S2, CC8S6

clearly deviant writing (e.g., scrawling letter formation), thereby providing a tangible product for study. However, handwriting, or penmanship, as it was once called, is a means to an end, a tool. It should not be stressed at the expense of other important skills, such as those necessary to speak, listen, read, spell, or compose well.

Sometimes handwriting problems are known as **dysgraphia,** which is "a written-language disorder that concerns the mechanical writing skill. It manifests itself in poor writing performance in children of at least average intelligence who do not have a distinct neurological disability and/or an overt perceptual-motor handicap" (Hamstra-Bletz & Blote, 1993, as cited in Bos & Vaughn, 2002, p. 264).

Students with dysgraphia may exhibit any or all of the following characteristics:

1. Poor letter formation
2. Letters that are too large, too small, or inconsistent in size
3. Incorrect use of capital and lower case letters
4. Letters that are crowded and cramped
5. Inconsistent spacing between letters
6. Incorrect alignment (letters do not rest on a base line)
7. Incorrect or inconsistent slant of cursive letters
8. Lack of fluency in writing
9. Slow writing even when asked to write as quickly as possible (Weintraub and Graham, 1998, as cited in Bos & Vaughn, 2002, pp. 264–265)

## Problems with Letter Formation

Handwriting problems include malformation of letters, poor spacing (both vertically and horizontally), and extremely slow writing. Everyone occasionally produces some illegible letters, but some students do so frequently enough that understanding what they have written is difficult. In such cases, handwriting is considered a problem. Also, most children write quite slowly when they are first learning to print or write in cursive. Slow handwriting is a problem, however, when students' writing speed interferes with their other work. Jamal's teacher explains:

**Jamal**

It takes Jamal a long time to complete any written task . . . much longer than the other students. He doesn't like to write. I think it's because it's so difficult for him. He gets very frustrated when he's unable to form certain letters.

*Alice Hamilton, Jamal's first-grade teacher*

**far-point copying** copying material from a distant source to a piece of paper

**near-point copying** copying material from a model on one's desk to a piece of paper

Students sometimes have difficulty simply copying materials from one source to another. Copying material from a chalkboard to a piece of paper is sometimes called **far-point copying.** Its complement is **near-point copying,** which involves copying from a model the student has on the desk. Some children have greater difficulty with far-point copying than near-point copying, perhaps (but not necessarily) due to problems with visual acuity.

Students sometimes write letters backward or reverse letters, seeming to substitute one for another (e.g., *b* for *d*). The substituted letter looks like the correct letter, except it is rotated. For example, a student might write *bog* for the word *dog*. **Reversal errors** are common when children are first learning to read and write (Bos & Vaughn, 2002). When students continue to reverse letters, it is sometimes taken as an indicator of underlying psychological or physiological disability. Some children with learning disabilities continue to experience reversals, but most do not. These facts undermine the mistaken contention that reversal errors indicate fundamental learning problems.

**reversal errors** the apparent substitution of one letter for another (*b* for *d*); these types of mistakes are common when children are first learning to read and write

## Problems with Fluency

A common handwriting problem for some students with learning disabilities is fluency. Many such students write so slowly and laboriously that they appear to be drawing each letter (Moats, 1983). Slow and labored handwriting will probably have negative effects on performance in other areas of written expression. Students who write slowly may lose their place more frequently; their slow writing makes it harder—especially for students with memory problems—to remember where they were.

## Causes and Effects of Handwriting Problems

Handwriting skills are related to some perceptual and perceptual-motor skills. Young students with handwriting problems have greater difficulties with items requiring them to find a picture of items in the same spatial orientation as shown in a sample, draw poorly when drawing requires crossing from one side of their bodies to the other, and do not benefit as much as other students from practice or handwritinglike tasks (Chapman & Wedell, 1972; Wedell & Home, 1969).

Students with poor handwriting are likely to lack spelling skills. There are at least two ways in which handwriting may contribute to misspellings. The first is legibility; the second is speed. Handwriting errors may make a word look like another word. Labored writing of letters may cause students to forget the word they are trying to spell or lose their place partway through spelling it.

# How Is Handwriting Performance Assessed?

Experienced teachers can readily recognize poor handwriting, so formal tests are not essential. In fact, testing for spelling and composition often provides samples suitable for at least preliminary evaluation. The examples of handwriting in Figure 13.1 (page 410) illustrate different degrees of poor handwriting. On the first two examples, the teacher wrote clarifications to help the students.

## Planning Handwriting Instruction

Students with handwriting problems—even those with dysgraphia—should not avoid writing altogether, as "writing is an important life skill necessary for signing

**FIGURE 13.1** Three Samples of Young Children's Handwriting

A

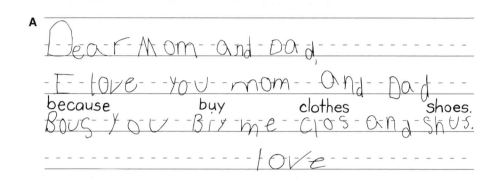

Dear Mom and Dad,
I love you mom and Dad
because          buy          clothes          shoes.
Bous you Biy me clos and shus.
love

B

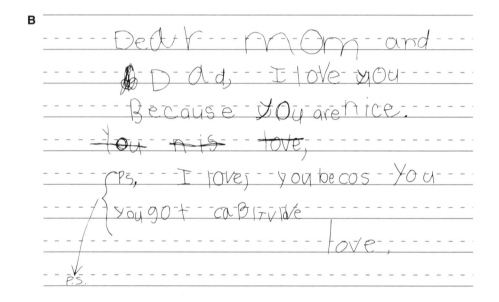

Dear mom and
Dad, I love you
Because you are nice.
You nis love,
PS, I love you be cos you
you got caBltvlve
love,
P.S.

C

On niet ther wus a Gray and in that Gray
Thr wa brk brk has and in that brk brk
haus thr wus a brk brk sar'a up tos sras
Th wos a brk brk rom and in that brk brk
rom Thr wos a brk brk bed and in that brk brk
bed wass a Pirosn and that Pros was
a mrstr.

documents, filling out forms, writing checks, taking telephone messages or writing a grocery list" (Richards, 1999, p. 2). To plan an instructional program, teachers need to determine which specific letters, types of letters, letter combinations, or other features of handwriting cause individual students difficulty. The *Basic School Skills Inventory—Diagnostic* (Hammill & Leigh, 1983) includes a writing test that assesses aspects of handwriting, including posture and holding a pencil as well as forming letters; the test is norm referenced and includes remedial recommendations.

As with screening, formal diagnostic testing of handwriting is usually unnecessary. Teachers can simply examine samples of students' writing and identify those parts of writing that need further instructional work. To conduct a diagnostic evaluation, a teacher first examines existing samples of students' writing to judge whether there are general legibility problems (e.g., inconsistent spacing between letters or excessive erasures). Second, the teacher determines whether the sample contains any of the more common types of handwriting errors (refer to Figure 13.1 for examples). Third, the teacher directs the student to produce another handwriting sample (copying from prepared materials) that includes areas not assessed in the first sample or areas that the first assessment has revealed might become problems for the student.

Students' performances on different writing tasks will vary. For example, far-point copying may be more difficult than near-point copying for some students, and both may be easier (or harder) for some students than producing letters when no model is available. Assessment should evaluate these different possibilities. Table 13.1 (page 412) describes assessment using various writing tasks and gives guidelines for judging accuracy and fluency on them. The activities teachers prescribe should depend on the kinds of mistakes students make.

## Monitoring Handwriting Progress

Teachers can use **curriculum-based assessment** to evaluate both the legibility and the speed of handwriting. Brief time periods for assessment can be set aside each day. Teachers can give students probes (i.e., short tests designed to assess the specific skill on which they need to work) and then ask them to write for a specified period of time (perhaps 1 or 2 minutes). The resulting writing samples can be scored for the percentage of letters written legibly (each letter to be judged as either legible or illegible) and the rate of letters written legibly (legible letters per minute). Table 13.1 provides general guidelines for appropriate rates.

Teachers can teach students to evaluate their own progress. The accuracy of students' judgments about their writing's legibility can be enhanced by using plastic overlays showing correctly formed letters or other self-correcting devices (Beck, Conrad, & Anderson, 1996; Jones, Trap, & Cooper, 1977; Stowitschek & Stowitschek, 1979). Self-evaluation improves the handwriting of students with learning disabilities (Kosiewicz, Hallahan, Lloyd, & Graves, 1982; Sweeney, Salva, Cooper, & Talbert-Johnson, 1993). Some commercial products, such as Basic Skill Builders (Beck et al., 1996), incorporate self-evaluation to utilize its beneficial effects on performance. As already emphasized, a teacher's major concerns about handwriting should be that it is legible and not so slow that production is impaired.

**curriculum-based assessment (CBA)** a formative evaluation method designed to evaluate performance in the particular curriculum to which students are exposed; usually involves giving students a small sample of items from the curriculum in use in their schools; proponents argue that CBA is preferable to comparing students with national norms or using tests that do not reflect the curriculum content learned by students

Council for
Exceptional
Children

**CEC Knowledge Check**
Self-evaluation of handwriting seems to enhance student remediation efforts. What priority do you place on self-evaluation? CC4S2, CC4S5, LD6K6

## TABLE 13.1    Guidelines for Assessing Handwriting

| PURPOSE | DIRECTIONS | ACCURACY STANDARD | SPEED STANDARD |
|---|---|---|---|
| • Free Writing<br><br>To provide a baseline for evaluating other tasks and for assessing progress | Identify the letters (e.g., alphabet) or words (e.g., names and familiar words) that the student can write readily. Direct the student to write the identified materials repeatedly, as quickly but as neatly as possible. | 95–100% | 60 characters per minute (cpm); 100 cpm, better |
| • Dictation<br><br>To evaluate a student's production of writing when she or he does not know what will come next | Decide whether to test individual letters, words, or phrases. Identify items you are sure the student can write without requiring much thinking (i.e., "known" items); you can use the same item several times in a test. Direct the student to write items as you say them. Watch closely, and, as the student finishes an item, say the next one. | 90–100% | 70% of standard for free writing |
| • Near-Point Copying<br><br>To evaluate a student's production of writing when she or he copies from materials on the desk | 1. Familiar: Select highly familiar material for the student to copy.<br><br>2. Unfamiliar: Select material the student has not previously seen but that is at about the same difficulty level as in the familiar condition.<br><br>Compare performances to estimate the contribution of familiarity. | 95–100% | 75–80% of standard for free writing |
| • Far-Point Copying<br><br>To evaluate a student's production of writing when she or he copies from a distant source (e.g., the chalkboard) | 1. Familiar: Select highly familiar material for the student to copy.<br><br>2. Unfamiliar: Select material the student has not previously seen but that is at about the same difficulty level as in the familiar condition.<br><br>Compare performances to estimate the contribution of familiarity. | 90–100% | 75–80% of standard for free writing |

# What Interventions Can Help with Handwriting Difficulties?

Teachers regularly confront the question of whether to teach manuscript or cursive. This fundamental question has yet to be resolved (Graham, 1999).

> Many learning-disability specialists advocate the use of instruction in only one form of handwriting, either manuscript or cursive. Some argue that manuscript is easier to learn, is more like book print, is more legible, requires less difficulty in making movement (Johnson and Myklebust, 1967), and should be the only writing form taught. Others feel cursive is faster, is continuous and connected, is more difficult to reverse letters, teaches the student to perceive whole words, and is easier to write. They feel cursive should be taught first as the only writing form. (Bos & Vaughn, 2002, p. 265)

Research does not show conclusively that a manuscript system is particularly easier to learn than a cursive system or that children write faster in either. In fact, by high school, most students have apparently developed a hybrid writing style that mixes printing and cursive and resembles italics (Duval, 1985). In the absence of solid research evidence substantiating the effectiveness of one script over another for students with learning disabilities, we support the recommendations of Graham (1999), who suggests that instruction begin with traditional manuscript letters. Further, "if cursive is introduced to students with LD, it should be taught after they have mastered manuscript" (Graham, 1999, p. 84).

## Teacher Modeling and Student Practice

For young students with reading and writing difficulties, effective handwriting instruction includes the following elements:

- teacher modeling
- teaching of letter names as students copied and wrote letters
- independent student practice
- tracing and writing letters with (then without) numbered arrow cues
- writing words
- copying sentences quickly to improve writing fluency (Edwards, 2003)

Jamal's teacher has had some success:

> Right now, Jamal very much dislikes writing, but I think that as he notices improvement, he'll be more confident that he can do it, and he'll like it more. He seems to enjoy tracing letters . . . especially the ones with arrow cues . . . with those, he knows exactly what to do.
>
> *Alice Hamilton, Jamal's first-grade teacher*

Council for Exceptional Children

**CEC Knowledge Check**

How important is this statement by Graham for students with learning disabilities? CC7K2

Council for Exceptional Children

**CEC Knowledge Check**

In this list of effective elements of instruction, where is self-evaluation? How would you include self-evaluation in this list? CC4S2, CC6S1

 Jamal

Council for
Exceptional
Children

**CEC Knowledge Check**

Would it be more effective for the teacher or for the student to graph results? Why?
CC4S2, CC4S5, LD6K7

Council for
Exceptional
Children

**CEC Knowledge Check**

All of this research was done in the 1970s. Why do you think so many students still have problems with handwriting? (Hint: Look at the next margin note)
LD3K2, LD4S11

**cognitive-behavioral techniques**  strategies through which individuals learn to think about, change, monitor, and track their behavior

**self-instruction**  a cognitive training method in which the teacher and then the student verbalize questions or instructions for performing a task

**self-recording**  a cognitive training method that requires individuals to track their behavior and document it on a sheet or graph

**phoneme**  any of the abstract units of the phonetic system of a language that correspond to a set of similar speech sounds that are perceived to be a single distinctive sound in the language

**grapheme**  the set of units of a writing system (letters and letter combinations) that represent a phoneme

In their handwriting instruction, teachers should focus on helping

> students develop writing that is legible and that can be produced quickly with little conscious attention. . . . Some teachers are not sure how much time students should spend practicing individual letters. It is not a good idea to apply massed practice procedures, where students practice the same letter over and over again in a single setting. Instead, once a letter is introduced, students should spend a short time carefully practicing it under the teacher's direction and evaluate the quality of their efforts (e.g., circle your two best formed letters). The letter should then be reviewed and practiced in subsequent sessions as needed. (Graham, 1999, pp. 84–85)

To increase handwriting speed, students need frequent opportunities to write. Teachers may want to try combining self-competition on timed exercises with reinforcement to increase motivation (Graham, 1999). In addition, teachers may want to keep graphs of the timed exercises to monitor students' progress. Graphing progress can be very reinforcing for students (Bos & Vaughn, 2002).

## Reinforcement

There is much evidence for a behaviorally oriented "near cure" for handwriting problems such as reversals. The procedure is simple: First, when the student writes a target letter, numeral, or word correctly, the teacher provides reinforcement (e.g., praise). Second, when the student writes an item incorrectly, the teacher requires the student to correct it. At least six studies have reported the successful use of this or a similar procedure (Fauke, Burnett, Powers, & Sulzer-Azaroff, 1973; Hasazi & Hasazi, 1972; Lahey, Busemeyer, O'Hara, & Beggs, 1977; Smith & Lovitt, 1973; Stromer, 1975, 1977).

## Self-Instruction Training

**Cognitive-behavioral techniques** such as **self-instruction** (Graham, 1982) and **self-recording** (Blandford & Lloyd, 1987) have also been used extensively for remediating handwriting problems. These techniques have proved effective with both younger students and high school students. For example, adolescents with learning disabilities received specialized instruction in using self-guiding statements and self-correction procedures (Sweeney et al., 1993). The instruction improved their performances markedly, as shown in Figure 13.2.

## What Spelling Problems Do Students Experience?

Because the English language appears irregular in its spellings, it is difficult to learn to spell. Spelling would be much easier if each **phoneme** of our language had one and only one **grapheme,** but that is not the case. There are 251 different spellings for the 44 sounds of English (Hull, 1981), and the language contains many irregularly

## FIGURE 13.2  Handwriting Improvement after Specialized Instruction

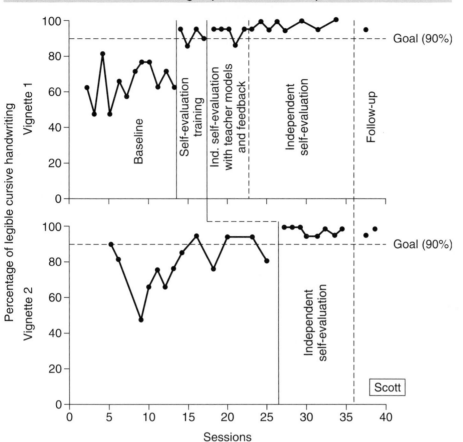

*Source:* From "Using Self-Evaluation to Improve Difficult-to-Read Handwriting of Secondary Students" by W. J. Sweeney, E. Salva, J. O. Cooper, and C. Talbert-Johnson, 1993, *Journal of Behavioral Education, 3,* p. 436. Copyright 1993 by Kluwer Academic/Plenum Publishers. Reprinted by permission.

spelled words. For example, *cough, tough, though,* and *through* all end with the same four letters but have different ending pronunciations. Teachers need to know not only how these and other oddities of English spelling work, but also enough about them to help students learn similarities and differences in words. Unfortunately, too few teacher education programs provide sufficient instruction for future teachers to develop a command of the relations between English sounds and their written equivalents (Moats, 1995).

The formal name for the system of representing spoken language in a written form is **orthography,** which comes from the Greek *ortho* ("straight," "regular," or "correct") and *graphy* ("process or manner of writing"). Thus, when students learn the orthography of English, they are learning the system for the correct spelling of English.

Council for Exceptional Children

**CEC Knowledge Check**
If this is the reality in education today, what can you do in your school to help remedy the situation for future students? When and who will turn this around? University faculty? General education teachers? Parents? LD4S1, LD9K1

**orthography**  the formal name for the system of representing spoken language in a written form; comes from the Greek ortho ("straight," "regular," or "correct") and graphy ("process or manner of writing")

## Spelling Errors

Spelling is a complex task requiring "the integration of phonological and orthographic knowledge" (Kamhi & Hinton, 2000, p. 38). Most of our knowledge about spelling problems comes from studies of the kinds of errors people make when they spell. Analyses of misspellings reveal that most errors are phonetically acceptable, made in the middle of words, and involve alterations of a single phoneme (Graham & Miller, 1979).

Figure 13.3 shows the results of a spelling test of a young student with learning disabilities. The words are drawn from the *Wide Range Achievement Test* (Jastak & Jastak, 1978); the correct words are (1) *go,* (2) *cat,* (3) *in,* (4) *baby,* (5) *and,* (6) *will,* (7) *make,* (8) *him,* (9) *say,* (10) *cut,* (11) *cook,* (12) *light,* (13) *must,* (14) *dress,* (15) *reach,* (16) *order,* (17) *watch,* and (18) *enter.* The girl who wrote the words was 8 years old. According to the test manual, her spelling performance was at the sixth month of the first grade; her score was at the tenth percentile. How many mistakes appear to be phonetically acceptable, made in the middle of the words, or show problems with just one phoneme? How many mistakes might simply reflect the quality of the girl's handwriting?

**FIGURE 13.3** Spelling Test of a Student with Learning Disabilities

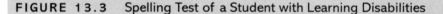

1. poy          16. unin
2. cat          17. ys
3. in           18. intn
4. bubu         19.
5. bna          20.
6. will         21.
7. mac          22.
8. Him          23.
9. Sa           24.
10. cot         25.
11. cuc         26.
12. ltat        27.
13. most        28.
14. nuis        29.
15. nis         30.

*Source:* From *Introduction to Learning Disabilities,* 2nd ed. (p. 246) by D. P. Hallahan, J. M. Kauffman, and J. W Lloyd, 1985, Boston: Allyn and Bacon. Copyright © 1985 by Pearson Education. Reprinted by permission of the publisher.

Children progress through a series of developmental stages as they learn to spell words (see Edwards, 2003; Treiman & Bourassa, 2000). Initially, they spell words quite simply (e.g., *type* as *TP*). Later, students represent all the phonemes of the word, although they might do so incorrectly (e.g., spelling *type* as *TIP*, a spelling that reads correctly if the letter *i* "says its name"). This strategy works well as long as the words are regularly pronounced consonant-vowel-consonant words. Still later, students may represent all the sounds and employ some of the conventions of orthography, although they still may not spell correctly (e.g., spelling *type* as *TIPE*). By the time they have reached the fifth grade, students have learned to use additional letters to indicate the pronunciation of parts of words (e.g., using the "silent *e*" rule) and appear to work by analogy (e.g., in trying to spell the word *criticize,* realizing it has a second *c* because they know the word *critic* has a second *c*).

The most consistent findings about the spelling of children with learning disabilities come from studies comparing normally achieving students with those who have reading problems (Barron, 1980; Bruck, 1988; Bruck & Treiman, 1990; Carlisle, 1987; Carpenter, 1983; Carpenter & Miller, 1982; Frith, 1980; Gerber & Hall, 1981; Lennox & Siegel, 1993, 1998; Moats, 1983; Nelson, 1980; Worthy & Invernizzi, 1990). Students with learning disabilities or severe reading problems

- do not necessarily produce unrecognizable spellings; "even when the errors are nonphonetic, they usually have a phonological basis" (Kamhi & Hinton, 2000, p. 42)
- have difficulty segmenting words and syllables into phonemes and their conventional, corresponding grapheme(s)
- seem to have particular difficulty with consonant clusters
- spell fewer words correctly than do their normally achieving age-mates, even when IQ differences are taken into account
- write words in ways that are more similar to those of younger students and show particular difficulty with morphological structure
- do not necessarily misspell words by making reversal errors

Indeed, the processes students with reading disabilities use to read and spell do not appear to differ qualitatively from those used by nondisabled students. However, older students with reading problems appear to produce errors that are better visual matches for the words than the errors of their peers at the same grade level (Lennox & Siegel, 1998). To date, evidence indicates that spelling, like reading, is very much of a language-based skill. In fact,

little evidence has been found for the importance of nonlinguistic factors such as visual memory. Individual differences in spelling ability are primarily caused by differences in the knowledge and use of sound-spelling information rather than differences in some nonlinguistic factor. Poor spellers may rely more on visual strategies than good spellers, but this is only because of their limited phonological knowledge. (Kamhi & Hinton, 2000, p. 48)

**phonemic awareness**
the ability to manipulate
the smallest units (i.e.,
phonemes) in spoken
words (e.g., What is the
first sound in *dog*? Say *smile*
without the /s/. What word
is /c/ /a/ /t/? How many
sounds do you hear in the
word *bike*?).

## Effects of Spelling Problems

Teachers working with students who have substantial spelling problems can expect these students to have difficulties in reading, in part, because of their difficulties with phonemic awareness. **Phonemic awareness** seems to be important in both the **decoding** aspect of reading and the **encoding** aspect of spelling (Hulme & Joshi, 1998). Jamal's teacher is aware of this relationship:

> I'm concerned about Jamal's spelling because of the problems he's having with letter sounds. He has a lot of trouble with segmenting tasks. He does well with beginning consonants—and fairly well with ending consonants—but he doesn't seem to hear the sounds in the middle of words.
>
> *Alice Hamilton, Jamal's first-grade teacher*

Jamal

**decoding**   the aspects of
reading that happen as the
reader converts the printed
words on the page into
more familiar spoken or
heard language

**encoding**   to express
and send a message; in
oral language or writing,
the ability to make oneself
understood

Council for
Exceptional
Children

**CEC Knowledge Check**

If one skill hampers the other, is it also true that if one skill is remediated the other will be affected positively? Why, or why not?
LD3K2, CC4S4

Spelling problems may actually hamper handwriting. A student who does not know how to spell a word automatically may experience a delay of the motor activity involved in writing the word. Stopping to think about the spelling of a word disrupts the smooth flow of handwriting or keyboarding. This illustrates the reciprocal nature of many learning problems: Handwriting fluency probably negatively affects spelling, and spelling problems probably negatively affect handwriting. Reciprocal relationships such as these are probably part of the reason learning disabilities are so difficult to correct and may help explain why simplistic, unidimensional approaches are insufficient. See the Case Connections box on page 419 for an interview with Jamal's first-grade teacher, Alice Hamilton, regarding the difficulties Jamal is having with handwriting and spelling.

## How Is Spelling Performance Assessed?

Assessment is the necessary first step in identifying students with spelling disabilities before interventions can be implemented.

Council for
Exceptional
Children

**CEC Knowledge Check**

Is it possible that a student may have deficiencies in writing, spelling, and fluency due to an undetected partial hearing loss? Would any of these assessments be able to detect it?
LD3K3

> There are three basic methods used to determine the status of a student's spelling skills. In the first, *dictation,* the examiner reads aloud a list of words and the student is instructed to write the spelling for each. In the second, *connected writing,* the student is asked to generate text in response to a picture or as a story retell. In the third, *recognition,* the student is given a group of words that contain the correct spelling along with a few misspellings, or foils. The student is asked to indicate which spelling is correct. (Masterson & Apel, 2000, p. 51)

### Standardized Assessment

Most standardized achievement batteries include measures of spelling skills. For example, the *California Achievement Tests—5th Edition* (CTB/Macmillan/McGraw-Hill,

CASE
CONNECTIONS

Jamal

## An Interview with Ms. Hamilton

The following interview was conducted with Ms. Hamilton, Jamal's first-grade teacher, regarding his difficulties with handwriting and spelling:

*Question:* When did you notice that Jamal was having difficulty with handwriting?

*Ms. Hamilton:* I could tell from the first day of school. I became suspicious when I asked the students to write their names, and Jamal only wrote J. I asked him if his family and friends call him J, and he said "no." Writing is such a chore for Jamal. It takes him a long time to form letters, and he gets annoyed when they don't look right. He also gets frustrated when he's the last one to finish. He knows he's behind.

*Question:* What are you doing to address Jamal's difficulties?

*Ms. Hamilton:* First of all, I think handwriting is important, so I won't let Jamal avoid the task, even if he doesn't like it. I do a lot of modeling, and then he practices. I like to mix in letters that are not too difficult for him with letters that are more challenging. That way, he experiences some success. Eventually, I want him to start enjoying writing. He also seems to like tracing letters with numbered arrow cues.

*Question:* What can you tell me about Jamal's progress in spelling?

*Ms. Hamilton:* It's slow going right now. Jamal seems to have difficulty hearing the sounds in words, especially the medial vowel sounds. For example, when I asked him to spell *can, mop,* and *run,* he wrote, *kn, mq,* and *rn.* As you can see, he seems to hear beginning and ending sounds (though he doesn't always identify the correct letter . . . and, sometimes, he makes reversal errors), but he rarely identifies the correct medial vowel. Jamal works on a few words each week, and we don't move on until he's mastered them.

1993), the *Peabody Individual Achievement Test—Revised,* or PIAT (Markwardt, 1989), and the *Wechsler Individual Achievement Test,* or WIAT (Psychological Corporation, 1992) all have spelling subtests. Because students who have spelling problems are very likely to have low scores on any of these tests, using them makes it possible to identify students with spelling deficits.

Examples of achievement batteries requiring students to write the spellings for words as the examiner dictates include the *Metropolitan Achievement Test—7th Edition* (Prescott, Balow, Hogan, & Farr, 1992), the *Wide Range Achievement Test—3* (Wilkinson, 1993), the WIAT, and the *Woodcock-Johnson—III* (Woodcock, McGrew, & Mather, 2001). Tests that require students to write spellings may seem more difficult, but they test skills that are closer to those required in actual schoolwork.

The Spontaneous Writing subtest from the *Test of Written Language,* or TOWL (Hammill & Larsen, 1996), is designed to measure a student's spelling skills in connected writing. The student generates a written story in response to a stimulus picture, and the examiner calculates a standard score based on the number of misspelled words and total number of words in the story. However, "such subtests simply do not contain a sufficient number of words representing the necessary orthographic patterns to make the scores meaningful or helpful" (Masterson & Apel, 2000, p. 52).

Many major achievement tests assess spelling skills by having students select the correct spelling from several choices or indicate whether a spelling is correct or incorrect. Because students' performance on this type of task may differ from their performance when required to produce the correct spellings of words, further testing for spelling skills is usually well advised. When students choose a correct spelling for a word, they may use a different strategy than they use when generating the spelling of that word.

Some tests that are designed specifically to measure spelling skill may also be useful for screening. For example, the *Test of Written Spelling—3,* or TWS–3 (Larsen & Hammill, 1994), provides several scores that allow comparison to norm groups so that a teacher can determine whether and to what extent a student is behind his or her peers. In practice, most teachers who test students to determine whether they are eligible for special education use an individually administered achievement test, such as the *Woodcock-Johnson—III* or TWS–3, that requires students to write words from dictation.

## Planning Spelling Instruction

Planning programs requires information about where to begin instruction, what skill areas need teaching, and so forth. For the purpose of placement, the most useful diagnostic tests are probably those that accompany the spelling program being used. Other methods for diagnosing spelling problems are formal tests, analysis of spelling errors, and informal spelling inventories.

Several formal tests assess different aspects of spelling skill. For example, the TWS–3 is composed of two types of words: those that follow regular spelling patterns (are spelled the way they sound) and those that have irregular spellings. Presumably, if students do well on the regularly spelled words but poorly on the irregularly spelled words, instruction in how to remember some words as wholes would be appropriate.

Some older instruments assess different parts of spelling skill. For example, the *Gates-Russell Spelling Diagnostic Test* (Gates & Russell, 1940) has sections for testing sound-symbol relationships, pronunciation of words, and other areas, as well as skill in spelling words. For students who have difficulty with certain areas of the subtests but not with others, an instructional plan that emphasizes the subareas on which they need to work would be prepared.

By classifying the words used on other tests, such as the WIAT, teachers can develop preliminary hypotheses about students' needs in spelling. However, such a strategy requires further evaluation of the students' performances, to sample them across types of words. Another time-honored approach is to analyze students' spelling errors.

## Error Analysis

Analyzing spelling errors involves looking for consistent patterns in a student's mistakes. One purpose of **error analysis** is to identify mistaken strategies—to "get inside the head" of a student and determine what is going wrong. Presumably, if teachers can do this, they can prescribe appropriate remedies.

One approach is to record types of errors, such as where in the word the mistake occurs. Teachers should examine students' spelling tests and written work for errors (Bos & Vaughn, 2002). If students repeatedly make the same types of errors, these error patterns probably form a good basis for monitoring progress. Teachers could record the percentage of time students make the same types of errors and determine whether instruction is appropriately affecting them.

Teachers often base their error analyses on the data they get from informal spelling inventories. Although this is a solid strategy, it must be exercised with caution. As with analyses of students' responses on formal spelling tests, teachers should be certain to sample performance across types of words.

## Informal Spelling Inventories

**Informal spelling inventories** are so called because they do not have norms and are administered under nonstandard conditions. Teachers can construct informal spelling inventories by selecting a sample of words from each level of an available language arts or spelling program. Students can be tested on their spelling of the words from the sample lists, and the level at which they make 20% or more mistakes is usually considered their instructional spelling level. However, those who use this approach to diagnosis should be aware that some students may happen to know (or not know) how to spell only those words on the given lists. When placement decisions are made on the basis of an informal spelling inventory, teachers should be certain to use information gained from progress-monitoring tests to adjust the placements as the school year proceeds.

## Monitoring Progress in Spelling

Spelling is an area in which the traditional teaching methods come closest to incorporating **progress monitoring.** Using curriculum-based assessment makes students more aware of their spelling goals and of teacher feedback about progress in spelling (Fuchs, Butterworth, & Fuchs, 1989).

Recording weekly spelling test scores provides teachers with regularly collected data about how well their students are doing in spelling. However, because the lists of words on which the students are tested usually change each week, scores may be at least partially influenced by the difficulty of a particular list. Also, students may be tested on words they already know and not get enough practice on words they do not know. Furthermore, such tests do not assess performance under authentic conditions for spelling, one of the emphases in learning disabilities today.

**error analysis** an informal method of teacher assessment that involves the teacher noting the particular kinds of errors a student makes when doing academic work

Council for Exceptional Children

**CEC Knowledge Check**

Why are authentic assessments such a good method for diagnosing student spelling deficiencies? CC7S4, CC8S2, CC8S5, CC6S1, LD4S6

**informal spelling inventories** a sample of words from each level of an available language arts or spelling program; the words are then used to test students in an effort to determine their instructional spelling level

**progress monitoring** the regular assessment of students' academic performance to determine whether they are benefiting from the instructional program

Council for Exceptional Children

**CEC Knowledge Check**

Given the benefits for student self-monitoring, how would you incorporate this strategy into your spelling remediation program? LD4S7, CC7K1

# What Interventions Help Students' Spelling Difficulties?

Even though some of the ability to spell has a genetic component (DeFries, Stevenson, Gillis, & Wadsworth, 1991), spelling ability is not fixed or unchangeable. Spelling performance is affected by many factors and is thus open to instruction.

Some programs for teaching spelling are designed to develop the spelling ability of young children who have not previously been exposed to instruction. As in reading, these are called developmental programs. Other programs are designed to improve the spelling competence of students who have failed to learn to spell well. These are usually called corrective or remedial programs.

Regardless of whether an intervention is designed for teaching beginning or remedial spelling, it should incorporate what research shows are effective practices in spelling instruction. Careful reviews of spelling research have identified many practices that are important for students with learning disabilities (Gordon, Vaughn, & Schumm, 1993; Graham, 1999; Graham & Miller, 1979; Kerr & Lambert, 1982; McNaughton, Hughes, & Clark, 1994). Table 13.2 describes practices that have been tested with students with learning disabilities and found to be more effective and less effective.

**TABLE 13.2   Effective and Ineffective Spelling Instructional Practices**

| LESS EFFECTIVE | MORE EFFECTIVE |
| --- | --- |
| Using a memorization approach | Using an approach in which students learn phoneme-grapheme correspondences |
| Presenting words in sentences or paragraphs | Presenting words in lists |
| Using the study-test method | Using the test-study-test method |
| Ignoring errors | Requiring students to practice mistaken words, pointing out (even imitating) mistakes |
| Presenting extensive lists of words to be learned each week | Using brief lists of only three words per day |
| Having students devise their own methods of studying | Providing specific strategies for studying, including structured peer tutoring |
| Treating spelling as an uninteresting and unimportant activity | Rewarding achievement, using spelling games |
| Having students practice writing words in the air | Having students practice writing words on paper, tracing letter tiles, or typing words on a computer |

## Developmental Interventions

It is estimated that an adult writer knows how to spell between 10,000 and 20,000 words. By way of contrast, in the most conscientious spelling curriculum (i.e., weekly "spelling lists" of words to be memorized), a child is explicitly taught approximately 3,800 words during the elementary years (Graham, Harris, & Loynachan, 1996). In this discrepancy lies the crux of much of the debate on spelling instruction. How much of spelling is "taught" and how much is "caught"? Those on the "caught" side of the fence argue that spelling will develop naturally in a literacy-rich environment where students are immersed in authentic reading and writing activities. They point out that some of the spelling "skills" taught (e.g., the schwa) are not used even by good spellers and that such instruction is not only boring, but fails to transfer to text-level writing. Proponents of "taught" spelling instruction, however, point to the lack of evidence for and confidence in naturalistic methods. (Scott, 2000, pp. 67–68)

Today, many favor balanced spelling instruction, whereby the teaching of spelling skills is direct and students engage in text-level writing to employ their skills in an effort to become strategic spellers (Scott, 2000).

Spelling is not simply a matter of learning and applying symbols for the sounds one hears. Sound-symbol spelling gets one started, but the multiple ways a sound can be written in English present problems. For example, the *s* sound can be written with *s* (*s*ent), *c* (*c*ent), or *sc* (*sc*ent), and the first sound in the word *cat* can be written with a *c* (*c*an), *k* (*k*in), *ch* (*ch*ord), or *kh* (*kh*aki). When spelling words, people apparently use not just their knowledge of sound-symbol relationships, but also some knowledge of the probability that certain spellings occur under certain conditions. Furthermore, when spelling words, they apparently use other strategies, such as analogy and, to a lesser extent, simple memory for visual patterns. Particularly important, they use their knowledge of the underlying structure of English. As a consequence, teachers should be prepared to promote flexible use of several different strategies.

To teach efficiently, teachers need to resolve some of this ambiguity for students. One approach is to build word lists for spelling practice. Choosing words to be used in teaching spelling is an important step in designing effective spelling instruction. There are several important kinds of words:

- *regular words,* which most closely approximate spelling-to-sound correspondences, such as *cat, cake, pinch, milk,* and *run*
- *high-frequency, less regular words,* which, although they approximate spelling-to-sound correspondences in part, are slightly irregular in their orthography, such as *was, said,* and *come*
- *homophonous words,* which require context for the speller to resolve which spelling is correct, such as *there, their,* and *they're*
- *demon words,* which are most often misspelled in English, such as *misspell*

Word lists for spelling should probably incorporate selections from each of these types. Spelling lists based on words that are both frequently used in children's writing and illustrate useful phoneme-grapheme relationships are available (Graham, Harris, & Loynachan, 1994). Learning to spell the words on such lists should help students learn the underlying orthography of English and acquire correct spellings for some words they will use often.

Another important feature of English should be represented in words chosen for spelling instruction. Teaching students building blocks that are slightly larger than sound-symbol relations is one good way to reduce the ambiguity of English orthography. Morphographs are one useful building block (Dixon, 1993). **Morphograph** refers to bases and affixes (prefixes and suffixes) and is based on morphemes. The idea behind using morphographs is deceptively simple but extremely powerful:

**morphograph** bases and affixes (prefixes and suffixes)

> Let's pretend that you can spell only three morphographs:
>
> | *Prefix* | *Base* | *Suffix* |
> |----------|--------|----------|
> | re | cover | ed |
>
> You can't make very many words from just these three morphographs: *recover, covered, recovered.* Now let's raise your knowledge from three to seven morphographs:
>
> | *Prefix* | *Base* | *Suffix* |
> |----------|--------|----------|
> | re | cover | ed |
> | dis | pute | able |
> | un | | |
>
> Take a look at the words you can form when you increase from three to just seven morphographs: *recover, recoverable, recovered, unrecoverable, unrecovered, repute, reputable, reputed, disreputable, disrepute, coverable, covered, uncover, uncoverable, uncovered, discover, discoverable, discovered, undiscoverable, undiscovered, disputable, disputed, indisputable, undisputed,* and so on.
>
> Now let's increase the number of morphographs you can use from 7 to 750. The different combinations they make should give us somewhere in the neighborhood of 12,000 to 15,000 words. Not bad, considering there's a good chance you can already spell many of the 750 morphographs. (Dixon, 1993, p. 30)

Special education teachers of students with learning disabilities in the primary and elementary grades should study the spelling program used in their students' general education classrooms. It is important to coordinate their work on spelling closely with the instruction delivered there (Kulieke & Jones, 1993). Important adaptations will probably have to include providing for extra practice, making the orthographic relationships among words more explicit (i.e., big ideas), promoting consistent use of effective cognitive strategies, and providing **scaffolding,** whereby the teacher provides assistance as the student is first learning a task but gradually removes help so that the student can do the task independently.

**scaffolding** an instructional technique in which the teacher provides assistance as the student is first learning a task but gradually removes help so that the student can do the task independently

## Remedial Interventions

Many of the same issues that arise in developmental instruction also are apparent in remedial instruction. For example, teachers must decide what words to teach in remedying spelling problems. Using spelling lists composed of words students have misspelled in their compositions does not do much to improve spelling; when students write, they generally choose words they already know how to spell. Thus, this kind of list would not reflect a student's spelling problems. Lists made up of words that many students misspell will be little better because students, especially older ones, vary so much in the words they use. Specially selected word lists probably would not include words that lend themselves to illustrating spelling patterns. Without sufficient examples of spelling patterns, students are unlikely to learn generalized spelling skills (Kerr & Lambert, 1982).

Other practices have empirical support. Chief among these are the ones described in Table 13.2 (Gordon et al., 1993; Graham & Miller, 1979; McNaughton et al., 1994). In addition, researchers (e.g., Anderson-Inman, 1981; Bryant, Drabin, & Gettinger, 1981; Gettinger, Bryant, & Fayne, 1982; Graham, 1999; McNeish, Heron, & Okyere, 1992; Van Houten & Van Houten, 1991) have found the following practices helpful with students who have learning disabilities:

- Present only a few spelling words on each day of instruction, and encourage students to break them into morphographs.
- Provide distributed practice (repeat words at different times).
- Teach for generalization by focusing on phonemic spelling patterns (i.e., illustrating the big ideas underlying spelling).
- Maximize the effects of training in one setting to induce transfer to other settings.
- Promote self-correction of spelling words as a means of practicing correct responses.

Jamal's mother agrees:

> Jamal is having a lot of trouble with spelling. I'm so glad he's in Ms. Hamilton's class. She gives him a few words to learn every other day and really has him practice. We also practice at home. I know that's what he needs, because if not, he'd forget the words after he supposedly "learned" them.
>
> *Irene Smith, Jamal's mother*

 Jamal

## Effective Teaching Procedures

Regardless of the many complexities of spelling, teachers can draw from research about effective practices to guide instruction. Some methods with a long history of use in learning disabilities have preliminary support in research. For example, the Orton-Gillingham methods have produced beneficial effects with students both in elementary schools and in college (Guyer, Banks, & Guyer, 1993; Vickery, Reynolds, & Cochran, 1987). In addition to those practices listed previously (see Table 13.2 and related text), teachers can use the five techniques described in the following sections.

**Council for Exceptional Children**

**CEC Knowledge Check**
How do you decide which words students have to know, should know, are optional to know?
CC4S3, LD6K5

### Test-Study-Test

With the test-study-test method, teachers pretest students to identify which words need to be learned. After instruction and study, teachers test students again to determine which words have been mastered.

> Although the efficacy of the test-study-test procedure has not been specifically examined with students with LD, this format is likely to benefit these children when their spelling lists contain a mix of known and unknown spellings, as they gain information about which words need to be studied and which words are subsequently mastered. A pretest provides little, if any, advantage, though, when students are unable to spell all or most of the words on their spelling lists, and some children will surely resent taking such tests. (Graham, 1999, p. 87)

### Practice Procedures

The old adage "practice makes perfect" appears to be very applicable to spelling, especially when combined with reinforcement of correct spelling behavior. Studies lead to recommendations that teachers

- present daily practice tests on parts of a weekly spelling test before presenting the weekly test itself (Rieth et al., 1974)
- require students to rewrite several times those words they missed on practice tests (Foxx & Jones, 1978; Matson, Esveldt-Dawson, & Kazdin, 1982; Ollendick, Matson, Esveldt-Dawson, & Shapiro, 1980)
- imitate students' errors and then require them to write the words correctly (Gerber, 1986; Kauffman, Hallahan, Haas, Brame, & Boren, 1978)
- practice fewer words, more often, over a longer period of time (Graham, 1999; Scott, 2000)
- arrange for tutoring by parents or peers (Broden, Beasley, & Hall, 1978; Harris, Sherman, Henderson, & Harris, 1972)

Some commercial products incorporate various practice procedures that are helpful to students with learning disabilities. Basic Skill Builders (Beck et al., 1996) and Speed Spelling (Proff, 1978) are examples. These programs include features of curriculum-based assessment, such as timing and graphing of student performance, as well.

### Time Delay

**progressive time delay**
a teaching practice in which the teacher presents an item, pauses briefly (3 seconds), and then gives the answer; if the student answers correctly during the pause, the teacher provides a reward; the teacher gradually shortens the pause

One technique from the behavioral literature that has been the focus of considerable study is **progressive time delay.** In it, the teacher pauses briefly (about 3 seconds) after asking a question. If the student responds correctly during the pause, the teacher provides a reward. If the student does not respond (or responds incorrectly), the teacher gives the correct answer but no reward. Gradually, the teacher increases the delay (the duration of the pause). The technique has had beneficial effects when used while students practice spelling, even with a computer (e.g., Stevens, Blackhurst, & Slaton, 1991; Stevens & Schuster, 1987; Winterling, 1990).

### Morphographic Spelling

Morphographic Spelling (Dixon, 1976, 1991) is an intensive, highly structured, teacher-directed remedial spelling program for use with fourth- through twelfth-graders and adults. Students placed in the program are assumed to know the basic spelling skills (sound-symbol relationships, etc.), so the program begins instruction with morphographs, small units of meaningful writing. Students are taught to spell morphographs and to use five rules for combining them. After about a year of 20-minute lessons five times a week, they are capable of spelling over 12,000 words. Research reveals that the program is quite effective with students who have been achieving well below their expected levels of spelling (Maggs, McMillan, Patching, & Hawke, 1981).

### Add-a-Word

Add-a-word is a spelling procedure that uses **flow lists.** In this approach, teachers create individualized lists and test students on their personal lists each day. When a student demonstrates mastery of a word on the list, it is removed and another one is substituted. Researchers have found that this type of procedure aids in the remediation of spelling problems (McLaughlin, Reiter, Mabee, & Byram, 1991). Furthermore, "an element common to both the add-a-word program and practicing a portion of the weekly words each day is daily testing. This component should not be neglected" (Graham, 1999, p. 89).

## What Composition Problems Do Students Experience?

Initially, children focus on learning and mastering mechanical skills—handwriting and spelling. In later grades, they are given short writing assignments that require them to organize and present their ideas in writing. By high school, students should have mastered the mechanical skills of handwriting, spelling, and grammar so that writing can focus on communicating the idea and refining style. See the Current Trends and Issues box on page 428 for highlights of contemporary issues in these areas.

Written expression requires the coordination of many different matters at the same time. Figure 13.4 (page 429) illustrates the complexity of the task. As it shows, there are many critical features in written products. These not only describe ways to measure performance, but also imply that students need to learn many things to become effective written communicators. Students may have problems in any of these areas.

Few studies of the characteristics of students who have writing disabilities were reported in the early years of the learning disabilities field. Myklebust (1965, 1973) conducted the most extensive analyses. In his 1973 study, he had students write stories about a picture of a little boy playing with dolls and reported that, compared to normally achieving students, those identified as having learning

**flow lists** a spelling list made up of words a student has not mastered; when the student masters a word, the word is dropped from the list and another added

**CEC Knowledge Check**
Using principles listed in this section, describe how you would use peer tutoring in your spelling program. Could you combine the add-a-word method with peer tutoring and self-monitoring? LD4S1, LD4S2, LD4S5

**CEC Knowledge Check**
Written language is expression of thought. For students with LD in early grades, could recorded oral language be used as a substitute to teach organizational thinking skills until writing skills improve? LD4K4, LD4K5, LD4S10

CURRENT
TRENDS
&
ISSUES

## Handwriting, Spelling, and Expressive Writing

Following is a brief discussion of current issues in the areas of handwriting, spelling, and expressive writing (see discussion of some of these issues in other parts of this chapter):

### Handwriting

*Issue:* Should students with learning disabilities be taught manuscript, cursive, D'Nealian (i.e., slanted manuscript letters), or italics? Should they learn manuscript only? Should they learn cursive only?

These basic questions have actually been around for a long time. Despite certain claims, no research evidence exists "clearly favoring one script over another" (Graham & Weintraub, 1996, as cited in Graham, 1999, p. 83). Similarly, "commonly assumed distinctions between manuscript and cursive are [now] being questioned" (Graham, 1999, p. 84). Regardless of the method chosen for instruction, children ultimately develop their own style; still, some authorities (e.g., Graham, 1999) recommend that handwriting instruction begin with traditional manuscript.

### Spelling

*Issue:* Should the natural learning approach replace spelling instruction?

No. "Although children acquire some of their facility with handwriting and spelling through incidental and informal methods of learning, by writing and reading frequently, students with LD tend to be much more reliant on systematic instruction" (Baker, Gersten, & Graham, 2003, p. 119).

### Expressive Writing

*Issue:* Should students who struggle with writing dictate their thoughts rather than write them down (or type them)?

As more students with learning disabilities take state assessments, this question will become increasingly important (Gersten & Baker, 2001). Some research findings (e.g., La Paz & Graham, 1997) indicate that when students dictate to an adult, writing performance increases. Such findings warrant further research in this area. However, it is important to emphasize that students with learning disabilities need, and should receive, explicit instruction in handwriting, spelling, and written expression (Baker et al., 2003).

---

disabilities scored lower on measures of total number of words written, words per sentence, syntactic accuracy, and abstraction. Students who had moderate learning disabilities did not differ from their nondisabled peers on gross writing production (numbers of words and sentences), but those who had severe learning disabilities did.

Results of many studies conducted since Myklebust's investigations make clear that students with learning disabilities have substantial problems in written expression that go beyond simply writing shorter passages. Although older students use more complex syntax and vocabulary than younger students, regardless of whether they have learning disabilities (Morris & Crump, 1982), students with learning disabilities

- engage in little or no planning when they write (Englert, Raphael, Fear, & Anderson, 1988; Graham & Harris, 1997a)
- produce writing with errors in spelling, capitalization, punctuation, and handwriting (Graham, Harris, MacArthur, & Schwartz, 1991)

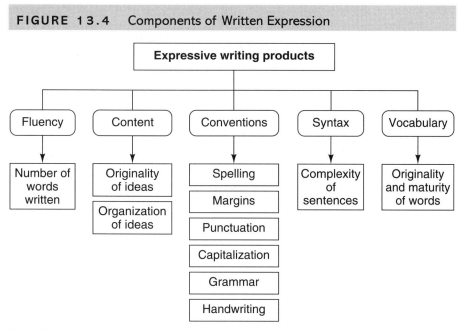

**FIGURE 13.4** Components of Written Expression

*Source:* From *Designing Instructional Strategies: The Prevention of Academic Learning Problems* (p. 427) by E. J. Kame'enui and D. Simmons, 1990. Copyright © 1990, 1st ed. Reprinted by permission of Pearson Education, Inc., Upper Saddle River, NJ.

- lack effective skills for revising writing (Graham, 1997)
- score lower in vocabulary and thematic maturity as well as in word usage, style, and overall writing skill (Poplin, Gray, Larsen, Banikowski, & Mehring, 1980)
- use less complex sentence structures and include fewer types of words (Morris & Crump, 1982; Tindal & Parker, 1991)
- write paragraphs that are less well organized (Englert, Raphael, Anderson, Gregg, & Anthony, 1989; Thomas, Englert, & Gregg, 1987; Tindal & Parker, 1991)
- include fewer ideas in their written products (Englert et al., 1989; Montague, Graves, & Leavell, 1991)
- write stories that have fewer important components, such as introducing main characters, setting scenes, describing a conflict to be resolved, and so forth (Laughton & Morris, 1989)

Overall, these studies imply that students with learning disabilities lag behind their nondisabled classmates in many aspects of written expression. The differences are not always consistent, but students with learning disabilities are likely to be weak in both the conventional (e.g., grammar) and the more meaningful aspects of composition (i.e., content). Such students will likely have difficulty with each of the components of written expression shown in Figure 13.4.

Although there is some disagreement in the research about whether students with learning disabilities fall further behind as they get older (Morris & Crump,

Council for Exceptional Children

**CEC Knowledge Check**
Are poor writing skills a symptom of poor thinking skills? Are there ways to improve organization of thoughts, sentence structure, and word choice?

1982; Poplin et al., 1980), they are unlikely to catch up with their peers in the absence of powerful instruction. Before providing corrective instruction, teachers must identify students who need it and plan programs for them.

## How Is Composition Performance Assessed?

Powerful assessment of written expression incorporates ways of evaluating all the features illustrated in Figure 13.4. Such assessment should clearly require several writing samples and careful scoring.

The main reason most widely used general achievement batteries do not require writing samples is that scoring them is time consuming and unreliable. Thus, there is little hope that general achievement instruments will ever be adequate for screening for writing disabilities. Teachers will have to make an initial judgment of their students' writing and may have to formally identify writing disabilities by administering one of the instruments designed as a diagnostic device.

### Screening

Screening for writing disabilities is difficult because many students other than those with learning disabilities write poorly. Broad standardized tests focus on achievement in other areas (e.g., reading and mathematics) as well, so they often measure only editorial or mechanical skills. For example, the *Metropolitan Achievement Test—7th Edition* (Prescott et al., 1992) has sections on punctuation, capitalization, and word usage but does not include other measures of writing performance. The *Sequential Tests of Educational Progress* (Educational Testing Service, 1972) and the written expression section of the *Tests of Achievement and Proficiency* (Scannell, Haugh, Schild, & Ulmer, 1978) require students to answer multiple-choice and true-false questions, most of which have to do with mechanics (e.g., punctuation and capitalization), though some relate to organization and style.

Facility in editing material and answering true-false or multiple choice questions about written material may be important, but it should not be confused with skill in composing material spontaneously. Better tests of composition require that students provide a sample of their writing.

Tests specifically designed to assess writing provide more detailed information. For example, the *Test of Written Language* (Hammill & Larsen, 1996) has norms that permit teachers to judge to what extent students' writing corresponds to average. In addition to measuring spelling, it incorporates measures of vocabulary, style, logical sentence formation, facility in combining sentences, competence in mechanics, sentence construction, and overall story quality.

### Planning Composition Instruction

Planning instruction also requires more detailed information about students' skills than a teacher gets from broad-focused achievement batteries. The *Picture Story Language Test,* or PSLT (Myklebust, 1965), and the *Test of Written Language* (Hammill &

Larsen, 1996) are two norm-referenced instruments that require students to compose writing samples. On the PSLT, students write a story about a picture of a boy playing. Aspects of the sample (number of words, average number of words per sentence, syntactic correctness, and degree of abstractness) are judged and compared with norms. On the TOWL, some subtests measure correct word usage and style, and students are asked to compose a writing sample about three cartoon panels showing a space adventure. Assessments of the writing sample provide scores for vocabulary and maturity of theme (paragraphing, characterization, beginning-middle-ending structure, etc.). Presumably, students with unusually low scores in any of these areas on either the PSLT or the TOWL should receive remedial instruction in the relevant skills.

Council for
Exceptional
Children

CEC Knowledge Check
What are some of the major problems associated with assessment of writing?
CC8K4, CC8S2, CC8S5, LD8S1

## Monitoring Progress in Composition

Progress in composition skills can be easily evaluated by regularly sampling students' writing (Parker, Tindal, & Hasbrouck, 1991). The teacher can then judge whether they represent improvement. Judgments of the samples usually are based on analysis of the given task.

> The task of "writing a paragraph" could be reduced to subtasks comprising "developing the ideational content," "developing paragraph structure," "writing sentences," and "using formal codes." To complete the task analysis, each of these larger components is reduced to subtasks thought to be prerequisite to successful use of each major component of paragraph composition. A component like "using formal codes" may be analyzed into "capitalization" and "punctuation," whereas "writing sentences" may be reduced to "expressing complete thoughts" and "composing sentences. . . ." Developing a progress monitoring system based on a task-analytic approach consists of creating measurement procedures for each of the subtasks that generate data on whether the standard or "criterion" for performance on that task has been met. (Deno, 1997, p. 80)

The resulting task analysis reinforces the importance of the components shown in Figure 13.4. Systems for monitoring increasing facility in these areas would be important in helping teachers adjust instruction to meet individual students' needs.

Teachers can assess improvement in overall quality of writing by simply comparing writing samples taken at different times. Figure 13.5 (page 432) shows two writing samples from students who had received extensive remedial teaching. Although there are some mistakes in the first sample, the second sample has many more mistakes and many of the characteristics of poor writing discussed in the previous section. Teachers can evaluate the quality of a sample such as the one in part B by noting whether it expresses complete ideas, has complex sentences, is well organized, and includes essential ideas and important components. For example, the second sentence in sample B mixes two different ideas in a disjointed way. The last sentence runs together too many ideas and misrepresents the idea of migration as "going east." Overall, the paragraph omits the important relationship between food and migration. Although these evaluations may seem subjective, in comparison with the sample by the more skillful writer, such evaluations are obvious.

**FIGURE 13.5**   Samples of Student Writing

A   Winter is difficult for some animals because it is hard to find food. Two ways animals can survive winter are migration and hibernation. When animals migrate they go find somewhere warm to spend the winter. In the spring they go back to their original home. Whale migrate to escape the winter's cold. Mosts birds migrate.

Hibernation is when an animal finds somewhere warm to stay for the winter and they fall into a deep sleep. In the spring they start waking up.

B   This is about hibernation and migration. Different animals that in the winter the animals go into a deep sleep and when it gets warm the animals wake up. But they have to do a lot of things to start, Ground hogs have to far dig far in the earth to a warm spot. Bears have to find a warm place like in a hole or something lik that. Whales have to go east and get to a warm spot and when spot turns cold they go to the old spot where they firt was

*Note:* These samples summarize a lesson on how animals adjust to cold and less abundant food. Panel A shows how the summary of a competent writer might look; panel B shows how the work of a less competent writer might look.

*Source:* Content of summaries from "Exposition: Reading, Writing, and the Metacognitive Knowledge of Learning Disabled Students" by C. S. Englert, T. E. Raphael, L. M. Anderson, S. L. Gregg, and H. M. Anthony, 1989, *Learning Disabilities Research, 5,* pp. 14–15. Copyright 1989 by Division for Learning Disabilities. Reprinted by permission.

# What Interventions Help Students with Composition Difficulties?

Some argue that instruction on the mechanical aspects of writing should be eliminated because it suppresses students' creativity. Although this is an appealing notion, one must be cautious about accepting it too readily. The teaching of writing should certainly encourage people to express the ideas they want to express. But the fundamental aspects of writing must not be disregarded; they are essential to competent, clear communication (Graham & Harris, 1997b). Too often we overlook the importance of formal work as a prerequisite to creative products. But jazz musicians know how to play simple scales and other exercises, and the poems of e. e. cummings are creative in part because he knew enough about the conventions of capitalization and punctuation to mock them.

However, this does not necessarily mean that instruction should be restricted to simple drills on grammatical rules. Programs must teach certain traditional aspects of grammar (nouns, verbs, etc.) because these are useful in identifying parts of speech when constructing and editing sentences, but mechanics should not overshadow instruction in communicating by writing. See the Multicultural Considerations box on page 434 for a discussion of writing instruction in bilingual special education settings.

## Developmental Interventions

Few programs have been explicitly designed to teach students writing skills. In lieu of specific directions, many authorities on writing have recommended that students learn to write simply by extensive practice in writing.

Many of the recommendations about developing writing facility echo books that provide general directions to teachers. For example, one approach begins by having the students write labels and captions for pictures they have cut out of magazines or drawn and put in their books (Sealey, Sealey, & Millmore, 1979). Later the teacher leads them into writing one-sentence descriptions of the pictures or drawings. At the third stage, the children are required to write two-sentence descriptions; here the conventions of punctuation and capitalization are introduced. In the fourth stage, the children write three-sentence or longer descriptions of the pictures; the sentences do not have to relate to one another. At the fifth stage, the children are asked to write thematically.

Other programs provide more explicit directions about instruction. For example, Reasoning and Writing (Engelmann, Arbogast, Davis, Grossen, & Silbert, 1993) includes specific instruction for writing simple sentences, understanding the story structure, resolving ambiguities, analyzing sentences, punctuating written materials, editing and revising, correcting unclear sentences, expressing specific concerns, and writing extended critiques. The program is founded on the idea that logical thinking and clear expression are intimately linked. The daily lessons of this program, although very structured and directive, focus on the specific skills that make up coherent written communication.

Several broad recommendations about instruction can be made on the basis of research on writing (see Baker, Gersten, & Graham, 2003; Gersten & Baker, 2001; Graham, Harris, & Troia, 2000):

# Investigating Writing Instruction for Students with Learning Disabilities in Bilingual Special Education Settings

Do we know which approach to writing instruction yields the best results for elementary school students with disabilities who speak a first language other than English? Consider the approaches in the following four classrooms investigated in a research study (i.e., Graves, Valles, & Rueda, 2000) and think about which would most benefit such students:

1. *Classroom 1.* In this self-contained special education classroom, students write in journals daily, and the teacher provides written responses to each entry. Instead of making overt corrections to spelling and grammar, the teacher addresses the errors indirectly (i.e., by modeling the correct spelling and grammar in his response to the student). During sharing, the students read their entries to the teacher. The teacher writes back immediately and reads his comments to the students.

2. *Classroom 2.* In this resource classroom, the teacher uses the Optimal Learning Environment program. Students write in journals daily, and the teacher provides written responses to each entry. In addition, students use Writer's Workshop to plan, write, edit, and revise their work. Each student's final copy becomes a page in a book that is laminated and kept in the classroom for sharing and reading. Students also engage in various reading activities.

3. *Classroom 3.* In this resource classroom, the focus is on Writer's Workshop. The students gather information on a topic, take notes on index cards, share and work with the teacher (who helps with editing and revising), and continue until a final copy is produced. The students illustrate their work, which is compiled into a book or displayed in the hall or in the classroom.

4. *Classroom 4.* In this resource room, students write in journals daily, but the teacher is unable to respond every day. She models webbing or mapping and has students do the same before writing their stories. In addition, the students engage in spelling practice, and the teacher gives weekly spelling tests.

Results of the above-mentioned study indicate that English-language learners with disabilities benefit from the Optimal Learning Environment (OLE) program (Graves et al., 2000). Other studies show similar results (e.g., Ruiz, 1995; Ruiz & Figueroa, 1995). The OLE program, which was designed specifically for bilingual students, includes elements such as

interactive journals, in which the teacher responds to students' daily entries to provide modeling of written dialogue . . . Writer's Workshop (D. Graves, 1983) based on writing-as-a-process, in which students go through planning, drafting, editing, revising, final drafting, and publishing each time they produce a written product, . . . strategic writing, . . . patterned writing and reading, . . . creating text for wordless books, . . . shared reading with predictable text, . . . literature conversation with read-alouds, . . . literature study with response journals, . . . student-made alphabet wall charts, and . . . drop-everything-and-read (d.e.a.r.) time. (Graves et al., 2000, pp. 1–2)

It is important to note that students experience writing improvement with other approaches (e.g., interactive journals alone, Writer's Workshop alone); however, they appear to experience longer-term improvement in writing performance with the OLE program. As more studies with more students are conducted in this area, our knowledge with respect to the relative strengths and weaknesses of elements used with different approaches will increase. Additional research will also shed light on when, and under what conditions, students should make the transition from writing in their native language to writing in English (Graves et al., 2000). (For a more detailed description of the OLE program and the activities in each classroom, see Graves et al., 2000.)

- Have students plan what they will write. Planning may range from simply making notes to preparing webs or outlines.
- Have students translate their plans into a written product. Translating should focus mostly on getting a written product, a rough draft.
- Have students edit what they have written. Editing should include reading the product to evaluate whether it communicates what they want to say and improving it. During editing, students might want to use a checklist to make certain they have followed the conventions of punctuation, capitalization, and grammar. Working with peers and using computers while editing may be beneficial (MacArthur, 1994).

One team of authorities offers six principles designed to prevent and address writing difficulties:

1. Provide effective writing instruction [see Table 13.3];
2. Tailor writing instruction to meet the individual needs of children with LD;

**Council** for **Exceptional Children**

**CEC Knowledge Check**
How important is the skill of thinking, in the writing process? Can thinking skills be taught?
CC4S2, LD4K4

---

**TABLE 13.3**    Features of Exemplary Writing Instruction

- A literate classroom environment where students' written work is prominently displayed, the room is packed with writing and reading material, and word lists adorn the walls.
- Daily writing with students working on a wide range of writing tasks for multiple audiences, including writing at home.
- Extensive efforts to make writing motivating by setting an exciting mood, creating a risk-free environment, allowing students to select their own writing topics or modify teacher assignments, developing assigned topics compatible with students' interests, reinforcing children's accomplishments, specifying the goal for each lesson, and promoting an "I can" attitude.
- Regular teacher-student conferences concerning the writing topic the student is currently working on, including the establishment of goals or criteria to guide the child's writing and revising efforts.
- A predictable writing routine where students are encouraged to think, reflect, and revise.
- Overt teacher modeling of the process of writing as well as positive attitudes toward writing.
- Cooperative arrangements where students help each other plan, draft, revise, edit, or publish their written work.
- Group or individual sharing where students present work in progress or completed papers to their peers for feedback.
- Instruction covering a broad range of skills, knowledge, and strategies, including phonological awareness, handwriting and spelling, writing conventions, sentence-level skills, text structure, the functions of writing, and planning and revising.
- Follow-up instruction to ensure mastery of targeted writing skills, knowledge, and strategies.
- Integration of writing activities across the curriculum and the use of reading to support writing development.
- Frequent opportunities for students to self-regulate their behavior during writing, including working independently, arranging their own space, and seeking help from others.
- Teacher and student assessment of writing progress, strengths, and needs.
- Periodic conferences with parents and frequent communications with home about the writing program and students' progress as writers.

---

*Source:* From "Prevention and Intervention of Writing Difficulties for Students with Learning Disabilities" (table 1: Features of Exemplary Writing Instruction, p. 77) by S. Graham, K. R. Harris, and L. Larsen, 2001, *Learning Disabilities Research and Practice, 16,* 74–84. Copyright 2001 by Blackwell Publishing. Reprinted by permission.

TODAY'S TECHNOLOGY

FOR LEARNING DISABILITIES

## What Research Says about Computer Technologies

A review of research on the use of computer technologies to help students with writing difficulties reveals the following:

### Word Processing

Word processors are flexible writing tools that may assist struggling writers with many aspects of composing, particularly handwriting and revising. The ability to correct errors and produce an attractive publication can be highly motivating to students who find handwriting and spelling difficult. Writers can focus on substantive matters while writing a first draft, confident that errors can be corrected later without tedious recopying. The editing power of the computer can also facilitate substantive revision. Typing can facilitate transcription, but it is important to note that it may also impose new burdens if the student has not received typing instruction. Research findings seem to indicate that simply providing students with word processors will not substantially change their writing, but word processing can facilitate instruction about writing processes and enhance motivation in ways that improve students' writing achievement over time.

### Word Processing and Revising

Instruction in revising strategies in combination with word processing can improve students' revising and overall writing. The studies under review did not reveal whether the strategy would work without the word processor. However, it seems likely that the word processing, at a minimum, enhanced motivation for revising.

### Spell Checkers

Research has demonstrated, as one might expect, that spell checkers help students with writing problems correct more of their errors, but they have significant limitations. The most serious limitation is that they fail to detect spelling errors that are other words, including homophones (e.g., *there, their,* and *they're*) and other real words (e.g., *sad* for *said* or *whet* for *went*). A second serious limitation is that the correct spelling may not appear in the list of suggestions, especially when words are severely misspelled. Other limitations of spell checkers include the possibility that students may not recognize the correct spelling in the list of suggestions and that proper names may be falsely identified as errors.

Council for Exceptional Children

**CEC Knowledge Check**

For students that do not respond well to spelling remediation, when do you rely on technology to help them cope with their transition to work? How many adults or teachers do you know spell well?

CC7S9, CC4S6, LD6K6

---

3. Intervene early, providing a coherent and sustained effort to improve the writing skills of children with LD;
4. Expect that each child will learn to write;
5. Identify and address academic and nonacademic roadblocks to writing and school success; and
6. Employ technological tools that improve writing performance. (Graham, Harris, & Larsen, 2001, p. 75)

See the Today's Technology box above for a discussion on the use of computer technologies to help students write more effectively.

Council for Exceptional Children

**CEC Knowledge Check**

When you plan or redesign spelling curriculum, how important will it be to incorporate the three recommendations and six principles listed here?

CC7K1, CC7K2

## Remedial Interventions

Many of the issues in developmental writing instruction are relevant to remedial instruction, too. As noted, teachers who are working to remedy composition skills

### Grammar Checkers

A grammar checker sensitive to the types of morphological and syntactic errors made by students with language and learning disabilities could be of considerable value. A team of researchers (Lewis, Ashton, Haapa, Kieley, & Fielden, 1999) investigated the effects of a grammar checker specifically designed for students with disabilities, but the use of the grammar checker did not result in any reduction in grammatical errors. The grammar checker accurately diagnosed less than half of students' errors, and students and teachers complained that the feedback was confusing.

### Word Prediction

Word prediction programs "predict" what word the writer intends to use based on the initial letters typed. For example, if a student types, "I went to the s," the program might offer a list of predictions, including *store, show,* and *same.* If the student continues adding a *t* to the *s,* the program updates the list, thus eliminating words that do not start with *st* and adding new words. The student could then insert the word in the text by typing the number of the word or clicking on it. Depending on the sophistication of the program, predictions will be based on spelling alone or on spelling plus syntax and words recently used by the writer. Research supports the use of word-prediction software with students with learning disabilities, particularly those who have severe spelling problems. Design issues, such as the size of the vocabulary, its match to the writing task, and the complexity of the interface, clearly make a difference in the impact.

### Other Technologies

Further research is needed on speech synthesis and speech recognition. In the case of speech synthesis, research is needed on instructional methods that help students take advantage of the speech capabilities to revise their work. In the case of speech recognition, issues of feasibility (e.g., accuracy and editing) must be considered along with evaluation of its impact on the quality of writing. Many promising applications have not been investigated. In particular, there has been almost no work on applications that might support more effective planning. Research has not examined the impact of mapping software on planning for writing, nor have researchers investigated outlining software. Another promising area for research is the use of technology to support the social aspects of writing. Many students are involved in projects that incorporate writing on the Internet. However, researchers have not investigated the impact of such activities on students with disabilities.

*Source:* Adapted from "New Tools for Writing: Assistive Technology for Students with Writing Difficulties" by C. A. MacArthur, 2000, *Topics in Language Disorders, 20,* 85–100. Copyright 2000 by Lippincott Williams & Wilkins. Reprinted by permission.

will have to coordinate their instruction with the programs used in students' general education classrooms (Kulieke & Jones, 1993).

One remedial intervention developed for students with writing problems or learning disabilities is called Expressive Writing (Englemann & Silbert, 1983). Students are taught how to indent at the beginning of paragraphs, use topic sentences, describe a temporal series of events, and evaluate their own written products for a variety of features (e.g., run-on sentences, capitalization, punctuation, and topic relevance).

## Effective Teaching Procedures

Research about effective practices has shown that many other techniques for teaching composition have benefits. These are especially important for students with learning disabilities. Many of these procedures address problems of cognition and metacognition and, thus, are similar to approaches we discussed in Chapter 8.

## Instructional Stages in the Self-Regulated Strategy Development Model

Teachers use Self-Regulated Strategy Development (SRSD) to teach a variety of writing strategies. The use of SRSD has resulted in

significant and meaningful differences in children's development of a variety of planning and revising strategies, including brainstorming, self-monitoring, reading for information and semantic webbing, generating and organizing writing content using story structure, advanced planning and dictation, goal setting, revising using peer feedback, and revising for both mechanics and substance. (De La Paz, Owen, Harris, & Graham, 2000, p. 107)

The effectiveness of SRSD is well documented (see Graham, Harris, & Larsen, 2001, for citations). Following is a brief description of the six instructional stages that provide the basic framework of SRSD:

1. *Develop background knowledge.* The teacher helps students develop the preskills, including knowledge of the criteria for good writing, which are important to understanding, acquiring, or executing the writing strategy and self-regulation procedures targeted for instruction.
2. *Initial conference: strategy goals and significance.* Teacher and student examine and discuss current writing performance and strategies used to accomplish specific assignments. The writing strategy, its purpose and benefits, and how and when to use it are examined, and students are asked to make a commitment to learn the strategy and act as a partner in this endeavor. Negative or ineffective self-statements or beliefs used by students may also be addressed at this time.
3. *Modeling of the strategy.* The teacher models aloud how to use the writing strategy, using appropriate self-instructions (e.g., self-evaluation statements). After analyzing the teacher's performance, teacher and students may collaborate on how to change the strategy to make it more effective. Students then develop personal self-statements they plan to use during writing.
4. *Memorization of the strategy.* The steps of the writing strategy and any accompanying mnemonic for remembering them as well as the personalized self-statements are memorized. Paraphrasing is allowed as long as the original meaning is maintained.
5. *Collaborative practice.* Students and teachers use the writing strategy and self-instructions collaboratively to complete specific writing assignments. Self-regulation procedures, including goal-setting or self-assessment, may be introduced at this point.
6. *Independent practice.* Students use the writing strategy independently. If goal-setting or self-assessment procedures are in use, students and the teacher may decide to fade them out; students are also encouraged to say their self-statements covertly in "their head."

Instructional procedures for promoting maintenance and generalization are integrated throughout the SRSD model. These include (1) discussing opportunities to use, and the results of using, the writing strategy; (2) self-regulation procedures with other tasks and in other settings; (3) asking other teachers and parents to comment on the student's success in using the writing strategy; and (4) working with other teachers to prompt the use of the writing strategy in their classsrooms.

*Source:* From "Prevention and Intervention of Writing Difficulties for Students with Learning Disabilities" by K. R. Harris and L. Larsen, 2001, *Learning Disabilities Research and Practice, 16,* 74–84. Copyright 2001 by Blackwell Publishing. Reprinted by permission.

### Self-Regulated Strategy Development

In this approach, teachers explicitly teach strategies for planning or revising text. They also teach self-regulation procedures similar to those we discussed in Chapter 8, such as goal setting, self-monitoring, self-instructions, and self-reinforcement

(Graham et al., 2000). See the Effective Practices box on page 438 for a description of the six instructional stages that provide the basic framework of Self-Regulated Strategy Development (SRSD). Teachers can use SRSD to teach strategies such as POWER: Plan, Organize, Write, Edit, and Revise (Englert, Raphael, Anderson, Anthony, & Stevens, 1991) and COPS: Capitalization, Organization, Punctuation, and Spelling (Schumaker, Nolan, & Deshler, 1985).

### Learning Strategy Interventions

As we discussed in Chapter 8, a team of researchers at the University of Kansas Center for Research in Learning (KU-CRL) has designed effective instructional strategies to address difficulties adolescents with learning disabilities experience in general education and postsecondary employment settings. The extensive interventions cover a wide variety of areas including reading, memorizing, note-taking, and test-taking (see Tralli, Columbo, Deshler, & Schumaker, 1999). In writing, students learn various strategies including the following:

- Sentence writing: Students learn how to recognize and write simple, compound, complex, and compound-complex sentences.
- Paragraph writing: Students learn how to outline ideas, select a point of view, select appropriate tense, and sequence ideas in an effort to compose organized, complete paragraphs.
- Error monitoring: Students learn how to find and correct errors in their writing.
- Theme writing: Students learn how to write a five-paragraph theme.

### Explicit Teaching of the Steps in the Writing Process

Explicitly teaching the steps of the writing process (i.e., planning, writing a first draft, and revising) produces strong effects on the quality of students' writing (Baker et al., 2003; Gersten & Baker, 2001). Teachers should use

> several examples and varying levels of support. Teaching students to use think sheets, planning sheets, prompt cards, or some other type of mnemonic aid is essential. These concrete reminders of critical steps provide students with a structure that prompts and encourages them to complete critical steps involved in developing a written product. They provide guidance on what to do when the students feel stuck or overwhelmed. (Baker et al., 2003, p. 111)

See Figure 13.6 (page 440) for an example of a prompt card for use in composing an opinion essay and Figure 13.7 (page 441) for an example of a planning sheet for compare-and-contrast essays.

### Explicit Teaching of the Conventions of a Writing Genre

What elements does a persuasive essay contain? What, exactly, does it mean to compare and contrast? Explicit instruction in the conventions of a writing genre is important, because "different types of writing are based on different structural

Council for
Exceptional
Children

**CEC Knowledge Check**

When teaching compare and contrast, would it be helpful to use a graphic organizer such as a Venn diagram? LD4K5, LD4S10

FIGURE 13.6    Prompt Card for Use in Composing Opinion Essays

**Prompt Card**
**Opinion Essay: Signal Words**

**Introductory Phrases**
In my opinion
I (dis)agree
From my point of view
I believe

**Countering Phrases**
Although
On the other hand
On the contrary
However, someone who disagreed
   with my opinion might argue

**Concluding Phrases**
After considering both sides
Even though
To sum up
In conclusion

**Supporting Words and Phrases**
First, Second, Finally
Equally important
For instance
As well

*Source:* From "Research on Genre-Specific Strategies for Enhancing Writing in Adolescents with Learning Disabilities" by B. Y. L. Wong, 1997, *Learning Disability Quarterly, 20,* 140–159. Copyright 1997 by the Council for Learning Disabilities. Reprinted by permission.

elements" (Baker et al., 2003, p. 116). Teachers should use a number of explicit models, examples, and prompts (see Figure 13.7). This instruction should be included with instruction about the writing process (Baker et al., 2003).

### Guided Feedback

Like the aforementioned techniques, guided feedback produces strong effects on the quality of students' writing (Baker et al., 2003; Gersten & Baker, 2001). In fact, "the successful application of procedural facilitators is enhanced considerably when they are linked to focused dialogue among students and teachers. In particular, extended

**FIGURE 13.7** Planning Sheet for Compare-and-Contrast Essays

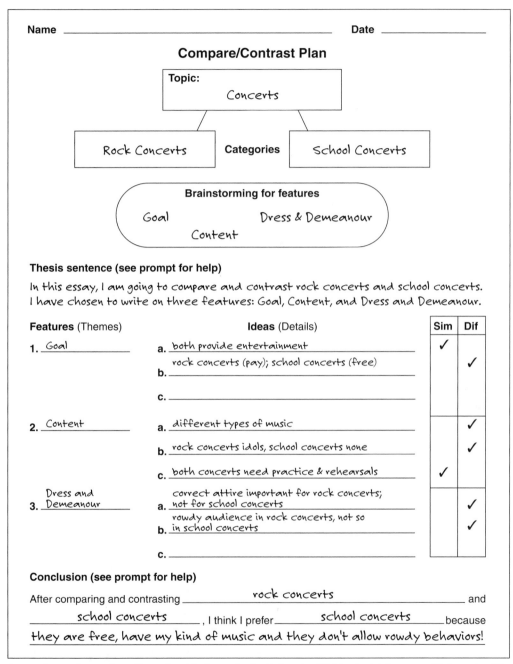

Name _____   Date _____

## Compare/Contrast Plan

Topic:
Concerts

Rock Concerts | Categories | School Concerts

**Brainstorming for features**
Goal            Dress & Demeanour
        Content

**Thesis sentence (see prompt for help)**

In this essay, I am going to compare and contrast rock concerts and school concerts.
I have chosen to write on three features: Goal, Content, and Dress and Demeanour.

| Features (Themes) | Ideas (Details) | Sim | Dif |
|---|---|---|---|
| 1. Goal | a. both provide entertainment | ✓ | |
| | b. rock concerts (pay); school concerts (free) | | ✓ |
| | c. | | |
| 2. Content | a. different types of music | | ✓ |
| | b. rock concerts idols, school concerts none | | ✓ |
| | c. both concerts need practice & rehearsals | ✓ | |
| 3. Dress and Demeanour | a. correct attire important for rock concerts; not for school concerts | | ✓ |
| | b. rowdy audience in rock concerts, not so in school concerts | | ✓ |
| | c. | | |

**Conclusion (see prompt for help)**

After comparing and contrasting _____ rock concerts _____ and
_____ school concerts _____, I think I prefer _____ school concerts _____ because
they are free, have my kind of music and they don't allow rowdy behaviors!

*Source:* From "Research on Genre-Specific Strategies for Enhancing Writing in Adolescents with Learning Disabilities" by B. Y. L. Wong, 1997, *Learning Disability Quarterly, 20,* 140–159. Copyright 1997 by the Council for Learning Disabilities. Reprinted by permission.

**FIGURE 13.8**   Writing Checklist

Before writing:

1. Have I chosen a topic appropriate for the assignment? (not too broad, not too narrow)   Yes   No

2. If I needed to, did I research and gather enough information in order to adequately cover my topic?   Yes   No

3. Have I organized my thoughts by using an outline, a web, or index cards?   Yes   No

*Note: Please do not go on until you have answered "yes" to each question above. Remember, you must be able to provide evidence for each step.*

After writing a first draft:

1. Is my introduction clear and interesting? (It should catch the reader's attention)   Yes   No

2. Does my introduction lead to a thesis that is stated completely, clearly, and correctly?   Yes   No

3. Are my supporting paragraphs logically organized?   Yes   No

4. Does the information in each body paragraph support the thesis?   Yes   No

5. Have I started each supporting paragraph with a topic sentence?   Yes   No

6. Have I ended each supporting paragraph with a concluding sentence?   Yes   No

7. Have I used good transitions (e.g., "however," "therefore," "in addition")?   Yes   No

8. Do I have enough supporting details in each body paragraph?   Yes   No

9. Does my concluding paragraph summarize the content of the paper?   Yes   No

10. In the conclusion, have I restated the thesis in different words?   Yes   No

11. Have I explained the significance of my topic in the conclusion?   Yes   No

12. Have I used complete sentences throughout my paper?   Yes   No

13. Have I used correct tenses?   Yes   No

14. Have I used proper spelling, capitalization, and punctuation?   Yes   No

15. Have I asked at least one other person to read my paper and make comments?   Yes   No

16. Have I met my teacher's specific requirements for this assignment?   Yes   No

*If you have answered "yes" to every question, you are now ready to type your final draft.*

dialogue and feedback can be another means for helping students significantly improve quality" (Baker et al., 2003, p. 114). The checklist in Figure 13.8 is an example of a **procedural facilitator** that can be used during guided feedback.

### Reinforcement

It is well established that rewarding young students' writing performance has positive benefits (Brigham, Graubard, & Stans, 1972; Maloney & Hopkins, 1973; Maloney, Jacobson, & Hopkins, 1975). When teachers make reinforcement contingent on writing more words, students write more words. When using more action verbs is rewarded, students use more action verbs in their compositions. (*Run, swing,* and *throw* are action verbs: *think, are,* and *want* are not.) When using a variety of words is reinforced, students write essays that show a wider vocabulary. However, rewarding performance on a certain part of writing may not affect performance on the other parts. Thus, the reward system must result in improvement in many different aspects of composition. Moreover, as effective as reinforcement has been shown to be, it is not a complete teaching program and should be used with other techniques.

### Story Grammar

One technique that has gained great currency in helping students with learning disabilities to write better compositions is story grammar. **Story grammar** refers to teaching students the basic components of a story (or essay) and then having them use a skeleton outline as a part of the planning stage in composing their products. Story grammar is sometimes called "procedural facilitation" because it is a strategy that facilitates the procedures of writing. Abundant research indicates that this technique is easy to implement and helps students produce higher-quality written products (Graves, Montague, & Wong, 1990; Montague et al., 1991; Montague & Graves, 1993; Schumm, 1992).

### Cognitive-Behavioral Techniques

Advocates of cognitive-behavioral approaches to learning disabilities often recommend that teachers combine components of other methods—story grammar (Martin & Manno, 1995), peer editing (Karegianes, Pascarella, & Pflaum, 1980), and self-evaluation (Harris & Graham, 1985)—when developing instructional programs for improving writing.

Self-evaluation and self-monitoring are particularly effective techniques. When monitoring students' progress in writing, teachers often count the number and different types of words in each essay and plot these counts on graphs. Interestingly, when students receive feedback about these and other features of their compositions, their writing often improves dramatically (Van Houten, Morrison, Jarvis, & McDonald, 1974), particularly when they evaluate their own writing (Ballard & Glynn, 1975).

For example, third-graders can learn to check their writing assignments according to specific guidelines. In one study, the self-evaluation procedure required

**procedural facilitator** think sheets, planning sheets, checklists, and the like used to help individuals with steps of the writing process

Council for Exceptional Children

**CEC Knowledge Check**
What are some of the limitations of rewards for performance (extrinsic motivation)? CC4S4, CC5S9

**story grammar** teaching students the basic components of a story (or essay) and then having them use a skeleton outline as part of the planning stage in composing their products

Council for Exceptional Children

**CEC Knowledge Check**
Is this technique similar to a graphic organizer, only showing students how the parts are put together? Explain. CC4S3, CC4S4, LD4S10

them to count the number of sentences written, words written, and various types of words used and to take other simple measures of their writing. According to these measures, the students assigned themselves points according to a reward system. This combination of self-evaluation and self-reward had positive effects on their writing (Ballard & Glynn, 1975). Similarly, secondary-school students with low achievement scores have learned to use an editing and rating system for evaluating their peers' essays. Later, these students scored higher on a posttest than those whose essays had been edited and rated by teachers.

Effective instructional approaches for improving the expressive writing skills of students with learning disabilities include teaching big ideas (planning, writing, and editing are fundamental features of writing) and strategies (e.g., story grammar), using scaffolding (i.e., gradually removing the overt aspects of the procedural facilitation), and providing extensive practice. In combination with handwriting and spelling instruction, these approaches make for "an effective, comprehensive writing program for students with LD" (Baker et al., 2003, p. 110).

As we have discussed in this chapter, students with learning disabilities experience a variety of problems in handwriting, spelling, and written expression. Effective teaching practices in handwriting emphasize teacher modeling and student practice. The teaching of spelling skills should be direct, and students should engage in text-level writing to employ their skills in an effort to become strategic spellers. Spelling instruction is likely to be more effective if it includes only a few spelling words on each day, provides distributed practice, teaches for generalization, and promotes self-correction. The problems experienced by students with learning disabilities in other areas (e.g., reading, spelling, and handwriting) are related to their difficulties in composition. To combat these difficulties, teachers should employ effective teaching procedures as they teach the writing process (i.e., plan, write, edit, and revise) without neglecting the fundamental aspects of writing.

**Council for Exceptional Children**

**CEC Knowledge Check**

Why would peer evaluation produce higher test scores than teacher evaluation? Could peer evaluation create problems in the classroom if students tease each other about results? What would you say or do? CC5K5, CC5S1, CC5S4

**Council for Exceptional Children**

**CEC Content Standards**

4. Instructional Strategies
5. Learning Environments and Social Interactions
6. Communication
7. Instructional Planning
8. Assessment

## PORTFOLIO-BUILDING ACTIVITY

### Demonstrating Mastery of the CEC Standards

Refer to the Case Connections box (page 419), Table 13.1 (page 412), Table 13.2 (page 422), and Figure 13.2 (page 415) in answering the following two questions:

How would you address Jamal's difficulties in handwriting? and spelling?

- Explain three methods that Jamal's teacher is using to teach handwriting that are supported by research.

- Choose three additional methods you would use to help Jamal improve his handwriting skills, and explain why you have chosen these methods.

- Explain two methods that Jamal's teacher is using to teach spelling that are supported by research.

- Choose two additional methods you would use to help Jamal improve his spelling skills, and explain why you have chosen these methods.

How would you monitor Jamal's progress in handwriting? In spelling?

- Describe two methods you would use to monitor progress in handwriting, and explain why you are choosing these methods.
- Describe two methods you would use to monitor progress in spelling, and explain why you are choosing these methods.

Questions to think about as you progress:

- What written language research-based interventions can be used to improve the performance skills of students with learning disabilities?
- How can learning environments be structured so that students with learning disabilities can increase meaningful self-management and active engagement?
- Why are assistive technologies important to the support and enhancement of teaching written communication skills?
- What is the importance of explicit modeling and efficient guided practice to ensure acquisition and fluency as powerful instructional variables? and
- How can regularly monitoring progress in written language performance improve instruction?

# SUMMARY

## What handwriting problems do students experience?

- Handwriting problems include difficulties with letter formation and fluency.
- These problems are often associated with other problems, particularly in spelling and composition.

## How is handwriting performance assessed?

- Experienced teachers can readily recognize poor handwriting, so formal tests are not essential.
- Testing for spelling and composition often provides samples suitable for at least preliminary evaluation.

## What interventions can help with handwriting difficulties?

- Effective teaching practices in handwriting emphasize teacher modeling and student practice.
- Other effective practices include reinforcement and self-instruction training.

## What spelling problems do students experience?

- English orthography is difficult because of the inconsistencies in it.
- Students with learning disabilities or severe reading problems do not necessarily produce unrecognizable

spelling. Many have difficulty segmenting words and syllables and seem to have particular difficulty when spelling involves consonant clusters.

- Students with spelling problems are very likely to have difficulty with the decoding aspects of reading. They also have problems in composition.

## How is spelling performance assessed?

- Three basic methods for assessing spelling skills are dictation, connected writing, and recognition.
- Most standardized achievement batteries include measures of spelling skills.
- Teachers sometimes analyze spelling errors, looking for consistent patterns in students' mistakes. Teachers should examine spelling tests and written work for errors. Informal spelling inventories and monitoring spelling progress are two instructional methods.

## What interventions help students' spelling difficulties?

- Spelling in English is made more difficult by the irregularities in the language.
- Spelling instruction at either the developmental or remedial level requires that teachers help students learn the alphabetic code for English.

- The teaching of spelling skills should be direct, and students should engage in text-level writing to employ their skills in an effort to become strategic spellers.
- Spelling instruction is likely to be more effective if it includes only a few spelling words on each day, provides distributed practice, teaches for generalization, and promotes self-correction.
- Effective teaching procedures include test-study-test, practice procedures, time delay, morphographic spelling, and add-a-word.

### What composition problems do students experience?

- Students with learning disabilities have more difficulty than their peers with planning, basic writing skills, revising, vocabulary, thematic maturity, word usage, style, sentence complexity, paragraph organization, and incorporation of important elements (e.g., characters, settings).
- The problems of students with learning disabilities in other areas (reading, spelling, and handwriting) are related to their difficulties in composition.

### How is composition performance assessed?

- Writing competence is not assessed well by reliance on tests of facility in editing material and answering true-false or multiple-choice questions about written material.

- Planning composition instruction requires detailed information about students' writing skills. For example, when students compose writing samples, teachers can assess elements such as number of words, average number of words per sentence, syntactic correctness, degree of abstractness, vocabulary, and maturity of theme.
- To evaluate progress, teachers can regularly sample students' writing to judge whether improvement has occurred. Teachers can assess improvement in overall quality of writing by comparing writing samples taken at different times.

### What interventions help students with composition difficulties?

- Teachers should encourage students to express the ideas they want to express, but they should not neglect the fundamental aspects of writing.
- Students should plan, write, edit, and revise.
- Effective teaching procedures include Self-Regulated Strategy Development, learning strategy interventions, explicit teaching of the steps in the writing process, explicit teaching of the conventions of a writing genre, guided feedback, reinforcement, story grammar, and cognitive-behavioral techniques.

## REFLECTIONS ON THE CASES

1. How would you address Jamal's difficulties in handwriting and spelling?
2. How would you monitor Jamal's progress in handwriting and spelling?
3. What do you think about the manner in which Ms. Hamilton is addressing Jamal's difficulties in handwriting and spelling?

## *Focus On* Writing

### *Do Now* Activities for Planning for Writing

### Think Sheets

● *What are they?*

Writing instruction presents many challenges for the student with learning disabilities. Students with learning disabilities experience difficulty with both the technical aspects (e.g., grammar, spelling, handwriting) and the conceptual aspects (concept development, organization, main idea, etc.) of writing. Recently, researchers have advocated that teachers of students with learning disabilities focus less on mechanics and more on cognitive processes when teaching students to write (Baker, Gersten, & Scanlon, 2002). The overemphasis on correct spelling and grammar take the focus away from student development of organized, interesting text. One technique that has been shown to assist secondary students with learning disabilities in developing their writing skills is the think sheet (Englert et al., 1991).

Think sheets are prewriting guides that make text structure explicit for students. They provide a visual guide for students to process what they need to do. Since think sheets are more visually spatial than traditional outlines, it is easier for students to see the whole project as well as how each part fits into the whole. For narratives, students would complete sheets that include information on characters, themes, setting, and plot. If students are writing a persuasive paper, they would write on their think sheet their statement of belief, the reasons for their belief, and the facts to support their belief. Thus, the format of the think sheet will vary, based on the text structure being taught.

● *How to implement them*

Think sheets assist students in the three main processes of writing—planning, writing, and revision. Think sheets can be commercially produced (see the Additional Resources) or teacher generated. Sheets should include the critical writing steps for the particular type of text structure being taught. Two examples of think sheets follow:

Compare/Contrast Think Sheet

---

What is being compared/contrasted?

_____

Feature: _____

| Similarities | Differences |

Feature: _____

| Similarities | Differences |

Feature: _____

| Similarities | Differences |

Summary statement:

_____

---

Persuasive Writing Think Sheet

Controlling argument:

_____

_____

Proof #1:

Proof #2:

Proof #3:

Summary statement:

_____

_____

Writing check:

Transition words  _____

Spelling  _____

Punctuation  _____

Capitalization  _____

Think sheets can be used for a variety of purposes. One way to introduce think sheets is for students to use them to analyze text selections. For example, students would read text representative of the type of structure to be taught (e.g., compare-contrast, persuasive, descriptive essays) and then use the think sheet to identify the critical features of the writing selection.

Teachers can also use think sheets to assist students in planning for writing. To do this, teachers should first model using think sheets several times prior to guiding students through the sheets. Next, students should have ample opportunity to complete the sheets independently. Finally, teachers should then model how to incorporate information from the sheet into connected text. Teachers often overlook this critical step!

A final use of the think sheet is for revision or writing evaluation. For this purpose, students use the think sheet in order to evaluate their writing piece and make sure the critical elements are included. Teachers can include features such as transition words, spelling, and punctuation as well into their think sheets.

## ● *Additional Resources*

**Stack the Deck Writing Program**
P.O. Box 429
Tinley Park, IL 60477-0429
Phone: 1-800-253-5737
Fax: 1-708-429-9516
E-mail: staff@stackthedeck.com
www.stackthedeck.com/order.html

**Masterminds, LLC**
P.O. Box 20433
Tuscaloosa, AL 35402-0433
E-mail: masterminds@graphicorganizers.com
www.graphicorganizers.com/

*Source:* Kristin L. Sayeski

How Does Mathematical Knowledge
Develop Normally?

What Problems in Mathematics
Do Students Experience?
- Problems in Cognitive Development
- Problems in Arithmetic Performance

How Are Mathematics Abilities Assessed?
- Achievement Tests
- Formal Diagnostic Testing

- Informal Inventories
- Error Analysis
- Monitoring Progress

What Interventions Help Students
with Mathematics Difficulties?
- Developmental Interventions
- Remedial Interventions
- Technology
- Effective Teaching Procedures

**Council for Exceptional Children**

See Companion Website
for detailed correlations
between chapter content
and Council for Excep-
tional Children Standards;
**www.ablongman.com/
hallahanLD3e**

**CEC Knowledge and Skills Discussed in This Chapter**

**1** Theories and models of special education instruction and curriculum that intersect
with human growth and development in mathematical abilities.

**2** The development and usage of individualized math assessment procedures, which
are based on prioritized general and special curricula, student needs, and instrument
limitation considerations.

**3** Instruction in mathematics, grounded in research-based methods, guided by results of
student data, incorporating the principles of task analysis, and used to facilitate generalization across settings.

**4** Methods for increasing accuracy and proficiency in math calculations and applications
that take into consideration necessary individual accommodations and inclusion of assistive technology in the curriculum.

# Students Who Experience Difficulties with Mathematics

**14**

> Math just doesn't make sense to me. Do I really have to know how to multiply binomials? I get very confused when I have to do a lot of calculations for one problem. I've learned to take my time and write out each step. Now, I don't make as many careless mistakes. Also, it helps when I have steps to follow for solving a problem.
>
> *Shannon*

In mathematics, students learn not just how to compute, but also how to reason and how to apply reason to solve real-life problems. Comprehension of concepts such as number, equality, sets, proportionality, and functional relationships are important aspects of competence in mathematics. Other skills are also important, such as counting money, telling time, and measuring size and weight.

Today, there is growing concern about students' deficits in mathematics. National organizations such as the National Council of Teachers of Mathematics have issued strong statements about the need for mathematical competence. Although research in mathematics disabilities still lags behind research in reading disabilities (Geary, 1999), math difficulties are receiving more and more attention in the field of learning disabilities (e.g., Robinson, Menchetti, & Torgesen, 2002; Woodward & Montague, 2002). This attention is spurred on by the low levels of achievement for students with learning disabilities (Cawley & Miller, 1989; Fuchs & Fuchs, 2001).

Part of the increased attention may also be related to increased interest in the cognitive aspects of learning. During the 1980s, extensive research focused on the cognitive aspects of acquisition of arithmetic skills (e.g., Resnick, 1983). Interest in this area has also grown out of the practical experience of teachers revealing that many children with learning disabilities have problems in mathematics.

# How Does Mathematical Knowledge Develop Normally?

**conservation** the preservation of a physical quantity during transformations or reactions

Some of the most influential approaches to development, based on the work of Piaget (1952), stress the relationship of the concept of **conservation** to mathematical knowledge and ability. Students have a concept of conservation if they understand, for example, that lengths of objects do not change when they are moved or that the amount of a liquid does not change when it is poured into a container of a different size or shape. These general rules of development help in understanding mathematical concepts.

In addition to general development, it also helps to look at mathematical development specifically. In what order do children and adolescents acquire concepts and operations? How does a student's approach to arithmetic change with age? Many authors have discussed these transformations and presented developmental theories of children's understanding of mathematical concepts (Carpenter & Moser, 1982; Geary, 1994).

Contemporary theory about mathematical development holds that students match new information with what they already know. Most of what they know about mathematics is intuitive and is often called informal mathematical knowledge (Geary, 1994; Ginsberg, 1977, 1997). Formal mathematical knowledge, in contrast, is the system of symbols, concepts, procedures, and so forth that form the content of mathematics instruction.

Normally developing young children usually come to school with some informal knowledge. In fact, infants as young as 4 or 5 months of age can discriminate between arrays of two and three objects. By about 18 months, they appear to understand something about numerical order (3 comes after 2). Thus, throughout the preschool years, children learn much about counting and numbers. Twin studies reveal that some mathematics skills are innate (Alarcón, DeFries, Light, & Pennington, 1997) but that they are also influenced by the environment. For example, children and parents often play counting games such as "One, two, buckle my shoe." Shannon's father recalls his daughter's difficulty with this nursery rhyme:

**Shannon**

> Shannon enjoyed hearing nursery rhymes when she was a preschooler, but she had trouble catching on when she'd try reciting them on her own. She seemed to have particular trouble with rhymes that involved numbers. I remember demonstrating the rhythmic pattern for her. I'd say, "Listen, Shannon . . . three, four, shut the door, five, six, pick up sticks . . . do you hear the rhyming? Now, you try." She'd try, but she seemed so confused. She often mixed up the phrases.
>
> *Daniel Ireland, Shannon's father*

By age 3 or 4 years, many children actually use number names to identify the number of objects in a group, although they can do so only when the group has a few items (Geary, 1994).

## Understanding Math Disabilities

Do we have a clear understanding of the causes of math disabilities? Are we able to identify children at risk for math disabilities? Researchers are working diligently to answer these questions. Robinson and colleagues (2002) propose a two-factor theory to explain a common difficulty of mastering basic number facts experienced by many students with math disabilities. In much the same way that many struggling readers have poor phonological processing skills, many who struggle with math may have phonological-processing problems. This may be

> because an almost universal method of teaching number facts in our educational culture is to have students orally practice repeating the facts to be learned. . . . The student hears and repeats a statement such as "nine times eight is 72" or "six eights are 48" until the recitation of the fact becomes automatic. During this period of acquisition, phonological information about the number fact is being generated and stored, and each repetition of the fact strengthens the association between the fact and its solution. In other words, what is being learned when number facts are rehearsed orally are connections or associations between the phonological representations of all the words included in the number fact. In a real sense, the child is memorizing a string of phonological representations. Highly overlearned connections between the elements of the number fact (the phonological representations that are memorized as a specific sequence) facilitate rapid recall.

If children have only "fuzzy" or degraded phonological representations of number names available to them, it follows that it should be more difficult to establish reliable connections between these representations when memorizing a specific sequence of them as a math fact. For example, if a child's phonological representations of the numbers "six" and "eight" and "48" are degraded or imprecise, then it will be harder for that child to commit to memory the sequence of phonological representations in the math fact "six eights are 48." (Robinson et al., 2002, p. 84)

However, because reading disabilities are not always accompanied by math disabilities, it is not likely that phonological-processing weaknesses cause all math disabilities. For some children, reading skills develop normally, but math disabilities still emerge. Robinson and colleagues (2002) point to poorly developed number sense as a possible explanation for the difficulties some students experience in learning math facts. The two-factor theory "suggests that difficulties in learning math facts might result from either weaknesses in phonological processing or weakly developed number sense" (Robinson et al., 2002, p. 86).

What does all this mean? Robinson and colleagues (2002) suggest that this theory, if verified, could have instructional implications (i.e., in the type of intervention teachers choose). Further, verification of this theory could lead to the early identification of children at risk for difficulties in acquiring number facts.

Researchers (e.g., Gersten & Chard, 1999) use the term **number sense** to describe a conceptual structure critical for mathematics learning. Number sense "refers to a child's fluidity and flexibility with numbers, the sense of what numbers mean, and an ability to perform mental mathematics and to look at the world and make comparisons" (Gersten & Chard, 1999, pp. 19–20). Most children develop this sense before kindergarten through informal interactions with family members. Number sense leads to greater facility with math information and the ability to solve arithmetic computations (Gersten & Chard, 1999). The Current Trends and Issues box above provides insight into how phonological processing skills and number sense might be related to our understanding of math disabilities.

**number sense** fluidity and flexibility with numbers; an understanding of what numbers mean; the ability to perform mental mathematics and make comparisons (most children develop number sense before kindergarten)

**CEC Knowledge Check**
When children have not played counting games and rhymes at home, what math skills will these children bring to their first day of school? CC1K1

When they arrive at school, many children use their number sense to solve simple arithmetic problems (Resnick, 1983; Resnick & Ford, 1981). These skills are probably based on a rudimentary understanding of the relationships between counting, numbers, and numerals. The concepts can be represented as a number line, shown in Figure 14.1. The concept of a mental number line holds that each number is conceptually linked to the next higher one in the way that it might be after extensive practice with counting. Each number is also linked to a concept of the number of "things" it represents (as represented by the drawings of dots). Thus, the mental number line represents children's understanding of the fundamental concepts that numbers occur in order and that numerals are used to represent numbers of objects. This concept is further discussed in Focus on Mathematics on pages 485–487. As young children grow more sophisticated, they learn other concepts to go with the mental number line. For example, they learn the related concepts of equality (in the mathematical sense) and correspondence.

Very young children typically have simple addition skills. By the time they begin to progress through the primary grades, children show further development of addition concepts. Regardless of culture, addition skills appear to be based on counting (Geary, 1994). Initially, children employ very simple strategies to add two sets or groups. For example, they count out the objects for one group ("one, two, three"), count out the objects for the second group ("one, two, three, four"), and then physically move the groups together. Once the groups are combined, they count the total ("One, two three, four, five, six, seven . . . seven eggs! Don't wanna drop 'em.").

In addition to the concept of a number line, primary-school children learn to think about numbers as wholes that are composed of parts. For example, the number 7 may also be thought of as being composed of the numbers 4 and 3, 5 and 2, and 6 and 1. Understanding the part-whole concept of numbers allows school-age

**FIGURE 14.1    The Mental Number Line Concept**

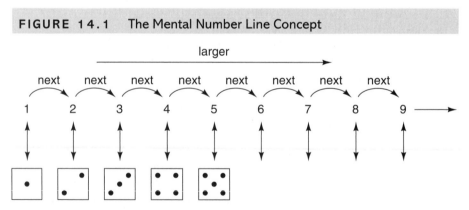

*Source:* From "A Developmental Theory of Number Understanding" (p. 110) by L. B. Resnick, 1983, in H. Ginsberg (Ed.), *The Development of Mathematical Thinking,* New York: Academic Press. Copyright 1983 by Academic Press. Reprinted by permission.

children to interpret and solve more sophisticated problems than preschoolers. Some instructional programs—for example, Connecting Math Concepts (Engelmann, Carnine, Engelmann, & Kelly, 1991)—base instruction on simple computation and even on problem solving or mastery of part-whole relationships.

As they develop greater facility with mathematics, children gradually adopt different strategies. For example, for addition, they progress from the counting of **manipulatives** to more and more efficient strategies, which require fewer cognitive actions. Table 14.1 (page 456) shows the usual developmental pattern of strategies through which most children go as they become more efficient with addition. Similar patterns also emerge for other forms of computation, such as subtraction (Geary, 1994).

Unfortunately, many educational methods for teaching arithmetic do not conform to the normal development of computation skill. The sequence of development shown in Table 14.1 illustrates this problem. Many education methods encourage young children to work with manipulatives when learning addition. First, they are shown the "counting manipulatives" strategy illustrated in Table 14.1. This system of instruction works well for students who have a lot of knowledge of mathematical concepts and competency with numbers. For students who lack those skills, skipping from a counting-manipulatives to a fact-retrieval strategy likely will cause problems.

Another major developmental step in understanding numbers is learning the working of the decimal, or base-10, system. At first, children are taught to treat two-digit numbers (e.g., 17) as composed of two parts (10 + 7); then they are instructed to extend this to other numbers, with the requirement that one of the parts must be a multiple of 10 (e.g., 43 is 40 and 3). Handling numbers in this manner (later extended to 100s, 1,000s, and so forth) is sometimes called the concept of **place value.** Development of this concept allows students to perform more complex computations "in their heads" by using strategies related to those they acquired earlier. For example, 147 + 265 is composed of (100 + 200), (40 + 60), and (7 + 5); these resolve to (300) + (100) + (12), which is 412.

As shown in Table 14.1, older students who solve more difficult problems also gradually adopt more efficient strategies. Their informal knowledge about more sophisticated topics gradually changes as they learn formal mathematics. For example, most young children can understand the meaning of "half" when it refers to a cookie. However, as they learn more, they understand that the concept of "half" does not stand only for physical relationships. They must learn that the idea of "half" can be applied to "half of the boys whom I know" (and that it does not require that each boy is cut into two pieces).

More sophisticated concepts in mathematics develop later. Computational skill and conceptual knowledge continue to change with age. Many of the advances in competence have to do with acquiring and using more sophisticated strategies. Students who do not advance beyond using elementary strategies (e.g., counting manipulatives or counting fingers, as illustrated in Table 14.1) have greater trouble with advanced concepts. For students with learning disabilities, acquiring advanced concepts is a particularly important problem.

Council for Exceptional Children

**CEC Knowledge Check**

What role do television programs such as "Sesame Street" play in developing children's understanding of basic math concepts? CC2K1

**manipulatives** physical materials (e.g., pattern blocks, base 10 blocks, rods, color tiles, linking cubes) used to facilitate an understanding of mathematical concepts

Council for Exceptional Children

**CEC Knowledge Check**

Do you think the constructivist model works for math instruction? Why, or why not? Which primitive culture first developed the concept of zero? CC1K1, CC2K1

**place value** a developmental step in number conceptualization in which children learn that numbers can be multiples of 10; also called the decimal, or base-10, system

**TABLE 14.1**     Commonly Used Addition Strategies

| STRATEGY | DESCRIPTION | EXAMPLE |
|---|---|---|
| **Simple Addition** | | |
| Counting manipulatives | The problem's augend and addend are represented by objects. The objects are then counted, starting from 1. | To solve 2 + 3, two blocks are counted out, then three blocks are counted out, and finally all five blocks are counted. |
| Counting fingers | The problem's augend and addend are represented by fingers. The fingers are then counted, usually starting from 1. | To solve 2 + 3, two fingers are lifted on the left hand, and three fingers are then lifted on the right hand. The child then moves each finger in succession as he or she counts them. |
| Verbal counting   Counting all (sum) | The child counts the augend and addend in succession starting from 1. | To solve 2 + 3, the child counts "1, 2, 3, 4, 5; the answer is 5." |
| Counting on first | The child states the value of the augend and then counts a number of times equal to the value of the addend. | To solve 2 + 3, the child counts "2, 3, 4, 5; the answer is 5." |
| Counting on larger (min) | The child states the value of the larger addend and then counts a number of times equal to the value of the smaller addend. | To solve 2 + 3, the child counts "3, 4, 5; the answer is 5." |
| Derived facts (decomposition) | One of the addends is decomposed into two smaller numbers, so that one of these numbers can be added to the other to produce a sum of 10. The remaining number is then added to 10. | To solve 8 + 7: Step 1. 7 = 5 + 2 Step 2. 8 + 2 = 10 Step 3. 10 + 5 = 15 |
| Fact retrieval | Direct retrieval of basic facts from long-term memory | Retrieving 5 to solve 2 + 3. |
| **Complex Addition** | | |
| Verbal counting   Counting on larger | Same as above | To solve 23 + 2, the child counts "23, 24, 25; the answer is 25." |
| Regrouping | The addends are decomposed into tens and units values. The tens and units values are summed separately. The two provisional sums are then added together. | To solve 25 + 42: Step 1. 25 = 20 + 5 Step 2. 42 = 40 + 2 Step 3. 20 + 40 = 60 Step 4. 5 + 2 = 7 Step 5. 60 + 7 = 67 |
| Columnar retrieval | The problem is solved by retrieving columnwise sums. | To solve 27 + 38: Step 1. 7 + 8 = 15 Step 2. Note trade (carry) Step 3. 2 + 3 = 5 Step 4. 5 + 1 (from trade) = 6 Step 5. Combined 6 from tens column to 5 from ones column to produce 65 |

*Source:* From *Children's Mathematical Development: Research and Practical Applications* (pp. 62–63) by D. C. Geary, 1994, Washington, DC: American Psychological Association. Copyright © 1994 by American Psychological Association. Reprinted by permission.

# What Problems in Mathematics Do Students Experience?

Students with learning disabilities experience a wide variety of problems in mathematics (Strang & Rourke, 1985; Geary, Hamson, & Hoard, 2000). Thus, just as with reading or writing disabilities, any effort to characterize "the math disabled child" is a mistake; students who have mathematics disabilities are too heterogeneous to constitute a type. **Dyscalculia** is the most widely used term for disabilities in mathematics. In general, dyscalculia means a severe or complete inability to calculate.

Studies indicate that "between 6 and 7% of school-age children show persistent, grade-to-grade, difficulties in learning some aspects of arithmetic or related areas" (Geary, 1999, p. 2). More than half of students with learning disabilities have individual education program goals in math (Kavale & Reece as cited in Fuchs & Fuchs, 2001). Students with learning disabilities who are in the third and fourth grades often score at a first-grade level in arithmetic. Things do not get better later; high school students often score at about the fifth-grade level (Cawley & Miller, 1989), and difficulties continue in postsecondary educational settings (Strawser & Miller, 2001). Clearly, students with such deficits deserve special education.

Some students with learning disabilities have problems in both mathematics and reading (Robinson et al., 2002). Others have problems in only one area (Lewis, Hitch, & Walker, 1994). The performance of students who have only mathematics problems differs from that of those who have problems in both reading and mathematics. For example, when tests are timed, students with only mathematics problems make about as many mistakes on simple story and number-fact problems as their peers who have both mathematics and reading problems. However, when tests are untimed, those with only mathematics problems make fewer mistakes and get just about as many problems correct as nondisabled students (Jordon & Montani, 1997).

**dyscalculia** the inability to perform mathematical calculations

Council for Exceptional Children

**CEC Knowledge Check**
What does this finding tell you about how to conduct your math tests?
CC4S3, LD4K1

## Problems in Cognitive Development

Authorities in learning disabilities have suggested many types of problems that may be associated with disabilities in learning mathematics. Many of these difficulties are not directly related to arithmetic performance but fall into the categories of developmental problems and information-processing disorders. Research in cognitive science indicates that students must have an understanding of mathematical facts (i.e., declarative knowledge), rules and procedures (i.e., procedural knowledge), and relationships (i.e., conceptual knowledge) in order to develop mathematical literacy. Students who have difficulty with math, for example, typically approach word problems in a mechanical fashion (e.g., by looking for key words) rather than attempting to understand the problem. In doing so, they often use irrelevant information and are unable to determine if their answer makes sense

(Goldman, Hasselbring, & the Cognition and Technology Group at Vanderbilt, 1997). Shannon's mother observes:

Shannon

> It seems like Shannon's always had problems with math. She just can't grasp the concepts. I remember she'd do problems like "If a bus holds 30 students, how many buses would be needed to take 100 students on a field trip?" and, with help, she'd do the calculations right—100 divided by 30 is 3 1/3. But then she'd say that 3 1/3 was her answer. I'd try to explain that they wouldn't be able to take one third of a bus along, that they'd need 4.
>
> *Kerrie Ireland, Shannon's mother*

As Goldman and colleagues (1997) note, mathematical competence

involves far more than fluent retrieval of basic math facts and the execution of computational procedures. To be sure, learners must possess a sufficient and efficient knowledge base from which to draw information. The retrieval of facts and basic procedural steps necessary to solve a problem depends on recognizing their appropriate use—a skill that requires the coordination of relationships among declarative, procedural, and conceptual knowledge. (p. 202)

## Problems in Arithmetic Performance

Some of the mathematical difficulties that students with learning disabilities have are directly associated with performance of arithmetic tasks. For example, students with dyscalculia often have problems with such skills as (1) writing numerals and mathematical symbols correctly, (2) recalling the meanings of symbols and the answers to basic facts, (3) counting, and (4) following the steps in a strategy for solving multistep problems (Glennon & Cruickshank, 1981).

### Performance on Basic Arithmetic Tasks

Students rarely make random mistakes in answering arithmetic problems. Classic studies have documented that the errors are usually systematic and indicate that students are consistently applying a mistaken strategy to solve the problems (Cox, 1975; Ginsberg, 1977; Lankford, 1972). The analysis of computational errors has a long history (Buswell & John, 1926). Extensive analyses of "bugs," or errors in computation, have also been made by educators and psychologists interested in children's thinking during solution of arithmetic problems (Ashlock, 1994; Woodward & Howard, 1994; Young & O'Shea, 1981).

Cognitive research on mathematical difficulties reveals that such students have deficits in fact retrieval (Garnett & Fleishner, 1983; Geary, 1994; Geary, Hoard, & Hamson, 1999). They make more mistakes in giving simple answers in various

Council for
Exceptional
Children

**CEC Knowledge Check**

Can consistency of math problem layout (vertical vs. horizontal alignment) help students? If you ask students to copy problems onto paper from the board, are you setting up some students for failure?
LD4K1, LD4K3, LD4S12

areas of arithmetic and sometimes recall facts more slowly than their peers. Such fact retrieval problems are probably related to deficits in working memory (see Chapter 8).

Students also make mistakes in applying strategies or procedures (Geary, 1994; Jordon & Montani, 1997). They may not only choose inefficient strategies, but also poorly use those they choose. For example, students with problems are more likely to depend on the counting-all strategy (see Table 14.1), even though it is less efficient than strategies developed later. When they revert to using this strategy, they may also make mistakes in counting, leading to wrong answers.

### Difficulties with Story Problems

Difficulties with computation will have obvious effects on whether students can solve story problems correctly. Problems reading the stories will affect performance, too, but students' difficulties with these kinds of tasks are more complex than one would predict because of reading or computation deficits alone.

Certain aspects of story problems make them difficult for many students. For example, story problems given in reverse order and beginning with the missing number (e.g., ones for which an equation might be written in this way: $? - 5 = 3$) are considerably harder than other story problem arrangements (Rosenthal & Resnick, 1974). The difficulties unique to solving story problem arrangements by students with learning disabilities reveal that these students' performances are adversely affected by such features of story problems as (1) presence of extraneous information, (2) use of complex syntactic structures, (3) change of number and type of noun used, and (4) use of verbs such as "purchased" or "bought" rather than "was given" (Blankenship & Lovitt, 1976; Jitendra, DiPipi, & Perron-Jones, 2002; Parmar, Cawley, & Frazita, 1996; Trenholme, Larsen, & Parker, 1978). The implication of these findings is not that teachers of students with learning disabilities should avoid assigning problems with these features. Instead, they should teach their students how to solve them by applying strategies such as Solve It! (Montague, Warger, & Morgan, 2000) and STAR (Maccini & Hughes, 2000). See the Case Connections box on pages 460–461 for an example of how Shannon uses the STAR strategy.

Students with learning disabilities are vulnerable to inadequate instructional programs and practices. For example, if a program for teaching fractions does not use both **proper fractions** and **improper fractions** when demonstrating how to work with fractions, students with learning disabilities are far more likely to make mistakes on problems involving improper fractions (Kelly, Gersten, & Carnine, 1990). Fractions is not the only area in which problems are likely to occur. Figure 14.2 (page 462) illustrates the range of problem areas in which students are likely to have trouble. If instructional practices, including both curriculum and teaching behavior, do not correct for problems in these areas, students with learning disabilities will be most likely to suffer. "Low-achieving students are often casualties of curricula that assume too much and teach too little. Difficulties are related to learners' fragile preskills and the subsequent failure of the curriculum to explicitly address those skills" (Kame'enui & Simmons, 1990, p. 393).

Council for Exceptional Children

**CEC Knowledge Check**

Should story problems be introduced before students have learned basic math concepts? Why, or why not? How is the Solve It! strategy an aid in story problem instruction? CC7K2, CC7S1

**proper fraction** a fraction wherein the value of the numerator is less than the value of the denominator; these fractions have a value between 0 and 1

**improper fraction** a fraction wherein the value of the numerator is greater than the value of the denominator; these fractions have a value greater than 1

Council for Exceptional Children

**CEC Knowledge Check**

Do "low-achieving students" in math only include students with learning disabilities? What should be done for these low achievers? CC2K1, CC2K5

## Applying a Problem-Solving Strategy:
## Shannon Ireland Explains

Teachers have used the STAR strategy (see Figure A) successfully with secondary school students with learning disabilities (Maccini & Hughes, 2000). Students are taught to read the problem, self-question, and write down facts. Then they learn to translate the words into an equation by progressing through three phases of instruction. In the first phase (i.e., concrete application), students represent the problem using Algebra Lab Gear. In the second phase (i.e., semiconcrete application), they represent the problem by drawing a picture. In the third phase (i.e., abstract application), they use numerical symbols. With the help of her teachers, Shannon has progressed through the first two phases. She is now in the third phase, where she is able to represent equations using numerical symbols. Here, Shannon explains how she uses the STAR strategy:

> I've learned the STAR strategy. I use it for word problems in algebra, like this one: "Monday, the temperature was –8° F. By Wednesday, the temperature had risen 15°F. What was the temperature on Wednesday?" First, I search the problem. That means I read it over carefully and figure out what facts I know and what I need to find. I know that the temperature was –8 on Monday, and it rose 15° by Wednesday. I need to figure out what the temperature was on Wednesday. Now, I have to translate the words into an equation. Let's see . . . I'm going to use $x$ as the temperature on Wednesday, so the equation would be $-8 + 15 = x$ . . . is that right? –8 on Monday plus 15 . . . that's how much the temperature rose . . . equals $x$ . . . the temperature on Wednesday. Yes, that looks right. Okay, so now I answer. I have different signs, so I subtract and keep the sign of the bigger number. 15 minus 8 is 7 . . . positive 7, since the sign of the bigger number, 15, is positive. The temperature on Wednesday was 7° F. Now, I review. The problem was: "Monday, the temperature was –8° F. By Wednesday, the temperature had risen 15° F. What was the temperature on Wednesday?" Does my answer make sense? I think so, but I'm not sure why. Let me check . . . negative 8 plus positive 15 is 7 because when you're adding, and you have different signs, you subtract and take the sign of the bigger number . . . positive 7 . . . that's right. There, that's how I use the STAR strategy!

## How Are Mathematics Abilities Assessed?

Mathematics learning problems are assessed in much the same way as deficits in other areas of academic learning. Teachers may make referrals because students appear to be having difficulties, and students may be administered screening tests to determine

## FIGURE A  STAR Strategy

1. **S**earch the word problem.
   a. Read the problem carefully.
   b. Ask yourself questions: "What facts do I know?" "What do I need to find?"
   c. Write down facts.
2. **T**ranslate the words into an equation in picture form.
   a. Choose a variable.
   b. Identify the operation(s).
   c. Represent the problem with Algebra Lab Gear. (*Concrete Application*)
      Draw a picture of the representation. (*Semiconcrete Application*)
      Write an algebraic equation. (*Abstract Application*)
3. **A**nswer the problem.

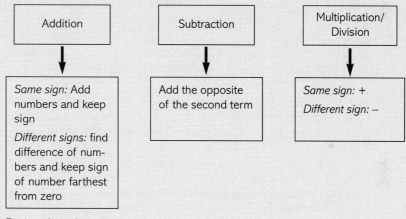

| Addition | Subtraction | Multiplication/Division |
|---|---|---|
| *Same sign:* Add numbers and keep sign<br><br>*Different signs:* find difference of numbers and keep sign of number farthest from zero | Add the opposite of the second term | *Same sign:* +<br>*Different sign:* – |

4. **R**eview the solution.
   a. Reread the problem.
   b. Ask question "Does the answer make sense? Why?"
   c. Check answer.

whether further assessment is needed. Another type of assessment includes testing used to guide program planning. This form of assessment is designed to help determine what specific arithmetic learning problems students have and what kind of educational program will be needed to remedy them. When remediation is under way, assessment continues in the form of **progress monitoring** (Bryant & Rivera, 1997).

**progress monitoring**
the regular assessment of students' academic performance to determine whether they are benefiting from the instructional program

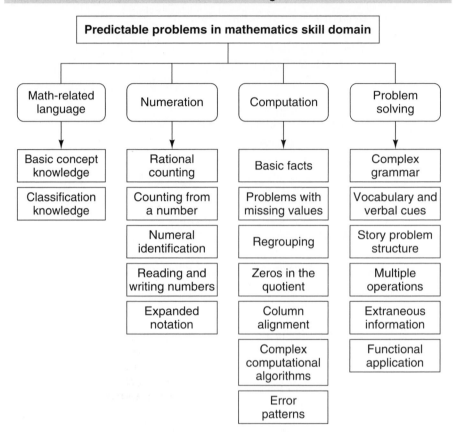

**FIGURE 14.2** Predictable Problems in Mathematics Skill Domain for Students with Learning Disabilities

*Source:* From *Designing Instructional Strategies: The Prevention of Academic Learning Problems* (p. 512) by E. J. Kame'enui and D. C. Simmons, 1990. Copyright © 1990, 1st ed. Reprinted by permission of Pearson Education, Inc., Upper Saddle River, NJ.

Unfortunately, most of the work on assessing mathematical competence of students with learning disabilities focuses almost exclusively on computation. Too little work has been done on assessing mathematical concepts. Because knowledge of underlying concepts facilitates mastery of arithmetic computation, students' understanding of concepts is an appropriate area for assessment. Similarly, students' strategies in solving problems are worthy of assessment (Ginsburg, 1991, 1997).

## Achievement Tests

To identify students who might need additional services, schools may screen large groups of students in mathematics. Administration of a screening test helps educators decide whether students should be tested further to determine if they have a mathematics learning problem or, if one is suspected, to confirm it.

Screening usually consists of administering a norm-referenced test to compare the referred student to normally performing age- and grade-males. When a student is greatly behind age- or grade-mates on arithmetic screening tests, an arithmetic learning disability is suspected. Commonly used screening tests include most of the general achievement batteries: the *California Achievement Test—5th Edition* (Teigs & Clark, 1992), the *Iowa Tests of Basic Skills* (Hieronymus, Lindquist, & Hoover, 1978), the *Metropolitan Achievement Test—7th Edition* (Prescott, Balow, Hogan, & Farr, 1992), and the *Stanford Achievement Test—8th Edition* (Gardner, Rudman, Karlsen, & Merwin, 1988). However, individually administered achievement batteries such as the *Peabody Individual Achievement Test—Revised* (Markwardt, 1989) and the *Woodcock-Johnson—III* (Woodcock, McGrew, & Mather, 2001), as well as some tests devoted specifically to diagnosing arithmetic and mathematics (discussed in the following section on formal diagnostic testing), probably are the instruments most commonly used when identifying students.

Some screening instruments may provide preliminary diagnostic information. For example, the *Metropolitan Achievement Tests* (Prescott et al., 1992) contain two subtests related to mathematics: one that assesses computation skills and one that assesses knowledge of concepts. If a student performs poorly on one of these but not on the other, the difference probably reflects something about his or her difficulties with mathematics. Some authors (e.g., Trembley, Caponiqro, & Gaffrey, 1980) suggest programming based on common achievement tests such as the PIAT and the *Wide Range Achievement Test—3* (Wilkinson, 1993). However, when planning instructional programs, teachers need much more fine-grained assessment measures than tests of this sort offer.

## Formal Diagnostic Testing

**Diagnostic tests** should allow the teacher to determine in which areas of mathematics a student is having difficulties. Table 14.2 (page 464) identifies some of these areas and gives examples of them. Diagnostic tests sample from some or all of these.

*Key Math Revised: A Diagnostic Inventory of Essential Mathematics* (Connolly, 1998) is a very widely used diagnostic instrument for grades kindergarten through 8. Its 14 subtests are arranged into three general areas: content, operations, and applications. The test covers most of the areas of knowledge and skill listed in Table 14.2 and provides different types of scores, ranging from a norm-referenced total test score to scores on individual items that can be used as program-planning aids. An extensive list of instructional objectives corresponding to the items on the test is included, making it easy to program instruction according to a student's performance on the test.

The *Stanford Diagnostic Mathematics Test* (Beatty, Madden, Gardner, & Karlsen, 1984) is another diagnostic instrument. It includes four levels, each designed for administration to a different age group ranging from first grade through high school. Three general areas of skill and knowledge—number system and numeration, computation, and applications—are assessed at each level (these include most of the

**diagnostic tests** tests used to determine in which of the many areas of mathematics a student is having difficulties

## TABLE 14.2    Areas of Arithmetic and Mathematics Learning

| AREA | EXAMPLES |
| --- | --- |
| *Basic information* | Number-numeral relationships, counting, equality, symbol names |
| *Computation skills* | Addition, subtraction, multiplication, division |
| *Problem solving* | Writing algorithms for "story problems" |
| *Fractions* | Regular, decimals, percentages, renaming, computation using fractions, ratios, proportions, probability |
| *Measurement* | Meters and derivatives; inches, feet, miles, etc.; grams and derivatives; ounces, pounds, bushels, pecks, etc.; seconds, minutes |
| *Money* | Coin values, equivalencies |
| *Algebra* | Linear and quadratic equations |
| *Geometry* | Shape names, theorems |

*Source:* From *Introduction to Learning Disabilities,* 2nd ed. (p. 274) by D. P. Hallahan, J. M. Kauffman, and J. W. Lloyd, 1985, Boston: Allyn and Bacon. Copyright © 1985 by Pearson Education. Reprinted by permission of the publisher.

areas shown in Table 14.2). Because you can administer this test to groups of students, you can also use it as a screening instrument.

Some commercial instruments cover diverse mathematical concepts quite thoroughly. For example, the *Multilevel Academic Survey Test* (Howell, Zucker, & Morehead, 1985) is based on a comprehensive analysis of the concepts that underlie mathematics and provides a valuable means of identifying areas of difficulty for students. Several other commercially available instruments may be used to diagnose problems in mathematics. *Diagnosis: An Instructional Aid in Mathematics* (Guzaitis, Carlin, & Juda, 1972) is a system of probes for use with primary- and elementary-school students; items on the probes are based on instructional objectives and are keyed to sections of instructional materials for teachers to use in remediating problems. The *Buswell-John Test* (Buswell & John, 1926) is a test of computation on which students write the answers to many items representing various levels of difficulty for each of the computational operations. The *Diagnostic Mathematics Inventory* (Gessell, 1983) is a test based on instructional objectives in mathematics; the manual provides detailed information about mistaken answers for each item and specific recommendations for remedial activities and materials.

**informal inventory**
a method of assessing mathematics in which the teacher has the student complete representative examples of different kinds of problems; informal inventories can be commercially developed or created by teachers and should be aligned with the curriculum in use

## Informal Inventories

Most teachers have students with widely differing skill levels in their classes and must teach each one how to solve different types of problems. Teachers can determine which kinds of mathematics problems are appropriate for each student by using **informal inventories.** These inventories can be particularly useful to the teacher of students with learning disabilities.

Informal inventories should include representative examples of different kinds of problems. They may be commercially developed or created by teachers themselves. Many of the diagnostic tests described previously, such as the *Buswell-John Test* (Buswell & John, 1926), do this in a broad way. One important consideration in choosing a commercial informal inventory or creating one is the extent to which it aligns with the curriculum used with the students to be tested. If an informal inventory does not assess the skills the students are expected to acquire, it will not be very helpful in determining what to teach them.

Other informal inventories assess performance in a more detailed way and allow teachers to make precise decisions about planning programs for students. Figure 14.3 (pages 466–469) shows a placement test for geometry knowledge. Each type of task assessed is associated with a general grade level. The grade levels should not be considered exact or fixed; they simply provide rough guidance about when certain topics might be taught.

Because these tests are designed to assess what a student can do, they are given without time limits or teacher assistance. Their purpose is to allow a teacher to determine what students have learned and what they should be taught next. Teachers can modify inventories such as these so that they align with the curriculum. Because these inventories are fairly comprehensive, they can even guide curricular decisions (Stein, Silbert, & Carnine, 1997). Stein and colleagues have provided explicit instructional procedures for teaching each of the skills assessed in the inventories shown in Figure 14.3.

**CEC Knowledge Check**
What are some of the limitations of informal math inventories? Why is there no time limit? CC7S4

## Error Analysis

Teachers can perform an **error analysis,** or analyze students' mistaken answers to determine what to teach. Student errors may include the following:

**error analysis** an informal method of teacher assessment that involves the teacher noting the particular kinds of errors a student makes when doing academic work

1. *Incorrect fact.* The student consistently recalls a fact incorrectly (e.g., $7 \times 8 = 57$).
2. *Incorrect operation.* The student executes the incorrect operation (e.g., consistently performs addition when the operation should be multiplication).
3. *Incorrect execution of procedures.* The student applies the steps to an algorithm incorrectly. The procedure may not be known or may be executed in the wrong sequence, or a necessary step may be omitted (e.g., the steps necessary to execute a long-division problem or subtraction with borrowing).
4. *No pattern errors.* The responses are incorrect but appear to be random.
5. *Combinations of incorrect facts and incorrectly employed operations and/or algorithms.* (Mastropieri & Scruggs, 2002a, pp. 164–165)

**CEC Knowledge Check**
What can you do for a student who continues to copy problems from the book incorrectly? LD4S6

Teachers can use instruments such as the *Diagnostic Inventory of Basic Arithmetic Skills* (Enright, 1983) and consult books (e.g., Ashlock, 1994) that provide extensive examples of students' mistaken answers, interpretations of them, and general suggestions for their remediation. For example, when a student's answers indicate that the student has failed to "carry," the teacher can employ manipulative aids, such as using bundles of ten sticks and single sticks, drawing boxes in the answer spaces for problems to prompt students to write only one numeral in each column, and playing games requiring the student to trade many chips of lesser value for a single, more valuable chip (Ashlock, 1994).

## FIGURE 14.3 Instructional Sequence and Assessment Chart

| Grade level | Problem type | Performance indicator |
|---|---|---|
| 1a | Identify circle. | Mark each circle with X. |
| 1b | Identify rectangle. | Mark each rectangle with X. |
| 1c | Identify triangle. | Mark each triangle with X. |
| 1d | Identify square. | Mark each square with X. |
| 1e | Identify interior of closed figure. | Tell me when I touch the interior of this figure. |
| 1f | Identify exterior of closed figure. | Tell me when I touch the exterior of this figure. |
| 2a | Identify cube. | Mark each cube with X. |
| 2b | Identify sphere. | Mark each sphere with X. |
| 2c | Identify cone. | Mark each cone with X. |
| 2d | Identify the diameter of a circle. | What is a diameter? Put X on each line that is the diameter of a circle. |

**FIGURE 14.3** Continued

| Grade level | Problem type | Performance indicator |
|---|---|---|
| 2e | Draw a line segment. | Draw the line segment CD. |

       C

A

      B

D

| 3a | Measure perimeter. | Find the perimeter of this square. |

◻ 4"

4"

| 3b | Measure area of rectangle or square. | Find the area of this rectangle. |

▭ 3"

6"

| 3c | Identify pyramid. | Mark each pyramid with X. |

| 3d | Identify cylinder. | Mark each cylinder with X. |

| 4a | Define/identify radius. | What is the radius of a circle? Mark each line that is a radius with X. |

| 4b | Using a compass, construct a circle, when given a radius. | Draw a circle that has a radius of 2 inches. Use a compass. |

| 4c | Label angles. | For each example, write the name of the angle. |

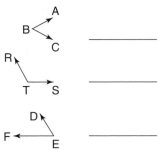

            A

B          _____

         C

R

           _____

T    S

        D

F        _____

        E

FIGURE 14.3 Continued

| Grade level | Problem type | Performance indicator |
|---|---|---|
| 4d | Define degree/measure angles, using a protractor. | Measure each of the following angles. |
| 4e | Construct angles, using a protractor. | Construct the following angles.<br><br>90° ————<br><br>45° ———— |
| 4f | Define/identify right angle. | What is a right angle? Circle each right angle. |
| 4g | Define/identify acute angle. | What is an acute angle? Circle each acute angle. |
| 4h | Define/identify obtuse angle. | What is an obtuse angle? Circle each obtuse angle. |
| 4i | Define/identify right triangle. | What is a right triangle? Circle each right triangle. |
| 4j | Define/identify equilateral triangle. | What is an equilateral triangle? Circle each equilateral triangle. |
| 4k | Define/identify isosceles triangle. | What is an isosceles triangle? Circle each isosceles triangle. |
| 4l | Define/identify scalene triangle. | What is a scalene triangle? Circle each scalene triangle. |

**FIGURE 14.3**   Continued

| Grade level | Problem type | Performance indicator |
|---|---|---|
| 4m | Identify the following polygons: pentagon hexagon octagon | Draw a P over the pentagon. Draw an H over the hexagon. Draw an O over the octagon. |
| 4n | Measure the volume of a cube. | What is the volume of a figure that is 5 inches long, 3 inches wide, and 6 inches high? |
| 5a | Identify parallel lines. | Circle each group of parallel lines. |
| 5b | Identify perpendicular lines. | Circle each group of perpendicular lines. |
| 5c | Identify a parallelogram. | Circle each parallelogram. |

*Source:* From *Designing Effective Mathematics Instruction: A Direct Instruction Approach,* 3rd ed., by M. Stein, J. Silbert, and D. Carnine, 1997, Upper Saddle River, NJ: Prentice Hall. Copyright © 1997. Reprinted by permission of Pearson Education, Inc., Upper Saddle River, NJ.

## Monitoring Progress

Some of the assessment instruments described in the preceding section may be readministered to determine if a student is making progress. For example, an achievement test may be given in the fall and spring of each year to assess how much progress students are making. Most formal standardized instruments, however, are not designed to be readministered more than once a year. They are not fine-grained enough to be sensitive to small amounts of student progress, and they do not have enough test items at each level to be readministered frequently. If students take these tests repeatedly, they may begin to answer items correctly, not because they have learned the skills, but because they have become familiar with the items. Furthermore, a formal test often takes over 30 minutes, making frequent testing excessively time consuming.

One appropriate means for evaluating progress is to assess students' performances on curricular materials. This approach has many advantages, not the least of which is that the teacher learns how well students are doing on the materials they

Council for
Exceptional
Children

**CEC Knowledge Check**
What is the problem with assessing students too often? How can you solve this problem? CC8K4

**curriculum-based assessment (CBA)**
a formative evaluation method designed to evaluate performance in the particular curriculum to which students are exposed; usually involves giving students a small sample of items from the curriculum in use in their schools; proponents argue that CBA is preferable to comparing students with national norms or using tests that do not reflect the curriculum content learned by students

are expected to master. Both computation and problem-solving aspects of mathematics competence can be measured using **curriculum-based assessment** (Shinn & Hubbard, 1992). Furthermore, a combination of curriculum-based assessment and consultation (e.g., recommendations about using peer tutoring) produces higher arithmetic achievement (Fuchs, Fuchs, Hamlett, & Stecker, 1991). It is particularly important for teachers to have instructional plans tied to their curriculum-based assessments (Fuchs, Fuchs, Hamlett, Phillips, & Bentz, 1994).

Another appropriate means of overcoming the difficulties of readministering tests is to adopt or create a set of short tests. These short tests, or probes, are similar to curriculum-based assessments in that they are brief (i.e., take only 1 or 2 minutes to administer) and assess actual student performance. They differ from curriculum-based assessment in not being directly linked to the curriculum in use. Probes should include many examples of problems that require specific skills and should be constructed so they can be readministered repeatedly and quickly. Several alternative probes for each type of problem should be created so that different probes can be used rather than repeatedly using the same one. This practice avoids the problem of students learning the answers to the problems used on one probe (see Howell, Fox, & Morehead, 1993; Howell & Morehead, 1987). Examples of some probes for addition problems are shown in Figure 14.4.

## What Interventions Help Students with Mathematics Difficulties?

Effective instruction has several features: "(a) It takes place in groups, (b) it is teacher directed, (c) it is academically focused, and (d) it is individualized" (Stevens & Rosenshine, 1981, p. 1). The Missouri Mathematics Program typifies this approach. It devotes nearly the entire arithmetic period to working on arithmetic problems, provides a daily review, demonstrates new skills, and offers extended opportunities to practice the new skills under individualized teacher supervision and correction. Students using this program learn significantly more than students in traditional programs (Good & Grouws, 1979; Good, Grouws, & Ebmeier, 1983). Mr. Shein, Shannon's special education teacher, explains some benefits:

Shannon

> Students like Shannon really benefit from demonstration and practice. It's important to present a variety of examples and explain in a step-by-step . . . think-aloud fashion . . . how I approach and solve each problem. I have high expectations for my students, and they know that. They want my feedback. They're eager to know if they're on the right track.
>
> *Martin Shein, Shannon's special education teacher*

See the Effective Practices box on page 472 for other features of effective instruction.

Unfortunately, many math programs in use today are not considerate of students with mathematical problems. For example, in teaching fractions, they

FIGURE 14.4    Probes for Monitoring Student Progress

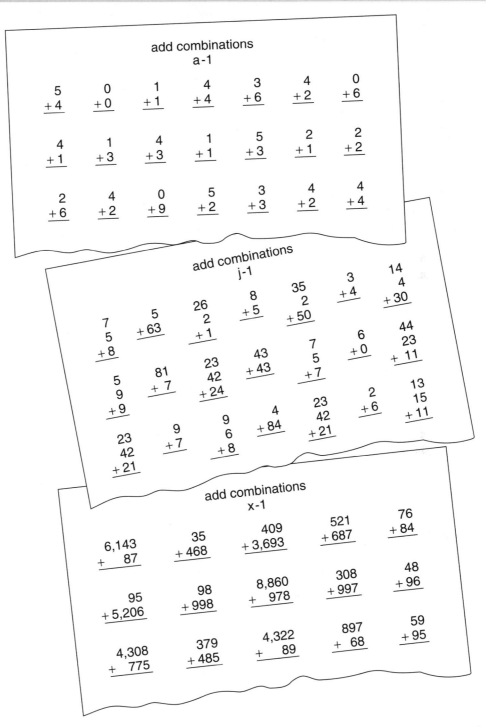

add combinations
a-1

| 5 | 0 | 1 | 4 | 3 | 4 | 0 |
|---|---|---|---|---|---|---|
| +4 | +0 | +1 | +4 | +6 | +2 | +6 |

| 4 | 1 | 4 | 1 | 5 | 2 | 2 |
|---|---|---|---|---|---|---|
| +1 | +3 | +3 | +1 | +3 | +1 | +2 |

| 2 | 4 | 0 | 5 | 3 | 4 | 4 |
|---|---|---|---|---|---|---|
| +6 | +2 | +9 | +2 | +3 | +2 | +4 |

add combinations
j-1

7
5
+8          5
+63         26
2
+1          8
+5          35
2
+50         3
+4          14
4
+30

5
9
+9          81
+7          23
42
+24         43
+43         7
5
+7          6
+0          44
23
+11

23
42
+21         9
+7          9
6
+8          4
+84         23
42
+21         2
+6          13
15
+11

add combinations
x-1

| 6,143 | 35 | 409 | 521 | 76 |
|---|---|---|---|---|
| + 87 | + 468 | + 3,693 | + 687 | + 84 |

| 95 | 98 | 8,860 | 308 | 48 |
|---|---|---|---|---|
| + 5,206 | + 998 | + 978 | + 997 | + 96 |

| 4,308 | 379 | 4,322 | 897 | 59 |
|---|---|---|---|---|
| + 775 | + 485 | + 89 | + 68 | + 95 |

**Effective Practices**

**FOR LEARNING DISABILITIES**

# Prevention and Intervention of Mathematics Difficulties

Researchers have derived four principles of prevention and intervention in the area of mathematics. Each principle meets the following criteria: (1) its effectiveness has been demonstrated in math, (2) research supports its use with students with learning disabilities, and (3) research supports its use with students without learning disabilities and its feasibility for use in general education settings (Fuchs & Fuchs, 2001). The four principles, along with teacher behaviors and student outcomes, are outlined here:

## Principle 1: Quick Pace, Varied Activities, and Engagement

The effective teacher . . .

- uses quick instructional pacing
- incorporates a variety of instructional formats
- uses a range of grouping arrangements

In doing so, students . . .

- spend almost 100% of the lesson discussing, writing, computing, and problem solving, rather than spending an inordinate amount of time sitting and listening

## Principle 2: Challenging Achievement Standards

The effective teacher . . .

- devotes time to motivating students by communicating high expectations

In doing so, the students are more likely to . . .

- be eager to learn
- be highly engaged
- perform at higher levels

## Principle 3: Self-Verbalization

The effective teacher . . .

- teaches explicit steps for approaching and solving problems (e.g., via self-questions on cards, structured worksheets, teacher modeling, feedback, reinforcement, etc.)

In doing so, students . . .

- improve their math performance

## Principle 4: Physical and Visual Representations

The effective teacher . . .

- uses physical and visual representations to facilitate conceptual understanding

In doing so, students are more likely to . . .

- master and maintain mathematical competence

Fuchs, Fuchs, and their research team at Vanderbilt University have developed Peer-Assisted Learning Strategies (PALS) in math and reading for students with and without learning disabilities in general education settings. This effective, research-based intervention includes elements of each of the above-mentioned principles, including "strong motivational system; quick pace, varied activities, and high levels of engagement; self-verbalization methods; and physical and visual representations of number concepts or problem-solving situations" (Fuchs & Fuchs, 2001, p. 88). See www.peerassisted learningstrategies.org for more information on PALS.

Council for Exceptional Children

**CEC Knowledge Check**
What would you predict about strategy effectiveness of the PALS in helping all students reach their math and reading potential?
LD4S1, CC7K1

*Source:* From "Principles for the Prevention and Intervention of Mathematics Difficulties" by L. S. Fuchs and D. Fuchs, 2001, *Learning Disabilities Research and Practice, 16,* 85–95. Copyright 2001 by Blackwell Publishing. Reprinted by permission

introduce content too rapidly, rarely identify and teach fundamental concepts ("big ideas"), use demonstrations that are convoluted and inefficient, and give students too little chance to practice what the programs are teaching (Carnine, Jitendra, & Silbert, 1997). Given such instruction, students—especially those with learning disabilities—naturally have trouble learning arithmetic and mathematics.

Few teachers have the time to design and implement a program such as the Missouri Mathematics Program on their own. Instead, they must depend on programs adopted by state or local education agencies. Teachers usually must adapt programs to make them suitable for students with learning disabilities. Adaptation requires modifying teaching behaviors (e.g., scheduling plenty of time for mathematics lessons) as well as instructional programming techniques (e.g., sequencing of lessons). The Multicultural Considerations box on page 474 provides suggestions for working with culturally and linguistically diverse students to develop their math skills.

**CEC Knowledge Check**
When will you find time to adapt materials for all your students? CC4S3, CC8S4

## Developmental Interventions

Major publishing companies offer **developmental programs** in mathematics. Among the most frequently used are Scott, Foresman's *Exploring Mathematics* (1991), Houghton Mifflin's *The Mathematics Experience* (1992), and Addison-Wesley's *Explorations* (1991) series. (From the titles of these programs, one can get an idea of how publishers position their products to stress popular themes; notice the emphasis on "exploration," with a hint of "discovery," in these titles.)

**developmental programs**
programs designed to foster the growth and improvement of math skills

Developmental programs introduce basic skills such as addition, subtraction, multiplication, and division. Most also introduce other important content areas, such as place value, measurement, geometry, and fractions. Despite the many similarities in what they cover, **basal programs** differ markedly in when they present material. For example, during the first grade, one program may devote a unit to fractions, but others may wait until a later grade to do so.

**basal programs**
programs used for teaching beginners fundamental math concepts

Connecting Math Concepts (Engelmann et al., 1991) is a basal program designed for use in primary through elementary school and is based on the Direct Instruction (DI) model. In highly structured lessons involving frequent teacher questions and student answers, students learn fundamental skills for solving mathematical problems. One important feature of this approach is that teachers explicitly teach students strategies to use in solving problems.

**CEC Knowledge Check**
How can you work with math teachers to sequence concepts that are appropriate for students with learning disabilities? CC7K2, CC7S6, CC7S1

The forerunner of Connecting Math Concepts was DISTAR Arithmetic (Engelmann & Carnine, 1975, 1976). Students whose teachers used DISTAR Arithmetic had higher levels of achievement in arithmetic than those in any of eight other model programs evaluated in one large national study. Not only did the students excel in basic skills such as computation, but they also scored higher on tests of mathematical concepts and problem solving (Abt Associates, 1976, 1977). Similar results have been obtained in comparisons of Connecting Math Concepts with other curricula (Vreeland et al., 1994; Wellington, 1994). Students taught using the DI program not only learn more computation skills, but also learn more concepts.

The Structural Arithmetic program (Stern & Stern, 1971) is designed to develop students' understanding of arithmetic principles by giving them extensive experience with manipulating objects. The program is designed for use in kindergarten through third grade and includes different colored blocks and sticks that represent numbers from 1 to 10. The 1 block is a cube, the 3 stick is the equivalent of laying three 1's in a line, and the 10 is the equivalent of laying ten 1's (or two 5's) in a line. Thus, numerical relationships are represented by different lengths. (Similar blocks are used in other approaches, particularly the Cuisenaire rods advocated by Gattegno, 1963).

██ MULTICULTURAL
   CONSIDERATIONS

## Ten Ways to Enhance the Math Skills of Culturally and Linguistically Diverse Students

Today, more than ever, we can expect to encounter diversity in classrooms throughout the United States. How can teachers enhance the math skills of their culturally and linguistically diverse students? Here are some suggestions to consider:

1. Continually consider ways to infuse the various cultures of students in your classroom and the cultures of students not represented in your mathematics curriculum. Students will appreciate, feel accepted, and learn a great deal about other cultures when cultural diversity is infused in their daily learning routines.

2. Develop story problems that reflect events from diverse cultures. Encourage students to design story problems that are reflective of the happenings of other cultures.

3. Read books about individuals from other cultures. Use the stories and data from these books to design story problems.

4. In designing mathematical problems, use the data from newspapers or magazines that provide information about individuals or events representing other cultures.

5. Design mathematical studies that address real problems of individuals or groups who are not from the mainstream culture. Assign these studies to individuals, students in pairs, or small groups.

6. Ensure that goals are challenging for all students and provide adequate support for their participation and effort. These challenges should provide opportunities for success, with infrequent failure.

7. Model an enthusiastic and positive attitude about appreciating and learning more about the cultures and languages of other groups.

8. Use manipulatives to concretely explore the meaning of mathematical symbols and problems. Manipulatives enhance learning and provide an easy means of crossing potential language barriers.

9. Use culturally relevant materials to learn about the ways in which mathematics are practiced in various cultures and mathematical games that are played.

10. Use the languages of your students throughout your instruction. Ask students to provide the word that means the same as "_____" and then use both words when referring to the term. Encourage all of the students in the room to use and apply multiple terms that represent the languages of the students in the class. Communicate to students that you value their home language. (Bos & Vaughn, 2002, pp. 341–342)

*Source:* Adapted from *Strategies for Teaching Students with Learning and Behavior Problems,* 5th ed., (pp. 341–342) by C. S. Bos and S. Vaughn, 2002, Boston: Allyn and Bacon. Copyright © 2002 by Pearson Education. Reprinted by permission of the publisher.

Children work with the blocks to discover relationships among numbers; for example, the program includes exercises to help them understand part-whole relationships by showing that the 7 block can be matched by a 6 block and a 1 block, a 4 and a 3, or a 5 and a 2. Although experimental evidence about the effectiveness of Structural Arithmetic is not available, many teachers use this program in working with students who have learning disabilities.

### Remedial Interventions

Remedial programs should have the same characteristics as effective developmental programs. Features such as introducing new concepts systematically, providing adequate practice and review, and teaching big ideas are critical (Carnine, Jones, &

Dixon, 1994; Kame'enui & Carnine, 1998). These features are probably especially important for adolescents with learning disabilities (Jones, Wilson, & Bhojwani, 1997).

The Computational Arithmetic Program, or CAP (Smith & Lovitt, 1982), is designed for use with students who need to learn basic addition, subtraction, multiplication, or division of whole numbers. The program includes directions for monitoring progress, suggestions and materials for reinforcing progress, and an extensive set of carefully sequenced worksheets. It is based on what Smith and Lovitt learned from their research with students who have learning disabilities (Lovitt & Smith, 1974; Smith & Lovitt, 1975, 1976; Smith, Lovitt, & Kidder, 1972).

The Corrective Mathematics program (Engelmann & Carnine, 1981) is composed of several modules, each of which covers a specific area of mathematics skill. These areas include addition, subtraction, multiplication, division, money, and measurement. The program includes scripts for daily lessons, and accompanying workbooks provide students with extensive opportunities for practice. Programs similar to Corrective Mathematics are Fractions (Engelmann & Steely, 1980) and Ratios and Equations (Engelmann & Steely, 1981).

## Technology

Arithmetic and mathematics lend themselves well to the use of technology. Their regularity and the value of drill and practice in learning computational skills probably contribute to the popularity of using technology in arithmetic instruction. People may also simply associate computers with mathematics and hence consider arithmetic a "natural" area for applying computer technology.

### Calculators

One of the first questions many teachers have about technology and arithmetic is whether it is advisable for students to use calculators. Calculators are common in classrooms today and provide many new learning opportunities. For example, some states provide graphing calculators for students so they can learn how to use them to solve problems. Students with disabilities benefit from using calculators in solving computation problems (Horton, Lovitt, & White, 1992). Of course, teachers must teach their students how to use the calculators. "What remains for many practitioners and researchers, however, is the question of exactly how calculators should complement or substitute for paper-and-pencil practice" (Woodward & Montague, 2002, p. 95). Shannon's father voices his concerns:

> I think calculators are great, but I was afraid that today's students—including Shannon—were relying on them too heavily. Some use them for basic facts! I remember how hard I worked to learn my multiplication facts when I was young. I wondered if teachers have stopped expecting their students to memorize multiplication facts. But Shannon's teachers reassured me. They explained that, even as high school teachers, they continue to work with their students on learning basic facts and mental math skills.
>
> *Daniel Ireland, Shannon's father*

**Council** for **Exceptional Children**

**CEC Knowledge Check**
How important is knowledge of percentage, interest, checkbook balancing, and use of calculator for high school students when making a transition plan? CC7S9, CC4S6

Shannon

**Council** for **Exceptional Children**

**CEC Knowledge Check**
If students can show that they understand math concepts (authentic assessments), should they be allowed to use calculators for daily work? For tests? LD4K3, CC7S9

TODAY'S TECHNOLOGY

FOR LEARNING DISABILITIES

## Ten Tips for Choosing Math Software

"The broad impact of techno-logical advancements over the past 30 years has been startling and well documented" (Woodward & Montague, 2002, p. 91). However, this means that educators have a vast, sometimes confusing, array of instructional software available to them. Here are tips for teachers and parents on selecting instructional math software:

### 1. The less clutter on the screen, the better.

Most students with LD are distracted by too much stimuli coming at them at the same time. Moreover, cluttered screens often distract from the math concept or procedure being studied. Choose programs that use simple screen displays.

### 2. Procedures should match those being taught in school.

Council for Exceptional Children

**CEC Knowledge Check**

Could students with learning disabilities have problems entering the answers of addition and subtraction problems on the computer screen from left to right vs. the normal procedure of right to left? CC4S3, CC7S9

Many students with LD get confused if the same task is presented in different ways, particularly in the early stages of learning. Some computation procedures used in software differ from standard classroom presentations. Weigh the other advantages of the software before introducing this conflict into math instruction. If you decide to use the software with differ-ing procedures, take the time to carefully point out the differences and be ready to assist if confusion arises.

### 3. Choose modifiable software.

Software in which speed, number of problems, and instructional levels can be modified will serve the needs of a wide range of students in a single class-room or an individual student over a long period of time.

### 4. Choose software with small increments between levels.

Most math software designed for all students makes rather large jumps in difficulty from one level to the next. This is particularly true of retail math software that purports to cover the entire K–8 math curriculum. Students with LD often test out of level 1 but then fail miserably on level 2 because the problems have gotten too difficult too fast. Special education publishers, such as Edmark (www.edmark.com), are more aware of this difficulty and incorporate smaller difficulty increments between levels.

### 5. Choose software with helpful feedback.

Math software should provide clues to the correct answer when a student makes an error. Software might indicate the range within which the answer should lie or show a diagram to indicate the underlying concept that could help students solve the problem on their own. Software that simply indicates a student is wrong is less helpful. Fraction Fireworks (from Ed-

### Computer-Assisted Instruction

Teachers who see a natural fit between mathematics and computers may find some support in evidence about drill-and-practice programs. Drill and practice refers to the repeated presentation of and response to a limited number of facts. Although constructivists view drill and practice as undesirable, facility with the automatic re-trieval of facts is important in solving problems. Computers can provide the practice opportunities many students with learning disabilities need to master basic facts (Hasselbring, Goin, & Bransford, 1987, 1988).

Computers can also be useful in teaching more conceptual arithmetic content. Instructional programs such as Mastering Fractions (Systems Impact, 1986) and Mastering Equations, Roots, and Exponents (Systems Impact, 1988) illustrate the

mark) incorporates an interesting and useful feedback technique. The fireworks celebration after a correct answer illustrates the fraction chosen.

6. **Choose software that limits the number of wrong answers for a single problem.**
   A sure formula for creating student frustration is to require students to repeatedly guess on a problem they don't know. The best software will limit the number of attempts, give clues as to the correct answer, provide the correct answer, and then reintroduce the same item at a later time. Test this feature on a software program by making deliberate errors.

7. **Choose software with good record-keeping capabilities.**
   We know that informative performance feedback can help students understand their errors and help them set realistic but challenging goals. Software should keep records for each student. Information should be made available on the types of problems or the exact problems that caused difficulties.

8. **Choose software with built-in instructional aids.**
   The ability to accurately represent word problems can increase problem-solving performance. Software that incorporates built-in instructional aids such as counters, number lines, base-10 blocks, hundreds charts, or fraction strips can give the student tools to represent a given problem and then go on to solve it. These virtual manipulatives are incorporated in such programs as Equivalent Fractions by Sunburst (www.sunburst.com).

9. **Select software that simulates real-life solutions.**
   In real life, there is usually more than one way to solve a problem. Money, time, and problem-solving software is more effective if it allows multiple roads to problem solution. Making Change by Attainment Company, Inc. (www.attainment-inc.com), for example, combines decisions with multiple solution routes.

10. **Remember, software is a learning tool—not the total solution!**
    Instructional software is a tool in effective math instruction and learning. With color, graphics, animation, sound, and interactivity, it can capture and hold the attention of students so that they persist in mathematics tasks. It is important, however, to combine direct teacher instruction with technology-assisted instruction. In most instances, concept development with concrete materials and clear procedural instruction should precede software use. Pencil-and-paper tasks still have a role in student learning (Babbitt, 1999).

*Source:* Adapted from *10 tips for software selection for math instruction* by B. C. Babbitt, 1999, retrieved June 10, 2003, from http://www.ldonline.org/ld_indepth/technology/babbitt_math_tips.html. Reprinted with permission.

application of technology to learning more than basic facts. Examples of concepts and operations are presented on videodisks, and colorful, animated demonstrations show how, for example, to determine whether a fraction is less than, equal to, or greater than 1 or how to subtract fractions with unlike denominators. While circulating among the students, the teacher controls the videodisk with a remote control device, and the students answer questions posed by the presenters on video monitors showing the program. As is typical of Direct Instruction programs, the questions are rapid, the demonstrations change in subtle but important ways, and the students answer specific questions either chorally or in writing.

The Mastering Fractions program produces substantially greater achievement by students with learning disabilities and those in remedial education than do other

Council for
Exceptional
Children

**CEC Knowledge Check**

Is there another method that is as efficient in delivery of math concepts as Direct Instruction? CC10S8, LD4K2, LD4K3, LD4S1

published instructional programs that cover the same content. In fact, this program helps students master about the same percentage of the objectives for instruction in prealgebra as their non-LD peers master in general education (Grossen & Ewing, 1994; Kelly, Carnine, Gersten, & Grossen, 1986; Lubke, Rogers, & Evans, 1989). The Today's Technology box on pages 476–477 provides tips for choosing math software.

The instructional technology of such programs is more important than the computer technology used in them. One team of researchers compared the effectiveness of the Mastering Fractions program when it was presented using the videodisk technology to the same program when a teacher presented the lessons according to the scripts but without the colorful animation (Hasselbring, Sherwood, & Bransford, 1986). Although teachers preferred to use the videodisk version (it was easier for them), student achievement did not differ under the two conditions. Similar results from other studies (e.g., Gleason, Carnine, & Boriero, 1990) support the idea that the means of delivering instruction is not the critical variable in raising the achievement of students with learning disabilities.

Video technology can also be used to simulate authentic context in which students use mathematics knowledge. Shannon's math teacher explains:

Shannon

> I've gotten some good ideas from research studies I've read by Bottge and others *[e.g., Bottge, 2001a; Bottge, 2001b; Bottge, Heinrichs, Chan, & Serlin, 2001]*. They've conducted studies where students work on video-based math problems . . . the videos present realistic scenarios, and the students work in groups to solve the problems. I've had great success with this approach. I explicitly teach the students the skills they'll need, and, then, they apply what they've learned by solving the problems presented via video. The students identify with the individuals in the videos, and they've been much more motivated!
>
> *Winn Taylor, Shannon's math teacher*

## Effective Teaching Procedures

Council for
Exceptional
Children

**CEC Knowledge Check**
Even though direct instruction should be a cornerstone of math instruction for students with learning disabilities, are there benefits to integrating math into other subject areas (such as earth science, weather, music)?
LD4S1, CC4S4, LD4S12

To benefit students with learning disabilities, beginning math instruction should focus, in part, on developing students' number sense (Gersten & Chard, 1999). Research-based strategies for teaching mathematics include modeling, reinforcement, strategy training, and self-instruction training (see Table 14.3).

### Modeling

A mainstay in teaching, modeling may be used in any of several ways:

- The teacher demonstrates for the student (e.g., "Watch me; here's how I do a division problem").
- The teacher has another student demonstrate (e.g., "Watch Judy; she's going to bisect that line").

**TABLE 14.3**    Algebra Instruction for Students with Learning Disabilities

| INSTRUCTIONAL FEATURES | EFFECTIVE TEACHING BEHAVIORS |
|---|---|
| **Before** | |
| Review | Administer daily quiz of previously learned skills (Kitz & Thorpe, 1995). |
| General orientation | Discuss with individual or in group to introduce the strategy; explain difficulties with problem-solving; explain rationale of self-questioning strategies for problem representation and solution of various problem types (Huntington, 1994; Hutchinson, 1989, 1993). |
| **During** | |
| Teacher modeling | Provide clear and precise presentation of the concept, skill, and/or strategy, using a wide range of examples and nonexamples and manipulatives and computer-assisted instruction (Huntington, 1994; Hutchinson, 1989, 1993; Kitz & Thorpe, 1995). |
| Guided practice | Direct students to important problem-solving steps via structured worksheets (Huntington, 1994; Hutchinson, 1989, 1993). |
| Feedback and reinforcement | Teach students to ask themselves questions during problem representation and solution (Huntington, 1994; Hutchinson, 1989, 1993). |
| | Provide opportunities for guided practice, including a wide range of examples and nonexamples (Huntington, 1994; Hutchinson, 1989, 1993). |
| | Monitor students' level of understanding (Huntington, 1994; Hutchinson, 1989, 1993; Kitz & Thorpe, 1995; Zawaiza & Gerber, 1993). |
| | Provide immediate corrective and positive reinforcement (Huntington, 1994; Hutchinson, 1989, 1993; Kitz & Thorpe, 1995). |
| Mastery learning | Require a set criterion level of mastery (Huntington, 1994; Hutchinson, 1989, 1993; Kitz & Thorpe, 1995; Zawaiza & Gerber, 1993). |
| Independent practice | Provide independent practice on a variety of word problems (Huntington, 1994; Hutchinson, 1989, 1993; Kitz & Thorpe, 1995). |
| Assessment | Assess students frequently, using a variety of measures (e.g., tests and quizzes that require written and oral responses) (Huntington, 1994; Hutchinson, 1989, 1993). |
| **After** | |
| Cumulative reviews/standard instruction | Provide extensive cumulative reviews (Kitz & Thorpe, 1995). |
| Closure | Show and discuss graph of student progress (Huntington, 1994; Hutchinson, 1989, 1993). |
| | Explain purpose for next lesson (Huntington, 1994; Hutchinson, 1989, 1993). |

*Source:* From "Algebra Instruction for Students with Learning Disabilities: Implications from a Research Review" (table 4, p. 124) by P. Maccini, D. McNaughton, and K. L. Ruhl, 1999, *Learning Disability Quarterly, 22,* 113–126. Copyright 1999 by the Council for Learning Disabilities. Reprinted by permission.

Council for
Exceptional
Children

**CEC Knowledge Check**

Does this mean that you should provide a correct math problem on all handouts? Why? LD4K3

- The teacher simply tells students a factual answer (e.g., "9 plus 5 equals 14").
- The teacher uses or constructs materials that include demonstrations and leaves these for students to consult while solving problems.

Researchers have found that providing a demonstration and a permanent model (a problem with a written solution on the students' arithmetic sheets) results in greatly improved performance (Smith & Lovitt, 1975). Moreover, the students' performance improvements generalize to other problems for which they received no demonstrations. Teachers can also use modeling not only with simple arithmetic computation (see Rivera & Smith, 1988), but also in correcting procedural errors in complex applications such as algebra (Silver & Smith, 1989). Shannon explains some benefits:

Shannon

> I really like when teachers show me how to do problems before they expect me to try them. It's especially helpful if they go through more than one. I like when they explain what strategies they use for each part. My math teacher showed me how to go back and check my steps . . . that helps me find mistakes I make.
>
> *Shannon*

### Reinforcement

Providing reinforcement for correct answers, or reinforcing responses, is another proven method of improving performance. However, arranging reinforcement contingencies for students who do not know how to perform tasks is of little value. Reinforcement is beneficial when prerequisite skills are in place (Mastropieri, Scruggs, & Shiah, 1991). However, when students do know how to answer problems but do so inconsistently or at too slow a pace, reinforcing accuracy or faster work is an effective way to improve performance (Hasazi & Hasazi, 1972; Smith et al., 1972). Reinforcement does not have to take the form of tangible rewards. Simply having students maintain graphs showing their performance can have beneficial effects on their arithmetic progress (Fink & Carnine, 1975).

### Strategy Training

**strategy training** a broad range of methods whereby students are taught component skills required to attack a given type of problem

**task analysis** the procedure of breaking down an academic task into its component parts for the purpose of instruction; a major feature of Direct Instruction

**Strategy training,** which covers a broad range of methods, is also effective in improving students' performance in mathematics (Miller, Butler, & Lee, 1998). When teachers model the steps involved in attacking a specific type of arithmetic problem, they usually are modeling a strategy (Cullinan, Lloyd, & Epstein, 1981; Lloyd, 1980; Lloyd & deBettencourt, 1982). In strategy training, a **task analysis** of a cognitive operation is performed so that the steps leading to the solution can be identified. Then students are taught the skills required by each of the steps. When students have mastered the component skills, they are taught how to put them together in order to attack a given type of problem. Students from preschool to college can benefit from strategy training (Grimm, Bijou, & Parsons, 1973; Montague &

Bos, 1986; Smith & Lovitt, 1975; Zawaiza & Gerber, 1993). Mastery of the component skills prior to strategy introduction leads to more rapid learning of the strategy and greater generalization of it to related problems (Carnine, 1980; Kame'enui & Carnine, 1998; Lloyd, Saltzman, & Kauffman, 1981).

Today in learning disabilities, strategy training continues to be an important means of teaching mathematics skills. Teachers can help students learn cognitive strategies for representing problems and solving them using modeling, practice, and reinforcement (Montague, 1997). To help students use strategies in many different situations, teachers may ask themselves questions that evaluate application. Table 14.4 shows evaluation questions for strategy training.

## Self-Instruction Training

**Self-instructional techniques** are another effective approach to teaching arithmetic and mathematics. Self-instructional programs have been reported to be successful

Council for Exceptional Children

**CEC Knowledge Check**
If strategy training and task analysis have such a wide-range impact, what should you know about strategy training? CC7S5, CC4S3, CC4S4

**self-instructional techniques** cognitive training techniques in which the teacher and then the student verbalize questions or instructions for performing a task

---

**TABLE 14.4**  Evaluation Questions for Strategy Training

| STRATEGY ACQUISITION | STRATEGY APPLICATION | STRATEGY MAINTENANCE | STRATEGY GENERALIZATION |
|---|---|---|---|
| • Can the student recite the strategy from memory and/or paraphrase the strategy (depending on the goal)? <br><br> • Can the student explain or define the terms of the strategy? <br><br> • Does the student understand the rationale for learning the strategy? | • How does the student's performance on domain-specific tasks (e.g., mathematical word problems, paraphrasing passages) following instruction compare with his or her performance prior to instruction (posttest vs. baseline)? <br><br> • Has the student reached a mastery by achieving a certain preset criterion for acceptable performance? <br><br> • Can the student use the strategy to detect and correct errors (self-monitor performance)? | • Did the student maintain performance levels on domain-specific tasks over time? <br><br> • Can the student explain how the strategy was used to solve the problem or complete the task? <br><br> • If the student did not maintain performance levels, did a booster session improve performance to mastery level? | • Did the student use the strategy successfully in other tasks? <br><br> • Did the student use the strategy successfully in other situations or settings? <br><br> • Can the student verbalize his or her rationale for selecting and using the strategy? |

*Source:* From "Cognitive Strategy Instruction in Mathematics for Students with Learning Disabilities" by M. Montague, 1997, *Journal of Learning Disabilities, 30,* 164–177. Copyright 1997 by PRO-ED, Inc. Reprinted by permission.

FIGURE 14.5 Example of a Solution Algorithm for Finding Equivalent Fractions

| Step | Description | Action | |
|---|---|---|---|
| 1: Read | Pupil reads problem to him- or herself. | "Let's see . . . um, 9/17ths is equal to how many 102nds?" | $\dfrac{9}{17} = \dfrac{?}{102}$ |
| 2: Plan | Pupil describes general process to him- or herself. | "Okay, I've got to multiply 9/17ths by some fraction that's the same as 1, and then I can get the number of 102nds that it equals." | $\dfrac{9}{17} = \dfrac{?}{102}$ |
| 3: Rewrite | Pupil rewrites problem, providing space for work. Note: This step can be completed while performing Step 2. | "Here's my workspace . . ." | $\dfrac{9}{17}\left(-\right) = \dfrac{?}{102}$ |
| 4: Identify known part | Pupil identifies part of equivalence for which numbers are known. | "Okay, I've got two out of three numbers here (pointing to denominators), so I can start on that part." | $\dfrac{9}{17}\left(-\right) = \dfrac{?}{102}$ |
| 5: Solve known part | Pupil uses prior knowledge to solve for missing multiplier. | "So, 17 times something equals 102 . . . um . . . I'll just figure that out . . .17 is almost 20, and 20 goes into 100 five times, so I'll try that . . . nope, 17 leftover, so it's 6 times . . . great! It's even." | $\dfrac{9}{17}\left(-\right) = \dfrac{?}{102}$  $17\overline{)102}$ $\dfrac{5}{\ }$ $\dfrac{95}{17}$ |
| 6: Substitute | Pupil uses information derived in Step 5 to complete fraction in equation. | "And that means this (writing) is 6 over 6 . . . which is the same as 1, so . . ." | $\dfrac{9}{17}\left(\dfrac{6}{6}\right) = \dfrac{?}{102}$ |
| 7: Derive missing numerator | Pupil solves for missing numerator using information from Step 6. | "Now, I can just multiply these 'cause I've got two out of three and . . . 6 times 9 is 54, sooo. . ." | $\dfrac{9}{17}\left(\dfrac{6}{6}\right) = \dfrac{?}{102}$ |
| 8: Read | Pupil reads completed problem. | "9/17ths is equal to 54/102nds." | $\dfrac{9}{17}\left(\dfrac{6}{6}\right) = \dfrac{54}{102}$ |

*Source:* From "Effective Mathematics Instruction" by J. W. Lloyd and C. E. Keller, 1989, *Focus on Exceptional Children, 21*(7), pp. 1–10. Copyright 1989 by Love Publishing Co. Reprinted by permission.

with learners with disabilities (see Johnston, Whitman, & Johnson, 1981; Whitman & Johnston, 1983). Specific types of self-instruction that have been tested have also shown some promise. For example, the teacher can have students read math problems aloud (self-verbalization) before writing their answers, or they can ask students to circle the operation sign (e.g., +) and name it before attempting to solve arithmetic problems (Parsons, 1972).

More general self-regulation training also has had beneficial effects on students' performances in arithmetic (Miller, Butler, & Lee, 1998). For example, having adolescents with learning disabilities actively use aspects of cognitive-behavioral interventions (goal-setting, self-monitoring, and self-reinforcement) helps students with learning disabilities complete more mathematics assignments (Seabaugh & Schumaker, 1993).

Self-instructional training often requires that students learn a strategy such as those taught in strategy training. This provides another illustration of how the lines between the models described in Chapter 4 can become blurred. Cognitive-behavioral modification and strategy training share many characteristics (Lloyd, 1980). For example, a teacher might teach students how to guide themselves (self-instruction) through a series of steps to solve problems of a certain sort (task-analytic strategy training). Figure 14.5 illustrates how a student might implement a self-instruction plan to solve the mathematical task of finding equivalent fractions.

As we have discussed in this chapter, students with learning disabilities experience a wide variety of problems in mathematics. Some students approach math problems in a mechanical fashion (e.g., by looking for key words) rather than attempting to understand the problem. Others have difficulty with writing numerals and symbols correctly, recalling the meaning of symbols, and following steps in a strategy for solving multistep problems. To combat these and other mathematics difficulties experienced by students with learning disabilities, teachers should assess students' abilities, employ effective instructional methods, and monitor progress frequently.

Council for Exceptional Children

**CEC Knowledge Check**

As mentioned in other chapters, more effective student learning is often achieved through combining models. Is this also true for math interventions? CC1K1, LD1K2

## PORTFOLIO-BUILDING ACTIVITY

### Demonstrating Mastery of the CEC Standards

Search the Internet for three free math software programs teachers can use in teaching math to their students. If you cannot locate any on the Internet, go to a school in your area and ask if you can review some of the math software programs they use. Design an evaluation tool based on (1) what research says about effective math instruction, and (2) the Today's Technology box (pages 476–477). After designing your evaluation tool and choosing three math software programs, evaluate each program (using your tool) as to its effectiveness and usefulness. Write this information up in a brief summative narration. This information will be valuable to you as a teacher. Questions to think about as you progress:

Council for Exceptional Children

**CEC Content Standards**

4. Instructional Strategies
5. Learning Environments and Social Interactions
6. Communication
7. Instructional Planning
8. Assessment
9. Professional and Ethical Practice

- What are the necessary factors in math instruction to improve student performance that are supported by research?

- How can math instruction and curriculum encourage student independence and personal empowerment?

- What assistive technologies can be used to support the mathematical needs of individuals with learning disabilities in terms of instruction and assessment?

- How important are efficient guided practice and ongoing analysis of the individual's learning progress to the instruction and curriculum process?

- Why should special education professionals seek to keep current with evidence-based best practices; what is available as resources for them to use with their students?

# SUMMARY

## How does mathematical knowledge develop normally?

■ Normally developing children learn many arithmetic operations and mathematical concepts before reaching school age. This is called informal knowledge.

■ Researchers are using the term *number sense* to describe a conceptual structure critical for mathematical learning.

■ During the school years, a student's knowledge of arithmetic operations and mathematical concepts changes gradually, partially because of aging and partially because of instruction. This is more formal knowledge.

■ Generally, children progress from using more primitive strategies to using more sophisticated and efficient strategies to solve problems.

■ Instruction in schools often does not match the progression from primitive to sophisticated strategies.

## What mathematics problems do students with learning disabilities experience?

■ About 6 to 7% of all students have problems learning arithmetic skills. Many students with learning disabilities have individual education program goals in math.

■ Some students with learning disabilities have problems in both arithmetic and reading.

■ Students with learning disabilities in arithmetic and mathematics may have difficulty with computation, problem solving, or both.

■ For some students with learning disabilities in arithmetic and mathematics, problems are mitigated when tests are not timed.

■ When solving computational problems, students with difficulties in arithmetic make more mistakes in giving simple answers in various areas of arithmetic and sometimes recall facts more slowly than their peers.

■ Students with learning disabilities also make mistakes in applying strategies or procedures, choosing inefficient strategies, and poorly using those they choose.

## How are mathematics abilities assessed?

■ Skills and deficits in arithmetic and mathematics are best assessed by using both tests and less formal, direct measurement methods, such as performance samples.

■ Comprehensive tests of arithmetic and mathematics performance may be used to assess general ability (grade level).

■ Teachers often use specific tests for more specific arithmetic and mathematics skill areas such as computation in each of the major areas (e.g., addition) and problem solving (e.g., word problems).

■ Teachers can perform an error analysis, or analyze students' mistaken answers, to determine what to teach.

■ Teachers need to be able to assess progress in arithmetic and mathematics skills and usually do so by devising informal inventories (e.g., probes to assess speed and accuracy in computation).

## What interventions help students with mathematics difficulties?

■ Choices of instructional methods should be based on whether the methods are effective.

■ There are benefits to teaching children both fundamental computation skills (adding, subtracting, etc.) and problem-solving skills (e.g., how to think through a problem clearly, set up a strategy for solving it, execute that plan, and monitor its completion).

■ Debates continue with respect to how calculators should be used. Computer software can provide the practice opportunities many students with learning disabilities need.

■ Specific teaching techniques that have research support are modeling, explicitly teaching students to use strategies, reinforcing responses, and self-instruction.

## REFLECTIONS ON THE CASES

1. How would you address Shannon's difficulties in mathematics?

2. How would you monitor Shannon's progress in mathematics?

3. How would you have responded to Mr. Ireland's concern about the use of calculators?

# Mathematics

## *Do Now* Activities to Promote Fluency and Build Number Sense

## Mathematical Fluency—Mad Minutes

### ● *What is it?*

Mathematical fluency is a student's ability to answer a mathematical question quickly and accurately. For students with learning disabilities, the importance of automaticity of basic mathematics facts can be overlooked as teachers focus on the array of other math skills needs—problem solving, numeration, and accuracy of computation. The speed in which students answer questions, however, has important implications for learning. Fluency in mathematics can lead to improved maintenance and generalization, ability to focus on more complex problem solving, and skill in making real-world applications (Miller & Heward, 1992).

To increase students' mathematical fluency, teachers can employ frequent, timed trials. In addition to skill building, charting students' correct responses on basic facts over time (e.g., one minute) creates a complete picture of students' mathematical skills for the teacher. For example, if two students each complete a page of math problems correctly but one student completes the page in 2 minutes and the other in 5 minutes, the instructional needs of these students vary. If a teacher were only looking at correct responses, these students would look very similar. Thus, timed trials serve both assessment and skill-building functions.

One form of timed trials is Mad Minutes. The object of a Mad Minute is to complete as many problems as possible in 1 minute. This timed trial assists students by providing them the opportunity to practice their skills at a fast rate. The worksheet provides teachers with a direct measure of student learning. In order for Mad Minutes to be effective, they should be administered frequently—at least three times per week. Some research has shown that daily timed trials are the most effective (Miller & Heward, 1992).

### ● *How to implement it*

- **Assess**

  Before beginning, run one Mad Minute timed trial in order to assess students' present levels of accuracy and speed. It is important to note that the skills assessed on the Mad Minute should be skills the students have already been taught. The purpose of Mad Minutes is to improve students' proficiency of already learned skills. You don't want students to respond quickly but incorrectly!

- **Run Mad Minute Timed Trials**

  A good time to run Mad Minutes is either at the beginning or end of the class period. Creating a consistent set of procedures to follow will make the trial more efficient and effective. Conduct the trial at the same time each day and follow the same directions for starting and finishing—for example, "Worksheets turned over. Ready, set, flip to start" and "Time. Pencils down."

- **Score and Chart**

  After the students have completed their sheets, teachers can have students score their own sheets. Self-scoring saves time and provides immediate feedback to students on how they are doing. Self-scoring also encourages students to compete against themselves rather than compare themselves to others. Teachers can use an overhead projector to guide students while correcting their sheets. In order for students to get a visual picture of their growth, students should also chart their progress on a graph. Typically, students will have two graphs on a page—one for speed (total number completed) and one for accuracy (total number correct). The date should be placed along the *x*-axis and the number (correct or total) along the *y*-axis. Connecting the dots will give students a clear picture of their progress.

### ● *Additional Resources*

Shoecraft, P. J., & Clukey, T. J. (1981). *The Mad Minute: A race to master the number facts.* Pearson Learning.

*Minute math drills grades 1–2* and *Minute Math drills grades 3–6.* Available online at www.tttools.com/

## Number Sense—Creating a Mental Number Line

### ● *What is it?*

Number sense is a person's comfort level with numbers. Although difficult to define, number sense is easily spotted by a teacher. Students who invent solutions to story problems, are not dependent on following the teacher-taught algorithm, or are comfortable using strategies for simple arithmetic, such as bridging ten, have a strong sense of numbers and how they relate (Gersten & Chard, 1999).

Students with learning disabilities have difficulty developing number sense on their own and frequently require specific activities designed to support the development of number sense. By teaching students strategies for basic arithmetic, such as bridging ten, or by having them engage in other number-line activities, teachers can foster the development of this critical ability. By age 6, students should have developed a schema for counting and comparing whole numbers (Fuchs, Fuchs, & Karns, 2001). Researchers have found that the mental number line is a critical concept for solving addition and subtraction problems (Gersten & Chard, 1999).

- **Bridging Ten**

  When applying the bridging ten strategy, the student looks at the first addend and decides, "What number do I need to add to this number to get 10?" The student then determines what is left from the second addend once the "bridge-to-ten number" is subtracted. The remaining numbers are added to 10 for the solution.

  For example, a student solving the problem 7 + 6 would go about the problem in this way: 7 + 3 = 10; 6 – 3 = 3; therefore, 10 + 3 = 13. For many students, computing the problem in this way is an easier way for them to "see the problem." It is their sense of numbers that allows them to add, subtract, and basically rearrange the quantities in order to solve the problem.

### ● *How to implement it*

To assist in the development of students' mental number line, provide students with number-line activities. Gersten and Chard (1999) recommend that teachers begin with a vertical number line (similar to a thermometer). The vertical number line reinforces the concept that greater numbers are higher and smaller numbers are lower. Once students are comfortable with the vertical number line, teachers can move to traditional number lines or to serpentine-shape Candyland number lines. Students should be given multiple opportunities to problem solve using these various representations.

- *Activity 1: Creating a Thermometer Number Line (grades K–1)*
  1. Create a vertical number line (thermometer) and add demarcations for 20 numbers.
  2. With your students, label the bottom demarcation 1 and the top demarcation 20.
  3. Ask your students a series of questions relating to the number line:
     a. Where do you think the 10 should be placed? Why?
     b. Where should we place the 2?
     c. Is 18 more than 10? If so, would it go above or below the 10?
  4. Continue to ask questions, using contrasting terms like *more* and *less, above* and *below,* and *higher* and *lower.*
  5. To extend the activity, you can ask students more challenging questions, such as "How many spaces are there between the 10 and 12?" or "How much more is 8 than 3?" or "How many fewer is 2 than 5?"
  6. For each of these activities, students can physically place the numbers on the number line or touch the number line to count out spaces.

- *Activity 2: Find the Missing Number (Adding and Subtracting) (grades 2–4)*
  1. Create a series of number lines 0 through 20.
  2. Leave one number blank on each number line.
  3. Have each student (or student pairs) create number sentences whose answer is the missing number.
  4. For example, if the missing number is 15, one pair may create the number sentence $10 + 5 = 15$. They can then physically demonstrate this using their number line. Other examples could include: $8 + 7 = 15$, $16 - 1 = 15$, or $1 + 14 = 15$.

## ● Additional Resources

McIntosh, A., Reys, B., & Reys, R. (1997). *Number sense: Simple effective number sense experiences (grades 1–2).* New Jersey: Dale Seymour.
Family Educational Network. (2002–2003). Line jump. An online number line activity available at www.funbrain.com/linejump/

*Source:* Kristin L. Sayeski

## What Are the Legal Mandates for Placement?
- IDEA
- No Child Left Behind Act

## How Do Students with Learning Disabilities Receive Special Education Services in General Education Classrooms?
- Co-Teaching
- Resource Rooms

## How Can Placement and Instructional Decisions Be Made?
- Assessing the Instructional Ecology
- Monitoring Student Progress

## What Are Modifications for Students with Learning Disabilities in General Education Classrooms?
- Modifications Defined
- Instructional Accommodations
- Instructional Adaptations

## What Are Effective Instructional Practices for Students with Learning Disabilities in General Education Classrooms?
- A Few Notes before We Begin
- Synthesis of Instructional Interventions
- Graphic Organizers
- Peer-Mediated Instruction
- Note-Taking
- General Recommendations for Science Instruction
- General Recommendations for Social Studies Instruction

Council for Exceptional Children

See Companion Website for detailed correlations between chapter content and Council for Exceptional Children Standards;
**www.ablongman.com/ hallahanLD3e**

### CEC Knowledge and Skills Discussed in This Chapter

**1** Laws and policies governing special education for students with learning disabilities, which guide the determination of appropriate individualized instruction, curriculum, and placement.

**2** Exercising sound judgment in advocating for strategies to successfully integrate students into various settings, including the use of instructional and environmental modifications, as part of special educators' responsibilities.

**3** Appropriate teacher attitudes, knowledge, and skills—as well as student social skills—which are necessary for successful implementation of research-based peer-mediated instruction.

**4** Commitment to high standards of competence and quality-of-life potential for students with learning disabilities, which requires educators to reflect on practice in creating a positive environment, using research to guide practice, prioritizing of learning needs, and advocating for appropriate services.

# Participation in General Education Classrooms for Students with Learning Disabilities

15

When I first began in school, I couldn't read very well. I got lots of help from my special education teacher. Now, after working so hard to learn to read, I'm finally beginning to feel like I belong in regular classes with other students. With help from my special education teacher and modifications in the classroom, I can do the work now.

*Shannon*

In recent years, a greater percentage of students with learning disabilities have received the majority of their instruction in the general education classroom at both the elementary and secondary levels. For example, in the 2000–2001 school year, 44% of students with learning disabilities (ages 6 to 21) received instruction in special education settings for less than 21% of the day (originally termed *regular education instruction*), and 40% of the students with learning disabilities received 21 to 60% of their instruction in special education classrooms (originally termed *resource room instruction*) (U.S. Department of Education, 2003). These percentages are up from earlier (1993–1994), when 39% of students with learning disabilities received instruction in general classrooms, and 41% received instruction in resource rooms (U.S. Department of Education, 1996). This increase in participation in the general education classroom has occurred for a variety of reasons and has been accompanied by a change in the cultural makeup of today's classrooms. (For more about effective and culturally responsive instruction in inclusive classrooms, see the Multicultural Considerations box on page 490.) In this chapter, we address the mandates taken directly from IDEA for inclusion of students with disabilities in the general curriculum and describe effective instructional practices for students with learning disabilities in the general education classroom.

## Effective and Culturally Responsive Instruction in Inclusive Classrooms

As most teachers know, today's classrooms contain many students from culturally and linguistically diverse backgrounds, in addition to students with disabilities. The general education teacher must be responsive to all of these students' needs. Culturally responsive instruction is often synonomous with effective instruction for students with learning disabilities. Recent recommendations for creating a culturally responsive inclusive classroom include the following:

1. Conduct a self-assessment of your (the teacher's) attitudes toward students from different cultures.
2. Use a range of culturally sensitive instructional methods and materials, including
   a. explicit, strategic instruction
   b. interdisciplinary units
   c. instructional scaffolding
   d. journal writing
   e. open-ended projects
3. Establish a classroom atmosphere that respects individuals and their cultures, using
   a. current and relevant bulletin boards
   b. book corners
   c. cross-cultural literature discussion groups
   d. language arts and social studies programs
4. Foster an interactive classroom learning environment, using
   a. cooperative learning groups
   b. guided and informal group discussions
   c. the Internet

5. Employ ongoing and culturally aware assessments, including
   a. daily observation of students' social and learning behaviors
   b. portfolio assessment
   c. teacher-made tests that are closely tied to the instructional program
   d. student self-assessment
   e. teacher self-evaluation
6. Collaborate with other professionals and families. (Montgomery, 2001)

Most of the teaching strategies on this list—including strategic instruction, instructional scaffolding, peer-mediated instruction, and frequent, direct measurement of student progress—are the same strategies identified in research and in this chapter as effective for students with learning disabilities. Therefore, even though these techniques and teacher behaviors take training and time to implement, they may encourage the success of both students with learning disabilities and those from culturally and linguistically diverse backgrounds, making teaching all groups of students a little bit easier.

**Council for Exceptional Children**

**CEC Knowledge Check**
Research has shown what is effective for these students to be successful. Why are these students not experiencing success? CC9S2, CC9S11, CC9S12, LD9K1, LD9S2

---

**general education curriculum** the curriculum for nondisabled peers set by state or district guidelines

**least restrictive environment (LRE)** a legal term referring to the fact that exceptional children must be educated in as normal an environment as possible

## What Are the Legal Mandates for Placement?

As discussed in Chapter 3, the emphasis in IDEA is to provide access to the general curriculum for students with disabilities. The **general education curriculum** and the general education classroom are often misconstrued as the same thing. They, in fact, are not. In this chapter, we argue that instruction is the most important variable in determining where students with learning disabilities receive their education. The environment that provides the most appropriate instruction, or can be modified to provide that instruction, for each student with learning disabilities is, in fact, the most appropriate placement, or **least restrictive environment (LRE).**

# IDEA

IDEA regulations regarding the least restrictive environment include the following statements:

1. That to the maximum extent appropriate, children with disabilities, including children in public or private institutions or other care facilities, are educated with children who are not disabled; and
2. That special classes, separate schooling or other removal of children with disabilities from the regular educational environment occurs only when the nature or severity of the disability is such that education in regular classes with the use of supplementary aids and services cannot be achieved satisfactorily. (U.S. Department of Education, 1999, p. 12457)

The regulations go on to say that when determining placements, "a child with a disability is not removed from education in age-appropriate regular classrooms solely because of needed modifications in the general curriculum" (U.S. Department of Education, 1999, p. 12458). Of course, the regulations require that the **continuum of alternative placements** be made available to students and decisions of placement are made on an individual basis. However, the emphasis since the **Regular Education Initiative** and subsequent **full inclusion** movements began (e.g., Pugach, 1995; Skrtic, Sailor, & Gee, 1996; Stainback & Stainback, 1984) has been on getting students with learning disabilities into the general education classroom and having them receive their special education instruction there. As stated previously, the instruction, not the place, is the variable that most affects a student with learning disabilities, and no one answer is correct for all students.

## No Child Left Behind Act

It will be interesting to follow the impact of the requirements of the No Child Left Behind Act (NCLB) on the placement and instruction of students with learning disabilities. The NCLB requires students with disabilities to participate in the state accountability systems for math and reading in grades 3 through 8 and in science. The act does allow for **accommodations** to the standardized tests as long as the tests remain reliable and valid so that students with disabilities can be included in the testing data reported. **Alternate assessments** for students with disabilities must include similar information as the standard forms.

NCLB requires that special educators be "highly qualified" teachers, just as general educators are. Further defined in IDEA, special educators who teach content area classes (e.g., science, social studies) must show qualifications similar to those of the general educator. Teachers who provide accommodations or consultation to a "highly qualified" general educator are not required to show the same content knowledge but must show they are highly qualified in special education (IDEA, S.1248, 2003, Sec 602(a–f)).

In addition, NCLB requires that the schools must show adequate yearly progress toward *all* students being proficient in reading and math or they will face penalties. This includes students with disabilities. Finally, NCLB requires that

**continuum of alternative placements** a legal term referring to the placement options available to students with disabilities, based on their unique individual needs (including instruction in regular classes, special classes, special schools, home instruction, and instruction in hospitals and institutions)

**Regular Education Initiative** a philosophy that maintains that general education, rather than special education, should be primarily responsible for the education of students with disabilities

**full inclusion** all students with disabilities are placed in their neighborhood schools in general education classrooms for the entire day

Council for
Exceptional
Children

**CEC Knowledge Check**
What primary factor determines educational placement for students with learning disabilities?
LD1K4

**accommodations** changes to the delivery of instruction, method of student performance, or method of assessment that do not significantly change the content or conceptual difficulty level of the curriculum

**alternate assessments** evaluations of student skills that are different from those given to nondisabled students

Council for
Exceptional
Children

**CEC Knowledge Check**

What is one requirement for all students that special education teachers need to document for NCLB?
CC8K2

teachers use "scientifically-based instruction" in their classrooms (U.S. Department of Education, 2002a). Only time will tell what the impact of NCLB will be on individual classrooms.

## How Do Students with Learning Disabilities Receive Special Education Services in General Education Classrooms?

With the advent of ideas such as full inclusion, schools have restructured their service delivery models so that special educators move with their students into the general education environment, redefine professional roles, drop professional labels, and establish collaborative partnerships with other teachers (Thousand & Villa, 1989). These instructional partnerships between special and general education exist under the umbrella term *collaboration*. We can define collaboration as "the interaction that occurs between two professionals, often between the special education teacher and the general education teacher, and the roles that they play as equal partners in a problem solving endeavor" for students with disabilities (Bos & Vaughn, 2002, p. 481).

Generally, two forms of instructional collaboration exist in the schools: collaborative consultation and co-teaching. **Collaborative consultation** involves the special educator acting as an expert consultant to the general educator, who is primarily responsible for the instruction of students with disabilities. The two share responsibility for the student and work together to meet the child's special education needs. The special educator, however, does not necessarily provide direct services to that child in the general education classroom. **Co-teaching,** on the other hand, puts the special educator into the general education classroom, working side by side with the general educator to provide instruction. According to the National Center on Educational Restructuring and Inclusion (1995), co-teaching is the collaborative model used most often by schools.

**collaborative consultation** the special educator acts as an expert consultant to the general educator, who is primarily responsible for instruction of students with disabilities

**co-teaching** the special educator works side by side with the general educator in the general education classroom to provide instruction

### Co-Teaching

In addition to other services, Shannon's current special education teacher works with her in a co-teaching arrangement. (For more information about Shannon's services and present level of performance, see the Case Connections box on pages 494–495.) This is how Shannon's special education teacher describes the class:

Shannon

> Shannon participates in a collaborative math class with me. In this class, I work with the general education teacher to modify assignments, give tests, and generally to help the students understand the material. This is the first course in algebra for these students so I end up helping everyone in the class by outlining notes while the

teacher lectures, providing additional examples when I see puzzled faces, and explaining things individually to students. It works out on most occasions because the math teacher has the expertise in algebra and I have the expertise in learning.

*Martin Schein, Shannon's special education teacher*

Co-teaching is "an educational approach in which general and special educators work in a coactive and coordinated fashion to jointly teach academically and behaviorally heterogeneous groups of students in educationally integrated settings" (Bauwens, Hourcade, & Friend, 1989, p. 18). Proponents argue that coteaching is an effective use of the specific and unique skills each professional brings to the classroom.

There are five basic models of co-teaching in the classroom (Vaughn, Schumm, & Arguelles, 1997). The models are flexible in that they are chosen to meet the needs of the students and the instructional task. The models are:

- *One teach–one assist*—Both teachers are present but one teacher takes the lead in delivering instruction. The other teacher then observes or moves around the room to monitor or assist students individually.
- *Station teaching*—Teachers divide the content to be delivered, and each takes responsibility for teaching their part to smaller groups of students who move between stations. Teachers divide students into three groups; two groups work with teachers, and one group works independently at all times.
- *Parallel teaching*—Teachers plan instruction together but split the class up and deliver the same instruction to smaller groups within the same classroom.
- *Alternative teaching*—One teacher works with a smaller group of students to reteach, preteach, or supplement the instruction received by the larger group.
- *Team teaching*—Both teachers share the instruction of all students at the same time.

Additionally, team teaching can be broken into four parts:

1. *Tag team*—One teaches a part, and the other follows.
2. *Speak and add*—One teaches, one adds information.
3. *Speak and chart*—One teaches, one records on overhead, easel, etc.
4. *Duet*—Teachers work in unison, finishing each other's sentences and ideas. (Sands, Kozleski, and French, 2000)

These models are not differentiated by grade level or disability category of students; rather, they are flexible and based on teacher planning time and instructional purpose.

Research on the effectiveness of co-teaching is still in its infancy (Weiss & Brigham, 2000). There are a few qualitative and descriptive studies of co-teaching that indicate there is great variety in the implementation of co-teaching programs (Reinhiller, 1996). For example, some have reported successful case studies of

Council for
Exceptional
Children

**CEC Knowledge Check**
Of the five co-teaching models presented, which is Shannon's special education teacher using? Why?
CC10K1

## Shannon's IEP and Her General Education Performance

According to IDEA, the IEP of each student with a disability must include information about how a student's disability impacts the student's performance in the general education curriculum, the special education services to be provided, and the accommodations/modifications necessary for the general education classroom. Here are examples of those components from Shannon's IEP.

**Present Level of Educational Performance**

According to an informal *Washington Informal Spelling Assessment* done 5/01, Shannon scored 100% on level 1, 84% on level 2, 84% on level 3, 81% on level 4, and 77% on level 5. Shannon is a conscientious worker who wants to please her teachers. She has improved in her reading fluency and comprehension this year, even though it was good to start with. She has made progress despite a significant processing deficit in the area of memory and the retrieval of factual information. This deficit impedes her progress in written language and math, as well as the retrieval of information on content-related tests/quizzes. Although she has strong conceptual writing abilities, she continues to need assistance with the mechanics of the writing process. Even though she is able to maintain topic cohesion, she continues to write run-on sentences. Although her foundation skills are strong, Shannon still struggles with the correct spellings of both familiar and unknown words. She struggles more with adding morphographs to words (such as following the "final *e*," "doubling," and "changing *y* to *i*" rules) than she does with vowel and consonant patterns. Math concepts are not fully understood, however, and math facts are not yet automatic. Therefore, Shannon requires more time allotment in math to finish class work, quizzes, and tests. Shannon takes content tests, as needed, with the resource teacher, because the retrieval of content "facts" is difficult for her. On tests and quizzes, she is more successful with some prompting or uses a word list for "fill-in-the-blanks." This helps her retrieve facts that are asked on tests. Self-esteem has been low this year. She is a very sensitive student

co-teachers who planned together, solved differences together, and instructed together for varying portions of the school day (e.g., Johnston, 1994; Nowacek, 1992; Phillips, Sapona, & Lubic, 1995). These teachers monitored their instruction and adapted to individual students' needs. However, others have reported co-teaching partnerships in which there was a lack of understanding of responsibilities, a continuing ownership struggle, and, at times, disruptive classroom events (e.g., Trent, 1998; Wood, 1998). In these reports, general educators concluded that the only

and wants to do her best all the time. She daydreams less, but it still happens. She complains that she does not have friends.

## Accommodations

1. small-group/individualized instruction, when necessary
2. tests taken with the resource teacher, as necessary
3. modifications regarding length of written assignments, when needed
4. additional time to complete written assignments and projects, if necessary
5. word list to be used during content tests, when appropriate
6. use of spell check, when needed
7. multimodel presentation of new information

## Educational Programs

A. *General Education*                                    % of instructional week: __86%__

Homeroom, Math, Science

Social Studies, Exploratories, Lunch

Assemblies, Physical Education, and

Language Arts

B. *Special Education and Related Services*

| Amount of Instructional Time (per week) | Date to Begin Services | Date to End Services | Percentage of Instruction Time (per week) |
|---|---|---|---|
| Special education instruction (225 mins.) | 8/26/99 | 6/5/00 | 14 |
| Math collaboration (225 mins.) | 8/26/99 | 6/5/00 | 14 |

Council for Exceptional Children

**CEC Knowledge Check**
Given the information about Shannon in this box and in this chapter, is 45 minutes per day enough time for Shannon to spend on math? If so, why? If not, what amount? Defend.
CC4S1, CC4S3, CC7S1

Council for Exceptional Children

**CEC Knowledge Check**
What are some of the factors that promote positive co-teaching outcomes? What factors contribute to negative outcomes?
LD10K

benefit students received was not from professional collaboration but because there was another person to help in the classroom.

At the secondary level, there is evidence that teachers use models of co-teaching that are not described in the literature (e.g., teaching different parts of a content area in a separate classroom), because the conditions of co-teaching (i.e., administrative support, scheduling, number of teachers collaborating) vary quite a bit (Weiss & Lloyd, 2002).

Another way that students with learning disabilities participate in the general education classroom is by attending general education classes and receiving supportive instruction in the resource classroom setting. Again, there is much variability in the instruction received in resource settings. Students can receive instruction in specific content areas (e.g., reading or language arts), in study and organizational skills, or in remediation of all content areas. Research on instruction in the resource room is mixed, indicating that much of the effectiveness and the perceptions of the students are determined by skill of the teacher, goals of the program, and conditions (e.g., discipline, variety of student needs) within the classroom (e.g., Le Mare & de la Ronde, 2000; Moody, Vaughn, Hughes, & Fischer, 2000; Padeliadu & Zigmond, 1996; Rea, McLaughlin, & Walther-Thomas, 2002; Vaughn & Klingner, 1998).

**Council for Exceptional Children**

**CEC Knowledge Check**
Is Shannon receiving "appropriate" instruction in the special education resource room? LD4K2

### Resource Rooms

Unfortunately, some special education resource room teachers simply concentrate on having students finish their homework. This can be appropriate for some students some of the time. But students should also receive instruction in the resource room setting, as is the case for Shannon:

Shannon

> Ms. Regents doesn't let us finish homework in the resource room. Most of the time, we work on things that we're not so good at, like math for me. Occasionally, we organize our notebooks, but Ms. Regents is pretty tough on us sticking to work. There aren't as many students in that class as there are in other classes. But I learn better that way.
>
> *Shannon*

## How Can Placement and Instructional Decisions Be Made?

Placement decisions for students with learning disabilities must be made on an individual basis and must be tailored to the student's unique individual needs. Any or all of the characteristics described in previous chapters could affect a student's performance in the general education classroom. Therefore, assessment of the instructional ecology of classrooms and continuous progress monitoring of student performance must be part of the decision-making process.

### Assessing the Instructional Ecology

**instructional ecology** includes the relationships between students and their instructional environments

**Instructional ecology** includes "the relationships between students and their instructional environments" (Salvia & Ysseldyke, 1998, p. 222). The purpose of assessing an instructional ecology is to determine what types of student behaviors, teacher behaviors, activities, tasks, and structures occur in a classroom situation; what characteristics of the individual student may interact with these variables for success or failure; and what modifications may need to be made to any or all of the variables so that the student can be successful. For example, here is what Shannon's school psychologist told us just prior to a meeting to decide her placement in eighth grade:

Shannon

Shannon is an eighth-grade student with a learning disability who has difficulties in the areas of listening comprehension, attention, and note-taking. We are considering placement in one of two general education classrooms. In the first classroom, observations of the teacher across lessons indicate that the major mode of instruction is lecture with few visual cues or guides. Students listen to the teacher, ask some questions, and then individually complete work, based on the lecture and supplemental readings. The teacher includes grades for homework completion, quizzes, and tests in a student's course grade.

In the second classroom, the teacher's major mode of instruction is split between lecture and student collaborative work groups. During the lecture, the teacher moves around the room, asks students questions, and provides an outline on the overhead of major points. Included in students' grades are homework completion, quizzes, tests, participation, and projects.

Given this information, I am going to recommend choosing the second classroom, based on evidence that the instruction is qualitatively different from the first classroom, not based on irrelevant factors, such as it fits into her schedule or there are open seats in that classroom.

*Mark Chang, Shannon's school psychologist*

## *Ecobehavioral Assessment Systems Software*

The evaluation of instructional ecology can take place in a variety of ways, some standardized, some informal. Greenwood and colleagues at the Juniper Gardens Center of the University of Kansas have developed the Ecobehavioral Assessment Systems Software (EBASS), now in its third edition (Greenwood, Carta, Kamps, Terry, & Delquadri, 1994). The EBASS program has three main coding systems: Code for Instructional Structure and Student Academic Response (CISSAR), Ecobehavioral System for Complex Analyses of Preschool Environments (ES-CAPE), and Mainstream Version of CISSAR (MS-CISSAR).

The EBASS programs use **time sampling** methods to evaluate student behaviors, teacher behaviors, instructional activities, instructional tasks, instructional structure, and settings. The program is loaded onto a laptop computer for data collection, analysis, and developing recommendations.

**time sampling** a term that refers to obtaining behavioral observation samples (i.e., did this behavior occur during this time) that occur through a day or class period

Research on the EBASS system indicates it is a reliable and valid measure of instructional ecology for students with disabilities and it has been used in many research studies (e.g., Greenwood et al., 1994; Wallace, Anderson, Bartholomay, & Hupp, 2002). The EBASS system provides teachers and IEP teams with information and recommendations about classrooms; however, it does require training and software for use. For more information about the EBASS system, see the Effective Practices box on page 499.

### Informal Checklists

There are many informal checklists that have been developed by teachers and others to guide observation of general education classrooms. These include many of the same topic areas as the standardized assessment devices and provide direction for informal observations or narrative descriptions of the events in the classroom. In order to use these checklists, teachers or others make repeated observations of classrooms and take notes on the occurrence (or lack of occurrence) of specific teacher actions, student actions, instructional tasks, classroom routines, and so on. Intervention checklists provide a more informal account of what is happening in the classroom, which must then be interpreted by the IEP team. Figure 15.1 (pages 500–501) provides an example of a portion of one such checklist.

The purpose of assessing instructional ecologies is not to evaluate teachers or pass judgment on classroom practices. Rather, the purpose is to identify the best possible placement for students who have a variety of strengths and weaknesses. Additionally, an assessment of the environment provides a wealth of information for the special education teacher, who must work with the general educator to provide appropriate instruction to the student with learning disabilities.

## Monitoring Student Progress

Equally important to the instructional ecology in the decision-making process is the continuous assessment of student performance. Once a placement decision is made, student performance toward IEP goals and performance in the general education curriculum should be evaluated on a regular basis. One of the best ways to do this is through the use of **curriculum-based assessment (CBA)** measures, as described in Chapter 3.

Curriculum-based assessment is

> a process of evaluating the relationships between instructional interventions and student performance . . . a process of systematically developing and implementing standards for (a) identifying academic behaviors from the curriculum that provide meaningful indicators of achievement, (b) frequently measuring changes in those behaviors, (c) displaying the results of testings, and (d) using the test data to make defensible instructional decisions. (Jones, Southern, & Brigham, 1998, p. 239)

For example, CBA can be used in science and social studies for topics such as vocabulary, problem solving, and graphic aids (Choate, Enright, Miller, Poteet, & Rakes, 1995). The key to effective CBA is for the teacher to do a thorough analysis of

**CEC Knowledge Check**
What kinds of information does an ecobehavioral assessment provide?
CC8S1

**CEC Knowledge Check**
Why are ecobehavioral assessments useful to special educators?
CC5K1, CC5S3

**curriculum-based assessment (CBA)**
the process of determining students' instructional needs within a curriculum by directly assessing specific curriculum skills

### Effective Practices

### FOR LEARNING DISABILITIES

## Where to Find Out More about Research-Based Practices

Listed below are Websites for additional information about research-based, effective teaching practices for students with learning disabilities in general education classrooms.

### EBASS

Juniper Gardens Children's Project at University of Kansas
www.jgcp.ku.edu/EBASS/index.htm

### Curriculum-Based Measurement

U.S. Department of Education
www.ed.gov/offices/OESE/SASA/aypstr/slide001.html

Measurement Tools for Academic Success and Assessment
sss.usf.edu/cbm/SiteMap.htm

Assessing Educational Outcomes
www.vanderbilt.edu/kennedy/topics/assess.html

### Content Enhancement

University of Kansas Center for Research and Learning
www.ku-crl.org

Strategic Instruction Model
www.ku-crl.org/htmfiles/sim.html

### PALS

National Center on Accelerating Student Learning
www.vanderbilt.edu/CASL

PALS Website
www.peerassistedlearningstrategies.org/index.asp

### Collaborative Strategic Reading

Interview with Developers
www.ncset.org/teleconferences/transcripts/2002_09.asp

Manual to Assist in Staff Development
www.calstat.org/manual.pdf

### Classwide Peer Tutoring

Classwide Peer Tutoring-Learning Management System Homepage
www.lsi.ku.edu/jgprojects/cwptlms/html2002/

Juniper Gardens Children's Project
www.jgcp.ku.edu/

### Science

Math and science instruction for students with learning disabilities
www.nwrel.org/msec/book7.pdf

### Social Studies

Institute for Academic Access
www.academicaccess.org

ERIC Digest—Learning Disabilities and Social Studies
Ericec.org/faq/so-stud.html

---

the curriculum and the expected outcome behaviors. Probes at similar difficulty levels can be administered to students quickly and efficiently to measure progress toward these end goals. Assessments occur on a frequent basis, perhaps even a couple of times a week, so that progress can be charted and instructional decisions can be made based on these data, not on individual end-of-unit test scores or homework grades.

A subset of CBA is called **curriculum-based measurement (CBM).** Student achievement has been measured and improved using CBM as an alternative form of evaluation. Shinn and Bamonto (1998) describe CBM as "a set of standard simple, short-duration fluency measures of reading, spelling, written expression, and mathematics computation . . . developed to serve as general outcome indicators measuring 'vital signs' of student achievement in important areas of basic skills or literacy" (p. 1).

**curriculum-based measurement (CBM)**
a set of standard simple, short-duration fluency measures of reading, spelling, written expression, and mathematics computation developed to serve as general outcome indicators measuring vital signs of student achievement in important areas of basic skills or literacy

**FIGURE 15.1**   Informal Checklist for Content Area Classroom

Student Name _____

Educator completing observation _____

Date _____

Class _____

| Characteristics of Setting | Check if it Applies | Student's Present Performance Level | Mastered? | Working on? | Unable to Perform? |
|---|---|---|---|---|---|
| Student Interaction | | Interacts appropriately? | | | |
| • Individual | | Individual | | | |
| • Cooperative | | Cooperative | | | |
| • Competitive | | Competitive | | | |
| Physical Environment | | Works well in: | | | |
| • Large group | | Large group? | | | |
| • Small group | | Small group? | | | |
| • One-to-one | | One-to-one? | | | |
| • Alone | | Alone? | | | |
| | | Works well in: | | | |
| • Traditional seating | | Traditional? | | | |
| • Circular or horseshoe | | Circular? | | | |
| • Cubicles/carrels | | Cubicles? | | | |
| • Other | | Can adapt? | | | |
| • No talking allowed | | Works silently? | | | |
| • Minor distractions | | Works with minor distractions? | | | |
| • Noisy environment | | Works with many distractions? | | | |
| • Provision for individual study space | | Works in individual study space? | | | |
| Teaching techniques | | | | | |
| • Structured class | | Works well in structure? | | | |
| • Student requires self-structure | | Can impose self-structure? | | | |
| • Lecture | | Retains material from lectures? | | | |
| • Explanation | | Comprehends group explanations? | | | |
| • Audiovisual presentations | | Retains audiovisual presentations? | | | |
| • Discussion | | Participates in class discussion? | | | |
| • Asking questions | | Responds to questioning appropriately? | | | |

FIGURE 15.1    Continued

| Characteristics of Setting | Check if it Applies | Student's Present Performance Level | Mastered? | Working on? | Unable to Perform? |
|---|---|---|---|---|---|
| • Self-directed study | | Works on independent projects? | | | |
| • Experiments | | Performs lab experiments? | | | |
| • Constructing | | Builds projects independently? | | | |
| • Group work | | Works in small groups? | | | |
| • Other | | Adapts to other teaching techniques? | | | |
| Academic transition | | | | | |
| • Notice is provided when making transition | | Makes transitions smoothly? | | | |
| • Notice is not provided when making transition | | | | | |
| Homework | | | | | |
| • Assignments copied from board | | Copies accurately? | | | |
| • Written assignments provided | | Reads assignments accurately? | | | |
| • Oral assignments provided | | Follows oral directions? | | | |
| • Kept in notebook | | Keeps homework in notebook? | | | |
| • Other requirements | | Completes homework? | | | |

*Source:* Adapted from *Adapting Instruction to Accommodate Students in Inclusive Settings,* 4th ed. (Appendix A), by J. W. Wood, 2002. Copyright © 2002. Adapted by permission of Pearson Education, Inc., Upper Saddle River, NJ.

CBM probes are constructed using state or school district curriculum and are administered in minutes by teachers on a frequent basis so that they can evaluate how students are performing and whether instructional changes are necessary. For example, a standard reading fluency CBM probe includes a passage of 250 words taken from a grade-level text. The teacher asks students to read as many words as possible in one minute while noting both words read correctly and errors. For reading comprehension, a teacher chooses a passage of 250 words taken from a grade-level text. Every seventh word is deleted and three

Council for
Exceptional
Children

CEC Knowledge Check

What are the major differences between CBA and CBM?
CC8K1, CC8K4

alternatives are provided. Students are given 5 minutes to read and select the correct words to fill in the blanks.

In both of these types of tasks—reading fluency and reading comprehension—history or science texts as well as literature or reading texts can be used. These measures provide teachers with an estimate of how well a student reads and understands material as well as information about improvement in those skills over time.

Studies have shown that students with learning disabilities in classrooms where teachers use CBM have shown greater increases in achievement than students with learning disabilities whose teachers do not use CBM (Fuchs et al., 1994; Hasbrouck, Woldbeck, Ihnot, & Parker, 1999; Stecker & Fuchs, 2000). CBM requires teachers to set goals for students, continually assess their progress, and change instructional methods when improvement is not made. For additional information about CBM, see Chapter 10 and the Effective Practices box on page 499.

Shannon's special education resource teacher has been using CBM with her, and she has responded positively.

**Council for Exceptional Children**

**CEC Knowledge Check**

Why is CBM an essential tool for special education teachers? LD4S6, CC8S8

Shannon

> Every couple of days in my resource class, Ms. Regents has me read from a book for 1 minute. When I'm done, I count the number of words I've read and chart it on a piece of graph paper. If my line goes up, Ms. Regents lets me help other students with their reading. If my line goes down, I do some more reading practice. I like the challenge, and my Mom likes knowing how I'm doing. At the beginning of the year, my science teacher did the same kind of thing with test questions about safety. We had to keep getting more questions right before we could use the lab equipment, and we had to get *all* of the answers right before we could use the equipment by ourselves!
>
> *Shannon*

## What Are Modifications for Students with Learning Disabilities in General Education Classrooms?

IDEA guarantees that the IEP of students with learning disabilities include "a statement of the program modifications or supports for school personnel that will be provided for the child (aa) to advance appropriately toward attaining the annual goals; (bb) to be involved and make progress in the general curriculum . . . ; (cc) to be educated and participate with other children with disabilities and nondisabled children in these activities." (IDEA, S.1248, 2003, Sec 614(d)(1)(A)(i)(iv)). The IEP team should determine what modifications are necessary for the student, based on the student's unique individual needs.

Research on the individual impact of program and testing modifications is hindered by the fact that students with learning disabilities are such a heterogeneous group. Thus, modifications may show fewer results for a large heterogeneous sample of students with learning disabilities than for a smaller, more homogeneous sub-group. Also, many of the decisions made by the IEP team about modifications can be haphazard, anecdotal, or convenient; some may benefit the student and others may not. This points out the importance of carefully assessing the instructional ecology and the student's educational characteristics.

However, modifications that are integral parts of specific teaching methods have been more thoroughly researched. In this section, we describe common modifications that may be used for any type of instruction or assessment for students with learning disabilities in the general education classroom.

**CEC Knowledge Check**
On what basis should IEP team members determine what modifications a student should receive?
CC5S6

## Modifications Defined

**Modifications** can occur in either instruction or assessment or in both. Modifications usually take the form of accommodation or adaptation. Accommodations "are changes to the delivery of instruction, method of student performance, or method of assessment that do not significantly change the content or conceptual difficulty level of the curriculum" (Miller, 2002, p. 292). Alternatively, **adaptations**

> typically involve more significant changes or modifications to the instructional process than accommodations. Routine adaptations are the instructional variations that teachers plan for at the beginning of the year because they anticipate the need for ongoing differentiated instruction. Specialized adaptations are created and used when unique difficulties emerge among individual students. (Miller, 2002, p. 299)

Teachers may incorporate accommodations and adaptations in isolation or in some combination. Obviously, adaptations are more difficult for teachers to implement, because they include differences in instruction or grouping. See Table 15.1 (page 504) for descriptions of nine types of common modifications.

**modifications** changes to instruction or assessment

**adaptations** involve changes to the curricular content, changes to the conceptual difficulty level of the curriculum, or changes to the instructional objectives and methodology

## Instructional Accommodations

Instructional accommodations most often include changes in time, input, output, participation, and level of support. For example, during a history lecture, the teacher may use a graphic organizer to indicate important points and to graphically display how information is related. For a math problem-solving project, a teacher may give a student a few extra days to complete the requirements. Instead of doing individual reports on the themes in *Romeo and Juliet,* a teacher may have students work in groups to develop a theme topic and to gather examples from the play. To teach story writing, a teacher may allow students to use computers to write the stories out or have students dictate stories to recorders and then write them down on paper. In science, a teacher may provide a copy of a proficient note-taker's notes for a student who has difficulty with note-taking. In all of these examples, the objective is the same: students will master the same information; how they go about mastering that information may be different.

It is often the case that teachers who make instructional accommodations for students with learning disabilities find that those accommodations also benefit

**TABLE 15.1    Nine Types of Modifications**

Council for
Exceptional
Children

| TYPE OF MODIFICATION | DESCRIPTION | EXAMPLES |
|---|---|---|
| Size | Change the amount or number of items the student is expected to learn or complete. | Have student complete the even-numbered problems in their math text. <br><br> Have student learn 10 rather than 20 vocabulary terms. |
| Time | Change the amount of time allowed for learning; change amount of time for completing assignments or tests. | Give student extra week to complete science project. <br><br> Give student 1½ hours instead of 1 hour to complete unit exam. |
| Input | Change the way instruction is presented. | Use cooperative learning. <br> Use visual displays. <br> Use computer-assisted instruction. |
| Output | Change the way students respond. | Allow student to say answers into a tape recorder rather than writing responses. <br> Allow students to complete projects rather than take tests. |
| Difficulty | Change the skill level required for task completion. | Allow open-book test. <br> Allow students to use spell checker. |
| Participation | Allow for various levels of student involvement. | One student counts and distributes 20 manipulative devices to each student; other students use the devices to solve subtraction problems. <br><br> One student writes report; another student draws accompanying illustrations. |
| Level of support | Change the amount of individual assistance. | Have paraeducator work one-to-one with student needing additional help with assignment. <br> Arrange peer tutoring. |
| Alternative goals | Use same materials, but change the expected outcomes. | Given a diagram of the parts of the eye, one student labels the parts; others label the parts and their function. <br><br> One student identifies the ingredients in a recipe; other students identify, measure, and mix the ingredients. |
| Substitute curriculum | Change the materials and instruction. | Some students read and discuss novel; some students participate in Reading Mastery lessons. |

> **CEC Knowledge Check**
>
> Which modification do you think would be easiest to implement for general education? Which would be the most difficult? Defend your answer.
> CC9S3, CC9S5

*Source:* From *Validated Practices for Teaching Students with Diverse Needs and Abilities* (p. 290) by S. P. Miller, 2002, Boston: Allyn and Bacon. Copyright © 2002 by Pearson Education. Reprinted by permission of the publisher.

many of the rest of the students in the class. (For a discussion of the concept of universal design for students, see the Today's Technology box on page 506.) For example, Shannon's social studies teacher reports:

Shannon

> In Shannon's case, I realize that she can often "drift off" from my instruction and that she does not make connections well. There are others in the classroom who have similar difficulties. Social studies is pretty easy to modify in that at random times, I can directly ask Shannon or others questions about the material we are reviewing. I have gotten in the habit of using graphic organizers or outlines on the overhead during lectures. These allow me to stop and make sure everyone is with me. It really helps to know about any misconceptions before the students move to working in collaborative groups.
>
> *Sylvia Rajam, Shannon's social studies teacher*

Council for Exceptional Children

**CEC Knowledge Check**

Is it important to list needed accommodations on an individual's IEP? Defend your answer. CC10S6, CC10S8

The critical feature of accommodations is that the content of instruction is not changed. The objective remains the same, though the route to the objective may have to be changed or adjusted for students with learning disabilities. Examples of Shannon's accommodations are shown in Table 15.2.

## Instructional Adaptations

Instructional adaptations, on the other hand, set different objectives for students with learning disabilities than those of their peers. Changes may be made by creating alternative goals or using a substitute curriculum. For example, a teacher may allow a student with learning disabilities to use notes or an open book for an activity in

### TABLE 15.2 Modifications for Shannon

| MODIFICATION LISTED IN IEP | TYPE OF MODIFICATION |
| --- | --- |
| Small-group/individualized instruction when necessary | Level of support |
| Tests taken with the resource teacher as necessary | Level of support |
| Modifications regarding length of written assignments when needed | Size |
| Additional time to complete written assignments and projects if necessary | Time |
| Word list to be used during content tests when appropriate | Difficulty |
| Use of spell check when needed | Difficulty |
| Multimodel presentation of new information | Input |

# Universal Design for Learning: Linking Technology and Access to the General Curriculum

**universal design**
the design of products
and environments to be
usable by all people, to
the greatest extent possible, without the need for
adaptation or specialized
design

Education has expanded the ar-
chitectural concept of universal
design to increase the accessibility of curriculum to students
with disabilities. **Universal design** is "the design of products
and environments to be usable
by all people, to the greatest extent possible, without the need
for adaptation or specialized design" (Center for Universal Design, 1997). In architecture, an example of universal design is the inclusion of ramps for entrances into
buildings. Originally intended to make buildings accessible to people using wheelchairs, ramps are also helpful
for people using baby strollers, dollies, and other wheeled
vehicles.

The same concepts can be applied to instruction in
general education classrooms. The Center for Applied
Special Technology (CAST), supported in part by the
U.S. Department of Education, has begun several initiatives to introduce ways in which technology can help
teachers make the general education classroom accessible
for all learners. CAST is an educational, not-for-profit organization that uses technology to expand opportunities
for all people, especially those with disabilities. CAST, in
a collaborative agreement with the U.S. Department of
Education's Office of Special Programs, has developed an
initiative called the National Center on Accessing the
General Curriculum (NCAC).

NCAC's main goal is to provide teachers with alternatives to text-based instruction, which can be difficult to
access for many students, including those with disabilities. In pursuit of this goal, NCAC has developed three
main principles of universally designed learning environments for use by teachers, as follows:

1. To support diverse recognition networks, provide
   multiple, flexible methods of presentation. For example: when introducing students to a new concept or unit, the teacher may provide multiple
   structures to present the information such as a lecture, digitized text, activity-based exploration, or
   demonstration.
2. To support diverse strategic networks, provide multiple, flexible methods of expression and apprenticeship. For example, when teachers request student
   responses to demonstrate understanding and knowledge, they could provide a range of tools that allow
   students to respond in various formats, such as written, oral, slide show, video, or drawing.
3. To support diverse affective networks, provide multiple flexible options for engagement. Allow students
   to select an area of interest within the topic or concept to research or study. For example, select versus
   assign one of the natural resources in a geographic
   area under study and obtain in-depth information.
   (Jackson & Harper, 2002, p. 6)

In an example unit, Endangered Species, provided
on the Website, examples of the technology used include
making print accessible through text-to-speech, enlarged
font, greater color contrasts, enhanced graphics, alternative tags, captioned video, electronic newspapers; making information accessible through the use of graphic
organizers, note-taking de-
vices, pre-video questioning;
and others. (See www.cast.
org/ncac/index.cfm?i=1941
for the sample unit.)

The project is still in its
infancy, but research has
begun on its principles of
curriculum and lesson de-
sign. You can access CAST
at www.cast.org and NCAC
at www.cast.org/ncac.

Council for
Exceptional
Children

**CEC Knowledge Check**

Were any of NCA's three
principles provided
during your teacher
training? If not, how
would you advocate
for change?
CC9S3, LD9K1

which other students are not permitted to do so. In this case, the objective is for the
student to have access to information when needed, rather than having to memorize
the information.

Varying the levels of reading instruction in the classroom is another example of an instructional adaptation. For example, the Bluebirds reading group may work toward the objective of identifying all 26 letters by name and sound, while the Cardinals group may work toward decoding words with medial vowel sounds.

**Tiered assignments** (Tomlinson, 2001) are another example of adaptations. In tiered assignments, teachers provide choices for assignments on a single topic that vary in difficulty. For example, when studying *Huck Finn,* some students may write paragraphs that identify and describe the characters, while others may write paragraphs that analyze the traits of each character. Both the assignment and subsequent grading will be different.

Shannon receives some instructional adaptations in science:

**tiered assignments**
assignments created around one topic that vary in difficulty

Council for
Exceptional
Children

**CEC Knowledge Check**

Do you think it is "fair" to make these adaptations for some students and not others? What is "fair"? Defend your answer.
CC9S2, LD9K1

Shannon

> In science, Shannon has a difficult time remembering all of the terms I introduce. So for her tests, I provide a word bank for her to use. No one else in the class gets a word bank, so it's unique for her. I'm not sure it always helps, because some of the words are so difficult for her.
>
> *David Hightower, Shannon's science teacher*

(For examples of Shannon's instructional adaptations, see Table 15.2.)

## What Are Effective Instructional Practices for Students with Learning Disabilities in General Education Classrooms?

Because more students with learning disabilities are receiving more of their instruction in the general education classroom, special education researchers have spent a great deal of time devising and testing instructional methods that are effective in this setting. In this section, we present information about some of the most effective strategies. In addition to the descriptions given, the Effective Practices box includes further resources and training information for each strategy.

### A Few Notes before We Begin

In today's general education classroom, there are many students with many needs at varying levels and often only one or two teachers to provide instruction to meet all of these students' needs in progressing toward state or district curriculum standards. Planning in a different way for each individual child is impossible. Planning with the inclusion of modifications is hard work and requires collaboration with other professionals. For more on teacher planning, see the Current Trends and Issues box on page 508.

## CURRENT TRENDS & ISSUES

## Teacher Planning: Critical Component of Including Students with Learning Disabilities

Teacher planning is a critical component to the successful inclusion of students with learning disabilities in the general education classroom. Collaboration with other professionals and accommodation and adaptation of instruction require that teachers determine critical elements of content and ways to convey information effectively and efficiently. Planning is so critical to success that "opportunities for planning must never be assumed but instead designed" (Jackson & Harper, 2002, p. 5).

Teacher planning includes three basic stages: preplanning (before instruction), interactive planning (during instruction), and postplanning (after instruction) (Vaughn, Bos, & Schumm, 2000). Bulgren and Lenz (1996) have suggested a multipart strategy for teachers to effectively preplan and interactively plan for all students. The process is called ReflActive Planning and includes the acronym, SMARTER, to help teachers remember the strategy.

Step 1. *Select* the critical content outcomes and develop a set of critical questions that all students should be able to answer by the end of instruction.

Step 2. *Map* the organization of the critical content in a way that will show the structure of the content and will be meaningful to all students.

Step 3. *Analyze* why the critical content might be difficult to learn based on amount, interest, relevance, abstractness, complexity, student background, organization, and external conditions.

Step 4. *Reach* decisions about *how the content will be taught* and how the content might be enhanced during instruction to reduce potential learning difficulties through specific teaching devices, alternative teaching routines, instruction in learning strategies, or curriculum revisions.

Step 5. *Teach* students about the enhancements in ways that will inform students about how to use the devices, routines, strategies, or curriculum revision, and explicitly guide students to become actively involved in exploring and using the enhancements to improve learning.

Step 6. *Evaluate* mastery of critical content and related processes for high-achievers, average-achievers, low-achievers, and others.

Step 7. *Reevaluate* planning and teaching decisions for the next step in learning. (Bulgren & Lenz, 1996, p. 432, emphasis added)

Teachers can apply the SMARTER steps to all levels of planning (e.g., course, unit, lesson). According to the authors, secondary teachers have used the SMARTER steps to increase the amount of time spent teaching the interconnectedness and critical features of content material (Bulgren & Lenz, 1996). Using the SMARTER steps requires time, practice, and training to become proficient. For more information, see www.ku-crl.org/htmlfiles/cecurriculum/ce description.html#course.

Council for Exceptional Children

CEC Knowledge Check

Why is reflection after planning and teaching a critical part of successful inclusive teaching? CC9S9, CC9S11

*Source:* From "Strategic Instruction in the Content Areas," by J. Bulgren and B. K. Lenz, 1996, in D. Deshler, E. S. Ellis, and K. Lenz, *Teaching Adolescents with Learning Disabilities,* Denver: Love Publishing. Copyright 1996 by Love Publishing Company. Reprinted by permission.

Our purpose in this section is to provide information about strategies for instruction that, when incorporated appropriately, will help meet the needs of many students in the classroom, particularly those with learning disabilities. We are under no illusions that these methods will solve every teacher's problems, and we realize that these approaches require additional planning and effort until they become part of a teacher's repertoire. However, we strongly encourage teachers to pursue a thorough understanding of the methods in order to make their classroom instruction more efficient and effective.

## Synthesis of Instructional Interventions

In a review of intervention research with students with learning disabilities, Swanson (2000) examined 180 studies. These studies included some type of instructional intervention and a control group of students with learning disabilities that did not receive the intervention. Though there were some design flaws within the various studies, Swanson's analysis generated findings that describe elements of effective instruction, regardless of setting, for students with learning disabilities. First, Swanson found that reading-related measures (e.g., comprehension) received the most attention, and instruction in reading-related areas generated the greatest change in student achievement when compared to non-reading-related measures (e.g., math). Second, Swanson found ten components of instruction important for students with learning disabilities, as described below.

### *Sequencing*

Sequencing includes breaking a task down into constituent parts; teaching each part with support, including step-by-step prompts; and fading the prompts or cues as the student masters the activities. For example, before asking students to write a report on a topic, the teacher must teach students (or verify that students know how) to conduct research, take notes, develop a hypothesis, and write about their findings.

### *Drill-Repetition and Practice-Review*

This includes daily testing of skills, distributed review and practice, use of redundant materials or tests, repeated practice, sequenced review, and daily feedback. Examples include using curriculum-based assessment on a frequent basis, asking questions of *all* students, and linking new knowledge to previous learning.

### *Segmentation*

Segmentation is breaking down a targeted skill (e.g., research on the Internet) into smaller units, teaching those smaller units, and then making sure the student can put the units together to accomplish the task. Segmentation is similar to sequencing but places the emphasis on putting the parts together to accomplish the whole task. An example would be using decoding skills to define unknown words in a text. The subskills in decoding are used together to make meaning of the word.

### *Directed Questioning and Responses*

Students with learning disabilities need to be engaged with the material they are learning. Therefore, directly questioning them and providing feedback to them during instruction allows a teacher to verify their engagement. For example, pausing and asking questions during a lecture or requiring **exit slips** for students to write about what they learned in class provides a teacher with the opportunity to give feedback and resolve misunderstandings.

**exit slips** students must write down what they have learned on a slip of paper before exiting the class

### Controlling Difficulty or Processing Demands of a Task

**scaffold** adjusting instruction so that the student is challenged to develop new skills but with appropriate support

The learning of new concepts requires varying levels of support, or **scaffolds,** for all students. Teachers control the complexity of tasks and understanding by providing different types of scaffolds at different points in instruction. An example includes the types of examples and the range of examples given to students. In early learning, students with learning disabilities need a broad range of examples that explicitly identify the critical elements of the concept. As they acquire knowledge of the concept, students with learning disabilities are more able to discriminate between examples and nonexamples of a concept on their own.

### Technology

The use of assistive technology allows students with learning difficulties in one area (e.g., writing or reading) to participate in instruction in another (e.g., social studies or science). For example, a screen reader may be useful for a student with reading problems who is doing research on the Internet about the government of Tahiti.

### Modeling of Problem-Solving Steps by the Teacher

Students with learning disabilities must be explicitly taught to use efficient and effective problem-solving strategies. Teachers need to provide instruction in how to accomplish tasks in a step-by-step fashion that is consistent over time. An effective way to do this is by using think-alouds and demonstrations. For example, a teacher can provide students with a demonstration of how to take notes during one of the teacher's own lectures. The students can use the same format and steps for subsequent lectures.

### Group Instruction

Flexible grouping is important to students with learning disabilities so they can learn from their peers in different grouping formats (e.g., heterogeneous groups, homogeneous groups). Instruction in smaller groups, with either teachers or peers, allows for increased participation and engagement with material.

### Supplements to Teacher and Peer Involvement

Supplements may include homework or involving parents or paraeducators in assisting in instruction.

Council for Exceptional Children

**CEC Knowledge Check**

In teaching reading comprehension, what three of Swanson's ten instructional components would you use? Explain.
CC4S1, LD4K2, LD4S5, LD4S9

### Strategy Cues

Strategy cues are reminders for students with learning disabilities to use the strategies or procedures they have been taught. These cues may take the form of verbal reminders from teachers ("I'm going to begin talking about the Civil War. Everyone please take out a note-taking sheet and label it . . . ") or in the form of checklists or written prompts (Swanson, 2000).

www.ablongman.com/hallahanLD3e

## Graphic Organizers

**Graphic organizers** provide students with visual representations of both concepts and facts. The purpose of graphic organizers is to show visually how information is related. Effective graphic organizers contain only important information, have a logical structure, and show conceptual relationships by their structure. Researchers and teachers have used graphic organizers successfully in all content areas.

**graphic organizers** aids that provide students with visual representations of both concepts and facts

### *Unit Organizer*

The **unit organizer** is an example of how a graphic organizer can relate concepts and facts from an entire unit to make the information memorable for students. The unit organizer is part of a **content enhancement routine** (Boudah, Lenz, Bulgren, Schumaker, & Deshler, 2000; Lenz et al., 1994) developed to engage teachers in making planning decisions about what critical content to emphasize in teaching, how to transform the content into a learner-friendly format, and how to memorably present the content to academically diverse groups of students.

**unit organizer** graphic organizer that visually displays main concepts, activities, and ideas about a unit of study

**content enhancement routine** a routine used by a teacher to provide organization and clarity of concepts for students in any content area

The unit organizer routine is used to help teachers plan for, introduce, and build a unit. All students can (1) understand how the unit is part of bigger course ideas or a sequence of units, (2) understand the "gist," or central idea, of the unit through a meaningful paraphrase of the unit title, (3) see a structure or organization of the critical unit information, (4) define the relationships of the critical information, (5) generate and answer questions regarding key unit information, (6) monitor progress and accomplishments in learning, and (7) keep the "big ideas" and structure of the unit in mind as the unit content is learned. Figure 15.2 (page 512) is an example of a unit organizer in social studies.

Research has indicated that teacher planning is enhanced by using content enhancement routines; the performance of low-achieving students, students with learning disabilities, and average-achieving students is improved substantially in regard to understanding and retaining information (Lenz et al., 1994). In fact, among these groups, students of teachers who used this routine regularly consistently scored an average of 15 percentage points higher on unit tests than students of teachers who used the method only irregularly. Teachers also reported that the unit organizer routine helped students with language problems and whose first language was not English to acquire secondary content. For more information on content enhancement devices, see the Effective Practices box (page 499). Graphic organizers have proved invaluable for Shannon.

Shannon

For Shannon, graphic organizers are imperative. In the collaborative math class, I find they do two things: help the teacher determine what is really the most important "stuff" to teach *and* help students (all students) figure out how the "stuff" is related and not just a jumble of facts.

*Martin Schein, Shannon's special education teacher*

FIGURE 15.2    Unit Organizer in Social Studies

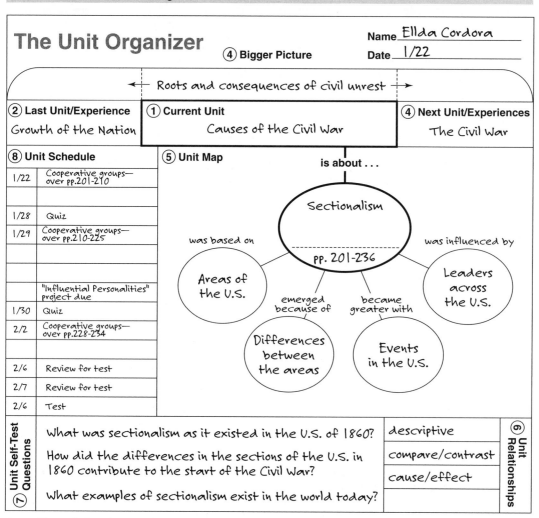

**The Unit Organizer**

④ **Bigger Picture**

Name ___Ellda Cordora___

Date ___1/22___

⟵ ┊ Roots and consequences of civil unrest ┊ ⟶

② **Last Unit/Experience**

Growth of the Nation

① **Current Unit**

Causes of the Civil War

④ **Next Unit/Experiences**

The Civil War

⑧ **Unit Schedule**

| | |
|---|---|
| 1/22 | Cooperative groups— over pp.201-210 |
| 1/28 | Quiz |
| 1/29 | Cooperative groups— over pp.210-225 |
| | |
| | "Influential Personalities" project due |
| 1/30 | Quiz |
| 2/2 | Cooperative groups— over pp.228-234 |
| | |
| 2/6 | Review for test |
| 2/7 | Review for test |
| 2/6 | Test |

⑤ **Unit Map**

is about . . .

Sectionalism
- - - - - - - - - -
pp. 201-236

was based on → Areas of the U.S.

was influenced by → Leaders across the U.S.

emerged because of → Differences between the areas

became greater with → Events in the U.S.

⑦ **Unit Self-Test Questions**

What was sectionalism as it existed in the U.S. of 1860?

How did the differences in the sections of the U.S. in 1860 contribute to the start of the Civil War?

What examples of sectionalism exist in the world today?

⑥ **Unit Relationships**

descriptive

compare/contrast

cause/effect

*Source:* From *The Unit Organizer Routine* by B. K. Lenz, J. A. Bulgren, J. B. Schumaker, D. D. Deshler, and D. A. Boudah, 1997, Lawrence, KS: Edge Enterprises. Copyright 1997 by Edge Enterprises. Reprinted by permission.

### Concept Diagram

**concept diagram**
a graphic organizer that visually displays the critical features of a concept in any content area

A **concept diagram** (Bulgren & Lenz, 1996) is another example of a graphic organizer. In the concept diagram, the important components of a concept and how those components are related are visually depicted. These components include key words related to the concept; characteristics that are always present, sometimes present, and never present; examples and nonexamples of the concept; practice with a new example; and a definition of the concept in the student's own words. When combined with the content enhancement planning routine, the concept diagram

## FIGURE 15.3    Concept Diagram for Science

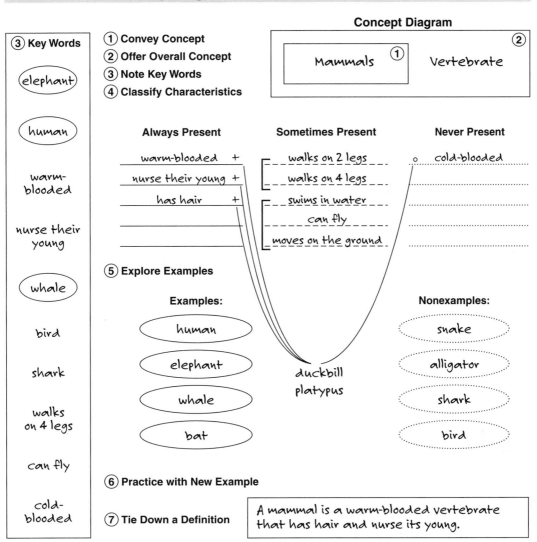

Source: From *The Content Enhancement Series: The Concept Mastery Routine* by J. A. Bulgren, D. D. Deshler, and J. B. Shumaker, 1993, Lawrence, KS: Edge Enterprises. Copyright 1993 by Edge Enterprises, Inc. Reprinted by permission.

eliminates irrelevant facts and helps students focus on understanding the critical features of a topic. See Figure 15.3 for an example of a concept diagram used in science.

The success of graphic organizers for students with learning disabilities is not linked merely to the visual representation of concepts. Rather, their effectiveness comes from their appropriate use by teachers. Graphic organizers require teachers to (1) identify the critical components of a unit, concept, or topic; (2) describe how

Council for
Exceptional
Children

CEC Knowledge Check

What must teachers
do to make graphic or-
ganizers beneficial to
students?
LD4S6, CC10S8

**peer-mediated instruction**
involves the use of peers
in structured activities to
provide increased opportunities for student practice
with content material

Council for
Exceptional
Children

CEC Knowledge Check

How is peer-mediated
instruction different from
cooperative learning?
LD5S1

the components are related to the unit and to each other; and (3) decide on how best to visually display the relationships. Only after teachers complete this planning process can they begin to teach the organizer to their students. Graphic organizers are only successful for students with learning disabilities when they are incorporated into instruction. In other words, teachers must teach students how to use the organizers by using modeling, guided practice, and corrective feedback. They must also provide students with cues as to when to use the organizers and how to use them independently. (*Note:* We appreciate the help provided by Dan Boudah in the preparation of this section.)

## Peer-Mediated Instruction

**Peer-mediated instruction** involves the use of peers in structured activities to provide increased opportunities for student practice with content material. Peer-mediated instruction is different from cooperative learning in that peer-mediated instruction requires the teacher to teach students how to conduct the required activities together and also requires that students act as both tutors and tutees. Three examples follow:

### Peer-Assisted Learning Strategies (PALS)

The PALS program is a student-mediated learning program designed to develop student skills, particularly in reading but also in math. PALS "incorporates structured activities that require peers to engage in frequent interaction, provide each other with immediate corrective feedback, and take turns as tutor and tutee" (Fuchs, Fuchs, & Burish, 2000, p. 85).

For example, after teacher-directed instruction on what to do and how to provide corrective feedback, teachers place students in pairs that include a higher-level reader and a lower-level reader. The dyads work together on three structured activities: partner reading, paragraph shrinking, and prediction relay. In partner reading, the higher-performing reader reads text for 5 minutes, after which the lower-performing student rereads the same material. The lower-performing student then retells what has occurred, with feedback from the higher-performing student.

In paragraph shrinking, students read aloud paragraph by paragraph; each stops to identify the main idea after reading and receives feedback from the partner.

Finally, in prediction relay, students make a prediction about what will be read in the next half page. The student reads a half page and summarizes the main idea. Both students then decide whether the prediction was correct or whether it needed revision, and then the next student reads. As the dyads work, they earn points for words read correctly, main ideas identified, and predictions. The dyads are included in larger class teams, which encourages students to work hard to get as many points as possible.

In reading, PALS has been investigated at the elementary level and found to improve both reading fluency and reading comprehension for students who are average, low achieving, and have learning disabilities (e.g., Fuchs, Fuchs, Mathes, and Simmons, 1997). PALS has also been evaluated at the high school level and found to improve reading comprehension skills (Fuchs, Fuchs, & Kazdan, 1999). The results for reading growth "compare favorably with more complicated and labor-intensive versions of collaborative learning" (Fuchs, Fuchs, & Burish, 2000, p. 88). Figure 15.4 gives an example of PALS cues for reading activities. For more information on PALS, see the Effective Practices box (page 499).

### Collaborative Strategic Reading

**Collaborative strategic reading (CSR)** is a method developed and researched by Vaughn and colleagues in both general education reading classrooms and in content area classrooms (e.g., Vaughn & Klingner, 1999; Vaughn, Klingner, & Bryant, 2001). CSR is made up of four reading comprehension strategies that teachers teach to students in a whole-group format. Students then use the strategies to guide their reading in small groups or in student pairs. The students act as both teachers and participants in the small-group situations.

The four comprehension strategies include previewing the text (activating background knowledge), click and clunk (monitoring reading and vocabulary understanding during reading), get the gist (identifying main ideas during reading), and wrap-up (summarizing key ideas after reading) (Vaughn, Klingner, & Bryant, 2001). Each student within a group is assigned a task. The leader keeps the group on task. The clunk expert helps students use strategies to fix their comprehension difficulties.

Council for
Exceptional
Children

**CEC Knowledge Check**
What academic skills can be improved by using the PALS intervention? LD4S5, LD4S8, LD4S9, LD4S11

**collaborative strategic reading (CSR)** peer-mediated instruction in reading groups that involves structured activities such as click and clunk and get the gist

---

### FIGURE 15.4    PALS Activities

**Retell**
1. What did you learn first?
1. What did you learn next?

**Paragraph shrinking**
1. Name the who or what.
2. Tell the most important thing about the who or what.
3. Say the main idea in ten word or less.

**Prediction relay**

| | |
|---|---|
| Predict _____ | What do you predict will happen next? |
| Read _____ | Read half a page. |
| Check _____ | Did the prediction come true? |

*Source:* From *PALS Reading for Grades 2–6: Teacher Manual* by L. S. Fuchs, D. Fuchs, K. Karns, and N. Phillips, 2000, Nashville, TN: Author. Reprinted by permission of the author.

---

The gist expert reminds everyone how to find the main idea. The announcer chooses students to read or answer questions and represents the group when the teacher brings groups back together (Vaughn & Klingner, 1999). Teachers have used collaborative strategic reading effectively in both elementary- and middle-school general education classrooms. Again, the success of the groups depends on how well students are able to perform the tasks (e.g., click and clunk) and how well they understand their roles. For more information on CSR, see the Effective Practices box.

### Classwide Peer Tutoring

classwide peer tutoring (CWPT)   peer-mediated instruction that includes reciprocal, structured roles for tutor and tutee

Both PALS and CSR are rooted in the success of **classwide peer tutoring,** or **CWPT** (Greenwood, Delquadri, & Carta, 1997). CWPT uses a gamelike format to pair diverse learners for practice in the acquisition and use of facts in any content area, particularly vocabulary, reading, and basic skills. As in the other programs, students are initially taught by the teacher how to participate in the activities, award points, and provide feedback. Then, teachers pair students of differing abilities, place the pairs on teams, and provide materials for students to complete.

Examples of uses of CWPT include practice for vocabulary or spelling words, basic math facts, and reading in the content areas. Tutors provide support for tutees as they complete the teacher-designed activities, as well as awarding points and giving feedback. After a given period of time, the tutors and tutees switch roles. The dyad is part of a larger class team and works toward earning points for the group as well. For more information on CWPT, see the Effective Practices box.

Peer-mediated instruction requires a great deal of instruction from the teacher in order to be effective. In all of the programs described here, teachers must teach students what their roles are in the group, how to carry out those roles, how to provide feedback to their peers, and how to maintain focus on the task. Students with learning disabilities, in particular, have a difficult time being placed in a group and told to "work together." Therefore, teachers must plan to spend instructional time teaching students how to work together appropriately. Shannon's teachers have not all been equally successful in structuring peer-mediated instruction. For example, her science teacher admits that maybe he has not provided enough structure.

Shannon

Council for Exceptional Children

**CEC Knowledge Check**

If research supports improved achievement using peer-mediated instruction, why is Shannon's teacher not experiencing success with his students? CC5K4, CC5K5, CC5S4

> Everyone talks about how great collaborative learning groups are. I just can't get them to work, particularly for students like Shannon. I hear from my team that in social studies, collaborative groups are a great success. I'm just not sure I could make mine as structured as Ms. Rajam does—with everyone having a role and a practiced activity to complete.
>
> *David Hightower, Shannon's science teacher*

### Note-Taking

Students with learning disabilities differ from their nondisabled peers in their ability to identify important information during lectures, their ability to write with speed, and their ability to make sense of notes they have taken in classes (Boyle, 2001). Even though note-taking is a skill that is used extensively in a student's academic career, little research has been done on the topic with students with learning disabilities. What we do know about note-taking is that it engages students in the content being presented and allows them to clarify confusing information. There is also a correlation between the amount of notes taken and student scores on tests of that information (Boyle, 2001).

A popular adaptation for students with learning disabilities is to provide another student's notes or the teacher's notes for the student. Unfortunately, if students do not try to take notes on their own, they will often not engage with the material, and other adaptations (e.g., directed questioning, summarizing orally) may be needed. Accommodations for notes include altering the teacher's lecture format by chunking material into smaller conceptual pieces, slowing the lecture pace, providing verbal and nonverbal cues (e.g., "The next important point is . . . ), and providing outlines or other visual cues (Boyle & Weishaar, 2001). Guided notes have also been used with students with learning disabilities. Guided notes can either provide strategy cues for note-taking or provide specific content information so that students can fill in additional material during the lecture.

Shannon's language arts teacher, for example, has used some of these accommodations.

> Shannon can take notes during class but often just doesn't even think about doing it. That's where cuing her to do it and then providing explicit statements about what to jot down are important. For example, I'll see Shannon (and other students) aren't really with me, so I'll say, "The next important point is . . . "
>
> *Jill Cartwright, Shannon's language arts teacher*

**Shannon**

Teachers can teach students to use a strategic note-taking process that includes a note-taking sheet (Boyle, 2001; Boyle & Weishaar, 2001) (see Figure 15.5, page 518). Students were taught to use this strategic note-taking sheet during practice lectures and then in real classrooms. The researchers found a significant difference between high school students with learning disabilities who used this strategy and those who did not on the number of words recorded, immediate recall of lecture material, long-term recall of lecture material, and understanding of new vocabulary (Boyle & Weishaar, 2001).

There are also strategies for use in note-taking. The first is LINKS (*L*isten, *I*dentify verbal cues, *N*ote information, *K*eywords, *S*tack into outline form (Suritsky & Hughes, 1997). The second is AWARE (*A*rrange to take notes, *W*rite quickly, *A*pply cues, *R*eview notes, *E*dit notes). Both of these strategies require that teachers teach students what the mnemonics mean, what activities they must complete in each step, and how to put the steps together. Instruction in these strategies *must* progress through all appropriate stages. Teaching the steps of the

Council for
Exceptional
Children

**CEC Knowledge Check**
Why is it important for some students to be directly taught how to take lecture notes? LD4S13

**FIGURE 15.5** Strategic Note-Taking Sheet

**Strategic Note-Taking Form**

*Fill in this portion before the lecture begins.*

Page 1

What is today's topic?

Describe what you know about the topic.

*As the instructor lectures, use these pages to take notes of the lecture.*

Today's topic?

Name three to seven main points with details of today's topic as they are being discussed.

Summary—Quickly describe how the ideas are related.

New Vocabulary or Terms:

- - - - - - - - - - - - - - - - - - - - - - - - - - - - - - - - - - - - - - - - - - - -

Page 2

Name three to seven *new* main points with details as they are being discussed.

New Vocabulary or Terms:

Summary—Quickly describe how the ideas are related.

- - - - - - - - - - - - - - - - - - - - - - - - - - - - - - - - - - - - - - - - - - - -

Page x

Name three to seven *new* main points with details as they are being discussed.

New Vocabulary or Terms:

Summary—Quickly describe how the ideas are related.

- - - - - - - - - - - - - - - - - - - - - - - - - - - - - - - - - - - - - - - - - - - -

Last Page

*At End of Lecture*

Write five main points of the lecture and describe each point.

1.

2.

3.

4.

5.

*Source:* From "The Effects of Strategic Notetaking on the Recall and Comprehension of Lecture Information for High School Students with Learning Disabilities" by J. R. Boyle and M. Weishaar, 2001, *Learning Disabilities Research and Practice,* 16, 133–141. Copyright 2001 by Blackwell Publishing. Reprinted by permission.

strategy alone will be insufficient to bring about meaningful student change. (For more information, contact Edge Enterprises, 708 W. Ninth Street, Suite 107, Lawrence, KS 66044.)

## General Recommendations for Science Instruction

Students with learning disabilities tend to get worse grades in secondary science classes than their peers (Cawley & Parmar, 2001). This is often attributed to the fact that science teachers still rely on text-based instruction for their classrooms and that many students with learning disabilities have weaknesses in the areas of language and literacy. In addition, science textbooks have been criticized for their reading difficulty, rapid introduction of new vocabulary, and superficial treatment of topics (Cawley & Parmar, 2001). For general education teachers who use texts most often in their instruction, here are recommendations to help include students with learning disabilities:

1. Prioritize material in the text for students.
2. Preteach vocabulary.
3. Have students paraphrase passages as they read.
4. Provide study guides, visual aids, and graphic organizers.
5. Supplement instruction with audiotaped texts.

During instruction (Munk, Bruckert, Call, Stoehrmann, & Radandt, 1998),

1. Use mnemonics to help students with vocabulary.
2. Try using guided notes during lecture.
3. Use cooperative learning groups for some material.

Much of the research literature about science instruction in general education classrooms advocates an activities-based approach to learning. **Activities-based learning** in this sense means using a guided inquiry approach, one that maintains structure and consistency in the learning cycle but allows students to work with real-life problems and to investigate phenomena instead of just reading about them (Mastropieri & Scruggs, 2000).

One example of a guided inquiry process includes the stages of (1) engaging students in learning about a phenomenon; (2) investigating that phenomenon by conducting experiments and finding information about it; (3) explaining the phenomenon in groups, using the information gathered; and (4) reporting hypotheses to the class (Palincsar, Magnusson, Collins, & Cutler, 2001). In this scenario, the teacher's role in the classroom is to help with literacy issues, evaluate student understanding so that no misconceptions are present, and help students work in groups.

A similar inquiry model includes **teacher modeling** and **structured coaching** as students progress through activities in cooperative learning groups (Cawley & Parmar, 2001). In this type of instruction, accommodations will have to be made in lab settings. These may include using checklists for lab steps, modifying materials,

**activities-based learning** using a guided inquiry approach, one that maintains structure and consistency in the learning cycle but allows students to work with real-life problems and investigate phenomena instead of just reading about them

**teacher modeling** teacher demonstrating what learners are about to learn

**structured coaching** provides sequenced prompts that help students proceed in an appropriate direction without directly providing answers

Council for
Exceptional
Children

**CEC Knowledge Check**

How can you assess the structure of another teacher's classroom for the benefit of a student with learning disabilities? If the teacher uses primarily lecture, how will you collaborate with the teacher to accommodate the student? CC5K1, CC5K3, CC5S3, CC5S4, CC10S6, CC10S9

**anchor** usually a video, used in instruction to present students with a real-life scenario that includes multiple subproblems for students to solve in a content area determined by the teacher

providing demonstrations, allowing students to work with partners, requiring lab journals, and frequently verifying student understanding (Salend, 1998). In such cases, rubrics that are objective and identify necessary skills for the evaluation of lab work are necessary to monitor student progress (Finson and Ormsbee, 1998). For more resources on teaching science, see the Effective Practices box (page 499).

## General Recommendations for Social Studies Instruction

Recommendations for social studies instruction for students with learning disabilities are similar to those for science: (1) increase student engagement, (2) teach using a problem-solving model, and (3) relate the concepts to real-life issues or events. For example, Ferretti, MacArthur, and Okolo (2001) used all of these components to engage middle-school students (with and without learning disabilities) in learning about westward expansion. They began by using a video describing a family's struggle as they moved west as an **anchor** for learning. The family included children of about the same age as the students. The teachers then explicitly taught students specific strategies to use to research and discuss who went west, why they went west, how they went west, and the outcomes of moving west. The students completed their research in collaborative structured groups using primary sources. The results indicated that everyone in the classroom, including students with learning disabilities, improved from pre- to posttest on knowledge, understanding, and inquiry skills measures (Ferretti, MacArthur, & Okolo, 2001).

Social studies instruction can be structured around a problem-solving model that is explicitly taught to students and then used to address any topical area (O'Brien, 2000). The problem-solving model includes:

1. Provide context and introduce background to the problem/question.
2. Generate the problem/question and familiarize students with the use of primary sources.
3. Generate possible solutions and raise questions about how to solve the problem.
4. Research possible solutions.
5. Reconsider possible solutions.
6. Explain a solution.
7. Reestablish the context of the problem.
8. Act upon the decision.
9. Evaluate the results.
10. Redefine the problem.

This cycle is similar to one described as a problem-solution-effect approach to teaching social studies (Carnine, Crawford, Harniss, Hollenbeck, & Miller, 1998). In both cycles, students define a problem, determine how the people of the time solved the problem, and then evaluate the problems generated by those solutions. In each case, students are taught an organized approach to learning facts and concepts, which are often the focus of text-based instruction. They are also all engaged in academic tasks by the group involvement and the discourse about problems in which the entire class participates.

As in science, social studies teachers are encouraged to make adaptations and accommodations in their use of textbooks. Providing study guides, prioritizing material, and providing graphic organizers and visual aids as well as teaching students how to use organizational structures within texts (e.g., headings, subheadings, summaries) are helpful for students with learning disabilities. (Examples of study guides can be found at www.educ.andrews.edu/program_tlc.html) In addition, the use of mnemonics to help students remember factual material, particularly material that occurs in a certain order (e.g., presidents), has proven effective (e.g., Mastropieri, Scruggs, & Whedon, 1997; Mastropieri, Sweda, & Scruggs, 2000). Finally, social studies teachers should consider changing how they lecture. When teachers chunk their lectures into conceptual units, stop after each unit, engage students in questioning and providing feedback, and then begin the next conceptual unit, students with learning disabilities improve their outcomes on curriculum-based measures, unit tests, and maintenance tests at a later time (Hudson, 1997). For more information on teaching social studies, see the Effective Practices box (page 499).

**CEC Knowledge Check**

When teaching using this structure, what problems might occur? How could you proactively avoid them? CC5K5, CC5S1, CC5S4

## PORTFOLIO-BUILDING ACTIVITY

### Demonstrating Mastery of the CEC Standards

Use the Case Connections box (pages 494–495) as well as information on Shannon provided in this chapter to design a spelling, reading comprehension, or math lesson, along with teacher and student instruction and curriculum support materials. Use the Effective Practices box (page 499) and the Websites listed in this box as well. Create materials of professional quality that you can later use in your classroom. Make sure to include all of the research-supported instructional steps for effective teaching described in this chapter. Questions to think about as you progress:

**CEC Content Standards**

3. Individual Learning Differences
4. Instructional Strategies
5. Learning Environments and Social Interactions
7. Instructional Planning

- Why must students with learning disabilities have individualized instruction planning in order to provide meaningful and challenging educational opportunities?

- What research-based instructional interventions exist that can promote achievement gains in general education classrooms and curricula for students with learning disabilities?

- How can special education professionals help general education colleagues integrate individuals with learning disabilities into general education environments and engage them in meaningful learning activities and interactions?

- In what ways can instruction plans, anchored in general and special curricula, address student needs and emphasize explicit modeling, guided practice, and ongoing progress analysis in a collaborative context?

# SUMMARY

## What are the legal mandates for placement?

- IDEA provides for specialized instruction in the least restrictive environment (LRE). Though some would describe LRE as the general education classroom for all students, IDEA requires a decision based on the individual needs of each student.
- The No Child Left Behind Act (NCLB) requires that all students participate in assessments of yearly progress. IEP teams determine whether or not students with disabilities will participate in the standardized assessments for the general education curriculum.

## How do students with LD receive special education services in general education classrooms?

- Co-teaching occurs when the special and general educators work together to teach students in the general education classroom.
- Special educators provide individualized instruction to students with learning disabilities in resource rooms.

## How can placement and instructional decisions be made?

- In order to make decisions about placement, IEP teams must gather data about classroom environments, including teacher behavior, expectations, routines, grading, and behavior management.
- Once placement and instructional decisions are made by the IEP team, teachers must monitor student progress on an ongoing basis to make sure that the student is making adequate progress. Teachers often use curriculum-based assessment.

## What are modifications for students with learning disabilities in general education classrooms?

- Modifications include accommodations and adaptations. Accommodations are changes to instruction, assignments, or assessment that do not radically change the content or level of material. Adaptations, on the other hand, change the content or level of the material.
- Instructional accommodations may include working in groups, providing a note-taker, or providing outlines or study guides of the material.
- Instructional adaptations may include varying levels of instruction in reading or tiered assignments.

## What are effective instructional practices for students with learning disabilities in general education classrooms?

- In a synthesis of instructional interventions, the following components were found effective for students with learning disabilities: sequencing, drill-repetition and practice-review, segmentation, directed questioning and responses, controlling difficulty or processing demands of a task, technology, modeling of problem-solving steps by teacher, group instruction, a supplement to teacher and peer involvement, and strategy cues.
- Graphic organizers, such as the unit organizer and concept diagram, provide clear guidance about how concepts and ideas are related.
- Peer-mediated instruction, such as peer-assisted learning strategies, collaborative strategic reading, and classwide peer tutoring, provide an alternative and effective way to reinforce both math and reading skills.
- Structured note-taking gives students with learning disabilities direct instruction in how to follow along and identify main ideas in lecture situations.
- General recommendations for science instruction include using activities-based learning and providing teacher modeling and structured coaching.
- General recommendations for social studies instruction include providing anchors and context for instruction and teaching "big ideas" such as a problem-solution-effect cycle.

## REFLECTIONS ON THE CASES

1. What are two areas of difficulty for Shannon in the general education classroom?
2. In what area does Shannon do well?
3. Which of the instruction strategies suggested in this chapter would benefit Shannon specifically? Why?

4. Choose one of the strategies you identified in the previous question. How would you implement that strategy in Shannon's math class?

5. How does Shannon's reading ability impact her other academic courses?

---

*Focus On* Inclusion in General Education
*Do Now* Activities for Making Accommodations

## Accommodations—Reading Road Maps for Content Area Texts

### ● *What are they?*

Reading road maps are guides that students can use to help them navigate reading non-narrative (expository) text such as that found in most social studies and science classrooms. Roe, Stoodt, and Burns (1995) define study guides as "a set of suggestions designed to lead the student through a reading assignment by directing attention to the key ideas in a passage and suggesting the application of skills needed to read a passage successfully" (pp. 267–268). Reading road maps make excellent strategies for general educators to use for students with learning disabilities who are included in content area classes.

Students with learning disabilities frequently encounter difficulty with reading and comprehending content area textbooks. Expository materials can present information in a variety of formats (e.g., description, compare-contrast, problem-solution, cause-effect). Without direct teaching on how to identify key information (main ideas and supporting facts or definitions) from the text, students with disabilities have difficulty focusing on key themes or content and can become overwhelmed by the amount of information and material within the text. Teachers find reading road maps valuable tools for both general education students and students with learning disabilities. Reading road maps also facilitate studying for exams!

### ● *How to implement them*

Teachers can use a variety of formats when developing their maps. To begin development, teachers should:

- **Determine text structure.**
  If the text is set up as descriptive, the teacher may design a map that includes focusing questions, terms and definitions, and reflection points. (See sample below.) If the text is set up as problem-solution-effect, the teachers can create a graphic organizer to support student connections.

- **Create the map using the text as a guide.**

- **Select from a variety of ideas for map activities.**
  - Identify key vocabulary and create a short phrase that illustrates the concept.
  - Prompt students to create summary sentences that summarize the section in one sentence.

• Create questions at the literal, inferential or applied, and critical-thinking levels. For example, with a cause-and-effect pattern, state some effects and ask students to identify the causes. Or, scramble the events or facts and have students classify them into "Causes" and "Effects" columns.

• Prompt students to reflect on key points or issues; connect prompts to previously learned material.

● *Sample reading road map*

| Reading selection: Chapter 3 (section 1–4) | | |
|---|---|---|
| Text | How to read? | Activity |
| Page 102 (intro.) | Read quickly **GO** | none |
| 103–105 | Read slowly. Pay attention to new vocabulary. **slow** | Define the three terms in bold. For each term write the example. 1. 2. 3. |
| 106 Purple box: Famous person feature | Read slowly and then stop to reflect. **slow** | Write a response of why you think this person is important. |
| 106–108 | Read slowly. **slow** | Restate paragraphs 1 and 2 in your own words. |
| 108–109 | Read slowly until the end of section 4. **slow** | In what ways do the two people in the reading differ? Complete a compare-contrast chart. |

*Source:* Kristin L. Sayeski

# Mastering the Council for Exceptional Children (CEC) Standards

- ● CEC Special Education Content Standards

- ● CEC Knowledge and Skills Base Standards for All Beginning Special Education Teachers of Students with Learning Disabilities (Common Core and Specialty Area)

The Special Education Content Standards are addressed throughout this textbook and referenced specifically in the *Portfolio-Based Activities* that appear at the end of each chapter. The Common Core and Learning Disability Knowledge and Skills are referenced specifically in the questions that appear in the *CEC Knowledge Check* margin notes throughout each chapter.

Additional infwormation about CEC Standards may be found at www.cec.sped.org/ps/nw_perf_based_stds.html

## CEC Special Education Content Standard 1: Foundations

Special educators understand the field as an evolving and changing discipline based on philosophies, evidence-based principles and theories, relevant laws and policies, diverse and historical points of view, and human issues that have historically influenced and continue to influence the field of special education and the education and treatment of individuals with exceptional needs both in school and society. Special educators understand how these influence professional practice, including assessment, instructional planning, implementation, and program evaluation. Special educators understand how issues of human diversity can impact families, cultures, and schools, and how these complex human issues can interact with issues in the delivery of special education services. They understand the relationships of organizations of special education to the organizations and functions of schools, school systems, and other agencies. Special educators use this knowledge as a ground upon which to construct their own personal understandings and philosophies of special education.

### COMMON CORE

*Knowledge:*

- CC1K1    Models, theories, and philosophies that form the basis for special education practice.
- CC1K2    Laws, policies, and ethical principles regarding behavior management planning and implementation.
- CC1K3    Relationship of special education to the organization and function of educational agencies.

- CC1K4    Rights and responsibilities of students, parents, teachers, and other professionals, and schools related to exceptional learning needs.
- CC1K5    Issues in definition and identification of individuals with exceptional learning needs, including those from culturally and linguistically diverse backgrounds.
- CC1K6    Issues, assurances and due process rights related to assessment, eligibility, and placement within a continuum of services.
- CC1K7    Family systems and the role of families in the educational process.
- CC1K8    Historical points of view and contribution of culturally diverse groups.
- CC1K9    Impact of the dominant culture on shaping schools and the individuals who study and work in them.
- CC1K10    Potential impact of differences in values, languages, and customs that can exist between the home and school.

*Skill:*
- CC1S1    Articulate personal philosophy of special education.

## LEARNING DISABILITIES

*Knowledge:*
- LD1K1    Historical foundations, classical studies, and major contributors in the field of learning disabilities.
- LD1K2    Philosophies, theories, models and issues related to individuals with learning disabilities.
- LD1K3    Impact of legislation on the education of individuals with learning disabilities.
- LD1K4    Laws and policies regarding pre-referral, referral, and placement procedures for individuals who may have learning disabilities.
- LD1K5    Current definitions and issues related to the identification of individuals with learning disabilities.

*Skills:*
None in Addition to Common Core

## CEC Special Education Content Standard 2: Development and Characteristics of Learners

Special educators know and demonstrate respect for their students first as unique human beings. Special educators understand the similarities and differences in human development and the characteristics between and among individuals with and without exceptional learning needs (ELN). Moreover, special educators understand how exceptional conditions can interact with the domains of human development and they use this knowledge to respond to the varying abilities and behaviors of individuals with ELN. Special educators understand how the experiences of individuals with ELN can impact families, as well as the individual's ability to learn, interact socially, and live as fulfilled contributing members of the community.

## COMMON CORE

*Knowledge:*

- CC2K1    Typical and atypical human growth and development.
- CC2K2    Educational implications of characteristics of various exceptionalities.
- CC2K3    Characteristics and effects of the cultural and environmental milieu of the individual with exceptional learning needs and the family.
- CC2K4    Family systems and the role of families in supporting development.
- CC2K5    Similarities and differences of individuals with and without exceptional learning needs.
- CC2K6    Similarities and differences among individuals with exceptional learning needs.
- CC2K7    Effects of various medications on individuals with exceptional learning needs.

## LEARNING DISABILITIES

*Knowledge:*

- LD2K1    Etiologies of learning disabilities.
- LD2K2    Neurobiological and medical factors that may impact the learning of individuals with learning disabilities.
- LD2K3    Psychological, social, and emotional characteristics of individuals with learning disabilities.

*Skills:*

None in addition to Common Core

## CEC Special Education Content Standard 3: Individual Learning Differences

Special educators understand the effects that an exceptional condition can have on an individual's learning in school and throughout life. Special educators understand that the beliefs, traditions, and values across and within cultures can affect relationships among and between students, their families, and the school community. Moreover, special educators are active and resourceful in seeking to understand how primary language, culture, and familial backgrounds interact with the individual's exceptional condition to impact the individual's academic and social abilities, attitudes, values, interests, and career options. The understanding of these learning differences and their possible interactions provide the foundation upon which special educators individualize instruction to provide meaningful and challenging learning for individuals with ELN.

## COMMON CORE

*Knowledge:*

- CC3K1    Effects an exceptional condition(s) can have on an individual's life.
- CC3K2    Impact of learners' academic and social abilities, attitudes, interests, and values on instruction and career development.

- CC3K3    Variations in beliefs, traditions, and values across and within cultures and their effects on relationships among individuals with exceptional learning needs. Family, and schooling.

- CC3K4    Cultural perspectives influencing the relationships among families, schools and communities as related to instruction.

- CC3K5    Differing ways of learning of individuals with exceptional learning needs including those from culturally diverse backgrounds and strategies for addressing these differences.

### LEARNING DISABILITIES

*Knowledge:*

- LD3K1    Impact of co-existing conditions and exceptionalities on individuals with learning disabilities.

- LD3K2    Effects of phonological awareness on the reading abilities of individuals with learning disabilities.

- LD3K3    Impact learning disabilities may have on auditory and information processing skills.

*Skills:*

None in Addition to Common Core

## CEC Special Education Content Standard 4: Instructional Strategies

Special educators possess a repertoire of evidence-based instructional strategies to individualize instruction for individuals with ELN. Special educators select, adapt, and use these instructional strategies to promote challenging learning results in general and special curricula and to appropriately modify learning environments for individuals with ELN. They enhance the learning of critical thinking, problem solving, and performance skills of individuals with ELN, and increase their self-awareness, self-management, self-control, self-reliance, and self-esteem. Moreover, special educators emphasize the development, maintenance, and generalization of knowledge and skills across environments, settings, and the lifespan.

### COMMON CORE

*Skills:*

- CC4S1    Use strategies to facilitate integration into various settings.

- CC4S2    Teach individuals to use self-assessment, problem solving, and other cognitive strategies to meet their needs.

- CC4S3    Select, adapt, and use instructional strategies and materials according to characteristics of the individual with exceptional learning needs.

- CC4S4    Use strategies to facilitate maintenance and generalization of skills across learning environments.

- CC4S5    Use procedures to increase the individual's self-awareness, self-management, self-control, self-reliance, and self-esteem.

- CC4S6    Use strategies that promote successful transitions for individuals with exceptional learning needs.

## LEARNING DISABILITIES

*Knowledge:*

- LD4K1    Strategies to prepare for and take tests.
- LD4K2    Methods for ensuring individual academic success in one-to-one, small-group, and large-group settings.
- LD4K3    Methods for increasing accuracy and proficiency in math calculations and applications.
- LD4K4    Methods for teaching individuals to independently use cognitive processing to solve problems.
- LD4K5    Methods for guiding individuals in identifying and organizing critical content.

*Skills:*

- LD4S1    Use research-supported methods for academic and nonacademic instruction of individuals with learning disabilities.
- LD4S2    Use specialized methods for teaching basic skills.
- LD4S3    Modify the pace of instruction and provide organizational cues.
- LD4S4    Identify and teach basic structures and relationships within and across curricula.
- LD4S5    Use instructional methods to strengthen and compensate for deficits in perception, comprehension, memory, and retrieval.
- LD4S6    Use responses and errors to guide instructional decisions and provide feedback to learners.
- LD4S7    Identify and teach essential concepts, vocabulary, and content across the general curriculum.
- LD4S8    Use reading methods appropriate to the individual with learning disabilities.
- LD4S9    Implement systematic instruction in teaching reading comprehension and monitoring strategies.
- LD4S10   Teach strategies for organizing and composing written products.
- LD4S11   Implement systematic instruction to teach accuracy, fluency, and comprehension in content area reading and written language.
- LD4S12   Use methods to teach mathematics appropriate to the individual with learning disabilities.
- LD4S13   Teach learning strategies and study skills to acquire academic content.

## CEC Special Education Content Standard 5: Learning Environments and Social Interactions

Special educators actively create learning environments for individuals with ELN that foster cultural understanding, safety and emotional well being, positive social interactions, and active engagement of individuals with ELN. In addition, special educators foster environments in which diversity is valued and individuals are taught to live harmoniously and productively in a culturally diverse world. Special educators shape environments to encourage the independence, self-motivation, self-direction, personal empowerment, and self-advocacy of individuals with ELN. Special educators help their general education colleagues integrate individuals with ELN in regular environments and engage them in meaningful learning activities and interactions. Special educators use direct motivational and instructional interventions with individuals with ELN to teach them to respond effectively to current expectations. When necessary, special educators can safely intervene with individuals with ELN in crisis. Special educators coordinate all these efforts and provide guidance and direction to paraeducators and others, such as classroom volunteers and tutors.

## COMMON CORE

*Knowledge:*

- CC5K1   Demands of learning environments.
- CC5K2   Basic classroom management theories and strategies for individuals with exceptional learning needs.
- CC5K3   Effective management of teaching and learning.
- CC5K4   Teacher attitudes and behaviors that influence behavior of individuals with exceptional learning needs.
- CC5K5   Social skills needed for educational and other environments.
- CC5K6   Strategies for crisis prevention and intervention.
- CC5K7   Strategies for preparing individuals to live harmoniously and productively in a culturally diverse world.
- CC5K8   Ways to create learning environments that allow individuals to retain and appreciate their own and each other's respective language and cultural heritage.
- CC5K9   Ways specific cultures are negatively stereotyped.
- CC5K10   Strategies used by diverse populations to cope with a legacy of former and continuing racism.

*Skills:*

- CC5S1   Create a safe, equitable, positive, and supportive learning environment in which diversities are valued.
- CC5S2   Identify realistic expectations for personal and social behavior in various settings.
- CC5S3   Identify supports needed for integration into various program placements.
- CC5S4   Design learning environments that encourage active participation in individual and group activities.
- CC5S5   Modify the learning environment to manage behaviors.
- CC5S6   Use performance data and information from all stakeholders to make or suggest modifications in learning environments.
- CC5S7   Establish and maintain rapport with individuals with and without exceptional learning needs.
- CC5S8   Teach self-advocacy.

- CC5S9     Create an environment that encourages self-advocacy and increased independence.
- CC5S10     Use effective and varied behavior management strategies.
- CC5S11     Use the least intensive behavior management strategy consistent with the needs of the individual with exceptional learning needs.
- CC5S12     Design and manage daily routines.
- CC5S13     Organize, develop, and sustain learning environments that support positive intracultural and intercultural experiences.
- CC5S14     Mediate controversial intercultural issues among students within the learning environment in ways that enhance any culture, group, or person.
- CC5S15     Structure, direct, and support the activities of paraeducators, volunteers, and tutors.
- CC5S16     Use universal precautions.

### LEARNING DISABILITIES

*Knowledge:*

None in addition to Common Core

*Skills:*

- LD5S1     Teach individuals with learning disabilities to give and receive meaningful feedback from peers and adults.

## CEC Special Education Content Standard 6: Language

Special educators understand typical and atypical language development and the ways in which exceptional conditions can interact with an individual's experience with and use of language. Special educators use individualized strategies to enhance language development and teach communication skills to individuals with ELN. Special educators are familiar with augmentative, alternative, and assistive technologies to support and enhance communication of individuals with exceptional needs. Special educators match their communication methods to an individual's language proficiency and cultural and linguistic differences. Special educators provide effective language models, and they use communication strategies and resources to facilitate understanding of subject matter for individuals with ELN whose primary language is not English.

### COMMON CORE

*Knowledge:*

- CC6K1     Effects of cultural and linguistic differences on growth and development.
- CC6K2     Characteristics of one's own culture and use of language and the ways in which these can differ from other cultures and uses of languages.
- CC6K3     Ways of behaving and communicating among cultures that can lead to misinterpretation and misunderstanding.
- CC6K4     Augmentative and assistive communication strategies.

- CC6S1    Use strategies to support and enhance communication skills of individuals with exceptional learning needs.

- CC6S2    Use communication strategies and resources to facilitate understanding of subject matter for students whose primary language is not the dominant language.

## LEARNING DISABILITIES

*Knowledge:*

- LD6K1    Typical language development and how that may differ for individuals with learning disabilities.

- LD6K2    Impact of language development and listening comprehension on academic and non-academic learning of individuals with learning disabilities.

- LD6K3

- LD6K4    Enhance vocabulary development.

- LD6K5    Teach strategies for spelling accuracy and generalization.

- LD6K6    Teach methods and strategies for producing legible documents.

- LD6K7    Teach individuals with learning disabilities to monitor for errors in oral and written communications.

## CEC Special Education Content Standard 7: Instructional Planning

Individualized decision-making and instruction is at the center of special education practice. Special educators develop long-range individualized instructional plans anchored in both general and special curricula. In addition, special educators systematically translate these individualized plans into carefully selected shorter-range goals and objectives taking into consideration an individual's abilities and needs, the learning environment, and a myriad of cultural and linguistic factors. Individualized instructional plans emphasize explicit modeling and efficient guided practice to assure acquisition and fluency through maintenance and generalization. Understanding of these factors as well as the implications of an individual's exceptional condition, guides the special educator's selection, adaptation, and creation of materials, and the use of powerful instructional variables. Instructional plans are modified based on ongoing analysis of the individual's learning progress. Moreover, special educators facilitate this instructional planning in a collaborative context including the individuals with exceptionalities, families, professional colleagues, and personnel from other agencies as appropriate. Special educators also develop a variety of individualized transition plans, such as transitions from preschool to elementary school and from secondary settings to a variety of postsecondary work and learning contexts. Special educators are comfortable using appropriate technologies to support instructional planning and individualized instruction.

## COMMON CORE

*Knowledge:*

- CC7K1    Theories and research that form the basis of curriculum development and instructional practice.

- CC7K2    Scope and sequences of general and special curricula.

- CC7K3  National, state or provincial, and local curricula standards.
- CC7K4  Technology for planning and managing the teaching and learning environment.
- CC7K5  Roles and responsibilities of the paraeducator related to instruction, intervention, and direct service.

*Skills:*
- CC7S1  Identify and prioritize areas of the general curriculum and accommodations for individuals with exceptional learning needs.
- CC7S2  Develop and implement comprehensive, longitudinal individualized programs in collaboration with team members.
- CC7S3  Involve the individual and family in setting instructional goals and monitoring progress.
- CC7S4  Use functional assessments to develop intervention plans.
- CC7S5  Use task analysis.
- CC7S6  Sequence, implement, and evaluate individualized learning objectives.
- CC7S7  Integrate affective, social, and life skills with academic curricula.
- CC7S8  Develop and select instructional content, resources, and strategies that respond to cultural, linguistic, and gender differences.
- CC7S9  Incorporate and implement instructional and assistive technology into the educational program.
- CC7S10  Prepare lesson plans.
- CC7S11  Prepare and organize materials to implement daily lesson plans.
- CC7S12  Use instructional time effectively.
- CC7S13  Make responsive adjustments to instruction based on continual observations.
- CC7S14  Prepare individuals to exhibit self-enhancing behavior in response to societal attitudes and actions.

## LEARNING DISABILITIES

*Knowledge:*
- LD7K1  Relationships among reading instruction methods and learning disabilities.
- LD7K2  Sources of specialized curricula, materials, and resources for individuals with learning disabilities.
- LD7K3  Interventions and services for children who may be at risk for learning disabilities.

*Skills:*
None in Addition to Common Core

## CEC Special Education Content Standard 8: Assessment

Assessment is integral to the decision-making and teaching of special educators and special educators use multiple types of assessment information for a variety of educational decisions. Special educators use the results of assessments to help identify exceptional learning needs and to develop and implement individualized instructional programs, as well as to adjust instruction in response to ongoing learning progress. Special educators understand the legal policies and ethical principles of measurement and assessment related to referral, eligibility, program planning, instruction, and placement for individuals with ELN, including those from culturally and linguistically diverse backgrounds. Special educators understand measurement theory and practices for addressing issues of validity, reliability, norms, bias, and interpretation of assessment results. In addition, special educators understand the appropriate use and limitations of various types of assessments. Special educators collaborate with families and other colleagues to assure non-biased, meaningful assessments and decision-making. Special educators conduct formal and informal assessments of behavior, learning, achievement, and environments to design learning experiences that support the growth and development of individuals with ELN. Special educators use assessment information to identify supports and adaptations required for individuals with ELN to access the general curriculum and to participate in school, system, and statewide assessment programs. Special educators regularly monitor the progress of individuals with ELN in general and special curricula. Special educators use appropriate technologies to support their assessments.

## COMMON CORE

### Knowledge:

- CC8K1    Basic terminology used in assessment.
- CC8K2    Legal provisions and ethical principles regarding assessment of individuals.
- CC8K3    Screening, pre-referral, referral, and classification procedures.
- CC8K4    Use and limitations of assessment instruments.
- CC8K5    National, state or provincial, and local accommodations and modifications.

### Skills:

- CC8S1    Gather relevant background information.
- CC8S2    Administer nonbiased formal and informal assessments.
- CC8S3    Use technology to conduct assessments.
- CC8S4    Develop or modify individualized assessment strategies.
- CC8S5    Interpret information from formal and informal assessments.
- CC8S6    Use assessment information in making eligibility, program, and placement decisions for individuals with exceptional learning needs, including those from culturally and/or linguistically diverse backgrounds.
- CC8S7    Report assessment results to all stakeholders using effective communication skills.
- CC8S8    Evaluate instruction and monitor progress of individuals with exceptional learning needs.
- CC8S9    Develop or modify individualized assessment strategies.
- CC8S10   Create and maintain records.

## LEARNING DISABILITIES

### Knowledge:

- LD8K1    Terminology and procedures used in the assessment of individuals with learning disabilities.

- LD8K2     Factors that could lead to misidentification of individuals as having learning disabilities.

- LD8K3     Procedures to identify young children who may be at risk for learning disabilities.

*Skills:*

- LD8S1     Choose and administer assessment instruments appropriate to the individual with learning disabilities.

## CEC Special Education Content Standard 9: Professional and Ethical Practice

Special educators are guided by the profession's ethical and professional practice standards. Special educators practice in multiple roles and complex situations across wide age and developmental ranges. Their practice requires ongoing attention to legal matters along with serious professional and ethical considerations. Special educators engage in professional activities and participate in learning communities that benefit individuals with ELN, their families, colleagues, and their own professional growth. Special educators view themselves as lifelong learners and regularly reflect on and adjust their practice. Special educators are aware of how their own and others' attitudes, behaviors, and ways of communicating can influence their practice. Special educators understand that culture and language can interact with exceptionalities, and are sensitive to the many aspects of diversity of individuals with ELN and their families. Special educators actively plan and engage in activities that foster their professional growth and keep them current with evidence-based best practices. Special educators know their own limits of practice and practice within them.

### COMMON CORE

*Knowledge:*

- CC9K1     Personal cultural biases and differences that affect one's teaching.

- CC9K2     Importance of the teacher serving as a model for individuals with exceptional learning needs.

- CC9K3     Continuum of lifelong professional development.

- CC9K4     Methods to remain current regarding research-validated practice.

*Skills:*

- CC9S1     Practice within the CEC Code of Ethics and other standards of the profession.

- CC9S2     Uphold high standards of competence and integrity and exercise sound judgment in the practice of the professional.

- CC9S3     Act ethically in advocating for appropriate services.

- CC9S4     Conduct professional activities in compliance with applicable laws and policies.

- CC9S5     Demonstrate commitment to developing the highest education and quality-of-life potential of individuals with exceptional learning needs.

- CC9S6     Demonstrate sensitivity for the culture, language, religion, gender, disability, socio-economic status, and sexual orientation of individuals.

- CC9S7    Practice within one's skill limit and obtain assistance as needed.
- CC9S8    Use verbal, nonverbal, and written language effectively.
- CC9S9    Conduct self-evaluation of instruction.
- CC9S10    Access information on exceptionalities.
- CC9S11    Reflect on one's practice to improve instruction and guide professional growth.
- CC9S12    Engage in professional activities that benefit individuals with exceptional learning needs, their families, and one's colleagues.

### LEARNING DISABILITIES

*Knowledge:*

- LD9K1    Ethical responsibility to advocate for appropriate services for individuals with learning disabilities.
- LD9K2    Professional organizations and sources of information relevant to the field of learning disabilities.

*Skills:*

- LD9S1    Participate in activities of professional organizations relevant to the field of learning disabilities.
- LD9S2    Use research findings and theories to guide practice.

## CEC Special Education Content Standard 10: Collaboration

Special educators routinely and effectively collaborate with families, other educators, related service providers, and personnel from community agencies in culturally responsive ways. This collaboration assures that the needs of individuals with ELN are addressed throughout schooling. Moreover, special educators embrace their special role as advocate for individuals with ELN. Special educators promote and advocate the learning and well being of individuals with ELN across a wide range of settings and a range of different learning experiences. Special educators are viewed as specialists by a myriad of people who actively seek their collaboration to effectively include and teach individuals with ELN. Special educators are a resource to their colleagues in understanding the laws and policies relevant to individuals with ELN. Special educators use collaboration to facilitate the successful transitions of individuals with ELN across settings and services.

### COMMON CORE

*Knowledge:*

- CC10K1    Models and strategies of consultation and collaboration.
- CC10K2    Roles of individuals with exceptional learning needs, families, and school and community personnel in planning of an individualized program.
- CC10K3    Concerns of families of individuals with exceptional learning needs and strategies to help address these concerns.
- CC10K4    Culturally responsive factors that promote effective communication and collaboration with individuals with exceptional learning needs, families, school personnel, and community members.

*Skills:*

- CC10S1  Maintain confidential communication about individuals with exceptional learning needs.
- CC10S2  Collaborate with families and others in assessment of individuals with exceptional learning needs.
- CC10S3  Foster respectful and beneficial relationships between families and professionals.
- CC10S4  Assist individuals with exceptional learning needs and their families in becoming active participants in the educational team.
- CC10S5  Plan and conduct collaborative conferences with individuals with exceptional learning needs and their families.
- CC10S6  Collaborate with school personnel and community members in integrating individuals with exceptional learning needs into various settings.
- CC10S7  Use group problem solving skills to develop, implement and evaluate collaborative activities.
- CC10S8  Model techniques and coach others in the use of instructional methods and accommodations.
- CC10S9  Communicate with school personnel about the characteristics and needs of individuals with exceptional learning needs.
- CC10S10  Communicate effectively with families of individuals with exceptional learning needs from diverse backgrounds.
- CC10S11  Observe, evaluate and provide feedback to paraeducators.

## LEARNING DISABILITIES

*Knowledge:*

- LD10K1  Co-planning and co-teaching methods to strengthen content acquisition of individuals with learning disabilities.
- LD10K2  Services, networks, and organizations that provide support across the life span for individuals with learning disabilities.

*Skills:*

None in addition to Common Core

Abt Associates. (1976). *Education as experimentation: A planned variation model* (Vol. 3A). Cambridge, MA: Author.

Abt Associates. (1977). *Education as experimentation: A planned variation model* (Vol. 4). Cambridge, MA: Author.

Ackerman, P. T., Dykman, R. A., & Gardner, M. Y. (1990). Counting rate, naming rate, phonological sensitivity, and memory span: Major factors in dyslexia. *Journal of Learning Disabilities, 23,* 325–327.

Ackerman, P. T., Peters, J. E., & Dykman, R. A. (1971). Children with specific learning disabilities: WISC profiles. *Journal of Learning Disabilities, 4,* 150–166.

Adams, G., & Carnine, D. (2003). Direct Instruction. In H. L. Swanson, K. Harris, & S. Graham (Eds.), *Handbook of learning disabilities* (pp. 403–416). New York: Guilford Press.

Adams, G., & Engelmann, S. (1996). *Research on Direct Instruction: 25 years beyond DISTAR.* Seattle: Educational Achievement Systems.

Adams, M. J. (1990). *Beginning to read: Thinking and learning about print.* Cambridge, MA: MIT Press.

Adams, M. J., Foorman, B. R., Lunberg, I., & Beeler, T. (1998). *Phonemic awareness in young children: A classroom curriculum.* Baltimore: Brookes.

Addison-Wesley. (1991). *Explorations.* Menlo Park, CA: Author.

Adelman, P. B., & Vogel, S. A. (1993). Issues in the employment of adults with learning disabilities. *Learning Disability Quarterly, 16*(3), 219–232.

Alarcón, M., DeFries, J. C., Light, J. G., & Pennington, B. F. (1997). A twin study of mathematics disability. *Journal of Learning Disabilities, 30,* 617–623.

Alberto, P., & Troutman, A. (2003). *Applied behavior analysis for teachers* (6th ed.). Upper Saddle River, NJ: Merrill/Prentice Hall.

Algozzine, B., Christenson, S., & Ysseldyke, J. E. (1982). Probabilities associated with the referral to placement process. *Teacher Education and Special Education, 5,* 19–23.

Algozzine, B., & Ysseldyke, J. E. (1983). Learning disabilities as a subset of school failure: The oversophistication of a concept. *Exceptional Children, 50,* 242–246.

Allor, J. H. (2002) The relationships of phonemic awareness and rapid naming to reading development. *Learning Disability Quarterly, 25,* 47–57.

American Psychiatric Association. (2000). *Diagnostic and statistical manual of mental disorders* (4th ed., text rev.). Washington, DC: Author.

Anderson, I. H. (1980). Study strategies and adjunct aids. In P. J. Spiro, B. C. Bruce, & W. F. Brewer (Eds.), *Theoretical issues in reading comprehension* (pp. 483–502). Hillsdale, NJ: Erlbaum.

Anderson, R. C., Hiebert, E. F., Wilkinson, I. A. G., & Scott, J. (1985). *Becoming a nation of readers.* Champaign, IL: National Academy of Education and Center for the Study of Reading.

Anderson-Inman, L. (1981). Transenvironmental programming: Promoting success in the regular classroom by maximizing effect of resource room instruction. *Journal of Special Education Technology, 4*(4), 3–12.

Archer, A. L., Gleason, M. M., & Vachon, B. L. (2003). Decoding and fluency: Foundation skills for struggling older readers. *Learning Disability Quarterly, 26,* 89–101.

Armbruster, B. B., Lehr, F., & Osborne, J. (2001). *Putting reading first: The research building blocks for teaching children to read: Kindergarten through grade 3.* Washington, DC: Partnership for Literacy. Retrieved February 7, 2003, from http://www.nifl.gov/partnershipforreading/publications/reading_first1.html

Armstrong, F. D., Seidel, J. F., & Swales, T. P. (1993). Pediatric HIV infection: A neuropsychological and educational challenge. *Journal of Learning Disabilities, 26*(2), 92–103.

Ashlock, R. B. (1994). *Error patterns in computation* (6th ed.). Columbus, OH: Merrill.

Association for Children with Learning Disabilities. (1986). ACLD definition: Specific learning disabilities. *ACLD Newsbriefs,* pp. 15–16.

Aune, E. P., & Johnson, J. M. (1992). Transition takes teamwork! A collaborative model for college-bound students with LD. *Intervention in School and Clinic, 27*(4), 222–227.

Babbitt, B. C. (1999). *10 tips for software selection for math instruction.* Retrieved June 10, 2003, from http://www.ldonline.org/ld_indepth/technology/babbitt_math_tips.html

Bailey, D. B. (2000). The federal role in early intervention: Prospects for the future. *Topics in Early Childhood Special Education, 20,* 71–78.

Baker, L., & Anderson, R. I. (1982). Effects of inconsistent information on text processing: Evidence for comprehension monitoring. *Reading Research Quarterly, 17,* 281–294.

Baker, S., Gersten, R., & Graham, S. (2003). Teaching expressive writing to students with learning disabilities: Research-based applications and examples. *Journal of Learning Disabilities, 36,* 109–123.

Baker, S., Gersten, R., & Scanlon, D. (2002). Procedural facilitators and cognitive strategies: Tools for unraveling the mysteries of comprehension and the writing process and for providing meaningful access to the general education curriculum. *Learning Disabilities Research and Practice, 17*(1), 65–77.

Ballard, K. D., & Glynn, T. (1975). Behavioral self-management in story writing with elementary school children. *Journal of Applied Behavior Analysis, 8,* 387–398.

Bandura, A. (1986). *Social foundations of thought and action: A social cognitive theory.* Upper Saddle River, NJ: Prentice Hall.

Bandura, A. (1995). Comments on the crusade against the causal efficacy of human thought. *Journal of Behavior Therapy and Experimental Psychiatry, 26,* 179–190.

Barkley, R. A. (1997). Behavioral inhibition, sustained attention, and executive functions: Constructing a unifying theory of ADHD. *Psychological Bulletin, 121,* 65–94.

Barkley, R. A. (1998). *Attention-deficit hyperactivity disorder: A handbook for diagnosis and treatment.* New York: Guilford Press.

Barkley, R. A. (2000a). *A new look at ADHD: Inhibition, time, and self-control* (video manual). Baltimore: Guilford Press.

Barkley, R. A. (2000b). *Taking charge of ADHD: The complete, authoritative guide for parents* (rev. ed.). NY: Guilford Press.

Barrera, I., & Corso, R. M. (2002). Cultural competency as skilled dialogue. *Topics in Early Childhood Special Education, 22,* 103–113.

Barron, R. W. (1980). Visual and phonological strategies in reading and spelling. In U. Frith (Ed.), *Cognitive processes in spelling* (pp. 195–213). New York: Academic Press.

Barsch, J., & Creson, B. (1980). *Barsch Learning Style Inventory.* Novato, CA: Academic Therapy Publications.

Bassett, D. S., Jackson, L., Ferrell, K. A., Luckner, J., Hagerty, P. J., Busesn, T. D., & MacIsaac, D. (1996). Multiple perspectives on inclusive education: Reflections of a university faculty. *Teacher Education and Special Education, 19,* 355–386.

Bateman, B. D. (1965). An educator's view of a diagnostic approach to learning disorders. In J. Hellmuth (Ed.), *Learning disorders* (Vol. 1, pp. 219–239). Seattle, WA: Special Child Publications.

Bateman, B. D. (1965). An educator's view of a diagnostic approach to learning disorders. In J. Hellmuth (Ed.), *Learning disorders* (Vol. 1, pp. 219–239). Seattle, WA: Special Child Publications.

Bateman, B. D. (1994). Who, how, and where: Special education's issues in perpetuity. *Journal of Special Education, 27,* 509–520.

Bateman, B. D. (1996). *Better IEPs* (2nd ed.). Longmont, CO: Sopris West.

Bateman, B. D., & Linden, M. A. (1998). *Better IEPs: How to develop legally correct and educationally useful programs* (3rd ed.). Longmont, CO: Sopris West.

Baumeister, A. A., Kupstas, F., & Klindworth, L. M. (1990). New morbidity: Implications for prevention of children's disabilities. *Exceptionality, 1,* 1–16.

Baumeister, R. F., Cambell, J. D., Krueger, J. I., & Vohs, K. D. (2003). Does high self-esteem cause better performance, interpersonal success, happiness, or healthier lifestyles? *Psychological Science in the Public Interest, 4,* 1–44.

Baumgartner, D., Bryan, T., Donahue, M., & Nelson, C. (1993). Thanks for asking: Parent comments about homework, tests, and grades. *Exceptionality, 4,* 177–185.

Bauwens, J., Hourcade, J. J., & Friend, M. (1989). Cooperative teaching: A model for general and special education integration. *Remedial and Special Education, 10,* 17–22.

Beale, I. L., & Tippett, L. J. (1992). Remediation of psychological process deficits in learning disabilities. In N. Singh & I. L. Beale (Eds.), *Learning disabilities: Nature, theory, and treatment* (pp. 526–568). New York: Springer-Verlag.

Beatty, L. S., Madden, R., Gardner, E. G., & Karlsen, B. (1984). *Stanford Diagnostic Mathematics Test.* New York: Harcourt Brace Jovanovich.

Beck, R., Conrad, D., & Anderson, P. (1996). *Basic skill builders: Helping students become fluent in basic skills.* Longmont, CO: Sopris West.

Becker, W. C. (1977). Teaching reading and language to the disadvantaged: What we have learned from field research. *Harvard Educational Review, 47,* 518–543.

Becker, W. C., & Gersten, R. (2001). Follow-up of Follow Through: The later effects of the direct instruction model on children in fifth and sixth grades. *Journal of Direct Instruction, 1*(1), 57–71.

Beichtman, J. H., Hood, J., & Inglis, A. (1992). Familial transmission of speech and language impairment: A preliminary investigation. *Canadian Journal of Psychiatry, 37,* 151–156.

Bell, R. Q., & Harper, L. V. (1977). *Child effects on adults.* Hillsdale, NJ: Erlbaum.

Bender, W., Rosenkrans, C. B., & Crane, M. K. (1999.). Stress, depression, and suicide among adolescents with learning disabilities: Assessing the risk. *Learning Disability Quarterly, 22,* 143–156.

Bialostok, S. (1997). Offering the olive branch: The rhetoric of insincerity. *Language Arts, 74,* 618–629.

Bialystok, E. (1993). Metalinguistic awareness: The development of children's representations in language. In C. Pratt and A. F. Garton (Eds.), *Systems of representation in children: Development and use.* Chichester: Wiley.

Biederman, J., Faraone, S. V., & Monuteaux, M. C. (2002). Impact of exposure to parental attention-deficit hyperactivity disorder on clinical features and dysfunction in the offspring. *Psychological Medicine, 32,* 817–827.

Biederman, J., Wilens, T., Mick, E., Spencer, T., & Faraone, S. V. (1999). Pharmacotherapy of attention-deficit/hyperactivity disorder reduces risk for substance abuse disorder. *Pediatrics, 104,* 20.

Birnie-Selwyn, B., & Guerin, B. (1997). Teaching children to spell: Decreasing consonant cluster errors by eliminating selective stimulus control. *Journal of Applied Behavior Analysis, 30,* 69–91.

Bisanz, J., Ho, E., Kachan, M., Rasmussen, C., & Sherman, J. (2003). Cognitive and information processing. In J. W. Guthrie (Ed.), *Encyclopedia of education* (2nd ed., pp. 567–570). New York: Macmillan Reference.

Blachman, B. (2001). Phonological awareness. In P. D. Pearson (Ed.), *Handbook of reading research* (pp. 483–502). Mahwah, NJ: Erlbaum.

Blachman, B. A. (1997). Early intervention and phonological awareness: A cautionary tale. In B. A. Blachman (Ed.), *Foundations of reading acquisition and dyslexia: Implications for early intervention* (pp. 409–430). Mahwah, NJ: Erlbaum.

Blachman, B. A., Ball, E. W., Black, R., & Tangel, D. M. (2000). *Road to the code: A phonological awareness program for young children.* Baltimore: Brookes.

Blachman, B. A., Tangel, D. M., Ball, E. W., Black, R., & McGraw, C. K. (1999). Developing phonological awareness and word recognition skills: A two-year intervention with low-income, inner-city children. *Reading & Writing, 11,* 239–273.

Blackman, S., & Goldstein, K. M. (1982). Cognitive styles and learning disabilities. *Journal of Learning Disabilities, 15,* 106–115.

Blackorby, J., & Wagner, M. (1996). Longitudinal postschool outcomes of youth with disabilities: Findings from the National Longitudinal Transition Study. *Exceptional Children, 62,* 399–413.

Blandford, B. J., & Lloyd, J. W. (1987). Effects of a self-instructional procedure on handwriting. *Journal of Learning Disabilities, 20,* 342–346.

Blankenship, C., & Lovitt, T. C. (1976). Story problems: Merely confusing or downright befuddling? *Journal for Research in Mathematics Education, 7,* 290–298.

Blaylock, G., & Patton, J. R. (1996). Transition and students with learning disabilities: Creating sound futures. *Journal of Learning Disabilities, 29,* 7–16.

Blum, H. T., Lipsett, L. A., & Vocom, D. J. (2002). Literature circles: A tool for self-determination in one middle school inclusive classroom. *Remedial and Special Education, 23,* 99–108.

Board of Trustees of the Council for Learning Disabilities. (1986). Use of discrepancy formulas in the identification of learning disabled individuals. *Learning Disability Quarterly, 9*(3), 245.

Bocian, K. M., Beebe, M. E., MacMillan, D. L., & Gresham, F. M. (1999). Competing paradigms in learning disabilities classification by schools and the variations in the meaning of discrepant achievement. *Learning Disabilities Research and Practice, 14,* 1–14.

Borkowski, J. G. (1992). Metacognitive theory: A framework for teaching literacy, writing, and math skills. *Journal of Learning Disabilities, 25,* 253–257.

Borkowski, J. G., & Burke, J. E. (1996). Theories, models, and measurements of executive functioning: An information processing perspective. In G. R. Lyon & N. A. Krasnegor (Eds.), *Attention, memory, and executive function* (pp. 235–262). Baltimore, MD: Brookes.

Borkowski, J. G., Wehring, R. S., & Carr, M. (1988). Effects of attributional retraining on strategy-based reading comprehension in learning-disabled students. *Journal of Educational Psychology, 7,* 46–53.

Bos, C. (1982). Getting past decoding: Assisted and repeated readings as remedial methods for learning disabled students. *Topics in Learning and Learning Disabilities, 1* (4), 51–57.

Bos, C. S., & Anders, P. L. (1990). Effects of interactive vocabulary instruction on the vocabulary learning and reading comprehension of junior-high learning disabled students. *Learning Disability Quarterly, 13,* 31–42.

Bos, C. S., & Filip, D. (1982). Comprehension monitoring skills in learning disabled and average students. *Topics in Learning and Learning Disabilities, 2*(1), 79–85.

Bos, C. S., & Vaughn, S. (1994). *Strategies for teaching students with learning and behavior problems* (3rd ed.). Boston: Allyn & Bacon.

Bos, C. S., & Vaughn, S. (2002). *Strategies for teaching students with learning and behavior problems* (5th ed.). Boston: Allyn & Bacon.

Bottge, B. A. (2001a). Reconceptualizing math problem solving for low-achieving students. *Remedial and Special Education, 22,* 102–112.

Bottge, B. A. (2001b). Using intriguing problems to improve math skills. *Educational Leadership, 58*(6), 68–72.

Bottge, B. A., Heinrichs, M., Chan, S., & Serlin, R. (2001). Anchoring adolescents' understanding of math concepts in rich problem solving environments. *Remedial and Special Education, 22,* 299–314.

Boudah, D. J., Lenz, B. K., Bulgren, J. A., Schumaker, J. B., & Deshler, D. D. (2000). Don't water down! Enhance content learning through the unit organizer routine. *Teaching Exceptional Children, 32*(3), 48–56.

Boyle, J. R. (1996). The effects of a cognitive mapping strategy on the literal and inferential comprehension of students with mild disabilities. *Learning Disabilities Quarterly, 19,* 86–98.

Boyle, J. R. (2001). Enhancing the note-taking skills of students with mild disabilities. *Intervention in School and Clinic, 36,* 221–224.

Boyle, J. R., & Weishaar, M. (2001). The effects of strategic notetaking on the recall and comprehension of lecture information for high school students with learning disabilities. *Learning Disabilities Research and Practice, 16,* 133–141.

Bradley, L., & Bryant, R. E. (1983). Categorizing sounds and learning to read: A causal connection. *Nature, 303,* 419–421.

Bradley, R., Danielson, L., & Hallahan, D. P. (Eds.). (2002). *Identification of learning disabilities: Research to practice.* Mahwah, NJ: Erlbaum.

Brady, S. A. (1997). Ability to encode phonological representations: An underlying difficulty of poor readers. In B. A. Blachman (Ed.), *Foundations of reading acquisition and dyslexia: Implications for early intervention* (pp. 21–47). Mahwah, NJ: Erlbaum.

Bredekamp, S. (Ed.). (1987). *Developmentally appropriate practice in early childhood programs serving children from birth through age 8.* Washington, DC: National Association for the Education of Young Children.

Brigham, F. J., Scruggs, T. E., & Mastropieri, M. A. (1995). Elaborative maps for enhanced learning of historical information: Uniting spatial, verbal, and imaginal information. *Journal of Special Education, 28,* 440–460.

Brigham, T. H., Graubard, P. S., & Stans, A. (1972). Analysis of the effects of sequential reinforcement contingencies on aspects of composition. *Journal of Applied Behavior Analysis, 5,* 421–429.

Brinckerhoff, L. C. (1996). Making the transition to higher education: Opportunities for student empowerment. *Journal of Learning Disabilities, 29,* 118–136.

Brinckerhoff, L. C., McGuire, J. M., & Shaw, S. F. (2002). *Postsecondary education and transition for students with learning disabilities* (2nd ed.). Austin, TX: PRO-ED.

Brinckerhoff, L. C., Shaw, S. F., & McGuire, J. M. (1992). Promoting access, accommodations, and independence for college students with learning disabilities. *Journal of Learning Disabilities, 25*(7), 417–429.

Broden, M., Beasley, A., & Hall, R. V. (1978). In class spelling performance: Effects of home tutoring by a parent. *Behavior Modification, 2,* 511–530.

Brody, L. E., & Mills, C. J. (1997). Gifted children with learning disabilities: A review of the issues. *Journal of Learning Disabilities, 30,* 282–296.

Brody-Hasazi, S., Salembier, G., & Finck, K. (1983). Directions for the 80's: Vocational preparation for secondary mildly handicapped students. *Teaching Exceptional Children, 15*(4), 206–209.

Bronfenbrenner, U. (1979). *The ecology of human development: Experiments by nature and design.* Cambridge, MA: Harvard University Press.

Brooks, J. G., & Brooks, M. (1993). *In search of understanding: The case for constructivist classrooms.* Alexandria, VA: Association for Supervision and Curriculum Development.

Brooks-Gunn, J., & Lewis, M. (1984). Maternal responsivity in interactions with handicapped infants. *Child Development, 55,* 858–868.

Brophy, J., & Good, T. L. (1986). Teacher behavior and student achievement. In M. C. Whittrock (Ed.), *Handbook of research on teaching* (3rd ed., pp. 328–375). New York: Macmillan.

Brotherson, M. J., Berdine, W. H., & Sartini, V. (1993). Transition to adult services: Support for ongoing parent participation. *Remedial and Special Education, 14*(4), 44–51.

Browder, D. M., Wood, W. M., Test, D. W., Karvonen, M., & Algozzine, B. (2001). Reviewing resources on self-determination: A map for teachers. *Remedial and Special Education, 22,* 233–244.

Brown, D. S., & Gerber, P. J. (1994). Employing people with learning disabilities. In P. J. Gerber & H. B. Reiff (Eds.), *Learning disabilities in adulthood: Persisting problems and evolving issues* (pp. 195–203). Boston: Andover Medical Publishers.

Brown, D. S., Gerber, P. J., & Dowdy, C. (1990). *Pathways to employment for people with learning disabilities: A plan for action.* Washington, DC: President's Committee on Employment of People with Disabilities.

Brown, W. H., Odom, S. L., & Conroy, M. A. (2001). Intervention hierarchy for promoting young children's peer interactions in natural environments. *Topics in Early Childhood Special Education, 21,* 162–175.

Bruck, M. (1988). The word recognition and spelling of dyslexic children. *Reading Research Quarterly, 23,* 51–69.

Bruck, M. (1998). Outcomes of adults with childhood histories of dyslexia. In C. Hulme & R. M. Joshi (Eds.), *Reading and spelling: Development and disorders* (pp. 179–200). Mahway, NJ: Erlbaum.

Bruck, M., & Treiman, R. (1990). Phonological awareness and spelling in normal children and dyslexics: The case of initial consonant clusters. *Journal of Experimental Child Psychology, 50,* 156–178.

Bruder, M. B. (2000). Family-centered early intervention: Clarifying our values for the new millennium. *Topics in Early Childhood Special Education, 20,* 105–115, 122.

Bryan, T. (1991). Social problems and learning disabilities. In B. Y. L. Wong (Ed.), *Learning about learning disabilities* (pp. 195–229). New York: Academic Press.

Bryan, T. H. (1974a). An observational analysis of classroom behaviors of children with learning disabilities. *Journal of Learning Disabilities, 7,* 26–34.

Bryan, T. H. (1974b). Peer popularity of learning disabled children. *Journal of Learning Disabilities, 7,* 621–625.

Bryan, T. H. (1986). Self-concept and attributions of the learning disabled. *Learning Disabilities Focus, 1,* 82–89.

Bryan, T. H., & Sullivan-Burstein, K. (1997). Homework how-to's. *Teaching Exceptional Children, 29*(6), 32–37.

Bryan, T. H., Wheeler, R., Felcan, J., & Henek, T. (1976). "Come on Dummy": An observational analysis of children's communications. *Journal of Learning Disabilities, 9,* 661–669.

Bryan, T., Bay, M., Lopez-Reyna, N., & Donahue, M. (1991). Characteristics of students with learning disabilities: A summary of the extant data base and its implications for educational programs. In J. W. Lloyd, N. N. Singh, & A. C. Repp (Eds.), *The regular education initiative: Alternative perspectives on concepts, issues, and models* (pp. 113–131). Sycamore, IL: Sycamore.

Bryan, T., Nelson, C., & Mathur, S. (1995). Homework: A survey of primary students in regular, resource, and self-con-tained classrooms. *Learning Disabilities Research and Practice, 10,* 85–90.

Bryant, B. R., & Rivera, D. P. (1997). Educational assessment of mathematics skills and abilities. *Journal of Learning Disabilities, 30,* 57–68.

Bryant, B. R., Bryant, D. P., & Rieth, H. J. (2002). The use of assistive technology in postsecondary education. In L. C. Brinckerhoff, J. M. McGuire, & S. F. Shaw, *Postsecondary education and transition for students with learning disabilities* (2nd ed., pp. 389–429). Austin, TX: PRO-ED.

Bryant, N. D., Drabin, I. R., & Gettlinger, M. (1981). Effects of varying unit size on spelling achievement in learning disabled children. *Journal of Learning Disabilities, 14,* 200–203.

Buck, J., & Torgesen, J. (n.d.). *The relationship between performance on a measure of oral reading fluency and performance on the Florida comprehensive assessment test* (Technical Report 1). Florida Center for Reading Research, Florida State University. Retrieved 1 July 2003, from http://www.fcrr.org/TechnicalReports/TechnicalReport1.pdf

Budoff, M. (1987). Measures for assessing learning potential. In C. S. Lidz (Ed.), *Dynamic assessment* (pp. 173–195). New York: Guilford Press.

Bulgren, J., & Lenz., B. K. (1996). Strategic instruction in the content areas. In D. D. Deshler, E. S. Ellis, & B. K. Lenz (Eds.), *Teaching adolescents with learning disabilities: Strategies and methods* (2nd ed.). Denver, CO: Love.

Bulgren, J. A., Deshler, D. D., & Shumaker, J. B. (1993). *The content enhancement series: The concept mastery routine.* Lawrence, KS: Edge Enterprises.

Bulgren, J. A., Schumaker, J. B., & Deshler, D. D. (1988). Effectiveness of a concept teaching routine in enhancing the performance of LD students in secondary-level mainstream classes. *Learning Disability Quarterly, 11*(1), 3–17.

Bulgren, J. A., Schumaker, J. B., & Deshler, D. D. (1994). The effects of a recall enhancement routine on the test performance of secondary students with and without learning disabilities. *Learning Disabilities Research and Practice, 9*(1), 2–11.

Buswell, G. T., & John, L. (1926). *Diagnostic studies in arithmetic.* Chicago: University of Chicago Press.

Byers, R. K., & Lord, E. E. (1943). Late effects of lead poisoning on mental development. *American Journal of Diseases of Children, 66,* 471–494.

Byrne, B., & Fielding-Barnsley, R. (1991). Evaluation of a program to teach phonemic awareness to young children. *Journal of Educational Psychology, 83,* 451–455.

Byrne, B., & Fielding-Barnsley, R. (1993). Evaluation of a program to teach phonemic awareness to young children: A 1-year follow-up. *Journal of Educational Psychology, 85,* 104–111.

Camarata, S., Hughes, C. A., & Ruhl, K. (1988). Mild/moderately behaviorally disordered students: A population at risk for language disorders. *Language, Speech, and Hearing Services in Schools, 19,* 191–200.

Campbell, P. H., Milbourne, S. A., & Lilverman, C. (2001). Strengths-based child portfolios: A professional development activity to alter perspectives of children with special needs. *Topics in Early Childhood Special Education, 21,* 151–161.

Campione, J. C., & Brown, A. L. (1987). Linking dynamic assessment with school achievement. In C. S. Lidz (Ed.), *Dynamic assessment* (pp. 82–115). New York: Guilford Press.

Cantwell, D. P. (1979). The "hyperactive child." *Hospital Practice, 14,* 65–73.

Caplan, D. (1992). *Language: Structure, processing, and disorders.* Cambridge, MA: MIT Press.

Caplan, N., Choy, M. H., & Whitmore, J. K. (1992, February). Indochinese refugee families and academic achievement. *Scientific American, 266,* 36–42.

Carlisle, J. F. (1987). The use of morphological knowledge in spelling derived forms by learning-disabled and normal students. *Annals of Dyslexia, 37,* 90–108.

Carlson, J. S., & Wiedl, K. H. (1992). The dynamic assessment of intelligence. In H. C. Haywood & D. Tzuriel (Eds.), *Interactive assessment* (pp. 167–186). New York: Springer-Verlag.

Carlson, N. R. (2001). *Physiology of behavior* (7th ed.). Boston: Allyn & Bacon.

Carnine, D. (1976). Similar sound separation and cumulative introduction in learning letter-sound correspondences. *Journal of Educational Research, 69,* 368–372.

Carnine, D. (1993, December 8). Facts, not fads. *Education Week,* p. 40.

Carnine, D. W. (1980). Preteaching versus concurrent teaching of the component skills of a multiplication problem-solving strategy. *Journal for Research in Mathematics Education, 11,* 375–379.

Carnine, D. W., Crawford, D. B., Harniss, M. K., Hollenbeck, K. L., & Miller, S. K. (1998). Effective strategies for teaching social studies. In E. J. Kame'enui & D. W. Carnine, *Effective teaching strategies that accommodate diverse learners.* Upper Saddle River, NJ: Merrill.

Carnine, D. W., Prill, N., & Armstrong, J. (1978). *Teaching slower performing students general case strategies for solving comprehension items.* Eugene: University of Oregon Follow-Through Project.

Carnine, D., & Kame'enui, E. J. (Eds.). (1992). *Higher order thinking: Designing curriculum for mainstreamed students.* Austin, TX: PRO-ED.

Carnine, D., & Kinder, D. (1985). Teaching low performing students to apply generative and schema strategies to narrative and expository material. *Remedial and Special Education, 6* (1), 20–30.

Carnine, D., Jitendra, A. K., & Silbert, J. (1997). A descriptive analysis of mathematics curricular materials from a pedagogical perspective: A case study of fractions. *Remedial and Special Education, 18* (2), 66–81.

Carnine, D., Jones, E. D., & Dixon, R. (1994). Mathematics: Educational tools for diverse learners. *School Psychology Review, 23,* 406–427.

Carnine, D., Silbert, J., & Kame'enui, E. J. (1996). *Direct instruction reading* (3rd ed.). Columbus, OH: Merrill.

Carnine, D., Silbert, J., Kame'enui, E. J., & Tarver, S. (2004). *Direct instruction reading* (4th ed.). Columbus, OH: Merrill.

Carpenter, D. (1983). Spelling error profiles of able and disabled readers. *Journal of Learning Disabilities, 16,* 102–104.

Carpenter, D., & Miller, L. J. (1982). Spelling ability of reading disabled LD students and able readers. *Learning Disability Quarterly, 5,* 65–70.

Carpenter, T. P., & Moser, T. M. (1982). The development of addition and subtraction problem-solving skills. In T. P. Carpenter, J. M. Moser, & T. A. Romberg (Eds.), *Addition and subtraction: A cognitive perspective* (pp. 9–24). Hillsdale, NJ: Erlbaum.

Carrier, J. G. (1986). *Learning disability: Social class and the construction of inequality in American education.* Westport, CN: Greenwood.

Carrow-Woolfolk, E. (1988). *Theory, assessment, and intervention in language disorders: An integrative approach.* Philadelphia: Grune & Stratton.

Carrow-Woolfolk, E. (1999). *Test for Auditory Comprehension of Language* (3rd ed.). Austin, TX: PRO-ED.

Cartledge, G., & Kiarie, M. W. (2001). Learning social skills through literature for children and adolescents. *Teaching Exceptional Children, 34*(2), 40–47.

Castellanos, F. X. (2001). Neural substrates of attention-deficit hyperactivity disorder. *Advances in Neurology, 85,* 197–206.

Castellanos, F. X., Lee, P. P., Sharp, W., Jeffries, N. O., Greenstein, D. K., Clasen, L. S., Blumenthal, J. D., James, R. S., Ebens, C. L., Walter, J. M., Zijdenbos, A., Evans, A. C., Giedd, J. N., & Rapoport, J. L. (2002). Developmental trajectories of brain volume abnormalities in children and adolescents with attention-deficit/hyperactivity disorder. *Journal of the American Medical Association, 288,* 1740–1748.

Cawley, J., & Miller, J. H. (1989). Cross-sectional comparisons of the mathematical performance of children with learning disabilities: Are we on the right track toward comprehensive programming? *Journal of Learning Disabilities, 22,* 250–254, 259.

Cawley, J. F., & Parmar, R. S. (2001). Literacy proficiency and science for students with learning disabilities. *Reading and Writing Quarterly: Overcoming Learning Disabilities, 17,* 105–125.

Cazden, C. (2001). *Classroom discourse: The language of teaching and learning* (2nd ed.). Portsmouth, NH: Heinemann.

Center for Universal Design. (1997). *The principles of universal design.* Retrieved March 9, 2003, from www.design.ncsu.edu: 8120/cud/univ_design/principle/udprinciples.htm

Cepeda, N. J., Cepeda, M. L., & Kramer, A. F. (2000). Task switching and attention deficit hyperactivity disorder. *Journal of Abnormal Child Psychology, 28,* 213–226.

Chalfant, J. C., Pysh, M. V., & Moultrie, R. (1979). Teacher assistance teams: A model of within-building problem solving. *Learning Disability Quarterly, 2*(3), 85–96.

Chall, J. (1967). *Learning to read: The great debate.* San Francisco: McGraw-Hill.

Chall, J., Roswell, F. E., & Blumenthal, S. H. (1963). Auditory blending ability: A factor in success in beginning reading. *Reading Teacher, 17,* 113–118.

Chapman, J. W., Tunmer, W. E., & Prochnow, J. E. (2001). Does success in the reading recovery program depend on developing proficiency in phonological-processing skills? A longitudinal study in a whole language instructional context. *Scientific Studies of Reading, 15,* 141–176.

Chapman, L. J., & Wedell, K. (1972). Perceptual-motor abilities and reversal errors in children's handwriting. *Journal of Learning Disabilities, 5,* 321–325.

Chard, D. J., Vaughn, S., & Tyler, B. (2002). A synthesis of research on effective interventions for building reading fluency with elementary students with learning disabilities. *Journal of Learning Disabilities, 35,* 386–406.

Children's Defense Fund. (2003). *Children in the United States.* Retrieved February 25, 2003, from http://www.childrens defense.org/states/all_states.pdf

Choate, J. S., & Evans, S. S. (1992). Authentic assessment of special learners: Problem or promise? *Preventing School Failure, 37*(1), 69.

Choate, J. S, Enright, B. E., Miller, L. J., Poteet, J. A., & Rakes, T. A. (1995). *Curriculum-based assessment and programming* (3rd ed.). Boston: Allyn & Bacon.

Clarizio, H. F., & Phillips, S. E. (1986). Sex bias in the diagnosis of learning disabled students. *Psychology in the Schools, 23*(1), 44–52.

Clay, M. M. (1985). *The early detection of reading difficulties.* Auckland, NZ: Heinemann.

Clay, M. M., & Imlach, R. H. (1971). Juncture, pitch and stress as reading behavior variables. *Journal of Verbal Learning and Verbal Behavior, 10,* 133–139.

Clements, S. D. (1970). *Minimal brain dysfunction in children: Educational, medical, and health related services.* Washington, DC: U.S. Public Health Service.

Clements, S. D., & Peters, J. E. (1962). Minimal brain dysfunctions in the school-age child. *Archives of General Psychiatry, 6,* 185–197.

Cognition and Technology Group at Vanderbilt. (1997). *The Jasper Project: Lessons in curriculum, instruction, assessment, and professional development.* Mahwah, NJ: Erlbaum.

Cohen, A. L., Torgesen, J. K., & Torgesen, J. L. (1988). Improving speed and accuracy of word recognition in reading disabled children: An evaluation of two computer program variations. *Learning Disability Quarterly, 11,* 333–341.

Cohen, S. A. (1971). Dyspedagogia as a cause of reading retardation: Definition and treatment. In B. Bateman (Ed.), *Learning disorders:* Vol. 4. *Reading* (pp. 269–291). Seattle, WA: Special Child Publications.

Colarusso, R. P., Keel, M. C., & Dangle, H. L. (2001). A comparison of eleigibility criteria and their impact on minority representation in LD programs. *Learning Disabilities Research and Practice, 16,* 1–7.

Coleman, J. M., & Minnett, A. M. (1992). Learning disabilities and social competence: A social ecological perspective. *Exceptional Children, 59,* 234–246.

Coleman, J. M., McHam, L. A., & Minnett, A. M. (1992). Similarities in the social competencies of learning disabled and low-achieving elementary school children. *Journal of Learning Disabilities, 25,* 671–677.

Coles, G. (1987). *The learning mystique: A critical look at "learning disabilities."* New York: Pantheon.

Colvin, G. (1992). *Managing acting-out behavior* (video lecture and workbook). Eugene, OR: Behavior Associates.

Colvin, G., Sugai, G., & Patching, B. (1993). Pre-correction: An instructional approach for managing predictable problem behaviors. *Intervention in School and Clinic, 28,* 143–150.

Compton, D. L. (2003). Modeling the relationship between growth in rapid naming speed and growth in decoding skill in first-grade children. *Journal of Educational Psychology, 95,* 225–239.

Conners, C. K. (1997). *Conners' Teacher Rating Scale—Revised (S).* North Tonawanda, NY: Multi-Health Systems.

Connolly, A. (1998). *Key Math revised: A diagnostic inventory of essential mathematics.* Circle Pines, MN: American Guidance Service.

Conte, R. (1991). Attention disorders. In B. Y. L. Wong (Ed.), *Learning about learning disabilities* (pp. 55–101). New York: Academic Press.

Content, A., Kolinski, R., Morais, J., & Bertelson, P. (1986). Phonetic segmentation in prereaders: Effect of corrective information. *Journal of Experimental Child Psychology, 42,* 49–72.

Cooper, D. H., & Speece, D. L. (1988). A novel methodology for the study of children at risk for school failure. *Journal of Special Education 22,* 186–198.

Cooper, H. M. (1989). *Homework.* White Plains, NY: Longman.

Cooper, H. M., & Hedges, L. V. (1994). *Handbook of research synthesis.* New York: Russell Sage.

Cooper, P. (1999). ADHD and effective learning: Principles and practical approaches. In P. Cooper & K. Bilton (Eds.), *ADHD: Research, practice and opinion* (pp. 138–157). London: Whurr.

Cosden, M., Brown, C., & Elliott, K. (2002). Development of self-understanding and self-esteem in children and adults with learning disabilities. In B. Y. L. Wong & M. Donahue (Eds.), *The social dimensions of learning disabilities: Essays in honor of Tanis Bryan* (pp. 33–51). Mahwah, NJ: Erlbaum.

Cox, L. S. (1975). Diagnosing and remediating systematic errors in addition and subtraction computations. *Arithmetic Teacher, 22,* 151–157.

Coyne, M. D., Kame'enui, E. J., & Simmons, D.C. (2001). Prevention and intervention in beginning reading: Two complex systems. *Learning Disabilities Research and Practice, 16,* 62–73.

Crawford, L., & Tindal, G. (2002). Curriculum-based collaboration in secondary schools. In M. R. Shinn, H. M. Walker, & G. Stoner (Eds.), *Interventions for academic and behavior problems:* II. *Preventive and remedial approaches* (pp. 825–852). Bethesda, MD: National Association of School Psychologists.

Crawford, V. (2002). *Embracing the monster: Overcoming the challenges of hidden disabilities.* Baltimore: MD: Brookes.

Crockett, J. B., & Kauffman, J. M. (1999). *The least restrictive environment: Its origins and interpretations in special education.* Hillsdale, NJ: Erlbaum.

Cruickshank, W. M., Bentsen, F. A., Ratzburg, F. H., & Tannhauser, M. T. (1961). *A teaching method for brain-injured and hyperactive children: A demonstration-pilot study.* Syracuse, NY: Syracuse University Press.

Cruickshank, W. M., Bice, H. V., & Wallen, N. E. (1957). *Perception and cerebral palsy.* Syracuse: Syracuse University Press.

CTB/Macmillan/McGraw-Hill. (1993). *CAT/5.* Monterey, CA: CTB/McGraw-Hill.

Cullinan, D. (2002). *Students with emotional and behavior disorders: An introduction for teachers and other helping professionals.* Upper Saddle River, NJ: Merrill/Prentice-Hall.

Cullinan, D., Lloyd, J., & Epstein, M. H. (1981). Strategy training: A structured approach to arithmetic instruction. *Exceptional Education Quarterly, 2*(1), 41–49.

Cummings, R., Maddux, C. D., & Casey, J. (2000). Individualized transition planning for students with learning disabilities. *Career Development Quarterly, 49,* 60–72.

Cunningham, A. E. (1990). Explicit versus implicit instruction in phonemic awareness. *Journal of Experimental Child Psychology, 50,* 429–444.

Davies, S., & Witte, R. (2000). Self-management and peer monitoring within a group contingency to decrease uncontrolled verbalizations of children with attention-deficit/hyperactivity disorder. *Psychology in the Schools, 37,* 135–147.

Davis, S. (1997). The Human Genome Project: Examining the Arc's concerns regarding the Human Genome Project's ethical, legal, and social implications. Address presented at the DOE Human Genome Program Contractor-Grantee Workshop VI. Retrieved July 29, 2001, from http://www.ornl.gov/hgmis/resource/arc.html

de Hirsch, K., Jansky, J., & Langford, W. S. (1966). *Predicting reading failure.* New York: Harper & Row.

De La Paz, S., Owen, B., Harris, K. R., & Graham, S. (2000). Riding Elvis's motorcycle: Using Self-Regulated Strategy Development to PLAN and WRITE for a state writing exam. *Learning Disabilities Research and Practice, 15,* 101–109.

de Mesquita, P. B., & Gilliam, W. S. (1994). Differential diagnosis of childhood depression: Using comorbidity and symptom overlap to generate multiple hypotheses. *Child Psychiatry and Human Development, 24,* 157–172.

deBettencourt, L. U. (1987). Strategy training: A need for clarification. *Exceptional Children, 54,* 24–30.

DeFries, J. C., Gillis, J. J., & Wadsworth, S. J. (1993). Genes and genders: A twin study of reading disability. In A. M. Galaburda (Ed.), *Dyslexia and development: Neurological aspects of extraordinary brains* (pp. 187–204). Cambridge, MA: Harvard University Press.

DeFries, J. C., Stevenson, J., Gillis, J. J., & Wadsworth, S. J. (1991). Genetic etiology of spelling deficits in the Colorado and London twin studies of reading disability. *Reading and Writing* (Special issue: Genetic and neurological influences on reading disability), *3,* 271–283.

Delacato, C. H. (1959). *The treatment and prevention of reading problems.* Springfield, IL: Thomas.

Denckla, M. B. (1993). The child with developmental disabilities grown up: Adult residua of childhood disorders. *Behavioral Neurology, 1,* 105–125.

Deno, S. L. (1997). Whether thou goest . . . Perspectives on progress monitoring. In J. W. Lloyd, E. J. Kame'enui, & D. Chard (Eds.), *Issues in educating students with disabilities* (pp. 77–99). Mahwah, NJ: Erlbaum.

Deno, S. L., & Fuchs, L. S. (1987). Developing curriculum-based measurement systems for data-based special education problem solving. *Focus on Exceptional Children, 19*(2),1–16.

Deno, S. L., & Mirkin, P. K. (1977). *Data-based program modification: A manual.* Reston, VA: Council for Exceptional Children.

Deno, S. L., Foegen, A., Robinson, S., & Espin, C. (1996). Commentary: Facing the realities of inclusion for students with mild disabilities. *Journal of Special Education, 30,* 345–357.

Denton, C. A., & Mathes, P. G. (2002). A focus on reading recovery: Use caution. *Current Practice Alerts, 7.* Available online at http://www.teachingld.org/ld_resources/alerts/

Denton, C. A., Vaughn, S., & Fletcher, J. M. (2003). Bringing research-based practice in reading intervention to scale. *Learning Disability Quarterly, 18,* 201–211.

Deshler, D. D., Ellis, E. S., & Lenz, B. (1996). *Teaching adolescents with learning disabilities: Strategies and methods.* Denver: Love.

DeStefano, L., & Wermuth, T. R. (1992). IDEA (P.L. 101-476): Defining a second generation of transition services. In F. R. Rusch, L. DeStefano, J. Chadsey-Rusch, L. A. Phelps, & E. Szymanski (Eds.), *Transition from school to adult life: Models,* *linkages, and policy* (pp. 537–549). Sycamore, IL: Sycamore Publishing.

Dickman, G. E., Hennessy, N. L., Moats, L. C., Rooney, K. J., & Tomey, H. A., III. (2002). *Response to OSEP Summit on Learning Disabilities: The nature of learning disabilities, identification process, eligibility criteria for services, intervention, professional development.* Baltimore, MD: International Dyslexia Society. Retrieved February 14, 2003, from http://www.interdys.org/docs/OSEP918.doc.

DiGangi, S. A., Maag, J. W., & Rutherford, R. B. (1991). Self-graphing of on-task behavior: Enhancing the reactive effects of self-monitoring on on-task behavior and academic performance. *Learning Disability Quarterly, 14,* 221–230.

Dixon, R. (1976). *Morphographic spelling.* Chicago: Science Research Associates.

Dixon, R. C. (1991). The application of sameness analysis to spelling. *Journal of Learning Disabilities, 24,* 285–291, 310.

Dixon, R. C. (1993). *The surefire way to better spelling: A revolutionary new approach to turn poor spellers into pros.* New York: St. Martins.

Dixon, R., & Carnine, D. (1994). Ideologies, practices, and their implications for special education. *Journal of Special Education, 28,* 356–367.

Dodge, B. *Semantic feature analysis.* Available online at http://edweb.sdsu.edu/people/bdodge/scaffold/compare.html

Donovan, M. S., & Cross, C. T. (Eds.). (2002). *Minority students in special and gifted education.* Washington, DC: National Research Council.

Drotar, D., Baskiewicz, A., Irvin, N., Kennell, J., & Klaus, M. (1975). The adaptation of parents to the birth of an infant with a congenital malformation: A hypothetical model. *Pediatrics, 56,* 710–717.

Dunn, L. M., Dunn, L. M., Williams, K. T., & Wang, J. J. (1997). *Peabody Picture Vocabulary Test—III.* Circle Pines, MN: American Guidance Service.

Dunn, R., Dunn, K., & Price, G. E. (1976). *Learning Style Inventory.* Lawrence, KS: Price Systems.

Dunst, C. J. (2002). Family-centered practices: Birth through high school. *Journal of Special Education, 36,* 139–147.

Dunst, C. J., Trivette, C. M., & Jodry, W. (1997). Influences of social support on children with disabilities and their families. In M. J. Guralnick (Ed.), *The effectiveness of early intervention* (pp. 499–522). Baltimore: Brookes.

DuPaul, G. J., Eckert, T. L., & McGoey, K. E. (1997). Interventions for students with attention-deficit/hyperactivity disorder: One size does not fit all. *School Psychology Review, 26,* 369–381.

Dupre, A. P. (1997). Disability and the public schools: The case against "inclusion." *Washington Law Review, 72* (whole no. 3).

Dupre, A. P. (2000). A study in double standards, discipline, and the disabled student. *Washington Law Review, 75,* 1–96.

Durlak, C. M., Rose, E., & Bursuck, W. D. (1994). Preparing high school students with learning disabilities for the transition to postsecondary education: Teaching the skills of self-determination. *Journal of Learning Disabilities, 27*(1), 51–59.

Duval, B. (1985). *Evaluation of eleventh grade students' writing supports teaching italic handwriting* (ERIC Document Reproduction Services No. ED 263 608).

Dyson, L. L. (1996). The experiences of families of children with learning disabilities: Parental stress, family functioning, and sibling self-concept. *Journal of Learning Disabilities, 29*, 280–286.

Eaton, M. D., & Lovitt, T. C. (1972). Achievement tests vs. direct and daily measurement. In G. Semb (Ed.), *Behavioral analysis and education* (pp. 78–87). Lawrence: University of Kansas.

Educational Testing Service. (1972). *Sequential Tests of Educational Progress.* Princeton, NJ: Author.

Edwads, L. (2003). Writing instruction in kindergarten: Examining an emerging area of research for children with writing and reading difficulties. *Journal of Learning Disabilities, 36*, 136–148.

Ehri, L. C. (1998). Grapheme-phoneme knowledge is essential to learning to read words in English. In J. L. Metsala & L. C. Ehri (Eds.), *Word recognition in beginning literacy* (pp. 3–40). Mahwah, NJ: Erlbaum.

Ehri, L. C., & Robbins, C. (1992). Beginners need some decoding skill to read words by analogy. *Reading Research Quarterly, 27*, 13–25.

Eisenson, J. (1972). *Aphasia in children.* New York: Harper & Row.

Elbaum, B., Vaughn, S., Hughes, M. T., & Moody, S. M. (2000). How effective are one-to-one tutoring programs in reading for elementary students at risk for reading failure? A meta-analysis of the intervention research. *Journal of Educational Psychology, 92*, 605–619.

Ellis, E. S. (1996). Reading strategy instruction. In D. D. Deshler, E. S. Ellis, & B. K. Lenz (Eds.), *Teaching adolescents with learning disabilities: Strategies and methods* 2nd ed., pp. 61–126. Denver, CO: Love.

Ellis, E. S., & Lenz, B. K. (1996). Perspectives on instruction in learning strategies. In D. D. Deshler, E. S. Ellis, & B. K. Lenz, *Teaching adolescents with learning disabilities: Strategies and methods* (2nd ed., pp. 9–60). Denver, CO: Love.

Elswit, L. S., Geetter, E., & Goldberg, J. A. (1999). Between passion and policy: Litigating the Guckenberger case. *Journal of Learning Disabilities, 32*, 292–303.

Ely, R. (2001). Language and literacy in the school years. In J. B. Gleason (Ed.), *The development of language* (pp. 409–454). Boston: Allyn & Bacon.

Engelmann, S. (1967a). Relationship between psychological theories and the act of teaching. *Journal of School Psychology, 5*, 92–100.

Engelmann, S. (1967b). Teaching reading to children with low MAs. *Education and Training of the Mentally Retarded, 2*, 193–201.

Engelmann, S. (1969). *Preventing failure in the primary grades.* Chicago: Science Research Associates.

Engelmann, S. (1997). Theory of mastery and acceleration. In J. W. Lloyd, E. J. Kame'enui, & D. Chard (Eds.), *Issues in educating students with disabilities* (pp. 177–195). Mahwah, NJ: Erlbaum.

Engelmann, S., & Carnine, D. W. (1975). *DISTAR arithmetic I* (2nd ed.). Chicago: Science Research Associates.

Engelmann, S., & Carnine, D. W. (1976). *DISTAR arithmetic II* (2nd ed.). Chicago: Science Research Associates.

Engelmann, S., & Carnine, D. W. (1981). *Corrective mathematics.* Chicago: Science Research Associates.

Engelmann, S., & Carnine, D. W. (1982). *Theory of instruction: Principles and applications.* New York: Irvington.

Engelmann, S., & Steely, D. (1980). *Fractions I and II.* Chicago: Science Research Associates.

Engelmann, S., & Steely, D. (1981). *Ratios and equations.* Chicago: Science Research Associates.

Engelmann, S., Arbogast, A. B., Davis, K. L. S., Grossen, B., & Silbert, J. (1993). Reasoning and writing. Chicago: Science Research Associates.

Engelmann, S., Carnine, D., Engelmann, O., & Kelly, B. (1991). *Connecting math concepts.* Chicago: Science Research Associates.

Engelmann, S., Hanner, S., & Johnson, G. (1999). *Corrective reading program: Series guide.* Chicago: Science Research Associates.

Engelmann, S., & Silbert, J. (1983). *Expressive writing.* Tigard, OR: C. C. Publications.

Engelmann, S., Haddox, P., Hanner, S., & Osborn, J. (1978). *Thinking basics: Corrective reading comprehension A.* Chicago: Science Research Associates.

Englert, C. S., & Mariage, T. V. (1991). Making students partners in the comprehension process: Organizing the reading "POSSE." *Learning Disability Quarterly, 14*, 123–138.

Englert, C. S., Raphael, T. E., Anderson, L. M., Anthony, H. M., & Stevens, D. D. (1991). Making writing strategies and self-talk visible: Cognitive strategy instruction in regular and special education classrooms. *American Educational Research Journal, 28*, 337–372.

Englert, C. S., Raphael, T. E., Anderson, L. M., Anthony, H. M., & Stevens, D. D. (1991). Making writing strategies and self-talk visible: Cognitive strategy instruction in regular and special education classrooms. *American Educational Research Journal, 28*, 337–372.

Englert, C. S., Raphael, T. E., Anderson, L. M., Gregg, S. L., & Anthony, H. M. (1989). Exposition: Reading, writing, and the metacognitive knowledge of learning disabled students. *Learning Disabilities Research, 5*, 5–24.

Englert, C., Raphael, T., Fear, K., & Anderson, L. (1988). Students' metacognitive knowledge about how to write informational texts. *Learning Disability Quarterly, 11*, 18–46.

Enright, B. C. (1983). *Diagnostic inventory of basic arithmetic skills.* North Billerica, MA: Curriculum Associates.

Epstein, M. H., Hallahan, D. P., & Kauffman, J. M. (1975). Implications for the reflectivity-impulsivity dimension for special education. *Journal of Special Education, 9*, 1–25.

Epstein, M. H., Polloway, E. A., Foley, R. M., & Patton, J. R. (1993). Homework: A comparison of teachers' and parents' perceptions of the problems experienced by students identified as having behavioral disorders, learning disabilities, or no disabilities. *Remedial and Special Education, 14*(5), 40–50.

Epstein, M., Munk, D., Bursuck, W., Polloway, E., & Jayanthi, M. (1999). Strategies for improving home-school communication about homework for students with disabilities. *Journal of Special Education, 33*, 166–176.

Ervin, R. A., DuPaul, G. J., Kern, L., & Friman, P. C. (1998). Classroom-based functional and adjunctive assessments: Proactive approaches to intervention selection for adolescents with attention deficit hyperactivity disorder. *Journal of Applied Behavior Analysis, 31*, 65–78.

Evers, R. B. (1996). The positive force of vocational education: Transition outcomes for youth with learning disabilities. *Journal of Learning Disabilities, 29*, 69–78.

Faraone, S. V., & Doyle, A. E. (2001). The nature and heritability of attention-deficit/hyperactivity disorder. *Child and Adolescent Psychiatric Clinics of North America, 10,* 299–316.

Faraone, S. V., Pliszka, S. R., Olvera, R. L., Skolnik, R., & Biederman, J. (2001). Efficacy of Adderall and methylphenidate in attention deficit hyperactivity disorder: A reanalysis using drug-placebo and drug-drug response curve methodology. *Journal of Child and Adolescent Psychopharmacology, 11,* 171–180.

Farmer, M. E., Klein, B., & Bryson, S. E. (1992). Computer-assisted reading: Effects of whole-word feedback on fluency and comprehension in readers with severe disabilities. *Remedial and Special Education, 13* (2), 50–60.

Fauke, J., Burnett, J., Powers, M. A., & Sulzer-Azaroff, B. (1973). Improvement of handwriting and letter recognition skills: A behavior modification procedure. *Journal of Learning Disabilities, 6,* 296–300.

Fawcett, A. J., Nicolson, R. I., Moss, H., Nicolson, M. K., & Reason, R. (2001). Effectiveness of reading intervention in junior school. *Educational Psychology, 21,* 299–312.

Fayne, H. R. (1981). A comparison of learning disabled adolescents with normal learners on an anaphoric pronominal reference task. *Journal of Learning Disabilities, 14,* 597–599.

Feil, E. G., Severson, H. H., & Walker, H. M. (2002). Early screening and intervention to prevent the development of aggressive, destructive behavior patterns among at-risk children. In M. R. Shinn, H. M. Walker, & G. Stoner (Eds.), *Interventions for academic and behavior problems: II. Preventive and remedial approaches* (pp. 143–166). Bethesda, MD: National Association of School Psychologists.

Feingold, B. F. (1975). *Why your child is hyperactive.* New York: Random House.

Feldman, R. G., & White, R. F. (1992). Lead neurotoxicity and disorders of learning. *Journal of Child Neurology, 7,* 354–359.

Fernald, G. M. (1943). *Remedial techniques in basic school subjects.* New York: McGraw-Hill.

Ferretti, R. P., MacArthur, C. D., & Okolo, C. M. (2001). Teaching for historical understanding in inclusive classrooms. *Learning Disability Quarterly, 24,* 59–71.

Feuerstein, R. (1979). *The dynamic assessment of retarded performers.* Baltimore: University Park Press.

Field, S., & Hoffman, A. (1996). *Steps to self-determination.* Austin, TX: PRO-ED.

Field, S., & Hoffman, A. (2002). Lessons learned from implementing the Steps to Self-Determination curriculum. *Remedial and Special Education, 23,* 90–98.

Filipek, P. A., Semrud-Clikeman, M., Steingard, R. J., Renshaw, P. F., Kennedy, D. N., & Biederman, J. (1997). Volumetric MRI analysis comparing subjects having attention-deficit hyperactivity disorder with normal controls. *Neurology, 48,* 589–601.

Fink, W. T., & Carnine, D. W. (1975). Control of arithmetic errors using informational feedback and graphing. *Journal of Applied Behavior Analysis, 8,* 461 (abstract).

Finlan, M. (1994). *Learning disabilities: The imaginary disease.* Westport, CT: Gergin & Garvey.

Finson, K. D., & Ormsbee, C. K. (1998). Rubrics and their use in inclusive science. *Intervention in School and Clinic, 34,* 79–88.

Fischer, F. W., Liberman, I. Y., & Shankweiler, D. (1978). Reading reversals and developmental dyslexia: A further study. *Cortex, 14,* 496–510.

Fletcher, J. M., Francis, D. J., Rourke, B. P., Shaywitz, S. E., & Shaywitz, B. A. (1992). The validity of discrepancy-based definitions of reading disabilities. *Journal of Learning Disabilities, 25*(9), 555–561, 573.

Fletcher, J. M., Lyon, G. R., Barnes, M., Stuebing, K. K., Francis, D. J., Olson. R. K., Shaywitz, S. E., & Shaywitz, B. A. (2002). Classification of learning disabilities: An evidence-based evaluation. In R. Bradley, L. Danielson, & D. P. Hallahan (Eds.), *Identification of learning disabilities: Research to practice.* (pp. 185–250). Mahwah, NJ: Erlbaum.

Fletcher, J. M., Shaywitz, S. E., Shankweiler, D. P., Katz, L., Liberman, I. Y., Stuebing, K. K., Francis, D. J., Fowler, A. E., & Shaywitz, B. A. (1994). Cognitive profiles of reading disability: Comparisons of discrepancy and low achievement definitions. *Journal of Educational Psychology, 86,* 6–23.

Foorman, B. R., Francis, D. J., Novy, D. M., & Liberman, D. (1991). How letter-sound instruction mediates progress in first-grade reading and spelling. *Journal of Educational Psychology, 83,* 456–469.

Forness, S. R., & Kavale, K. A. (1994). Meta-analysis in intervention research: Methods and implications. In J. Rothman & J. Thomas (Eds.), *Intervention research: Effective methods for professional practice* (pp. 117–131). Chicago: Haworth Press.

Forness, S. R., & Kavale, K. A. (1997). Defining emotional or behavioral disorders in school and related services. In J. W. Lloyd, E. J. Kame'enui, & D. Chard (Eds.), *Issues in educating students with disabilities* (pp. 45–61). Mahwah, NJ: Erlbaum.

Forness, S. R., & Kavale, K. A. (2001). Ignoring the odds: Hazards of not adding the new medical model to special education decisions. *Behavioral Disorders, 26,* 269–281.

Forness, S. R., Kavale, K. A., & Crenshaw, T. M. (1999). Stimulant medication revisited: Effective treatment of children with ADHD. *Journal of Emotional and Behavioral Problems, 7,* 230–235.

Forness, S. R., Kavale, K. A., Blum, I. M., & Lloyd, J. W. (1997). What works in special education and related services: Using meta-analysis to guide practice. *Teaching Exceptional Children, 29*(6), 4–9.

Forrest, D. L., & Waller, I. G. (1981, April). Reading ability and knowledge of important information. Paper presented at the meeting of the Society for Research in Child Development, Boston.

Foxx, R. M., & Jones, J. R. (1978). A remediation program for increasing the spelling achievement of elementary and junior high school students. *Behavior Modification, 2,* 211–230.

Friend, M., & Cook, L. (2003). *Interactions: Collaboration skills for school professionals* (4th ed.). Boston: Allyn & Bacon.

Frisby, C. L., & Braden, J. P. (1992). Feuerstein's dynamic assessment approach: A semantic, logical, and empirical critique. *Journal of Special Education, 26,* 281–301.

Frith, U. (1980). Unexpected spelling problems. In U. Frith (Ed.), *Cognitive processes in spelling* (pp. 495–515). New York: Academic Press.

Fuchs, D., & Fuchs, L. S. (1995a). Inclusive schools movement and the radicalization of special education reform. *Exceptional Children, 60,* 294–309.

Fuchs, D., & Fuchs, L. S. (1995b). What's "special" about special education? *Phi Delta Kappan, 76,* 522–530.

Fuchs, D., Fuchs, L. S., & Burish, P. (2000). Peer-assisted learning strategies: An evidence-based practice to promote reading achievement. *Learning Disabilities Research and Practice, 15,* 85–91.

Fuchs, D., Fuchs, L. S., Mathes, P. G., & Simmons, D.C. (1997). Peer-assisted learning strategies: Making classrooms more responsive to diversity. *American Educational Research Journal, 34,* 174–206.

Fuchs, D., Mock, D., Morgan, P. L., & Young, C. L. (2003). Responsiveness-to-intervention: Definitions, evidence, and implications for the learning disabilities construct. *Learning Disabilities Research and Practice, 18,* 157–171.

Fuchs, L. S. (2003). Assessing intervention responsiveness: Conceptual and technical issues. *Learning Disabilities Research and Practice, 18,* 172–186.

Fuchs, L. S., & Deno, S. L. (1991). Paradigmatic distinctions between instructionally relevant measurement models. *Exceptional Children, 57,* 488–500.

Fuchs, L. S., & Deno, S. L. (1994). Must instructionally useful performance assessment be based on the curriculum? *Exceptional Children, 61,* 15–24.

Fuchs, L. S., & Fuchs, D. (1986). Effects of systematic formative evaluation: A meta-analysis. *Exceptional Children, 53,* 199–208.

Fuchs, L. S., & Fuchs, D. (1998). Treatment validity: A unifying concept for reconceptualizing the identification of learning disabilities. *Learning Disabilities Research and Practice, 13,* 204–219.

Fuchs, L. S., & Fuchs, D. (2001). Principles for the prevention and intervention of mathematics difficulties. *Learning Disabilities Research and Practice, 16,* 85–95.

Fuchs, L. S., & Fuchs, D. (2002). Mathematical problem-solving profiles of students with mathematics disabilities with and without comorbid reading disabilities. *Journal of Learning Disabilities, 35,* 564–574.

Fuchs, L. S., Butterworth, J. R., & Fuchs, D. (1989). Effects of ongoing curriculum-based measurement on student awareness of goals and progress. *Education and Treatment of Children, 12,* 63–72.

Fuchs, L. S., Fuchs, D., & Karns, K. (2001). Enhancing kindergartners' mathematical development: Effects of peer-assisted learning strategies. *Elementary School Journal, 101* (5), 494–510.

Fuchs, L. S., Fuchs, D., & Kazdan, S. (1999). Effects of peer-assisted learning strategies on high school students with serious reading problems. *Remedial and Special Education, 20,* 309–318.

Fuchs, L. S., Fuchs, D., Hamlett, C. L., & Stecker, P. M. (1991). Effects of curriculum-based measurement and consultation on teacher planning and student achievement. *American Educational Research Journal, 28,* 617–641.

Fuchs, L. S., Fuchs, D., Hamlett, C. L., Phillips, N. B., & Bentz, J. (1994). Classwide curriculum-based measurement: Helping general educators meet the challenge of student diversity. *Exceptional Children, 60,* 518–537.

Fulk, B. M. (1996). The effects of combined strategy and attribution training on LD adolescents' spelling performance. *Exceptionality, 6,* 13–27.

Fulk, B. M., Lohman, D., & Belfiore, P. J. (1997). Effects of integrated picture mnemonics on the letter recognition and letter-sound acquisition of transitional first-grade students with special needs. *Learning Disability Quarterly, 20,* 33–42.

Gajar, A. (1992). Adults with learning disabilities: Current and future research priorities. *Journal of Learning Disabilities, 25*(8), 507–519.

Gajria, M., & Salend, S. J. (1995). Homework practices of students with and without learning disabilities: A comparison. *Journal of Learning Disabilities, 28,* 291–296.

Galaburda, A. M., & Kemper, T. L. (1979). Cytoarchitectonic abnormalities in developmental dyslexia: A case study. *Annals of Neurology, 6,* 94–100.

Galaburda, A. M., Menard, M. T., & Rosen, G. D. (1994). Evidence for aberrant auditory anatomy in developmental dyslexia. *Proceedings of the National Academy of Science USA, 91,* 8010–8013.

Galaburda, A. M., Sherman, G. F., Rosen, G. D., Aboitiz, F., & Geschwind, N. (1985). Developmental dyslexia: Four consecutive patients with cortical anomalies. *Annals of Neurology, 18,* 222–233.

Gallagher, J. J. (1994). The pull of societal forces on special education. *Journal of Special Education, 27,* 521–530.

Gallagher, J. J. (2000). The beginnings of federal help for young children with disabilities. *Topics in Early Childhood Special Education, 20,* 3–6.

Gardill, M. C., & Jitendra, A. K. (1999). Advanced story map instruction: Effects on the reading comprehension of students with learning disabilities. *Journal of Special Education, 33,* 2–17, 28.

Gardner, E. R., Rudman, H. C., Karlsen, B., & Merwin, J. C. (1988). *Stanford Achievement Test—eighth edition.* New York: Harcourt Brace Jovanovich.

Garnett, K., & Fleishner, J. E. (1983). Automatization and basic fact performance of normal and learning disabled children. *Learning Disability Quarterly, 6,* 223–230.

Garton, A., & Pratt, C. (1998). *Learning to be literate: The development of spoken and written language.* London: Blackwell.

Gates, A. I., & Russell, D. (1940). *Gates-Russell Spelling Diagnostic Test.* New York: Columbia University Press.

Gattegno, C. (1963). *For the teaching of elementary mathematics.* Mt. Vernon, NY: Cuisenaire Company of America.

Gazzaniga, M. S., & LeDoux, J. E. (1978). *The integrated mind.* New York: Plenum Press.

Geary, D. C. (1994). Children's mathematical development: Research and practical applications. Washington, DC: American Psychological Association.

Geary, D. C. (1999). *Mathematical disabilities: What we know and don't know.* Retrieved June 10, 2003, from http://www.ld online.org/ld_indepth/math_skills/geary_math_dis.html

Geary, D. C., Hamson, C. O., & Hoard, M. K. (2000). Numerical and arithmetical cognition: A longitudinal study of process and concept deficits in children with learning disability. *Journal of Experimental Child Psychology, 77,* 236–263.

Geary, D. C., Hoard, M. K., & Hamson, C. O. (1999). Numerical and arithmetical cognition: Patterns of functions and deficits in children at risk for a mathematical disability. *Journal of Experimental Child Psychology, 74,* 213–239.

Geenen, S., Powers, L. E., & Lopez-Vasquez, A. (2001). Multicultural aspects of parent involvement in transition planning. *Exceptional Children, 67,* 265–282.

Gerber, M. M. (1986). Generalization of spelling strategies by LD students as a result of contingent imitation/modeling and mastery criteria. *Journal of Learning Disabilities, 19,* 530–537.

Gerber, M. M. (2000). An appreciation of learning disabilities: The value of blue-green algae. *Exceptionality, 8,* 29–42.

Gerber, M. M., & Hall, R. J. (1981). Development of spelling in learning disabled and normally achieving children. Unpublished manuscript, Learning Disabilities Research Institute, University of Virginia.

Gerber, M. M., & Semmel, M. I. (1984). Teacher as imperfect test: Reconceptualizing the referral process. *Educational Psychologist, 19,* 137–148.

Gerber, P. J. (1992). At first glance: Employment for people with learning disabilities at the beginning of the Americans-with-Learning-Disabilities-Act era. *Learning Disability Quarterly, 15*(4), 330–332.

Gerber, P. J., & Reiff, H. B. (1991). *Speaking for themselves: Ethnographic interviews with adults with learning disabilities.* Ann Arbor: University of Michigan Press.

Gerber, P. J., Ginsberg, R., & Reiff, H. B. (1992). Identifying alterable patterns in employment success for highly successful adults with learning disabilities. *Journal of Learning Disabilities, 25*(8), 475–487.

Gershon, J. (2002). A meta-analytic review of gender differences in ADHD. *Journal of Attention Disorders, 5,* 143–154.

Gersten, R. & Baker, S. (2000). The professional knowledge base on instructional practices that support cognitive growth for English-language learners. In R. Gersten, E. P. Schiller, & S. Vaughn (Eds.), *Contemporary special education research: Syntheses of the knowledge base on critical instructional issues* (pp. 31–80). Mahwah, NJ: Erlbaum.

Gersten, R., & Baker, S. (2001). Teaching expressive writing to students with learning disabilities: A meta-analysis. *Elementary School Journal, 101,* 251–272.

Gersten, R., & Chard, D. (1999). Number sense: Rethinking arithmetic instruction for students with mathematical disabilities. *Journal of Special Education, 33,* 18–28.

Gersten, R., Fuchs, L. S., Williams, J. P., & Baker, S. (2001). Teaching reading comprehension strategies to students with learning disabilities: A review of research. *Review of Educational Research, 71,* 279–320.

Gersten, R., Irvin, L., & Keating, T. (2002). Critical issues in research on families: Introduction to the special issue. *Journal of Special Education, 36,* 122–123.

Geschwind N., & Levitsky, W. (1968). Human brain: Left-right asymmetries in temporal speech. *Science, 161,* 186–187.

Gessell, J. (1983). *Diagnostic Mathematics Inventory.* Monterey, CA: CTB/McGraw-Hill.

Gettinger, M. (1993). Effects of invented spelling and direct instruction on spelling performance of second-grade boys. *Journal of Applied Behavior Analysis, 26,* 281–291.

Gettinger, M., Bryant, N. D., & Fayne, H. R. (1982). Designing spelling instruction for learning-disabled children: An emphasis on unit size, distributed practice, and training for transfer. *Journal of Special Education, 16,* 439–448.

Gillingham, A., & Stillman, B. (1965). *Remedial training for children with specific disability in reading, spelling and penmanship* (7th ed.). Cambridge, MA: Educators Publishing Service.

Gillis, J. J., Gilger, J. W., Pennington, B. F., & DeFries, C. (1992). Attention deficit disorder in reading-disabled twins:

Evidence for a gentic etiology. *Journal of Abnormal Child Psychology, 20,* 303–315.

Ginsberg, H. (1977). *Children's arithmetic: The learning process.* New York: Van Nostrand.

Ginsberg, H. P. (1997). Mathematical learning disabilities: A view from developmental psychology. *Journal of Learning Disabilities, 30,* 20–33.

Ginsburg, H. P. (1991). A cognitive approach to assessing the mathematical difficulties of children labeled "learning disabled." In H. L. Swanson (Ed.), *Handbook on the assessment of learning disabilities: Theory, research, and practice* (pp. 177–227). Austin, TX: PRO-ED.

Gleason, M., Carnine, D., & Boriero, D. (1990). Improving CAI effectiveness with attention to instructional design in teaching story problems to mildly handicapped students. *Journal of Special Education Technology, 10,* 129–136.

Glennon, V. J., & Cruickshank, W. M. (1981). Teaching mathematics to children and youth with perceptual and cognitive deficits. In V. J. Glennon (Ed.), *The mathematical education of exceptional children and youth: An interdisciplinary approach* (pp. 50–94). Reston, VA: National Council of Teachers of Mathematics.

Goldberger, S., & Kazis, R. (1996). Revitalizing high schools: What the school-to-career movement can contribute. *Phi Delta Kappan, 77,* 547–554.

Goldman, R., & Fristoe, M. (2000). *Goldman Fristoe Test of Articulation* (2nd ed.). Circle Pines, MN: American Guidance Service.

Goldman, S. R., Hasselbring, T. S., & the Cognition and Technology Group at Vanderbilt. (1997). Achieving meaningful mathematics literacy for students with learning disabilities. *Journal of Learning Disabilities, 30,* 198–208.

Goldstein, D. E., Murray, C., & Edgar, E. (1998). Employment earning and hours of high school graduates with learning disabilities through the first decade after graduation. *Learning Disabilities Research and Practice, 13,* 53–64.

Golinkoff, R. M., & Rosinski, R. R. (1976). Decoding, semantic processing, and reading comprehension skill. *Child Development, 47,* 252–258.

Good, R. H. (2003). *DIBELS benchmark levels.* University of Oregon. Retrieved July 27, 2003, from http://dibels.uoregon.edu/benchmark.php

Good, R. H., Simmons, D.C., & Kame'enui, E. J. (2001). The importance and decision-making utility of a continuum of fluency-based indicators of foundational reading skills for third-grade high-stakes outcomes. *Scientific Studies of Reading, 5,* 257–288.

Good, T. L., & Grouws, D. A. (1979). The Missouri Mathematics Effectiveness Project: An experimental study in fourth-grade classrooms. *Journal of Educational Psychology, 71,* 355–362.

Good, T. L., Grouws, D. A., & Ebmeier, H. (1983). *Active mathematics teaching.* New York: Longman.

Goodman, K. S. (1965). A linguistic study of cues and miscues in reading. *Elementary English, 42,* 639–643.

Goodman, K. S. (1986). *What's whole in whole language: A parent-teacher guide.* Portsmouth, NH: Heinemann.

Goodman, K. S. (1992). I didn't found whole language. *Reading Teacher, 46,* 188–199.

Goodman, K. S., & Goodman, Y. M. (1979). Learning to read is natural. In L. B. Resnick & P. A. Weaver (Eds.), *Theory and practice for early reading* (vol. 1, 137–154). Hillsdale, NJ: Erlbaum.

Gordon, J., Vaughn, S., & Schumm, J. S. (1993). Spelling interventions: A review of literature and implications for instruction for students with learning disabilities. *Learning Disabilities Research and Practice, 8,* 175–181.

Gottlieb, J., Alter, M., Gottlieb, B. W., & Wishner, J. (1994). Special education in urban America: It's not justifiable for many. *Journal of Special Education, 27,* 453–465.

Gough, P. B. (1996). How children learn to read and why they fail. *Annals of Dyslexia, 46,* 3–20.

Gough, P. B., & Tunmer, W. E. (1986). Decoding, reading, and reading disability. *Remedial and Special Education, 7*(1), 6–10.

Graham, S. (1982). Composition research and practice: A unified approach. *Focus on Exceptional Children, 14*(8), 1–16.

Graham, S. (1997). Executive control in the revising of students with learning and writing difficulties. *Journal of Educational Psychology, 82,* 223–234.

Graham, S. (1999). Handwriting and spelling instruction for students with learning disabilities: A review. *Learning Disability Quarterly, 22,* 78–98.

Graham, S., & Harris, K. R. (1997a). Self-regulation and writing: Where do we go from here? *Contemporary Educational Psychology, 22,* 102–114.

Graham, S., & Harris, K. R. (1997b). Whole language and process writing: Does one approach fit all? In J. W. Lloyd, E. J. Kame'enui, & D. Chard (Eds.), *Issues in educating students with disabilities* (pp. 239–258). Mahwah, NJ: Erlbaum.

Graham, S., & Harris, K. R. (2002). Prevention and intervention for struggling writers. In M. R. Shinn, H. M. Walker, & G. Stoner (Eds.), *Interventions for academic and behavior problems: II. Preventive and remedial approaches* (pp. 589–610). Bethesda, MD: National Association of School Psychologists.

Graham, S., & Miller, L. (1979). Spelling research and practice: A unified approach. *Focus on Exceptional Children, 12*(2), 1–16.

Graham, S., Harris, K. R., & Larsen, L. (2001). Prevention and intervention of writing difficulties for students with learning disabilities. *Learning Disabilities Research and Practice, 16,* 74–84.

Graham, S., Harris, K. R., & Loynachan, C. (1994). The spelling for writing list. *Journal of Learning Disabilities, 27,* 210–214.

Graham, S., Harris, K. R., & Troia, G. A. (2000). Self-Regulated Strategy Development revisited: Teaching writing strategies to struggling writers. *Topics in Language Disorders, 20,* 1–14.

Graham, S., Harris, K. R., MacArthur, C., & Schwartz, S. (1991). Writing instruction. In B. Wong, (Ed.), *Learning about learning disabilities* (2nd ed., pp. 391–423). New York: Academic Press.

Graham, S., Harris, K., & Loynachan, C. (1996). The Directed Spelling Thinking Activity: Application with high-frequency words. *Learning Disabilities Research and Practice, 11,* 34–40.

Graves, A. W., Valles, E. C., & Rueda, R. (2000). Variations in interactive writing instruction: A study in four bilingual special education settings. *Learning Disabilities Research and Practice, 15,* 1–9.

Graves, A., Montague, M., & Wong, Y. (1990). The effects of procedural facilitation on the story composition of learning disabled students. *Learning Disabilities Research, 5,* 88–93.

Graves, D. (1983). *Writing: Teachers and children at work.* Portsmouth, NH: Heinemann.

Green, R. (1992). "Learning to learn" and the family system: New perspectives on underachievement and learning disorders. In M. J. Fine & C. Carlson (Eds.), *The handbook of family-school intervention: A systems perspective* (pp. 157–174). Boston: Allyn & Bacon.

Greenbaum, B., Graham, S., & Scales, W. (1996). Adults with learning disabilities: Occupational and social status after college. *Journal of Learning Disabilities, 29,* 167–173.

Greenwood, C. R., Carta, J. J., Kamps, D., Terry, B., & Delquadri, J. (1994). Development and validation of standard classroom observation systems for school practitioners: Ecobehavioral assessment systems software (EBASS). *Exceptional Children, 61,* 197–210.

Greenwood, C. R., Delquadri, J. S., & Carta, J. J. (1997). *Together we can! Classwide peer tutoring to improve basic academic skills.* Longmont, CO: Sopris West.

Greenwood, C. R., Delquadri, J., & Carta, J. J., (1998). *Classwide peer tutoring.* Seattle: Educational Achievement Systems.

Greenwood, S. C. (2002). Making words matter: Vocabulary study in the content areas. *Clearing House, 75*(5), 258–263.

Greer, J. V. (1990). The drug babies. *Exceptional Children, 56,* 382–384.

Gresham, F. M. (2002). Responsiveness to intervention: An alternative approach to identification of learning disabilities. In R. Bradley, L. Danielson, & D. P. Hallahan (Eds.), *Identification of learning disabilities: Research to practice* (pp. 467–519). Mahwah, NJ: Erlbaum.

Grigorenko, E. L. (2001). Developmental dyslexia: An update on genes, brains, and environments. *Journal of Child Psychology and Psychiatry, 42,* 91–125.

Grigorenko, E. L., Wood, F. B., Meyer, M. S., & Pauls, D. L. (2000). Chromosome 6p influences on different dyslexia-related cognitive processes: Further confirmation.

Grimm, J. A., Bijou, S. W., & Parsons, J. A. (1973). A problem solving model for teaching remedial arithmetic to handicapped young children. *Journal of Abnormal Child Psychology, 1,* 26–39.

Grossen, B. (1993a). Child-directed teaching methods: A discriminatory practice of Western education. *Effective School Practices, 12*(2), 9–20.

Grossen, B. (1993b). Focus: Heterogeneous grouping and curriculum design. *Effective School Practices, 12*(1), 5–8.

Grossen, B., & Ewing, S. (1994). Raising mathematical problem-solving performance: Do the NCTM teaching standards help? *Effective School Practices, 13*(2), 79–91.

Grossen, B., Coulter, G., & Ruggles, B. (1996). Reading recovery: An evaluation of benefits and costs. *Effective School Practices, 15*(3), 6–24.

Grotclushchen, A. K., Borkowski, J. G., & Hale, C. (1991). Strategy instruction is often insufficient: Addressing the interdependency of executive and attributional processes. In T. E. Scruggs & B. Y. L. Wong (Eds.), *Intervention research in learning disabilities* (pp. 81–101). New York: Springer-Verlag.

*Guckenberger v. Boston University,* 974 F. Supp. 106 (D. Mass. 1977).

Gurney, D., Gersten, R., Dimino, J., & Carnine, D. (1990). Story grammar: Effective literature instruction for high school students with learning disabilities. *Journal of Learning Disabilities, 23,* 335–342, 348.

Guyer, B. P., Banks, S. R., & Guyer, K. E. (1993). Spelling improvement for college students who are dyslexic. *Annals of Dyslexia, 43,* 186–193.

Guzaitis, J., Carlin, J. A., & Juda, S. (1972). Diagnosis: An instructional aid in mathematics. Chicago: Science Research Associates.

Haager, D., & Vaughn, S. (1997). Assessment of social competence in students with learning disabilities. In J. W. Lloyd, E. J. Kame'enui, & D. Chard (Eds.), *Issues in educating students with disabilities* (pp. 129–152). Mahwah, NJ: Erlbaum.

Haberlandt, K. (1996). *Cognitive psychology.* Boston: Allyn & Bacon.

Habib, M. (2000). The neurological basis of developmental dyslexia: An overview and working hypothesis. *Brain, 123,* 2373–2399.

Hains, A. H., Belland, J., Conceicao-Runlee, S., Santos, R.M., & Rothenberg, D. (2000). Instructional technology and personnel preparation. *Topics in Early Childhood Special Education, 20,* 132–144.

Hale, J. B., Hoeppner, J. B., DeWitt, M. B., Coury, D. L., Ritacco, D. G., & Trommer, B. (1998). Evaluating medication response to ADHD: Cognitive, behavioral, and single-subject methodology. *Journal of Learning Disabilities, 31,* 595–607.

Hallahan, D. P. (1992). Some thoughts on why the prevalence of learning disabilities has increased. *Journal of Learning Disabilities, 25*(8), 523–528.

Hallahan, D. P., & Cruickshank, W. M. (1973). *Psycho-educational foundations of learning disabilities.* Englewood Cliffs, NJ: Prentice-Hall.

Hallahan, D. P., & Hudson, K. G. (2002). *Teaching tutorial 2: Self-monitoring of attention.* Division for Learning Disabilities of the Council for Exceptional Children. Available online at www.Teaching.LD.org.

Hallahan, D. P., & Kauffman, J. M. (1977). Labels, categories, behaviors: ED, LD, and EMR reconsidered. *Journal of Special Education, 11,* 139–149.

Hallahan, D. P., & Kauffman, J. M. (1994). Toward a culture of disability in the aftermath of Deno and Dunn. *Journal of Special Education, 27,* 496–508.

Hallahan, D. P., & Kauffman, J. M. (2003). *Exceptional learners: Introduction to special education* (7th ed.). Boston: Allyn & Bacon.

Hallahan, D. P., & Martinez, E. A. (2002). Working with families. In J. M. Kauffman, M. Mostert, S. C. Trent, & D. P. Hallahan (Eds.), *Managing classroom behavior: A reflective case-based approach* (3rd ed., pp. 124–140). Boston: Allyn & Bacon.

Hallahan, D. P., & Mercer, C. D. (2002). Learning disabilities: Historical perspectives. In R. Bradley, L. Danielson, & D. P. Hallahan (Eds.), *Identification of learning disabilities: Research to practice* (pp. 1–67). Mahwah, NJ: Erlbaum.

Hallahan, D. P., & Reeve, R. E. (1980). Selective attention and distractibility. In B. K. Keogh (Ed.), *Advances in special education* (Vol. 1, pp. 141–181). Greenwich, CT: JAI Press.

Hallahan, D. P., Gajar, A. H., Cohen, S. B., & Tarver, S. G. (1978). Selective attention and locus of control in learning disabled children. *Journal of Learning Disabilities, 4,* 47–52.

Hallahan, D. P., Kauffman, J. M., & Ball, D. W. (1973). Selective attention and cognitive tempo of low achieving and high achieving sixth grade males. *Perceptual and Motor Skills, 36,* 579–583.

Hallahan, D. P., Kauffman, J. M., & Lloyd, J. W. (1985). *Introduction to learning disabilities* (2nd ed.). Englewood Cliffs, NJ: Prentice-Hall.

Hallahan, D. P., Kneedler, R. D., & Lloyd, J. W. (1983). Cognitive behavior modification techniques for learning disabled children: Self-instruction and self-monitoring. In J. D. McKinney & L. Feagans (Eds.), *Current topics in learning disabilities* (Vol. 1, pp. 207–244). New York: Ablex.

Hallahan, D. P., Lloyd, J. W., Kosiewicz, M. M., Kauffman, J. M., & Graves, A. W. (1979). Self-monitoring of attention as a treatment for a learning disabled boy's off-task behavior. *Learning Disability Quarterly, 2,* 24–32.

Hallenbeck, B. A., & Kauffman, J. M. (1995). How does observational learning affect the behavior of students with emotional or behavioral disorders? A review of research. *Journal of Special Education, 29,* 45–71.

Hallgren, B. (1950). Specific dyslexia (congenital word blindness): A clinical and genetic study. *Acta Psychiatrica et Neurologica, 65,* 1–279.

Halpern, A. S. (1993). Quality of life as a conceptual framework for evaluating transition outcomes. *Exceptional Children, 59*(6), 486–498.

Halpern, A. S. (1994). The transition of youth with disabilities to adult life: A position statement of the Division on Career Development and Transition, the Council for Exceptional Children. *Career Development for Exceptional Individuals, 17,* 115–124.

Halpern, D. F., & Donaghey, B. (2003). Learning theory: Historical overview. In J. W. Guthrie (Ed.), *Encyclopedia of education* (2nd ed., pp. 1458–1463). New York: Macmillan Reference.

Hammill, D. D. (1990). On defining learning disabilities: An emerging consensus. *Journal of Learning Disabilities, 23*(2), 74–84.

Hammill, D. D., & Bryant, B. R. (1991). The role of standardized tests in planning academic instruction. In H. L. Swanson (Ed.), *Handbook on the assessment of learning disabilities* (pp. 373–406). Austin, TX: PRO-ED.

Hammill, D. D., & Larsen, S. C. (1996). *Test of Written Language* (3rd ed.). Austin, TX: PRO-ED.

Hammill, D. D., & Leigh, J. E. (1983). *Basic School Skills Inventory—Diagnostic.* Austin, TX: PRO-ED.

Hammill, D. D., & Newcomer, P. (1997). *Test of Language Development—3.* Austin, TX: PRO-ED.

Hammill, D. D., & Newcomer, P. L. (1997). *Test of Language Development—Intermediate* (3rd ed.). Austin, TX: PRO-ED.

Hammill, D. D., Leigh, J. E., McNutt, G., & Larsen, S. C. (1981). A new definition of learning disabilities. *Learning Disability Quarterly, 4,* 336–342.

Hammill, D. D., Mather, N., & Roberts, R. (2001). *The Illinois Test of Psycholinguistic Abilities* (3rd ed.). Austin, TX: PRO-ED.

Hammill, D., Brown, V. L., Larsen, S. C., & Wiederholt L. (1994). *Test of Adolescent and Adult Language* (3rd ed.). Austin, TX: PRO-ED.

Hammitte, D. J., & Nelson, B. M. (2001). Families of children in early childhood special education. In D. J. O'Shea, L. J. O'Shea, R. Algozzine, & D. J. Hammitte (Eds.), *Families and teachers of individuals with disabilities: Collaborative orientations and responsive practices* (pp. 129–154). Boston: Allyn & Bacon.

Hanson, M. J., & Carta, J. J. (1996). Addressing the challenges of families with multiple risks. *Exceptional Children, 62,* 201–212.

Haring, K. A., Lovett, D. L., & Smith, D. D. (1990). A follow-up of recent special education graduates of learning disabilities programs. *Journal of Learning Disabilities, 23*(2), 108–113.

Haring, K. A., Lovett, D. L., Haney, K. F., Algozzine, B., Smith, D. D., & Clarke, J. (1992). Labeling preschoolers as learning disabled: A cautionary position. *Topics in Early Childhood Special Education, 12,* 151–173.

Haring, N. G., Lovitt, T. C., Eaton, M. D., & Hansen, C. L. (1978). *The fourth R: Research in the classroom.* Columbus, OH: Merrill.

Harris, K. R., & Graham, S. (1985). Improving learning disabled students' composition skills: A self-control strategy training approach. *Learning Disability Quarterly, 8,* 27–36.

Harris, K. R., & Larson, L. (2001). Prevention and intervention of writing difficulties for students with learning disabilities. *Learning Disabilities Research and Practice, 16,* 74–84.

Harris, K. R., Graham, S., Reid, R., McElroy, K., & Hamby, R. S. (1994). Self-monitoring of attention versus self-monitoring of performance: Replication and cross-task comparison studies. *Learning Disability Quarterly, 17,* 121–139.

Harris, R. E., Marchand-Martella, N., & Martella, R. C. (2000). Effects of a peer-delivered corrective reading program. *Journal of Behavioral Education, 10,* 21–36.

Harris, V. W., Sherman, J. A., Henderson, D. G., & Harris, M. S. (1972). Effects of peer tutoring on the spelling performance of elementary classroom students. In G. Semb (Ed.), *Behavior analysis and education—1972* (pp. 222–231). Lawrence: Department of Human Development, University of Kansas.

Hart, B. (2000). A natural history of early language experience. *Topics in Early Childhood Special Education, 20,* 28–32.

Hart, B., & Risley, T. (1995). *Meaningful differences in the everyday experiences of young American children.* Baltimore: Paul H. Brooks.

Hasazi, J. E., & Hasazi, S. E. (1972). Effects of teacher attention on digit-reversal behavior in an elementary school child. *Journal of Applied Behavior Analysis, 5,* 157–162.

Hasbrouck, J. E., Woldbeck, T., Ihnot, C., & Parker, R. I. (1999). One teacher's use of curriculum-based measurement: A changed opinion. *Learning Disabilities Research and Practice, 14,* 118–126.

Hasselbring, T. S., Goin, L. I., & Bransford, J. (1987). Developing automaticity. *Teaching Exceptional Children, 19,* 30–33.

Hasselbring, T. S., Goin, L. I., & Bransford, J. (1988). Developing math automaticity in learning handicapped children: The role of computerized drill and practice. *Focus on Exceptional Children, 20*(2), 1–7.

Hasselbring, T., Sherwood, R., & Bransford, J. (1986). Evaluation of the Mastering Fractions level one instructional videodisc program. Unpublished manuscript, Tennessee Valley Authority.

Haywood, H. C. (1992). Interactive assessment: A special issue. *Journal of Special Education, 26,* 233–234.

Hebbeler, K., Wagner, M., Spiker, D., Scarborough, A., Simeonsson, R., & Collier, M. (2001). *National Early Intervention Longitudinal Study: A first look at the characteristics of children and families entering early intervention services* (NEILS data report no. 1). Menlo Park, CA: SRI International. Available online at http://www.sri.com/neils/FormAreport.pdf

Hegge, T. G., Kirk, S. A., & Kirk, W. D. (1970). *Remedial reading drills.* Ann Arbor, MI: Wahr.

Heibert, E. H., & Taylor, B. M. (2002). Beginning reading instruction: Research on early interventions. In *Handbook of reading research* (pp. 455–482). Mahwah, NJ: Erlbaum.

Henley, M., Ramsey S. R., & Algozzine, R. (1996). *Characteristics of and strategies for teaching students with mild disabilities* (2nd ed.). Boston: Allyn & Bacon.

Heron, T. E., & Catera, R. (1980). Teacher consultation: A functional approach. *School Psychology Review, 9,* 283–289.

Heshusius, L. (1989). The Newtonian mechanistic paradigm, special education, and contours of alternatives: An overview. *Journal of Learning Disabilities, 22,* 403–415.

Heshusius, L. (1994). Freeing ourselves from objectivity: Managing subjectivity or turning toward a participation mode of consciousness. *Educational Researcher, 23* (3), 15–22.

Heshusius, L. (2004). From creative discontent toward epistemological freedom in special education: Reflections on a 25-year journey. In D. J. Gallagher (Ed.), *Challenging orthodoxy in special education: Dissenting voices* (pp. 169–230). Denver, CO: Love.

Hessler, G., & Kitchen, D. (1980). Language characteristics of a purposive sample of early elementary learning disabled students. *Learning Disability Quarterly, 3*(3), 36–41.

Heward, W. L. (2003). Ten faulty notions about teaching and learning that hinder the effectiveness of special education. *Journal of Special Education, 36,* 186–205.

Heward, W. L., & Silvestri, S. M. (2003). The neutralization of special education. In J. W. Jacobson, J. A. Mulick, & R. M. Foxx (Eds.), *Fads: Dubious and improbable treatments for developmental disabilities.* Mahwah, NJ: Erlbaum.

Hiebert, E. (1994). Reading recovery in the United States: What difference does it make to an age cohort? *Educational Researcher, 23* (9), 15–25.

Hieronymus, A. N., Lindquist, E. F., & Hoover, H. D. (1978). *Iowa Tests of Basic Skills.* Lombard, IL: Riverside.

Hinshelwood, J. (1907). Four cases of congenital word-blindness occurring in the same family. *British Medical Journal, 2,* 1229–1232.

Hirsch, E. D., Jr. (1996). *The schools we need and why we don't have them.* New York: Anchor.

Hitchcock, C. H., & Noonan, J. J. (2000). Computer-assisted instruction of early academic skills. *Topics in Early Childhood Special Education, 20,* 145–158.

Hitchings, W. E., Luzzo, D. A., Ristow, R., Horvath, M., Retish, P., & Tanners, A. (2001). The career development needs of college students with learning disabilities: In their own words. *Learning Disabilities Research and Practice, 16,* 8–17.

Hobbs, F., & Stoops, N. (2002). *Demographic trends in the 20th century*. Washington, DC: U.S. Government Printing Office.

Hodges, A., & Balow, B. (1961). Learning disability in relation to family constellation. *Journal of Educational Research, 55,* 41–42.

Holahan, A., & Costenbader, V. (2000). A comparison of developmental gains for preschool children with disabilities in inclusive and self-contained classrooms. *Topics in Early Childhood Special Education, 20,* 224–235.

Holmes, D. L., & Peper, R. J. (1977). An evaluation of the use of spelling error analysis in the diagnosis of reading disabilities. *Child Development, 48,* 1708–1711.

Hoover, H. D., Dunbar, S. B., & Frisbie, D. A. (2001). *Iowa Tests of Basic Skills.* Itasca, IL: Riverside.

Horner, R. H. (1994). Functional assessment: Contributions and future directions. *Journal of Applied Behavior Analysis, 27,* 401–404.

Horton, S. V., Lovitt, T. C., & White, O. R. (1992). Teaching mathematics to adolescents classified as mentally handicapped: Using calculators to remove the onus. *Remedial and Special Education, 13*(3), 36–61.

Hosp, J. L., & Reschly, D. J. (2002). Predictors of restrictiveness of placement for African-American and Caucasian students. *Exceptional Children, 68,* 225–238.

Houghton Mifflin. (1992). *The mathematics experience.* Boston: Author.

Howell, K. W., & Davidson, M. R. (1997). Aligning teacher thought processes with the curriculum. In J. W. Lloyd, E. J. Kame'enui, & D. Chard (Eds.), *Issues in educating students with disabilities* (pp. 101–128). Mahwah, NJ: Erlbaum.

Howell, K. W., & Morehead, M. K. (1987). *Curriculum-based evaluation for special and remedial education: A handbook for deciding what to teach.* Columbus, OH: Merrill.

Howell, K. W., & Nolet, V. (2000). *Curriculum-based evaluation: Teaching and decision making.* Belmont, CA: Wadsworth.

Howell, K. W., Fox, S. L., & Morehead, M. K. (1993). *Curriculum-based evaluation: Teaching and decision making* (2nd ed.). Pacific Grove, CA: Brooks/Cole.

Howell, K. W., Zucker, S. H., & Morehead, M. K. (1985). *MAST: Multilevel Academic Survey Test.* San Antonio, TX: Psychological Corporation.

Howell, K. W., Fox, S. L., & Morehead, M. K. (1997). *Curriculum-based evaluation for special and remedial education: A handbook for deciding what to teach* (2nd ed.). Pacific Grove, CA: Brooks/Cole.

Hoy, A. W. (2003). Educational psychology. In J. W. Guthrie (Ed.), *Encyclopedia of education* (2nd ed., pp. 676–683). New York: Macmillan Reference.

Hresko, W. (1979). Elicited imitation ability of children from learning disabled and regular classes. *Journal of Learning Disabilities, 12,* 456–461.

Hresko, W. P., Reid, K., & Hammill, D. D. (1999). *Test of Early Language Development* (3rd ed.). Austin, TX: PRO-ED.

Hudson, P. (1997). Using teacher-guided practice to help students with learning disabilities acquire and retain social studies content. *Learning Disability Quarterly, 20,* 23–31.

Huefner, D. S. (2000). *Getting comfortable with special education law: A framework for working with children with disabilities.* Norwood, MA: Christopher-Gordon.

Huey, E. B. (1908). *The psychology and pedagogy of reading: With a brief review of the history of reading and writing and of methods, texts, and hygiene in reading.* New York: Macmillan.

Hughes, C. A. (1996). Memory and test-taking strategies. In D. D. Deshler, E. S. Ellis, & B. K. Lenz (Eds.), *Teaching adolescents with learning disabilities: Strategies and methods* (2nd ed., pp. 209–266). Denver, CO: Love.

Hughes, C. A., & Schumaker, J. B. (1991). Test-taking strategy instruction for adolescents with learning disabilities. *Exceptionality, 2,* 205–221.

Hughes, C. A., Ruhl, K. L., Deshler, D. D., & Schumaker, J. B. (1993). Test-taking strategy instruction for adolescents with emotional and behavioral disorders. *Journal of Emotional and Behavioral Disorders, 1,* 189–198.

Hughes, C. A., Ruhl, K. L., Schumaker, J. B., & Deshler, D. D. (2002). Effects of instruction in an assignment completion strategy on the homework performance of students with learning disabilities in general education classes. *Learning Disabilities Research and Practice, 17,* 1–18.

Hughes, J. N., & Baker, D. B. (1990). *The clinical child interview.* New York: Guilford Press.

Hull, M. A. (1981). Phonics for the teacher of reading: Programmed for self-instruction (3rd ed.). Columbus, OH: Merrill.

Hulme, C. (2002). Phonemes, rimes, and the mechanisms of reading development. *Journal of Experimental Child Psychology, 82,* 58–64.

Hulme, C., & Joshi, R. M. (Eds.). (1998). *Reading and spelling: Development and disorders.* Mahwah, NJ: Erlbaum.

Hulme, C., & Snowling, M. (1992). Phonological deficit in dyslexia: A "sound" reappraisal of the verbal deficit hypothesis. In N. N. Singh & I. I. Beale (Eds.), *Learning disabilities: Nature, theory, and treatment* (pp. 270–301). New York: Springer-Verlag.

Human Genome Project information. (2003). Retrieved May 26, 2003, from http://www.doegenomes.org

Humphreys, P., Kaufmann, W. E., & Galaburda, A. M. (1990). Developmental dyslexia in women: Neuropathological findings in three patients. *Annals of Neurology, 28,* 727–738.

Hunt, J. McV. (1961). *Intelligence and experience.* New York: Ronald Press.

Huntington, D. J. (1994). Instruction in concrete, semi-concrete, and abstract representation as an aid to the solution of relational problems by adolescents with learning disabilities (doctoral dissertation, University of Georgia, 1994). *Dissertation Abstracts International, 56/02,* 512.

Hurford, D. P., Schauf, J. D., Bunce, L., Blaich, T., & Moore, K. (1994). Early identification of children at risk for reading disabilities. *Journal of Learning Disabilities, 27,* 371–382.

Hutchinson, N. L. (1989, April). *The effects of small group instruction in algebra problem solving.* Paper presented at the annual meeting of the American Educational Research Association, San Francisco, CA.

Hutchinson, N. L. (1993). Effects of cognitive strategy instruction on algebra problem solving of adolescents with learning disabilities. *Learning Disability Quarterly, 16,* 34–63.

Hynd, G. W., Hern, K. L., Novey, E. S., Eliopulos, D., Marshall, R., Gonzalez, J. J., & Voeller, K. K. (1993). Attention deficit hyperactivity disorder and asymmetry of the caudate nucleus. *Journal of Child Neurology, 8,* 339–347.

Iano, R. (1986). The study and development of teaching with implications for the advancement of special education. *Remedial and Special Education, 7*(5), 50–61.

Iano, R. P. (2004). The tale of a reluctant empiricist. In D. J. Gallagher (Ed.), *Challenging orthodoxy in special education: Dissenting voices* (pp. 231–249). Denver, CO: Love.

Idol, L., & Croll, V. (1987). Story mapping training as a means of improving reading comprehension. *Learning Disability Quarterly, 10,* 214–230.

Idol-Maestas, L., & Ritter, S. (1985). A follow-up study of resource consulting teachers. *Teacher Education and Special Education, 8,* 121–131.

Individuals with Disabilities Education Act (IDEA) Amendments of 1997. (1997). Public Law 105-17.

Individuals with Disabilities Education Improvement Act (IDEA) of 2003. (2003). Senate Bill 1248.

Invernizzi, M., Meier, J. D., Juel, C., & Swank, L. K. (1997). *PALS II: Phonological awareness and literacy screening.* Charlottesville: University of Virginia.

Iverson, S., & Tunmer, W. E. (1993). Phonological processing skills and the Reading Recovery program. *Journal of Educational Psychology, 85,* 112–126.

Jackson, R., & Harper, K. (2002). *Teacher planning and the universal design for learning environments.* Retrieved March 9, 2003, from http://www.cast.org/ncac/index.cfm?i=1941

Jacobs, A. E., & Hendricks, D. J. (1992). Job accommodations for adults with learning disabilities: Brilliantly disguised opportunities. *Learning Disability Quarterly, 15*(4), 274–285.

Jakubecy, J. J., Mock, D. R., & Kauffman, J. M. (2003). Special education, current trends. In J. W. Guthrie (Ed.), *Encyclopedia of education* (2nd ed., pp. 2284–2290). New York: Macmillan Reference.

Janiga, S. J., & Costenbader, V. (2002). The transition from high school to postsecondary education for students with learning disabilities: A survey of college service coordinators. *Journal of Learning Disabilities, 35,* 462–468, 479.

Jastak, J., & Jastak, S. (1978). *Wide Range Achievement Test.* Wilmington, DE: Guidance Associates.

Jenkins, J. R., & O'Connor, R. E. (2002). Early identification and intervention for young children with reading/learning disabilities. In R. Bradley, L. Danielson, & D. P. Hallahan (Eds.), *Identification of learning disabilities: Research to practice* (pp. 99–149). Mahwah, NJ: Erlbaum.

Jerome, A. C., Frijiki, M., Brinton, B., & James, S. (2002). Self-esteem in children with specific language impairments. *Journal of Speech, Language, and Hearing Research, 45,* 700–714.

Jitendra, A. K., Hoppes, M. K., & Xin, Y. P. (2000). Enhancing main idea comprehension for students with learning problems: The role of a summarization strategy and self-monitoring instruction. *Journal of Special Education, 34,* 127–139.

Jitendra, A., DiPipi, C. M., & Perron-Jones, N. (2002). An exploratory study of schema-based word-problem-solving instruction for middle school students with learning disabilities: An emphasis on conceptual and procedural understanding. *Journal of Special Education, 36,* 23–38.

Johnson, D. J., & Myklebust, H. R. (1967). *Learning disabilities: Educational principles and practices.* New York: Grune & Stratton.

Johnson, D. R., Stodden, R. A., Emanuel, E. J., Luecking, R. L., & Mack, M. (2002). Current challenges facing secondary education and transition services: What research tells us. *Exceptional Children, 68,* 519–531.

Johnson, L., Graham, S., & Harris, K. R. (1997). The effects of goal setting and self-instruction on learning a reading comprehension strategy: A study of students with learning disabilities. *Journal of Learning Disabilities, 30,* 80–91.

Johnston, M. B., Whitman, T. L., & Johnson, M. (1981). Teaching addition and subtraction to mentally retarded children: A self-instructional program. *Applied Research in Mental Retardation, 1,* 141–160.

Johnston, W. F. (1994). How to educate all the students . . . together. *Schools in the Middle, 3,* 3–12.

Jolivette, K., Wehby, J. H., Canale, J., & Massey, N. G. (2001). Effects of choice-making opportunities on the behavior of students with emotional and behavioral disorders. *Behavioral Disorders, 26,* 131–145.

Jones, E. D., Southern, W. T., & Brigham, F. J. (1998). Curriculum-based assessment: Testing what is taught and teaching what is tested. *Intervention in School and Clinic, 33,* 239–249.

Jones, E. D., Wilson, R., & Bhojwani, S. (1997). Mathematics instruction for secondary students with learning disabilities. *Journal of Learning Disabilities, 30,* 151–163.

Jones, J. C., Trap, J., & Cooper, J. O. (1977). Technical report: Students' self-recording of manuscript letter strokes. *Journal of Applied Behavior Analysis, 10,* 509–514.

Jordon, N. C., & Montani, T. O. (1997). Cognitive arithmetic and problem solving: A comparison of children with specific and general mathematics difficulties. *Journal of Learning Disabilities, 30,* 624–634, 684.

Jorgenson, G. W. (2002). Gray, William Scott (1885–1960). In J. W. Guthrie (Ed.), *Encyclopedia of education* (2nd ed., pp. 970–971). New York: Macmillan Reference.

Joshi, R. M., Dahlgren, M., & Boulware-Gooden, R. (2002). Teaching reading in an inner city school through a multi-sensory teaching approach. *Annals of Dyslexia, 52,* 229–242.

Joshi, R. M., Williams, K. A., & Wood, J. R. (1998). Predicting reading comprehension from listening comprehension: Is this the answer to the IQ debate? In C. Hulme & R. M. Joshi (Eds.), *Reading and spelling: Development and disorders* (pp. 319–327). Mahwah, NJ: Erlbaum.

Juel, C. (1988). Learning to read and write: A longitundinal study of fifty-four children from first through fourth grade. *Journal of Educational Psychology, 80,* 437–447.

Juel, C. (1991). Beginning reading. In R. Barr, M. L. Kamil, P. B. Mosenthal, & P. D. Pearson (Eds.), *Handbook of reading research* (Vol. 2, pp. 759–788). New York: Longman.

Juel, C., Griffith, P. L., & Gough, P. B. (1986). Acquisition of literacy: A longitudinal study of children in first and second grade. *Journal of Educational Psychology, 78,* 243–255.

Kagan, J., Rosman, B. L., Day, D., Albert, J., & Phillips, W. (1964). Information processing in the child: Significance of analytic and reflective attitudes. *Psychological Monographs, 78*(1).

Kail, R. V., & Leonard, L. B. (1986). Word-finding abilities in language-impaired children. Rockville, MD: American Speech-Language-Hearing Association.

Kame'enui, E. J. (2002). *Final Report: An Analysis of Reading Assessment Instruments for K–3.* University of Oregon. Retrieved July 27, 2003, from http://idea.uoregon.edu/assessment/final_report.pdf

Kame'enui, E. J., & Carnine, D. W. (1998). *Effective teaching strategies that accommodate diverse leaners.* Upper Saddle River, NJ: Merrill.

Kame'enui, E. J., & Carnine, D. W. (1998). *Effective teaching strategies that accommodate diverse learners.* Upper Saddle River, NJ: Merrill.

Kame'enui, E. J., & Simmons, D. C. (1990). *Designing instructional strategies: The prevention of academic learning problems.* Columbus, OH: Merrill.

Kame'enui, E. J., Carnine, D. W., Dixon, R. C., Simmons, D. C., & Coyne, M. D. (2002). *Effective teaching strategies that accommodate diverse learners* (2nd ed.). Upper Saddle River, NJ: Merrill/Prentice Hall.

Kame'enui, E., Carnine, D., & Maggs, A. (1980). Instructional procedures for teaching reversible passive voice and clause constructions to three mildly handicapped children. *Exceptional Child, 27*(1), 29–41.

Kamhi, A. G., & Hinton, L. N. (2000). Explaining individual differences in spelling ability. *Topics in Language Disorders, 20,* 37–49.

Kamps, D. M., & Tankersley, M. (1996). Prevention of behavioral and conduct disorders: Trends and research issues. *Behavioral Disorders, 22,* 41–48.

Kanbayashi, Y., Nakata, Y., Fujii, K., Kita, M., & Wada, K. (1994). ADHD-related behavior among non-referred children: Parents' ratings of DSM-III-R symptoms. *Child Psychiatry and Human Development, 25*(1), 13–29.

Kaplan, D. E., Gayan, J., Ahn, T.-W., Won, T.-W., Pauls, D. L., Olson, R. K., DeFries, C., Wood, F. B., Pennington, B. F., Page, G. P., Smith, S. D., & Gruen, J. R. (2002). Evidence for linkage and association with reading disability, on 6p21.3–22. *American Journal of Human Genetics, 70,* 1287–1298.

Karegianes, M. L., Pascarella, E. T., & Pflaum, S. W. (1980). The effects of peer editing on the writing proficiency of low-achieving tenth grade students. *Journal of Educational Research, 73,* 203–207.

Kass, C. E. (1966). Psycholinguistic disabilities of children with reading problems. *Exceptional Children, 32,* 533–539.

Katsiyannis, A., & Maag, J. W. (2001). Manifestation determination as a golden fleece. *Exceptional Children, 68,* 85–96.

Katz, L. G. (1994). Perspectives on the quality of early childhood programs. *Phi Delta Kappan, 76,* 200–205.

Kauffman, J. M. (1989). The regular education initiative as Reagan-Bush education policy: A trickle-down theory of education of the hard-to-teach. *Journal of Special Education, 23,* 256–278.

Kauffman, J. M. (1993a). *Characteristics of emotional and behavioral disorders of children and youth* (5th ed.). Columbus, OH: Merrill/Macmillan.

Kauffman, J. M. (1993b). How we might achieve the radical reform of special education. *Exceptional Children, 60,* 6–16.

Kauffman, J. M. (1994). Places of change: Special education's power and identity in an era of educational reform. *Journal of Learning Disabilities, 27,* 610–618.

Kauffman, J. M. (1995). Why we must celebrate a diversity of restrictive environments. *Learning Disabilities Research and Practice, 10*(4), 225–232.

Kauffman, J. M. (1997). *Characteristics of emotional and behavioral disorders of children and youth* (6th ed.). Upper Saddle River, NJ: Prentice-Hall.

Kauffman, J. M. (1997). How we prevent the prevention of emotional and behavioral disorders. *Exceptional Children, 65,* 448–468.

Kauffman, J. M. (1999). How we prevent the prevention of emotional and behavioral disorders. *Exceptional Children, 65,* 448–468.

Kauffman, J. M. (2002). *Education deform: Bright people sometimes say stupid things about education.* Lanham, MD: Scarecrow Education.

Kauffman, J. M. (2003). Appearances, stigma, and prevention. *Remedial and Special Education, 24,* 195–198.

Kauffman, J. M. (2004). How we prevent the prevention of emotional and behavioral difficulties in education. In P. Garner, F. Yuen, P. Clough, & T. Pardeck (Eds.), *Handbook of emotional and behavioral difficulties in education.* London: Sage Publications.

Kauffman, J. M. (2005). *Characteristics of emotional and behavioral disorders of children and youth* (8th ed.). Upper Saddle River, NJ: Prentice Hall.

Kauffman, J. M., & Hallahan, D. P. (1974). The medical model and the science of special education. *Exceptional Children, 41,* 97–102.

Kauffman, J. M., & Hallahan, D. P. (1993). Toward a comprehensive delivery system for special education. In J. I. Goodlad & T. C. Lovitt (Eds.), *Integrating general and special education* (pp. 73–102). Columbus, OH: Merrill/Macmillan.

Kauffman, J. M., & Hallahan, D. P. (1997). A diversity of restrictive environments: Placement as a problem of social ecology. In J. W. Lloyd, E. J. Kame'enui, & D. Chard (Eds.), *Issues in educating students with disabilities* (pp. 325–342). Hillsdale, NJ: Erlbaum.

Kauffman, J. M., & Landrum, T. J. (in press). Educational service interventions and reforms. In J. W. Jacobson & J. A. Mulick (Eds.), *Handbook of mental retardation and developmental disabilities.* New York: Kluwer.

Kauffman, J. M., & Lloyd, J. W. (1995). A sense of place: The importance of placement issues in contemporary special education. In J. M. Kauffman, J. W. Lloyd, D. P. Hallahan, & T. A. Astuto (Eds.), *Issues in educational placement: Students with emotional and behavioral disorders* (pp. 3–19). Hillsdale, NJ: Erlbaum.

Kauffman, J. M., Bantz, J., & McCullough, J. (2002). Separate and better: A special public school class for students with emotional and behavioral disorders. *Exceptionality, 10,* 149–170.

Kauffman, J. M., Hallahan, D. P., Haas, K., Brame, T., & Boren, R. (1978). Imitating children's errors to improve their spelling performance. *Journal of Learning Disabilities, 11,* 217–222.

Kauffman, J. M., Lloyd, J. W., Astuto, T. A., & Hallahan, D. P. (1995). Toward a sense of place for special education in the 21st century. In J. M. Kauffman, J. W. Lloyd, D. P. Hallahan, & T. A. Astuto (Eds.), *Issues in educational placement: Students with emotional and behavioral disorders* (pp. 379–385). Hillsdale, NJ: Erlbaum.

Kauffman, J. M., Mostert, M. P., Trent, S. C., & Hallahan, D. P. (1998). *Managing classroom behavior: A reflective case-based approach.* Boston: Allyn & Bacon.

Kauffman, J. M., Mostert, M. P., Trent, S. C., & Hallahan, D. P. (2002). *Managing classroom behavior: A reflective case-based approach* (3rd ed.).Boston: Allyn & Bacon.

Kavale, K. (1981). The relationship between auditory perceptual skills and reading ability: A meta-analysis. *Journal of Learning Disabilities, 14,* 539–546.

Kavale, K. A. (1980). The reasoning abilities of normal and learning disabled readers on measures of reading comprehension. *Learning Disability Quarterly, 3* (4), 34–45.

Kavale, K. A. (1988). The long-term consequences of learning disabilities. In M. C. Wang, M. C. Reynolds, & H. J. Walberg (Eds.), *Handbook of special education: Research and practice:* Vol. 2. *Mildly handicapped conditions.* New York: Pergamon.

Kavale, K. A. (2002). Discrepancy models in the identification of learning disability. In R. Bradley, L. Danielson, & D. P. Hallahan (Eds.), *Identification of learning disabilities: Research to practice* (pp. 369–426). Mahwah, NJ: Erlbaum.

Kavale, K. A., & Forness, S. R. (1983). Hyperactivity and diet treatment: A meta-analysis of the Feingold hypothesis. *Journal of Learning Disabilities, 16,* 324–330.

Kavale, K. A., & Forness, S. R. (1985). *The science of learning disabilities.* San Diego, CA: College Hill Press.

Kavale, K. A., & Forness, S. R. (1987a). History, politics, and the general education initiative: Sleeter's reinterpretation of learning disabilities as a case study. *Remedial and Special Education, 8*(5), 6–12.

Kavale, K. A., & Forness, S. R. (1987b). Substance over style: A quantitative synthesis assessing the efficacy of modality testing and teaching. *Exceptional Children, 54,* 228–234.

Kavale, K. A., & Forness, S. R. (1992). History, definition, and diagnosis. In N. N. Singh & I. L. Beale (Eds.), *Learning disabilities: Nature, theory, and treatment* (pp. 3–41). New York: Springer-Verlag.

Kavale, K. A., & Forness, S. R. (1995a). *The nature of learning disabilities.* Hillsdale, NJ: Erlbaum.

Kavale, K. A., & Forness, S. R. (1995b). Social skill deficits and training: A meta-analysis of the research in learning disabilities. In T. E. Scruggs & M. A. Mastropieri (Eds.), *Advances in learning and behavioral disabilities* (pp. 119–160). Greenwich, CT: JAI Press.

Kavale, K. A., & Forness, S. R. (1997). Defining learning disabilities: Consonance and dissonance. In J. W. Lloyd, E. J. Kame'enui, & D. Chard (Eds.), *Issues in educating students with disabilities* (pp. 3–25). Mahwah, NJ: Erlbaum.

Kavale, K. A., & Forness, S. R. (2000). What definitions of learning disability do and don't say: A critical analysis. *Journal of Learning Disabilities, 33,* 239–256.

Kavale, K. A., Fuchs, D., & Scruggs, T. E. (1994). Setting the record straight on learning disability and low achievement: Implications for policymaking. *Learning Disabilities Research and Practice, 9,* 70–77.

Kelley, M. L. (1990). *School-home notes: Promoting children's classroom success.* New York: Guilford Press.

Kelley, M. L., & McCain, A. P. (1995). Promoting academic performance in inattentive children. *Behavior Modification, 19,* 357–375.

Kelly, B. F., Gersten, R., & Carnine, D. (1990). Student error patterns as a function of curriculum design: Teaching fractions to remedial high school students and high school students with learning disabilities. *Journal of Learning Disabilities, 23,* 23–29.

Kelly, B., Carnine, D., Gersten, R., & Grossen, B. (1986). The effectiveness of videodisc instruction in teaching fractions to learning-disabled and remedial high school students. *Journal of Special Education Technology, 8*(2), 5–17.

Keogh, B. K. (1987). Learning disabilities: In defense of a construct. *Learning Disabilities Research, 3*(1), 4–9.

Keogh, B. K. (2003). *Temperament in the classroom: Understanding individual differences.* Baltimore: Brookes.

Keogh, B. K., & Becker, L. D. (1973). Early detection of learning problems: Questions, cautions, and guidelines. *Exceptional Children, 40,* 5–11.

Keogh, B. K., & Sears, S. (1991). Learning disabilities from a developmental perspective: Early identification and prediction. In B. Y. L. Wong (Ed.), *Learning about learning disabilities* (pp. 485–503). New York: Academic Press.

Kern, L., Bambara, L., & Fogt, J. (2002). Class-wide curricular modification to improve the behavior of students with emotional or behavioral disorders. *Behavioral Disorders, 27,* 317–326.

Kerr, M. M., & Lambert, D. L. (1982). Behavior modification of children's written language. In M. Hersen, R. M. Eisler, & P. M. Miller (Eds.), *Progress in behavior modification* (Vol. 13, pp. 79–108). New York: Academic Press.

Kerr, M. M., & Nelson, C. M. (1998). *Strategies for managing behavior problems in the classroom* (3rd ed.). Upper Saddle River, NJ: Prentice-Hall.

Kerr, M. M., & Nelson, C. M. (2002). *Strategies for addressing behavior problems in the classroom* (4th ed.). Upper Saddle River, NJ: Prentice Hall.

King-Sears, M. E., & Carpenter, S. L. (1997). *Innovations: Teaching self-management to elementary students with developmental disabilities.* Washington, DC: American Association on Mental Retardation.

Kirk, S. A. & Bateman, B. (1962). Diagnosis and remediation of learning disabilities. *Exceptional Children, 29,* 73–78.

Kirk, S. A. (1962). *Educating exceptional children.* Boston: Houghton Mifflin.

Kirk, S. A. (1963). Behavioral diagnosis and remediation of learning disabilities. In *Proceedings of the conference on exploration into problems of the perceptually handicapped child.* Chicago: Perceptually Handicapped Children.

Kirk, S. A. (1969). Illinois Test of Psycholinguistic Abilities: Its origin and implications. In J. Hellmuth (Ed.), *Learning disorders* (Vol. 3, pp. 395–427). Seattle, WA: Special Child Publications.

Kirk, S. A. (1975). Behavioral diagnosis and remediation of learning disabilities. In S. A. Kirk & J. M. McCarthy (Eds.), *Learning disabilities: Selected ACLD papers* (pp. 7–10). Boston: Houghton Mifflin.

Kirk, S. A. (1976). S. A. Kirk. In D. P. Hallahan & J. M. Kauffman (Eds.), *Teaching children with learning disabilities: Personal perspectives* (pp. 238–269). Columbus, OH: Merrill.

Kirk, S. A., & Elkins, J. (1975). Characteristics of children enrolled in the child service demonstration centers. *Journal of Learning Disabilities, 8,* 630–637.

Kirk, S. A., Kirk, W. E., & Minskoff, E. H. (1985). *Phonic remedial reading lessons.* Novato, CA: Academic Therapy Publishing.

Kirk, S. A., McCarthy, J., & Kirk, W. E. (1968). *Illinois Test of Psycholinguistic Abilities.* Urbana: University of Illinois Press.

Kitz, W. R., & Thorpe, H. W. (1995). A comparison of the effectiveness of videodisk and traditional algebra instruction for college-age students with learning disabilities. *Remedial and Special Education, 16,* 295–306.

Kline, C. L., & Kline, C. L. (1975). Follow-up study of 216 dyslexic children. *Bulletin of the Orton Society, 25,* 127–144.

Klingner, J. K., & Vaughn, S. (1998). Reciprocal teaching of reading comprehension strategies for students with learning disabilities who use English as a second language. *Elementary School Journal, 96,* 275–293.

Knapp, T. R. (2003). *Review of Learning Style Inventory.* Retrieved March 30, 2003, from Mental Measurements Yearbook at http:// spweb.silverplatter.com/c133231?sp.form.first.p=src hmain.htm&sp.dbid.p=S(YB)

Kosiewicz, M. M., Hallahan, D. P., Lloyd, J., & Graves, A. W. (1982). Effects of self-instruction and self-correction procedures on handwriting performance. *Learning Disability Quarterly, 5,* 71–78.

Kotsonis, M. E., & Patterson, C. J. (1980). Comprehension-monitoring skills in learning disabled children. *Developmental Psychology, 16,* 541–542.

Kratochwill, T. R., & McGivern, J. F. (1996). Clinical diagnosis, behavioral assessment, and functional analysis: Examining the connection between assessment and intervention. *School Psychology Review, 25,* 342–355.

Kuhn, M., & Stahl, S. (2003). Fluency: A review of developmental and remedial practices. *Journal of Educational Psychology, 95,* 3–21.

Kulieke, M., & Jones, B. (1993). Cognitive instructional techniques in relation to whole language approaches. *Remedial and Special Education, 14,* 26–29.

La Paz, S., & Graham, S. (1997). Effects of dictations and advanced planning instruction on the composing of students with learning problems. *Journal of Educational Psychology, 89*(2), 203–222.

LaBerge, D., & Samuels, S. J. (1973). Toward a theory of automatic information processing in reading. *Cognitive Psychology, 6,* 293–233.

Lahey, B. B., Busemeyer, M. K., O'Hara, C., & Beggs, V. E. (1977). Treatment of severe perceptual-motor disorders in children diagnosed as learning disabled. *Behavior Modification, 1,* 123–140.

Lamon, M. (2003). Learning theory: Constructivist approach. In J. W. Guthrie (Ed.), *Encyclopedia of education* (2nd ed., pp. 1463–1466). New York: Macmillan Reference.

Landerl, K., Wimmer, H., & Frith, U. (1997). The impact of orthographic consistency on dyslexia: A German-English comparison. *Cognition, 63,* 315–334.

Lane, H. B., & Pullen, P. C. (2004). *Phonological awareness assessment and instruction: A sound beginning.* Boston: Allyn & Bacon.

Lankford, F. C., Jr. (1972). Some computational strategies of seventh grade pupils (Final Report of Project No. 2-C 013, U.S. Department of Health, Education, and Welfare Grant No. OEG-3-72-0035). Charlottesville: Center for Advanced Studies, University of Virginia.

Lardieri, L. A., Blacher, J., & Swanson, H. L. (2000). Sibling relationships and parent stress in families of children with and without learning disabilities. *Learning Disability Quarterly, 23,* 105–116.

Larsen, S., & Hammill, D. D. (1994). *Test of Written Spelling—3.* Austin, TX: PRO-ED.

Larson, K. A., & Gerber, M. M. (1992). Metacognition. In N. N. Singh & I. L. Beale (Eds.), *Learning disabilities: Nature, theory, and treatment* (pp. 126–169). New York: Springer-Verlag.

Laughon, P. (1990). The dynamic assessment of intelligence: A review of three approaches. *School Psychology Review, 19,* 459–470.

Laughton, J., & Morris, N. T. (1989). Story grammar knowledge of learning disabled students. *Learning Disabilities Research, 4,* 87–95.

Lawrence, V., Houghton, S., Tannock, R., Douglas, G., Durkin, K., & Whiting, K. (2002). ADHD outside the laboratory: Boys' executive function performance on tasks in video-game play and on a visit to the zoo. *Journal of Abnormal Child Psychology, 30,* 447–462.

Le Mare, L., & de la Ronde, M. (2000). Links among social status, service delivery mode, and service delivery preference in LD, low-achieving, and normally achieving elementary-aged children. *Learning Disability Quarterly, 23,* 52–62.

Leach, J. M., Scarborough, H. S., & Rescorla, L. (2003). Late-emerging reading disabilities. *Journal of Educational Psychology, 95,* 211–224.

Learning Disabilities Council. (2002). *Understanding learning disabilities: A parent guide and workbook* (3rd ed.). Richmond, VA: Learning Disabilities Council.

Learning Disability Study Group. (1997). *Assessment and decision making: Technical assistance guide for learning disability.* Des Moines, IA: State of Iowa Department of Education.

Leete-Guy, L., & Schor, J. B. (1992). *The great American time squeeze: Trends in work and leisure, 1969–1989.* (Briefing paper for the Economic Policy Institute, Washington, DC.)

Leinhardt, G., Seewald, A., & Zigmond, N. (1982). Sex and race differences in learning disabilities classrooms. *Journal of Educational Psychology, 74,* 835–845.

Lennox, C., & Siegel, L. S. (1993). Visual and phonological spelling errors in subtypes of children with learning disabilities. *Applied Psycholinguistics, 14,* 473–488.

Lennox, C., & Siegel, L. S. (1998). Phonological and orthographic processes in good and poor spellers. In C. Hulme & R. M. Joshi (Eds.), *Reading and spelling: Development and disorders* (pp. 395–404). Mahwah, NJ: Erlbaum.

Lenz, B. K. (2000). *The content enhancement series.* Lawrence: University of Kansas, Center for Research on Learning.

Lenz, B. K., Bulgren, J. A., Schumaker, J. B., Deshler, D. D., & Boudah, D. J. (1994). *The content enhancement series: The unit organizer routine.* Lawrence, KS: Edge Enterprises.

Lerman, D. C., & Vorndran, C. M. (2002). On the status of knowledge for using punishment: Implications for treating behavior disorders. *Journal of Applied Behavior Analysis, 35,* 431–464.

Leviton, A., Bellinger, D., Allred, E. N., Rabinowitz, M., Needleman, H., & Schoenbaum, S. (1993). Pre- and post-natal low-level lead exposure and children's dysfunction in school. *Environmental Research, 60,* 30–43.

Lewis, B. A. (1992). Pedigree analysis of children with phonology disorders. *Journal of Learning Disabilities, 25*(9), 586–597.

Lewis, B. A., & Thompson, L. A. (1992). A study of developmental speech and language disorders in twins. *Journal of Speech and Hearing Research, 35,* 1086–1094.

Lewis, C., Hitch, G. J., & Walker, P. (1994). The prevalence of specific arithmetic difficulties and specific reading difficulties in 9- to 10-year-old boys and girls. *Journal of Child Psychology and Psychiatry and Allied Disciplines, 35,* 283–292.

Lewis, R. B., Ashton, T. M., Haapa, B., Kieley, C. L., & Fielden, C. (1999). Improving the writing skills of students with learning disabilities: Are word processors with spelling and grammar checkers useful? *Learning Disabilities, 9,* 87–98.

Liberman, I. Y. (1970). Segmentation of the spoken word and reading acquisition. *Bulletin of the Orton Society, 23,* 65–77.

Liberman, I. Y. (1971). Basic research in speech and lateralization of language: Some implications for reading disability. *Bulletin of the Orton Society, 21,* 71–87.

Liberman, I. Y., & Shankweiler, D. (1991). Phonology and beginning reading: A tutorial. In L. Rieben & C. A. Perfetti (Eds.), *Learning to read: Basic research and its implications* (pp. 3–17). Hillsdale, NJ: Erlbaum.

Liberman, I. Y., Shankweiler, D., Fischer, F. W., & Carter, B. (1974). Explicit syllable and phoneme segmentation in the young child. *Journal of Experimental Child Psychology, 18,* 201–212.

Lidz, C., & Elliott, J. G. (2000). *Dynamic assessment: Prevailing models and applications.* New York: Elsevier Science.

Linan-Thompson, S., & Jean, R. E. (1997). Completing the parent participation puzzle: Accepting diversity. *Teaching Exceptional Children, 30*(2), 46–50.

Lloyd, J. (1980). Academic instruction and cognitive-behavior modification: The need for attack strategy training. *Exceptional Education Quarterly, 1*(1), 53–63.

Lloyd, J. W. (2002). There's more to identifying learning disability than discrepancy. In R. Bradley, L. Danielson, & D. P. Hallahan (Eds.), *Identification of learning disabilities: Research to practice* (pp. 427–435). Mahwah, NJ: Lawrence Erlbaum.

Lloyd, J. W., & Blanford, B. J. (1991). Assessment for instructional planning. In H. L. Swanson (Ed.), *Handbook on the assessment of learning disabilities: Theory, research, and practice* (pp. 45–58). Boston: Little, Brown.

Lloyd, J. W., & deBettencourt, L. U. (1982). *Academic strategy training: A manual for teachers.* Charlottesville: Learning Disabilities Research Institute, University of Virginia.

Lloyd, J. W., & Keller, C. E. (1989). Effective mathematics instruction. *Focus on Exceptional Children, 21* (7), 1–10.

Lloyd, J. W., Cawley, P., Kohler, F., & Strain, P. S. (1988). Redefining the applied research agenda: Cooperative learning, prereferral, teacher consultation, and peer-mediated interventions. *Journal of Learning Disabilites, 21,* 43–52.

Lloyd, J. W., Forness, S. R., & Kavale, K. A. (1998). Some methods are more effective than others. *Intervention in School and Clinic, 33,* 195–200.

Lloyd, J. W., Kauffman, J. M., Landrum, T. J., & Roe, D. L. (1991). Why do teachers refer pupils for special education? An analysis of referral records. *Exceptionality, 2,* 115–126.

Lloyd, J., Epstein, M. H., & Cullinan, D. (1981). Direct teaching for learning disabilities. In J. Gottlieb & S. S. Strichart (Eds.), *Developmental theory and research in learning disabilities* (pp. 278–309). Baltimore: University Park Press.

Lloyd, J., Hallahan, D. P., & Kauffman, J. M. (1980). Learning disabilities: A review of selected topics. In L. Mann & D. A. Sabatino (Eds.), *Fourth review of special education* (pp. 35–60). New York: Grune & Stratton.

Lloyd, J., Sabatino, D., Miller, T., & Miller, S. (1977). Proposed federal guidelines: Some open questions. *Journal of Learning Disabilities, 11,* 65–67.

Lloyd, J., Saltzman, N.J., & Kauffman, J. M. (1981). Predictable generalization in academic learning as a result of preskills and strategy training. *Learning Disability Quarterly, 4,* 203–216.

Lo, Y., Loe, S. A., & Cartledge, G. (2002). The effects of social skills instruction on the social behaviors of students at risk for emotional or behavioral disorders. *Behavioral Disorders, 27,* 371–385.

Lock, R. H., & Layton, C. A. (2001). Succeeding in postsecondary ed through self-advocacy. *Teaching Exceptional Children, 34*(2), 66–71.

Lomax, R. G. (1983). Applying structural modeling to some component processes of reading comprehension development. *Journal of Experimental Education, 52,* 33–40.

Lopez-Reyna, N. A., & Bay, M. (1997). Enriching assessment using varied assessments for diverse learners. *Teaching Exceptional Children, 29*(4), 33–37.

Lopez-Reyna, N. A., Bay, M., & Patrikakou, E. N. (1996). Use of assessment procedures: Learning disabilities teachers' perspectives. *Diagnostique, 21*(2), 35–49.

Lorsbach, T. C., & Frymier, J. (1992). A comparison of learning disabled and nondisabled students on five at-risk factors. *Learning Disabilities Research and Practice, 7,* 137–141.

Lou, H. C., Henriksen, L., & Bruhn, P. (1984). Focal cerebral hypoperfusion in children with dysphasia and/or attention deficit disorder. *Archives of Neurology, 41,* 825–829.

Lou, H. C., Henriksen, L., Bruhn, P., Borner, H., & Nielsen, J. B. (1989). Striatal dysfunction in attention deficit and hyperkinetic disorder. *Archives of Neurology, 46,* 48–52.

Lovett, M. W. (1987). A developmental approach to reading disability: Accuracy and speed criteria of normal and deficient reading skill. *Child Development, 58,* 234–260.

Lovett, M. W., Barron, R. W., & Benson, N.J. (2003). Effective remediation of word identification and decoding difficulties in school-age children with reading disabilities. In H. L. Swanson, K. R. Harris, & S. Graham (Eds.), *Handbook of learning disabilities* (pp. 273–292). New York: Guilford Press.

Lovett, M. W., Lacerenza, L., Borden, S. L., Frijters, J. C., Steinbach, K. A., & De Palma, M. (2000). Components of effective remediation for developmental reading disabilities: Combining phonological and strategy-based instruction to improve outcomes. *Journal of Educational Psychology, 92,* 263–283.

Lovitt, T. C. (1967). Assessment of children with learning disabilities. *Exceptional Children, 34,* 233–239.

Lovitt, T. C. (1975). Applied behavior analysis and learning disabilities: Part 1. Characteristics of ABA, general recommendations, and methodological limitations. *Journal of Learning Disabilities, 8,* 432–443.

Lovitt, T. C. (1978). New applications and new techniques in behavior modification. *Journal of Special Education, 12,* 89–93.

Lovitt, T. C. (1991). Behavioral assessment of learning disabilities. In H. L. Swanson (Ed.), *Handbook for the assessment of* learning disabilities: Theory, research, and practice (pp. 95–119). Austin, TX: PRO-ED.

Lovitt, T. C. (1995). *Tactics for teaching*. New York: Merrill.

Lovitt, T. C., & Fantasia, K. (1980). Two approaches to reading program evaluation: A standardized test and direct assessment. *Learning Disability Quarterly, 3*(4), 77–87.

Lovitt, T. C., & Hansen, C. L. (1976a). Round one: Placing the child in the right reader. *Journal of Learning Disabilities, 9,* 347–353.

Lovitt, T. C., & Hansen. C. L. (1976b). The use of contingent skipping and drilling to improve oral reading and comprehension. *Journal of Learning Disabilities, 9,* 481–487.

Lovitt, T. C., & Smith, D. D. (1974). Using withdrawal of positive reinforcement to alter subtraction performance. *Exceptional Children, 40,* 357–358.

Lubke, M. M., Rogers, B., & Evans, K. T. (1989). Teaching fractions with videodiscs. *Teaching Exceptional Children, 21,* 55–56.

Luecking, R. G., Tilson, G., & Willner, M. (1991). *Corporate employee assistance for workers with learning disabilities.* Rockville, MD: TransCen.

Lundberg, I. (2002). Second language learning and reading with the additional load of dyslexia. *Annals of Dyslexia, 52,* 165–187.

Lundberg, I., Frost, J., & Peterson, O. R. (1988). Effects of an extensive program for stimulating phonological awareness in preschool children. *Reading Research Quarterly, 23,* 263–285.

Luria, A. (1961). *The role of speech in the regulation of normal and abnormal behaviors.* New York: Liveright.

Lyon, G. R. (1995). Research initiatives in learning disabilities: Contributions from scientists supported by the National Institute of Child Health and Human Development. *Journal of Child Neurology, 10* (Suppl. 1), 120–126.

Lyon, G. R. (1997, December 28). *Testimony of G. Reid Lyon, Ph.D. on children's literacy.* (Online). Available at: http://www.apa.org/ppo/lyon.html.

Lyon, G. R. (1999). *The NICHD research program in reading development, reading disorders, and reading instruction.* Retrieved February 7, 2003, from http://www.ncld.org/research/keys99_nichd.cfm

Lyon, G. R., Fletcher, J. M., Shaywitz, S. E., Shaywitz, B. A., Torgesen, J. K., Wood, F. B., Schulte, A., & Olson, R. (2001). *Rethinking learning disabilities.* Hudson Institute.

Lyon, R. (2002, November). The current status and impact of U.S. reading research. Keynote address to the National Association of University Centers for Excellence in Developmental Disabilities, Bethesda, MD.

MacArthur, C. A. (1994). Peers + word processing + strategies = a powerful combination for revising student writing. *Teaching Exceptional Children, 27,* 24–29.

MacArthur, C. A. (2000). New tools for writing: Assistive technology for students with writing difficulties. *Topics in Language Disorders, 20,* 85–100.

MacArthur, C. A., Ferretti, R. P., Okolo, C. M., & Cavalier, A. R. (2001). Technology applications for students with literacy problems: A critical review. *Elementary School Journal, 101,* 273–301.

Maccini, P., & Hughes, C. A. (2000). Effects of a problem-solving strategy on the introductory algebra performance of secondary school students with learning disabilities. *Learning Disabilities Research and Practice, 15,* 10–21.

Maccini, P., McNaughton, D., & Ruhl, K. L. (1999). Algebra instruction for students with learning disabilities: Implications from a research review. *Learning Disability Quarterly, 22,* 113–126.

MacMillan, D. L., & Reschly, D. J. (1998). Overrepresentation of minority students: The case for greater specificity or reconsideration of variables examined. *Journal of Special Education, 32,* 15–24.

MacMillan, D. L., & Siperstein, G. N. (2002). Learning disabilities as operationally defined by schools. In R. Bradley, L. Danielson, & D. P. Hallahan (Eds.), *Identification of learning disabilities: Research to practice* (pp. 287–333). Mahwah, NJ: Erlbaum.

MacMillan, D. L., & Speece, D. L. (1999). Utility of current diagnostic categories for research and practice. In R. Gallimore, L. P. Bernheimer, D. L. MacMillan, D. L. Speece, & S. Vaughn (Eds.), *Developmental perspectives on children with high-incidence disabilities* (pp. 111–133). Mahwah, NJ: Erlbaum.

MacMillan, D. L., Gresham, F. M., Lopez, M. F., & Bocian, K. M. (1996). Comparison of students nominated for prereferral interventions by ethnicity and gender. *Journal of Special Education, 30,* 133–151.

MacMillan, D. L., Gresham, F. M., Siperstein, G. N., & Bocian, K. M. (1996). The labyrinth of IDEA: School decisions on referred students with subaverage general intelligence. *American Journal on Mental Retardation, 101,* 161–174.

MacMillan, D. L., Siperstein, G. N., & Gresham, F. M. (1996). A challenge to the viability of mild mental retardation as a diagnostic category. *Exceptional Children, 62,* 356–371.

Maggs, A., & Maggs, R. (1979). Review of direct instruction research in Australia. *Journal of Special Education Technology, 2* (3), 26–34.

Maggs, A., McMillan, K., Patching, W., & Hawke, H. (1981). Accelerating spelling skills using morphographs. *Educational Psychology, 1,* 49–56.

Maheady, L. Harper, G. F., & Mallette, B. (2003). A focus on class wide peer tutoring: Go for it. *Current Practice Alerts, 8.* Available online at http://www.teachingld.org/ld_resources/alerts/

Mahoney, G., & Robenalt, K. (1986). A comparison of conversational patterns between mothers and their Down syndrome and normal infants. *Journal of the Division for Early Childhood, 10,* 172–180.

Mahoney, M. J. (1974). *Cognition and behavior modification.* Cambridge, MA: Ballinger.

Malian, I., & Nevin, A. (2002). A review of self-determination literature: Implications for practitioners. *Remedial and Special Education, 23,* 68–74.

Maloney, K. B., & Hopkins, B. L. (1973). The modification of sentence structure and its relationship to subjective judgment of creativity in writing. *Journal of Applied Behavior Analysis, 6,* 425–433.

Maloney, K. B., Jacobson, C. R., & Hopkins, B. L. (1975). An analysis of the effects of lectures, requests, teacher praise, and free time on the creative writing behaviors of third-grade children. In E. Ramp & G. Semb (Eds.), *Behavior analysis: Areas of research and application* (pp. 244–260). Englewood Cliffs, NJ: Prentice-Hall.

Mann, L. (1971). Psychometric phrenology and the new faculty psychology. *Journal of Special Education, 5,* 3–14.

Mann, L. (1979). *On the trail of process: A historical perspective on cognitive processes and their training.* New York: Grune & Stratton.

Mann, L., & Phillips, W. (1967). Fractional practices in special education. *Journal of Special Education, 5,* 3–14.

Manos, M. J., Short, E. J., & Findling, R. L. (1999). Differential effectiveness of methylphenidate and Adderall in school-age youths with attention-deficit/hyperactivity disorder. *Journal of the American Academy of Child and Adolescent Psychiatry, 38,* 813–819.

Manset, G., & Semmel, M. I. (1997). Are inclusive programs for students with mild disabilities effective? A comparative review of model programs. *Journal of Special Education, 31,* 155–180.

Marchand-Martella, N. E., Slocum, T. A., & Martella, R. C. (2004). *Introduction to Direct Instruction.* Boston: Allyn & Bacon.

Margalit, M., & Almougy, K. (1991). Classroom behavior and family climate in students with learning disabilities and hyperactive behavior. *Journal of Learning Disabilities, 24,* 406–412.

Margalit, M., & Al-Yagon, M. (2002). The loneliness experience of children with learning disabilities. In B. Y. L. Wong & M. Donahue (Eds.), *The social dimensions of learning disabilities: Essays in honor of Tanis Bryan* (pp. 53–75). Mahwah, NJ: Erlbaum.

Margalit, M., Raviv, A., & Ankonina, D. B. (1992). Coping and coherence among parents with disabled children. *Journal of Clinical Child Psychology, 21,* 202–209.

Markwardt, F. C. (1989). *Peabody Individual Achievement Test—Revised.* Circle Pines, MN: American Guidance Service.

Marston, D. (1989). Curriculum-based measurement: What is it and why do it? In M. R. Shinn (Ed.), *Curriculum-based measurement: Assessing special children* (pp.18–78). New York: Guilford Press.

Marston, D. (1996). A comparison of inclusion only, pull-out only, and combined service models for students with mild disabilities. *Journal of Special Education, 30,* 121–132.

Marston, D. (2002). A functional and intervention-based assessment approach to establishing discrepancy for students with learning disabilities. In R. Bradley, L. Danielsson, & D. P. Hallahan (Eds.), *Identification of learning disabilities: Research to practice* (pp. 437–447). Mahwah, NJ: Erlbaum.

Martin, E. W., Martin, R., & Terman, D. (1996). The legislative and litigation history of special education. *Future of Children, 6,* 25–39.

Martin, K. F., & Manno, C. (1995). Use of a check-off system to improve story compositions by middle school students. *Journal of Learning Disabilities, 28,* 139–149.

Masterson, J. J., & Apel, K. (2000). Spelling assessment: Charting a path to optimal intervention. *Topics in Language Disorders, 20,* 50–65.

Mastropieri, M. A., & Scruggs, T. E. (1991). *Teaching students ways to remember: Strategies for learning mnemonically.* Cambridge, MA: Brookline Books.

Mastropieri, M. A., & Scruggs, T. E. (1998). Enhancing school success with mnemonic strategies. *Intervention in School and Clinic, 33,* 201–208.

Mastropieri, M. A., & Scruggs, T. E. (2000). *The inclusive classroom: Strategies for effective instruction.* Upper Saddle River, NJ: Merrill.

Mastropieri, M. A., & Scruggs, T. E. (2002a). *Effective instruction for special education* (3rd ed.). Austin, TX: PRO-ED.

Mastropieri, M. A., & Scruggs, T. E. (2002b). *Mnemonic instruction: A teaching tutorial.* Retrieved February 7, 2003, from http://www.teachingld.org/members_only/teaching_tutorials/default.cfm

Mastropieri, M. A., Scruggs, T. E., & Graetz, J. E. (2003). Reading comprehension instruction for secondary students: Challenges for struggling students and teachers. *Learning Disability Quarterly, 226,* 103–116.

Mastropieri, M. A., Scruggs, T. E., & Shiah, S. (1991). Mathematics instruction for learning disabled students: A review of research. *Learning Disabilities Research and Practice, 6,* 89–98.

Mastropieri, M. A., Scruggs, T. E., & Whedon, C. (1997). Using mnemonic strategies to teach information about U.S. presidents: A classroom-based investigation. *Learning Disability Quarterly, 20,* 13–21.

Mastropieri, M. A., Scruggs, T. E., Spencer, V., & Fontana, J. (2003). Promoting success in high school world history: Peer tutoring versus guided notes. *Learning Disabilities Research and Practice, 18,* 52–65.

Mastropieri, M. A., Scruggs, T., Mohler, L., Beranek, M., Spencer, V., Boon, R. T., & Talbott, E. (2001). Can middle school students with serious reading difficulties help each other and learn anything? *Learning Disabilities Research and Practice, 16,* 21–29.

Mastropieri, M. A., Sweda, J., & Scruggs, T. E. (2000). Putting mnemonic strategies to work in an inclusive classroom. *Learning Disabilities Research and Practice, 15,* 69–74.

Mather, N., & Goldstein, S. (1999). *Learning disabilities and challenging behaviors: A guide to intervention and classroom management.* Baltimore: Brookes.

Mather, N., & Roberts, R. (1994). Learning disabilities: A field in danger of extinction? *Learning Disabilities Research and Practice, 9*(1), 49–58.

Mathes, M. Y., & Bender, W. N. (1997). The effects of self-monitoring on children with attention-deficit/hyperactivity disorder. *Remedial and Special Education, 18,* 121–128.

Mathes, P. G., & Fuchs, L. S. (1993). Peer-mediated reading instruction in special education resource rooms. *Learning Disabilities Research and Practice, 8,* 233–243.

Mathes, P. G., Fuchs, D., Fuchs, L. S., Henley, A. M., & Sanders, A. (1994). Increasing strategic reading practice with Peabody Classwide Peer Tutoring. *Learning Disabilities Research and Practice, 9,* 44–48.

Mathes, P. G., Torgesen, J. K, & Allor, J. H. (2001). The effects of peer-assisted literacy strategies for first-grade readers with and without additional computer-assisted instruction in phonological awareness. *American Educational Research Journal, 38,* 371–410.

Matson, J., Esveldt-Dawson, K., & Kazdin, A. E. (1982). Treatment of spelling deficits in mentally retarded children. *Mental Retardation, 20,* 76–81.

Mazurek, K., & Winzer, M. A. (Eds.). (1994). *Comparative studies in special education.* Washington, DC: Gallaudet University Press.

McArthur, G. M., & Hogben, J. H. (2001). Auditory backward recognition masking in children with specific language impairments and children with specific reading disabilities. *Journal of the Acoustical Society of America, 109,* 1092–1100.

McCain, A. P., & Kelley, M. L. (1994). Improving classroom performance in underachieving adolescents: The additive effects of response cost to a school-home note program. *Child and Family Behavior Therapy, 16,* 27–41.

McConnell, S. R. (2000). Assessment in early intervention and early childhood special education: Building on the past to project into our future. *Topics in Early Childhood Special Education, 20,* 43–48.

McDonnell, L. M., McLaughlin, M. J., & Morison, P. (Eds.). (1997). *Educating one and all: Students with disabilities and standards-based reform.* Washington, DC: National Academy Press.

McGregor, K. K., Newman, R. M., Reilly, R. M., & Capone, N. M. (2002). Semantic representations and naming in children with specific language impairments. *Journal of Speech, Language, and Hearing Research, 45,* 998–1014.

McInerney, D. M. (1999). What should teachers do to get children to want to read and write? Motivation for literacy acquisition. In A. J. Watson & L. R. Giorcelli (Eds.), *Accepting the literacy challenge* (pp. 95–115). Sydney, Australia: Scholastic.

McKinney, J. D. (1983). Contributions of the institutes for research on learning disabilities. *Exceptional Education Quarterly, 4*(1), 129–144.

McLaughlin, T. F., Reiter, S. M., Mabee, W. S., & Byram, B. J. (1991). An analysis and replication of the Add-A-Word Spelling Program with mildly handicapped middle school students. *Journal of Behavioral Education, 1,* 413–426.

McMaster, K., Fuchs, D., Fuchs, L. S., & Copton, D. L. (2002). Monitoring the academic progress of children who are unresponsive to generally effective early reading intervention. *Assessment for Effective Intervention, 27*(4), 23–34.

McNamara, K. M., & Hollinger, C. L. (1997). Intervention-based assessment: Rates of evaluation and eligibility for specific learning disability classification. *Psychological Reports, 81,* 620–622.

McNaughton, D., Hughes, C. A., & Clark, K. (1994). Spelling instruction for students with learning disabilities: Implications for research and practice. *Learning Disability Quarterly, 17,* 169–185.

McNeish, J., Heron, T. E., & Okyere, B. (1992). Effects of self-correction on the spelling performance of junior high school students with learning disabilities. *Journal of Behavioral Education, 2,* 17–27.

McNulty, M. A. (2003). Dyslexia and the life course. *Journal of Learning Disabilities, 36,* 363–381.

McNutt, J. C., & Li, J. C.-Y. (1980). Repetition of time-altered sentences by normal and learning disabled children. *Journal of Learning Disabilities, 13,* 25–29.

Meichenbaum, D. (1977). *Cognitive-behavior modification: An integrative approach.* New York: Plenum Press.

Meichenbaum, D. (1981, April). Teaching thinking: A cognitive behavioral approach. Paper presented at the meeting of the Society for Learning Disabilities and Remedial Education, New York.

Meichenbaum, D., & Goodman, J. (1971). Training impulsive children to talk to themselves: A means of developing self-control. *Journal of Abnormal Psychology, 77,* 115–126.

Mellard, D. F., & Hazel, J. S. (1992). Social competencies as a pathway to successful life transitions. *Learning Disability Quarterly, 15*(4), 251–271.

Meltzer, L. (1994). Assessment of learning disabilities: The challenge of evaluating the cognitive strategies and processes underlying learning. In G. R. Lyon (Ed.), *Frames of reference for the assessment of learning disabilities: New views on measurement issues* (pp. 571–606). Baltimore: Brookes.

Meltzer, L., & Montague, M. (2001). Strategic learning in students with learning disabilities: What have we learned? In D. P. Hallahan & B. K. Keogh (Eds.), *Research and global perspectives in learning disabilities: Essays in honor of William M. Cruickshank.* Mahwah, NJ: Erlbaum.

Meltzer, L., & Reid, D. K. (1994). New direction in the assessment of students with special needs: The shift toward a constructivist perspective. *Journal of Special Education, 28,* 338–345.

Meltzer, L., Katzir-Cohen, T., Miller, L., & Roditi, B. (2001). The impact of effort and strategy use on academic performance: Student and teacher perceptions. *Learning Disability Quarterly, 24,* 85–98.

Menn, L, & Stoel-Gammon, C. (2001). Phonological development: Learning sounds and sound patterns. In J. B. Gleason (Ed.), *The development of language* (pp. 70–124). Boston: Allyn & Bacon.

Menyuk, P. (1972). *The development of speech.* New York: Bobbs-Merrill.

Mercer, C. D., Jordan, L., Allsopp, D. H., & Mercer, A. R. (1996). Learning disabilities definitions and criteria used by state education departments. *Learning Disability Quarterly, 19,* 217–232.

Michaels, C. R., & Lewandowski, L. J. (1990). Psychological adjustment and family functioning of boys with learning disabilities. *Journal of Learning Disabilities, 23,* 446–450.

Miller (Eds.), *Progress in behavior modification* (Vol. 13, pp. 79–108). New York: Academic Press.

Miller, A. D., & Heward, W. L. (1992). Do your students really know their math facts? Using daily time trials to build fluency. *Intervention in School and Clinic, 28,* 98–104.

Miller, S. P. (2002). *Validated practices for teaching students with diverse needs and abilities.* Boston: Allyn & Bacon.

Miller, S. P., & Mercer, C. D. (1997). Educational aspects of mathematics disabilities. *Journal of Learning Disabilities, 30,* 57–68.

Miller, S. P., Butler, F. M., & Lee, K. (1998). Validated practices for teaching mathematics to students with learning disabilities: A review of literature. *Focus on Exceptional Children, 31,* 1–24.

Milner, B. (1974). Hemispheric specialization: Scope and limits. In F. O. Schmitt & F. G. Worden (Eds.), *The neurosciences: Third study program* (pp. 75–89). Cambridge, MA: MIT Press.

Minder, B., Das-Smaal, E. A., Brand, E. F., & Orlebeke, J. F. (1994). Exposure to lead and specific attentional problems in schoolchildren. *Journal of Learning Disabilities, 27*(6), 393–399.

Mithaug, D. K., & Mithaug, D. E. (2003). Effects of teacher-directed versus self-management of young children with disabilities. *Journal of Applied Behavior Analysis, 36,* 133–136.

Moats, L. C. (1983). A comparison of the spelling errors of older dyslexic and second-grade normal children. *Annals of Dyslexia, 33,* 121–140.

Moats, L. C. (1995). The missing foundation in teacher education. *American Educator, 19*(2), 9, 43–51.

Moats, L. C. (1998). Teaching decoding. *American Educator, 22*(1–2), 42–49, 95.

Moats, L. C. (2000). *Speech to print: Language essentials for teachers.* Baltimore, MD: Brookes.

Moats, L. C., & Lyon, G. R. (1993). Learning disabilities in the United States: Advocacy, science, and the future of the field. *Journal of Learning Disabilities, 26,* 282–294.

Mock, D. R., & Kauffman, J. M. (2002). Preparing teachers for full inclusion: Is it possible? *Teacher Educator, 37.* 202–215.

Mock, D. R., & Kauffman, J. M. (in press). The delusion of full inclusion. In J. W. Jacobson, J. A. Mulick, & R. M. Foxx (Eds.), *Fads: Dubious and Improbable Treatments for Developmental Disabilities.* Mahwah, NJ: Erlbaum.

Montague, M. (1997). Cognitive strategy instruction in mathematics for students with learning disabilities. *Journal of Learning Disabilities, 30,* 164–177.

Montague, M., & Bos, C. (1986). The effect of cognitive strategy training on verbal math problem solving performance of learning disabled adolescents. *Journal of Learning Disabilities, 19,* 26–33.

Montague, M., & Graves, A. (1993). Improving students' story writing. *Teaching Exceptional Children, 25,* 36–37.

Montague, M., Graves, A., & Leavell, A. (1991). Planning, procedural facilitation, and narrative composition of junior high students with learning disabilities. *Learning Disabilities Research and Practice, 6,* 219–224.

Montague, M., Warger, C., & Morgan, T. H. (2000). Solve it! Strategy instruction to improve mathematical problem solving. *Learning Disabilities Research and Practice, 15,* 110–116.

Montgomery, W. (2001). Creating culturally responsive, inclusive classrooms. *Teaching Exceptional Children, 33,*(4), 4–9.

Moody, S. W., Vaughn, S., Hughes, M. T., & Fischer, M. (2000). Reading instruction in the resource room: Set up for failure. *Exceptional Children, 66,* 305–316.

Morgan, D. P., & Jenson, W. R. (1988). *Teaching behaviorally disordered students.* Columbus, OH: Merrill/Macmillan.

Morningstar, M. E. (1997). Critical issues in career development and employment preparation for adolescents with disabilities. *Remedial and Special Education, 18,* 307–320.

Morris, N. T., & Crump, W. D. (1982). Syntactic and vocabulary development in the written language of learning disabled and non-learning disabled students at four age levels. *Learning Disability Quarterly, 5,* 163–172.

Morris, R. D., Krawiecki, N. S., Wright, J. A., & Walter, L. W. (1993). Neuropsychological, academic, and adaptive functioning in children who survive in-hospital cardiac arrest and resuscitation. *Journal of Learning Disabilities, 26,* 46–51.

Morrison, G. M., & Zetlin, A. (1992). Family profiles of adaptability, cohesion, and communication for learning handicapped and nonhandicapped adolescents. *Journal of Youth and Adolescents, 21,* 225–240.

Mosenthal, P. B., & Kamil, M. L. (1991). Epilogue: Understanding progress in reading research. In R. Barr, M. L. Kamil, P. Mosenthal, & P. D. Pearson (Eds.), *Handbook of reading research* (Vol. 2; pp. 1013–1046). Mahwah, NJ: Erlbaum.

Mull, C., Sitlington, P. L., & Alper, S. (2001). Postsecondary education for students with learning disabilities: A synthesis of the literature. *Exceptional Children, 68,* 97–118.

Munk, D. D., Bruckert, J., Call, D. T., Stoehrmann, T., & Radandt, E. (1998). Strategies for enhancing the performance of students with learning disabilities in inclusive science classes. *Intervention in School and Clinic, 34,* 73–78.

Murray, C., Goldstein, D. E., & Edgar, E. (1997). The employment and engagement status of high school graduates with learning disabilities through the first decade after graduation. *Learning Disabilities Research and Practice, 12,* 151–160.

Murray, C., Goldstein, D. E., Nourse, S., & Edgar, E. (2000). The postsecondary school attendance and completion rates of high school graduates with learning disabilities. *Learning Disabilities Research and Practice, 15,* 119–127.

Muter, V. (1998). Phonological awareness: Its nature and its influence over early literacy development. In C. Hulme & R. M. Joshi (Eds.), *Reading and spelling: Development and disorders* (pp. 113–125). Mahwah, NJ: Erlbaum.

Myklebust, H. R. (1965). *Development and disorders of written language:* Vol. 1. *Picture Story Language Test.* New York: Grune & Stratton.

Myklebust, H. R. (1973). *Development and disorders of written language:* Vol. 2. *Studies of normal and exceptional children.* New York: Grune & Stratton.

Myklebust, H. R. (1975). Nonverbal learning disabilities: Assessment and intervention. In H. R. Myklebust (Ed.), *Progress in learning disabilities* (Vol. 3, pp. 85–121). New York: Grune & Stratton.

Myklebust, H. R., Bannochie, M. N., & Killen, J. R. (1971). Learning disabilities and cognitive processes. In H. R. Myklebust (Ed.), *Progress in learning disabilities* (Vol. 2, pp. 213–251). New York: Grune & Stratton.

Nation, K., Marshall, C. M., & Snowling, M. J. (2001). Phonological and semantic contributions to children's picture naming skill: Evidence from children with developmental reading disorders. *Language and Cognitive Processes, 16,* 241–259.

National Center for Education Statistics (2002). *Schools and staffing survey,* from National Center for Education Statistics (2001a), *Digest of Educational Statistics* (table 42). Retrieved April 18, 2003, from http://nces.ed.gov/pubs2002/digest2001/tables/dt042.asp

National Center for Education Statistics (2001a). *Digest of educational statistics* (table 42). Retrieved April 18, 2003, from http://nces.ed.gov/pubs2002/digest2001/tables/dt042.asp

National Center for Education Statistics (2001b). *Digest of educational statistics* (table 70). Retrieved April 18, 2003, from http://nces.ed.gov/pubs2002/digest2001/tables/dt070.asp

National Center for Education Statistics. (2001c). *Dropout rates in the United States: 2000.* (Executive Summary). Retrieved May 22, 2003, from http://nces.ed.gov/pubs2002/drop pub_2001/

National Center on Educational Restructuring and Inclusion. (1995). National study on inclusion: Overview and summary report. *National Center on Educational Restructuring and Inclusion Bulletin, 2*(2), 1–10.

National Institute for Literacy. (2003). *Definition of reading.* Retrieved June 28, 2003, from http://www.nifl.gov/partnershipforreading/explore/reading_defined.html

National Institutes of Health. (November, 1998). *Diagnosis and treatment of attention deficit hyperactivity disorder, NIH Consensus Statement, 16*(2).

National Reading Panel. (2000). Teaching children to read: An evidence-based assessment of the scientific research literature on reading and its implications for reading instruction (NIH Publication No. 00-4769). Washington, DC: U.S. Government Printing Office. Retrieved February 7, 2003, from http://www.nichd.nih.gov/publications/nrp/smallbook.htm

National Research Council, Committee on Minority Representation in Special Education (M. Suzanne Donovan and Christopher T. Cross, Eds.). (2002). *Minority Students in Special and Gifted Education.* Washington, DC: National Academy Press.

Neef, N. A., Bicard, D. F., & Endo, S. (2001). Assessment of impulsivity and the development of self-control in students with attention deficit hyperactivity disorder. *Journal of Applied Behavior Analysis, 34,* 397–408.

Nelson, H. E. (1980). Analysis of spelling errors in normal and dyslexic children. In U. Frith (Ed.), *Cognitive process in spelling* (pp. 475–493). London: Academic Press.

Newcomer, P. L., & Hammill, D. D. (1997). *Test of Language Development—3, Primary.* Austin, TX: PRO-ED.

Newcomer, P. L., & Hammill, D. D. (1997). *Test of Language Development—Primary* (3rd ed.). Austin, TX: PRO-ED.

Nicholson, T. (1991). Do children read words better in context or in lists? A classic study revisited. *Journal of Educational Psychology, 83,* 444–450.

Nippold, M. A. (1998). *Later language development: The school-age and adolescent years.* Austin, TX: PRO-ED.

Noel, M. M. (1980). Referential communication abilities of learning disabled children. *Learning Disability Quarterly, 3*(3), 70–87.

Notari-Syverson, A., O'Connor, E. O., & Vadasy, P. F. (1998). *Ladders to literacy: A preschool activity book.* Baltimore: Brookes.

Nowacek, E. J. (1992). Professionals talk about teaching together: Interviews with five collaborating teachers. *Intervention in School and Clinic, 27,* 262–276.

O'Brien, J. (2000). Enabling all students to learn in the laboratory of democracy. *Intervention in School and Clinic, 35,* 195–205.

O'Connor, E. O., Notari-Syverson, A., & Vadasy, P. F. (1998). *Ladders to literacy: A kindergarten activity book.* Baltimore: Brookes.

O'Connor, R. E., Bell, K. M., Harty, K. R., Larkin, L. K., Sackor, S. M., & Zigmond, N. (2002). Teaching reading to poor readers in the intermediate grades: A comparison of text difficulty. *Journal of Educational Psychology, 94,* 474–485.

O'Connor, R. E., Notari-Syverson, A., & Vadasy, P. (1998). First grade effects of teacher-led phonological activities in kindergarten for children with mild disabilities: A follow-up study. *Learning Disabilities Research and Practice, 13,* 43–52.

O'Connor, R. E., Notari-Syverson, A., & Vadasy, P. F. (1996). Ladders to literacy: The effects of teacher-led phonological activities for kindergarten children with and without disabilities. *Exceptional Children, 63,* 117–130.

O'Neill, R. E., Horner, R. H., Albin, R. W., Sprague, J. R., Storey, K., & Newton, J. S. (1997). *Functional assessment and program development for problem behavior.* Pacific Grove, CA: Brooks/Cole.

O'Shea, D. J., & Lancaster, P. L. (2001). Families of students from diverse backgrounds. In D. J. O'Shea, L. J. O'Shea, R. Algozzine, & D. J. Hammitte (Eds.), *Families and teachers of individuals with disabilities: Collaborative orientations and responsive practices* (pp. 51–76). Boston: Allyn & Bacon.

Oakland, T., Black, J. L., Stanford, G., Nussbaum, N. L., & Balise, R. R. (1998). An evaluation of the dyslexia training program: A multisensory method for promoting reading in students with reading disabilities. *Journal of Learning Disabilities, 31,* 140–147.

Obrzut, J. E., & Bolick, C. A. (1991). Neuropsychological assessment of childhood learning disabilities. In H. L. Swanson (Ed.), *Handbook on the assessment of learning disabilities* (pp. 121–145). Austin, TX: PRO-ED.

Ochoa, S. H., Rivera, B. D., & Ford, L. (1997). An investigation of school psychology training pertaining to bilingual psycho-educational assessment of primarily Hispanic students: Twenty-five years after Diana v. California. *Journal of School Psychology, 35,* 329–349.

Ochoa, S. H., Rivera, B. D., & Ford, L. (1997). An investigation of school psychology training pertaining to bilingual psycho-educational assessment of primarily Hispanic students: Twenty-five years after *Diana v. California. Journal of School Psychology, 35,* 329–349.

Odom, S. L. (2000). Preschool inclusion: What we know and where we go from here. *Topics in Early Childhood Special Education, 20,* 20–27.

Okolo, C. M., Cavalier, A. R., Ferretti, R. P., & MacArthur, C. A. (2000). Technology, literacy, and disabilities: A review of the research. In R. Gersten, E. P. Schiller, & S. Vaughn (Eds.), *Contemporary special education research: Syntheses of the knowledge base on critical instructional issues* (pp. 179–250). Mahwah, NJ: Erlbaum.

Ollendick, T., Matson, J., Esveldt-Dawson, K., & Shapiro, T. (1980). Increasing spelling achievement: An analysis of treatment procedures utilizing an alternating treatments design. *Journal of Applied Behavior Analysis, 13,* 645–654.

Olson, R. K., Wise, B., Ring, J., & Johnson, M. (1997). Computer-based remedial training in phoneme awareness and phonological decoding: Effects on the posttraining development of word recognition. *Scientific Studies of Reading, 1,* 235–253.

Olympia, D. E., Sheridan, S. M., Jenson, W. R., & Andrews, D. (1994). Using student-managed interventions to increase homework completion and accuracy. *Journal of Applied Behavior Analysis, 27,* 85–99.

Opp, G. (2001). Learning disabilities in Germany: A retrospective analysis, current status and future trends. In D. P. Hallahan & B. K. Keogh (Eds.), *Research and global perspectives in learning disabilities: Essays in honor of W. M. Cruickshank* (pp. 217–238). Mahwah, NJ: Erlbaum.

Ortiz, A. A. (1997). Learning disabilities occurring concomitantly with linguistic differences. *Journal of Learning Disabilities, 30,* 321–332.

Orton, S. T. (1937). *Reading, writing and speech problems in children.* New York: Norton.

Oswald, D. P., Coutinho, M. J., Best, A. M., & Singh, N. N. (1999). Ethnic representation in special education: The influence of school-related economic and demographic variables. *Journal of Special Education, 32,* 194–206.

Overton, T. (2003). *Assessing learners with special needs: An applied approach* (4th ed.). Upper Saddle River, NJ: Merrill.

Owens, R. E. (2001). *Language development: An introduction* (5th ed.). Boston: Allyn & Bacon.

Padeliadu, S., & Zigmond, N. (1996). Perspectives of students with learning disabilities about special education placement. *Learning Disabilities Research and Practice, 11,* 15–23.

Palincsar, A. S., Brown, A. L., & Campione, J. C. (1991). Dynamic assessment. In H. L. Swanson (Ed.), *Handbook on the assessment of learning disabilities* (pp. 75–94). Austin, TX: PRO-ED.

Palincsar, A. S., & Klenk, L. (1992). Fostering literacy learning in supportive contexts. *Journal of Learning Disabilities, 2,* 211–225.

Palincsar, A. S., Magnusson, S. J., Collins, K. M., & Cutler, K. (2001). Making science accessible to all: Results of a design experiment in inclusive classrooms. *Learning Disability Quarterly, 24,* 15–32.

Palmer, S. B., & Wehmeyer, M. L. (2003). Promoting self-determination in early elementary school: Teaching self-regulated problem-solving and goal-setting skills. *Remedial and Special Education, 24,* 115–126.

Pan, B. A., & Gleason, J. B. (2001). Semantic development: Learning the meanings of words. In J. B. Gleason (Ed.), *The development of language* (pp. 125–161). Boston: Allyn & Bacon.

Paris, S. G., & Myers, M. (1981). Comprehension monitoring, memory, and study strategies of good and poor readers. *Journal of Reading Behavior, 13,* 5–22.

Parker, R., Tindal, G., & Hasbrouck, J. (1991). Progress monitoring with objective measures of writing performance for students with mild disabilities. *Exceptional Children, 58,* 61–73.

Parmar, R. S., Cawley, J. F., & Frazita, R. R. (1996). Word problem solving by students with and without mild disabilities. *Exceptional Children, 62,* 415–429.

Parmar, R. S., Deluca, C. B., & Janczak, T. M. (1994). Investigations into the relationship between science and language abilities of students with mild disabilities. *Remedial and Special Education, 15* (2), 117–126.

Parsons, J. A. (1972). The reciprocal modification of arithmetic behavior and program development. In G. Semb (Ed.), *Behavior analysis and education—1972* (pp. 185–199). Lawrence: Department of Human Development, University of Kansas.

Patton, J. (1998). The disproportionate representation of African Americans in special education: Looking behind the curtain for understandings and solutions. *Journal of Special Education, 32,* 25–31.

Paulesu, E., Démonet, J.-F., Fazio, F., McCrory, E., Chanolne, V., Brunswick, N., Cappa, S. F., Cossu, G., Habib, M., Frith, C. D., & Frith, U. (2001). Dyslexia: Cultural diversity and biological unity. *Science, 291,* 2165–2167.

Pearl, R. (2002). Students with learning disabilities and their classroom companions. In B. Y. L. Wong & M. Donahue (Eds.), *The social dimensions of learning disabilities: Essays in honor of Tanis Bryan* (pp. 77–91). Mahwah, NJ: Erlbaum.

Pearl, R., & Bay, M. (1999). Psychosocial correlates of learning disabilities. In D. H. Saklofske & V. L. Schwean (Eds.), *Handbook of psychosocial characteristics of exceptional children* (pp. 443–470). New York: Plenum.

Pelham, W. E. (1981). Attention deficits in hyperactive and learning-disabled children. *Exceptional Education Quarterly, 2*(3), 13–23.

Pennington, B. F. (1990). Annotation: The genetics of dyslexia. *Journal of Child Psychology and Child Psychiatry, 31*(2), 193–201.

Pennington, B. F., Gilger, J. W., Olson, R. K., & DeFries, J. C. (1992). The external validity of age-versus-IQ-discrepant definitions of reading disability: Lessons from a twin study. *Journal of Learning Disabilities, 25*(9), 562–573.

Perfetti, C. A. (1991). Representations and awareness in the acquisition of reading competence. In L. Rieben & C. A. Perfetti (Eds.), *Learning to read: Basic research and its implications* (pp. 33–44). Hillsdale, NJ: Erlbaum.

Perfetti, C. A., & Hogoboam, T. (1975). Relationship between single word decoding and reading comprehension skill. *Journal of Educational Psychology, 67,* 461–469.

Perfetti, C. A., Marron, M. A., & Foltz, P. W. (1996). Sources of comprehension failure: Theoretical perspectives and case studies. In C. Cornoldi & J. Oakhill (Eds.), *Reading comprehension difficulties: Processes and interventions* (pp. 137–165). Mahwah, NJ: Erlbaum.

Petryshen, T. L., Kaplan, B. J., Liu, M. F., deFrench, N. S., Tobias, R., Hughes, M. L., & Field, L. L. (2001). Evidence for a susceptibility locus on Chromosome 6q influencing phonological coding dyslexia. *American Journal of Medical Genetics (Neuropsychiatrica Genetics), 105,* 507–517.

Petti, V., Voelker, S. L., Shore, D. L., & Hayman-Abello, J. E. (2002). Perception of nonverbal emotion cues by children with nonverbal learning disabilities. *Journal of Developmental and Physical Disabilities, 15,* 23–36.

Pflaum, S. W., & Bryan, F. H. (1981). Oral reading behaviors in the learning disabled. *Journal of Educational Research, 73,* 252–258.

Pflaum, S. W., & Pascarella, E. T. (1980). Interactive effects of prior reading achievement and training in context on the reading of learning disabled children. *Reading Research Quarterly, 16,* 138–158.

Phillips, L., Sapona, R. H., & Lubic, B. L. (1995). Developing partnerships in inclusive education: One school's approach. *Intervention in School and Clinic, 30,* 262–272.

Piaget, J. (1952). *The shields conception of number.* New York: Norton. (Original work published 1941)

Pianta, R. C. (1990). Widening the debate on educational reform: Prevention as a viable alternative. *Exceptional Children, 56,* 306–313.

Pinel, J. P. J. (2000). *Biopsychology* (4th ed.). Boston: Allyn & Bacon.

Pinker, S. (2002). *The blank slate: The modern denial of human nature.* New York: Viking.

Pinnell, G. S. (1989). Reading recovery: Helping at-risk children learn to read. *Elementary School Journal, 90,* 159–181.

Pinnell, G. S. (1990). Success for low achievers through reading recovery. *Educational Leadership, 48*(1), 17–21.

Pittelman, S. D., Heimlich, J. E., Berglund, R. L., & French, M. P. (1999). *Semantic feature analysis: Classroom applications.* Newmark, DE: International Reading Association.

Pliszka, S. R., Browne, R. G., Olvera, R. L., & Wynne, S. K. (2000). A double-blind, placebo-controlled study of Adderall and methylphenidate in the treatment of attention-deficit/hyperactivity disorder. *Journal of the American Academy of Child and Adolescent Psychiatry, 39,* 619–626.

Polloway, E. J., Epstein, M. H., Polloway, C., Patton, J., & Ball, D. (1986). Corrective Reading Program: An analysis of effectiveness with learning disabled and mentally retarded students. *Remedial and Special Education, 7,* 41–47.

Polloway, E. J., Foley, R. M., & Epstein, M. H. (1992). A comparison of the homework problems of students with learning disabilities and nonhandicapped students. *Learning Disabilities Research and Practice, 7,* 203–209.

Poplin, M. S. (1988a). Holistic/constructivist principles of the teaching/learning process: Implications for the field of learning disabilities. *Journal of Learning Disabilities, 21,* 401–416.

Poplin, M. S. (1988b). The reductionist fallacy in learning disabilities: Replicating the past by reducing the present. *Journal of Learning Disabilities, 21,* 389–400.

Poplin, M. S., Gray, R., Larsen, S., Banikowski, A., & Mehring, R. (1980). A comparison of components of written expression abilities in learning disabled and non-learning disabled students at three grade levels. *Learning Disability Quarterly, 3*(4), 46–53.

Poteet, J. A., Choate, J. S., & Stewart, S. C. (1993). Performance assessment and special education: Practices and prospects. *Focus on Exceptional Children, 26*(1), 1–20.

Powell, S., & Nelson, B. (1997). Effects of choosing academic assignments on a student with attention deficit hyperactivity disorder. *Journal of Applied Behavior Analysis, 30,* 181–183.

Prater, M. A., Joy, R., Chilman, B., Temple, J., & Miller, S. R. (1991). Self-monitoring of on-task behavior by adolescents with learning disabilities. *Learning Disability Quarterly, 14,* 164–177.

Prescott, G. A., Balow, I. H., Hogan, T. R., & Farr, R. C. (1992). *Metropolitan Achievement Tests—7th Edition Survey Battery.* New York: Harcourt Brace Jovanovich.

President's Commission on Excellence in Special Education. (2002). *A new era: Revitalizing special education for children and their families.* Washington, DC: U.S. Department of Education, Office of Special Education and Rehabilitative Services. Available online at http://www.ed.gov/inits/commissionsboards/whspecialeducation/

Pressley, M., Symons, S., Snyder, B. L., & Cariglia-Bull, T. (1989). Strategy instruction comes of age. *Learning Disability Quarterly, 12,* 16–30.

Price, L. A., Wolensky, D., & Mulligan, R. (2002). Self-determination in action in the classroom. *Remedial and Special Education, 23,* 109–115.

Proff, J. (1978). *Speed spelling.* Tigard, OR: C. C. Publications.

Psychological Corporation. (1992). *Wechsler Individual Achievement Test.* San Antonio, TX: Harcourt Brace Jovanovich.

Pugach, M. C. (1995). On the failure of imagination in inclusive schooling. *Journal of Special Education, 29,* 212–223.

Pulgren, J. A., & Lenz, B. K. (1996). Strategic instruction in the content areas. In D. D. Deshler, E. S. Ellis, & B. K. Lenz (Eds.), *Teaching adolescents with learning disabilities: Strategies and Methods* (2nd ed., pp. 409–473). Denver: Love.

Pullen, P. C. (2002, October 1). Expert connection: Phonological awareness. *TeachingLD.org.* Available online at http://TeachingLD.org/expert_connection/phonological.html

Rabren, K., Darch, C., & Eaves, R. C. (1999). The differential effects of two systematic reading comprehension approaches with students with learning disabilities. *Journal of Learning Disabilities, 32,* 36–47.

Rack, J. P., Snowling, M. J., & Olson, R. K. (1992). The nonword reading deficit in developmental dyslexia: A review. *Reading Research Quarterly, 27,* 28–53.

Rashotte, C. A., & Torgesen, J. K. (1985). Repeated reading and reading fluency in learning disabled children. *Reading Research Quarterly, 20,* 180–188.

Raskind, M. (1993). Assistive technology and adults with learning disabilities: A blueprint for exploration and advancement. *Learning Disability Quarterly, 16*(3), 185–196.

Raynor, K., Foorman, B. R., Perfetti, C. A., Peretsky, D., & Seidenburg, M. S. (2001). How psychological science informs the teaching of reading. *Psychological Science in the Public Interest, 2,* 31–74.

Rea, P. J., McLaughlin, V. L., & Walther-Thomas, C. (2002). Outcomes for students with learning disabilities in inclusive and pullout programs. *Exceptional Children, 68,* 203–222.

Redden, S. C., Forness, S. R., Ramey, S. L., Ramey, C. T., & Brezausek, C. M. (2002). Mental health and special education outcomes of Head Start children followed into elementary school. *NHSA Dialog,* 71–94.

Redden, S. C., Forness, S. R., Ramey, S. L., Ramey, C. T., Brezausek, C. M., & Kavale, K. A. (in press). Head Start children with a putative diagnosis of ADHD: A four-year follow-up of special education placement. *Education and Treatment of Children.*

Reid, D. K., Hresko, W. P., & Swanson, H. L. (Eds.). (1996). *Cognitive approaches to learning disabilities* (3rd ed.). Austin, TX: PRO-ED.

Reid, R. (1996). Research in self-monitoring with students with learning disabilities: The present, the prospects, the pitfalls. *Journal of Learning Disabilities, 29,* 317–331.

Reid, R., Casat, C. D., Norton, H. J., Anastopolous, A. D., & Temple, E. P. (2001). Using behavior rating scales for ADHD across ethnic groups: The IOWA Conners. *Journal of Emotional and Behavioral Disorders, 9,* 210–218.

Reid, R., Riccio, C. A., Kessler, R. H., DuPaul, G. J., Power, T. J., Anastopolous, A. D., Rogers-Adkinson, D., & Noll, M. (2000). Gender and ethnic differences in ADHD as assessed by behavior ratings. *Journal of Emotional and Behavioral Disorders, 8,* 38–48.

Reiff, H. B., Gerber, P. J., & Ginsberg, R. (1997). *Exceeding expectations: Successful adults with learning disabilities.* Austin, TX: PRO-ED.

Reinhiller, N. (1996). Coteaching: New variations on a not-so-new practice. *Teacher Education and Special Education, 19,* 34–48.

Reis, E. M. (2002). Attention deficit hyperactivity disorder: Implications for the classroom teacher. *Journal of Instructional Psychology, 29,* 175–177.

Reis, S. M., Neu, T. W., & McGuire, J. M. (1997). Case studies of high-ability students with learning disabilities who have achieved. *Exceptional Children, 63,* 463–479.

Reith, H. J., Bryant, D. P., Kinzer, C. K., Colburn, L. K., Hur, S., Hartman, P., & Choi, H. S. (2003). An analysis of the impact of anchored instruction on teaching and learning activities in two ninth-grade language arts classes. *Remedial and Special Education, 24,* 173–184.

Reschly, D. J. (2002). Minority overrepresentation: The silent contributor to LD prevalence and diagnostic confusion. In R. Bradley, L. Danielson, & D. P. Hallahan (Eds.), *Identification of learning disabilities: Research to practice.* (pp. 361–368). Mahwah, NJ: Erlbaum.

Resnick, L. B. (1970). Relations between perceptual and syntactic control in oral reading. *Journal of Educational Psychology, 61,* 382–385.

Resnick, L. B. (1983). A developmental theory of number understanding. In H. P. Ginsburg (Ed.), *The development of mathematical thinking* (pp. 110–151). New York: Academic Press.

Resnick, L. B., & Ford, W. W. (1981). *The psychology of mathematics for instruction.* Hillsdale, NJ: Erlbaum.

Reynolds, C. A., Hewitt, J. K., Erickson, M. T., Silberg, J. L., Rutter, M., Simonoff, E., Meyer, J., & Eaves, L. J. (1996). The genetics of children's oral reading performance. *Journal of Child Psychology and Psychiatry and Allied Disciplines, 37,* 425–434.

Rhode, G., Jenson, W. R., & Reavis, H. K. (1992). *The tough kid book: Practical classroom management strategies.* Longmont, CO: Sopris West.

Riccio, C. A., Gonzalez, J. J., & Hynd, G. W (1994). Attention-deficit hyperactivity disorder (ADHD) and learning disabilities. *Learning Disability Quarterly, 17,* 311–322.

Rice, M. L., & Wexler, K. (1996). Toward tense as a clinical marker of specific language impairment in English-speaking children. *Journal of Speech and Hearing Research, 39,* 1239–1257.

Richards, R. G. (1999). *Strategies for dealing with dysgraphia.* Retrieved June 10, 2003, from http://www.ldonline.org/ld_indepth/writing/dysgraphia_strategies.html

Richardson, E., DiBenedetto, B., & Bradley, C. M. (1977). The relationship of sound blending to reading achievement. *Review of Educational Research, 47,* 319–334.

Richardson, E., DiBenedetto, B., Christ, A., & Press, M. (1980). Relationship of auditory and visual skills to reading retardation. *Journal of Learning Disabilities, 13,* 77–82.

Rieth, H. J., Axelrod, J., Anderson, R., Hathaway, F., Wood, K., & Fitzgerald, C. (1974). Influence of distributed practice and daily testing on weekly spelling tests. *Journal of Educational Research, 68*(2), 73–77.

Rieth, H. J., Bryant, D. P., Kinzer, C. K., Colburn, L. K., Hur, S., Hartman, P., & Choi, H. S. (2003). An analysis of the impact of anchored instruction on teaching and learning activities in two ninth-grade language arts classes. *Remedial and Special Education, 24,* 173–184.

Rivera, D., & Smith, D. D. (1988). Using a demonstration strategy to teach learning disabled midschool students how to compute long division. *Journal of Learning Disabilities, 21,* 77–81.

Robbins, M., & Glass, G. V. (1969). The Doman-Delacato rationale: A critical analysis. In J. Hellmuth (Ed.), *Educational therapy* (Vol. 2). Seattle, WA: Special Child Publications.

Robinson, C. S., Menchetti, B. M., & Torgesen, J. K. (2002). Toward a two-factor theory of one type of mathematics disabilities. *Learning Disabilities Research and Practice, 17,* 81–89.

Robison, L. M., Skaer, T. L., Sclar, D. A., & Galin, R. S. (2002). Is attention deficit hyperactivity disorder increasing among girls in the US? *CNS Drugs, 16,* 129–137.

Roe, B., Stoodt, B., & Burns, P. (1995). *The content area: Adjusting reading assignments to fit all students.* Boston: Houghton Mifflin.

Roffman, A. J., Herzog, J. E., & Wershba-Gershon, P. M. (1994). Helping young adults understand their learning disabilities. *Journal of Learning Disabilities, 27*(7), 413–419.

Romaniuk, C., Miltenberger, R., Conyers, C., Jenner, N., Jurgens, M., & Ringenberg, C. (2002). The influence of activity choice on problem behaviors maintained by escape versus attention. *Journal of Applied Behavior Analysis, 35,* 349–362.

Rooney, K. (1998). *Independent strategies for efficient study* (Upper elementary/middle school ed.). Richmond, VA: Educational Enterprises.

Rose, T. L. (1984a). Effects of previewing on the oral reading of mainstreamed behaviorally disordered students. *Behavioral Disorders, 10,* 33–39.

Rose, T. L. (1984b). The effects of previewing on retarded learners' oral reading. *Education and Training of the Mentally Retarded, 19,* 49-53.

Rose, T. L., & Beattie, J. R. (1986). Relative effects of teacher-directed and taped previewing on oral reading. *Learning Disability Quarterly, 9,* 193–199.

Rose, T. L., & Sherry, L. (1984). Relative effects of two previewing procedures on the oral reading performance of learning disabled adolescents. *Learning Disability Quarterly, 7,* 39–44.

Rosenberg, M. S. (1989). The effects of daily homework assignments on the acquisition of basic skills by students with learning disabilities. *Journal of Learning Disabilities, 22,* 314–323.

Rosenberg, M. S. (1997). Learning disabilities occurring concomitantly with other disability and exceptional conditions: Introduction to the series. *Journal of Learning Disabilities, 30,* 242–244.

Rosenkoetter, S. E., Whaley, K. T., Hains, A. H., & Pierce, L. (2001). The evolution of transition policy for young children with special needs and their families: Past, present, and future. *Topics in Early Childhood Special Education, 21,* 3–15.

Rosenshine, B. (1997). Advances in research on instruction. In J. W. Lloyd, E. J. Kame'enui, & D. Chard (Eds.), *Issues in educating students with disabilities* (pp. 197–220). Mahwah, NJ: Erlbaum.

Rosenshine, B., & Stevens, R. (1986). Teaching functions. In M. C. Wittrock (Ed.), *Handbook of research on teaching* (3rd ed., pp. 376–391). New York: Macmillan.

Rosenthal, D. J., & Resnick, L. B. (1974). Children's solution processes in arithmetic word problems. *Journal of Educational Psychology, 66,* 817–825.

Rosenzweig, M. R. (1966). Environmental complexity, cerebral change, and behavior. *American Psychologist, 21,* 321–332.

Rosewell, F. G., & Chall, J. S. (1997). *Roswell-Chall Auditory Blending Test.* Cambridge, MA: Educators Publishing Service.

Ross, G., Lipper, E. G., & Auld, P. A. M. (1991). Educational status and school-related abilities of very low birth weight premature children. *Pediatrics, 88*(6), 1125–1134.

Roswell, F. G., & Chall, J. C. (1978). *Roswell-Chall Diagnostic Reading Test of Word Analysis Skills* (rev. ed.). New York: Essay Press.

Roth, F. P., Speece, D. L., & Cooper, D. H. (2002). A longitudinal analysis of the connection between oral language and early reading. *Journal of Educational Research, 95,* 259–272.

Rourke, B. P. (1989). *Nonverbal learning disabilities: The syndrome and the model.* New York: Guilford.

Rourke, B. P. (Ed.). (1995). *Syndrome of non-verbal learning disabilities: Neurodevelopmental manifestations.* New York: Guilford.

Rourke, B. P., & Tsatsanis, K. D. (1996). Syndrome of nonverbal learning disabilities: Psycholinguistic assets and deficits. *Topics in Language Disorders, 16*(2), 30–44.

Rovet, J. F., Ehrlich, R. M., Czuchta, D., & Akler, M. (1993). Psychoeducational characteristics of children and adolescents with insulin-dependent diabetes mellitus. *Journal of Learning Disabilities, 26*(1), 7–22.

Rozin, P., & Gleitman, L. R. (1977). The structure and acquisition of Reading 11: The reading process and the acquisition of the alphabetic principle. In A. S. Reber & D. L. Scarborough (Eds.), *Toward a psychology of reading: The proceedings of the CUNY conferences* (pp. 55–141). Hillsdale, NJ: Erlbaum.

Ruddell, R. B. (2002). *Teaching children to read and write: Becoming an effective literacy teacher* (3rd ed.). Boston: Allyn & Bacon.

Rueckl, J. B., & Dror, I. E. (1994). The effect of orthographic-semantic systematicity on the acquisition of new words. In C. Umilta & M. Moscovitch (Eds.), *Attention and performance: Vol. 15. Conscious and nonconscious information processing* (pp. 571–588). Cambridge, MA: MIT Press.

Ruiz, N. T. (1995). The social construction of ability and disability: II. Optimal and at-risk lessons in a bilingual special education classroom. *Journal of Learning Disabilities, 28,* 491–502.

Ruiz, N. T., & Figueroa, R. A. (1995). Learning-handicapped classrooms with Latino students: The optimal learning environment (OLE) Project. *Education and Urban Society, 27,* 463–483.

Rumrill, P. D., & Cook, B. G. (2001). *Research in special education: Designs, methods, and applications.* Springfield, IL: Thomas.

Sachs, J. (1989). Communication development in infancy. In J. Gleason (Ed.), *The development of language* (pp. 35–58). Columbus, OH: Merrill.

Salend, S. (1998). Using an activities-based approach to teach science to students with disabilities. *Intervention in School and Clinic, 34,* 67–72.

Salend, S. J., & Nowack, M. R. (1988). Effects of peer previewing on LD students' oral reading skills. *Learning Disability Quarterly, 11,* 47–52.

Salend, S. J., & Schliff, J. (1989). An examination of the homework practices of teachers of students with learning disabilities. *Journal of Learning Disabilities, 22,* 621–623.

Salvia, J., & Ysseldyke, J. E. (1998). *Assessment* (7th ed.). Boston: Houghton Mifflin.

Salvia, J., & Ysseldyke, J. E. (2001). *Assessment* (8th ed.). Boston: Houghton Mifflin.

Samuels, S. J. (1979). The method of repeated readings. *Reading Teacher, 32,* 403–408.

Samuels, S. J. (1981). Some essentials of decoding. *Exceptional Education Quarterly, 2*(1), 11–25.

Samuels, S. J., Schermer, N., & Reinking, D. (1992). Reading fluency: Techniques for making decoding automatic. In S. J. Samuels & A. E. Farstrup (Eds.), *What research says about reading instruction* (2nd ed., pp. 124–144). Newark, DE: International Reading Association.

Sands, D. J., Kozleski, E. B., & French, K. (2000). *Inclusive education for the 21st century: A new introduction to special education.* Belmont, CA: Wadsworth.

Sasso, G. M. (2001). The retreat from inquiry and knowledge in special education. *Journal of Special Education, 34,* 178–193.

Satz, P., & Fletcher, J. M. (1988). Early identification of learning disabled children: An old problem revisited. *Journal of Consulting and Clinical Psychology, 56,* 824–829.

Sawyer, D. J., & Bernstein, S. E. (2002). Do discrepancy models satisfy either the letter or the spirit of IDEA? In R. Bradley, L. Danielson, & D. P. Hallahan (Eds.), *Identification of learning disabilities: Research to practice* (pp. 457–466). Mahwah, NJ: Erlbaum.

Sawyer, V., Nelson, J. S., Jayanthi, M., Bursuck, W. D., & Epstein, M. H. (1996). Views of students with learning disabilities of their homework in general education classes: Student interviews. *Learning Disability Quarterly, 19,* 70–85.

Scanlon, D., & Mellard, D. F. (2002). Academic and participation profiles of school-age dropouts with and without disabilities. *Exceptional Children, 68,* 239–258.

Scannell, D. P., Haugh, O. M., Schild, A. H., & Ulmer, G. (1978). *Tests of Achievement and Proficiency.* Boston: Houghton Mifflin.

Schatschneider, C., Carlson, C. D., Francis, D. J., Foorman, B. R., & Fletcher, J. M. (2002). Relationship of rapid automatic naming and phonological awareness in early reading development: Implications for the double deficit hypothesis. *Journal of Learning Disabilities, 35,* 245–256.

Schneider, W., Roth, E., & Ennemoser, M. (2000). Training phonological skills and letter knowledge in children at risk for dyslexia: A comparison of three kindergarten intervention programs. *Journal of Educational Psychology, 92,* 284–295.

Schrag, J. (2000). *Discrepancy approaches for identifying learning disabilities.* Alexandria, VA: NASDSE.

Schulte-Korne, G. (2001). Annotation: Genetics of reading and spelling disorders. *Journal of Child Psychology and Psychiatry, 42,* 985–997.

Schulte-Korne, G., Deimel, W., Muller, K., Gutenbrunner, C., & Remschmidt, H. (1996). Familial aggregation of spelling disability. *Journal of Child Psychology and Psychiatry, 37,* 817–822.

Schulz, E. (1994, October 5). Beyond behaviorism. *Education Week,* pp. 19–21, 24.

Schulz, J. B. (1987). *Parents and professionals in education.* Boston: Allyn & Bacon.

Schumaker, J. B., Nolan, S. M., & Deshler, D. D. (1985). *The error-monitoring strategy.* Lawrence: University of Kansas.

Schumaker, J., Deshler, D., Alley, G., Warner, M., & Denton, P. (1984). Multipass: A learning strategy for improving reading comprehension. *Learning Disability Quarterly, 5,* 295–304.

Schumm, J. S. (1992). Using story grammar with at-risk high school students. *Journal of Reading, 35,* 296.

Schumm, J. S., & Vaughn, S. (1992). Planning for mainstreamed special education students: Perceptions of general classroom teachers. *Exceptionality, 3,* 81–98.

Schumm, J. S., Vaughn, S., Gordon, J., & Rothlein, L. (1994). General education teachers' beliefs, skills, and practices in planning for mainstreamed students with learning disabilities. *Teacher Education and Special Education, 17,* 22–37.

Schwartz, I. S., Garfinkle, A. N., & Davis, C. (2002). Arranging preschool environments to facilitate valued social and educational outcomes. In M. R. Shinn, H. M. Walker, & G. Stoner (Eds.), *Interventions for academic and behavior problems: II. Preventive and remedial approaches* (pp. 455–468). Bethesda, MD: National Association of School Psychologists.

Scott, C. M. (2000). Principles and methods of spelling instruction: Applications for poor spellers. *Topics in Language Disorders, 20,* 66–82.

Scott, C. M., & Windsor, J. (2000). General language performance measures in spoken and written narrative and expository discourse of school-age children with language learning disabilities. *Journal of Speech, Language, and Hearing Research, 43,* 324–339.

Scott, Foresman. (1991). *Exploring mathematics.* Glenview, IL: Author.

Scott, S. (1994). Determining reasonable academic adjustments for college students with learning disabilities. *Journal of Learning Disabilities, 27*(7), 403–412.

Scruggs, T. E., & Mastropieri, M. A. (2002). On babies and bathwater: Addressing the problems of identification of learning disabilities. *Learning Disability Quarterly, 25,* 155–168.

Scruggs, T. E., & Mastropieri, M. A. (1992). Classroom applications of mnemonic instruction: Acquisition, maintenance, and generalization. *Exceptional Children, 58,* 219–229.

Scruggs, T. E., & Mastropieri, M. A. (2000). The effectiveness of mnemonic instruction for students with learning and behavior problems: An update and research synthesis. *Journal of Behavioral Education, 10,* 163–173.

Seabaugh, G. O., & Schumaker, J. B. (1993). The effects of self-regulation training on the academic productivity of secondary students with learning disabilities. *Journal of Behavioral Education, 4,* 109–133.

Sealey, L., Sealey, N., & Millmore, M. (1979). *Children's writing: An approach for the primary grades.* Newark, DE: International Reading Association.

Sedlak, R., & Weiner, P. (1973). Review of research on the Illinois Test of Psycholinguistic Abilities. In L. Mann & D. A. Sabatino (Eds.), *First review of special education* (Vol. 1, pp. 113–163). Philadelphia: Buttonwood Farms.

Seligman, M. E. (1992). *Helplessness: On depression, development and death.* San Francisco: Freeman.

Seligman, M., & Darling, R. B. (1989). *Ordinary families, special children: A systems approach to childhood disability.* New York: Guilford Press.

Semel, E. M., & Wiig, E. H. (1975). Comprehension of syntactic structures and critical verbal elements by children with learning disabilities. *Journal of Learning Disabilities, 8,* 46–51.

Semel, E., Wiig, E. H., & Secord, W. A. (1995). *Clinical Evaluation of Language Fundamentals* (3rd ed.). San Antonio, TX: Psychological Corporation.

Semrud-Clikeman, M., & Hynd, G. W. (1990). Right hemispheric dysfunction in nonverbal learning disabilities: Social, academic, and adaptive functioning in adults and children. *Psychological Bulletin, 107*(2), 196–209.

Semrud-Clikeman, M., & Hynd, G. W. (1990). Right hemispheric dysfunction in nonverbal learning disabilities: Social, academic, and adaptive functioning in adults and children. *Psychological Bulletin, 107*(2), 196–209.

Senapati, R., & Hayes, A. (1988). Sibling relationships of handicapped children: A review of conceptual and methodolog-

ical issues. *International Journal of Behavioral Development, 11,* 89–115.

Serna, L. A., Lambros, K., Nielsen, E., & Forness, S. R. (2002). Head Start children at risk for emotional or behavioral disorders: Behavior profiles and clinical implications of a primary prevention program. *Behavioral Disorders, 27,* 137–141.

Shapiro, E. S., DuPaul, G. J., & Bradley-Klug, K. L. (1998). Self-management as a strategy to improve the classroom behavior of adolescents with ADHD. *Journal of Learning Disabilities, 31,* 545–555.

Shapiro, E. S., Durnan, S. L., Post, E. E., & Levinson, T. S. (2002). Self-monitoring procedures for children and adolescents. In M. R. Shinn, H. M. Walker, & G. Stoner (Eds.), *Interventions for academic and behavior problems: II. Preventive and remedial approaches* (pp. 433–454). Bethesda, MD: National Association of School Psychologists.

Shapiro, J., & Rich, R. (1999). *Facing learning disabilities in the adult years.* New York: Oxford University Press.

Shattuck, R. (1999). *Candor and perversion: Literature, education, and the arts.* New York: Norton.

Shatz, M., & Gelman, R. (1973). The development of communication skills: Modifications in the speech of young children as a function of the listener. *Monographs of the Society for Research in Child Development, 38* (5, Serial no. 152).

Shaw, R. A. (1999). The case for course substitutions as a reasonable accommodation for students with foreign language learning difficulties. *Journal of Learning Disabilities, 32,* 320–328.

Shaywitz, B. A., Fletcher, J. M., & Shaywitz, S. E. (1995). Defining and classifying learning disabilities and attention-deficit/hyperactivity disorder. *Journal of Child Neurology, 10* (Supplement), S50–S57.

Shaywitz, S. (2003). *Overcoming dyslexia: A new and complete science-based program for overcoming reading problems at any level.* New York: Knopf.

Shaywitz, S. E., Shaywitz, B. A., Fletcher, J. M., & Escobar, M. D. (1990). Prevalence of reading disabilities in boys and girls: Results of the Connecticut Longitudinal Study. *Journal of the American Medical Association, 264*(8), 998–1002.

Shepard, G., & Koch, C. (1990). Introduction to synaptic circuits. In G. Shepard (Ed.), *The synaptic organization of the brain* (pp. 3–31). London: Oxford University Press.

Sheridan, S. M., Eagle, J. W., Cowan, R. J., & Mickelson, W. (2001). The effects of conjoint behavioral consultation: Results of a 4-year investigation. *Journal of School Psychology, 39,* 361–385.

Sheridan, S. M., Welch, M., & Orme, S. F. (1996). Is consultation effective? A review of outcome research. *Remedial and Special Education, 17,* 341–354.

Sheridan, S. M. (2000). Considerations of multiculturalism and diversity in behavioral consultation with parents and teachers. *School Psychology Review, 29,* 344–353.

Sherman, D. K., Iacono, W. G., & McGue, M. K. (1997). Attention-deficit hyperactivity disorder dimensions: A twin study of inattention and impulsivity-hyperactivity. *Journal of the American Academy of Child and Adolescent Psychiatry, 36,* 745–753.

Shimabukuro, S. M., Parker, M. A., Jenkins, A., & Edelen-Smith, P. (1999). The effects of self-monitoring of academic performance on students with learning disabilities. *Education and Treatment of Children, 22,* 397–414.

Shinn, M. R. (2003). *Curriculum-based measurement and its use in a problem-solving model.* Retrieved July 3, 2003, from http://www.edformation.com/benchdemo.htm

Shinn, M. R., & Bamonto, S. (1998). Advanced applications of curriculum-based measurement: "Big ideas" and avoiding confusion. In M. R. Shinn (Ed.), *Advanced applications of curriculum-based measurement.* New York: Guilford Press.

Shinn, M. R., & Hubbard, D. D. (1992). Curriculum-based measurement and problem-solving assessment: Basic procedures and outcomes. *Focus on Exceptional Children, 24*(5), 1–20.

Short, E. J., & Weissberg-Benchell, J. (1989). The triple alliance for learning: Cognition, metacognition, and motivation. In C. B. McCormick, G. E. Miller, & M. Pressley (Eds.), *Cognitive strategy research: From basic research to educational applications* (pp. 33–63). New York: Springer-Verlag.

Siegel, L. S. (1989). IQ is irrelevant to the definition of learning disabilities. *Journal of Learning Disabilities, 22*(8), 469–478, 486.

Siegel, S., & Gaylord-Ross, R. (1991). Factors associated with employment success among youths with learning disabilities. *Journal of Learning Disabilities, 24*(1), 48–64.

Silver, E. A., & Smith, M. S. (1989). Canceling cancellation: The role of worked-out examples in unlearning a procedural error. In C. A. Maher, G. A. Goldin, & R. B. Davis (Eds.), *Proceedings of the eleventh annual meeting of the North American Chapter of the International Group for the Psychology of Mathematics Education* (pp. 40–46). New Brunswick, NJ: Center for Math, Science and Computer Education, Rutgers University.

Simmons, D. C., & Kame'enui, E. J. (Eds.). (1998). *What reading research tells us about children with diverse learning needs.* Mahwah, NJ: Erlbaum.

Simmons, D. C., Kame'enui, E. J., Good, R. H., Harn, B. A., Cole, C., & Braun, D. (2002). Building, implementing, and sustaining a beginning reading improvement model: Lessons learned school by school. In M. R. Shinn, H. M. Walker, & G. Stoner (Eds.), *Interventions for academic and behavior problems: II. Preventive and remedial approaches* (pp. 537–570). Bethesda, MD: National Association of School Psychologists.

Simos, P. G., Fletcher, J. M., Bergman, E., Breier, J. I., Foorman, B. R., Castillo, E. M., Davis, R. N., Fitzgerald, M., & Papanicolaou, A. C. (2002). Dyslexia-specific brain activation profile becomes normal following successful remedial training. *Neurology, 58,* 1203–1213.

Sinclair, E. (1993). Early identification of preschoolers with special needs in Head Start. *Topics in Early Childhood Special Education, 13,* 184–201.

Sindelar, P. T., Lane, H. B., Pullen, P. C., & Hudson, R. F. (2002). Remedial interventions for students with reading and decoding problems. In M. R. Shinn, H. M. Walker, & G. Stoner (Eds.), *Interventions for academic and behavior problems: II. Preventive and remedial approaches* (pp. 703–727). Bethesda, MD: National Association of School Psychologists.

Sindelar, P. T., Monda, L. E., & O'Shea, L. J. (1990). Effects of repeated readings on instructional- and mastery-level readers. *Journal of Educational Research, 83,* 220–226.

Singer, J. D. (1988). Should special education merge with regular education? *Educational Policy, 2,* 409–424.

Singer, J. D., & Butler, J. A. (1987). The Education of All Handicapped Children Act: Schools as agents of social reform. *Harvard Educational Review, 57,* 125–152.

Sitlington, P. L., & Frank, A. R. (1999). Life outside of work for young adults with learning disabilities. *Journal for Vocational Special Needs Education, 22,* 3–22.

Skinner, M. E. (1998). Promoting self-advocacy among college students with learning disabilities. *Intervention in School and Clinic, 33,* 278–283.

Skrtic, T. M., Sailor, W., & Gee, K. (1996). Voice, collaboration, and inclusion: Democratic themes in educational and social reform initiatives. *Remedial and Special Education, 17,* 142–157.

Slavin, R. E. (2003). *Educational psychology: Theory and practice* (7th ed.). Boston: Allyn & Bacon.

Slavin, R. E., Madden, N. A., Dolan, L. J., & Wasik, B. A. (1994). Roots and wings: Inspiring academic excellence. *Educational Leadership, 52*(3), 10–14.

Sleator, E. K., & Ullmann, R. K. (1981). Can the physician diagnose hyperactivity in the office? *Pediatrics, 67,* 13–17.

Sleeter, C. E. (1986). Learning disabilities: The social construction of a special education category. *Exceptional Children, 53,* 46–54.

Slocum, T. A., O'Connor, R. E., & Jenkins, J. R. (1993). Transfer among phonological manipulation skills. *Journal of Educational Psychology, 85,* 618–630.

Smith, B. J. (2000). The federal role in early childhood special education policy in the next century: The responsibility of the individual. *Topics in Early Childhood Special Education, 20,* 7–13.

Smith, D. D., & Lovitt, T. C. (1973). The educational diagnosis and remediation of written *b* and *d* reversal problems: A case study. *Journal of Learning Disabilities, 6,* 356–363.

Smith, D. D., & Lovitt, T. C. (1975). The use of modeling techniques to influence the acquisition of computational arithmetic skills in reading-disabled children. In E. Ramp & G. Semb (Eds.), *Behavior analysis: Areas of research and application* (pp. 283–308). Englewood Cliffs, NJ: Prentice-Hall.

Smith, D. D., & Lovitt, T. C. (1976). The differential effects of reinforcement contingencies on arithmetic performance. *Journal of Learning Disabilities, 9,* 21–29.

Smith, D. D., & Lovitt, T. C. (1982). *The Computational Arithmetic Program.* Austin, TX: PRO-ED.

Smith, D. D., Lovitt, T. C., & Kidder, J. D. (1972). Using reinforcement contingencies and teaching aids to alter subtraction performance of children with learning disabilities. In G. Semb (Ed.), *Behavior analysis and education* (pp. 342–360). Lawrence: Department of Human Behavior, University of Kansas.

Smith, D. D., & Rivera, D. P. (1991). Mathematics. In B. Y. L. Wong (Ed.), *Learning about learning disabilities* (pp. 345–374). New York: Academic Press.

Smith, H. D., Baehner, R. L., Carney, T., & Majors, S. J. (1963). The sequelae of pica with and without lead poisoning: A comparison of the sequelae five or more years later: I. Clinical and laboratory observations. *American Journal of Diseases of Children, 105,* 609–616.

Smith, R. G., & Churchill, R. M. (2002). Identification of environmental determinants of behavior disorders through functional analysis of precursor behaviors. *Journal of Applied Behavior Analysis, 35,* 125–136.

Smith, T. J., Dittmer, K. L., & Skinner, C. H. (2002). Enhancing science performance in students with learning disabilities using cover, copy, and compare: A student shows the way. *Psychology in the Schools, 39,* 417–427.

Smythe, I., & Everatt, J. (2002). Dyslexia and the multilingual child: Policy into practice. *Topics in Language Disorders, 22*(5), 71–80.

Snell, M. E. (2003). Severe and multiple disabilities, education of individuals with. In J. W. Guthrie (Ed.), *Encyclopedia of education* (2nd ed., pp. 2210–2213). New York: Macmillan Reference.

Snider, V. E. (1992). Learning styles and learning to read: A critique. *Remedial and Special Education, 13*(1), 6–18.

Snider, V. E. (1995). A primer on phonemic awareness: What it is, why it's important, and how to teach it. *School Psychology Review, 24,* 443–455.

Snow, C., Burns, M., & Griffin, P. (1998). *Preventing reading difficulties in young children.* Washington, DC: National Academies Press.

Snowling, M. J., Gallagher, A., & Frith, U. (2003). Family risk of dyslexia is continuous: Individual differences in the precursors of reading skill. *Child Development, 74,* 358–373.

Solanto, M. V. (2002). Dopamine dysfunction in AD/HD: Integrating clinical and basic neuroscience research. *Behavioural Brain Research, 130,* 65–71.

Soodak, L. C., Erwin, E. J., Winton, P., Brotherson, M. J., Turnbull, A. P., Hanson, M. J., & Brault, L. M. J. (2002). Implementing inclusive early childhood education: A call for professional empowerment. *Topics in Early Childhood Special Education, 22,* 91–102.

*Southeastern Community College v. Davis,* 422 U.S. 397 (1979).

Sparks, R. L., & Javorsky, J. (1999). Students classified as LD and the college foreign language requirement: Replication and comparison studies. *Journal of Learning Disabilities, 32,* 329–349.

Sparks, R. L., Phillips, L. G., & Javorsky, J. (2002). Students classified as LD who received course substitutions for the college foreign language requirement: A replication study. *Journal of Learning Disabilities, 35,* 482–500.

Sparks, R. L., Phillips, L., Ganschow, L., & Javorsky, J. (1999a). Comparison of students classified as LD who petitioned for or fulfilled the college foreign language requirement. *Journal of Learning Disabilities, 32,* 553–565.

Sparks, R. L., Phillips, L., Ganschow, L., & Javorsky, J. (1999b). Students classified as LD and the college foreign language requirement: A quantitative analysis. *Journal of Learning Disabilities, 32,* 566–580.

Speece, D. L., & Cooper, D. H. (1990). Ontogeny of school failure: Classification of first-grade children. *American Educational Research Journal, 27,* 119–140.

Speece, D. L., & Shekitka, L. (2002). How should reading disabilities be operationalized: A survey of experts. *Learning Disability Research and Practice, 17,* 118–123.

Speece, D. L., Case, L. P., & Molloy, D. E. (2003). Responsiveness to general education instruction as the first gate to learning disabilities identification. *Learning Disabilities Research and Practice, 18,* 147–156.

Speece, D. L., Mills, C., Ritchey, K. D., & Hillman, E. (2002). Initial evidence that letter fluency tasks are valid indicators of early reading skill. *Journal of Special Education, 36,* 223–233.

Spencer, T., Biederman, J., Wilens, T., Harding, M., O'Donnell, D., & Griffin, S. (1996). Pharmacotherapy of attention-deficit hyperactivity disorder across the life cycle. *Journal of the American Academy of Child and Adolescent Psychiatry, 35,* 409–432.

Sperry, R. W. (1964). The great cerebral commissure. *Scientific American, 210,* 42–52.

Spillane, S. A., McGuire, J. M., & Norlander, K. A. (1992). Undergraduate admission policies, practices, and procedures for applicants with learning disabilities. *Journal of Learning Disabilities, 25*(10), 665–670, 677.

Spinelli, C. G. (1999). Breaking down barriers—building strong foundations: Parents and teachers of exceptional students working together. *Learning Disabilities: A Multidisciplinary Journal, 9,* 123–130.

Sridhar, D., & Vaughn, S. (2001). Social functioning of students with learning disabilities. In D. P. Hallahan & B. K. Keogh (Eds.), *Research and global perspectives in learning disabilities: Essays in honor of William M. Cruickshank* (pp. 65–91). Mahwah, NJ: Erlbaum.

Stainback, W., & Stainback, S. (1984). A rationale for the merger of special and regular education. *Exceptional Children, 51,* 102–111.

Stanovich, K. E. (1980). Toward an interactive compensatory model of individual differences in the development of reading fluency. *Reading Research Quarterly, 16,* 32–71.

Stanovich, K. E. (1986). Matthew effects in reading: Some consequences of individual differences in the acquisition of literacy. *Reading Research Quarterly, 21,* 360–407.

Stanovich, K. E. (1988). Science and learning disabilities. *Journal of Learning Disabilities, 21,* 210–214.

Stanovich, K. E. (1989). Has the learning disabilities field lost its intelligence? *Journal of Learning Disabilities, 22,* 465–528.

Stanovich, K. E. (1991). Discrepancy definitions of reading disability: Has intelligence led us astray? *Reading Research Quarterly, 26,* 7–29.

Stanovich, K. E., & Siegel, L. S. (1994). Phenotypic performance profile of children with reading disabilities: A regression-based test of the phonological-core variable-difference model. *Journal of Educational Psychology, 86*(1), 24–53.

Stanovich, K. E., Cunningham, A., & Freeman, D. (1984). The relationship between early reading acquisition and word decoding with and without context: A longitudinal study of first grade children. *Journal of Educational Psychology, 76,* 668–677.

Starlin, C. (1971). Evaluating progress toward reading proficiency. In B. Bateman (Ed.), *Learning disorders: Vol. 4. Reading* (pp. 389–465). Seattle, WA: Special Child Publications.

Stecker, P. M., & Fuchs, L. S. (2000). Effecting superior achievement using curriculum-based measurement: The importance of individual progress monitoring. *Learning Disabilities Research and Practice, 15,* 128–134.

Stein, M., Silbert, J., & Carnine, D. (1997). *Designing effective mathematics instruction: A Direct Instruction approach* (3rd ed.). Upper Saddle River, NJ: Merrill.

Stephenson, S. (1907). Six cases of congenital word-blindness affecting three generations in one family. *Ophthalmoscope, 5,* 482–484.

Stern, C. A., & Stern, M. B. (1971). Children discover arithmetic: An introduction to structural arithmetic (rev. ed.). New York: Harper & Row.

Stevens, K. B., & Schuster, J. W. (1987). Effects of a constant time-delay procedure on the written spelling performance of a reading disabled student. *Learning Disability Quarterly, 10,* 9–16.

Stevens, K. B., Blackhurst, A. E., & Slaton, D. B. (1991). Teaching memorized spelling with a microcomputer: Time delay and computer-assisted instruction. *Journal of Applied Behavior Analysis, 24,* 153–160.

Stevens, L. M., & Werkhoven, W. van. (2001). Learning disabilities in the Netherlands. In D. P. Hallahan & B. K. Keogh (Eds.), *Research and global perspectives in learning disabilities: Essays in honor of W. M. Cruickshank* (pp. 273–291). Mahwah, NJ: Erlbaum.

Stevens, R., & Rosenshine, B. (1981). Advances in research on teaching. *Exceptional Education Quarterly, 2*(1), 1–9.

Stevenson, J. (1992). Evidence for a genetic etiology in hyperactive children. *Behavior Genetics, 22,* 337–344.

Steventon, C. E., & Frederick, L. D. (2003). The effects of repeated readings on student performance in the Corrective Reading program. *Journal of Direct Instruction, 3,* 17–27.

Still, G. F. (1902). Some abnormal psychical conditions in children. *Lancet, 1,* 1008–1012, 1077–1082, 1163–1168.

Stowitschek, C. E., & Stowitschek, J. J. (1979). Evaluating handwriting performance: The student helps the teacher. *Journal of Learning Disabilities, 12,* 203–206.

Strain, P. S., & Timm, M. A. (2001). Remediation and prevention of aggression: An evaluation of the Regional Intervention Program over a quarter century. *Behavioral Disorders, 26,* 297–313.

Strang, J. D., & Rourke, B. P. (1985). Arithmetic disability subtypes: The neuropsychological significance of specific arithmetical impairment in childhood. In B. P. Rourke (Ed.), *Neuropsychology of learning disabilities: Essentials of subtype analysis* (pp. 167–183). New York: Guilford Press.

Strauss, A. A., & Kephart, N. C. (1955). *Psychopathology and education of the brain-injured child:* Vol. 2. *Progress in theory and clinic.* New York: Grune & Stratton.

Strauss, A. A., & Lehtinen, L. E. (1947). *Psychopathology and education of the brain-injured child.* New York: Grune & Stratton.

Strauss, A. A., & Werner, H. (1942). Disorders of conceptual thinking in the brain-injured child. *Journal of Nervous and Mental Disease, 96,* 153–172.

Strawser, S., & Miller, S. P. (2001). Math failure and learning disabilities in the postsecondary student population. *Topics in Language Disorders, 21,* 68–84.

Stromer, R. (1975). Modifying letter and number reversals in elementary school children. *Journal of Applied Behavior Analysis, 8,* 211.

Stromer, R. (1977). Remediating academic deficiencies in learning disabled children. *Exceptional Children, 43,* 432–440.

Suritsky, S. K., & Hughes, C. A. (1997). Notetaking strategy instruction. In D. D. Deshler, E. S. Ellis, & B. K. Lenz, *Teaching adolescents with learning disabilities: Strategies and methods* (2nd ed.). Denver, CO: Love.

Swank, L. K., Meier, J. D., Invernizzi, M., & Juel, C. L. (1997). *PALS I: Phonological awareness and literacy screening.* Charlottesville: University of Virginia.

Swanson, H. L. (1999a). Reading comprehension and working memory in learning-disabled readers: Is the phonological loop more important than the executive system? *Journal of Experimental Child Psychology, 72,* 1–31.

Swanson, H. L. (1999b). Reading research for students with LD: A meta-analysis in intervention outcomes. *Journal of Learning Disabilities, 32,* 504–532.

Swanson, H. L. (2000). What instruction works for students with learning disabilities? Summarizing the results from a meta-analysis of intervention studies. In R. Gersten, E. P. Schiller, & S. Vaughn (Eds.), *Contemporary special education research: Syntheses of the knowledge base on critical instructional issues.* Mahwah, NJ: Erlbaum.

Swanson, H. L. (2002). Learning disabilities is a specific processing deficit, but it is much more than phonological processing. In R. Bradley, L. Danielson, & D. P. Hallahan (Eds.), *Identification of learning disabilities: Research to practice* (pp. 643–651). Mahwah, NJ: Erlbaum.

Swanson, H. L., & Alexander, J. E. (1997). Cognitive processes as predictors of word recognition and reading comprehension in learning-disabled and skilled readers: Revisiting the specificity hypothesis. *Journal of Educational Psychology, 89,* 128–158.

Swanson, H. L., & Ashbaker, M. H. (2000). Working memory, short-term memory, speech rate, word recognition and reading comprehension in learning disabled readers: Does the executive system have a role? *Intelligence, 28,* 1–30.

Swanson, H. L., & Cooney, J. B. (1991). Learning disabilities and memory. In B. Y. L. Wong (Ed.), *Learning about learning disabilities* (pp. 103–127). New York: Academic Press.

Swanson, H. L., & Sachse-Lee, C. (2001). Mathematical problem solving and working memory in children with learning disabilities: Both executive and phonological processes are important. *Journal of Experimental Child Psychology, 79,* 294–321.

Swanson, P. N., & De La Paz, S. (1998). Teaching effective comprehension strategies to students with learning and reading disabilities. *Intervention in School and Clinic, 33,* 209–218.

Sweeney, W. J., Salva, E., Cooper, J. O., & Talbert-Johnson, C. (1993). Using self-evaluation to improve difficult-to-read handwriting of secondary students. *Journal of Behavioral Education, 3,* 427–443.

Symons, S., Snyder, B. L., Cariglia-Bull, T., & Pressley, M. (1989). Why be so optimistic about cognitive strategy instruction? In C. B. McCormick, G. E. Miller, & M. Pressley (Eds.), *Cognitive strategy research: From basic research to educational applications.* New York: Springer-Verlag.

Systems Impact. (1986). *Mastering fractions.* Washington, DC: Author.

Systems Impact. (1988). *Mastering equations, roots, and exponents.* Washington, DC: Author.

Szymanski, E. M. (1994). Transition: Life-span and life-space considerations for empowerment. *Exceptional Children, 60*(5), 402–410.

Tabassam, W., & Grainger, J. (2002). Self-concept, attributional style and self-efficacy beliefs of students with learning disabilities with and without Attention Deficit Hyperactivity Disorder. *Learning Disability Quarterly, 25,* 141–151.

Tager-Flusberg, H. (2001). Putting words together: Morphology and syntax in the preschool years. In J. B. Gleason (Ed.), *The development of language* (pp. 162–212). Boston: Allyn & Bacon.

Tarver, S. G. (1986). Cognitive behavior modification, direct instruction and holistic approaches to the education of students with learning disabilities. *Journal of Learning Disabilities, 19,* 368–375.

Tarver, S. G. (1994). In search of effective instruction. *Effective School Practices, 13*(4), 23–32.

Tarver, S. G., & Ellsworth, P. S. (1981). Written and oral language for verbal children. In J. M. Kauffman & D. P. Hallahan (Eds.), *Handbook of special education* (pp. 491–511). Englewood Cliffs, NJ: Prentice-Hall.

Tarver, S. G., Hallahan, D. P., Kauffman, J. M., & Ball, D. W. (1976). Verbal rehearsal and selective attention in children with learning disabilities: A developmental lag. *Journal of Experimental Child Psychology, 22,* 375–385.

Taylor, H. G., & Schatschneider, C. (1992). Academic achievement following childhood brain disease: Implications for the concept of learning disabilities. *Journal of Learning Disabilities, 25,* 630–638.

Taylor, R. L. (1997). *Assessment of exceptional students: Educational and psychological procedures* (4th ed.). Boston: Allyn & Bacon.

Teicher, M. H., Anderson, C. M., Polcarl, A., Glod, C. A., Maas, L. C., & Renshaw, P. F. (2000). Functional deficits in basal ganglia of children with attention-deficit/hyperactivity disorder shown with functional magnetic resonance imaging relaxometry. *Nature Medicine, 6,* 470–473.

Teigs, E. W., & Clark, W. W. (1992). *The California Achievement Tests—Fifth Edition.* Monterey, CA: CTB/McGraw-Hill.

Temple, E., Deutsch, G. K., Poldrack, R. A., Miller, S. L., Tallal, P., Merzenich, M. M., & Garrieli, J. D. E. (2003). Neural deficits in children with dyslexia ameliorated by behavioral remediation: Evidence from functional MRI. *Proceedings of National Academy of Sciences, 100,* 2860–2865.

Terwilliger, J. (1997). Semantics, psychometrics, and assessment reform: A close look at "authentic" assessments. *Educational Researcher, 26*(8), 24–27.

Thelander, H. E., Phelps, J. K., & Walton, K. (1958). Learning disabilities associated with lesser brain damage. *Journal of Pediatrics, 53,* 405–409.

Thomas, A., & Grimes, J. (Eds.). (1995). *Best practices in school psychology, III.* Washington, DC: National Association of School Psychologists.

Thomas, B. (1994). Education should be special for all. *Phi Delta Kappan, 75,* 716–717.

Thomas, C. C., Englert, C. S., & Gregg, S. (1987). An analysis of errors and strategies in the expository writing of learning disabled students. *Remedial and Special Education, 8,* 21–30.

Thomas, C. J. (1905). Congenital "word-blindness" and its treatment. *Ophthalmoscope, 3,* 380–385.

Thompson, J. R., Fulk, B. M., & Piercy, S. W. (2000). Do individualized transition plans match the postschool projections of students with learning disabilities and their parents? *Career Development for Exceptional Individuals, 23,* 3–25.

Thompson, L. (1997). *Children talking: The development of pragmatic competence.* Philadelphia: Multilingual Matters.

Thorpe, H. W., Lampe, S., Nash, R. T., & Chiang, B. (1981). The effects of the kinesthetic-tactile component of the VAKT procedure on secondary LD students' reading performance. *Psychology in the Schools, 18,* 334–340.

Thousand, J. S., & Villa, R. A. (1989). Enhancing success in heterogeneous schools. In S. Stainback, W. Stainback, & M. Forest (Eds.), *Educating all students in the mainstream of regular education* (pp. 89–103). New York: Brookes.

Tilson, G. P., Luecking, R. G., & Donovan, M. R. (1994). Involving employers in transition: The Bridges Model. *Career Development for Exceptional Individuals, 17,* 77–89.

Tindal, G. A., & Marston, D. B. (1990). *Classroom-based assessment: Evaluating instructional outcomes.* Columbus, OH: Merrill/Macmillan.

Tindal, G., & Parker, R. (1991). Identifying measures for evaluating written expression. *Learning Disabilities Research and Practice, 6,* 211–218.

Tomlinson, C. A. (2001). *How to differentiate instruction in mixed-ability classrooms* (2nd ed.). Alexandria, VA: ASCD.

Torgesen, J. K. (1977). The role of nonspecific factors in the task performance of learning disabled children: A theoretical assessment. *Journal of Learning Disabilities, 10,* 27–34.

Torgesen, J. K. (1979). Factors related to poor performance in reading disabled children. *Learning Disability Quarterly, 2,* 17–23.

Torgesen, J. K. (1991). Learning disabilities: Historical and conceptual issues. In B. Y. L. Wong (Ed.), *Learning about learning disabilities* (pp. 3–37). New York: Academic Press.

Torgesen, J. K. (2002a). Empirical and theoretical support for direct diagnosis of learning disabilities by assessment of intrinsic processing weaknesses. In R. Bradley, L. Danielson, & D. P. Hallahan (Eds.), *Identification of learning disabilities: Research to practice* (pp. 565–613). Mahwah, NJ: Erlbaum.

Torgesen, J. K. (2002b). The prevention of reading difficulties. *Journal of School Psychology, 40,* 7–26.

Torgesen, J. K., & Bryant, B. T. (1994). *Phonological awareness training for reading.* Austin, TX: PRO-ED.

Torgesen, J. K., & Bryant, B. R. (1994). *Test of Phonological Awareness.* Austin, TX: PRO-ED.

Torgesen, J. K., Morgan, S. T., & Davis, C. (1992). Effects of two types of phonological awareness training on word learning in kindergarten children. *Journal of Educational Psychology, 84,* 364–370.

Torgesen, J. K., Waters, M. D., Cohen, A. L., & Torgesen, J. L. (1988). Improving sight-word recognition skills in LD children: An evaluation of three computer program variations. *Learning Disability Quarterly, 11,* 125–132.

Torgeson, J. K., & Mathes, P. (1999). What every teacher should know about phonological awareness. In *Consortium on Reading Excellence, Reading research: Anthology—The why? of reading instruction* (pp. 54–61). Emeryville, CA: Author.

Tralli, R., Columbo, B., Deshler, D. D., & Schumaker, J. B. (1999). The Strategies Intervention Model: A model for supported inclusion at the secondary level. In D. D. Deshler, J. B. Schumaker, K. R. Harris, & S. Graham (Eds.), *Teaching every adolescent every day: Learning in diverse middle and high school classrooms* (pp. 250–280). Cambridge, MA: Brookline Books.

Treiman, R., & Bourassa, D. C. (2000). The development of spelling skill. *Topics in Language Disorders, 20,* 1–18.

Trembley, P., Caponiqro, J., & Gaffrey, V. (1980). Effects of programming from the WRAT and PIAT for students determined to have learning disabilities in arithmetic. *Journal of Learning Disabilities, 13,* 291–293.

Trenholme, B., Larsen, S. C., & Parker, R. (1978). The effects of syntactic complexity upon arithmetic performance. *Learning Disability Quarterly, 1*(4), 80–85.

Trent, S. C. (1998). False starts and other dilemmas of a secondary general education collaborative teacher: A case study. *Journal of Learning Disabilities, 31,* 503–513.

Turnbull, A. P., & Turnbull, H. R. (2001). *Families, professionals, and exceptionality: Collaborating for empowerment* (4th ed.). Upper Saddle River, NJ: Prentice-Hall.

U.S. Census Bureau. (2002). *Poverty rate rises, household income declines, census bureau reports.* Retrieved February 25, 2003, from http://www.census.gov/Press-Release/www/2002/cb02-124.html

U.S. Department of Education. (1992). *Fourteenth annual report to Congress on the implementation of the Individuals with Disabilities Education Act.* Washington, DC: Author.

U.S. Department of Education. (1996). *Eighteenth annual report to Congress on the implementation of the Individuals with Disabilities Education Act.* Washington, DC: Author. Retrieved February 25, 2003, from http://www.ed.gov/pubs/OSEP96AnlRpt

U.S. Department of Education. (1999, March 12). Assistance to states for the education of children with disabilities and the early intervention program for infants and toddlers with disabilities: Final regulations. *Federal Register, 64* (48), 12406–12672.

U.S. Department of Education. (2001a). Family involvement in the education of elementary and middle school students receiving special education. In *Twenty-third annual report to Congress on the implementation of the Individuals with Disabilities Education Act* (Section III: *Programs and Services,* pp. 7–34). Washington, DC: Author.

U.S. Department of Education. (2001b). *Twenty-third annual report to Congress on the implementation of the Individuals with Disabilities Education Act.* Washington, DC: Author.

U.S. Department of Education. (2002a). *The No Child Left Behind Act Title I: Improving the academic achievement of the disadvantaged—Summary of final regulations.* Retrieved February 25, 2003, from http://www.ed.gov/PressReleases/11-2002/regs_sum.html

U.S. Department of Education. (2002b). *Twenty-fourth annual report to Congress on the implementation of the Individuals with Disabilities Education Act.* Washington, DC: U.S. Department of Education, Office of Special Education Programs.

U.S. Department of Education. (2003). *IDEA data.* Retrieved September 7, 2003, from www.ideadata.org/arc_toc3.asp#partbLRE

U.S. Office of Education. (1968). *First annual report of National Advisory Committee on Handicapped Children.* Washington, DC: U.S. Department of Health, Education, and Welfare.

U.S. Office of Education. (1977, December 29). Assistance to states for education of handicapped children: Procedures for evaluating specific learning disabilities. *Federal Register, 42*(250), 65082–65085. Washington, DC: U.S. Government Printing Office.

Unger, D. G., Jones, C. W., Park, E., & Tressell, P. A. (2001). Promoting involvement between low-income single caregivers and urban early intervention programs. *Topics in Early Childhood Special Education, 21,* 197–212.

Utley, C. A., Delquadri, J. C., Obiako, F. E., & Mims, V. A. (2000). General and special educators' perceptions of teaching strategies for multicutural students. *Teacher Education and Special Education, 23,* 34–50.

Valle, J. W., & Aponte, E. (2002). IDEA and collaboration: A Bakhtinian perspective on parent and professional discourse. *Journal of Learning Disabilities, 35,* 469–479.

Van Houten, R., & Van Houten, J. (1991). The effects of breaking new spelling words into small segments on the spelling performance of students with learning disabilities. *Journal of Behavioral Education, 1,* 399–411.

Van Houten, R., Morrison, E., Jarvis, R., & McDonald, M. (1974). The effects of explicit timing and feedback on compositional response rate in elementary school children. *Journal of Applied Behavior Analysis, 7,* 547–555.

van Keulen, J. E., Weddington, G. T., & DeBose, C. E. (1998). *Speech, language, learning, and the African American child.* Boston: Allyn & Bacon.

Vaughn, S., & Fuchs, L. S. (2003). Redefining learning disabilities as inadequate response to instruction: The promise and potential pitfalls. *Learning Disabilities: Research and Practice, 18,* 137–146.

Vaughn, S., & Klinger, J. K. (1999). Teaching reading comprehension through collaborative strategic reading. *Intervention in School and Clinic, 34,* 284–292.

Vaughn, S., & Klinger, J. K. (1998). Students' perceptions of inclusion and resource room settings. *Journal of Special Education, 32,* 79–88.

Vaughn, S., & Linan-Thompson, S. (in press). Group size and time allotted to intervention: Effects for students with reading difficulties. *Learning Disabilities Research and Practice.*

Vaughn, S., Bos, C. S., & Schumm, J. S. (2000). *Teaching exceptional, diverse, and at-risk students in the general education classroom* (2nd ed.). Boston: Allyn & Bacon.

Vaughn, S., Bos, C., & Schumm, J. S. (1997). *Teaching mainstreamed, diverse, and at-risk students in the general education classroom.* Boston: Allyn & Bacon.

Vaughn, S., Kim, A., Sloan, C. V. M., Hughes, M. T., Elbaum, B., & Sridhar, D. (2003). Social skills interventions for young children with disabilities: A synthesis of group design studies. *Remedial and Special Education, 24,* 2–15.

Vaughn, S., Klinger, J. K., & Bryant, D. P. (2001). Collaborative strategic reading as a means to enhance peer-mediated instruction for reading comprehension and content-area learning. *Remedial and Special Education, 22,* 66–75.

Vaughn, S., Levy, S., Coleman, M., & Bos, C. S. (2002). Reading instruction for students with LD and EBD: A synthesis of observation studies. *Journal of Special Education, 36,* 2–13.

Vaughn, S., Schumm, J. S., & Arguelles, M. E. (1997). The ABCDEs of Co-teaching. *Teaching Exceptional Children, 30,* 4–10.

Vellutino, E. R., & Scanlon, D. M. (1987). Phonological coding, phonological awareness, and reading ability: Evidence from a longitudinal and experimental study. *Merrill-Palmer Quarterly, 33,* 321–363.

Vellutino, F. R., Steger, J. A., & Kandel, G. (1972). Reading disability: An investigation of the perceptual deficit hypothesis. *Cortex, 8,* 106–118.

Venkatagiri, H. S. (2002). Speech recognition technology applications in communication disorders. *American Journal of Speech-Language Pathology, 11,* 323–332.

Vickery, K. S., Reynolds, V. A., & Cochran, S. W. (1987). Multisensory teaching approach for reading, spelling, and handwriting. Orton-Gillingham based curriculum in a public school setting. *Annals of Dyslexia, 37,* 189–200.

Vogel, S. A. (1974). Syntactic abilities in normal and dyslexic children. *Journal of Learning Disabilities, 7,* 103–109.

Vogel, S. A. (1977). Morphological ability in normal and dyslexic children. *Journal of Learning Disabilities, 10,* 41–49.

Vogel, S. A., & Adelman, P. B. (1992). The success of college students with learning disabilities: Factors related to educational attainment. *Journal of Learning Disabilities, 25*(7), 430–441.

Vollmer, T. R. (2002). Punishment happens: Some comments on Lerman and Vorndran's review. *Journal of Applied Behavior Analysis, 35,* 469–473.

Vreeland, M., Vail, J., Bradley, L., Buetow, C., Cipriano, K., Green, C., Henshaw, P., & Huth, E. (1994). Accelerating cognitive growth: The Edison School math project. *Effective School Practices, 13*(2), 64–69.

Vye, N. J. (2003). Anchored instruction. In J. W. Guthrie (Ed.), *Encyclopedia of education* (2nd ed., pp. 1151–1154). New York: Macmillan Reference.

Vygotsky, L. (1962). *Thought and language.* New York: Wiley.

Waber, D. P., Weiler, M. D., Wolff, P. H., Bellinger, D., Marcus, D. J., Ariel, R., Forbes, P., & Wijpy, D. (2001). Processing of rapid auditory stimuli in school-age children referred for evaluation of learning disorders. *Child Development, 72,* 37–49.

Wagner, M., Blackorby, J., Cameto, R., Hebbeler, K., & Newman, L. (1993). *The transition experiences of young people with disabilities: A summary of findings from the National Longitudinal Transition Study of special education students.* Menlo Park, CA: SRI International.

Wagner, M., Marder, C., & Blackorby, J. (with Cardoso, D.). (2002). *The children we serve: The demographic characteristics of elementary and middle school students with disabilities and their households.* Menlo Park, CA: SRI International. Available online at http://www.seels.net/designdocs/SEELS_Children_We_Serve_Report.pdf

Wagner, M., Spiker, D., & Linn, M. I. (2002). The effectiveness of the parents as teachers program with low-income parents and children. *Topics in Early Childhood Special Education, 22,* 67–81.

Wagner, R. K., & Torgesen, J. K. (1987). The nature of phonological processing and its causal role in the acquisition of reading skills. *Psychological Bulletin, 101,* 192–212.

Wagner, R. K., Torgesen, J. K., & Rashotte, C. A. (1994). Development of reading-related phonological processing abilities: New evidence of bidirectional causality from a latent variable longitudinal study. *Developmental Psychology, 30,* 73–87.

Wagner, R. K., Torgesen, J. K., Rashotte, C. A., Hecht, S. A., Barker, T. A., Burgess, S. R., Donahue, J., & Garon, T. (1997). Changing relations between phonological processing abilities and word-level reading as children develop from beginning to skilled readers: A 5 year longitudinal study. *Developmental Psychology, 33,* 468–479.

Walker, H. M. (1995). *The acting-out child: Coping with classroom disruption.* Longmont, CO: Sopris West.

Walker, H. M., & Severson, H. H. (1990). *Systematic Screening for Behavior Disorders (SSBD): A multiple gating procedure.* Longmont, CO: Sopris West.

Walker, H. M., & Shinn, M. R. (2002). Structuring school-based interventions to achieve integrated primary, secondary, and tertiary prevention goals for safe and effective schools. In M. R. Shinn, H. M. Walker, & G. Stoner (Eds.), *Interventions for academic and behavior problems: II. Preventive and remedial approaches* (pp. 1–26). Bethesda, MD: National Association of School Psychologists.

Walker, H. M., Block-Pedego, A., Todis, B., & Severson, H. (1991). *School Archival Records Search (SARS).* Longmont, CO: Sopris West.

Walker, H. M., Calvin, G., & Ramsey, E. (1995). *Antisocial behavior in school: Strategies and best practices.* Pacific Grove, CA: Brooks/Cole.

Walker, H. M., Ramsey, E., & Gresham, F. M. (2004). *Antisocial behavior in school: Strategies and best practices* (2nd ed.). Pacific Grove, CA: Brooks/Cole.

Wallace, C., Larsen, S. C., & Elksnin, L. K. (1992). *Educational assessment of learning problems: Testing for teaching* (2nd ed.). Boston: Allyn & Bacon.

Wallace, G., & Hammill, D. D. (2002). *Comprehensive Receptive and Expressive Vocabulary Test* (2nd ed.). Austin, TX: PRO-ED.

Wallace, T., Anderson, A. R., Batholomay, T., & Hupp, S. (2002). An ecobehavioral examination of high school classrooms that include students with disabilities. *Exceptional Children, 68,* 345–359.

Waugh, R. (1975). The ITPA: Ballast or bonanza for the school psychologist? *Journal of School Psychology, 13,* 201–208.

Wechsler, D. (1991). *Wechsler Intelligence Scale for Children—III.* San Antonio, TX: Psychological Corporation.

Wedell, K., & Home, L. E. (1969). Some aspects of perceptual-motor disability in 5-year-old children. *British Journal of Educational Psychology, 39,* 174–182.

Wehman, P. (2001). *Life beyond the classroom: Transition strategies for young people with disabilities* (3rd ed.). Baltimore: Brookes.

Wehmeyer, M. L., Agran, M., & Hughes, C. (1998). *Teaching self-determination to students with disabilities.* Baltimore: Brookes.

Weiss, M. P., & Brigham, F. J. (2000). Co-teaching and the model of shared responsibility: What does the research support? In T. E. Scruggs & M. A. Mastropieri (Eds.), *Advances in learning and behavioral disabilities: Educational interventions.* Stamford, CT: JAI Press.

Weiss, M. P., & Lloyd, J. W. (2001). Structure and effective teaching. In D. P. Hallahan & B. K. Keogh (Eds.), *Research and global perspectives in learning disabilities: Essays in honor of William M. Cruickshank* (pp. 131–145). Mahwah, NJ: Erlbaum.

Weiss, M. P., & Lloyd, J. W. (2002). Congruence between roles and actions of secondary special educators in co-taught and special education settings. *Journal of Special Education, 36*(2), 58–68.

Weiss, M. P., & Lloyd, J. W. (2003). Conditions for co-teaching: Lessons from a case study. *Teacher Education and Special Education, 26,* 27–41.

Wellington, J. (1994). Evaluating a mathematics program for adoption: Connecting math concepts. *Effective School Practices, 13*(2), 70–75.

Werner, H., & Strauss, A. A. (1939). Types of visuo-motor activity in their relation to low and high performance ages. *Proceedings of the American Association on Mental Deficiency, 44,* 163–168.

Werner, H., & Strauss, A. A. (1940). Causal factors in low performance. *American Journal of Mental Deficiency, 45,* 213–218.

Werner, H., & Strauss, A. A. (1941). Pathology of figure-background relation in the child. *Journal of Abnormal and Social Psychology, 36,* 236–248.

Westby, C. (2000). Who are adults with learning disabilities and what do we know about them? *Topics in Language Disorders, 21,* 1–14.

White, T. G., Graves, M. F., & Slater, W. H. (1990). Growth of reading vocabulary in diverse elementary schools: Decoding and word meaning. *Journal of Educational Psychology, 82,* 281–290.

White, W. A. T. (1988). A meta-analysis of the effects of direct instruction in special education. *Education and Treatment of Children, 11,* 364–374.

Whitman, T., & Johnston, M. B. (1983). Teaching addition and subtraction with regrouping to educable mentally retarded children: A group self-instructional training program. *Behavior Therapy, 14,* 127–143.

Wiederholt, J. L. (1974). Historical perspectives on the education of the learning disabled. In L. Mann & D. Sabatino (Eds.), *The second review of special education* (pp. 103–152). Philadelphia: Journal of Special Education Press.

Wiggins, G. P. (1993). *Assessing student performance: Exploring the purpose and limits of testing.* San Francisco: Jossey-Bass.

Wiig, E. H. (2001). Multi-perspective, clinical-educational assessments of language disorders. In A. S. Kaufman and N. L. Kaufman (Eds.), *Specific learning disabilities and difficulties in children and adolescents: Psychological assessment and evaluation* (pp. 247–279). New York: Cambridge University Press.

Wiig, E. H., & Roach, M. A. (1975). Immediate recall of semantically varied "sentences" by learning disabled adolescents. *Perceptual and Motor Skills, 40,* 119–125.

Wiig, E. H., & Semel, E. M. (1975). Productive language abilities in learning disabled adolescents. *Journal of Learning Disabilities, 8,* 578–586.

Wiig, E. H., Semel, E. M., & Abele, E. (1981). Perception of ambiguous sentences by learning disabled twelve-year-olds. *Learning Disability Quarterly, 4,* 3–12.

Wiig, E. H., Semel, E. M., & Crouse, M. A. (1973). The use of English morphology by high-risk and learning disabled children. *Journal of Learning Disabilities, 6,* 457–465.

Wilder, A. A., & Williams, J. P. (2001). Students with severe learning disabilities can learn higher order comprehension skills. *Journal of Educational Psychology, 93,* 268–278.

Wilens, T. E., Biederman, J., & Spencer, T. J. (2002). Attention deficit/hyperactivity disorder across the lifespan. *Annual Review of Medicine, 53,* 113–131.

Wilkinson, G. S. (1993). *The Wide Range Achievement Test—III.* Wilmington, DE: Wide Range.

Will, M. (1984). *OSERS programming for the transition of youth with disabilities: Bridges from school to working life.* Washington, DC: U.S. Department of Education, Office of Special Education and Rehabilitative Services.

Williams, J. P. (2003). Teaching text structure to improve reading comprehension. In H. L. Swanson, K. R. Harris, & S. Graham (Eds.), *Handbook of learning disabilities* (pp. 293–305). New York: Guilford Press.

Williams, J. P., Lauer, K. D., Hall, K. M., Lord, K. M., Gugga, S. S., Bak, S., Jacobs, P. R., & deCani, J. S. (2002). Teaching elementary school students to identify story themes. *Journal of Educational Psychology, 94,* 235–248.

Williams, J. R. (1977). Building perceptual and cognitive strategies into a reading curriculum. In A. S. Reber & D. L. Scarborough (Eds.), *Toward a psychology of reading: The proceedings of the CUNY conferences* (pp. 257–288). Hillsdale, NJ: Erlbaum.

Williams, J. R. (1980). Teaching decoding with an emphasis on phoneme analysis and phoneme blending. *Journal of Educational Psychology, 72,* 1–15.

Williams, J. R. (1991). The use of schema in research on the problem solving of learning disabled adolescents. In T. E. Scruggs & B. Y. L. Wong (Eds.), *Intervention research in learning disabilities* (pp. 302–321). New York: Springer-Verlag.

Williams, J. R., Brown, L. G., Silverstein, A. K., & deCani, J. S. (1994). An instructional program in comprehension of narrative themes for adolescents with learning disabilities. *Learning Disability Quarterly, 17,* 205–221.

Windsor, J., Scott, C. M., & Street, C. K. (2000). Verb and noun morphology in the spoken and written language of children with language learning disabilities. *Journal of Speech, Language, and Hearing Research, 43,* 1322–1336.

Wing, L., Leekam, S. R., Libby, S. J., Gould, J., & Larcombe, M. (2002). The diagnostic interview for social and communication disorders: Background, inter-rater reliability and clinical use. *Journal of Child Psychology and Psychiatry and Allied Disciplines, 43*(3), 307–325.

Winterling, V. (1990). The effects of constant time delay, practice in writing or spelling, and reinforcement on sight word recognition in a small group. *Journal of Special Education, 24,* 101–116.

Winzer, M. A. (1993). *The history of special education: From isolation to integration.* Washington, DC: Gallaudet University Press.

Wisconsin Department of Public Instruction. (2002). *Federal/state definitions/criteria for learning disabilities.* Madison: Author.

Wise, B., W., & Olson, R. K. (1998). Studies of computer-aided remediation for reading disabilities. In C. Hulme & R. M. Joshi (Eds.), *Reading and spelling: Development and disorders* (pp. 473–487). Mahwah, NJ: Erlbaum.

Wise, B., W., Olson, R. K., Ring, J., & Johnson, M. (1998). Interactive computer support for improving phonological skills. In J. Metsala & L. C. Ehri (Eds.), *Word recognition in beginning literacy* (pp. 189–208). Mahwah, NJ: Erlbaum.

Wise, B., W., Ring, J., & Olson, R. K. (2000). Individual differences in gains from computer-assisted remedial reading. *Journal of Experimental Child Psychology, 77,* 197–235.

Witkin, H. A., Goodenough, D. R., & Karp, S. A. (1967). Stability of cognitive style from childhood to young adulthood. *Journal of Personality and Social Psychology, 7,* 291–300.

Witte, R. H., Philips, L., & Kakela, M. (1998). Job satisfaction of college graduates with learning disabilities. *Journal of Learning Disabilities, 31,* 259–265.

Wolery, M., Brashers, M. S., & Neitzel, J. C. (2002). Ecological congruence assessment for classroom activities and routines: Identifying goals and intervention practices in childcare. *Topics in Early Childhood Special Education, 22,* 131–142.

Wolf, M. (1991). Naming speed and reading: The contribution of the cognitive neurosciences. *Reading Research Quarterly, 24,* 123–141.

Wolf, M. (1997). A provisional, integrative account of phonological and naming-speed deficits in dyslexia: Implications for diagnosis and intervention. In B. Blachman (Ed.), *Foun-*

dations of reading acquisition and dyslexia: Implications for early intervention (pp. 67–92). Mahwah, NJ: Erlbaum.

Wolf, M., & Bowers, P. G. (1999). The double-deficit hypothesis for the developmental dyslexias. *Journal of Educational Psychology, 91,* 415–438.

Wolinsky, S., & Whelan, S. (1999). Federal law and the accommodation of students with LD: The lawyer's look at the BU Decision. *Journal of Learning Disabilities, 32,* 286–291.

Wolraich, M. L., Wilson, D. B., & White, J. W. (1996). The effect of sugar on behavior or cognition in children: A meta-analysis. *Journal of the American Medical Association, 274,* 1617–1621.

Wong, B. Y. L. (1982). Understanding the learning disabled student's reading problems: Contributions from cognitive psychology. *Topics in Learning and Learning Disabilities, 1*(4), 43–50.

Wong, B. Y. L. (1991). The relevance of metacognition to learning disabilities. In B. Y. L. Wong (Ed.), *Learning about learning disabilities* (pp. 231–258). New York: Academic Press.

Wong, B. Y. L. (1996). *The ABCs of learning disabilities.* San Diego: Academic Press.

Wong, B. Y. L. (1997). Research on genre-specific strategies for enhancing writing in adolescents with learning disabilities. *Learning Disability Quarterly, 20,* 140–159.

Wong, B. Y. L., & Donahue, M. (Eds.). (2002). *The social dimensions of learning disabilities: Essays in honor of Tanis Bryan.* Mahwah, NJ: Erlbaum.

Wong, B. Y. L., & Roadhouse, A. (1978). The Test of Language Development (TOLD): A validation study. *Learning Disability Quarterly, 1*(3), 48–61.

Wood, C., & Farrington-Flint, L. (2001). Orthographic analogy use and phonological priming effects in non-word reading. *Cognitive Development, 16,* 951–963.

Wood, J. W. (2002). *Adapting instruction to accommodate students in inclusive settings* (4th ed.). Upper Saddle River, NJ: Merrill.

Wood, M. (1998). Whose job is it anyway? Educational roles in inclusion. *Exceptional Children, 64,* 181–195.

Woodcock, R. W. (1997). *Woodcock Diagnostic Reading Battery.* Circle Pines, MN: American Guidance Service.

Woodcock, R. W., McGrew, K. S., & Mather, N. (2001). *Woodcock-Johnson III.* Itasca, IL: Riverside Publishing.

Woodward, J., & Howard, L. (1994). The misconceptions of youth: Errors and their mathematical meaning. *Exceptional Children, 61,* 126–136.

Woodward, J., & Montague, M. (2002). Meeting the challenge of mathematics reform for students with LD. *Journal of Special Education, 36,* 89–101.

Worrall, R. S. (1990). Detecting health fraud in the field of learning disabilities. *Journal of Learning Disabilities, 23,* 207–212.

Worrall, R. S., & Carnine, D. (1994, March). *Lack of professional support undermines teachers and reform—A contrasting perspective from health and engineering.* Unpublished manuscript. National Center to Improve the Tools of Educators, College of Education, University of Oregon, Eugene.

Worthen, B. R. (1993). Critical issues that will determine the future of alternative assessment. *Phi Delta Kappan, 74,* 444–456.

Worthy, M. J., & Invernizzi, M. (1990). Spelling errors of normal and disabled students on achievement levels one through four: Instructional implications. *Annals of Dyslexia, 40,* 138–151.

Yell, M. L. (1998). *The law and special education.* Upper Saddle River, NJ: Prentice-Hall.

Yell, M. L., & Shriner, J. G. (1997). The IDEA amendments of 1997: Implications for special and general education teachers, administrators, and teacher trainers. *Focus on Exceptional Children, 30*(1), 1–19.

Yelland, N., & Siraj-Blatchford, J. (Eds.). (2002). *Contemporary Issues in Early Childhood* (technology special issue). Retrieved April 10, 2003, from www.triangle.co.uk/ciec/index.htm

Yopp, H. K. (1988). The validity and reliability of phonemic awareness tests. *Reading Research Quarterly, 23,* 159–177.

Young, R. M., & O'Shea, T. (1981). Errors in children's subtraction. *Cognitive Science, 5,* 153–177.

Ysseldyke, J. E., & Christenson, S. L. (1987). Evaluating students' instructional environments. *Remedial and Special Education, 8*(3), 17–24.

Ysseldyke, J. E., & Salvia, J. A. (1974). Diagnostic prescriptive teaching: Two models. *Exceptional Children, 41,* 181–186.

Ysseldyke, J. E., Algozzine, B., & Epps, S. (1983). A logical and empirical analysis of current practice in classifying students as handicapped. *Exceptional Children, 50,* 160–166.

Ysseldyke, J. E., Algozzine, B., & Thurlow, M. L. (1992). *Critical issues in special education* (2nd ed.). Boston: Houghton Mifflin.

Ysseldyke, J. E., Algozzine, B., Shinn, M. R., & McGue, M. (1982). Similarities and differences between low achievers and students classified as learning disabled. *Journal of Special Education, 16,* 73–85.

Zawaiza, T. R. W., & Gerber, M. M. (1993). Effects of explicit instruction on math word-problem-solving by community college students with learning disabilities. *Learning Disability Quarterly, 16,* 64–79.

Zigler, E., & Styfco, S. J. (2000). Pioneering steps (and fumbles) in developing a federal preschool intervention. *Topics in Early Childhood Special Education, 20,* 67–70, 78.

Zigmond, N. (1990). Rethinking secondary school programs for students with learning disabilities. *Focus on Exceptional Children, 23*(1), 1–22.

Zigmond, N. (1993). Learning disabilities from an educational perspective. In G. R. Lyon, D. B. Gray, J. F. Kavanagh, & N. A. Krasnegor (Eds.), *Better understanding learning disabilities: New views from research and their implications for education and public policies* (pp. 251–272). Baltimore: Brookes.

Zigmond, N. (1997). Educating students with disabilities: The future of special education. In J. W. Lloyd, E. J. Kame'enui, & D. Chard (Eds.), *Issues in educating students with disabilities* (pp. 377–390). Mahwah, NJ: Erlbaum.

Zigmond, N., & Baker, J. M. (1996). Full inclusion for students with learning disabilities: Too much of a good thing? *Theory into Practice, 35*(1), 26–34.

Zigmond, N., & Miller, S. E. (1986). Assessment for instructional planning. *Exceptional Children, 52,* 501–509.

Zigmond, N., & Miller, S. E. (1992). Improving high school programs for students with learning disabilities: A matter of substance as well as form. In F. R. Rusch, L. DeStefano, J. Chadsey-Rusch, L. A. Phelps, & E. Szymanski (Eds.), *Transition from school to adult life* (pp. 17–31). Sycamore, IL: Sycamore Publishing.

# SUBJECT INDEX

*Note: f* indicates a figure, and *t* indicates a table.

Blending, 369
Boston University, 327
Bottom-up programming, 318–319
Brain, 46–54, 49*f. See also* Neurological
    dysfunction; *specific parts of brain*
Brain research, 46, 47, 271–272, 396
Brain stem, 48, 49*f*
Brainstorming programs, 188
Broca's area, 52, 53*f*
Business-school partnerships, 182–183
*Buswell-John Test* (Buswell and John), 464

Calculators
    benefits of using, 475
    talking, 189
Cardiac arrest, 60
Caudate, 272, 274*f*, 275
CEC standards, 525–537
Celebrities with learning disabilities, 8
Cell body. *See* Soma
Center for Applied Special Technology
    (CAST), 506
Central fissure, 49*f*, 50
Cerebellum, 48, 49–50, 49*f*, 272, 273, 274*f*,
    275
Cerebral cortex, 48, 50–51
Cerebral dysfunction, 13, 16
Cerebral palsy, 262
Checklists, informal, 498, 500*f*–501*f*
Children and Adults with Attention
    Deficit/Hyperactivity Disorders
    (CHADD), 132, 272
Children with learning disabilities. *See also*
    Students with learning disabilities
    identifying, 149–152
    intervention programs for, 152–156
    risk factors, 146–147
Child study teams, 24, 74
Choices, 214, 215, 216*f*
Chunking, 224
Class size, 67
Classwide peer tutoring (CWPT), 397, 516
Clinical Evaluation of Language Funda-
    mentals–III, 343*t*
Clinical interview, 267
Clinical teaching, 378
Clustering, 224
Coaching, 519
Code for Instructional Structure and Stu-
    dent Academic Response (CISSAR),
    497
Cognition, 224
Cognitive abilities, 77
Cognitive-behavioral techniques, 414,
    443–444
Cognitive-behavior modification (CBM),
    308–309, 318, 319–320
Cognitive development, problems in,
    457–458
Cognitive model, 296*t*, 307–309, 318–319,
    320
Cognitive strategies, 248–251
Cognitive styles, 230–231
Cognitive training, 39, 238–253, 239*f*
Cohesion, 114–115
Collaboration, CEC standard on, 536–537
Collaborative consultation, 102*t*, 492

Collaborative strategic reading (CSR),
    515–516
College
    choosing, 177–179, 178*t*
    instructional accommodations in,
        180–181
    preparedness for, 175–176
    social skills in, 172
    success in, 176–181
Columnar retrieval, 456*t*
Committee on Employment of People
    with Disabilities, 184
Communication. *See also* Language
    assessment of. *See* Language assessment
    definition of, 76–77, 325, 328
    family-professional, 126–136, 139–141,
        159
Comorbidity, 13, 17, 35–36
Compensatory strategies, 187–188
Composition, 427–444
    assessment of, 430–431
    components of, 429*f*
    dictating, 428
    interventions for, 433–444
    problems with, 427–430
    teaching, 435*t*, 437–444
Comprehension, 364–367
    problems with, 371–375
    teaching, 388, 398–400, 402–403
Comprehensive Receptive and Expressive
    Vocabulary Test, 344*t*
Comprehensive standardized assessment,
    342–343, 343*t*
Computational Arithmetic Program
    (CAP), 475
Computational skills, 77
Computer-assisted instruction (CAI),
    162–163, 347, 395, 476–478
Concept diagram, 512–514, 513*f*
Conceptual definition, 70
Conceptual models, 295–313. *See also*
    *specific models*
    advantages of, 295–296
    definition of, 295
    disadvantages of, 295
Conduct problems, 198–199
Conferences, parent–teacher, 130–135, 134*t*
Confidentiality, 86–88
Connected writing, 418
Connecting Math Concepts, 473
*Conners' Teacher Rating Scale—Revised,* 268
Conservation, 452
Consistency, 201
Constant time delay (CTD), 163
Constructivist model, 296*t*, 309–312, 318,
    319
Consultative teacher model, 24
Contacts, 186
*Contemporary Issues in Early Childhood*
    (online journal), 163
Content enhancement routine, 511
Content textbook strategy, 248, 250–251
Context
    reading in, 374
    teaching in, 353
Contextual assessment, 79–80
Contingency-based self-management, 282

Continued reading, 385
Continuous performance tests (CPTs), 268
Continuum of alternative placements,
    104–105, 491
Conversation
    development of, 337–338
    teaching in, 353
Coordinated Campaign for Learning Dis-
    abilities (CCLD), 132
Corpus callosum, 55
Corrective Mathematics program, 475
Corrective reading, 389
Corrective Reading Program (CRP), 379,
    380*f*, 394–395
Co-teaching, 102*t*, 492–495
Council for Exceptional Children (CEC)
    standards, 525–537
Council for Learning Disabilities (CLD),
    132
Counting fingers, 456*t*
Counting manipulatives, 455, 456*t*
Crack cocaine, 59
Criterion-referenced tests, 82*f*
Cultural differences, *vs.* learning disabili-
    ties, 147–148
Culturally and linguistically diverse (CLD)
    children, 147–148
Culturally and linguistically diverse (CLD)
    parents, 174
Curriculum-based assessment (curriculum-
    based measurement) (CBA/CBM),
    25, 81–83
    in general education, 498–502
    in handwriting, 411
    in language, 346–347
    in mathematics, 470
    in reading, 379–380
Cursive system, 413

Decimal, 455
Decoding
    definition of, 318
    fluent, 385
    problems with, 369
    in reading, 364–367, 366*t*
    and spelling, 418
Dendrites, 46, 47, 48*f*
Dependency, 169
Derived facts, 456*t*
Developmental interventions, 423–424,
    433–436, 473–474
Developmentally appropriate practices
    (DAP), 158–159
Developmentally delayed, definition of,
    150
Developmental reading instruction, 389
Diabetes, 60
Diagnosis, 376
*Diagnosis: An Instructional Aid in Mathemat-
    ics* (Guzaitis et al.), 464
*Diagnostic and Statistical Manual of Mental
    Disorders* (DSM), 263–265
*Diagnostic Mathematics Inventory* (Gessell),
    464
Diagnostic-remedial model, 296*t*, 298–300
Diagnostic testing, 377, 463–464, 464*t*
Dictation, 412*t*, 418, 428

Difficulty, controlling, 510
Direct assessment, 320–321
Directed questioning, 509
Direct Instruction (DI), 39, 69–70, 301–306
  bottom-up programming in, 318
  *vs.* direct instruction, 301–302, 302*t*
  effectiveness of, 319–320
  specific strategies in, 318
  structure in, 319
  task analysis in, 305*f,* 306
  Thinking Operations in, 303*f*–304*f*
Direct instruction (di), 301–302, 302*t*
Direct teaching, 239*f*
Discrepancy
  dual, 96
  severe, 70, 72–73
Discrepancy formulas, 21–22
DISTAR Arithmetic, 473
Distributed practice, 251
Districtwide assessment, 99–100
Dizygotic twins, 58–59
Doctor's office effect, 267, 269
Dopamine, 273, 275, 286
Drill-repetition, 509
Dropout rates, 168
Drug abuse, in pregnant women, 59
Dual discrepancy, 96
Duet (team), 493
Dysarthia, 329
Dyscalculia, 6, 457
Dysgraphia, 408
Dyslexia, 44, 363, 367, 396
Dysnomia, 329
Dyspedagogia, 45

Early childhood learning impairment (ECLI), 163
Early intervention, 152–156, 213. *See also specific programs*
  legislation on, 154–155
  quality of, 155–156
  before referral for eligibility assessment, 23–24
  responsiveness to, 24–26
  trends in, 156–163
Ecobehavioral Assessment Systems Software (EBASS), 497–498
Educational approaches, 295–321. *See also* Direct Instruction
  behavioral model, 296*t,* 300–307
  cognitive model, 296*t,* 307–309, 318–319, 320
  constructivist model, 296*t,* 309–312, 318, 319
  diagnostic-remedial model, 296*t,* 298–300
  differences and similarities of, 317–321
  medical model, 296*t,* 297–298
  research on, 313–317
Education for All Handicapped Children Act (1975), 19*t,* 272
Effect size, 315–317, 316*f*
Effort, 243
Elaboration, 350
Electronic reference materials, 189

Eligibility for special education, 65–106
  alternative process of, 94–96
  decision on, 88–94
  determining, 23–27
  evaluation for. *See* Assessment
  traditional process of, 73–94
Emily Hall Tremaine Foundation, 132
Emotional problems, 195–219
  assessing characteristics of, 202–206
  causes of, 199–202
  educational methods for, 208–219
  learning disabilities and, 195–199
Emotions, self-regulation of, 279–280
Empirical validation, 67, 68–69
Employees with learning disabilities, 181–191
  preparedness for, 181–183
  school–business partnerships and, 182–183
  successful, 185–191
  technology and, 183, 188–189
  vocational training for, 175, 182
  workplace accommodations for, 184–185
Encephalitis, 261
Encoding, 418
English-language learners, 351
Environment, learning, 78, 529–531
Environmental factors of neurological dysfunction, 61
Environmentalism, 45, 46
Episodic memory, 225
Error analysis, 421, 465
Errors, 80
Ethical practice standards, 535–536
Ethnicity. *See* Race/ethnicity
Etiology, 43. *See also* Learning disabilities, causes/factors
Exceptional learning needs (ELN), 526
Executive control, 225, 234–236
Executive functions, 50, 278–279
Exit slips, 509
Expansion, 350
Expectancy formulas, 72
Expectations, 201
Expressive language, 329
Expressive writing. *See* Composition
Externalizing behavior, 202
External locus of control, 236
Eye-gaze Response Interface Aid (ERICA), 270–271, 270*f*
Eye-movement studies, 270–271

Fact retrieval, 456*t*
Familiality, 57–58, 119
Families, 109–136. *See also* Parents
  resources for, 132–133
Family-based education, 159–160
Family-centered models, 111
Family Education Network, 132
Family involvement, 113, 114, 159–160
Family life
  current trends in, 116–117, 159
  diversity and, 116–117, 118
  family characteristics, 113
  family functions, 115
  family interaction, 113–115

family unit, 116
  nontraditional families, 116
  single-parent families, 116
  socioeconomic status and, 117
Family life cycle, 115
Family role
  attitudes toward learning, 121
  communication, 126–136, 139–141, 159
  family adjustment, 118–121
  family reaction, 121
  homework, 122–125
  parental guilt, 119
  parental stress, 111, 119–120
  sibling reactions, 120–121
Family systems model, 113–115
Family Village, 132
Far-point copying, 408, 411, 412*t*
Feedback, guided, 440–443
Feingold diet, 275
Fernald approach, 389–390
Fetal alcohol syndrome, 59
Field independence–field dependence concept, 230
Flash cards, 405
Flexible strategy use, 384
Flow lists, 427
Fluency, 383–384
  enhancing, 395–397
  mathematical, 485–486
Fluency problems
  in handwriting, 409
  in reading, 370–371, 371*t*
Food additives, 275
Foreign language learning, 327
Foresight, 279
Formal diagnostic testing, 463–464, 464*t*
Formal mathematical knowledge, 452
Fractions, 459
Free and appropriate public education (FAPE), 66
Free writing, 412*t*
Frontal lobes, 48, 49*f,* 50, 272, 273, 274*f*
Full inclusion, 104–105, 491
Functional behavioral assessment (FBA), 85, 204–206, 281–282
Functional magnetic resonance imaging (fMRI), 46, 47, 55, 396

Gates-Russell Spelling Diagnostic Test, 420
Gender
  and ADHD, 266
  and learning disabilities, 34–35
  and reading problems, 382
General education classrooms, LD students in, 489–521
  co-teaching for, 492–495
  and culturally responsive instruction, 490
  decisions on, 496–502
  instructional practices for, 507–521
  legal mandates for, 490–492
  modifications for, 502–507
  and resource rooms, 496
  technology and, 506
General education curriculum, 490

Generic approach to early identification of learning disabilities, 150
Gene therapy, 60
Genetics, molecular, 59
Genres, 439–440
Gist comprehension, 375
Gist comprehension training, 399–400
Globus pallidus, 272, 274f, 275
Goals, 98–99
Goldman Fristoe Test of Articulation, 344t
Grade-level deviations, 72
Grammar checkers, 437
Grapheme, 414
Graphic organizers, 511–514, 512f, 513f
Grouping
    heterogeneous, 67
    homogeneous, 67
Group instruction, 510
Guided feedback, 440–443
Guilt, parental, 119

Handwriting, 407–414, 428
    assessment of, 409–411, 410f, 412t
    interventions for, 413–414, 415f
    problems with, 407–409
Head Start, 45, 153
*Heath Literacy* (Alvermann et al.), 379
Hegge-Kirk-Kirk approach, 391–392
Helplessness, learned, 237–238
Hereditary factors
    of ADHD, 275, 276–277
    of neurological dysfunction, 56–59
Heritability, 58–59, 119
Heterogeneous grouping, 67
Hindsight, 279
Hispanic Americans, 116–117, 232
    with learning disabilities, 32, 33, 33t, 97
    poverty rate for, 117
Historical figures with learning disabilities, 8
Holism, 309–310
Home-school communication systems, 139–141
Home-school note programs, 135–136, 136f
Homework, 122–125
    parents and, 122, 124
    students and, 125, 125t
    teachers and, 122–124, 123f
Homogeneous grouping, 67
Hyperactive child syndrome, 263

Illinois Test of Psycholinguistic Abilities (ITPA), 11f, 227–230
Improper fractions, 459
Improving Education Results for Children with Disabilities Act (2003), 19t, 25
Impulsivity–reflectivity concept, 230–231
Inactive learner, 237
Inclusive education, 156–158
Inclusive settings, 104–105
Individualized education program (IEP), 68, 96–106
    behavioral assessment and, 83
    behavior management plan in, 203, 204, 205f
    components of, 98–101

definition of, 7, 111
development of, 88
family involvement in, 114
parents approving, 96
transition plan in, 170
Individualized education program (IEP) meeting, 130–135
Individualized education program (IEP) planning form, 130, 131f
Individualized family service plan (IFSP), 111, 155
Individuals with Disabilities Education Act (IDEA), 19t
    on ADHD, 272
    on assistive technology, 347
    definition of learning disability in, 15t, 70–73, 382
    on early intervention, 154–155
    on eligibility process, 65–66
    on evaluation, 85–86
    on individualized education program, 98, 203
    on language problems, 328
    on parental involvement, 111
    on placement, 491
    on prereferral strategies, 74
    on referral, 75
    on special education service delivery, 101
    on timeline, 96
    on transition programs, 169–170, 173
Infancy
    learning disabilities identified in, 149–152
    risk factors in, 146–147
Informal checklists, 498, 500f–501f
Informal language assessment, 344–346, 345t, 346t
Informal mathematical knowledge, 452
Informal mathematics inventories, 464–465, 466f–469f
Informal reading inventories (IRI), 377–378
Informal spelling inventories, 421
Information-processing skills, 77, 307
Information-processing theory, 224–226
Inner speech, 279
Instruction, 200–201, 213. *See also* Direct Instruction; Self-instruction; Teaching
    anchored, 309, 310, 520
    CEC standards on, 528–529, 532–533
    computer-assisted, 162–163, 347, 395, 476–478
    in general classroom, 507–521
    group, 510
    mathematics, 478–483, 479t
    multiculturalism and, 308, 490
    peer-mediated, 397, 514–516
    reading. *See* Reading instruction
    remedial, 389
    scaffolded, 39, 398, 424, 510
    science, 519–520
    social science, 520–521
Instructional accommodations, 180–181, 503–505
Instructional adaptations, 505–507

Instructional ecology, 496–498
*Intelligence and Experience* (Hunt), 45
Intelligence tests, 18–20, 21, 22, 72, 73
Interactive assessment, 83–84, 84f
Interagency collaboration, 170–172
Interim alternative educational setting (IAES), 206
Internalizing behavior, 202
Internal locus of control, 236
International Academy for Research in Learning Disabilities, 10f
International Dyslexia Association (IDA), 26, 44
Intervention. *See* Early intervention; Language interventions; Reading interventions; Writing interventions
Interviews, 79–80, 267
Intonation, 339
Intra-individual differences, 13, 15–16
Iowa Test of Basic Skills, 376

*Journal of Learning Disabilities,* 8
Juvenile delinquency, 198–199

*Key Math Revised: A Diagnostic Inventory of Essential Mathematics* (Connolly), 463
Keyword mnemonic, 245–246, 245f, 351–352, 352f
Kindergarten, 151, 157
Kinesthetic modality, 389

Language
    CEC standard on, 531–532
    definition of, 77, 325, 328
    elements of, 325–326, 328–341
    expressive, 329
    foreign, learning, 327
    primary, 117
    receptive, 329
Language assessment, 76–77, 341–347
    informal, 344–346, 345t, 346t
    standardized, 341–344, 343t, 344t
Language differences, 147–148, 159, 160, 232, 434, 474
Language interventions, 347–356
    keyword mnemonics, 351–352, 352f
    phonemic awareness, 353–355, 354t
    semantic feature analysis, 350–351, 352f
    statement repetition, 355–356
    teaching in context or conversation, 353
Language problems, 325–356
    hereditary factors of, 58–59
    with metalinguistic awareness, 340–341
    with morphology, 334–335, 335f
    with phonology, 331–332
    with pragmatics, 338
    with receptive and expressive language, 329–330
    research on, 52
    with semantics, 336–337
    with syntax, 333–334
Lateral fissure, 49f, 50
Lead ingestion, 59
Learned helplessness, 237–238